D0192994

Beyond the American Pale

Beyond the American Pale

The Irish in the West, 1845–1910

David M. Emmons

University of Oklahoma Press : Norman

Also by David M. Emmons

Garden in the Grasslands: Boomer Literature of the Central Great Plains (Lincoln, Nebr., 1971)

The Butte Irish: Class and Ethnicity in an American Mining Town, 1875–1925 (Urbana, Ill., 1989)

Library of Congress Cataloging-in-Publication Data

Emmons, David M.
  Beyond the American pale : the Irish in the West, 1845–1910 / David M. Emmons
     p.   cm.
  Includes bibliographical references and index.
  ISBN 978-0-8061-4128-2 (hardcover : alk. paper)
  1. Irish Americans—West (U.S.)—History—19th century. 2. Irish Americans—West (U.S.)—History—20th century. 3. Catholics—West (U.S.)—History. 4. Immigrants—West (U.S.)—History. 5. Pioneers—West (U.S.)—History. 6. Frontier and pioneer life—West (U.S.) 7. Migration, Internal—United States—History. 8. West (U.S.)—Ethnic relations—History—19th century. 9. West (U.S.)—Ethnic relations—History—20th century. 10. West (U.S.)—History. I. Title.
  F593.3.I6E48 2010
  305.891'62073078—dc22

                                                                    2009052965

1 2 3 4 5 6 7 8 9 10

To Caroline Dollard Emmons,
whose last boat from Albany took her just far enough

Contents

Introduction

The American Pale

Between 1845 and 1910 approximately five million people left Ireland for the United States. The vast majority of them were Catholic, desperately poor, and without the work skills that could command decent wages. They were also a subject people, the refuse of an empire from which the United States had had the wisdom and grit to escape. They went almost everywhere in their new national home and did almost everything, though usually in the employ of someone else. But wherever and whenever they were found, they brought cultural habits and values that differed, often strikingly, from those of the "host society." The behavior of the Irish immigrants and of their descendants arose in large part from the intersection of Irish Catholic culture and society and the American Protestant versions of the same. The large differences that existed between the Irish and the Americans produced deep divisions. The Irish were as fearful and suspicious of Americans as the Americans were of them.[1]

This historical account, partial and selective as all such histories are, deals with aspects of the lives of Irish-born and Irish American Catholics who made their way to the western parts of the United States. These were the "two-boat Irish," a phrase the Irish used to describe those who had ventured from their initial seaboard landing sites. Their second vessels were of every conceivable kind—wagons, railroads, flatboats, bateaux, paddle-wheelers, even another ocean-going sailing ship or steamer. They need not have carried them far—need not, in fact, have carried them westward. Some second "boats" went only from New York City to Albany or from Boston to Springfield. But a great number of those inland transports took the Irish deep into the American interior. Still others navigated the full passage; tens of thousands of Irish were delivered to the Pacific Coast, putting an ocean once again on their western side.[2]

Historians have not paid a great deal of attention to the Irish American experience in western America. There are studies of the Irish in various western towns and cities but nothing on the western Irish in general or on the Irish in small western towns or on western farms. This neglect arises in part from at least two assumptions. The first of these is that the failure of the Irish potato crop from 1845 to 1849 and the appalling suffering of *an Gorta Mór*, "the Great Hunger," that followed had convinced the Irish that farming brought only isolation, misery, and death. "The Irish rejected the land," writes one historian, "for the land had rejected them." Their "experience with the potato blight," in the words of another, "had soured them on farming." The second assumption is that those who would not grow crops or pasture animals, whatever their reason might be, did not go west. Growing something was what the West was for. That was what westerners did; it was, in fact, about all that westerners did. But it was not just what they did; it was who they were. The West was the natural home of sturdy American yeomen and both a contrast and a reproach to the industrializing East.[3]

Both of these assumptions are false; it is time for historians to discard them. An Gorta Mór soured the Irish on further participation in a political union that let them starve, not on agriculture. The notion of a built-in aversion to farming is belied by the fact that Irish Catholics farmed in Australia and Canada. Many also farmed in America, and more would have if the American land system had not so closely resembled that of British-owned Ireland. The starving times did not make the Irish reluctant to farm; it made them hate the United Kingdom, the hoax that had joined them to it, and the great British land grab that had dispossessed them. This was the Famine's most enduring lesson. The starving times would remain a part of Ireland's remembered and anguished past, and even those Irish who emigrated a half-century and more after those terrible years carried with them "great hatred, . . . a fanatic heart." Less poetically, they brought all the bitterness and self-pity that went with their sense of themselves as exiles.[4]

As for the western idyll, it was a fiction, part of the very active and politically conscious myth-making of nineteenth-century America. It represented the West as imagined, not the West as found. Much of the West to which the Famine and post-Famine Irish immigrants had access was more urban and industrial than any other section of the country. It is no surprise that most of the Irish in the West were in western cities carrying out the hard labor of an industrializing economy and were in the company of the most racially and ethnically diverse workforce anywhere in America. That is what the real West was and that is what the real West did. And even the part that could be farmed was home to more agricultural tenants than independent freeholders. As to the numbers of two-boat western Irish, I grant at the outset that not many Irish moved West. I would point out, however, that not many others did either. The western movement may have been romantic, but it was not always very well attended. Understanding the Irish who were part of this movement will involve discussing what the Irish thought about the West and what they did once they got there. But it will also involve a discussion of what Americans, East and West, thought about these western wayfaring Irish and what they did to them.[5]

That simple statement, however, hides as much as it reveals, and some definitions and explanations are in order. Let me begin with my use of the word "pale." It had two meanings, and I use it in both ways. In its plainest geographical form, a pale was an enclosure bound by a line that could be drawn on a map. The same could be said of a county line or any other solely political or administrative border. In this sense, by "Irish beyond the pale" I mean simply those who had crossed outside and west of a boundary, those whose second and subsequent boats had carried them into the American interior. That is the plain and uncomplicated definition of a pale. It is also the less important definition. One could be outside a county, but seldom was anyone said to be "beyond" it.

This introduces that most famous of America's borders, the "frontier." It was regularly said that someone had gone beyond the frontier, and that meant more than just changing addresses. But the more common preposition with "frontier" was "on." Hardy sorts lived on the frontier. Those who went beyond it were daring greatly; they were fools or heroes or both. The frontier marked the line separating settled regions from unsettled, "civilized" peoples from "savages." The frontier was the battle zone between two distinct classifications of people: Anglo-American Strangers and American Indian Natives. The Strangers were cultural warriors: when they went beyond the frontier, they dragged the line marking it with them. They were changing places geographically, but they were also part of an ongoing historical process.[6]

Like frontiers, pales also had unfixed and movable borders that served to identify and separate different cultures. They were also like frontiers in that some few people or entire large groups of people could live within the line of the pale and still be outside and beyond it. The thresholds that marked the pale distinguished between two disparate social groups and then segregated them for a great variety of reasons, including religion and political culture. One group lived by the codes and rules enforced within the pale; the other lived by an entirely different set of codes and rules and was thus beyond it. By the mid-nineteenth century, literally millions of non-Indian peoples were in America but not of it. The American pale, as surely as the American frontier, was a limbic region, in the sense that those who occupied it were in limbo—that is, on "the edge of hell," in a "fool's paradise." And that definition applied to those on both sides of the border. It was the place where Natives and Strangers met and rubbed against and abraded one another.

But a pale/frontier not only marked off separate entities: it also joined them in an articulated relationship. Those on each side of the line functioned in response to those on the other side; in the modern language of literary criticism, each was Other to the other. All of this might have made for little more than interesting conversation between those on either side, except that the articulation along the line was never between equals. In Ireland—the obvious model for my usage—the pale was contained within an irregularly shaped zone that extended outward from its "capital" in Dublin. It enclosed within it those of pure heart, civilized manners, and steady habits who also happened to constitute the imperial class. The overwhelming majority of these palesmen were Protestants, all with a fine disdain for Catholics and all things Catholic. Protestantism was the source of their purity, civility, and steadiness; anti-Catholicism was a principal justification of their imperium. But religion was not their only defining characteristic. Palesmen were Britons, and though that definition was an invention, all knew that it meant Protestant and that it carried great weight. The Irish Others were both different and deficient.[7]

Since the Irish pale was a doctrinal rather than a political boundary, no one casually wandered back and forth across it. Those beyond it were not simply the ones who lived west of Dublin and its surrounds. They were Catholic Irish and thus had no claim to being Britons. That they had evinced no desire to be Britons, and had made manifest their aversion by holding tenaciously to their Catholicism, only confirmed the wisdom of their consignment beyond the pale. These Irish were literally "outlanders." Indeed, that word and its derivative, "outlandish," arose in the context of British descriptions of the Catholic and wayward Irish. The pale was a palisade (the etymological origin of that word), a fortified wall built to protect the imperial British settlers from the rebellious, or at least always potentially rebellious, native Irish.[8]

At times those within the pale wanted to extend its borders outward, to conquer but also to convert and bring in the intractable and unruly ones on the outside and beyond its civilizing influence. Predictably, the outlanders in turn wanted to push the line back and shrink the pale, though almost always for purposes of cultural defense and survival rather than conquest and conversion. Again, the similarity with the frontier as Americans perceived it is striking. A fair amount of mixing and blending took place in both directions across the pale, but only at the point of contact, where the articulated tug-of-war took place. Those deepest within the pale did not mix with those deepest without and most clearly beyond it.

If the pale was to be understood—if, in fact, the line marking it was even to be found—there had to be a fairly detailed rule book explaining what it meant to be on one or the other side of the line. The people on both sides had to define themselves; they needed standards of eligibility. On occasion this self-identification was quite conscious, especially on the part of palesmen, who used it as a means of justifying their dispossession of those beyond the pale. It was part of the "cant of conquest." Usually, however, the two sides revealed themselves un-self-consciously and visually through their color, or un-self-consciously and invisibly through their stories, their laws, their folkways, and, most particularly— in Ireland as in America—their religion. Each side knew who they were and knew also who the Others were. Little wonder that the articulated relationship across pales was often contentious. Pales mark cultural borders, and borderlands can be dark and menacing places.[9]

The American palesman was always a white male, usually native-born or of British "stock." If not themselves westward wanderers, the Americans within the pale were at least convinced that going westward was a very American thing to do and that a westerner was a very American thing to be. At this point, the two definitions of "pale" coalesced. The West as a place and westering as a process were joined. The West was God's gift to Americans; it distinguished them from other people. Going west defined them and proved that they were deserving of this providential favor. Providence, however, in America as in Britain and Ireland, assumed an inflexible and tenaciously held sectarian aspect. As in English-ruled Ireland, to be within the American pale, one had always to be a Protestant.[10]

That is a confined and confining list of qualifications, but until about the 1830s, with the obvious exception of African slaves, it accurately described most Americans, these new men residing within their well-guarded pale and governed by rigidly Protestant and anti-Catholic codes of conduct. The rule book, more-over, did not change, even as an expanding United States entered and took title to regions already inhabited by outlanders—American Indians always, but also the French Catholics around New Orleans and St. Louis and the Hispanic Catholics of the Southwest. Nor were changes made as outlandish immigrants began to arrive. Included in that list of deviant sorts were all those of whatever racial or national origin who were not Protestant Christians—both Anglican and Dissenter—or deists and hence respectably secular. The "frontiers" dividing those with proper credentials from all of these Others were as inflexible and well fortified as those of any pale, including Ireland's. Some of the deists and Dissenters directly challenged British imperial rule in Ireland. Many more merely muttered to themselves about that rule. A sizable number from both camps packed up to leave, usually for America. But whether active incendiaries or quiet grumblers, most of these Protestants from Ireland came to fit snugly inside the American pale.[11]

That was not true of the Catholic Irish. In Ireland their religion, not their politics, placed them beyond the pale. But once in America they ran into another cultural palisade and another set of religious eligibility rules that they could not meet. This New World palisade conflated religion and politics and left them twice outcast. And this raises an important historical point. It has been argued with increasing frequency of late that when the criteria for admission to the pale and to "true Americanism" were based on ethnicity or color or race rather than political or religious orthodoxy, the Irish tried to shed their status as outlanders by "becoming white." I do not dispute that the American Republic was the preserve of white men or that whiteness was privileged and the "wages of whiteness" were built into American pay scales, however "pay" may be defined.[12]

But true American republicanism was also based on Protestantism; it, too, was privileged, and the "wages of Protestantism" were also built into the system. The idea that the Irish American response to the other Others was part of the "alchemy of race," that it was how the Irish "became white," is not just reductionist; it is a form of historical imperialism, presuming a priori that adopting racist attitudes was how the Irish "became American." Why not complete the investigation and make fuller sense of it by inquiring into "how the Catholics became (or did not become) Protestant"? That said, I grant that the Irish accommodation to America—East and West—did require them to respond not just to the host society and its palesmen but also to those with whom they shared an outsider's status. That Irish response deserves to be studied, but without preconceptions.[13]

It is the reaction of the host society in America to the Irish that is presently at issue, however, not how the Irish dealt with America's various races, colors, and creeds. The American response to Irish Catholics was almost a mirror image of what had occurred in Britain. Why would it not be? Both societies were based on a self-conscious Protestantism and on the aggressive anti-Catholicism that was central to it. The initial English settlements in America had a powerful religious component, as did the disagreements that led to the American colonial separation from imperial Britain. But there was no disagreement between England and its new Englands on the monstrous nature of popery. The anti-Catholicism of Britain as mother country and of America as rebellious progeny were alike in style and substance.

The entire American experience from the Puritan City on a New England Hill to the Chesapeake Bay and the coastal islands of the Carolinas and Georgia was not just a beacon to the world but also marked off a pale that separated the new and unsullied from the old and corrupt. And the deeper into the continent the Americans moved, the more distance they could put between their robust young selves and the feeble old world and the more impenetrable the pale. But to the Americans—as assuredly Protestant as the Britons by whom they were spawned—nothing was older or more decrepit than the Church of Rome. The American Revolution and the republican ideology that propelled it solidified a sectarian partition. The American pale had a religious entrance test as surely as did the pale constructed by the British in Ireland.

Beginning in the 1840s, the American economy started its "take-off," its "spurt" toward industrial capitalism. A "market revolution" initiated the "passage" of American political culture from the artisanal republicanism of the revolutionary era to a new republicanism built on expanding labor, consumer, and resource markets. At the same time, and related to this fundamental shift in republicanism, came a second fundamental change. The American nation-state began to consolidate its political and cultural authority and vastly extend its geographical reach. A "righteous empire" of continental breadth would both sustain and be sustained by this new version of republicanism. I do not mean "empire" in the conventional, which is to say British, sense. American expansion westward was imperious but not technically imperial. The distinction, however, is slight.[14]

Protestantism would adjust nicely to every aspect of this modern project, from industrial capitalism to the governing class of the new nation-state to America's expansionist instincts. Shopkeepers would ally with millenarians; profits would be joined to piety; modernity would be wedded to morality. The nagging suspicion remained, however, that this alliance of God and Mammon was unnatural and came at the expense of the nation's innocence, that it broke the republican covenants that made Americans a providential people. Morality and cities on a hill aside, the realization also grew that the big changes carried big risks; that there were, among myriad issues, some fundamental disagreements between the providers of labor and the consumers of that labor and that those disagreements could also violate covenants, whatever their terms. Specifically, it forced Americans to ask whether republicanism could survive in a society in which disparities of wealth and asymmetries of power were so fully on display.[15]

This is when the West, both as a place and as a frontier/pale, took on a new, expanded, and quite manufactured and counterfeit identity. It was cast as America's last virginal landscape, becoming a constructed province, a deceptive and fanciful myth-world. None of this happened by chance; the mythical West was as much a product of the modern project as were steel rails and dynamos. This was a West that market capitalism and evangelical Protestantism both made and made up. It would be the natural home of the righteous and the underwriter of American righteousness; at a time when many feared that the nation had lost or squandered the moral and spiritual high ground, this was no transient and trifling matter. The West became a region enshrouded in myth, "the most strongly imagined section of the United States," according to one historian, a "fairy-tale land," according to another. Its settlement would be in the form of conquest. It was a place to be won.[16]

This, in briefest form, was the historical context in which the West was both found and imagined. History made the West, both the real one and the mythical one. The physical or environmental features of the various parts of this West were important, but not in deciding its boundaries. Those were determined by events in time, by the social and cultural values in play as its component parts were being settled and their social forms established. Those values shaped the guidebook by which the pale could be identified and by which eligibility for admission to it was decided. This guidebook had no entries under the heading "Catholic Irish." The story of the Irish in "fairy-tale land" is not merely undertold, and the telling of it involves more than just moving the historical stage settings from the East to the West. It is a fundamentally different story with different historical set pieces. Their next and last boats took them to places where history and its big changes literally had no room for them.

The Irish side of this story had a temporal element as well. In Ireland, the mid-1840s witnessed a demographic catastrophe. At least a million people died in an Gorta Mór; almost two million more emigrated—or, as the Irish would have had it, were exiled—most of them to America. The host society of New York and Boston may not have rushed to the docks to bid them welcome, but the modern project required—indeed begged for—willing workers, and beggars seldom can choose. They must accept what history gives them. America took the Irish and put them to hard labor, as it would the Irish immigrants after the Famine years. Thus did totally disconnected historical lines intersect. Modern, industrializing America needed workers; Ireland, both during and after the starving times, met and at times exceeded that need; call it an application of the law of unintended historical consequences.

History also shaped the Irish response to America. This was true wherever they settled, but the mixing of otherwise disconnected historical lines is of particular interest in the case of the Irish in western America, both the real West and the imagined one. At issue is what Kerby Miller has called the "exile motif," the Irish sense that they were not emigrants but forced exiles banished from their homes, and the deeper Irish and Catholic culture code that partly produced and partly arose from that motif. Miller's description deserves to be cited fully:

> Catholic Irish were more communal than individualistic, more dependent than independent, more fatalistic than optimistic, more prone to accept conditions passively than to take initiatives for change, and more sensitive to the weight of tradition than to innovative possibilities for

the future. Indeed, their perspectives seemed so premodern that to bourgeois observers from business-like cultures, the native Irish often appeared "feckless," "child-like," and "irresponsible."

This was the perception of the Irish held by Protestants hostile to them, particularly English and American Protestants. It had a cruel intent, but it was not entirely false, particularly in its more Catholic rather than Irish aspects. Catholicism *was* traditional, communal, dependent, fatalistic, and premodern; the Irish version was especially so. It was easy enough, then, to internalize those features of the faith, to turn them from negatives to positives, and to make them the Irish people's perception of themselves.[17]

It was also easy, as the Irish economy went through its own smaller-scale market revolution, for middle-class elements of Irish society to take the idea of exile and turn it to their social-class advantage. In other words, the exile motif, as surely as the American western myth—call it the frontier motif—was partly a manufactured product designed to serve the purpose of social control. As Miller puts it, "a large proportion" of those leaving Ireland between 1856 and 1921 were not exiles "but eager, ambitious emigrants seeking material and personal enhancement." These were Irish happy to be rid of the place; the gnashing of teeth that could still be heard at their leave-taking was for effect; it shielded them from the charge that they had abandoned their families. Exile assuaged some of their guilt. That is the Irish side of exile. The Irish American side is different. One of Miller's critics refers to his analysis of this Irish worldview— what I have called the Irish culture code—as Miller's "Irish Catholic disabilities variables." They were variables because Protestants did not share them, disabilities because they left the Irish at a distinct disadvantage when it came to meeting American conditions, particularly, I would add, those of the imagined American West.[18]

And, in fact, it must be asked what effect this Irish Catholic culture code, as well as the exile motif as a manifestation of it, had on their potential as manly frontiersmen. The American West, clearly, was not to be won by childlike Irish. This was not a hypothetical issue. For example, did the exile motif extend to the second boat? The immigrants' first westbound boat took them into exile; the next ones might well have seemed an extension of that exile. It may have been as wrenching for them to leave New York as it had been for them to leave Ireland. If any part of that gloomy playscript is true, then westward the majority of them did not go freely. That bit of American sloganeering was only for those who did in fact go freely. Those who went freely went also of their own accord.[19]

If the legacy of the West was of conquest, then the Irish clearly had a limited role: they could be the blunt instruments of conquest, the foot soldiers of the

American conquistadores, but not themselves conquerors. This was a distinctly subordinate role, but it was all that could be expected of passive exiles not thought to possess the plucky individualism necessary to frontier conquests. They would be the shock troops, first in time but last in claimant rights. There was a great irony in this. The agents of dispossession had themselves been dispossessed. The role did not always fit them very well, but conditions in Ireland, their own sense of themselves as exiles, and Americans' dismissal of them as beyond the pale left them little choice but to play it.[20]

The archaic usage "leaping the pale" means overstepping proper bounds and going where one does not meet the entrance requirements. This book is about more than just the Irish going to and living in the West. It is about Celtic pale-leapers, which means all of the Catholic Irish who joined in the national ethos of westering and ended up in a place they were not supposed to be. Telling that story raises some obvious and important questions. How far west and to what kind of West did the later boats go? Did westering Irish fare better than those who stayed in the East? Was their adjustment easier? Did the Irish component of their lives diminish or strengthen as they went deeper into the American interior? On related issues, was their commitment to Irish nationalism and worker rights different from that of the Irish for whom one boat was enough? More specifically, did western Irish American nationalism take a form different from the eastern form? Did moving West make the two-boat Irish more American and hence less Irish? How did their new western American world treat the Irish? Did it change them, or they it? How assimilable were these Irish—that is, how well did their cultural values align with those of western Americans? What was the gender balance among Irish in the West, and did Irish women respond to western America differently from men? How did Irish Americans differ from Irish immigrants? In sum, what was it like to be Catholic, Irish, and working class in the West of America between 1845 and 1910—always keeping in mind that by every known standard of western settlement they should not have been there?

A final issue needs to be addressed early and head on. This entire study is based on three related beliefs: first, culture counts; second, religion is a key component of a people's culture; and third, there were significant differences between Catholics and Protestants. Being Catholic was what put the Irish beyond the pale. Simply being from Ireland would not have been sufficient. The Catholic Irish were cultural strangers and were among the least assimilable of America's immigrants, notwithstanding their ability to speak English. The lives of Irish American Catholics were not determined solely by their material circumstances, a point of obvious importance given that they spent most of those lives in the American working class.[21]

The problem is that the assertions that religion mattered generally and that Catholicism mattered specifically are not self-evident truths to most historians, particularly to those who specialize in the history of American working people. I acknowledge that mine are contrarian views. Religion was not a reflection of a social infrastructure arising from the mode of production or any other "base." Neither was it a place to hide from economic and social realities. It was not a form of psychological escape and compensation. It did not suggest intellectual obtuseness, neuroses, alienation, or false consciousness. Religion was a part of the contemporary moral imagination of the vast majority of the men and women of all classes in the years and places here under discussion. And because it was central to most Americans' lives, it is central to the historical enterprise of describing those lives. This is particularly the case when the people of the time were not in positions of power, whether political or economic, or when—and this was frequently the cause of their underclass status—they were racial, ethnic, cultural, or ideological Others, leapers of the pale. The voices from beyond the pale are never as audible as those from within it.[22]

The idea that those underclasses are to be found and understood only in the context of their socioeconomic status and that their efforts at self-identification are irrelevant turns what should be a conversation into a soliloquy. The historian infers or imposes causal laws of explanation that leave the underclasses mute and powerless—precisely the condition in which their "masters" were alleged to have placed them. The problem with this kind of social-class analysis—which approaches a failure to analyze—is not just its relentless determinism. It involves a presumption by historians that the real truths of past lives were not understood by those who lived them. Historical truths are not found objects, but neither are they something that historians can construct by using their own theoretical patterns. Working people had "lives of their own"; there were, in fact, entire "worlds that slaves made." Working people, including the vast majority of the Catholic Irish in America, were not placed within a structure. They were not *placed* anywhere. Rather, employing their own moral and cultural compasses, they placed themselves within worlds at least partially of their own making. And they frequently described and validated their agency in their own overtly religious idiom. It will not do for historians to assign lines to working people and then reproach them for speaking their own lines or for missing cues that they either could not hear or did not understand.[23]

Finally, I must say something about the date that ends this partial and selective history. I mean 1910 only as a guidepost. There is no question that the mid-1840s saw major changes in both Irish and American society. My decision to begin with those changes was easy. But I know of nothing of moment that happened in 1910. The modern project did not end then; neither, in fact, did the Irish immigration. Nor, obviously, did the settlement of the American West or the telling of self-congratulatory hero-tales about the conflicts and conquests on the border that were a central part of that settlement. I chose 1910 because of what began then, not for what ended. In briefest terms, the intersecting lines of Irish and American history were always more tangled than the simple statement of their intersection would suggest. But after about 1910 the lines became incredibly jumbled. Irish as well as Irish American nationalism began a politically leftward tilt. So did the American labor movement, led by Irish Americans. On the labor side of the story was the powerful corporate counter-attack against labor, America's involvement in the Great War, the treaty that concluded that war, and the Bolshevik Revolution during it. The Irish side was no less busy. Add to the complex mix the 1916 Easter Rising, the Anglo-Irish War, and the Irish Civil War. This book is in part a historical prelude to those developments. It would take another book to try to explain them.

PART I

Unwelcome Strangers

The Irish and the West

CHAPTER 1

From Ireland to America's Mythic West

William L. O'Brien's Working-Class Grand Tour

I n early August 1914, four members of the U.S. Commission on Industrial Relations, recently formed by Congress and charged with "seek[ing] to discover the underlying causes" of industrial unrest nationwide, conducted hearings in the copper-mining town of Butte, Montana. The commissioners were in Butte for three days. They called a number of witnesses, including the governor of the state; the vice president, chief counsel, and director of mines of the city's largest mining company; doctors and other experts in occupational health issues; a representative sample of the city's many radical industrial unionists; and a wide variety of what in Butte were known simply as "practical miners," men who had spent many demanding years underground.[1]

One of those the commissioners called was an Irish-born miner by the name of William L. O'Brien. He was one of many Irishmen who would be asked to testify, something anyone who knew Butte could have predicted. The Irish dominated western hard-rock mining generally, but Butte was their capital city. It was the largest mining town in the world, had the largest local union in the world, and was the most Irish town in America. That was not all. In most of industrial America, immigrant and ethnic Catholics worked for Protestant Yankees; social class relations were based on ethnicity and culture as well as economics. That was not the pattern in Butte. The stable and established Irish ran the city, its mines, and its miners' union, often behaving as if Butte somehow belonged to them by proprietary right. By 1914 new immigrants—the Irish called them all "Bohunks" —were beginning to challenge those claims, creating the "industrial unrest" bordering on industrial anarchy that the commission had come to investigate.[2]

It would have been useful to the work of the commission if O'Brien had been asked to explain the situation in Butte and to comment on the larger lessons to be learned from it. That cannot, however, have been the reason the commissioners wanted to hear from him. They kept him only a short time and asked him no important or searching questions. His testimony takes up a bare two pages in the transcript, and one is left to wonder why he was called at all. He was not an officer of the old Butte Miners Union (BMU), but he had been nominated for the presidency of the recently formed and considerably more militant Butte Mine Workers' Union (BMWU), losing to another Irishman, Michael (Muckie) McDonald. O'Brien admitted not only to leadership in the BMWU but to personal involvement in the destruction of the Butte Miners Union Hall, the act that precipitated the crisis in industrial relations in Butte and brought the commission to town. He was not asked if he was a member of the militant Industrial Workers of the World and would probably not have revealed his membership if he had been.[3]

At that, there was no doubting his radicalism. He was an avowed "industrial unionist" and accused the BMU of "corruption" and class collaborationism. He did not repeat the charge that the union's Irish leaders colluded with capital to advance strictly Irish interests, but it is certain that he knew of the allegation and likely that he believed it. When asked how long he had been in Butte, he answered "ten months and seven days," the response of someone counting down the days of a prison sentence, and his general comments were those of a man who clearly saw himself as a casualty of the class wars. By 1914, however, if radicalism alone had been enough to be invited to testify, the commissioners would have had to call thousands of miners. O'Brien, moreover, had not been in Butte long (although his nomination for the presidency of the BMWU is strong evidence that he had lived there earlier), had worked in only one of its scores of mines, and had not worked at all for the previous six months. As he put it, "I took pneumonia." He may have, but in Butte respiratory illness in a miner was no more a distinguishing characteristic than militancy had become.[4]

What set O'Brien's comments apart was his response to a question posed by John R. Commons, the distinguished economist who was the commission's acting chair. Commons asked O'Brien where "had you worked in the mining business before you came here?" His response gave new meaning to the phrase "Irish rover." "All over the world," said O'Brien. "Africa, Australia, New Zealand, Tasmania, Canada, Alaska, Mexico, this country, and South America." The transcript gives no indication of whether O'Brien inflected his comment in any way or offered it up as offhandedly as it would appear. Neither does the transcript indicate the response of the commissioners. Commons's follow-up was routine: "And your birthplace is where?" "Ireland," O'Brien answered, "County Cork."[5]

I wish the commissioners had found O'Brien as interesting as I do and had been willing to listen to him for more than twenty minutes. This is a book about the Irish in the American West as well as about Irish ideas about the West; O'Brien's career is of more than passing interest to any such account. He was one of those who had moved through two middle passages, the first from Ireland to New Worlds, the second to the newest parts of those New Worlds. William O'Brien's entire working life was a series of middle passages. He had literally been all over the world and had memories from every part of it. He would have had many stories to tell; and, given the incredible and increasing ethnic diversity in the Butte mine workforce, those stories would have had a particular relevance. The commissioners, however, were not interested in O'Brien's past; their questions were all in the present tense. They wanted to know what O'Brien was at that moment in 1914, namely, a firsthand witness to the industrial and ethnic tensions in Butte. I grant that he was that. But I want to know what he had been, what had happened to him, and how he remembered what had happened to him as he wandered from continent to continent digging rocks. He derived his values and his politics from his history and his memory, and values and politics are historical facts. My questions are in the past tense.[6]

I cannot *know* what O'Brien's memories were, in large part because the commissioners did not share my interest in them. Like Commons, they asked no follow-up questions, leaving me to make what I hope are informed guesses. Guessing is risky, but O'Brien's past justifies the risk. Here was an Irish immigrant who had lived and worked in six of what historians once called frontiers and now call settler societies, contested regions where the "Strangers" met the "Natives" and the two determined their responses to one another. O'Brien had lived and worked only in old New Worlds, where established indigenous societies were displaced—frequently with great cruelty—by Europeans with conquest on their minds.[7]

Clearly, more than mere wandering is at issue in O'Brien's case. He was a "frontiersman," though it is unlikely that he or anyone else would have classified him as such. It is also unimportant. By 1914 Americans and Britons—the other of O'Brien's imperial "employers"—had constructed an entire master narrative whose chief themes included taming wild lands and wild people and expanding national borders. Frontiersmen were conquerors. I grant that O'Brien had conquered nothing. He dug rocks; and by the time we meet him, he was doing his digging for wages. That notwithstanding, he was a participant in an expansionist enterprise as brutal as the one that had ransacked Ireland and set its people to wandering. O'Brien was a frontiersman because he had lived on the borders. It is a generic label for those like him. The historical record is incomplete, but it is sufficient to allow us to wonder whether he ever understood that he was participating in a series of imperial conquests of Native peoples not unlike the one that had made a wreckage of Ireland.[8]

And what a range of peoples O'Brien had known. He had lived and worked with Asians, Maoris, Aborigines, Hispanics, American Indians, East Indians, Latin Americans, Africans, and African Americans—all people of color—as well as a wild assortment of ethnic and racial Others from every part of Europe. O'Brien's was an astonishing list of work companions. I know of no other working-class American, regardless of birthplace, who compiled anything like it. Of all the Irish who allegedly "became white," William L. O'Brien had the widest possible range of nonwhites from whom to choose to distance himself. If, as one historian has recently written, "the 'savage' resides at the borders of [the American] imagined national community," O'Brien would have qualified as a member of that community; he was intimately familiar with "the savage." The problem was that many in America would have considered him one.[9]

Whether a savage or not, William O'Brien was an outlander. The western America he knew was nothing like the carefully constructed mythic frontier, but clearly the fortifications of that imagined West were designed to keep those like him out and beyond. Westward, according to their national epic, Americans went free. They were border warriors, or at least pioneers pushing out the pale. Going west was a kind of culture test. When administered to immigrants, it indicated the extent of their assimilation. O'Brien would seem to have passed the test. He had blazed a trail of sorts. It did not lead to the West as promised land, however, and his assimilation was not to American values conventionally defined. As his testimony and his life made clear, he had assimilated from the bottom up. He understood and embraced American ideals, but they were the ideals of a sullen and vaguely menacing working class. The commissioners were uninterested.[10]

I cannot be so nonchalant, and not just on the question of social class discord. O'Brien was a lot more peripatetic than most of the diasporic Irish, but at that he was one of an identifiable type, part of a vast, hungry, and mobile army of Irish workers. Like the others, he was responding to America's "voracious appetite for cheap labor," immigrating to America and then joining in the equally vast internal migration within America. It is in this context of worker mobility that O'Brien's too brief testimony before the Industrial Commission deserves to be read. But more important, it deserves to be read into, to be teased out and made to reveal something more than it says and more than the commissioners made of it. This exercise will necessarily involve some speculative leaps, some "constructions" and inventions, both by me and by readers. But this is true of most historical interpretations. What else, then, can be said about the life of William L. O'Brien?[11]

We know that he was from County Cork, but O'Brien is a surname encountered almost everywhere in Ireland; it is impossible to use name/place association to fix his origins with any greater precision. We cannot know if he was from the western parts of Cork, identified even by other Corkonians as a remote place filled with *cabogues* (clodhoppers and ignoramuses), willing to work anywhere at any time at and for anything. O'Brien might once have been that hopelessly unsophisticated, although the world had taught him a lot by the time he got to Butte. But West Cork was also the place where Irish—*cabogues* included—had been mining copper for generations. O'Brien had "worked in the mining business" on four continents. He did not mention Europe, but that may have been from neglect. It is also possible that, though he had not mined in Ireland, members of his immediate family were among the many thousands who had. I think it entirely reasonable to assume that O'Brien knew something of "practical" mining's rhythms and dangers before he left Ireland and that he carried those lessons with him around the world.[12]

Only a few things about the name and the place can be known. "O'Brien" means descendant of Brian; for the overly romantic, the Brian in question may be imagined to have been Brian Boru or Boruma, the greatest of the Irish high kings. Whether descendant of Boru or not, William O'Brien carried a most distinguished name. I would also like to know what his parents were thinking when they named him. "William" was a fairly common Christian name in Cork, but not one associated with either Irish or Catholic fighters and martyrs. Perhaps he was the youngest son of a large family and his parents had run out of heroic names. In all events, it gives away nothing regarding the self-consciousness of the O'Briens. As for County Cork, in the language of one contemporary British observer, it was "the very capital of Irish nationality." William L. O'Brien could claim to be the legatee of the most celebrated of Ireland's kings and a product of "rebel Cork," the most passionately nationalistic and Anglophobic of its counties. It is doubtful, however, that either royal ancestry or any inherited or acquired commitment to Irish nationalism was much on O'Brien's mind when he came before the Industrial Commission.[13]

The commissioners did not ask O'Brien about his last memories of Ireland or any of the other places he had been. They neglected even to ask his age so that we might construct a plausible account of what those memories might have been. We do know that he had been a member of the Western Federation of Miners (WFM) for twelve years, and so we know that he had been in the United States and/or Canada since 1902. Aside from that, artful—and some not so artful—speculation is all we have left. Given his work history, he almost surely left Ireland as a young man, not as the dependent child of immigrant parents. He was on his own but almost surely not alone. The Irish emigrated in groups and as parts of extended chains of migration. O'Brien probably left with others of his family or friends and in response to letters from other Irish who had emigrated previously and were calling him to join them. There is no evidence that he had family with him in Butte in 1914—or many friends for that matter. But he did not begin his grand adventure that way.[14]

We can fix O'Brien in time by dating the boom periods in African, South American, and Antipodean hard-rock mining prior to 1902, because it is likely that he leapt from continent to continent in response to ore-strikes or the promise of high wages as new mines were exploited and that his roll call of places of employment was not in order of residence. His reference to Alaska almost certainly indicates that he joined hundreds, if not thousands, of other Irishmen in the great Klondike gold hunt of 1896–97. But the major ore strikes in South Africa occurred after 1902, suggesting that he went back and forth between continents—or mined in other and less well documented parts of Africa. Dating him is difficult. Without even pretending to strict accuracy, we can surmise that William O'Brien was probably born in the mid-1850s and emigrated along with more than 70,000 others from County Cork alone in the mid-1870s.[15]

The commissioners never asked if English was O'Brien's only language and took no notice of a revealing moment in his testimony when he closed a declarative sentence with an un-self-conscious "I don't say," a common Hiberno-English construction. This is hardly proof that he was or ever had been an Irish-speaker. The linguistic tag line indicates only that he carried some of its accents and syntax with him. We know that he was literate, but probably only in English. Certainly he was literate by the time he reached Butte; his testimony indicates that he was quite current in the literature of worker protest. It would be useful to know, however, in what language system he interpreted that literature. The Irish spoke in English, but many still thought in Irish. I prefer to think of O'Brien as one of those.[16]

Neither were the commissioners interested in O'Brien's reasons for leaving Ireland. He may have thought of himself as an unlucky and exploited exile or a fortunate and enterprising emigrant. Given his world-girdling grand tour, I am guessing that, at the least, he boarded his boats willingly. He doubtless was consigned to steerage, but no one travels that far or that often without having some dreams of making a fair living. The commissioners were not interested in his dreams, whether for himself, his social class, or his home place. In fact, they did not ask where exactly he considered himself to be from. They asked where he had lived and worked but not where his true home was or if he thought of himself as "uprooted" and, if so, whether he had been "transplanted" and to where. One of the commissioners, James O'Connell, upon hearing that O'Brien was from Cork, commented, "You come from a pretty good county." O'Brien replied only "Yes." Whether he said it defiantly, proudly, or matter-of-factly cannot be known. But that he mentioned his home county at all attests to the "profoundly localized mentality" of the Irish. Cork made a difference. It, not some abstract idea of an Ireland, was the land of O'Brien's birth. It was from Cork, not Ireland, that he emigrated.[17]

Still, if "Yes" was the best O'Brien could do in response to O'Connell's comment, why bring up Cork at all? Here was another opportunity for O'Brien to say something to fill in more of the historical record. Predictably, he did not take that opportunity, and the commissioners did not make him. O'Connell is also a name most closely associated with West Cork and neighboring County Kerry, and perhaps O'Brien's simple "Yes" was accompanied by some nonverbal acknowledgment of a shared county of origin. It is also possible that it was terse and unaccompanied, the only answer that O'Connell's effort at ethnic chumminess required or deserved. Maybe O'Connell and the others thought that an Irishman identifying his county was like an American identifying his state. But that was not the case in Ireland, and it is unfortunate that O'Brien did not take advantage of the chance to educate the commissioners on what Irish Americans—often derisively—called "countyism."[18]

O'Brien's New World experiences seem to have been of more interest to him. He told the commissioners that he was a "metalliferous" miner, a hard-rock man, and that he had never dug coal. It was important to him that they know that. The work that O'Brien had done set him apart. The occupational identity of hard-rock men contained more than a little vanity. Coal miners were miners of a kind—just not of the same or equal kind. They mined "soft" rock and always worked for wages in the collieries of other men. Many, probably most, of the hard-rock miners in the early placer years of the 1860s and 1870s thought of themselves as independent operators, "capitalists" of a kind. Their dreams were not of paychecks but of striking it rich. Given his remarkable tramping life, it is more than possible that O'Brien falls into this category.[19]

In this O'Brien was unlike most who left Ireland at about the same time, particularly if they had families. Striking it rich was a dream reserved for the footloose and unattached. So, for that matter, was labor militancy. The stable Irish miners of Butte wanted safe and steady work—nothing more, but nothing less. More than anything else about him, I would like to know if O'Brien had ever had a wife and children. Working-class dreams were highly contingent, Irish identities highly relational. Again, I am guessing—and hoping: there had to have been more to O'Brien's life than boat trips and deep mines. But by 1914 O'Brien was nearly sixty years old, almost surely unmarried, and living alone in a small boarding house in Butte, Montana. William Butler Yeats wrote in "Fergus and the Druid" that the Druid, though wise, was "like a wind-blown reed. / No woman's loved me, no man sought my help." Men had sought O'Brien's help; hard-rock miners helped one another. But that notwithstanding, when I think of O'Brien, I think of the Druid.[20]

O'Brien had dug hard rocks all over the world, sometimes for himself, more often for corporations. It may be assumed that the experience was not a pleasant one. He testified that he had been a member of miners' unions in "Australia,

Africa, New Zealand, [and] Tasmania" as well as the United States, suggesting that his dreams had gone bust in South America or the Klondike. O'Brien's testimony does not even hint at an event or a moment of insight that propelled him toward worker radicalism. He might well have left Ireland angry and disillusioned, but it was the decades spent in deep drifts putting rocks in the box for distant and faceless corporations that had radicalized him. The commissioners knew only that he was a radical; they never asked what had radicalized him, never posed a question in the past tense.[21]

Equally curious and frustrating is the fact that at no time during their three days in Butte did the commissioners—all four of whom were friends of labor and from the East—comment that the West was an unlikely place for O'Brien's brand of radicalism, that the West was where Americans were expected to go to escape industrial violence and radicalism, not to find it in its most angry and volatile form. The West was also supposed to be the natural home of the "true American," but one of the Butte miners' most intractable problems, as Joe Shannon, another Irish-born radical, told the commission, was that the mine workforce and hence the Butte Miners Union was so "cosmopolitan." Shannon was being semi-sarcastic, but he meant cosmopolitan in its most literal sense; Butte's miners came from everywhere.[22]

That was not the city's only departure from the norm. In the conventional metaphor, the West was expected to be industrial America's "safety valve," a place of refuge not just from the social class tensions of the East but from its ethnic and racial diversity as well. Perhaps by 1914 the commissioners had come to know better; the safety valve did not work—for the Irish or any other component of the American working class. Commons, writing in 1919, stated that "great corporations controlled [the West's] natural resources . . . and, if the workingman is to have any opportunity, he cannot secure it by going west . . . and settling on the soil." Perhaps O'Brien's testimony had been part of Commons's education. If so it is doubly unfortunate that more of America had not heard O'Brien—or Shannon and Dan Sullivan and Con Lowney and Dan Shovlin and any one of dozens of other western American Irishmen called before the commission. They all had lessons to teach about the West and its place in industrial America.[23]

There are limits to how much can be read into any text. Those limits have been nearly reached. But the most important part of this reconstruction of the life of William L. O'Brien has yet to be crafted. It affected every aspect of this singular roving Irishman, his sense of himself as Irish and as a worker and his response to the culture and society of the places in which he sojourned. Predictably, the commission did not inquire into it. No one asked him about his religion. In 1914, had he been asked, O'Brien might well have answered as Joe Shannon had answered the commissioners' question that same day. "This soul business is a kind of myth with me," Shannon had said. "We have enough to do to take care of the body." Shannon's hostility to organized religion was an important part of his radicalism, as it may have been of O'Brien's. But the "soul business" was one in which a variety of soul watchers were involved. As important as Shannon's hostility—and O'Brien's if he shared it—was the denominational perspective from which it came. In other words, it is one thing to tag both Irishmen as unchurched, even godless, in 1914, quite another to assume that such had always been the case.[24]

Let me state the obvious: it is possible that O'Brien came out of Ireland a confirmed, even a vocal, nonbeliever. It is more probable that he did not. It is even possible that he was born and raised a Presbyterian or an Anglican. Maybe his family of O'Briens had converted to Protestantism. Maybe his parents named him after the Protestant King William of Orange. These are possibilities—but highly unlikely ones. In 1861, 2,000 Presbyterians and 43,400 Anglicans lived in County Cork. But there were 494,000 Catholics, and they were of the devotional type unique to mid-nineteenth century Ireland. The safe guess is that with a name like O'Brien, and the work résumé he had compiled, William L. had been one of Cork's half-million Catholics, the source of the vast majority of its emigrants.[25]

Whether he remained such is an important question. Assuming that he had broken with the Catholic Church, the break probably occurred because the church's hostility to radicalism offended him. To a certain extent, every Irish Catholic worker, whether immigrant or descendant of immigrants, had to choose between being Catholic and being a labor militant. He may also have had to choose between being Irish and being a militant, though some would suggest that being Irish and being Catholic were the same thing. A few tried to finesse these issues; O'Brien may have been one of those. But it is far more likely that he saw the reconciliation of worker radicalism, Catholicism, and Irish nationalism as the equivalent of squaring a circle and opted for radicalism. In all events, these issues are beyond the reach of even the most freewheeling historical reconstruction.

That the religious dimensions of O'Brien's life are important historically, however, requires no reaching or teasing out of meaning. And so a couple of final points need to be made about William L. O'Brien before he is allowed to return to historical obscurity. We can be as certain of this as of anything else that O'Brien did not directly tell us: he was born, grew up, and, for a time at least, remained a Catholic. I think his story would be fascinating without his assumed Catholicism, or at least Catholic grounding, but it would not have the same historical traction or consequence. It is a story that cannot be stripped of its religious or irreligious aspects without sacrificing much of its meaning. O'Brien's presumed Catholicism and the avowed Catholicism of the overwhelming majority of the Irish in the American West were a profoundly important part of their adjustment to America and of America's adjustment to them.

Catholics and Protestants, including those who lived in Ireland, read and rendered their worlds in significantly different ways. It does not matter if these sectarian distinctions corresponded to "realities." They created the realities. There was a language of Protestantism, spoken in Britain and America, and a language of Catholicism, spoken in O'Brien's Ireland and in the new Irelands in which he traveled. Translating between these two languages was never easy. Putting the differences in cultural terms, the Catholic imagination was analogical, stressing community, the sacramental character of everyday life, and an institutional—and authoritative—expression of faith. The Protestant "culture code"—and American values were based on it—was dialectical, dismissive of both tradition and religious authority, and gave the privileged position to individualism rather than community. In theological terms, Protestants thought of themselves as "righteous"; America was their "righteous empire." For Catholics, righteousness was beyond reach; the best they could hope for was forgiveness, and the merely forgiven do not found empires—at least of a conventional sort.[26]

These rather arcane descriptions had profound political consequences, particularly when immigrants from Ireland were involved. Counting only nonsouthern states, in the century from 1820 to about 1920, 95 percent of the Protestant Irish voted the Whig or Republican ticket while 95 percent of the Catholic Irish voted Democratic. Partisan politics in America may have been more theatrical than ideological, but those remarkable voting percentages suggest some fundamental differences in the way the two peoples viewed their world and one another. "No Irish Need Apply" signs did not refer to Protestant immigrants from Ireland—the self-described "Scotch-Irish." Indeed, as the historian Kevin Kenny has recently written, "the 'Scotch-Irish' ceased to be Irish (in their own estimation as well as that of others) in the early nineteenth century." That could never be said of William O'Brien and his Irish comrades—whether they remained within the institutional Catholic Church or not, and however "comrade" is defined.[27]

For all the richness of William O'Brien's story, even the significant part of it that remains conjecture or invention, his life is no historical stand-in for the millions of other Irish whose western experience was markedly less nomadic and chancy—and melancholic—than his own. I have offered O'Brien's reconstructed life not because it supplies answers, but because of what it suggests about the general question of the Irish in America. O'Brien's ethnicity, like that of other Irish, is not a given. There was no such thing as "Irishness," whether essential or existential. About all that can be said is that the immigration of Irish Catholics was the longest-running immigration in American history and that Ireland changed during that century and a half during which it offered up its surplus sons and daughters for export. The Irish who emigrated from Allihies in West Cork in 1869 (it does not stretch credibility to include William O'Brien among them) were not the same as those who left Allihies in 1889 or 1909. And all three types need also to be distinguished from those who emigrated from Dennystown or

Gweedore in County Donegal, or Thurles in County Tipperary, or anywhere else in Ireland, whatever the timing of their leave-taking.[28]

This raises another of O'Brien's points. "Irish American" is a misleading label. O'Brien was a "Cork American." The Irish identified themselves by family, clan, townland, parish, or county. Maurice O'Sullivan in his wonderful *Twenty Years A-Growing* wanted it understood that "I am no Irishman . . . though I have Irish blood in me . . . I am a Blasket man." O'Sullivan's reference was to the Blasket Islands off the coast of County Kerry, no more than fifty miles from O'Brien's likely home village in Cork. It was on the Great Blasket that O'Sullivan found his home; from there that he took his identity. Irish blood was important, but it was not synonymous with an Irish nation. The far stronger association was with what Edmund Burke in 1790 had called the "little platoons" of Ireland, the leftovers of ancient faction fights. The more committed of the Irish nationalists in America railed against these local differences and reflexively wished them away. Historians are not allowed that privilege. Attention must be paid to those differences.[29]

So, too, those with Irish blood in them did not come to America but to New York; Worcester; Chicago; St. Paul; San Francisco; Melrose, Iowa; Butte, Montana; and thousands of other American places, large and small, East and West, rural and urban, industrial and agricultural. Each of these places had its own and distinct history and culture and its own civic identity. The Irish were not only well used to a local identity; their presence in each of those places played a critical role in the formation of it. Historians of Irish America are thus presented with constantly moving and often fragmented targets. Transporting a people and their culture— in this instance from the distinct parts of Ireland to the equally distinct parts of America—transfigured both cultures and produced a mix of Irish and American elements.[30]

This new hybrid culture, seasoned by the steady arrival of new immigrants from those multiple Irelands, was then passed down in various and altered states to succeeding generations, further mutating it. There was no straight-line cultural inheritance from one Irish American generation to the next. Add to that the commonplace reality that some Irish did well in America, some did not so well, while still others fared poorly. The first were often embarrassed by the third, who in their turn loathed the first. Those in the middle were hard pressed to know what to make of either. The result was ethnic fragmentation, centrifugal forces creating an Irish American world divided culturally, socially, and generationally. O'Brien seems to have felt those forces strongly.

Centripetal forces were at work as well. Each generation of immigrants and most of its sons and daughters continued to profess related faiths: Catholicism, some form of Irish nationalism, and a working-class consciousness. The ratios and percentages varied, but in every generation the Irish faced nativist and social-class prejudice as a consequence of each. Like everything else in Irish and Irish American worlds, history would work major changes in the secular faiths and minor changes in the religious ones, but the commitment to Irish nationalism would be as deep and as defining, and as oppositional in its visions and cultural effects, as the commitment to the church. As for their involvement in the fight for workers' rights—and, once again, O'Brien is an example—it sometimes buttressed, sometimes wrecked both.

The stages of Irish *emigration* were thus layered, overlapping, and regionally and socially selective phenomena. Countyism and the long-running nature of the Irish immigration were sources of ethnic division; Catholicism plus American anti-Catholicism, the often visceral connection to some abstract notion of "Ireland free," and the working-class culture shared by most were sources of ethnic solidarity. The stages of Irish *immigration* were similarly layered, overlapping, and selective, and for the same reasons of historical change and regional and social class distinctions. As each emigrant generation left a different Ireland, so each entered a different America, an America changed in some measure by previous Irish immigrations.

Thus did the history of America and the history of Ireland cross and conjoin. Each powerfully influenced the other. The Famine immigration coincided with the accelerated takeoff toward industrial capitalism. The agrarian distress in Ireland of the late 1870s and early 1880s contributed to a large emigration, O'Brien's included, that arrived just as the American economy was recovering from the devastating depression of 1873–78. The late immigrants arrived as the American economy was recovering from the even more devastating depression of 1893–97 and entering its fully mature industrial stage. During each of these eras, many Irish emigrant farmers became American immigrant workers.[31]

Let me make a brief general point. Historians are programmed to revise. It is their calling. The Great Hunger and the subsequent scattering of the Irish have come in for their share of revisionist attention. But no amount of revision can change the obvious: a million people should not have died in Ireland between 1846 and 1849. Two million more should not have been forced to emigrate. The Irish were never as desperately poor after the Hunger—the elimination of more than three million people from a population of barely more than eight million had a predictable effect—but they were not prospering and were often unable to keep their children. That said, Ireland's calamitous history had some quite unintended consequences. It aligned perfectly with America's takeoff to market capitalism. The axis of Irish history and that of American history came together and reinforced one another. The exodus from Ireland helped to fuel American industrialization, which, in turn, accelerated the exodus.[32]

There was a randomness to this historical intersection, but however haphazard the arrangement, the starving and abandoned island became a labor warehouse for the industrializing nation. Even when the intersection came to resemble a head-on collision, the reciprocity built into it was only marginally affected. The Irish may be forgiven if they missed some of the symmetry and balance of their emigration/immigration; they suffered cruelly at both ends of the process. Jonathan Swift's "Modest Proposal" suddenly had become less satirical; the industrializing economies of the Atlantic World were eating Ireland's young. Karl Marx's daughter Eleanor put the matter only slightly differently when she wrote that Ireland had become "the Niobe of the nations," a country that was weeping copiously for her sacrificed children. Her father was more specific; between 1855 and 1866, Marx wrote, "1,032,694 Irishmen were displaced by 996,877 cattle." O'Brien might well have been one of the million plus whose place was taken by a cow.[33]

Regardless of when they left Ireland and from where, regardless of where they went in America and how many boats it took them to get there, the Irish entered and became a part of an industrializing society, an America, according to Richard Slotkin, going through a "violent rite of passage between one stage of political-economic development and another." Industrialization was a transforming process and, like all such, a painful and unsettling one. It may well be that the modern project inverted, subverted, and/or perverted American republicanism, that the years from 1860 to 1900, as one writer recently put it, represented the "age of betrayal" of the republican values of the Revolution. "Taking off" occasioned big changes, and they could not be easily finessed.[34]

They could, however, be disguised and/or wished away. To this end and to an even greater extent than before, the West would become the protector of what still passed for republican virtue. As Slotkin has written, the "myth of the frontier" arose out of and became an indispensable part of "the age of industrialization." But which "frontier," the real one or the fanciful one? That question alone would have caused trouble enough. Compounding the issue was that there were two contradictory fairy-tales about the West. One emphasized its anarchic and violent—and hence manly and heroic—aspect. The other described its pastoral and edenic—hence domestic and mundane—aspect. It could not be both, at least not at the same time; in fact, it was neither. But myths die hard, and these hardest of all. Americans—but particularly easterners—clung to them tenaciously. "In [the easterners'] romantic view, the West was a . . . pristine world untouched by the . . . struggles" of the rest of an industrializing America.[35]

What further confused the issue was that the heroic myth—the "fatal environment"—placed or, rather, left the West beyond the pale, while the edenic myth positioned it at the center of the pale, indeed, as the heart of America. The West, wrote Theodore Roosevelt, wanting it both ways, was the home of the "true American." But who might he be? Roosevelt offered this list: "the Indian and the buffalo-hunter, the soldier and the cow-puncher . . . [the] reckless riders who unmoved looked in the eyes of life or of death. In that land we led a free and hardy life, with horse and with rifle. . . . We knew toil and hardship and hunger and thirst; and we saw men die violent deaths." That was a very odd and self-congratulatory definition of true Americanism. But then Roosevelt was only an occasional westerner. For a real one like William O'Brien, only the last sentence would have made sense.[36]

An Englishman, James Bryce, had a far truer understanding of the region than Roosevelt or any of his contemporaries did; truer because it cast O'Brien and his mates in central roles. The West, Bryce wrote, was "the most American part of America, the part where those features which distinguish America from Europe come out in the strongest relief." He was right about that, but not for the reasons Roosevelt had in mind. Bryce explained that it was not America's vaunted newness and innocence that the West revealed in strongest relief, but their opposites: "The heat and pressure and hurry of life always growing as we follow the path of the sun. In Eastern America there are still quiet spots. . . . In the West there are none." The West was to the East "what England [was] to the rest of Europe," bustling, noisy and noisome, grasping, a "whirlpool" of "reckless and heedless habits."[37]

All of this means that it would be useful to have some sense of where in America this unlovely West might be found. Unfortunately, drawing borders around ideograms is not a routine exercise. Fairy-tale lands are not easily placed within set geographical limits. The problem is compounded when, as was the case, the imagined West and the real West have different borders, or, as was also the case, when the West presents so bewildering an array of physical and environmental features. For these and a few other reasons, I think historians—and history—are better served by drawing temporal rather than spatial borders. The location of the West was a function of the timing of settlement and the changes over time of the ideas, policies, and cultural values that directed that settlement.

The West was formed by historically determined forces that can be analyzed. It would change internally, but it would not shrink or expand, which means that both process and place are important. The West of fact was a place; people lived and worked there. The West of the imagination was a mirage or, rather, a set of mirages. It was a frontier to be conquered; a meeting ground or a jousting field where the forces of civilization met those of savagery. It was a metaphor, a state of mind, a direction, a geographical ideogram, a symbol, a metaphysical construct, and a vision. At other times, it became a safety valve, a rural utopia, or an agricultural garden of delights. Historians must deal with both Wests, the real and the imagined, just as the Irish had to. Both were critical in forming the historical western province and the boundaries of time as well as space that defined and delimited it.[38]

If asked, then, whether a given place is in the West, let the response be: "When was this place settled?" rather than "Where was—or is—this place located?" This is not as eccentric as it might seem. David Hackett Fischer, for example, has argued that a "region . . . . might be defined primarily in historical terms, as a place in time" rather than "a physical entity formed by terrain, soil, climate, resources." Richard White is even bolder, insisting that "geography did not determine the boundaries of the West; rather, history created them." My Irish history begins in 1845, when the first rotten potato was dug out of the ground. My American history begins at the same time, at the beginning of the first stage of an industrializing process. I align the two histories. The American West was that part of the United States entered and settled by non-native peoples after 1845, the date that marked the beginnings of both the Great Hunger that pushed millions of Catholics out of Ireland and the "modern project," the great takeoff into industrial capitalism, that recast American ideas of republicanism, transformed the American economy, and redefined the role of the West in nurturing both.[39]

With that as introduction, what are the borders of the West beyond the 1845 meridian of time? They are slightly unconventional: based on when non-Indians began to enter and occupy the ground, the West's eastern edge starts at and includes the Upper Peninsula of Michigan and runs through northwestern Wisconsin. It takes in all of Minnesota and Iowa then proceeds southwesterly through the western half of Missouri (excluding St. Louis, which was settled long before 1845) and the westernmost section of Arkansas. From there it cuts diagonally across Texas, exiting the United States near Del Rio. There should be no dispute over the western border; the West, by definition, includes all the territory (Hawaii and Alaska included) lying west of that eastern border. On the north and the south, the American West ends at the Canadian and Mexican borders for the simple but compelling reason that Mexico and Canada, although they share similar environments with their nearest American neighbors (and despite the fact that O'Brien lived in both), had different—often distinctly different—histories.

As I define it, the region included parts of six states: Michigan, Wisconsin, Missouri, Arkansas, Oklahoma, and Texas. It included all of nineteen others: Minnesota, Iowa, Kansas, Nebraska, South Dakota, North Dakota, Montana, Wyoming, Colorado, New Mexico, Arizona, Utah, Nevada, Idaho, Washington, Oregon, California, Hawaii, and Alaska. I acknowledge some problems with this definition. First, if I were to be entirely consistent, I would have to include parts of Maine and Florida—but this would push the merely unconventional to the patently nonsensical. Second, Walter Nugent has argued that the West is the place where people who think of themselves as westerners live, and that could not be said of very many in the north woods of Michigan, Wisconsin, and Minnesota or even of the corn farmers of Iowa. I agree with Nugent's criterion.[40]

I would point out, however, that they may not have thought of themselves as western simply because the western myth was not applied to them. Theodore Roosevelt's "cowpunchers" and "restless riders" did not live there. Neither did John Wayne or the Marlboro Man, to make the myth somewhat more current. Historically, however, Iowans and Minnesotans did once think of themselves as western—we are back to the West as process again—and Roosevelt's cowboys were from the Dakotas, which are also frequently excluded from the West. Besides, "being western," or even thinking of oneself as western, was not as important as being subject to and constructed by certain historical forces—in this instance, the so-called modern project. Except that the word "frontier" creates problems of its own, I would call this West the "frontier that market capitalism made and made up."

By whatever name, this entire and contiguous region was settled and developed using some or all of the technological and professional advances of an industrializing society—by steamships, land and immigration agents, army personnel, dam builders, mining engineers, managerial elites, territorial administrators, and bureaucrats of myriad sorts. But mostly it was settled and developed by the railroad. In the words of Joseph Schumpeter, the "western and middle western parts of the U.S. were, economically speaking, *created* by the railroad." Schumpeter meant created economically, the physical act of building a social order. He was referring to the real West. I am as well. But I am also including those acts of creation that were literary, symbolic, and representational. In other words, I am referring to the figuratively as well as the literally created West—the myth as well as the reality. In both cases, it was a painful creation. To borrow the powerful imagery of Donald Worster, "far from being a child of nature, the West was actually given birth by modern technology and bears all the scars of that fierce gestation, like a baby born of an addict." I acknowledge the obvious: this constructed West was not a coherent whole. But neither was the postbellum American South, America's other historically constructed—or, in this instance, reconstructed—region.[41]

Also like the South, the West had a number of subregions; I count eight real ones as well as the two constructed ones previously identified, the edenic and the heroic. Not all of these subregions, both real and imagined, were geographically contained, and they all differed considerably from one another. But also like the subregions of the South, they were bound together by powerful historical forces. First was the corn-belt West of Minnesota, Iowa, western Missouri, and eastern Nebraska and Kansas. Moving west, the next two subregions are the wheat belt and the West of cattle and sheep. For these regions the old geographical borders are still definitive for the ecologically determined reason that both enterprises are unique to the traditional West. Fourth was the urban West, the one most favored by westering Irish. Western cities arose when and where they did because the production and movement of goods, the exchange of money, and the processing of new people—the imperatives of an industrializing society—required them.

The fifth subregion may be called the corporate/resource extractive West. It is this criterion that compels the inclusion of the Upper Peninsula of Michigan, the white pine forests of northern Michigan, Wisconsin, and Minnesota, and the Mesabi Range of northern Minnesota. The first industrial exploitation of the copper ores of the Upper Peninsula, the iron ores of the Mesabi, and the forests of the entire "North Country" began in the 1850s and represented the first incursion of white Americans into regions as undeveloped as any on the continent. Elizabeth Gurley Flynn, an Irish American radical with a fondness for western places, described the Iron Range as "like the primitive frontier days in the West . . . it was basic industry in the raw, in a rough wild country." This was in 1907.[42]

The sixth West was particularly important, particularly for the Irish, and it deserves more extended treatment. It arose directly from the fifth. The men and women who lived and worked in the corporate West shared the same culture of work, the same dependence on national and international markets for steady employment, and many of the same political and social ideas. Carlos Schwantes calls them part of a wageworkers' West consisting of two distinct classes: settled industrial workers—the homeguards—and transients—the bindlestiffs. These were distinctions based on timing of arrival, skill level, and social status. But they were also based on race and ethnicity. This was not a recipe for intraclass harmony. Rather it created the conditions for what Patricia Limerick calls the western "competition for legitimacy" at the intersection of "ethnic diversity and property allocation." The western wageworkers' frontier was more ethnically divided than any region in America, and capital played upon these divisions as imperial powers had once played upon the divisions among American Indians, or as Southern capital played on those between white and black—or as the English played on those between Irish Catholics and Irish Protestants.[43]

The pattern was not unlike that of the intertribal warfare among the Plains Indians for control of the buffalo grounds. I intend that more as an extended metaphor than as an analogy, but, that said, the wageworkers' frontier involved fierce interethnic warfare for the one resource the corporate West had: jobs digging rocks, laying rails, smelting ores, harvesting crops. Those jobs were as central to workers' lives as the buffalo herds were to those of the Lakotas or the Blackfeet. But I would stretch the metaphor even further: Western workers were often as seminomadic as the Lakotas and the Blackfeet. There were transient workers everywhere in industrial America, but they were a far more conspicuous part of the western workforce than the eastern one. All westerners were, or had been, transient or at least in transit, often moving in tribal or ethnic bands. The western workforce consisted of thousands of "industrial cowboys" (or Indians; the comparison fits almost as well) riding the rails from one mining town or lumber camp or corporate farming region to another.

The seventh and eighth subregions, like the urban, the corporate/resource extractive, and the wageworkers', are scattered and not contained within geographical borders. The seventh is obvious and routinely acknowledged: American Indians living on *tribal-based reservations,* the casualties of the righteous empire. The eighth is not so obvious, seldom acknowledged, and never acknowledged in quite this same way. My reference is to western *ethnic/religious communities,* both urban and rural. These enclaves were not unique to the West, but the western variety had more ethnic components and may have housed a larger percentage of the total population. To return to the extended metaphor above, there were some striking similarities between these ethnic clusters and Indian reservations.[44]

Clearly, nothing held these many Wests together except the timing of their occupancy. All were products of industrialization and were, in fact, themselves industrial, regardless of the nature of their economies. But this means as well that each of them was encased in myth; indeed, this West of the imagination might easily be appended as a ninth and tenth subregion, a constructed or invented province—either edenic or heroic—which bore faint if any resemblance to the real. That, it seems to me, is more than enough to tie together in one historical bundle everything west of the "1845 divide," from the northern forests to the tall-grass prairies and short- and mixed-grass Great Plains; from the Rocky Mountains to the Great Basin and the Southwest deserts; and from the Cascades, Sierras, and interior coastal ranges and valleys to the shores of the Pacific.

In many ways the most important of these Wests were the two that never existed: subregions nine and ten, the edenic and the heroic. The real West helped to create industrial America. Industrial America responded by creating the western legend. The ideological—they could almost be called psychological—resources of the western myth were among the most significant products of the takeoff and the industrialization consequent to it. What lends more interest to the myth was the fact that it contained elements that served the clearly defined interests of a range of social classes from the industrial elite to the emerging proletariat. The most careful student of the myth is Richard Slotkin. He quite correctly refers to western legends as key components in an emerging "bourgeois ideology." It was not an aspect of "a national folklore but the medium of the victorious party in an extended historical struggle generated by the social conflicts that attended the emergence of capitalist economies."[45]

It was certainly all of that. But the western myth was a supple and multisided phenomenon. It contained something for everyone. Capitalists may have favored those parts of it that offered clear counterrevolutionary alternatives to labor militancy; workers going west to pioneer rather than manning barricades, by way of obvious example. Those same workers, however, East and West, sorted through the myth and took different lessons from it. The image of wagon trains of eastern laborers docilely heading toward western farms was not just a myth created for purposes of social control. It was a pipe dream. More appealing to workers, particularly western workers, were the stories of outlawry, many of them as fictive as everything else in the catalog of western tall tales. Banditry had more glamor than sod-busting—and far more relevance to the nonascendant. The Irish favored those who were themselves Irish—or were said to be: the Doolin-Dalton gang, even Jesse James. These western American outlaws might not have had quite the dash of Ned Kelly, Australia's most famous Irish bushranger; but Irish epics were made to be embellished, and Doolin and the Daltons robbed trains with as much style as the Kelly bunch robbed banks. The western myth, however, did not serve class interests equally. Brigands ended up on the gallows; eastern laborers turned western farmers were monuments to American exceptionalism and righteousness.[46]

Making sturdy pioneers of surly proletarians was America's most impressive magic act. It was also one of its most important, particularly as the pace of industrialization accelerated after the Civil War. Whether that war was the last capitalist revolution can be debated. What cannot be debated is that the core values of the Republican Party were vindicated and that the Republicans were the party of capital as well as of emancipation. It was, in fact, their embrace of the former, and of the free labor market that it demanded, that gave rise to the latter. That "free-labor ideology" was dependent upon and sustained by the belief that the West was a place of infinite riches, both material and hegemonic, what I previously called psychological. As one writer has put it, "free land was . . . a prophylaxis against revolution." At least it was thought to be such.[47]

Listen to the following exchange between Thomas O'Donnell, an unemployed Irish mule spinner from Fall River, Massachusetts, and a member of a congressional committee investigating the deteriorating relations between labor and management. The year was 1883, but it could have been any time between 1845 and 1910. It was established that O'Donnell made about $150 a year and that he had to support himself and his wife and five children. O'Donnell was not certain how he could meet his responsibilities. One of the commissioners offered him a lesson in the political economy of the free labor system. "Why do you not go West on a farm?" he asked O'Donnell. "How could I go," O'Donnell replied, "walk it?" This is the exchange that ensued.

"Well, I want to know why you do not go out West . . . take up a homestead and break it and work it up, and then have it for yourself and family."

"I can't see how I could get out West. I have nothing to go with."

"It would not cost you over $1,500."

"I never see over a $20 bill, and that is when I have been getting a month's pay at once. If someone would give me $1,500, I will go."

O'Donnell was not threatening to lead a rebellion of disgruntled workers. He was more weary than mutinous. But I have to believe that America's corporate heads offered up the same lesson and that they were quite aware of how it might be used to suppress labor's insurgent instincts. Advising laborers to "go West and grow up with the country," as Horace Greeley did, was "as futile as a signboard pointing to the end of the rainbow." No one was going to give O'Donnell $1,500. The fact that he required it was evidence that he did not deserve it.[48]

In his wonderful book *The End of Hidden Ireland,* Robert Scally tells the painful story of the Irish in the townland of Ballykilcline during the Great Hunger of the 1840s. Scally is discussing the lesson plan and reading list for Irish children attending a British National School. The students were tested on subjects like "On Value" and "On Capital." In the latter course, they were told the story of the grasshopper and the bee, the moral of which was that "'those who do nothing but drink, and dance, and sing, in the summer, must expect to starve in the winter.'" This, Scally judges, must be counted among the "most . . . casually cruel of the fables of capitalism." I agree. It would have been that in the best of times. But I would contend that it had a close rival for casual cruelty in the uniquely American variation on the same theme, the fable that the solution to social class misery was migration to the West, not political reform and never militancy. To mix the fables, only the bees went West. That was one of the rules of engagement with second-chance countries. To change those rules was to change the nature of America's frontiers and leave them open to those who would defile them—the grasshoppers and all of those other summer-time drinkers, dancers, and singers.[49]

The West as a prophylaxis against revolution was the best known of the mythical powers assigned the region, but a number of other half-truths and nontruths arose from this central "myth of concern." Industrial safety valves, if they were to function properly, had to release the potentially mutinous into brave, new, and different worlds. Since the escape was from an urban and industrial East, that meant into a rural and small-town and agrarian West. This was where Americans would play out their second acts. But act two, if it were to have any meaning, could not be act one restaged with western set decorations. Recall that O'Donnell was not just advised to go west but to "take up a homestead." Shuffling him off to South Omaha to work in a packing house would have been of no use to him or to the cause of industrial peace. Similarly, dumping the unhappy workmen of the old America onto the semiarid and agriculturally barren lands of the new was no bargain either. Unfortunately, and contrary to the edenic myth, most of the West (particularly that part of it west of the 98th meridian) was, if not barren, far short of Arcadian. Western land promoters were undeterred, arguing that semiaridity was a transient annoyance and that constantly increasing rainfall would soon eliminate it. Casually cruel lessons and promises were not a monopoly of the British.[50]

Another of the component pieces of the frontier myth was that the West would be the place where true American values had freest play. By the 1840s the East was becoming ethnically polyglot and the South was irreversibly contaminated by slavery. As Samuel F. B. Morse graphically put it, there had been "a leak in the ship through which the muddy waters from without threaten to sink us." "From without" was the key; Morse was talking about Catholic, including Irish, "conspiracies" against American liberties. Fortunately, the leak could be patched— though it would take time and great effort to clarify the turbid water that had already contaminated the commonwealth. The immigrants who rushed in through the leak had to be assimilated, which, in the case of the Catholics Morse had in mind, meant converted. As for slavery, it would either be eradicated by external force or be destroyed by internal rot. But until those happy days, the hard truth was that the Northeast and the South had squandered their providential gifts and allowed themselves to become outlandish. Only the West remained pure and purely American.[51]

Of all the dreamlike descriptions of the West, this one was the most important, the most durable, and the most surreal. The real West was a place of many and mixed minds, the most ethnically and racially diverse of America's sections. It was also the most Catholic. In other words, even by the time Morse was writing, it was everything it could never be allowed to be. And it would only become more deviant in subsequent years. The result was regional schizophrenia, an identity crisis that must have left westerners wondering who they were, where they were, and how they were to reconcile what they knew with what they were told. Clearly, either they did not understand who they were or the easterners who limned them were delusional.[52]

In important ways, the California gold rush and the transcontinental railroad system, which California essentially called into being, were western America's dominant symbols as well as its inescapable reality. The West set the standard. Its settlement by Americans occurred at precisely the right time, for precisely the right reasons, and in precisely the right way. The takeoff had begun; the search was for gold; the settlement was chaotic if not anarchistic. The California template was broadly applied, particularly in the arid and semiarid sections of the West. In Walter Nugent's words, its "profile reappeared in a whole series of freshly discovered gold and silver bonanzas . . . for the next fifty years," including all of those on William O'Brien's world tour. In fact, it reappeared in a series of bonanzas of every sort, shape, and size. Mining was only the most obvious. The West of the "California model" was no place for Daniel Boone or for Jeffersonian yeomen marching last through the Cumberland Gap. It was rather a region where huge corporations hired tens of thousands from every corner of the globe to extract, process, and ship by rail the resources necessary to an industrializing society. California was the first of what would be many western anti-Wests.[53]

A great many of those early Californians were Catholic Irish. The real West was full of surprises; the percentage of papists of Irish descent was another of the unexpected and unwelcome realities of the Bonanza West. It may be difficult to define the borders of the West, but once they are defined, based on whatever criteria, it is not difficult to find the Irish and to establish an Irish regional presence that has previously been neglected. I am not suggesting, in the language of a recent and good book, that "the Irish won the West." The West was not "won," and the Irish knew better than to try to beat a place into submission. At that, however, they were far more active "pioneers" than has been previously acknowledged. "Western Irish American" is not an internally contradictory phrase. They may not have had any role in the West as imagined, but they had a starring one in the West as found; indeed, it was often they who found and/or founded significant parts of it.[54]

Whatever its exact "Irish Catholic quotient," however, the West had more of them than it was expected to have, and more of them than was thought good for it. Their presence in numbers, in fact, helps to explain some of the other areas where the West departed from what was expected of it. One obvious but unexpected characteristic was the number of Catholics. Another characteristic, but not so obvious, was the strange and unpredictable tendency to form western labor unions, which fluctuated wildly between militancy and pragmatism. This returns the story to William L. O'Brien. O'Brien seems not to have consciously identified himself on the basis of his Irishness, and certainly he did not identify himself on the basis of his presumed Catholicism or at least Catholic background. That, however, is not the point. What counts is that he would have found hundreds, even thousands of Irish at every one of his stopping-off places, the numbers varying only on the basis of the size of the mining camps in which he found himself. He could not have ignored the Irish even had he wanted to—and he may have. No western miner could have ignored them, and many clearly did want to. They were everywhere that rocks were being dug, and it is entirely likely that O'Brien was in Butte because of them.

It is certain that O'Brien was in Butte because it was industrial and provided jobs, not because it was in Montana and provided the promise of a farm. Butte was the ultimate anti-West; it violated every aspect of the western myth, mocked every pretension of the myth makers. It called itself "Butte, America," and that label alone, if even partly true (and it was more than that), was enough to have broken the heart of the eastern ascendancy. Montana was not supposed to have a Butte. It was supposed to look like Charlie Russell painted it, filled with cowboys, American Indians, horses, and bleached buffalo skulls. I wish that Russell had set up his easel on Big Butte and painted Butte's mines or on Smelter Hill and painted Anaconda's giant Washoe Smelter. I wish that he had painted O'Brien or someone like him, preferably Irish, being hoisted down into a working drift thousands of feet under the Montana ground. I wish, in other words, that he had painted Montana true.[55]

As already noted, the commissioners never asked O'Brien about any aspect of the contrast between the western promise and the western reality. He had opportunity enough to work a comment on myth and reality into his answers, but he did not take it. His testimony was laconic, even curt, and strangely passionless for all its bitterness. Fortunately, other Irishmen who spent time in Butte, including two "exiles of Erin" whom O'Brien almost certainly knew, were less restrained and considerably more poetic. Both composed their laments in the Irish language, describing their own experiences and those of thousands of other Irishmen like them. Their testimony should be entered into the record as necessary addenda to O'Brien's.

Seán Ruiséal (John Russell—the other Russell of this story) was a self-described *spailpín fánach* (itinerant worker). He admitted:

> I was too young to know what was good for me
> When I left lovely Ireland
> To walk the regions around Butte, Montana,
> Without a penny in the bottom of my purse. . . .
> it would be pleasant for me and my friends
> To be cosy back in Tralee
> Rather than wandering here like a helpless cripple,
> Without a woman to love me.[56]

In another poem Ruiséal wrote: "West to America I went / In my youth to hunt, / Looking for that well-known gold under the ground / On the slopes and edges of the mountains." He wanted it known by those considering emigration that

> The songs you'll most hear . . .
> Are the shouts and screams of the miners. . . .
> The boss will be standing there
> And next to him the lean foreman
> Driving all the wretches to work
> At the break of day.
> They'll soon take you down
> Where you can't see the light of day,
> And give you a shovel or a car
> Or a hammer or a little blunt axe;
> Your eyes will be blinded with dust
> At the break of day . . .
> It's a miserable way to earn a living
> For any strong, vigorous fellow;
> For you'll be so deep in the ground

That you'll never see the sun or the moon,
But only the light of the dim little candle in your hat
At the break of day.

Séamus Ó Muircheartaigh (James Moriarty), another *spailpín fanach,* told similar tales and like Ruiséal was in Butte during O'Brien's time in the mining city.

Alas that I ever came to this land,
And that I left my beloved Ireland behind. . . .
I well remember that fine fresh morning
When I bade farewell to my poor sad mother;
I never saw gold on the street corners—
Alas, I was a poor aimless person cast adrift.
That's how I spent part of my life,
Going from place to place, with no company at my side;
It's far better to be in Ireland.

I can imagine O'Brien feeling the same, even if he never expressed his feelings. Whether he also shared Ruiséal's and Ó Muircheartaigh's unstated but very real hatred of Britain for what they would have considered their forced exile is less certain; he was more a class than a national warrior.

But what truly distinguished Ruiséal's and Ó Muircheartaigh's poems is not that they were about Irish America but that they were about western America. Butte, Montana, was not the place to go to escape industrialism and its discontents. The same would have to be said of all the other of O'Brien's stopovers. Assuming that he knew something of the "promise of the West"—an altogether safe assumption—O'Brien and countless thousands of others, Irish and non-Irish, had been duped. That must have contributed to both the militancy and the pragmatism of the western American proletariat. Being exploited in the East was one thing; a worker could always escape to the West. That was the promise. Being exploited in the West left the disenchanted literally with no place to go. There was no relief to be found anywhere on earth.[57]

I remember well a conversation I had with the late Tony Lukas. He was working on the book that became *Big Trouble: A Murder in a Small Western Town Sets Off a Struggle for the Soul of America.* Mark particularly his insistence that the soul of the nation was being contested. He intended the book as the natural sequel to his prize-winning and brilliant *Common Ground: A Turbulent Decade in the Lives of Three American Families.* He wanted *Big Trouble* to do for social-class conflict what *Common Ground* had done for racial conflict, and he set about finding an event, an incident, a historical development that played out over time—anything in the nation's past that could be used to reveal the depth and the nature of social-class tensions in America. Because Lukas was a journalist, the field was open to him; he could have taken his topic from any place and any time.

Lukas chose the 1907 trial of three officers of the Western Federation of Miners for the murder of ex-governor Frank Steunenberg of Idaho. Steunenberg was killed in his hometown of Caldwell, Idaho; the trial took place in Boise; the Western Federation of Miners had been founded fourteen years earlier in Butte; its offices had only recently been moved from Butte to Denver. In other words, this battle for the soul of America not only had a western location but was at its core a western story. I had the chance to ask Lukas how he came to find the trouble he was looking for in Boise. In the usual way of journalists, he said. He began reading generally about the history of American workers. He then put together a list of a dozen possible topics and read carefully the secondary literature on each. He pared his list to six, read some more, then cut the list to three and finally to the one. Lukas was a New Yorker. He had seldom even traveled west, and he was utterly unprepared for where his search was taking him. Of the first twelve events, ten took place west of the Mississippi; of the second six, all were western.[58]

Lukas also said that he was looking for a topic that had not received the attention it deserved and for one that had dramatic as well as historical significance. This one was surely all of that. The defense was lead by Clarence Darrow; the prosecution by William Borah. One of the three defendants was "Big Bill" Haywood, who even then had an undeserved reputation for being one of western labor's hard men. Steunenberg, a Democrat and presumed friend of the working class, had turned against labor when he called out the National Guard during the 1899 strike in Idaho's Coeur d'Alene mining district. The Western Federation of Miners, led by the Irish-born Ed Boyce, accused him of the basest betrayal of principle. Six years later—or so it was alleged—the WFM got its revenge when Haywood and the other two officers hired Harry Orchard, western roustabout and general badman, to kill Frank Steunenberg.

Steunenberg certainly died violently enough to make the story interesting; he was bushwhacked, blown up by a bomb attached to the gate post of his house. Throw into the mix an astonishing array of characters—perjurers, informers, disappearing witnesses, industrial spies, a glamorous actress on tour, even a promising young baseball pitcher. Reporters came from every corner of America to cover the trial, and all, especially those on the political left, were stunned, maybe even a little disappointed, when the jury of tobacco-spitting Idaho farmers, after weeks of testimony in a sweltering Boise courtroom, found the three WFM officers innocent. The story was irresistible even without its western setting. Plot lines and characters aside, however, I repeat an earlier point: Lukas had winnowed the field looking for a contest of classes that might reveal the "soul" of industrial America. He found western stories; he selected one of the wildest of them, rendered it honestly and gracefully, and, in the process, shredded what was left of the western master narrative.

I never talked to Lukas about the other five events on his short list, except to learn that Butte during the years of its labor violence, strikes, and military "occupation" from 1912 to 1920 was one of them. But Lukas had an almost limitless range of western topics that he might have chosen, and I like to imagine that his list looked something like this: the 1910 bombing of the *Los Angeles Times* building, allegedly by the Irish American McNamara brothers; the 1916 Preparedness Day violence in San Francisco and the trial of the Irish American radical Tom Mooney; the general strikes in Minneapolis, Seattle, and San Francisco, the only such events in American history; the western "battalions" of Coxey's Army, larger and more militant than those of any other region. In fact, Lukas could have selected from scores of strikes, lockouts, deportations, and killings in the Coeur d'Alene mining district in Idaho; on the Minnesota Iron Range and in the copper towns of Michigan's Upper Peninsula; in Cripple Creek, Telluride, Leadville, and Ludlow, Colorado; in Bisbee, Jerome, and Morenci, Arizona; Goldfield, Nevada; Wheatland, California; Butte and Anaconda, Montana; Everett and Centralia, Washington. And this is a partial list.[59]

I would add, as Lukas did, other forms of western rebelliousness from agricultural protest movements like populism and the Nonpartisan League to western range wars. With the possible exception of the South, agrarian discontent was greater and more menacing in Minnesota, Kansas, Iowa, the Dakotas, West Texas, and Oklahoma than anywhere else in the nation—and that fact only strengthens the case for the West as the place where the dark soul of industrial America was most clearly and starkly exposed. The Irish presence in these western rural protests was less obvious, but only because there were fewer of them on the West's farms than in its mines and factories. At that it would be a mistake to ignore the Irish strain in American rural radicalism and its efforts to reach some sort of accord with the urban working class. Ignatius Donnelly's entire and long political career was spent inveighing against the exploiters of farmers and workers. Other Irishmen like James Manahan, Patrick Rahilly, and James Loftus gave Donnelly stout support in Minnesota, the only state where farm-labor movements came and—with a few fits and starts—stayed together.[60]

Consider, too—as Lukas did—the genuinely radical Industrial Workers of the World. The IWW was born in Chicago, but it was conceived in Butte. It arose from the Western Labor Union and the American Labor Union, both headquartered in Montana's mining city. The IWW organized from Massachusetts to California, but its lineage was western and its most militant actions took place in the West; indeed, it is hard to imagine it in any but a western setting, including a western agricultural setting where the IWW formed the Agricultural Workers' Organization in an effort to mobilize transient farm workers as well as a bronco busters union to represent western cowboys. The other important point is that if Lukas had chosen from any of the above, he would also have found—as he did in his Boise tale—a clear and unmistakable Irish presence.[61]

To understate considerably, "big trouble" is the last thing Americans were looking for when they looked westward. They expected to see—had been trained to see—billowing fields of grain; fat livestock; eastern workers throwing down their dynamite and picking up the plow; happy, barefoot, uniquely American boys with cheeks of tan; and Protestants. That all of these were to come from a region to which the vast majority of Americans would never go and about which a significant percentage knew very little adds to the West's significance. It was a mysterious place of talismanic powers—and, like most such places, the more one knew about it, the less magical and potent its gifts. The West was a national hallucination. That hallucinatory aspect, however, became an integral part of the real. To say that the imagined variant had a stronger and more durable hold on the American mind would be true, but this would be an incomplete version of the truth: the imagined was the true.[62]

But the West of romance and escape was not simply mythical. All peoples have myths of origin and development; they are the "lies that tell the truth," revealing much of the society that needed and created them. The Americans who went west after 1845, however, were not always the authors of their own legends. The western myths had gotten there before them. They arose from a variety of sources: dime novels as well as more "serious" literature; Wild West shows; explorers' journals; guidebooks and gazettes; travelers' accounts; art, including Russell's and Frederic Remington's; autobiographical fantasies; tall tales from the gold rush; and newspapers. As a character in the short story "The Man Who Shot Liberty Valance" told a newspaperman, "This is the West, sir. When the legend becomes fact, print the legend." Some of this myth-making was purposeful, some inadvertent; but either way, the mythical West accurately described eastern fears and ambitions, not western realities. It met eastern needs, not western ones, and was imposed upon the region by eastern patricians who did not live there and had no intention of moving there. Thus the nature of the imagined West would change depending on what easterners needed it to be. By as early as the 1880s, they needed it to be the cowboy West, the home of individualism, integrity, and indomitable courage. The two-boat Irish would have to adjust and accommodate themselves to both Wests. The real one presented its own set of problems, but the imagined one could never be totally ignored.

There was a certain unfairness in this. Imposing myths, assigning a role for a geographical space in advance of the settlement of that space, is clearly a form of colonization if not imperialism. Westerners would have been better served had they been allowed to design their own myths of origin and development. Legends that arise indigenously are no less "false" than those that are imposed externally, but they do at least spring from native soil and reflect, albeit in distorted or exaggerated ways, the society that composed them and passed them down. The western myth was not simply false. It was purposefully contrived. Its function was to settle the jangled nerves of an eastern cultural elite by providing it with cowboy campfire tales of a heroic time and place that was not industrial or urban or filled with mongrel "races." There were no William O'Brien types living there. It is the case that westerners contributed to the myths, both as they promoted the settlement of their region and as they reminisced about their pioneering pasts—the first an act of prophecy, the second of memory.[63]

Whether predicting or remembering, however, westerners gave often unconscious voice to what nonwesterners had said first and most wanted to hear. When a professor of classics at Harvard described the West in 1842 as a place where "each man is himself a sovereign by indefeasible right, and has no idea that another is his better in any one respect," he said far more about himself, Harvard, and Boston than about any known West. That was also true of Theodore Roosevelt and others of the eastern establishment when they grandiloquently trumpeted their western adventures. If the matter could have been left at that, these would simply have been examples of eastern silliness; the problem was that westerners heard these stories so often that some of them came to believe and repeat them. At that moment, what had been merely silly became also sad.[64]

By 1880 if not sooner, the American West had become a place where memory and history did not coincide. For all the eastern claims that the West was the key to America's future, it was always the eastern version of that future that was at stake. The West was not central but instrumental; its "history" would be written somewhere else and would ultimately be about someone else. The somewhere else, the "colonial" power, was the eastern United States going through the birth pangs of industrialization and the divisive debates with Southern slaveholders and Northern labor that accompanied that industrialization. In this context—and others—the East was Slotkin's "victorious party" in the conflicts that were part of the growth of industrial capitalism.

The guardians of free markets and free labor would win both wars. One of them, the competition with the South, had been fought over the control of the West, and the victors claimed the western regions as spoils of war. The other, the labor wars, required the defense and consolidation of that control. The new American ascendancy would make the western myth its medium, the instrument of its victory. It is in this context that the reconstructed life of William L. O'Brien ·must be considered. Everything about his testimony before the Commission on Industrial Relations was misaligned with the western myth and the master narrative that arose from it. I include Butte itself on that list of the misshapen and misplaced; consider its mile-deep mine shafts and 10,000 miles of underground— sometimes far underground—drifts and stopes; the radical industrial unionism of the IWW; the dynamiting of the Butte Miners Union Hall; the ethnic diversity and the ethnic—read tribal—conflict among the Irish, Finns, and Serbo-Croatians; the Irish-dominated politics. Finally, find a place in the West as imagined for Butte's fifteen Catholic parishes in a town of fewer than 60,000 people.

Much of this was known by 1914 when the commission came to Butte and talked with O'Brien and the other parties in Butte's industrial tensions (which were to escalate to full-scale industrial war over the next six years). But the mythical West was still a potent symbol of American identity, and it is unimaginable that the commissioners were completely free of its influence, whether consciously or not. Maybe, had they been able to get Charlie Russell's Montana out of their minds and replace it with Seán Ruiséal's, the commissioners would have asked O'Brien more searching questions. As it was, the western reality had became the aberrant form; neither O'Brien nor Butte had any business being in the West. They were phantoms in Charlie Russell's Montana, and the commissioners, like most of America, did not know how to deal with phantoms.[65]

CHAPTER 2

Irrepressible Conflicts

Systems of Slavery in the Civil War Era

"Never have I known the world without,
Nor ever stray'd beyond the pale."

—Alfred, Lord Tennyson, "The Holy Grail"

The emergence of national states and the system of industrial capitalism that later sustained and was sustained by them are among the most important and best-chronicled developments of modern history. These were the large structural adjustments, the "big changes" that defined Europe and later America. Since none could entirely escape them, one of the important questions confronting historians is trying to understand how the people lived those big changes. The ascendant classes lived them willingly, expectantly, even covetously. It was they, after all, who had initiated the changes and directed them in their own interests. The ordinary people, on the other hand, often lived the changes reluctantly and by not themselves changing very much, which makes for some interesting history. Their lives provided an often discordant counterpoint to the triumphalist narratives of the elite. Understanding those lives presents a different set of issues and problems.[1]

Beginning in the sixteenth century, the governing classes in Europe started to identify themselves on the basis of their participation in and allegiance to their nation and its institutions. It may now be debated if these nations were political contrivances—imagined communities that manufactured cultural particularities—or the parent lands of the "volk"—genuine reflections of distinct cultural identities already in place. This was seldom debated at the time the states were formed. Nations had a distinct cultural identity; they did not create that identity but were created by it. This was true, moreover, even in colonial or client states; indeed, it was an insistence on separate identities that gave legitimacy to many colonial rebellions and to the postcolonial nation building that followed the successful ones.[2]

These are important and tangled questions. Some of them may be skirted; they are far beyond the reach of this study. Others, however, must be addressed. The historical lines of two of those distinct national groups converged in the mid-nineteenth century, with profound effects on both. The two peoples were the Irish and the Americans. Like many of the stories that involve them, this one begins in the home country of neither, but in England/Britain, at one time the colonial master of both. As has already been alluded to, Britons, that assortment of English, Scots, and Welsh, were held together as a national people by their shared Protestantism. In the words of Linda Colley, "the invention of Britishness . . . was bound up with Protestantism." Britons "defined themselves as Protestants. . . . The Protestant world view was so ingrained in [their] culture that it influenced people's thinking irrespective of whether they went to church or not, . . . read the Bible or not, or whether, indeed, they were capable of reading at all." This was a multidenominational Protestantism with deep divisions within it, with such revolutionary consequences that it may be said that what truly held Britain together was not Protestantism but the intense and abiding hatred of Catholicism that was both cause and effect of it, whatever its denominational form.[3]

A second point arises from this first: the essential Protestantism and anti-Catholicism of the emerging British state found institutional expression and new sources of energy in the British monarchy and the British Empire. It is the latter that is of greater interest here. Building, defending, and managing empires put the British people and state in constant contact with those who were outlandish—non-British, non-Protestant, or nonwhite. And these outlanders, both near and far from the metropolis that invented them, were the "fringe" players, the people of the "peripheries" who provided the inverse mirrors with which the British tested and validated both their Britishness and their Protestantism. Included, sometimes prominently, in this list of the outlandish were the Catholic people of Ireland.[4]

But the imperial connection, however unequal the power relations, determined the self-understanding of the colonized as well as that of the colonizer. If the British invented and came to understand themselves as non-Irish and non-Catholic, then Irish Catholics came to understand themselves as non-British and quite Catholic and to invent an Irish nation, or at least an Irish identity, based in part on that understanding. The Irish clung desperately to this identity. It was all they had. But it was also something no one else had, and it could not be taken away. To call this a formula for clannishness is to understate. It was a formula for a profoundly exclusionary mentality that bordered on the xenophobic. But how could it have been otherwise? The resistance of conquered peoples whose lands were taken and colonized often took the form of dividing the world into the "we, who are the people" versus the "others, who are not." That required an Irish Catholic refusal to internalize any part of the culture of their British Protestant conquerors. The Irish continued to sing their own songs, dance their own dances, play their own games, and practice with even greater fervor their own religious faith. Success in achieving this separateness was usually mixed, but in all cases the culture of the imperial conquerors was the referent, the model of how not to behave and believe.[5]

There was, then, an entire culture of conquest and a separate and subaltern culture of being conquered, in this instance a culture of British Protestantism and another one of Irish Catholicism. For the Irish, however, the most essential of their "weapons of the weak," the Gaelic Irish language, came to be so severely compromised as to be nearly valueless. The British proscribed the use of Irish, as they did Irish songs, dances, and games. This "linguistic imperialism" also compelled the British to remap Ireland and rename everything in it. Mountains and hillocks, roads and coves, places the Irish had known all their lives, had new names and hence new histories and identities. This was more than just disorienting. It was disinheriting. The Irish almost literally did not know where they were or— and as a result—who they were. It made them "cultural emigrants," men and women who had "moved in their minds" long before they moved in space.[6]

They filled the cultural void with a devotional Catholicism, an attachment to the more recondite practices of the faith, in the process putting even more distance between their own religious lives and those of the Protestants who ruled them. That devotional form of Irish Catholicism, with origins that antedated the starving times of the late 1840s, replaced the Irish language as the principal expression of difference and the surest way to keep Ireland Irish, which was to say not English. Irish images of the past had been possessed and contained in vernacular speech. Now they were expressed in religious faith. Irish and Catholic became blurred, almost a single word denoting a recognizable cultural, social, and political type. Catholicism had become a national as well as a religious question. In the language of the contemporary Irish journalist Fintan O'Toole, the words "Irish Catholic" had "come to stand for some third thing born out of the fusion of the other two." As a result, Irish nationalism created not dead heroes but martyrs, and it demanded a violent retribution for their martyrdom. The public statements of Irish nationalists read like prayers, the supplications of mendicants rather than the manifestos of politicians. The English did not understand this, could not comprehend that the Irish had become their bad seed.[7]

The Americans understood these Irish no better than the British did—which brings us to the third set of players. Americans, David Hackett Fischer has argued, were "Albion's [good] Seed"; the sheer Englishness of American culture was everywhere apparent. It follows that since religion, in the sectarian shape of Reformed

Christianity, was the ultimate source of that Englishness, it was also the most important of the cultural folkways transferred from Britain to its American colonies. Americans were at least as self-consciously Protestant as any Briton, and the Revolution that took America out of Britain's empire arose in no small measure because of, not despite, that self-consciousness. Colley, in fact, refers to the Revolution as a "*civil war.*" Kevin Phillips goes further than that; he calls it a "cousins' war." Edmund Burke had it right when he wrote that all Protestantism was "a sort of dissent," but the Protestantism of Britain's American colonies was "a sort of dissidence of dissent, and the Protestantism of the Protestant religion." In time, Americans would come to take their identities from their westering as well as from this dissidence of dissent, but before the "significance of the frontier in American history"—to steal a phrase—and its significance in the formation of the American identity can be understood, the initial Protestant nature of that identity needs to be acknowledged and developed.[8]

Americans, moreover, did not become less self-consciously dissenting Protestant in breaking away from England. The Revolution was preceded and animated by an evangelical revival, and it never lost its near-apocalyptic Protestant aspect. Wars against monarchies involved, implicitly and explicitly, wars against religious monarchs. The Spirit of '76 was a rearguard action against Rome as well as London, against popes as well as kings. No wonder that in England the American Revolution was known as "a Presbyterian war." Lyman Beecher, who would have known, called the Revolution a religious revival, as well as a political revolt; and though grateful for the support provided by nominally Catholic France, American revolutionaries were not likely to become careless and forgetful of the Protestant purposes for which they fought. This is not to dispute the powerful assist given to the revolutionary impulse by the aggressively secular dogma of the Enlightenment—which included its own anti-Catholic credo—but simply to acknowledge the potency of dissenting Protestantism in shaping the ideology of revolution.[9]

The colonial response to the Quebec Act of 1774 was the perfect expression of this mix of Protestantism and westward expansion as the twin sources of an emerging American republican identity. By this act, the British Parliament extended religious toleration to French Catholics in the trans-Appalachian region. Popery was now at colonial Americans' western borders, blocking not only their way but their mission, imperiling not only the size of their purses but their very sense of themselves. Tom Paine, for whom anti-Catholicism came easily, was certain that the Quebec Act meant that "Popery and French laws in Canada are but a part of that system of despotism which has been prepared for the colonies," and Paine's reference was to what America would become as well as to what it was. Another patriot protested that the Quebec Act meant that "we may live to see our churches converted into mass houses and our lands plundered . . . for the support of the

Popish clergy." If nothing else, the Quebec Act represented a violation of the king's coronation oath to "maintain the protestant reformed religion." Its effect, said another rebel, was to make "friends with Babel's scarlet whore."[10]

More official remonstrances were less unrestrained but no less determined. The Declaration and Resolves of the First Continental Congress made specific reference to "the act . . . for establishing the Roman Catholick Religion." The Quebec Act did not establish Catholicism; it merely tolerated it. Even this was too much for the Continental Congress, which, in its declaration of the "Causes and Necessity of Taking Up Arms," spoke of Catholic Quebec as "a despotism dangerous to our very existence . . . erected in a neighbouring province." Thomas Jefferson, in the most famous of America's revolutionary declarations, used similar language and the same prophetic style. The king, he wrote, had abolished "the free System of English Laws in a neighbouring Province, establishing therein an Arbitrary government, . . . the fit instrument [of] absolute rule." It was beside the point that this instrument was outside the colonies, that there was no British effort to force the established Protestant colonies east of the Appalachians to tolerate Catholicism, and that the Quebec Act did not interfere with the rights of Protestants to enter Quebec. Quebec was in the path of American westward expansion, blocking access not only to the land but to America's righteous future. The toleration of Catholicism within its borders effectively closed it off to a people who defined themselves in considerable measure on the basis of their hostility to "Babel's scarlet whore."[11]

This fierce colonial resistance to the Quebec Act—and that act may have evoked more passionate protest than anything else Britain did in the run-up to the Revolution—gave very early expression to the foundations of American identity, to its sustaining spirit, and to its most obvious feature. Protestantism fit as snugly with republican America's western expansion as with monarchical Britain's world-girdling empire. America's emerging sense of itself had two quite compatible and related wellsprings: the Protestantism it inherited from Britain and the West it inherited from God. These were not rival claimants for the American soul but perfectly coordinated aspects of the same phenomenon. The American response to the Quebec Act reflected this still-developing sense of national identity and of the importance of the West to and as the nation's future.

That future as surely as the colonial past and the revolutionary present had to be kept unsullied. The Constitution itself, writes one historian, "was permeated with Protestant assumptions about history and society." The moral characteristics of religious belief and political ideology were fused, the linkage, as another recent historian has put it, "of American Protestantism and American republicanism." And when it came time in 1790 for the young Republic to decide who might legally immigrate to it, very serious consideration was given to the congressional motions to exclude Catholics. America needed their labor; it needed everyone's labor. "Tolerance" for Catholics belongs under the same heading as tolerance for slavery; both were "necessary evils." There would be Catholics in America, but they would not be of it. They could sit at the table of the American future, but only after they had served the meal and then only to eat the leftovers. The nation's secular holy days not only did not include them, they tacitly and sometimes overtly excluded them. Catholics, writes Robert Wiebe, were among "democracy's outcasts."[12]

By the 1830s it was accepted almost without question that the destiny of America was to remain Protestant and that this destiny would be revealed, literally made manifest, in the West. The spread-eagled expansionism of the period from 1803 to the Civil War made clear that a Protestant republic might trace its origins to Albion, but it would find its next and greater chapter inscribed in the newest parts of the New World. Alexis de Tocqueville wrote of those Americans who "plung[ed] into the West," observing that "the people of the United States [are] that portion of the English people who are commissioned to explore the forests of the New World," as neat a balancing of the internal and external sources of American identities as one could want. It is also the case that Tocqueville did not exclude Catholics from joining in the exploration of those forests, but this was a wayward opinion. The prevailing notion was that new men lived in new lands; that, in fact, the new lands created the new men, and that to be American was to fit oneself into a narrative of a national republic with its western reaches as well as its Protestant values as spiritual mainsprings.[13]

Tocqueville, moreover, was speaking more of the transfer of continental European Catholicism to America than of the transfer of the Irish; and when Irish Americans were factored in, they were of that pre-Famine immigrant generation that would appear almost genteel in comparison to the Irish who would follow it. Tocqueville would not have been so sanguine had he known that it was the devotional Famine and Post-Famine version of Irish Catholicism that would be imported to the American Republic. Two years after his visit to the United States, he paid a call on Ireland and reported in his notes on the condition and prospects of its people. He was appalled by the poverty of the Irish tenants and the wretchedness in which they lived. But at no time did he imagine that this squalid peasantry would ever make its way to America or that its attachment to the church, which he described as deeply affectionate, would soon become politically ferocious. He never linked his two books, never asked what might happen if impoverished Irish were to collide with American democracy, whether in the settled cities of the seaboard or the primordial forests of the interior. We may make that connection for him: Catholicism abstractly, even theologically, defined might survive in the New World republic, but that could not be said of its Irish variant.[14]

In all events, Tocqueville's was a distinctly minority voice. With the exception of Catholic prelates like the Irish-born bishop of New York, John Hughes, the only prominent American who spoke to the compatibility of Catholicism and American values was Orestes Brownson, a convert to Catholicism and a renegade, if not eccentric, thinker who essentially spoke only to himself. Americans, quite explicitly and self-consciously, continued to base their values and their institutions on a firm rejection of what they perceived to be Catholic and to insist that from the 1830s forward, "the American truth [was] . . . a distinctly Protestant one." Catholicism embodied traits that were squarely antithetical to American ideals, particularly as those ideals were subtly redefined and given increasingly frontier origins under the misleading label of Jacksonianism. Catholicism stood American values, by whatever name, on their head. The Catholic Church would impose rules on a ruleless society; restraints on a people in conscious flight from restraint. Even the symbols and iconography of the church seemed threatening. Catholicism was apostolic, hence hierarchical; it was Trinitarian, hence irrational; it gave its priests unlimited authority, hence was deterministic. It inhibited individual freedoms and rejected out of hand both the idea that freedoms were unalienable and that this or anything else was self-evidently true.[15]

Of the two Frenchmen who commented on American political culture in the 1830s, it was not Tocqueville but the lesser-known Michael Chevalier who spoke most directly to these points. I do not mean to suggest that Americans took their political cues from Frenchmen, however favorably disposed they may have been to American institutions; but Chevalier's comments reflected the way America's revolutionary legacy would be extended to a postrevolutionary society that would face severe challenges to that legacy. American republicans had never made fine distinctions between political and religious liberty and were not about to begin now; the two were, and were to remain, indistinguishable. Chevalier seemed to understand this intuitively: "There must be harmony between the political and religious schemes that are suited to any one people. Protestantism is republican; Puritanism is absolute self-government in religion and begets it in politics. The United States are Protestant. Catholicism is essentially monarchical."[16]

Chevalier doubtless had French Catholicism in mind when he offered his remarks. But other Catholic people, conspicuously the Irish, though they might display their faith less grandly, were no less obedient and thus no less subservient. "In countries which are Catholic," he continued, "a regular democracy is impracticable." The attempt to "apply . . . the political institutions of Protestant countries" to "Catholic nations" produced only "anarchy" and "bitter regrets." It may safely be assumed that the application of Catholic institutions to Protestant nations would be equally disastrous. As Chevalier concluded, "Protestantism, republicanism, and individualism are all one." He should have added "western expansionism" to his list of self-reinforcing values; perhaps he did not because he sensed that it was too imperial to comport well with republicanism. At that, his was a tidy synopsis.[17]

The advancement of Chevalier's Trinitarianism was America's revolutionary mission. Like all revolutions this one had its key players. Martin Luther was its "Mirabeau . . . Henry VIII was the Robespierre and the Napoleon." In other words, republicanism was a blended product, a mix of the secular and the divine. And, as with so much else in the American polity, it was a legacy of the Americans' Britishness, another offshoot of Albion's seed. "England," Chevalier explained, "was . . . big with those habits of industry and order. . . . Her children . . . carried with them the germ of those principles and institutions which were to secure to them . . . supremacy in the New [World]." This was especially the case with the American farmer, even more particularly the farmer who had moved deepest into the western interior. He was the most favored of the nation's children; he instinctively and "harmoniously combined in his mind . . . the doctrines of moral and religious independence . . . with the . . . more recent notions of political freedom." These were the basic components of the modern age. The American farmer had absorbed them all. "He is one of the initiated." Chevalier was writing more than a decade before the Great Hunger drove Irish by the millions to the United States, but nothing happened in Ireland during that decade that bestowed rites of "initiation" on Catholics. The radical, nearly utopian, vision of American republicanism could not be cut and tailored to fit everyone.[18]

These references to Catholicism as slavery were not intended metaphorically. Many Americans saw the Catholic Church in the same way they saw chattel slavery, whether in the abstract or as it manifested itself in the American South, and they used the same language in their attacks on both. I should say at the outset that it is too easy to dismiss the attacks on Catholicism and Catholics as well as the association of the church with slavery as parts of an irrational "Protestant crusade" or as the inevitable consequences of a "paranoid style." The truth, however, is that the Catholic Church was in fact almost totally incapable of comprehending the least part of America; it would concede nothing to these impious and insolent Americans. Pope Gregory XVI's 1832 denunciation of liberty of conscience as an "insanity" simply cannot be reconciled with anything Ralph Waldo Emerson ever wrote or with any part of Walt Whitman's self-reliant singers of self. Similarly, the Syllabus of Errors of 1864 and the 1870 Proclamation of Papal Infallibility cannot be adjusted to fit the Gettysburg Address. The fact that the Catholic Church identified the entire United States as "missionary" territory until 1908 speaks volumes.[19]

Some of the attacks on Catholicism arose from an uncomplicated religious prejudice and nothing more. But that cannot be said of all of them. It was easy enough, without any ascription of religious prejudice, for Protestant Americans to believe that republicanism and Catholicism simply could not coexist. But even if this were not the case, it would be impossible to distinguish between mindless

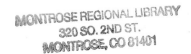

prejudice and thoughtful concern. It is safer to state the matter simply and without interpretive adornment: many Americans saw Catholicism and slavery as kindred both in their sinfulness and in their incompatibility with republicanism.[20]

Anti-Catholicism, moreover, was by far the more long-standing of the two "reforms." This is where the argument that race defined antebellum Americans misses an important point. Race was only part—and not always the "prevailing" part—of the vernacular of American citizenship. America was a republic, and that republic was inspired and girded by Protestantism as surely as by whiteness, by faith as surely as by race. Skin color became a politically loaded issue only when light-skinned papists began either to wash ashore or to be absorbed. By 1850, reflecting the enormous immigration from a starving Ireland and the annexation of the Southwest from Texas to California, Catholics were the largest denomination in the country. That did not matter—except to heighten the fears of the nativists. Not only did these Catholics have no claims on what was a Protestant republic, but they were outside it, were in fact its potential subverters.[21]

So, of course, were the slaveholders of the South, overwhelmingly Protestant and, in their minds at least, heirs of the Revolution as surely as Northerners. Clearly, by the 1840s many Northerners were of a different mind, often reviling Southerners in the name of that same revolutionary tradition and in the same language they used to describe Catholicism. "Slavery," said Anson Burlingame, ". . . denies the right of a man to his body." "Priestcraft," he added, ". . . denies . . . the right of a man to his soul." "American Republicanism is FREEDOM," wrote Thomas Whitney in 1856. "Romanism is *slavery*." That put the matter bluntly. Slavery and Catholicism had become metaphors for each other. Whitney, however, was speaking generally if not abstractly. His indictment was not offered up in the context of *Southern* slavery or *Irish American* Catholicism.[22]

Some of Whitney's abolitionist colleagues were more direct, their correlation of slavery and Catholicism more to the point of the emerging crisis between North and South and the coincident arrival of hundreds of thousands of ramshackle Irish. Theodore Parker, one of the most erudite of the Protestant antislavery reformers, wrote in 1850 that Catholicism meant "material and spiritual despotism." The ideas of the pope are "*pre-medieval*. He . . . can no more escape from being a reactionary and a despot than the Devil can help promoting *sin*." Fortunately, the nineteenth century belonged to Protestantism, and "the ideas of [that] century [will] shake his Pontifical State to pieces . . . his spiritual power will be worth little, except," Parker could not resist adding, "with the Paddies in Ireland." Seven years later Parker was even more direct. "There were two charges to be met," he insisted, "the *despotic Church* of the Irish, and the *despotic State* of the slaveholder." The issue for Parker and the many others of like mind did not require sophisticated analysis. In 1856 another abolitionist, Samuel Busey, drew the obvious conclusion that "a conflict must come."[23]

There was a lot of that kind of talk in America in 1856, much of it coming from abolitionists like Parker and Busey. The conflict that must come was between freedom and slavery. That was as elemental as it could be. The fact that Busey was not referring to the North and the South but rather to the inevitable conflict between Catholic and Protestant did not make it any less so. The issues were the same in both contests: Christian perfection versus the anti-Christ. Both would be bloody and to the death, as befitted Armageddon. As Edward Beecher put it, "one must exterminate the other." He, too, was talking about Protestant freedom and Catholic slavery. These predictions came only two short but busy years before William Seward referred to the conflict between North and South as "irrepressible." Obviously, Seward's was the more accurate prediction. Houses divide in different ways, however—to borrow from Lincoln's metaphorical reference. The nation could not survive "half slave and half free," but the years of sectional crisis were marked by sectarian as well as sectional hostility; and there were many who doubted the nation's ability to survive half Protestant and half papist—allowing in both instances for some imprecision in the assignment of shares.[24]

In 1856, just two years before Seward's "irrepressible conflict" speech, in a remarkable letter to Senator Charles Sumner, Theodore Parker revealed a means of dealing with both forms of slavery. He argued that the Constitution guaranteed to each state a "republican form of Government," a clause that put slavery "as completely in the power of Congress as it puts Papism." In a passage reminiscent of the Continental Congress's reminder to the Crown of its coronation oath, Parker then called on the Congress to honor its constitutional oath: "If South Carolina were to establish a government exactly like that of Rome . . . Congress would be bound to interfere and establish a republican form of Government." The idea that the Catholic Church was "completely in the power of Congress" and that Congress was constitutionally bound to proscribe it was fairly avant-garde even for Parker. The idea that there was an equation of interests between Catholicism and slavery, however, was routinely made and based on what were perceived to be features common to both.[25]

Harriet Beecher Stowe, to cite another obvious example, had to have known what she was doing when she created Uncle Tom's owners, the conspicuously Catholic St. Clare family. Little Eva St. Clare's attendance at Methodist services with Uncle Tom made clear that her emancipation was as much at issue as his. The St. Clares were not Irish, but though historians have paid too little attention to Stowe's association of slavery and Catholicism, it is unlikely that her contemporaries missed the point. What is intriguing about this is whether Margaret Mitchell, that other well-known novelist of the antebellum South, had this same association in mind when she wrote *Gone with the Wind*. Mitchell clearly did not share Stowe's animus toward either the South or Irish Catholicism, but she just as clearly thought the two went well with one another. She created the noticeably affluent O'Haras, named their plantation Tara after the residence of an Irish high king, gave Scarlett a quite Irish disregard for time, and had them all watch as the South was blown away. In the mid-1850s there were many in the North, Stowe included, who prayed that Irish Catholics would likewise be gone with the wind—or with whatever other primal force was available.[26]

C. B. Boynton's prayers were particularly fervent, but, like most of the abolitionists, he was very nearly convinced that they had already been answered. He directly "connect[ed] the slaveholder to the priest," but he had to have taken great comfort in the belief that "the [American] govt 'was designed for the overthrow of slavery'"—and he meant of both sorts. There were, Boynton knew, "two dangers which threaten our Noble Republic: 'the Papacy and Slavery.'" He meant them in that order. But he also knew that his noble Republic had God's blessings. That was what made it noble. And God's judgment was writ large: "the American eagle [would] never dwell in peace with the coiling serpent of slavery." Lest anyone be uncertain exactly which serpent he had in mind, Boynton explained that his nation "was not destined to be 'led in chains by a priesthood, nor betrayed by a jesuit.' America would be Protestant and Free!" Indeed, unless it were the one, it could never be the other.[27]

Destiny notwithstanding, however, the threat was real. The papists, after all, did not despoil just by their presence. They could and did vote; Boynton's "Protestant and Free" America had enfranchised Catholics; the Romanist threat bore a distinct and frightening political aspect. As the exquisitely patrician George Templeton Strong put it, Irish Catholics, like Southern slaveholders, were "fellow citizens," and they voted overwhelmingly for the Democrats, the party of slavery and the South. It was one thing for the "Catholic influence" to be "on the side of slavery," for the "Jesuit and Pro-Slavery politician" to be "natural allies." It was quite another and more menacing thing for these natural allies to come together politically in the Democratic Party and to join as co-conspirators in a "Romish [and slave power] Cabal" against American freedom and Americans' future.[28]

Moreover, for those whose suspicions of Catholicism were pushing them toward paranoia, there was unmistakable evidence that such a conspiracy was pending if it had not already begun and that the Irish were its unwitting agents. Jesuitical intriguing was likely beyond the reach of those whom the Jesuits had themselves enslaved, but this was hardly enough to excuse them. Irish Catholics, said William Lloyd Garrison, were "disposed to go with the accursed South for every purpose and to any extent." "The foreign Catholic vote," according to another antislavery spokesman, "is almost unanimously cast for slavery"—whether out of ignorance or mendacity was unimportant.[29]

Parker went so far as to identify Irish Catholics as the "vassals . . . of the slaveholders": "every Irishman in the United States is in favour of slavery." They were, he continued, "a wretched race of people for us to import and breed from in America." It would be "generations," Parker feared, before "we shall overcome the ignorance, stupidity, and superstition of the Irish Catholics in America. . . . All may be expected to be on the side of slavery. . . . I mean all in a body—their Romanism will lead them to support slavery." There is, I suppose, some irony in the fact that the Irish Catholic leader Daniel O'Connell was an abolitionist; that John Mitchell, Irish rebel in the Rising of 1848, then resident in the South and staunch defender of slavery, was a Protestant; and that the Orange Protestants in the north of Ireland would be avowedly pro-Confederate during the Civil War. The ironies escaped Parker, as they did Hinton Helper, the Alabama abolitionist. "There is little difference," Helper wrote in 1856, "between Slavery and Popery and the Negro-driving Democracy . . . we are not at all surprised to see them going hand in hand in their diabolical works of inhumanity and desolation." According to a Protestant minister, the political rallying cry of the Democrats in 1856 was "Slavery, Romanism, and Rum"—a slight if less alliterative variant on the 1884 Republican charge that the Democrats were the party of "rum, Romanism, and Rebellion."[30]

George Templeton Strong even managed to extend the alliance to include political style. "A parallel might be drawn," he confided to his diary, "between the South Carolina . . . fire-eater, and the Irish politician descended from Brian Boru." Both were secessionists of a kind, and both were "full of gas and brag and bosh." He was tired of this "long established firm of 'Celt, Doughface, and Chivalry.'" Strong was not alone in his weariness and frustration. As *Harper's Magazine* put it in 1851, there was a "broad consensus that [the Irish], . . . low-browed, brutish, simian, and with black tint to skin, . . . were constitutionally incapable of intelligent participation in the governance of the nation." They were, said Strong, "semi-humanized gorillas . . . pediculous . . . bogtrotters . . . and the like scum" who "crawl and eat dirt and poison every community they infest." They carried "in their very blood," said the Irish-born Protestant E. L. Godkin, "traditions which give universal suffrage an air of menace."[31]

When Irish went on a murderous rampage against African Americans in New York City in the summer of 1863, there were predictable and quite justifiable expressions of horror at just how menacing the Irish could be, but few expressions of surprise. These draft/race/social class riots occurred just days after the Battle of Gettysburg and with Robert E. Lee's army still in the North. Federal troops were dispatched to the "Battle of the Bowery"; many in the North were not only exceedingly anxious but convinced that these Irish-led assaults against innocent blacks as well as against the public order were an indication that the political alliance between Irish Catholics and Southern slave owners had taken on a quasi-military aspect. In fact, the Irish-led rioters had genuine grievances—none against the unoffending blacks whom they chose as targets, but legitimate nonetheless.

No matter. "The mob! The mob!" shouted *Harper's Magazine.* "The Irish have risen to resist the draft." Strong knew what was at stake. This was a "Copperhead insurrection," he wrote. The rioters were "lewd fellows . . . Irish at that." They were not just lewd. The Irish were described as "whooping, yelling, blaspheming, howling, demonic . . . none . . . seems to be American." "Irish" had come to be a symbol, a code word for riotous and barbaric. It was more a negative referent than a national designation.[32]

Barely six weeks after the riots, in the middle of the war being fought to limit and eradicate chattel slavery, Andrew Greenlees, a Protestant immigrant from Belfast, wrote from his farm in Illinois to his brother in Ireland. Greenlees reported on crop yields and prices, the birth of a son, and news of the family. But he also commented on the progress of the American Civil War, hoping to impress upon his brother the meaning and importance of a Union victory. He used a revealing analogy. Greenlees's brother in a previous letter had asked "to be excused for not entering into the spirit of the [American] war as enthusiastic as I [Greenlees] do." Greenlees understood. Belfast was a long way from Illinois and "I would not expect you to be quite So much interested in the success of our arms as if you were a Citizen of our Country."[33]

The issues, however, closed the distance and rejoined these two of Albion's scattered seeds. I will let Greenlees speak for himself: "Suerly no good Citizen Can feel indeferent as to the result had Smith O Brien and his Confederates Succeeded in their designs of rebelling against the British government and been so far successful as to raise a great and powerful army. . . . with the avowed purpose of putting down the British protestant government and establishing in its room a papal tyrannical despotism." Calling O'Brien and the other Irish rebels of 1848 "Confederates" cannot have been unintentional. It solidified the connection between those who would challenge the "British protestant government in Ireland" and replace it with a "papal tyrannical despotism" and those who would do almost the same in America. His brother would certainly have understood that threat, and Greenlees was sure he would "shoulder [his] knapsack and musket and march to the defense of [his] Countrys *dearest rights.* It is so with me."[34]

Through all of this, however, one essential difference between the attacks on slavery and the simultaneous and related attacks on Catholics remained: very few Southern slaveholders were Catholic. One of the most vigorous defenders of slavery, the Virginian George Fitzhugh, thought more of them should be, that Catholicism fit slavery better than did any of the Protestant denominations. Fitzhugh himself was not Catholic and not about to convert; he was simply offering a history lesson. That it happened to be the same one the abolitionists themselves had made was not lost on Fitzhugh's audience—both pro- and antislavery. But the fact remained that Southerners were co-religionists of their Northern critics and thus still among the elect, the initiated as Chevalier had defined it. Slavery had seduced them and made them indolent, and as such they were an immediate and formidable threat to republicanism. But once slavery was removed, Southerners would be restored to their full Protestant and republican vigor. As Theodore Parker put it in 1854, "Slavery is nothing. It exists only by whim." As for Southerners as slaveholders, "a breath unmakes them as a breath once made."[35]

The events of the next decade would make clear that it was going to take more than a gentle breath, but the point was unmistakable: Southerners had only abandoned the secular faith; theirs was an act of apostasy, sinful but correctable. Catholicism, however, did not exist only by whim. Catholics were not merely apostates. They could not forswear what they had never sworn. We know now—as Southerners sensed then—that slavery had insinuated itself into the culture of the white South and given it a distinct set of interests and values, including those counted as moral values. Slavery was more than a structural and existential flaw, the removal of which would be fully redemptive and restorative. It was the essence of the South. It could not be surgically removed without killing—figuratively in this instance—the patient.

That was not, however, the judgment of the Northern reformers at the time. The radical perfectionism that drove them, with its inspired attacks on all systems of slavery, demanded only that Southerners repent and reform, not that they transfigure themselves. Southerners needed reconstruction, not spiritual conversion or rebirth. This would require some strenuous evangelization, but at least they were not condemned by irredeemable error. That could not be said of Catholics. Their deformities were essential; their redemption required a metamorphosis, killing the Catholic to save the person. The Civil War—like the Revolution—was, then, a "cousins' war," preceded, as the Revolution had been, by an evangelical great awakening. It was a conflict that was quite literally internecine, fought within the Protestant family and in the name of its shared values. Irish Catholics participated in the war, but more as mercenaries, not as one of the "cousins." They had no familial stake in the fight, no real understanding even of what had provoked it and no understanding at all of republics "conceived in Liberty and dedicated to the proposition that all men are created equal." The Revolution had created a Protestant republic; the Civil War would defend and restore it. All of this was thought quite beyond the mental reach of Irish Catholics.[36]

The political and partisan response to the Irish and their church was predictable given the emotional heat that generated it. That response—what one recent historian has described as "an American-styled Kulturkampf"—has been well and frequently chronicled, most recently and compellingly by John McGreevy in his *Catholicism and American Freedom*. Anti-Catholicism came packaged as political reform; the implications of that, both short and long term, were enormous. The Republican Party's commitment to slavery's extinction and its immediate insistence that slavery not be allowed to expand into the western territories were matched by its more covert hostility to Catholicism and those who professed it. The historian David Potter perfectly captured the contradiction when he wrote:"The fact is that much of the rural, Protestant, Puritan-oriented population of the North was sympathetic to antislavery . . . and nativism and unsympathetic to the . . . Irish Catholics. . . . Thus it happened that nativism and antislavery operated in *conjunction.*" Potter added that "it may seem paradoxical . . . that the same people who opposed the oppression of a racial minority also favored discrimination against a religious minority, but history is frequently illogical." So, it would seem, are some historians, who, Potter continued, "have been slow to recognize . . . the fact that anti-slavery . . . and nativism should have operated in partnership."[37]

That partnership was first expressed in the Know-Nothing movement of the 1850s, but the Know-Nothing Party, as English observer Philip Bagenal put it in 1882, was the gate of entry, the "vestibule of the present Republican party." There was a general awareness that the vast majority of Know-Nothings moved seamlessly into the Republican Party. The linkage between "the politics of anti-Catholicism" and "anti-slavery feeling" was obvious enough that, in the words of the historian R. Laurence Moore, "one is inclined to agree with those who argue that the most important cause of the Civil War was the Irish potato famine," a conclusion that nicely answers Robert Scally's question concerning the nature of "the Irish ingredients in the stew that formed the antebellum republic on the eve of its bloodiest trial." For those then and later who prefer their politics uncluttered and predictable, the "Irish ingredient" produced a political system and culture that seemed maddeningly inconsistent—even internally contradictory.[38]

The relationship between the anti-Catholicism of the Know-Nothing Party and the new Republican Party that displaced it is of central importance. Potter identified what he saw as the obvious paradox that the party of antislavery was also the party of anti-Catholicism; but since both slavery and Catholicism were seen as forms of bondage the paradox disappears. The political confusion, however, does not. There had always been tension between secular and Protestant reformers and the Catholic Church—witness Thomas Paine. In these early years, however, the reformers' hostility was directed toward the institutional church, not the innocent and, by their reckoning, victimized laity. There could be no slavery without slaves, and slaves deserved the sympathy of the right thinking. The institutional church and its hierarchical clergy were the slaveholders; the laity were the slaves. The hope of the reformers was to liberate Catholics from Catholicism, as it was later to liberate slaves from slavery. As one Protestant clerical reformer put it in 1834 with black slavery much on his mind, once the Irish had experienced the free institutions of America they would "break the chains of priestcraft and be free!"[39]

That was the one hopeful part of the calculus. It proved unstable and without staying power but, prior to the Great Hunger, many Americans believed that if

Irish Catholics could only be converted to Protestantism—reconstructed, to use a word about to be made quite current—they would embrace both republicanism and the market values that were to be grafted to it. Josiah Nott, a Southern race theorist and defender of slavery, thought that the Irish were a "diseased stock," but that, like "our domestic animals," giving them better food would bring rapid improvement. With improvement, it may be presumed, would come a measure of wisdom, perhaps even enough that the Irish would understand that the Protestant societies formed to evangelize and convert them did so in the interest of saving Irish souls and improving Irish prospects. The Protestant minister who wrote in 1834 imploring them to break their chains was opposed to Catholicism but not to Catholics. He was proselytizing but only as a means of liberating. Each Catholic convert to Protestantism represented a "marvelous defection." By defecting, the Catholic was redeemed and delivered; the more the defections, the more the nation was made politically secure and economically prosperous.[40]

For a time at least even Theodore Parker thought the Irish might listen and understand. "Good," he argued in 1856, would "come out of evil. I think the Irish Catholics . . . could not so soon be emancipated in any country as in our dear blessed land." Simply being in the United States and subject to its laws would "clean, educate, and emancipate 'the gintleman from Carrrk'!" Parker's use of the word "emancipate" was as important as his burlesque of the Irish brogue. Their "primitive reverence" and "filial obedience," said Philip Bagenal, would give way in America, even among "the most catholic of the catholics." At issue was not simply the incompatibility of Catholicism and republicanism but the manifest superiority of republicanism over Catholicism.[41]

The Irish Catholic John Maguire, writing in the 1850s, acknowledged that the point was frequently made that "the moment the Irish touch the free soil of America they lose the old faith—that there is something in the very nature of Republican institutions fatal to the Church of Rome." Maguire did not mean to alarm, but he thought this was nonsense, the wishful thinking of bigots. He offered this up as good news, encouragement to those who feared that the hordes of Irish Catholics would corrupt America by defaming its values. Nativists would have taken no encouragement from his comments, would, in fact, have seen them as a slur on those values. If republicanism was compatible with Catholicism then the entire American experiment was discredited. Surely, the Catholic Irish arriving by the boatload would see the truth of that and act on it, shedding their popery as they shed their accents.[42]

It did not happen that way. The free institutions of America had no discernible effect on the Irish. In the face of all that was deemed rational and righteous, the Famine Irish immigrants clung tenaciously to their Catholicism. The total of marvelous defections was embarrassingly small and may in fact have been exceeded by the number of American converts to Catholicism. The consequences were disastrous. The fundamental assumption that Catholicism was reactionary and that it could never be otherwise was now applied with equal force to both the hierarchy in its resplendence and the laity in its squalor. It was hard for a people who believed that God had given them liberty as an inalienable right to feel any sympathy for those who when offered the choice of liberty or bondage chose bondage. The Irish had inflicted this wound on themselves.

At a time when Americans were beginning to think of themselves as a separate "volk," a distinct and superior subset of Anglo-Saxons or Caucasians, the Irish embrace of their own slavery suggested that they were genetically as well as culturally outlandish and depraved. Not only was their conversion not automatic, it was not even likely. Worse still, even those few Irish who defected would remain irredeemably Irish. As one champion of Anglo-Saxonism put it in the late 1840s, the "key to the supremacy of England and America was that in those countries there were few Celts." He made no reference to Catholics. It was not that the Irish had chosen Catholicism but that Catholicism had chosen them. There was some defective gene in the Celtic "race" that predisposed them to improvidence, servility, and ineradicable ignorance. The Anglo-Saxon, Parker believed, "loves liberty . . . hates equality." The Irishman, however, "cares little for liberty, but loves equality." The Celtic race, Parker concluded, was doomed by this defect and would "rapidly disappear." They were a flawed people. That being the case, Parker asked rhetorically, "is it to be expected that an ignorant, idle, turbulent, and vicious population will, by a mere [change] of . . . laws, become industrious, provident, moral, and intelligent?" Parker lapsed briefly in 1856 when he expressed his hope that America might emancipate the Irish, but by 1859 he was fully recovered from this fit of optimism. "The Irishman is always a Paddy," he wrote with no apparent regret. Nothing could make them palesmen.[43]

Those of this mind were coming perilously close to arguing that the Irish were ready-made slaves of Catholicism as surely as Africans, according to Southern defenders of slavery, were ready-made chattel slaves. For blacks, freedom would come hard if it was to come at all. But the Irish had only to walk away from the church, its priests, its inquisitional practices, and its mind-numbing rituals. This the Irish would not do, and many influential Americans began to believe, as one of them put it, that the "Irish heartily deserve their despotism." The slaves of the South, at least, *wanted* to be free. The slaves of Rome did not. Indeed, they seemed not even to know they were unfree. There were powerful and enduring lessons in this. As the nativist Joseph Berg put it in 1841, "I count the poor slave . . . under the lash of a heartless overseer, a freeman" compared with the man who lives free yet "voluntarily fetters his soul, and surrenders himself, bound hand and foot, to the sovereign will and pleasure of a popish priest." Abolitionists attacked both slavery as an institution and slaveholders as the immediate agents of enslavement; they did not attack slaves. Nativists, however, attacked the Catholic

Church as both an institution and an idea. They condemned the hierarchy as both conspirators and the makers and keepers of slaves. They then condemned individual Catholics as the willing and hence unredeemable participants in the whole sordid enterprise.[44]

Most of this criticism of Catholicism and Catholics arose from a deep-seated fear that neither the institutional church nor its benighted parishioners could be trusted with republican values. As was true of the simultaneous attacks on Southern slavery, there was a clear moral and ideological imperative behind these sectarian assaults. Both forms of slavery were seen as sinful and politically impure. But both were also seen as socially regressive, remnants of outmoded systems that the modern project would displace. The economic takeoff of the 1830s and 1840s, in other words, altered not just the nature of American republicanism and the role of the West in sustaining it but the way the crusade against Catholicism would be framed. The assumption of unending hostility between popery and republicanism survived the passage intact, perhaps even strengthened. Certainly it added to the list of Catholicism's critics; not only was it condemned as sinful and inherently antirepublican, but it was also inefficient and irrational. The assault on Catholics would now come from Protestant capitalists as well as Protestant moralists, from reactionaries on the political right as well as radical perfectionists on the left.

There were major differences between artisanal republicanism and the free-labor version that replaced it, but most of those differences were hidden behind the language of freedom and virtue that was common to both. Among the most important parts of that shared discourse was Protestantism. It had given moral order to republicanism; it would do the same for capitalism. As one historian has put it, the "creed that grew alongside this elemental Protestantism was that of laissez-faire capitalism." The Republican Party synthesized that elemental Protestantism with the free-market economy, blending piety with prosperity. In time, there would be tensions between the two, but in the 1850s this conjunction of moralist and modernizer troubled no one. Republicans were bringing together the ideals of the Revolution of 1776 and the market revolution of the 1840s and doing rhetorical justice to both. They had become the party of what another historian has dubbed "commercial Protestantism." Republicans themselves were not that crass; they said that theirs was the party of "free soil, free labor, and free men" and that their defense of the free market and their assaults on systems of slavery were both propelled by ideals, not by self-interest. There is little reason to doubt their sincerity; ample reason to doubt whether the Sermon on the Mount could, in fact, be reconciled to *The Wealth of Nations*.[45]

This assimilation of Protestant idealism with the new commercial ethic meant that once again Irish Catholics would find themselves leagued with Southern slave-holders as enemies, this time of capitalism as well as republicanism. It is the case

that Republicans chose new targets as they compiled their critiques of Southerners and papists, shifting their focus from tyranny and servility to sloth and
intemperance. Two things, however, did not change; first, popish impiety threatened
prosperity as surely as it did morality and virtue; and, second, there were no
meaningful distinctions to be made between the Catholic Church and the Southern
slavocracy. They not only thought alike but acted alike, and their social effects
were alike. Both were feudal, regressive, hierarchical, despotic, aristocratic, and
deeply conspiratorial. Both enslaved. Catholics and Southerners, from top to bottom,
were shiftless and dilatory in their habits. Republicans said and doubtless believed
that the Democratic Party represented an unholy coalition of Southern whites—
both slave owners and non–slave owners—and their Irish Catholic vassals in the
Northern states. Much divided them, not the least of which was the Protestantism
and anti-Catholicism of many Southerners, but systems of slavery were indiscriminate in their effects. They enslaved all who came into contact with them,
however remote the contact. At the least, they made a people derelict. They corrupted entire societies and made them base and ignoble.[46]

This Republican critique of the South and of Catholicism could have been
taken from any primer on political economy: national economic progress required
a wide-awake, individualistic, competitive, entrepreneurial, educated, frugal, and
sober populace. It was easy to identify the places where such people lived; the
barns were painted, the fences were in good repair. Farmers plowed straight
furrows. There were improvements everywhere—canals, waterways, roads, railroads. The villages were neat and orderly, with red schoolhouses, white Protestant
chapels, and civic meeting halls. The workshops of the tradesmen were well kept,
their tools cared for and put away in proper order. The shops of the merchants
were clean, the board sidewalks were swept, the merchandise was attractively
displayed. Work was honored; indolence was scorned. As Henry Adams learned as
a young boy in Quincy, Massachusetts, to "the New England mind, roads, schools,
clothes, and a clean face were connected as part of the law of order or divine
system. Bad roads meant bad morals." It made no difference which was cause and
which effect.[47]

The roads of the South, however, as well as everything else that indicated the
energy and enterprising spirit of a people, were bad beyond measure. Barns were
unpainted, fences were sagging and in disrepair; and no Southern farmer, it seemed,
could draw a straight line, much less plow one. William Seward made his first trip
from his native New York to Virginia in 1835. His visit left a lasting impression.
"It was necessary that I should travel in Virginia to have any idea of a slave State.
An exhausted soil, old and decaying towns, wretchedly-neglected roads, and, in
every respect, an absence of enterprise and improvements, distinguish the region
through which we have come, in contrast to that in which we live. Such has been
the effect of slavery." Sometime between 1850 and 1854 Henry Adams also had

occasion to travel through Virginia. The roads were horrible, one of them so bad it "amounted to a social crime." Adams knew the cause. "Slavery was wicked and slavery was the cause of this road's badness. . . . Slave states were dirty, unkempt, poverty-stricken, ignorant, vicious." And Seward and Adams were in Virginia. Mississippi or Louisiana would likely have appeared to them more brutish, more literally outlandish than any place they had ever known.[48]

T. H. Gladstone, brother of the future prime minister of Great Britain and Ireland and hence well schooled in distinguishing between the civilized and the barbarous, confirmed the judgment of Seward and Adams. In 1857 Gladstone toured Kansas, bloodied by the border war between anti- and proslavery forces for control of the territory and the rest of the West. He offered vivid parallel portraits of North and South. The free states and the slave states were characterized by "comfort and discomfort," "neatness and disorder," "cleanliness and filth," "farming the land and letting the land farm itself," "trade and stagnation," "stirring activity and reigning sloth," "wide-spread intelligence and almost universal ignorance," "general progress and an incapacity for all improvement or advancement." Which of these sectional archetypes the West would become was yet to be determined. Gladstone referred to Westerners as "border-men" and the "Western borderer[s]," terms that English often used to describe the semicivilized who lived in northern England, on the border with Scotland. But it was the South that really caught his attention. Southerners, white and black, rich and poor, were lazy, and slavery had made them so.[49]

Precisely the same arguments were made regarding Catholics in general and Irish Catholics in particular. Political nativists were convinced that the Catholic Church, by discouraging education, obstructed economic advance and material well-being. Theodore Parker called the church "the one great obstacle to human progress and welfare." A Know-Nothing publication noted that Italy, once tutor to the world, was now "sunk in ignorance." Catholicism was "the canker-worm that has eaten out her . . . vitals." Spain was little better than Italy, and Parker added France to the list; its "40,000 priests . . . steal in everywhere and spread their slime over the baby, the child, the maiden, and the man." No wonder France was "greatly demoralized." Mexico, recently and easily defeated in the Mexican War, was proof that even the bracing air of new worlds was not enough to make them immune from the cankerworm. Catholicism was no longer merely a theological or geopolitical threat; like slavery, it had a corrupting influence over both personal behavior and social values. Bad roads were not the only markers of bad morals.[50]

But Ireland specifically came in for the greatest share of comment. The pattern began early. The Venerable Bede, writing in the eighth century, said simply that "their plows do not run straight" and that the Celts were "wayward, idiosyncratic, argumentative, wilful, disorganized, incapable of settling down and following any Rule." They were like "errant children . . . requir[ing] discipline, admonition . . .

and instruction." Obviously Bede was not comparing Protestant and Catholic cultures; he was, however, clearly of the mind that the Irish church and hence the Irish people were quite unlike their English neighbors. For a more recent and sectarian example, the English Protestant John Ewing's 1823 account of conditions in the Catholic parish of Glencolumbkille in County Donegal, Ireland, is instructive; it begs comparison with Seward's indictment of Virginia:

> There are no plantations not one—in the parish. . . . No modern buildings; no towne or gentleman's Seats. No inn, roads horribly bad— not a perch of good road in the Parish. . . . There is neither lawyer, attorney, magistrate or policeman in the Parish, education here is very far bad indeed. No libraries or manuscripts. . . . There are very few ploughs here . . . no fairs or markets. . . . Tradesmen neither numerous nor good.[51]

British Protestants touring and reporting on Ireland were less confident or explicit than Northerners visiting the South in assigning blame. There was even some speculation that the climate, not the church, was Ireland's curse, that soft mists made a people shiftless. But it is also worth noting how different these English reports were from those describing the more northerly, which is to say Ulster-Scot Protestant, regions of Ireland. Even their cartoon caricatures of Catholic and Protestant in Ireland were different. The Catholics were simian and slovenly, stunted both physically and morally; the Protestants, though not quite as elegant in appearance as the English, were sturdy and enterprising, square jawed and determined in spirit and mien. The Protestant villages of northeastern Ireland were tidy; the people were clean, enterprising, eager for education. An English Protestant clergyman explained the differences to Americans: "The intelligence and thrift of Protestant Ulster are in strong contrast with the ignorance and discomfort of Roman Catholic Munster and Connaught." The English and American Protestants of the nineteenth century clearly needed no reminder that it was "Pilgrims" who "Progressed," that "Protestant peasant" was a contradiction in terms. The phrase was unknown to them, but they would have understood instinctively both the meaning of Protestant Work Ethic and that Catholics did not have one.[52]

This returns the discussion to the intersection of Irish and American history— of starving island and industrializing nation. Scally is correct when he writes that at the time of what he calls America's "great [industrial] transformation" it "seems almost self-evident that very large numbers of hungry and movable manual workers were essential." The Irish were the most likely of workers because they were the hungriest and most movable of all. They supplied the "surplus humanity," the "reserve army of labor" from the "periphery," in this instance the Celtic fringe, that propelled industrial capitalism. Scally is talking about the Famine emigrants, but those who went out of Ireland in subsequent years were every bit as useful. The process of American industrialization would have progressed without the Irish immigration, but the addition of two and a half million more Irish to the surplus humanity of those years was of enormous significance.[53]

This post-Famine Irish immigration was slightly more purposeful and orderly than the desperate and chaotic immigration of the late 1840s. British officials were aware from the 1830s forward that the emigration of the Irish—the shoveling out as they called it—relieved them of the responsibility of feeding or, more commonly, burying them, but that awareness grew after the Famine and the shoveling-out process became more systematic. For example, emigrant guides were distributed without charge throughout Ireland. Similar guidebooks, designed to stimulate immigration to the United States, made their way to Germany, Scandinavia, and Britain. These, however, tended to celebrate America's farmlands and the ease with which they could be had and cultivated. The best-known Irish guide was produced by the Englishman Vere Foster in 1855. Its title was instructive: *Work and Wages; or, the Penny Emigrant's Guide to the United States and Canada.*[54]

The Irish entered the emerging Atlantic economy in the mid- and late nineteenth century to work for wages. Ireland supplied a "mobile 'reserve army of labor' to provide . . . cheap muscle power" for the world's rapidly industrializing nations, including the United States. As noted earlier, it is not altogether certain that they would have been allowed to enter America under any other set of circumstances. There had never been a dearth of things to do in America, but the market revolution vastly expanded the list of chores. As a mid-nineteenth century newspaperman put it, "America demands for her development an inexhaustible fund of physical energy, and Ireland supplies the most part of it. There are several sorts of power—Waterpower, steam-power, and Irish-power. The last works hardest of all." It was that willingness to work—and nothing else—that commended them. As Orestes Brownson pointed out, the "old American people hated the Catholic religion as the devil does holy water; but business is business, and they were obliged to tolerate it, for the services of these Catholic Irish were indispensable to their industrial enterprises."[55]

For their part, the British were delighted to be rid of the Irish. They were a burden on the national treasury—if not the national conscience—and of no use at all to Britain's industrial enterprise, at least in 1847. In that worst year of the Hunger, three members of Parliament did express some concern about how the Irish would be received in America. After all, as the three put it in language that Brownson would later echo, "if ever two nationalities came into collision by meeting, it is the Irish and the American. . . . Everywhere in the United States, the Irish-born part of the population is only tolerated . . . as what has been termed 'a serviceable nuisance'; it is socially despised, and . . . ill-treated." Capitalist America did not like them any more than republican America did. But capitalist America needed them and so took them in. The best that could be said for this immigration was that it was well timed.[56]

Edward Everett Hale was fully aware that the Irish were both serviceable and a nuisance. In 1852 he wrote his *Letters on Irish Emigration,* published in pamphlet form. It is hard to imagine any other statement of the issue that gave more practical expression to America's new "business is business" credo or to what the transformation from artisanal republicanism to the free-labor ideology meant. These letters established the standard for how America would go about making its working class. The Irish were Hale's prototype, and fainter praise for a people would be difficult to imagine. As a Unitarian minister from Massachusetts, Hale did not figure to be well disposed to papists, but in his own strange way he was complimenting the Irish and celebrating the intersection of Irish and American history. As he put it, the Irish were coming to America "at just the needed moment." "It is clear enough, that there must, in any community, be manual labor. The soil is to be tilled and the roads built and repaired."[57]

This was precisely what the "Celtic Exodus" was for. Nicely joining piety and profit, Hale saw the hand of a kind providence in "the western faring" of the Irish, what he also referred to as their "plunge into the sea." It was the case that these Irish were distinctly premodern and unschooled in the new political economy; those Americans who thought the Irish were only "ignorant diggers and delvers" were right. They were also, however, shortsighted, for "God, when he supplied [the Irish], was freeing other laborers for . . . higher and wider uses." This was Ireland's (or God's) gift to America. "Their inferiority as a race compels them to go to the bottom; and the consequence is that we are, all of us, the higher lifted because they are here." No Southern defender of African slavery could have said it better or would have said it differently.[58]

Brownson was more sympathetic than Hale, but only slightly so and, one suspects, because it was important to him to demonstrate that Catholicism and republicanism and the industrial capitalism now grafted to it could coexist. His argument covered the same points that Hale had made. America had an adequate supply of "passable . . . engineers, overseers, mechanics, and teamsters." What America did not have was "laborers, to take the pick and spade and do the work of excavation. An American could invent but he could not or would not dig." For that Americans would "send to Ireland, where the supply of labor was largely in excess of the demand, and import Irish laborers," who knew only how to dig. Without them, and without "Bridget" and the other "female domestics . . . our public works, canals, and railroads could not have been constructed, our manufacturing industries sustained, or domestics be had." Brownson would have agreed with Hale's conclusion, that it was America's "duty to receive the scattered fugitives . . . the beaten Celts . . . and make of them what we can."[59]

For the moment, at least, that would not be much, mostly because the Irish cut so unprepared and squalid a figure. Hale said that "they were fugitives from defeat," adding that he meant his comment "without a metaphor." They were "fugitives from slavery," he continued, also likely without metaphor. Hale, whose friendship with Theodore Parker should be noted, believed that the "pure [Irish] race has done nothing positive for mankind, and been nothing but a monument of failure." But it was that failure, ironically, that so perfectly suited them to America's needs. They were thought the ideal unskilled industrial workers— hungry, movable, and stupid. Once they moved, whether to England or America, their "poverty made even the paltriest wages seductive." "The worst dwellings are good enough for them," Friedrich Engels wrote; " . . . their food consists of potatoes and potatoes only; whatever they earn beyond these needs they spend upon drink." Engels wondered aloud "what does such a race want with high wages?" Hale said the same thing. The "pure Celtic race . . . is . . . useless in the world, except as Mr. Emerson has said, for the guano that is in it." His reference to Ralph Waldo Emerson was accurate as far as it went. But, since Emerson also believed that the Irish immigration was "black vomit" and that the Irish, "deteriorated in size and shape, the nose sunk, the gum exposed, . . . operated with diminished brain," fertilizer was all that could be expected.[60]

Indeed, according to George Templeton Strong, their advantages went beyond their mere desperation. The Irish had "prehensile paws supplied them by nature," which made "the handling of the spade and the wielding of the pickaxe" easy and natural. They had "congenital hollows on the shoulder wonderfully adapted to make the carrying of the hod a luxury." Strong was probably half-kidding. Thomas Carlyle, whose social acuity Strong much admired, was not kidding at all when he wrote that the Irishman, in "his rags and laughing savagery . . . is there to undertake all work that can be done by mere strength of hand and back." It was the case, said a phrenologist in 1859, that the Irish should only work outside and at physical labor, "for they require a great amount of air and exercise." Fortunately, as another observer put it in 1864, there was plenty of that kind of work for them. "Irishmen have been a great help to America in supplying the demand for rough and heavy work on canals, railways, etc., and vast numbers of Irish girls have found employment as servants." After centuries, the Irish were finally useful.[61]

Southerners, understandably, watched the Northern use of the Irish with growing interest. They viewed themselves as experts on the ignorant, idle, turbulent, and vicious, as the Irish had been described, and on the problems that arose from dependence on the labor of such. The North was offering only slight variations on oft-played Southern themes. But Southerners also watched with some apprehension.

The great economic transformation begun in the 1840s did not entirely miss them; Southern cotton fueled some of it, Southern cotton growers prospered from most of it. But the evangelical fervor with which market capitalism was invested and the free-labor ideology that issued from it vastly widened the sectional breach between North and South. The Northern insistence that free labor was the essence of republicanism and hence morally and economically superior to slave labor forced a Southern response. Since many of the "free" laborers of the North were Irish, and since the Catholicism of those Irish was so frequently described in the same language that Northern critics reserved for their attacks on slavery, some of that Southern response inevitably came to take in the "Irish question" as well as the labor question.

The *herrenvolk* champions of slavery, those who defended it on the basis of theories of a master white race and black racial inferiority, had little to say on the Irishness of Northern labor. Their attack was not on market capitalism or the modern project generally, and they had no complaint with the free-labor ideology that arose from that emerging capitalist economy. They disputed that good roads were the measure of morality—but even Henry Adams came to admit that at the end of one particularly wretched Virginia road was Mount Vernon. Similarly, they had no quarrel with republicanism or democracy or egalitarianism or any of the other residual rhetoric of the Revolution. Those values, of course, applied only to whites, but the Revolution itself belonged to them as surely as to any Northerner, and they were unsparing in their attacks on those in the North who would turn those revolutionary principles into a historical justification for an attack on black slavery. The dispute between the *herrenvolk* defenders of slavery and the growing ranks of antislavery Northerners was bitter and impassioned. It would produce some monumental bloodletting, but it made no references to Irish or to Catholics, who were irrelevant to it.[62]

The same cannot be said of those who attempted to justify slavery in the abstract rather than simply in its racialized Southern form. These so-called seignorial defenders of slavery made few if any references to the Revolution, wanted nothing to do with the modern project in any of its forms, and condemned the system of free labor as barbarous. As one particularly indignant Southerner wrote to Theodore Parker, "Gentlemen, I am a slave-owner . . . but by God! no one should treat my negroes as you stand here and see these poor Irish treated." There was no recorded response from Parker. It is safe to assume that other Southerners felt and wrote similarly. But these Southern references to the treatment of Northern labor tended to be random and offhand. Of greater importance were the systematic assaults on free labor, with their frequent mention of Irish and Ireland, that distinguished the writings of the seignorialists. William Grayson, for example, in his 1855 narrative poem "The Hireling and the Slave," answered the abolitionists who "grieve that the slave is never taught to write." But the slaves, Grayson insisted, read as well as "the hireling white." More to the point, he asked, "Have Ireland's millions, flying from the rule / Of those who censure, ever known a school?" As to the punishment meted out to slaves, Grayson asked mockingly, "What gentle rule, in Britain's Isle, prevails . . . How much humaner than a master's whip, / Her penal colony and convict ship!"[63]

George Fitzhugh was even more explicit. The most skilled of the seignorialists, Fitzhugh wrote of the "sufferings of the Irish" and of "famine hover[ing] o'er the land. Emigrants, like a flock of hungry pigeons or Egyptian locusts, are alighting on the North." These Irish were escaping "freedom." Indeed, Ireland, according to Fitzhugh, was "the freest country in the world." Fitzhugh conceded nothing to Northern advocates of free labor. They were "engaged in the White Slave Trade," he said, and "it is more cruel than the Black Slave Trade, because it exacts more of its slaves, and neither protects nor governs them." "Was it not," Fitzhugh demanded, "this slavery to capital that occasioned the great Irish famine?"[64]

England had taken two islands, Ireland and Jamaica. In the first, they took the land but "left the people free." It was, however, an odd and distorted freedom. "The Irish became the subjects of capital—slaves with no masters obliged by law, self interest or domestic affections to provide for them." A half-million Irish died, Fitzhugh went on, because "in the eye of the law they were equals, and liberty had made them enemies, of their landlords and employers. Had they been vassals or serfs, they would have been beloved, cherished and taken care of by those same landlords and employers. Slaves never die of hunger, scarcely ever feel want." He was derisive of the 1833 emancipation of the black slaves of Jamaica. "Now," he jeered, "they enjoy Irish liberty." But Fitzhugh was not done. In his mind the ultimate occasion for this enslavement to capital was the Reformation, which "debased . . . the public taste . . . and tended to diminish the liberty of the mass of the people, and to impair their moral, social, and physical well-being." That a defender of slavery would attack the Reformation would have occasioned no surprise in the North.[65]

What compounds the tragedy of this era of strange political bedfellows is that the Civil War brought an end to chattel slavery but not to the related idea that Catholicism was also a form of slavery—but one in which the slaves blindly accepted their condition. The Civil War could not change that. The anti-Catholicism of the 1830s, 1840s, and 1850s would endure. "Like some of the subterranean rivers of America," Bagenal wrote, "it runs strong and deep." And it ran in the channels carved for it by the Republican Party. The dispute over slavery diverted attention from the Catholic question and in time eclipsed it, but it did not eradicate it. As one Know-Nothing put it, the fight against Catholicism would "not rust by being postponed a few years." He was right. It did not rust and would be taken up again. The result was that the American working class, disproportionately immigrant/ethnic and Catholic, was effectively cut off from the main currents of American reform. If American labor history was indeed "exceptional" it would be well for historians to look to the religious prejudice and other bad habits of elite reformers as well as to the alleged myopia of labor or the hegemony and avarice of capital.[66]

Some historians, most prominently Eric Foner, would argue that the opponents of slavery were not truly nativist and that after the Civil War their heirs formed an alliance with working-class Irish Americans. Indeed, Foner calls this informal alliance a "conjunction," the same word that Potter had used to describe the exact opposite of what Foner is intending. This conjunction of interests, moreover, extended from labor issues to the cause of Irish nationalism. I find no evidence of this. Foner, for example, centers his argument around the work of Irish-born Patrick Ford, who in the 1870s became the founding editor of the reformist *Irish World and American Industrial Liberator,* a paper read throughout Irish America. The title alone reflects a conjunction of sorts, but when Ford issued a full front-page condemnation of anti-Catholicism in 1880, concluding that most of it came from "*brothers in the fraternity of reform,*" he was acknowledging—and lamenting—the only conjunction that counted. Reform elements in America were never able to shed their reflexive anti-Catholicism. I wish they had been; the cause of social justice in America would have been advanced. That the reformers thought slavery a more formidable threat than Catholicism is not in dispute. But they did not believe that Catholicism was necessarily less malevolent; and once slavery was ended, liberal reformers reverted to form.[67]

This close association of liberal reform and anti-Catholicism would confound American politics for the next century. Indeed, it still marks and clutters American politics. It would also hopelessly confuse the Irish Catholics' accommodation to their new American home. The most obvious problem arose from the fact that Irish Catholics were a dominant element in the organization of the American working class, particularly after the Civil War. I agree entirely with Foner when he argues that many of the working-class Irish, including some of their priests, were genuinely radical in their politics. Their problem was that they had no allies among the radicals and reformers who were part of the Protestant and secular elite. The cause of labor should have been the obvious target of the reformers' energies—as it was everywhere else in the industrializing world. The postwar working class tried to make that the case in America as well—tried, in other words, to stretch the ideology of the Civil War "beyond [black] equality" and to make the Northern triumph over slavery a victory for oppressed workers of whatever color and section. This was the revolutionary promise of the war, and workers in the North claimed a part of it.[68]

They even used the familiar verbal imagery of antislavery to make their case. The irony in this was huge, if entirely unintended; the language of antislavery was also the language of anti-Catholicism. Reversible metaphors were a rhetorical stock-in-trade of both movements. It is unlikely that Irish Catholic laborers were unaware of this; but aware or not, they were undeterred. As in the case of the nativists before them, slavery and all of its attendant images became a linguistic device. Northern labor was "enslaved" to market-driven wages; their liberation from this "wage slavery" was no less a moral imperative than the emancipation of the chattel slaves of the South. They were "white slaves," "white niggers," as they occasionally tagged themselves, whose lives were as unrelentingly grim and hopeless as that of any black in the South, whether slave before the war or "free" after it.[69]

In 1882, to offer only one example, Patrick Ford praised John Brown in language that the staunchest abolitionist would have approved. "John Brown killed slavery," Ford said, "and White and Black stand equal To-Day in Industrial Servitude." So much for American industrial liberation. The fact that in Irish the word for laborer, *scláibhaí,* is also the word for slave (and that it is pronounced "sklavy" with a long *a*) was a part of all this. I have already noted that by this time the vast majority of Irish used English words. But the structure of their language and their thoughts was, I believe, still contained in the Irish. Even if the idea/word was used only figuratively the Irish understood that there were still *scláibhaí* in America; the 13th Amendment left them unaffected.[70]

Working Irish were not the only ones to use slavery—both the indisputable reality of it before 1865 and its de facto survival after the war—as an extended analogy for their own condition. Others speaking for the Northern working class did as well. Orestes Brownson was convinced that "the great mass of operatives" in the North were "virtually slaves—slaves . . . as much as are the Negroes on one of our Southern plantations." Terence Powderly—Irish, Catholic, and from 1879 to 1889 the General Master Workman of the Noble and Holy Order of the Knights of Labor—acknowledged that "the conditions of servitude were somewhat different between the white toiler of the North and his sable brother of the South, [but] the result was the same when the master decided to use his power." "No wonder," Powderly continued, " . . . that the desire to secure freedom for all . . . began to grow." Abolitionism and the organization of Northern workers proceeded apace; "both," Powderly insisted, "were revolutionary." The stakes for both were the same: "the freedom of the man who worked." Karl Marx knew precisely the context of his famous reference to workers having nothing to lose but their chains. Even the papacy, though it took until 1891 for Leo XIII to put it on the record, made the point, and less elliptically than Marx had. A "yoke little better than that of slavery itself," the pope said, had been laid "upon the teeming masses of the laboring poor."[71]

These were exaggerations, to be sure, whether for political effect or out of ignorance is unimportant. What counted was that there were labor union and other leaders who believed that industrial democracy was as central to the American promise as political democracy, but that the Civil War did little or nothing to advance either form. "'Life, liberty, and the pursuit of happiness,'" according to Powderly, were the watchwords not just of the Spirit of '76 but of antislavery and emancipation, and that most assuredly included the emancipation of those in the North who were "slave[s] to the whim or caprice" of those who owned their labor. The end of the war, however, pushed the champions of emancipation either into premature retirement, their labors done, or to more vigorous assaults on Irish Catholics, often in the guise of agitating for temperance or prohibition or for Civil Service reform.[72]

The only meaningful exceptions were Wendell Phillips and the Scottish-born James Redpath. After the Civil War, both transferred their considerable reformist energies from abolitionism to the cause of Northern labor and Irish freedom. Phillips, however, eventually came to distrust Irish Catholics and gave up the good fight in defense of their and labor's cause. Redpath's course was slightly more consistent, but even he did not entirely outgrow his earlier associations. His close allies in the abolitionist crusade in general and the Kansas struggles specifically included Anson Burlingame, Amos Lawrence, and C. W. Dana among other active anti-Catholics. By the 1870s and 1880s Redpath was touring Ireland and offering strong and apparently sincere support for the Irish Land League, though, like Marx before him and Henry George after him, it was to land reform in general, not the Irish version of it, that he committed himself. He had no special love of the Irish or of Catholics—nor should he have had. The point is that Redpath's postwar career, even had he dedicated it solely to advancing the rights of the Catholic Irish, is not enough to change the fact that the only conjunction that counted was the one between the reformers and the nativists.[73]

The consequences of this were tragic. If nothing else—and there was a good deal else—many Irish Catholics directed their frustration and anger not just at the abolitionists and postwar reformers who had scorned them but at the African Americans, slave and free—their "sable brothers," as Powderly called them—who had enjoyed the abolitionists' favor and support. It could, I suppose, be argued that racism or social-class insecurity led the Irish to reject Protestant reform, abolitionism included, "become white," and turn their enmity on their potential social-class allies in the black working class. The more compelling argument, however, is that the reformers rejected the Irish even prior to the Irish leaving Ireland and for reasons having to do with religious beliefs. In sum, American "liberalism," whether of secular or evangelical origin, was the declared enemy of the Irish faith and of those who embraced it. However it happened and in whatever order, Irish Catholic immigrant workers and native Protestant reformers each traduced and spurned the other.

But the power, and so the last word, belonged to the reformers. They had won the Civil War; Irish Catholics had "lost" it, or at least had no claims on it. As surely as the Revolution did, the Civil War represented a triumph of the Protestant republic, with industrial capitalism now securely grafted to it. Philip Bagenal went so far as to write that "since 1860 . . . , the effect of American ideas has been everywhere to break down the . . . power of the priest." He cannot have selected 1860 randomly. The victory over Southern slavery was a victory over all systems of slavery. The defeat of Southern slaveholders was a defeat as well for their Northern and Irish "vassals," particularly the working-class Irish whose 1863 attack on New York City offered material support to their "allies" and co-conspirators in the Confederacy. Writing from the perspective of 1882, Bagenal was sure of what the war had meant. Irish Americans were not sure of anything and would not be for years. Hallowed ground was not an alien concept to them, but they were denied entry to this patch of it.[74]

The dream that the emancipation of the Northern working class from market-driven wages might accompany the emancipation of the Southern working class had no chance. The revolution in labor systems that the Civil War might have brought remained unfinished. After offering up his hymn of praise to John Brown, Patrick Ford next told his readers that the United States had "yet to face the Labor Problem." The Civil War was no meaningless exercise in nation saving, but until the entire "labor problem" was confronted, its genuinely revolutionary promise would remain "unfinished." In this sense as in others, the Irish "lost" the Civil War. It left them politically orphaned. The North did not win the war; Republicans did. And the Republicans were not disposed to extend their victory to include working-class Irish papists. The party of capital and the modern project was not about to become the party of labor; the party of slave emancipation was not likely to embrace those who had voted with slaveholders; the party of righteous Protestantism was not going to conjoin with popery and barbarism.[75]

The Democratic Party was no more useful. It was dominated by conservative Southerners (the so-called Bourbons) who were indistinguishable from Northern Republicans in their support of industrialization and their antilabor policies—an instance of how Southerners became Northerners. The Northern working class, particularly its Irish component, had some access to the Democrats in the North's industrial cities, but this availed them little nationally. The unskilled working classes of both the North and the South, white in the one, black in the other, were made free and equal—and left all but powerless. As for the Irish specifically, Mark Noll describes their predicament after the war perfectly. They were, he writes, "beyond the pale . . . too thoroughly 'the Other' in the myth of a godly, Protestant America." Every part of Noll's formulation—"beyond the pale," "'Other,'" "myth," "Protestant"—is exactly to the point.[76]

Citing cartoon symbols of national identity as if they had historical validity is a risky thing to do. These figures are constantly shifting caricatures; they burlesque reality, and using them for more than illustrative purposes is a gloss on a gloss. It is also, however, a useful form of shorthand, and it is in that context and spirit that I present the players: John Bull, the Briton, was Protestant and imperial—often imperious. He took his identity from an amalgam of Anglo-Saxon self-consciousness, reformed Christianity, unyielding hostility to Catholicism, and a commercial empire of impressive sweep. The American Uncle Sam—or Brother Jonathan—was his natural issue. As militantly Protestant as the parent, he had nonetheless learned much and changed much from leaving home. Distance made him rebellious and estranged. His identity arose from his free institutions—political and commercial—from the Protestantism that gave strength to both and from his vast expanse of land, the frontier that fed him and shaped his character.

The third player had an entirely different set of symbols. Both its inventors and its exploiters saw Ireland as Catholic and irrational, a subaltern Other. Ireland had no share in either English or American triumphs, was in fact the victim of both and, largely because of that, the potential subverter of both. George Fitzhugh was a special pleader and as such must be read with care and a healthy skepticism. At that, he had it right when he implied that Britain had let Ireland starve and that starving Irish, as surely as African Americans, answered America's Help Wanted notices and provided that discordant counterpoint to America's righteous empire. As color distinguished the Southern working class, so religion distinguished the Northern. The great irony is that many of the reformers of the North reviled the exploiters of the one while joining in the simultaneous exploitation of the other. By their reckoning, there was no place in the American culture code for Irish papists. They were too priest-ridden to be republican, too lazy and irremediably ignorant to do more than fill the bottommost ranks of an industrializing economy.

It is appropriate to let an Englishman have the final word on the issue. In 1836, in a burst of inspired anti-Irish rhetoric, Benjamin Disraeli gave loud vent to attitudes that were centuries old among Britons. The Irish, Disraeli said, "hate our free and fertile isle. They hate our order, our civilization, our enterprising industry, our sustained courage, our decorous liberty, our pure religion." In this instance, as in others, the Irish hated what they could not possibly understand. The cultural differences between Irish and Briton could be neither traversed nor mediated. The Irish were a "wild, reckless, indolent, uncertain and superstitious race." They "have no sympathy with the English character. Their fair idea of human felicity is an alternative of clannish broils and coarse idolatry. Their history describes an unbroken circle of bigotry and blood." Disraeli's list of Irish inadequacies was fairly exhaustive; if he omitted anything it is not easily detected. But note in particular three references: Britons enjoyed a "pure religion"; the Irish were "superstitious"; their idea of happiness arose from a volatile mix of "clannish broils and coarse idolatry." Such people could have "no sympathy with" or even basic understanding of the superior "character" of the citizens of the larger and fairer isle.[77]

Neither could these Irish have understood Americans, a great number of whom were of precisely the same mind as Disraeli. The only thing that distinguished the American response to the Irish from that of the British was that the presence of slavery provided Americans with a ready-made organizational metaphor; the Catholicism of the Irish was like slavery, supported slavery, was slavery. This again raises the question of how it was that Irish Catholics were allowed to enter the United States at all. Their unrestricted immigration must have appeared to some like the equivalent of the reopening of the African slave trade. The answer to the question goes beyond the contention that the Irish were, for all their obvious deformities, white. They seemed particularly well suited, by reason of those same deformities, to work with tools with long handles. This and this alone commended them. The passage of the Republic required, as Hale and Emerson so elegantly phrased it, an abundance of industrial guano.

CHAPTER 3

Slavery, the Irish, and Western America

"But, too unruly deer, he broke the pale
And feeds from home."

　　　　　　　　　　　—*Shakespeare,* Comedy of Errors *(ii.1.100)*

Before anyone even knew its full extent or what much of it looked like, Americans knew that the West was the source of their national identity and that its development would have to be shaped and directed in accordance with well-defined republican principles. They had reason to be optimistic. Jefferson had written in 1801 that Americans could "look forward to distant times, when our rapid multiplication will expand itself and cover the whole northern, if not the southern continent, with a people speaking the same language, governed in similar forms, and by similar laws." He said nothing of religion. He had no need to. It was enough simply to note that he could not "contemplate with satisfaction either blot or mixture on that surface," however far that surface might extend. The "principles of the Declaration of Independence would become the recognized system for the whole continent . . . our endeavor should surely be, to make our hemisphere . . . the domicile of freedom." There was no room in that hemispheric plan for the ideologically deviant, that is, those who did not interpret the Declaration of Independence as containing self-evident truths.[1]

Of all the potential threats, two came to dominant American consciousness: Catholicism and Southern slavery. It was worrisome enough that both were part of American society. For Jefferson, according to one historian, the Catholic Church was "the most dangerous" of religions. It represented "the institutionalization of medieval superstition, sectarian narrowness, and monarchical despotism." Obviously, papist blots and mixtures were more than just eyesores. The Catholic Church was a small and feeble thing in Jefferson's America, certainly a less formidable threat than slavery. But that could change. It might grow and expand into the still unexplored parts of the continent. If left to nature's designs, the West would ensure that republicanism and democracy would flourish because monarchies and the trappings of aristocracy—read Catholicism and slavery—were so unsuited to western places as to be unthinkable. But nature's designs were frequently undone; the domicile of freedom was not guaranteed. If republicanism was to survive, Americans would have to remain as watchful as they had been at the time of the Quebec Act in 1774.[2]

Their vigilance was particularly critical during the market revolution of the 1830s and 1840s and the evangelical Protestant religious revival, the so-called Second Great Awakening, that accompanied and ministered to it. The accelerated pace of industrialization following the takeoff did not call social class and ethnic tensions into being, but it certainly made them more noticeable and threatening. During this time of transition, the West became a kind of national balance wheel. The free-labor ideology, later incorporated into the ideology of the Republican Party, would have made no sense without vast areas of "unsettled" lands beyond a so-called frontier line. It made little enough sense with those lands. The West— the idea, not the reality—allowed free-labor Republicans to promote industrial capitalism without having to deal with the less lovely aspects of it. "Frontiering" meant pushing out the borders of freedom and imposing a set of republican values to which newly made industrial workers—both immigrant and native, and whether they went west or not—would be asked to subscribe.[3]

They would not be asked gently, particularly after Americans began to turn themselves into a distinct people—not just Protestant and republican but a separate "volk." Those Western/American/Protestant Anglo-Saxon values—individualism, a conquering spirit, competition, manliness, and grit—became the soul of the "ascriptive civic myths" that Americans used to define themselves. The West would imprint these ascribed values on all who entered it, but the mythical vision remained that only Anglo-Saxons and Protestants could "conquer" the West, and only the West could reinforce the Anglo-Saxon and Protestant code of conquest.[4]

Going west was a part of the racialist alchemy of the volk and central to what was becoming a uniquely American cultural standard. The frontier was the playground of the Anglo-Saxons, and those most-favored people, "the wire-grass of nations," as one of their admirers called them, were destined to "extirpate . . . the . . . inferior races." But because going west in America as surely as going west to America was an act of self-cleansing, the abnegation of old and discredited values for newer and more righteous ones, these western paladins were of a specific and Protestant sort. Kit Carson, for example, was one of those heroes; his embarrassing conversion to Catholicism was air-brushed out of his portrait. The heart of America was not New York but the West, where the sanitized Kit Carsons lived. The light of the new world shone brighter the deeper into it one went, and it did not shine on popery.[5]

Horace Bushnell spoke for many Northern reformers when he wrote in 1835 that religious purity, by which he meant evangelical Protestantism and the anti-Catholicism that accompanied it, which he shared in full measure, had to "call up around it all its own proper institutions. He who apportions all events to their times with sovereign wisdom had reserved such a world unknown . . . a vast continent of forests still in the wilderness of nature. . . . It was Protestantism in religion that produced republicanism in government." This was a nice mix of Protestantism and the mythical West, but note the full reach of his comment: Protestantism produced republicanism; the Republic, for its part, had to protect its Protestant foundations and essence and advance its core values or cease to be. Luckily (though luck had nothing to do with it as far as Bushnell was concerned), God was so pleased that he gave to the American people the means to nurture and extend the fusion of secular and religious faiths, a "vast continent . . . a wilderness of nature."[6]

There was nothing uncommon about Bushnell's associations. The West was the seed ground for the emerging American character. In Hector St. John de Crèvecoeur's mind, for example, America was inhospitable ground for Catholics not just because of an inherited anti-Catholicism but because Americans were creatures of the forests, "new men" who rejected old ways and institutions. There was room for Catholics in America, but only if they became bad Catholics. The West was the place where the second act would be played out; Catholics who did not believe in second acts, being born again, or being witness to new truths would find it a most inhospitable place. Michael Chevalier agreed with Crèvecoeur. He said that Americans had no sense of the past; indeed, their rootlessness approached vulgarity. But this was a most creative vulgarity; it deserved most of the credit for American democracy and for the assured success of America's mission.[7]

"Mission" is a very interesting and loaded word. It is inseparable from destiny and so exists only in future time. Ordinarily, like everything in the future, it is entirely contingent. The American belief in a "*manifest* destiny" implied an assured future, a noncontingent mission. It was a contradiction in terms or extraordinarily arrogant or both. No one had to be bothered with the metaphysical implications of clairvoyance, of knowing the future with such absolute certainty. Even manifest destinies, however, had to be watched over and protected against enemies. The future was assured only for the wary.

Few in America were more certain of this missionary impulse or of the potential threats to its fulfillment than Samuel F. B. Morse and Lyman Beecher. Morse and Beecher could rightly be accused of stylistic extravagance, but they spoke for many when they warned of an irrepressible conflict between popish tyranny and

Protestant republicanism. A great number of Americans were of that mind, as the routine association of Southern slavery with Catholicism would attest. The difference with Morse and Beecher was that both believed that the conflict would center on the control of the West and would likely be fought out there. In 1834, the year before Bushnell mixed Protestantism and frontiers, Morse warned of a "foreign conspiracy against the liberties of the United States." The foreign enemy was popery, and it was at the gates. Morse was unrestrained. "The *house is on fire.* . . . may we sleep securely . . . while the sappers and miners of foreign despots are at work under our feet?" In less metaphorical terms, the despots and their unwitting and witless agents, namely Catholic immigrants, were moving into the Mississippi Valley. Should the Catholics capture the West, the Republic would surely fall. This was no time for indolence, and in 1835 Morse sounded reveille: "Up! Up! I beseech you. Awake! To your posts! . . . Place your guards. . . . Shut your gates." "It is *Liberty itself* that is in danger," and not just the liberty of the United States, "but the *liberty of the world* . . . and THE WORLD EXPECTS AMERICA, REPUBLICAN AMERICA, TO DO HER DUTY."[8]

While Morse was declaiming on America's duty, the Reverend Beecher was giving sermons also warning of the Catholic menace in the Mississippi Valley. In 1835 these sermons were published as *A Plea for the West.* The anti-Catholicism of these years had always contained an implied warning that popery imperiled the American future, but space and time were conjoined—the West was America's future. Beecher made that connection directly; his was a plea *for the West.* He did not make it as a humble supplicant. Beecher first confirmed his nation's providential mission. It was "plain," he said, "that the religious and political destiny of our nation is to be decided in the West." That vast region was "destined to be the great central power of the nation, and, under heaven, must affect powerfully the cause of free institutions and the liberty of the world." Those were high stakes. The West was a prized endowment, but title to it was not guaranteed. Like Morse, Beecher was not referring to America's European rivals. The threat to America was internal. Catholicism, Beecher sermonized, was inherently "adverse to liberty, . . . its clergy to a great extent are dependent on foreigners . . . opposed to the principles of our government . . . a dark-minded, vicious populace—a poor, uneducated reckless mass of infuriated animalism."[9]

Beecher can only have been speaking of those few pre-Famine Catholic Irish who had wandered into the Mississippi Valley, there to become the dupes of continental Catholic despots. The teachings of this imperious and impious church had to be combated. They were "capital offenses not to be tolerated, but punished by the civil power with disfranchisement, death and confiscation of goods." Nothing less would have been sufficient. Beecher detailed the many crimes of popery, including the power of the priests "to corroborate or cancel their [parishioners'] oath of allegiance and to sway them to obedience or insurrection by the power of life or death eternal." If, in fact, the priests still had such power, "if such, I say," and he was fairly screaming now,

> are the maxims *avowed by her pontiffs, sanctioned by her councils, stereotyped on her ancient records, advocated by her most approved authors, illustrated in all ages by her history, and still* UNREPEALED. . . . if these things are so, is it invidious and is it superfluous to call the attention of the nation to the bearing of such a denomination upon our civil and religious institutions . . . ? It is the *right of* SELF-PRESERVATION, and the denial of it is TREASON or the INFATUATION OF FOLLY.

There was little to distinguish between Beecher and Theodore Parker—except that Beecher's plea was more nearly a rant and he moved the foreign conspiracy from the dark places of America's eastern cities, where Parker confronted it, to the vestal lands of the West. Parker was describing a sacrilege—Catholicism's baleful influence on republicanism. Beecher was describing an unholy terror—the designs of Catholicism on the West, the wellspring of that republicanism. His was less a plea for the West than a declaration of godly war in defense of its and the nation's future.[10]

In 1846 Albert Barnes, another of the Northern reformers who mixed anti-slavery and anti-Catholicism, wrote that America's western regions were to be "the great battle-field of the world, the place where . . . the destinies of the world [were] to be decided." "If this nation is to be free," Barnes went on, "the population of the [Mississippi] valley is to preserve and perpetuate [that] freedom; if it is to be enslaved, the chains that are to fetter us are to be forged beyond the [Appalachian] mountains." Note that Barnes did not say forged south of the Ohio River. Slavery was the issue, but not the chattel slavery of the South. He was referring to the threat posed by Catholic designs on the Mississippi Valley. That threat had to be taken seriously, but Barnes was confident. "The moss-grown cathedral," he wrote, "the pompous ceremonial, the long train of priests" were "unseen where a man makes a western prairie his home." Barnes's optimism, his belief in what might be called the "natural limits" to Catholic expansion, was not, however, universally shared. As Beecher in particular had made clear, there were already far too many cathedrals on the western prairies and more— including, according to some, the one that would house the offices of the pope— were planned.[11]

This crusade against the spread of Catholicism bore a striking resemblance to the simultaneous campaign to check permanently the spread of slavery. How could it not have? How could those who fought so doggedly against the west-ward expansion of Southern slavery be expected to loll about and acquiesce in the westward expansion of European slavery? Slavery and Catholicism had been so closely associated in the public mind for so long that their images began to cross and transmutate. It followed that the fears and the methods of the holy warriors against both systems of slavery would be alike. Both systems were in open violation of America's emerging civic identity and the myths that accompanied it. But that identity also set boundaries. In ascribing values, it also proscribed and labeled those values that did not fit the cultural template and had expansionist tendencies that needed to be checked.

As with Catholicism in France or Italy, freedom-loving Americans could do little about slavery in South Carolina or Virginia. But there was much they could do to quarantine it and prevent its spread into America's new lands. Some believed that the expansion of Southern slavery had "natural limits" too, and these included climatological as well as cultural barriers. As Daniel Webster rather famously put it, the question of chattel slavery in the West had been decided by God—and God was not inclined to permit it. Webster's prediction, however, gave a false sense of security. The danger posed by an expansionist Southern slave power could not be left to chance or "natural limits"; it had to be met directly.[12]

In 1854 William Seward issued a bold challenge to the South during the debates on the Kansas-Nebraska Act: "Come on then," he dared the "Gentlemen of the Slave States." "We will engage in competition for the virgin soil of Kansas." The gentlemen of the slave states were no less combative. It would be quite a competition. Neither side, however, could escape its manifest destiny; neither had a choice but to engage the other. The national house had survived half-slave and half-free, but the West could not. That too was manifest. If slavery were to expand into the western regions, the northern free labor system would be effectively cut off from those same regions—with consequences too terrible to contemplate.[13]

Southerners faced exactly the same crisis; they knew precisely what quarantining slavery would mean to them. Richard Meade of Virginia warned in 1851 that the South had to "thin . . . [its] black population," a polite way of saying that a slave labor system had some internal hazards of its own that were not unlike those of the free-labor North. Meade's solution was to activate a Southern safety valve by bringing upward of 50,000 slaves to California. This would be "invaluable . . . as a means" of relieving the racial/social class tensions that bedeviled the South. The slave states lived in constant fear of "servile revolt," said another Southerner, without any apparent realization that Northerners were worrying about "servile" revolts as well. There were some, Meade admitted, who "say that the climate and productions [of California] are unsuited to slave labor," but "they are either endeavoring to deceive or are deceiving themselves." So much for "natural limits."[14]

Meade made clear the urgency of the crisis. The South was in grave danger: "my race and my country are . . . engaged in a death struggle." Southern whites faced a race war of apocalyptic scale and had to "retain the power of self-protection. . . .

What will give us this power?" Meade asked. The same thing that would give it to the North: "Space—empire. . . . I say, then, to the South, stretch your arm to the Pacific. . . . To the Pacific, then, I say—to the Pacific. Your future security depends entirely upon your strength; secure to yourselves while you can, an empire." The previous year, William Lowndes, with unconscious irony, had offered the frightening prospect that if the South failed in this effort, if Republicans had their way in blocking the expansion of slavery and closing the Southerners' safety valve, the relationship of the South to the North would be like that of "poor Ireland . . . to England."[15]

So be it, Northerners reasoned. An Ohio Republican stated simply in 1861 that "no more slavery in the territories and no more slave states must be our motto." George Templeton Strong explained what was at issue, writing in 1863 that the Civil War was "a struggle of two hostile and irreconcilable systems of society for the rule of this continent." Oliver Morton of Indiana knew that "if we do not exclude slavery from the Territories, it will exclude us"—and with devastating consequences. In this context, the 1857 *Dred Scott* decision, which theoretically opened up the West to slavery, was the equivalent of the Quebec Act of 1774. Once again a system of slavery was established on republican America's western border.[16]

But if the expansion of slavery could be blocked, what prizes the future would hold for the North. Salmon Chase made both the contrast and the stakes of the contest clear. A West from which slavery was prohibited would be characterized by "freedom not serfdom; freeholds not tenancies; democracy not despotism; education not ignorance . . . progress, not stagnation or retrogression." Chase was a politician, however, and so the implicit in his comments must also be considered. His remarks have to be read into as well as read. I do not dispute that Chase was talking about the chattel slavery of the Southern states; but if we consider his descriptions of the effects of slavery—serfdom, tenancies, despotism, ignorance, stagnation, and retrogression—and apply them to contemporary descriptions of Catholic Ireland, it is fair to conclude that it was all systems of slavery, not just the Southern version, that had to be restrained.[17]

By the 1850s there were other, nonpolitical types for whom the association between Southern slavery and the Catholic variety could be made explicit and direct and who knew instinctively that blocking the expansion of one into the West involved necessarily blocking the expansion of the other. Theodore Parker, perhaps believing his native Massachusetts was lost to invading Irish papists, was determined to save Kansas. America, he said in 1854 in a speech on the Nebraska question, was facing a crisis. Would the West, the future of the country, have as its symbols the "schools of Ohio, or the ignorance of Tennessee? . . . the public libraries, newspapers, lectures, lyceums, of Massachusetts; or the . . . ignoble sloth of Mississippi and Alabama?" In other words, was the West to have bad roads and bad morals? To this point in his address, even Parker's concern seems strictly limited to Southern slavery; but popery was never far from his mind, and he concluded these remarks on the West by saying that this was a "great religious question, that the Northern religion, the Northern faith in God," was being challenged. "America," he reminded his readers, "has a Church without a Bishop," it has "no 'Pope,' no 'King,' no 'Noble.'" In America "the monster dies."[18]

Precisely which monster was undefined and unimportant. Which of the systems of slavery was proxy for the other made no difference. What mattered was that "the mighty arm" of the Republic, as an Ohio Know-Nothing wrote in 1856 in regard to the Kansas-Nebraska Act, was being "prostituted to subserve the interests of papal power and slavery aggression." That was a curious and revealing comment. How the papal power could be subserved by the Kansas-Nebraska Act was not explained, but it was clear that both forms of slavery had to be resisted. This was also the message of the Reverend Henry Ward Beecher, son of Lyman and of the same mind regarding popery and the West. E. L. Godkin recalled hearing Henry Ward Beecher speak in 1856. "His subject was the connection between liberty and religion," and he called on all "Christians . . . to protest by their votes against the extension of any system which prevented a man's being as much of a man as he could possibly be in this world." Since Catholicism, as surely as Southern slavery, had repeatedly been described as just such a system, his reference is clear.[19]

The similar language used to describe Southern and Catholic expansionism was matched by similar methods in dealing with the threat posed by both. Slave owners had enough political power to block legislative attempts to restrict the spread of slavery and absolute power to block any antislavery campaigns in the South—power that they likely would have used with fierce determination. But they had no particular and immediate authority in those western territories where the issue of slavery and free labor was being openly contested. This was particularly the case with Kansas, opened to slavery by the Kansas-Nebraska Act of 1854. The churches of New England responded to the Kansas-Nebraska Act by forming the New England Emigrant Aid Society, arming its legions with rifles—known, appropriately, as "Beecher's Bibles"—and dispatching them to Kansas. "Bleeding Kansas," with much of the blood let by a militant John Brown, was the result.[20]

Anti-Catholicism offered no comparable western spectacle, partly because American Catholics were too few, too spread out, and too powerless to do much more than mutter their complaints and try to defend themselves from the more rabid of the nativists. At that, organizations were formed with the expressed intent of saving the West from Catholicism, and these organizations took their responsibilities at least as seriously as any of those set up to save the West from Southern slavery. A spokesman for the Home Missionary Society in Iowa in 1842 called specifically for the churches of New England to "station their men here, on these outposts of Zion to counteract [the] influence" of the Catholics then resident and those whom the "Catholics in Europe [could] afford to sustain . . . here, with a view to *future influence*." This was fifteen years before those same churches deployed the antislavery societies and directed them to Kansas for the same purpose of counteracting the future influence of Southern slaveholders.[21]

What form the Home Missionary Society's anti-Catholic counteraction might take was left indefinite, though the words "station" and "outposts" had a faintly martial and threatening tone to them. But even John Brown could not have exceeded the Reverend Thaddeus B. Hurlbut of the Home Missionary Society in intensity and passion. Indeed, rhetorically at least, if sheer venom—not to mention pathology—counted for anything, Hurlbut was as fanatical as a phalanx of John Browns. Hurlbut was writing in 1846 from somewhere in the West. "One formidable enemy with which we have to contend," he remarked, "is 'the Man of Sin,' 'speaking lies in hypocrisy.'" But the man of sin was not unaccompanied. Hurlbut spoke also of a "*strange* woman, sitting upon a scarlet-covered beast having seven heads and ten horns . . . having a golden cup in her hand full of abominations and filthiness of her fornications." She was "the mother of harlots. . . . she has drunk . . . the blood of *one hundred millions* of human beings! And yet her thirst is not abated or her tract gorged." It is uncertain if Hurlburt's reference was to the Virgin—the "Pope's Gal," as Parker had dubbed her—or to the whole feminized Catholic Church. Either way, one such as this would be a threat anywhere, for "her deadly wounds can never be healed." Hurlbut, however, noted with a singular horror that "with the desperation of a raging giant she seeks to renew the vigor of her youth, by breathing the free and balmy air, and traversing our wide and fertile plains of the great West."[22]

Slavery on occasions inspired the same kind of thunderous condemnation, but clearly this other "raging giant" and "mother of harlots" also had to be stopped. As with the effort to block the expansion of slavery, nativists used what weapons they had, plus a few others contrived for the occasion. Consider, for example, Parker's novel theory that Congress had a constitutional responsibility to ensure republican governments in each of the states. Obviously, it had a similar responsibility when it came to organizing western territories. Hence Congress had the full power to foreclose on both slavery and Catholicism in the West. Similarly, had the Know-Nothings succeeded in extending the probationary period for naturalization from six months to twenty-one years, immigrants would not only have been deprived of the suffrage but would have been denied the equal protection clause of the Constitution. In one sense their status would have been comparable to that of free blacks, stripped of their citizenship by the *Dred Scott* decision. Given the number of states that had prohibitions against black or mulatto immigration, the implications of a twenty-one-year probationary period are obvious. No state would have been under constitutional obligation to admit any immigrant,

Catholic or not. But it was Irish Catholic immigrants who were being targeted—
"raw, verdant[!], outlandish fellows," said one nativist, "with no more fitness to
act the great character of a Republic than a Chinese automaton."[23]

Consider as well the California Organizations of Vigilance, the Know-Nothings
of the Pacific, whose hostility to Irish Catholics was venomous and often lethal.
Although slightly more rambunctious than eastern Know-Nothings, the vigilantes
were standard-issue nativists. What makes California particularly interesting is that
the vigilantes were frequently allied with other nativists who were openly pro-
South and proslavery, the so-called Chivs (for chivalrous) Democrats. Although
not technically vigilantes, the Chivs were also the sworn enemies of California's
Irish. Fitzhugh and Grayson would have had a hard time with this pairing. It was,
by any accounting, a strange and fragile political alliance. Its focused violence
against Catholics in the 1850s openly contradicts the West's reputation for tolerance,
but it does more than break down a durable myth. The alliance of vigilante and
Chiv also confounds the related notions that Irish anxiety about their own whiteness made them especially cruel—if also pathetic—mimics of American racism and
that Irish Catholics were always and everywhere the "vassals" of the slave owners.[24]

The chivalrous proslavery Democrats of California had a particular dislike for
David Broderick, the son of Irish Catholics who had immigrated to Washington,
D.C., in the early 1820s. The vigilant ones shared this anti-Broderick enmity, if
for different reasons. Broderick was a Democrat who headed the "Irish machine"
in San Francisco and was a political power in state politics. Like the vast majority
of Californians, he was born and cut his political teeth in the East and brought
a certain eastern—and Irish—style of politics when he boarded his second boat.
He did not, however, bring any discernible racial insecurities; nor did he behave
like a liege subject of Southern slave owners. He was, in fact, a free soil Democrat
who as a senator broke with his party on the proslavery Lecompton Constitution for Kansas, led the opposition to a state bill to prevent "Free Negroes and
Persons of Color" from entering California, battled against nativist efforts to impose
a special tax on foreign miners, and fought to protect the rights of Mexicans
and Californios against nativist land grabbers.[25]

Broderick was said to control one faction of California's Democratic Party. That
control, it was also said, arose from Broderick's Irish connections and the willingness of the Irish to follow the "boss" blindly. The vigilante response, writes one
recent historian, was "to purge the city of 'corruption,' singling out twenty-nine
'cancerous' men to be eliminated through hanging, prison, or exile. Nearly all
twenty-nine were Democrats. Most were Irish Catholics and friends of Broderick's."
The Chivs' contribution to this nativist crusade was to have one of their own,
Judge David Terry, challenge Broderick to a duel, provide Broderick with a defective weapon, and observe as Terry shot him. The dying Broderick was alleged to
have said that he was killed because he "was opposed . . . to the extension of slavery."[26]

It is, of course, possible that the antislavery politics of California's Irish hid anti-black prejudices, that Broderick was hostile to the expansion of slavery because he was hostile to the expansion of blacks. I freely grant that the western alchemy of race was no less toxic than the eastern version, but the specifically Irish element in that alchemists' brew is more complicated than the whitening of the Irish version of the story would suggest. The safer and more charitable interpretation is to take Broderick at his word and assume that he and his Irish legions opposed slavery and did not want to see it fix itself on California or anywhere else in the West. That there were complex reasons for that opposition may be assumed and hardly distinguishes them from every other opponent of slavery, radical abolitionists included.[27]

The larger body of California vigilantes and nativists, however, did not line up with the Chivs in the Democratic Party but with the antislavery Know-Nothings and Republicans. Hinton Rowan Helper, who, as noted, believed that slavery and popery were hand in hand, was in California from 1851 to 1854. His book *The Land of Gold* praised the vigilantes and listed the Irish, along with the Chinese and Indians, among the "inferior races." William Gay, a Boston newspaper correspondent, reported from San Francisco on the urgency of congressional action to change immigration laws before California was "ruled by the rabble and the mob," whose type and shape were well known to his Boston readers. "Not a boy in our public schools of 14 . . . but is better acquainted with the institutions of our country than nine out of ten of these ignorant, bigoted Irish [who] are making great inroads."[28]

Fortunately, there was still time to stop them, but only if New Englanders took the lead and applied the lessons they had learned so painfully in dealing with their own "ignorant, bigoted Irish." Edward Everett, the president of Harvard, told those bound for California to "take the Bible in one hand and your New England civilization in the other." The Know-Nothing Stephen Webb, elected mayor of San Francisco with strong Vigilante support, noted with pride that "everywhere over our surface, in New England fashion, arise the spires of churches and schoolhouses; all the influences which have . . . crowned [San Francisco] with glory are New England influences." Needless to add, he did not mean by New England influences anything having to do with Boston and its Irish. Neither did Timothy Dwight Hunt, a Protestant minister in California, who had as his goal making "California the Massachusetts of the Pacific." He allowed that that would require a Cromwellian "cleansing," but such was "now in process."[29]

To the Vigilance Committees, the new Cromwellians, he wished "God speed" as they drove the Irish, presumably, to hell or (back to) Connacht; and "the *people* [of California], from the snows to the sea, say every day in thunder tones, Amen!" Their hallelujah shouts were earnest and timely. During his two years before the mast, Richard Henry Dana, an early convert to the antislavery principles of the

Republican Party, reported on his visit to San Francisco's "Cathedral of St. Mary
... where the Irish attend." It was "like one of our stifling Irish Catholic churches
in Boston or New York with intelligence in so small a proportion to the number
of faces." Stifling churches filled with the verdant ignorant were not as wicked
as slave auction houses, but the differences were of degree—and only a slight
degree, at that—not of kind. California could be defaced by Irish papists as surely
as Kansas could be corrupted by proslavery renegades from Missouri.[30]

Unfortunately, what Morse had referred to as the "leak in the ship" was filling
Northern cities with Irish as another and earlier leak had filled the South with
slaves. Systems of slavery had fixed themselves on the American past, but the
leaks could be stanched and America, with the help of God and some skillful
reconstructive plumbing, could be made pure again. The West would be the
American garden regained. The legacy of Appomattox involved far more than
emancipation and reunification. The defeated South would be reconstructed; the
West would be constructed. The blueprints, drawn from missionary zeal, traditional republican values, and market capitalism, were the same in both instances.
Saving the West from slavery was not just good for business—although it was
assuredly that. It was also a "holy enterprise" that "God had commissioned America
to undertake." Northern Republicans understood that unless they wanted the
West, and by definition America's future, to look like Mississippi and South
Carolina—or Italy and Ireland—they could not permit systems of slavery to
escape and corrupt the innocent.[31]

It is difficult to see William Gilpin as anything more than a parody of the
western promoter, so overly zealous was he in the claims he made for the West.
But in an age of extravagance—and many of the claims of the Republican Party
regarding the future of the West were nothing if not extravagant—Gilpin was a
representative type. He may have tended toward the lavish, but he spoke for many
when he wrote after the Civil War:

> The ... destiny of the American people is to subdue this continent ...
> to set the principle of self-government at work ... to establish a new
> order in human affairs—to set free the enslaved—to regenerate super-
> annuated nations—to change darkness into light—to teach old nations
> a new civilization—to confirm the destiny of the human race—to shed
> a new and resplendent glory upon mankind ... to dissolve the spell of
> tyranny ... to absolve the curse that weighs down humanity, and to
> shed blessings round the world. *Divine Task! immortal mission.*

This was not something one trifled with; though Gilpin made no specific reference
to Catholicism or to the Irish, it was clear that the American West had a nobler role
to play than that of providing cabin space for slaves or shanty space for papists.[32]

The war against the pope and his agents had a clear and unambiguous purpose but a number of contradictory aspects. The North needed Irish Catholics to fill out the bottom levels of its industrializing workforce. Dependence on "racially" inferior stock was not ideal—a point many Southern slave owners would have echoed in regard to African slaves—but it was unavoidable, and Northern capital knew it. And so the Irish continued to dig and delve, a cheap source of unskilled labor, like blacks. These emigrating Irish millions, the Celtic fringe's contribution to the surplus labor necessary to industrial development, did not just lift, haul, and dig in America's eastern cities, but even those who did remain in the East contributed vitally to the development of the West. Without their labor, there would not have been adequate capital and population for America's westward thrust. As Richard Slotkin put it, "the cheap land Frontier of the West was matched by a 'cheap labor' Frontier in the East."[33]

It was the cheap labor frontier in the East that was the more immediate source of trouble. Cheap labor was unhappy and hence potentially mutinous labor: unless those who relied on it wished to live in a constant state of high anxiety, a means had to be found to defuse its potential for militancy—which returns the discussion to the idea of the West as a safety valve, both as an abstract idea, a fable of capitalism, and as a semicredible means of dealing with labor and its discontents. Edward Everett had used the term "safety-valve" in connection with the West as early as 1829; Caleb Cushing repeated the phrase in 1839. Even Northern abolitionists embraced the idea of a safety valve; access to western lands, wrote one of them, was one of the central features distinguishing the truly free workers from the North from the slaves of the South. Neither Everett nor Cushing—nor, it would appear, any of the abolitionists—said anything about this safety valve ever closing or ever needing to be activated. For them it operated automatically and in perpetuity.[34]

Not all Northerners were that confident of the safety valve's efficiency. As early as 1830, before the great takeoff had fairly begun, Samuel C. Allen of Massachusetts warned that only the "unsettled lands in the West" "retard[ed]" social-class conflict, but that this was "an accidental circumstance" that could only "retard" the "celerity" of that conflict. It could not permanently avert it. Allen's was a minority voice, however, particularly after the Republican Party began to form its free-labor ideology around the availability of an open frontier. America's quite unique ability to dodge and escape, according to Republicans, was not a transient phenomenon. For the Republicans, it—and all knew what "it" meant—would never happen here. There were, however, some critics of the nonchalance and shortsightedness of the Republicans. Unsettled lands, they pointed out, became settled lands. The West was not inexhaustible; it could not hold off the inevitable.[35]

Among the first to comment on this inherent flaw in Republican thinking were radicals of various sorts both in America and in Europe, including Marx. The free-labor ideology, with its insistence on market-driven wages and support of the "cheap labor frontier," was for them an instrument of capitalist aggression. Attacks on the Republican creed from this source were to be expected. But the attacks came as well from another and less predictable source. There is paradox enough in the close association of nativists and abolitionists; that Southern defenders of slavery would be lecturing Northerners on the fatuousness of their safety-valve theories extends the definition of paradox. But when the eminent Virginian George Fitzhugh justified slavery he accompanied his defense of the Southern labor system with an ominous warning about the workings of the Northern one, a warning that would become increasingly familiar after the Civil War: Northern workers, Fitzhugh predicted, would not remain forever docile. In language that leagued him with other labor radicals, though without their sense of eager anticipation, he cautioned Northerners that, once the workers' patience and resources were exhausted, they would rise up and reveal the hollowness of the North's vaunted free-labor ideology.[36]

Fitzhugh was unsure when this working-class rebellion would begin, and even less certain when or how it would end. But he was certain that all that prevented it was the existence of a vast continent of unsettled lands in the American West. Robert Barnwell Rhett of South Carolina agreed, noting in 1838 that "it is the accident of our situation alone, having a continent to people, which has enabled us so long to maintain" our free institutions. "But the time is rapidly approaching . . . when the way to the West will be blocked up." Blocked up by what and with what consequences, Rhett did not say. It was Fitzhugh who took the argument and made it part of an extended attack on the free-labor ideology of the North, an attack in which he and Marx were in virtual lockstep. Marx had referred to America's western lands as an "anomaly," but one that gave American industrial capitalists a significant advantage over those of England and the continent. As one Englishman lamented, "if only it were possible to interpose Nova Scotia or New Zealand in the ocean space between Great Britain and Ireland."[37]

Geographical realities being what they were, England would have to deal with its labor problem as best it could, which included, in the minds of some Americans, dumping its unwanted Irish Catholics on the Protestant United States. In America, on the other hand, the legitimate demands of labor could be deflected simply by reminding workers that their grievances were only temporary, that mobility was built into the American system, and that immediate relief was a mere matter of moving out, moving on, and moving up. As noted, there was something cold blooded, not to mention illusory, about this remedy. Recall the almost slapstick exchange between Thomas O'Donnell and the congressional committee investigating industrial unrest. O'Donnell would "go west" and "take up a farm," in the process opening up his mill job to someone else who would labor for a time and then go west and take up a farm. It was all syncopated, like a game of musical chairs, but with enough chairs for everyone.

A certain logic did attach to the idea that covered wagons were preferable to street barricades. If there were too many workers in the East and low wages and misery resulted, and too few workers in the West with attendant high wages and the promise of independence, then let the government devise a system that gave eastern workers access to the West. The nascent labor movement also embraced part of this argument, demanding that Congress make western land cheaper or, better yet, free. Some workers would leave the East and take up those lands. Even those who stayed would benefit; their wages would go up in direct proportion to the number of workers who left. Capital's labor costs would increase, but so would its profits, and it would be rid of the looming threat of social-class upheaval. William Gilpin made it all sound so simple: America had only to "combine *idle* populations and *idle* lands . . . and fire up the stagnant torpidity of both." Was ever a social system so perfect and so self-activating in its operation?[38]

Even Fitzhugh was taken in by it. "The situation of the North," he wrote, "is abnormal and anomalous . . . in forty-eight hours, laborers may escape to the West, and become proprietors. It is a blessing to them to be thus expelled, and a blessing to those who expel them." It is difficult to reconcile his use of the word "escape" followed in the next sentence with the word "expel." It suggests a certain ambivalence—or carelessness and confusion. In all events, Fitzhugh wanted it understood that this was a "forc[ed] emigration to the West," evidence of "the despotism of capital." He also wanted it understood that even this despotic remedy would be available only temporarily. "Society will not fail in the Northeast," Fitzhugh admitted, "until the whole West is settled. The emigration to the West rids the East of a surplus population." Fitzhugh might well have added "potentially insurgent" to "surplus." But with settlement would come the reckoning; Northerners would have to pay an awful price for the folly of basing their social policy on "accidents" and "anomalies."[39]

Fitzhugh's contemporary James Henry Hammond of South Carolina was even more blunt. Hammond, like Fitzhugh, understood that he could not present a coherent defense of slavery without directly challenging the champions of wage labor in the North. He took particular offense at their smug and untested assumption that their system was based on a fundamental equality between the users and the providers of labor and was, as a consequence, inherently stable. Hammond allowed that "the whole world had abolished slavery. Aye, the *name*, but not the *thing*." He did not reproach the North for its slavery, only for its self-righteous refusal to admit that it engaged in it. As for the Northern claims that its workers were free and hence content, he was dismissive to the point of contemptuousness:

"There is afloat a fearful rumor that there have been consultations for Vigilance Committees." Surely, he added, "You know what that means." For the hopelessly dim-witted in the North, he offered this explanation. It was one with which Fitzhugh—and Marx—would have been in total accord. "Transient and temporary causes have thus far been your preservation," Hammond said. "The great West has been open to your surplus population," by which he meant the "hordes of semibarbarian immigrants, who are crowding in year by year."[40]

But these were semibarbarians of a particular sort. "Have you heard," Hammond asked Northern free-labor ideologues, "that the ghosts of Mendoza and Torquemada are stalking in the streets of your great cities? That the inquisition is at hand? you call it progress. Whither?" Whither indeed. Hammond was writing in 1858. His use of the images and specters of the Inquisition can only have been a reference to the two million Catholic Irish who had immigrated in the previous decade. His reference to vigilance committees was also revealing; there were no vigilantes in the East. Hammond was talking about California, the most glittering part of the golden West. If the West was what stood between Northern capital and, as Fitzhugh put it, societal failure, then the North was clearly doomed.[41]

It is fair to question the sincerity of Fitzhugh's (and Hammond's) advocacy of the rights of Northern laborers; Fitzhugh's so-called seignorial defense of slavery would, after all, have made chattel slaves of the Northern white working class, including its Irish component. Fitzhugh's point was that they were slaves anyway; their misery arose solely because they were "slaves without masters" to care for them. Southern slaveholders had better ethical instincts than Northern ones— witness the moral superiority of Southern slavery to Northern slavery. Witness, as well, the inane and craven Northern refusal to acknowledge even that its system also enslaved. But if one can put aside for the moment Fitzhugh's advocacy of the enslavement of the North's lower or working class, albeit in the name of kindness, a case can be made that the self-proclaimed white slaves of the North had a powerful champion in the aristocratic Virginian.

More than just irony is involved. As already noted, some Northerners tried to persuade the antislavery forces to take up the cause of the Northern working class with as much determination as they had shown in taking up the cause of the Southern. They tried, in other words, to split the union of nativism and abolitionism and align reform politics. These champions of Northern labor—though they cannot have liked the fact—found themselves on the side of the Fitzhughs. Those whom these labor reformers attempted to enlist in their cause were essentially being asked to join with seignorial defenders of slavery, at least long enough to take seriously the grievances of Northern "white slaves." This the forces of antislavery would not do. In their minds, Northern workers were *free;* they were not slaves of any kind and certainly not to wages. Only Southern workers were *slaves;* a system of wage labor would liberate them as Northern workers were liberated.

The Northern system was benevolent; the Southern was cruel. That was all that counted. Fitzhugh laughed, scorning these arguments as hypocritical. In a world in which attacks on slavery were accompanied by attacks on Catholicism, it was somehow fitting that the most ideologically consistent of the Southern defenses of slavery would read, sometimes quite literally, like a Communist manifesto.[42]

The only comfort free-labor ideologues could take from the alliance of Marx and Fitzhugh, other than the sheer incongruity of the pairing, was that it did offer capital a reprieve: the revolution might come, but not immediately, not until the safety valve of free land was closed. Until such time—and Republicans in particular thought it would be a very long time—the West provided them with a way to manage both their cheap labor and their cheap land frontiers by allowing the two to work synergistically, each solving the problems of the other. And this is what gave such urgency to the sectional debate over slavery in the western territories: the expansion of slavery would sabotage the safety valve. Northern laborers would not move West, as it was presumed every instinct of their being told them to do, if the region had been infected and profaned by the presence of slaveholders—and black slaves. If the West was to be a place of escape for free white workers, slave workers had to be excluded from it.[43]

But there was a problem with this North/West equipoise that went deeper than the charge that it was accidental and impermanent or that permitting Southern slavery to enter it would destroy the West's usefulness as a safety valve. If the priest-ridden Irish went west, what was to prevent *them* from contaminating the fairest part of America by their popery and their unwavering and mindless commitment to the Democratic Party and its proslavery policies? Massachusetts Republicans, for example, a great many of whom had entered the party through the "vestibule" of Know-Nothingism, ascribed John Charles Frémont's defeat in 1856 to the foreign vote in the West, making no distinction between Protestant and Catholic foreigners. In January 1857, less than three months after the Republican Frémont's defeat, Edward L. Pierce, a Chicago Republican, sent a quite public letter to the leaders of his party in Massachusetts in an attempt to educate them in the realities of mid-nineteenth century politics. Pierce explained that it was not western immigrants as such who had voted against Frémont, but immigrants (and their American-born sons) of a certain kind. Pierce used blunt language. Voting records from selected Illinois counties, he said, "may surprise some persons in Massachusetts, where the foreigners are generally Irish Catholics." "The foreigners of the West," he continued, "while including this class . . . are yet composed in a larger proportion of Germans, Scandinavians, and other nations. . . . A large mass of the Germans hate Catholicism more bitterly than even the Puritans of New England do." That must have been encouraging news. But Pierce had more. Those immigrants voted strongly for Frémont. So did some of the German Catholics "and even the most intelligent of the Catholic Irish."[44]

The problem, unhappily for Republican prospects, was that there were so few of the latter, but Pierce's points were clear. First, the Republican Party had to learn what the more politically savvy of the Know-Nothings had already learned and exercise some discretion on the immigrant question. The threat to freedom came not from immigrants generally but from Catholic, proslavery, Democratic immigrants—in a word, the Irish. And second, Easterners exaggerated even that threat. Nativist and Republican fears that the Catholic Irish would contaminate the West and win it for the Democratic Party and slavery were groundless. Protestant immigrants, particularly from Germany, would win the West for freedom and the Republican Party. Had Pierce and the other Republicans known of the looming and extensive immigration from Protestant Scandinavia, they would have had even more reason for optimism.[45]

Pierce made a good case for a more careful and denominationally sensitive approach to the issue of immigrants in the West. His words had to have been of comfort even to the anxious nativists of Massachusetts. But he could not answer the question of what to do with Edward Everett Hale's "refugees from defeat," the shoveled-out Irish of *an Gorta Mór*. Much of the cheap labor in the East consisted of Irish Catholics who answered the Help (unskilled) Wanted (desperately and now) notices. It was for just such as these that the safety valve was of greatest use. If the industrializing East was to escape the Terror that Marx and Fitzhugh had prophesied, the valve had to emit the Irish. They had to be expelled or allowed to escape, to borrow the language of Fitzhugh. But what of the prophecies of Morse and Beecher—or even those of Pierce? If the West was to be saved, and with it the freedom that was America's birthright, then those same Irish and the Catholicism with which they defined themselves had to be kept out. Did not the legacy of the Civil War require their exclusion as surely as the exclusion of Southern slavery? Clearly, the Republican Party was going to have to make up its mind.

On this issue, the historical record is indisputable; Republicans decided to save capitalism and hope that republicanism and democracy could somehow save themselves. In reality, of course, their position was neither as resigned nor as fatalistic as that sounds. First, they made no distinction between capitalism and democracy. They conflated the two then washed their hands of the ideological and social carnage that resulted. Second, the West was the place where even the most tenacious of the moss-covered habits of old worlds would be shed. It had been identified as central to America's future and as the source from which that future would arise and take form. It could not be allowed to fall to any system of slavery. The statement of the problem presaged a part of the solution. Systems of slavery were inconsonant in the West and unworthy of it. The South would have to be forcibly reminded of that truth; Irish Catholics were as truculent as Southerners but not as powerful or as well positioned. Because the West was America writ whole and writ pure, it would either throw out Irish Catholics or transfigure them. In all events, and even if the assimilative powers of the West should prove chimerical or not up to this admittedly challenging task, the immediate and pressing crisis was to keep the safety valve open and, should Irish pass through it, pray to the kind providence that had sustained America that the West would change their papist hearts.[46]

In her recent and very good book on the "reconstruction of America" after the Civil War, the historian Heather Cox Richardson writes of the moment when it "suddenly dawned on me: the nation's strongest cultural images of the postwar years came from the West." Indeed, "the reconstruction years [can] not be understood without acknowledging the central importance of the American West." It was not, however, the West as found that was central but "the blinding postwar image" of the West as invented. That image, as she makes clear, was not simply idealized; it was delusional, the result of a mixture of romanticized republicanism, pragmatic capitalism, and pixie dust. The western myth world masked the "harsh reality" of what had actually happened in America's second-chance country. It was, in other words, "casually cruel."[47]

In one sense, the Northern and Republican myth makers had no choice but to construct a western province. The Civil War had been fought over the future of the Republic and "the new birth of freedom" that victory would guarantee to it. That new birth would not just act itself out in the West; it was the West. The Republican triumph had validated and sanctified market capitalism, including the distorted republicanism that attended it, by removing the countervailing power of Southern slavery. The Republican victory gave the modern project a more open field. America could now truly be a more perfect union, even the greatest nation of the earth. This also was manifestly destined. But it was too frequently contradicted by what the Republican victory over the South had, in fact, produced. Americans would have to settle for a more powerful union; given the ugly realities of unchecked industrialization, North, South, East, and West, perfection was out of reach.[48]

To borrow from the title of Richard Slotkin's book, "the age of industrialization" now had greater traction and pace. It needed a "myth of the frontier" even more than it had before the Civil War. Republicans took the lead in supplying that myth. Their concept of the frontier "came to be . . . as jealously guarded a heritage as Plymouth Rock"—another nice mix of the two allied sources of the American soul. The West was not just a place to grow corn, it was a place to grow corn growers. The fear that these idealized types would be closed out of their western inheritance did not end with the Civil War, principally because one source of that fear had not disappeared. There were still papist "minds in the West." As surely as Plymouth Rock was the place to escape popery, so too was the frontier. The Irish profaned both places. The threat of the bad roads and the bad morals they signified had yet to be addressed.[49]

The Irish in America could do little to relieve these fears. Even if they had put themselves on their best behavior, they had for too long been dismissed as feckless or savage or both or worse. Theirs was not an image that could be suddenly recast. Nor, as it happened, did they behave in a fashion that suggested otherwise. The year after the Civil War ended, Irish American Fenians twice invaded Canada as a means of striking at Britain. The Fenian raids were a reminder to Americans that the Irish among them had not assimilated, however that often inappropriate word might be interpreted. There was something of the burlesque about the Fenians' raids, but they also had a vague nationalist and ideological component. Even that could not be said of the St. Patrick's Day riots in New York in 1867 or, on the surface, of the Molly Maguire campaigns of "retributive justice" in northeastern Pennsylvania in the 1860s and 1870s.[50]

Even more ominous were the events of 1870–71 in New York, when Americans witnessed yet another example of what many perceived as primitive and thickheaded Irish violence. In scenes eerily reminiscent of the 1863 draft/race riots, Irish Catholics and Protestants, many of the latter with strong ties to the militantly Protestant Orange Order in the north of Ireland, waged on the streets of New York what must have looked to Americans like a Celtic equivalent of a Chinese tong war. Catholic Irish saw the Orangemen as agents of the Republican Party and the Republicans as natural successors to the Orange-dominated Know-Nothings. They were the logical and predictable expression of "perfidious Albion" and the worst of its seed. The Orangemen, in their turn, saw the Irish Catholics as agents of Rome and a threat to republicanism and workers' rights. The basic outlines of the quarrel had not changed since the 1830s.[51]

Most of the Americans who witnessed or learned of the riots were not interested in what produced them, only in what they might produce, what sinister developments they foreshadowed. The Orange riots took place only three months after the Commune had engaged in similar outrages against civility and order in France and raised the red flag over Paris, which only heightened the fears. George Templeton Strong was as unrestrained as he had been in 1863, commenting in his diary on the behavior of "Celtic bogtrotters . . . and the like scum," of "these 'ferocious human pigs' (should we not substitute Irish for human?)." The problem was that these human pigs were politically ascendant. The "*Celtocracy*" of the North, Strong noted three years later, was "as bad as a *niggerocracy*" in the South, "and in some respects worse." The *New York Times* was only slightly more reflective (although it did add a proper note of anti-Catholicism), stating that "Celtic worship has always inclined to the sensuous . . . the social organization of the race has inevitably tended to the slavish subjection inherent in the clan, rather than to the personal independence that has come to us from the forests of Germania."[52]

The *Times'* smug mix of Celtic forms of worship and slavery recalled antebellum associations; the reference to Germania reflected the currently fashionable idea that the greatness of England was the result of the Teutonic sorts that had made their way to it. America was still Britain's seed, but Britain got its seed via Germania. It was all very confusing and very senseless. Not only that: America's forests were about to replace Germania's as the source of Americans' "personal independence." No matter; slavish subjection to the clan was unbefitting the forests of either. The Orange Riots, like those of 1863, were propelled in no small measure by Irish Catholic anxiety and desperation. Were these not precisely the sorts for whom the West was made? If the West and the safety valve it provided were to provide even a measure of protection for those in the East, the Irish would have to be given a place in the line. But if the West was to be tomorrow's country and underwrite all of those second chances, surely the Irish would either have to be kept out or forced to post the equivalent of a performance bond.

As before the Civil War, Americans had to figure out a way to relieve the East without imperiling the West. The Catholic Irish were the obvious first case in point. The West was a winnowing device. Its settlement was both a test of "racial" strength and a means of racial strengthening, the natural home of the American volk whose always assertive claims of Anglo-Saxon/Teutonic superiority had been fortified and hardened after the Civil War by a crude social Darwinism. Letting loose the hordes of Irish barbarians might save the East, but only at the expense of the West. E. L. Godkin, one of the "best men" of the postwar generation, pointed out in 1871 that with the threat from Southern slavery extinguished, "Catholic interests" were the "most portentous of all the 'interests' which [then threatened] American society and government." Four years later President Ulysses S. Grant, who spoke with some authority on the matter, returned momentarily to his Know-Nothing days and predicted that "if we are to have another contest the dividing line will not be Mason and Dixon's but between patriotism and intelligence on the one side and superstitions and ignorance on the other." Since Grant at the time was advocating mandatory public school attendance for immigrant children in order to thwart the designs of "the demagogue or priestcraft," little decryption of his remarks is required.[53]

The contest would doubtless have been less bloody than the previous one, but there was no mistaking the seriousness of this more recent division or its similarity to the earlier one. Somehow the United States had come to contain thousands of these Irish who, as Engels put it, brought their poverty with them. "Filth and drunkenness, too, they have brought with them." But more was involved than bad hygiene and insobriety. The Irish immigrant contingent included the politically insurgent, "incendiaries . . . from Tipperary . . . who are always at war with every form of government thus far known among civilized nations." As the British press put it, "Ireland is boiling over, and the scum"—Morse's "muddy waters" again—"flows across the Atlantic." There were still strangers in the land. The Civil War had not removed all the obstacles to a perfect union and a greatest nation.[54]

Obviously, no civilized nation could be expected to look kindly on these sorts wherever they might be found in it. The tension between the demands for immigrant labor and the political hazards posed by those immigrants—between the requirements of industrial capitalism and the requirements of republicanism—was as relentless as ever. As they had before the war, Americans chose to contend first with the perils to capitalism. They were more pressing and immediate, but the unoccupied lands of the West would both defuse them and teach republican virtues. There were some skeptics. Madison Grant, for example, whose anti-immigrant and anti-Catholic prejudices were based on an advanced and malignant form of Anglo-Saxon supremacy, was dismissive of those who would barter away the future of the American volk. The Civil War, he argued, had taken the best of Americans, men who, "with their descendants, would have populated the Western States," and replaced them with "the racial nondescripts who are now flocking there." "The American," Grant concluded, "sold his birthright in a continent to solve a labor problem."[55]

It was in this context that some of the more frightened Protestant Anglo-Saxons mounted their post–Civil War racial/religious counteroffensive against the Irish and other Catholics. That counteroffensive began in the late 1870s and concentrated much of its attention on the West, its present crisis, and its imperiled future. One of the first shots was fired by James Anthony Froude, English historian and adulatory biographer of Carlyle, dogged champion of the Anglo-Saxons, and vituperative anti-Catholic (particularly Catholicism of the Irish kind). Froude's principal criticism of English policy toward Ireland was that it was not forceful enough. It had not put a permanent end to Catholicism in Ireland and thus left the Irish in a fixed state of retarded savagery.

In two articles that appeared in the *North American Review*, Froude lauded America as "a land of wonders"; but most wonderful of all, it possessed a "vast virgin continent . . . unconstrained by tradition and superstitions," a place where "new ideas can organize themselves." As with Ulysses Grant's references to superstitions and ignorance, no one in the late nineteenth century would have had to decode Froude's use of "tradition" and "superstition"—or virginity. Americans, however, were overconfident if not arrogant; they "thought that they could absorb and assimilate [the] ignorant millions of ragged wretches" who had come from Ireland and decamped among them. This might be possible only if the government could send the Irish where "their priests could not follow," the corollary of the performance bond. Failing that, "the question would have to be fought out with bullets instead of with balloting papers," for "Romanism," and Froude was now quoting from an anonymous pamphlet, "is as inconsistent with a republican form of government as slavery was."[56]

That last statement contained nothing new—except the shifting verb tense. Slavery was past; Romanism and its Celtic advance guard were the crisis of the present. Seven years after Froude's screed, and a careful reading of it, the Reverend Josiah Strong of the American Home Missionary Society made clear how grave the crisis was. Strong called his book *Our Country: Its Possible Future and Its Present Crisis.* A product of the same society and the same mentality that gave the country the Reverend Thaddeus Hurlbut, Strong wrote of many national perils, but the one that most unnerved him was the threat of "Romanism" in the American West. "Rome," he wrote, "is concentrating her strength in the western territories. As the West is to dominate the nation, she intends to dominate the West."[57]

The gendering of Rome should be noted, but it was not its feminine—and effeminate—character that most troubled Strong. Romanists, it was true, were not as "energetic as the Protestants who are pushing into [the western] territories . . . but they are energetic enough to be counted. The most wretched members of society count as much at the polls as the best, and often *much more.*" This was Godkin's argument; it was what gave an air of "menace" to manhood suffrage. For "those degraded people," Strong continued, "are clay in the hands of the Jesuits," who, when driven out of Europe, "declared that they would plant themselves in the western territories of America. And they are there to-day with empires in their brains . . . they are free to colonize in the great West, and are there, purposing to Romanize and control our western empire." "Beyond a peradventure," Strong concluded, "the character, and hence the destiny, of the great West, for centuries to come, is now being determined. . . . What the final form . . . is likely to be, we may infer from the forces which are at work shaping it."[58]

In his introduction to the 1891 edition of *Our Country,* the Reverend Austin Phelps called specific attention to the similarity between Strong's plea and that of Lyman Beecher fifty years earlier. Like Beecher, Strong exposed "the multiform varieties of Western infidelity" while "thrill[ing] the hearts of Christian assemblies at the East with . . . pictures of Western greatness, and Western perils." Austin did not count Catholics among the Christian assemblies, East or West. They were idolaters and infidels. But they were "filling up" the West and "conspiring against Christian institutions." It was, said Austin, "a certainty that Christianity must go down in the struggle, if Eastern enterprise was not prompt in . . . preoccupying the land for Christ." By "preoccupying" Austin meant doing what the antislavery forces had done in Kansas before the Civil War. The historian George Fredrickson calls it "evangelical imperialism," getting there first and occupying the land before infidels with empires in their brains had a chance to fasten themselves upon it.[59]

As was true before the Civil War, this "evangelical imperialism" was the weapon of an equally evangelical republicanism, a merging of reformed Christianity and Americanism. It was a holy calling—indeed there were none holier—and only Anglo-Saxon Protestants were up to the task. They would be the lead warriors in what Strong clearly perceived as Armageddon, a struggle for the

soul of the most important part of the most important nation. Like Morse and
Beecher fifty years before him, Strong believed that the West would determine the
future of the nation and that the nation would determine the future of the world.
This was no time to be lackadaisical.

In making his late nineteenth-century plea, Josiah Strong cited a number of
authorities on the West, its importance to the nation, and its immediate future.
Many of these spoke to the question of open lands, their effects on American
institutions, and their rapid settlement. He quoted, for example, Thomas Carlyle,
who, in one of his playful moods, told an American that "'Ye may boast o' yer
dimocracy, or any ither 'cracy, or any kind o' poleetical roobish; but the reson
why yer laboring folk are so happy is thot ye have a *vost deal o' land for a verra
few people.*'" He quoted Thomas Macaulay in one of his thoughtful moods, who
wrote in 1857—about the same time Fitzhugh and Marx were offering quite
similar comments—that America's "fate [was] certain. As long as you have a boundless extent of fertile and occupied land, your laboring population will be far
more at ease than the laboring population of the Old World. But the time will
come when" these lands will be occupied: "then your institutions will be fairly
brought to the test." Note that these British observers, like the many Americans who
were offering identical warnings, dealt with more than just the so-called safety
valve. Carlyle counted democracy among the gifts of the West; Macaulay said
America's institutions, not just its wage scales, were about to be tested. Strong
quoted both with approval—and alarm. Phelps, in his introduction to *Our Country,*
said that Strong, like Beecher, was acting just "in the nick of time." The frontier was
about to end. The battle for our country was in its last and most critical stage.[60]

It was at this point that Frederick Jackson Turner added his voice to the conversation. He would, of course, come to dominate it. Born in 1861 in Portage,
Columbia County, Wisconsin, on the edge of the frontier he would immortalize
and the Civil War he would all but ignore, Turner developed the frontier thesis
that provided the master narrative for the entire American experience—while
managing to exclude a significant percentage of the entire American people. He
explained Americans to themselves in a way that gave them a reason to believe
that they were not only unique but uniquely blessed. Turner told them that they
were the people of the West, that moving west was the most distinctive feature
of their past, and that from the West came their most distinctive characteristics.
It was not the originality of his ideas that set him apart and gave his thesis its
special attraction. All of the ideas that came to be associated with Turner—the
West as safety valve, as wellspring of democracy, as source of the American spirit—
had found frequent expression long before he presented his 1893 paper on the
significance and the primacy of the frontier in American history.[61]

Turner's was a hymn to glory. Americans were not Albion's seeds. Their institutions owed nothing to the forests of Germania. Those institutions and the values

that surrounded them arose from native ground. What American would not have responded positively to comments like "American democracy is fundamentally the outcome of the experiences of the American people in dealing with the West" or "the men of the 'Western World' turned their backs upon the Atlantic Ocean, and with a grim energy and self-reliance began to build up a society free from the dominance of ancient forms"? The West, Turner wrote, was America's "gate of escape to the free conditions of the frontier." And the freedom of the frontier "promoted individualism, economic equality, freedom to rise, democracy. Men would not accept inferior wages and a permanent position of social subordination when this promised land of freedom and equality was theirs for the taking." It is true that in this same essay Turner said that there was very little good land left for anyone's taking and that Americans would have to make some major adjustments. But that was the point: the West had made Americans a resilient and adaptable people. Removing the source of their national strength did not make them less strong. The end of the frontier might require them to have to turn and face the Atlantic Ocean, but only at a sidelong angle and more as teachers than as students and never as supplicants.[62]

I suspect that one of the reasons Turner's ideas became so conspicuous a part of the popular culture was because he spoke so calmly; his contribution to this West as constructed province was always inadvertent, though no less real for being unintentional. It had nothing of the strident sectarianism and assertive Anglo-Saxonism that marked his predecessors from Beecher to Josiah Strong or successors such as Madison Grant. Neither was there any of the overstrung and slightly menacing fatuousness of Theodore Roosevelt. It was unthinkable that Turner would ever write, as Roosevelt had, of an old friend from the "cow camps . . . a huge, powerful man," Jim by name, "who . . . had been distinctly a fighting character." Roosevelt had invited Jim to join him and the British ambassador at lunch in the White House but had to warn Jim that if he "shot at the feet of the British Ambassador to make him dance, it would be likely to cause international complications." Jim—model westerner that he was—answered cowboy style: "Why Colonel, I shouldn't think of it, I shouldn't think of it!"[63]

Roosevelt did not say if Jim followed with a wink and a nudge. He did not need to; every part of the exchange with Jim was in code, the equivalent of handshakes, passwords, and the other ritualistic paraphernalia of secret brotherhoods. True Americans knew what it all meant. They knew that both Roosevelt and Jim were hospitable enough but that they were also dangerous characters and not to be trifled with. Turner would also have known what the code meant; he may even have believed in what it meant, that there was a bit of the dandy about Europeans and that Americans, particularly those from the far frontiers, liked to fun with them. It was one of the privileges of being among the initiated. But even if he believed Strong or Roosevelt, he did not sound like either. He was the young scholar, not the frightened agent of the Home Missionary Society or the bombastic sometimes western he-man. He sounded alarms, but from the perspective of a student of the past, not some self-appointed prophet of an imperiled future. Turner spoke more often of challenges than of crises. And he never spoke of shoot-outs or of making dudes dance.

Turner's sunny disposition aside, however, I do not know why those who have sought his precursors have neglected Josiah Strong and Lyman Beecher. It is inconceivable that Turner had not read *Our Country*. His family was Protestant and Republican. He grew up in Wisconsin, where W. H. McGuffey's *Eclectic Readers* were the primers of choice, as they were throughout the West. McGuffey was a close friend of the Beecher family and included parts of Lyman Beecher's *Plea for the West* in his postwar editions of the *Readers*. Turner read everything that had been written about the West, and Strong's book came out while he was a graduate student at Johns Hopkins and sharing office and boarding room space with Woodrow Wilson, who surely knew of Josiah Strong. The exclusion of Lyman Beecher's 1835 *A Plea for the West* from the list of Turner's precursors is even more curious. As will be seen, Turner had read Beecher carefully. Beecher's plea was an obvious primary source for a young graduate student interested in the history of western America in the years before the Civil War. Turner read it again before writing his 1893 paper. He read more critically this time, but no less approvingly.[64]

Turner's basic argument was that American institutions and attitudes arose specifically on that contested ground where the Old World met the New. On this constantly moving frontier, the cultural traditions of Europe and of the eastern United States shattered and evaporated, to be replaced by something fresh and unique. The Americans, said Turner, were "English in neither nationality nor characteristics." He was very sure of this. As he argued in his best-known essay, "The advance of the frontier has meant a steady movement away from the influence of Europe, a steady growth . . . along American lines." "American lines" meant western lines, and they were cleanly drawn. Essentially, Turner invented a West and then used it to invent an American culture. Had he ever thought to compile a catalog of folkways, the cultural patterns and attitudes it described would have been fairly similar to those of Britain, but their origins would have been entirely different. After all, the frontier was "a gate of escape from the bondage of the past," not a place where the past might put down new roots.[65]

But Turner ignored the deep Protestant roots of this new American culture, or at least made no specific reference to them. Perhaps he thought these Protestant roots too self-evident to require comment or too European in origin to merit it. He believed that the frontier influenced religion, but not that religion had much to do with the frontier. Perhaps his secularism led him to exclude it. There is very mixed and contradictory evidence that Turner knew that the Protestant emphasis on individualism perfectly suited his notion of frontier-inspired individualism, but he never made the connection explicit. It is the case that he dealt only with white men, a point frequently commented upon. But they were also exclusively Protestant white men, a point too infrequently commented upon. He was aware, for example, that religious oppression in Europe was the source of much immigration to America, but when it came to evaluate the case of Ireland, his only reference was to the "Presbyterians . . . in Ireland" who were "oppressed."[66]

None of this is easily explained. It is the case that Columbia County's immigrant population was overwhelmingly of British, German, and Scandinavian descent—all of whom Turner also basically ignored—but as late as 1910, there were more than a thousand Irish in the county and almost three thousand more in adjacent Dane County. In 1870, when Turner was a boy, a thousand Catholics lived in Columbia County, over seven thousand more in Dane. The young Turner was not exactly surrounded by outlanders, but he was the near neighbor of great numbers of people whom he later wrote out of his histories. His sole direct reference to Catholicism can only be described as bizarre: in 1891, the year that Strong issued the second edition of *Our Country*, Turner commented on "the titles, government, and ceremonials of the Roman Catholic church," aspects of Catholic practice that comported badly with "steady growth along American lines." But it was his next statement that was literally eccentric. "For when the Caesar passed away," Turner wrote, "his scepter fell to that new Pontifex Maximus, the Pope." This is certainly not what Catholics meant by the apostolic succession. But the coded language is also revealing: "Caesar" (and the charge that the pope had inherited the mantle of Caesarism), "scepters," and most obviously "Pontifex Maximus." These were alien and threatening concepts, and it is unimaginable that Turner did not know it.[67]

Why Turner chose to make his point so obliquely is puzzling. Perhaps it was because he was not entirely certain what point he was making. His 1893 article on the "Significance of the Frontier" has been subjected to more scrutiny than anything else Turner did—more scrutiny, in fact, than any short essay ever written by an American historian. But one passage in that essay has largely escaped attention. Turner was making his argument for the democratic character and democratizing power of the West, but his tone was ambivalent. "The rise of democracy," he wrote, "came in with western preponderance . . . and it meant the triumph of the frontier—*with all its good and all its evil elements.*" Or, later in the essay: "the democracy born of free land . . . has its dangers as well as its benefits." Those dangers included "the spoils system, lax business honor, . . . and lax financial integrity." The frontier, he went on, was a place of primitive society, and "a primitive society can hardly be expected to show [an] intelligent appreciation of the complexity of business interests" or, it would seem, of much else.[68]

Given this mixed legacy, given that the West was draining the East of its population and destroying old local allegiances, it was little wonder that "the East has always feared the result of an unregulated advance of the frontier, and has tried to check and guide it." Turner described some of the means the East had used, but the reader is left to wonder—or at least this reader was—whether Turner was quietly applauding the effort or cautiously criticizing it. Reference to a commitment to some sort of historical "objectivity" solves nothing. If I had to take a side, I would say that Turner thought the East was wise to try to "check and guide" frontier exuberance in the interests of national honor and integrity. There was a futility to the effort—the West was far too lusty and full of itself to be haltered and reined—but Turner understood why the effort had to be made.[69]

Less certainty attaches to Turner's discussion of what he called "the most effective" of these eastern attempts to restrain the West. Those attempts centered on the "educational and religious activity . . . of organized societies." It was at this critical point that Turner specifically mentioned the work of Lyman Beecher. Beecher, "speaking in 1835, . . . declared: 'It is . . . plain that the religious and political destiny of our nation is to be decided in the West.'" Turner certainly agreed with that, as he did with Beecher's warning that "no man at the East [could] . . . dream of liberty, whatever may become of the West. . . . Her destiny is our destiny." Turner did note that Beecher seemed to have some "fears lest other religious sects anticipate [his] own," but Turner did not go beyond that, concluding only that "the religious aspects of the frontier make a chapter in our history which needs study." He was right about that.[70]

But what Turner did not say about Beecher is more remarkable than what he did say. Beecher, of course, did not simply "speak" his thoughts; he published them in *A Plea for the West,* which Turner footnoted. The "religious sects" that Beecher feared included Unitarianism, at which he took a few polite swipes, and Catholicism, which he attacked with considerable ferocity. Turner made no reference to any of this. He offered no hint that Beecher's "plea for the West" was so incendiary. He did not quote Beecher on the Catholic system, its hostility to liberty, or its dependence on foreigners who neither understood nor could be made to understand American values. Turner said nothing regarding Beecher's remark that Catholics were a "dark-minded, vicious populace—a poor, uneducated reckless mass of infuriated animalism." Beecher hoped that these foreigners could be educated, and Turner believed that the frontier experience was a part of that educational process. By the time Turner was writing, Catholics were even more alien than the Irish that Beecher had confronted. Turner cannot have presumed that Italians, Croats, Poles, and others of the "new immigration" would be more educable than Beecher's Irish hordes or that their values would have more room for the "principles of our government." Turner had obviously studied *A Plea for the West.* Why did he skip the raging parts? Why, in fact, did he skip the rage?

Turner did provide an analysis of Beecher's plea, but his characterization of it was either disingenuous or purposefully misleading. Beecher, according to Turner, had a "dread" not of Catholicism that would subvert the nation but "of Western emancipation from New England's political and economic control." And this dread "was paralleled by [New England's] fears lest the West cut loose from her religion." Beecher, of course, was not the only one to express this specific concern, as all of those who congratulated Californians for having transplanted New England's institutions would attest. But how was it possible that Turner could have converted Beecher's impassioned plea for national self-preservation against the anti-Christ into a flaccid, almost banal effort by the East to "check and guide" the West?[71]

Answers do not come easily, but clearly the Catholic issue—including the compatibility of Catholicism and Turner's notions of the frontier—was best dealt with covertly. Maybe the fact that 1893 was the height of the anti-Catholic antics of the American Protective Association (APA) and that he was speaking in Chicago on the occasion of Christopher Columbus's voyage made a more detailed accounting of Beecher's—or Strong's—remarks impolitic or lacking in scholarly detachment. But using Beecher as he did and when he did suggests that Turner either knew that his readers would get the point or did not get it himself. However it is explained, Turner developed his master narrative without any direct reference to America's self-conscious Protestantism and the anti-Catholicism that accompanied it.[72]

Americanized meant Protestantized, whether Turner made that explicit or not. His language is filled with what Robert Bellah has called "the Protestant moral code." He came out of a time and place where that code was thought to govern the lives of westering Protestants. He was the direct descendant of these. Their lives were a part of his remembered past. Turner argued that Americans rose up as a separate people out of their own contested environment. But this was an environment that yielded to and rewarded Protestant values and habits, as Turner also argued, often without acknowledging or even knowing that that was what he was doing. This was the America he knew, and this was the America whose history he would tell. American lines, for Turner, had to run straight and true, unaccompanied by any other lines. He was wrong on all counts.[73]

Had Turner carried his story deeper into the nineteenth century and engaged more directly the coming of the Civil War—something he did later when he turned his scholarly attention from frontiers to sections—he might have made the connection between Lyman Beecher, the nativist moving toward abolitionist, and the various members of the Beecher family who had completed the move. Similarly, had Turner carried his story farther west, beyond the prairies, he would have confronted the new filaments of culture that intersected the existing ones. What would he have done with, say, Irish miners in the mountain West, or with Chinese, Japanese, Italians, Greeks, and others wherever the western railroads were being built? Turner, in other words, did not just "ignore the ladies" or the Native peoples or the working classes of the West. He ignored all those whom he did not understand or who did not fit his definition of western. His entire history of America is selective, not just his use of Beecher's plea for the West. I think it is possible that he knew that were he to be more inclusive his whole frontier theory would collapse. And so he cut off his story, both temporally and spatially, and was never able to write the final chapter of his frontier epic.[74]

In the end, however, it is Turner's good nature that dominates his American portrait. The others who feared and pled for the West were often ill-tempered and malicious. Their constructed West and its constructed enemies contained more than a little casual cruelty. Turner's West was marked more by casual omissions. It is the case that his selection of quotable sources—Beecher, to be sure, but also Robert Lowell and Rudyard Kipling—as well as his those he admired and who admired him—Woodrow Wilson, Theodore Roosevelt, John Fiske, among them—were all proclaiming America's (or England's) Anglo-Saxon and Protestant destiny. Roosevelt, who once described Irish Catholics as "low, venal, corrupt, and unintelligent brutes," congratulated Turner for having "struck some first class ideas." Wilson wrote that "Turner and I were close friends. He talked with me a great deal about his idea. All I ever wrote on the subject came from him." It is unfortunate that precisely which subject went unstated, for Wilson was a man of multiple interests, including Anglo-Saxon superiority, the incompatibility of Catholicism and "the principles of free government," the fact of a "Romish invasion of this country," the tendency of Irish and other Catholics—the "unwholesome deposits . . . outcasts and desperados," as he called them—to stay in the East, and the belief that "we had to have a frontier; we got into the habit and needed one." It is likely that Turner talked about the many component ideas that made up his singular Idea. It would also be interesting to know what Wilson taught Turner as well as what he learned from him. Nevertheless, Wilson's message is clear enough. Turner belonged in this company of scholars and policy makers. He was one of them.[75]

Turner, however, always showed more forbearance—or less candor—than most of his compatriots. This is not to surrender the major point: it is as likely that Turner was suspicious of Catholics as it is that a white American of that same era was suspicious of—if not overtly hateful to—African Americans. It came with the territory, and to condemn him for it would be anachronistic, although to ask that he give us more of his thoughts about Beecher is entirely fair. Still, there are large differences between Turner and Josiah Strong or Lyman Beecher—or Woodrow Wilson for that matter—and those large differences may, in fact, be the reason that Turner cited Beecher so selectively. Whatever "strange road" Turner was "going down," his reference to "Pontifex Maximus" was almost benign in comparison to Strong's discussion of the perils of Romanism. The West that Turner constructed was a model of cultural tolerance when set beside the others. But for all that, trying to fit Catholics and Catholic values into Turner's West is impossible. Even had they behaved with uncommon decorum, the Irish could not remake themselves into the chosen people. They would be the West's barbaric tamers. They would serve only to kick in the Turnerian door, not to cross over the threshold.[76]

CHAPTER 4

Most Unlikely Westerners

It would be helpful at this point to return to two seminal ideas introduced earlier. The first, borrowed from the work of Linda Colley, concerned Britons, the inhabitants of Albion and its surrounds. Britons were a blended people. The Great(er) British component of their united kingdom was an amalgam of English, Scots, and Welsh, hammered out on the "forge" of Protestantism and the anti-Catholicism that was part of it. Protestantism was what held Britons together, and their refusal to become Protestant was a large part of what made the Irish such cultural misfits. The second idea was taken from David Hackett Fischer, who held that Americans were Albion's seed, the spawn of those Protestant Britons, and formed by the folkways Britons brought with them to the various new Englands in the New World. The formula is simple: Britons were self-consciously Protestant and anti-Catholic; Americans were the cultural offspring of Britons; it followed that Americans were also self-consciously Protestant and anti-Catholic. As for the Irish, they were not the only Catholics, but they were the nearest to Britain and the first in numbers in America and as outlandish in the latter as they had been in the former.[1]

Fischer identified twenty-four of those folkways shared by Britains and their American kin. Merely to list and briefly define a few of them is to make clear how different the Irish were and how outside the Anglo-American cultural borders defined by those folkways. *Speech ways* included syntax and grammar. The Catholic Irish ability to understand English words, and to make themselves understood by using English words, did as much to make the Irish aware of how alien they were as it did to ease their adjustment to American society. Neither did the two peoples— Britons and their American offspring being one, the Irish another—practice the same *family ways, marriage ways, gender ways,* or *sex ways.* The Irish had different and at times quite contradictory *age* and *death ways.* Irish mortality rituals, mortuary customs, and mourning practices were uniquely theirs. So were their *magic ways, dress* and *food ways, wealth and rank ways,* and *sports ways.* Irish *order ways,* including ideas of order and forms of disorder, not only had room for social bandits but gave them a privileged place. Anglo-American and Irish *work ways* and *time ways* were so unalike as to be disjunctive. More will be said about both; but regarding time, consider Oliver MacDonagh's point that the Irish had no "developmental or sequential view of [the] past"; they lived "outside a chronologically calibrated, or indeed any, time scale." All of these are important; on such distinctions are pale lines drawn.[2]

But this is an account of Irish who not only moved (or were moved) to America but who continued to wander when they got there. A special significance attaches to *social ways,* under which heading Fischer includes "conventional patterns of migration, settlement, association and affiliation." In other words, the Irish determined when, why, where, how, and with whom to move through the world on the basis of social patterns solely their own. Fischer's next three related folkways are equally important and determinative: *power ways,* "attitudes toward authority and power, and patterns of political participation"; *freedom ways,* "prevailing ideas of liberty and restraint"; and finally, and most significantly because they drove most of the others, *religious ways,* "patterns of religious worship, theology, ecclesiology." Americans and Irish simply did not cohere. The two peoples occupied distinct if adjoining and overlapping cultural worlds. The result was that the intersection of Irish and American cultures occasioned considerable tensions. Neither side gave way; neither overwhelmed the other; both were changed.[3]

The strongest statement of the cultural divide between Catholic Ireland and Protestant America comes from Kerby Miller's massive and masterful *Emigrants and Exiles.* Miller believes that there were "basic distinctions" between "Irish Catholic culture and Protestant Irish, British, and American cultures." Those distinctions were of historical and religious origin; they created a fault line that divided Irish Catholics from American Protestants and created Irish cultural misfits. They were premodern leftovers—communal, dependent, fatalistic, passive, traditional—attempting to make their way in a modern industrial society that was individualistic, independent, optimistic, aggressive, and innovative. The Irish had only their prehensile paws to commend them to "bourgeois" societies with "business-like cultures." As will be seen, I think these Irish characteristics may have helped more than hindered their adjustment to western America, but I have no quarrel with the existence and relevance of Miller's Irish Catholic "variables," the basic distinctions between the Irish and the Anglo-Americans.[4]

I assume that Oliver MacDonagh, an Irish Australian historian, would join me in this assent. MacDonagh uses language remarkably similar to Miller's to describe Irish immigrants of the mid-nineteenth century, in the process adding to the list of variables. According to MacDonagh, Irish Catholics were "Occidental Orientals"; they "expressed a set of values and a scale of judging men and things which were altogether alien to the Yankee. . . . the Irish prized the group, and their political morality was crowd ethics. They placed loyalty above reason, the concrete above the abstract, hierarchy above equality, leadership above self-expression, compassion above justice." Irish cultural emphasis, MacDonagh goes on to write, "was antipathetic to . . . individual endeavor and achievement at the expense of familial duty and support." But individual endeavor and achievement were precisely the virtues of modern societies. The future belonged to these societies in part because the past had no hold on them, in larger part because their culture taught self-reliance, trying hard, taking risks, and maintaining high expectations of success.[5]

The Irish had come to a place inhabited by a people who had made up their minds about almost everything, a place that was without uncertainties, mysteries, or doubts. The Irish knew only uncertainties and the insecurity that went with them. Mystery and doubt were part of their cultural landscape, and they had made up their minds about almost nothing—except that they were comfortable enough without having to make up their minds. The two peoples, Irish and American, even defined equity differently. When the Irish referred to someone as a *sassenach* (their word for the English), the point was not that the object of scorn was disloyal; the person may have been that, too, but *sassenach* meant stingy, ungenerous, a seeker of the main chance. America was filled with the seed of the *sassenach*. Those and other behavioral differences could be neither averted nor finessed.[6]

The differences between Irish ways and American ways were apparent wherever the Catholic Irish ventured in American society. They revealed themselves in boldest relief, however, in the West. The point is not simply that the Irish were unwelcome, even unacceptable, in western America. They were also unfitted to western places. In some respects, this second consideration was a built-in corrective to the first. Those Americans who did not want them in the West could take some comfort in knowing that the Irish were incapable of meeting the challenges of living there. The theorists of western settlement and the myth makers—and they were frequently one and the same—said as much. The issue is not, then, that the American West was myth encrusted and literally unreal. The Irish were well used to myths. More than most cultures, theirs was made up of them. Let it be noted at the outset of this discussion that many of these Irish cultural habits, particularly those that indicated certain deformities of character, were assigned them by their nativist critics. They arose from vivid and prejudiced imaginations. But many of those habits were acknowledged by the Irish themselves and were real enough. They were the products of Irish history and society.

Whatever the source of the descriptions, some of these Irish cultural habits and the patterns of social behavior that arose from them derived purely from religion, from the faith traditions and practices that the Irish shared with all Catholics. Others were more nearly ethnic or national, arising from the essentials of Irish history, particularly poverty and scarcity, but including as well a few self-serving myths that the Irish middling classes invented. If some of the myth of the West was the creation of an ascendant class, so, to cite only two examples, were the myth or motif of Irish exile and the related assumption of premodern Irish innocence. And some of these Irish habits were a mix of the two, cultural derivatives from the Devotional Revolution and Catholicism's role as the arbiter of Irishness. Whatever their origin, their form of expression, or even the fairness and accuracy of their description, their values placed Irish Catholics beyond the pale. The idea that they might become permanent settlers in western America was outlandish.[7]

The American West—real and imagined, going to it and living in it—was solidly based on the American commitment to individual rights, private property, and the moral duty to guard both. This commitment could not be reconciled with the Irish agricultural system of rundale with land held jointly, its use governed by ancient traditions of cooperation and community obligation. The Irish economy was based on cooperation—"cooring" in the Irish—among interrelated kin groups and on the exchange of favors among them. Cooring, booleying (the Irish word for the seminomadic pasturing of animals), the codes and etiquette of the clachans (basically, a cluster of farmhouses), computing the value of land not in acres but in "collops" (the number of cows or sheep, goats, horses, geese, or ganders it could support): the whole elaborate if uncodified system of agricultural cooperation set the Irish apart from the self-consciously individualistic and independent western American farmer.[8]

The Irish "silent economy of friends" was not built on torts. The "plaintiff" in an Irish dispute was never the state but the individual against whom a civil wrong had been committed. There was something of the western (and southern) code duello about this, but the western code called individuals to conflict. The Irish defined "shoot-out" in their own unique way. They fought as families, septs, and tribes. When individual Irish were involved—even when they spoke for more than themselves—the Irish had some most peculiar "battle ways." When the dispute was between equals, this could produce some ferocious Irish tribal or faction fighting. But in the grotesquely imbalanced relationship between individual Irish and imperial Britain, battle ways took on a different form and meaning.[9]

The Irish had been cruelly treated by the British. The British were the "guests of the Irish nation," but they had behaved badly and had stolen from their hosts. The Irish were owed some form of compensation; Britain was in their debt. There was, however, an obvious problem. The British debtors/defendants were so superior in power, the aggrieved Irish "creditors" so utterly powerless, that justice could be had only by revealing the debtors' petty niggardliness and shaming them, calling down upon them the opprobrium of all those from whom they had taken and whom they had not compensated. The ultimate Irish vengeance—and this was no petty vengeance—was to force the British debtors to reveal their unwilling-ness to behave honorably and pay back what they owed. The Irish would do this by hunger striking, as W. B. Yeats wrote, by "biting at the grave" and sitting on British thresholds—even that of the king—and starving himself "till he die." And "while . . . perishing there, [the king's] good name in the world / Is perishing also." This was not a symbolic protest. The Irish would go on hunger strike in full view of the only ones who could feed them. Hunger striking must have seemed to Americans like a particularly gruesome kind of Irish bull; it made no sense— was, in fact, a contradiction of sense. It was not just a weapon of the weak, it defined weakness.[10]

It is, of course, the case that the Irish shed or were forced to abandon some of these social practices as they entered and progressed through the nineteenth and twentieth centuries. Words were changed; the Irish names were converted to English or to feeble Hiberno-English neologisms. Markets replaced cooring; land came to be owned by individuals and to be measured in acres not in collops. Changing the names unmoored the places from the community and from history. Even when used to describe the same parcel of land, an acre is one thing, a collop is another and different thing. The words were not simply a way of measuring and ordering units of land; they measured and ordered human relations. And there were other changes: villages—shabbier, to be sure, than those of England, but identifi-ably villages—replaced clachans. Cities—Dublin, Kilkenny, Wexford, Waterford, Cork, Killarney, Tralee, Limerick, Galway, Derry, and others—grew, if they did not quite prosper, and were a part of a new and more "modern" social reality.[11]

These were "big changes" that altered the social patterns of colonial Ireland. They did not, however, appreciably affect the cultural values of the Irish people. Renaming Ireland by redrawing the maps was easy. Reordering Irish society was a great deal more difficult, in part because these big changes were imposed or inflicted on the Irish by the *sassenach,* and resistance to them had a religious and ethnic as well as a social class dimension. This, too, the Irish brought with them to America. They were given no choice but to submit to the remapping—the translation—of their world from the Irish to English. But many did not submit to the translation of the ways they organized their lives, and even those who did submit likely felt a few atavistic tugs on their consciences. The values and patterns of behavior of the clachans—the booleying and cooring, the livestock on the collops—survived. Even the biting at the grave and the complex of feelings that produced it survived. The British and the Americans were not the only ones with pale lines; theirs just happened to be based on borders drawn to mark heroic victories. The Irish pale was more defensive; it was based on borders that marked heroic defeats.

The Irish pale also enclosed and marked off a people who defined themselves almost entirely on the basis of relationships, of associations outside and larger than themselves. The Daniel Boone types of the American frontier who were said to pack up and move whenever they could see the smoke of their neighbors' cabin made no sense to them. To the Irish, this behavior was clear evidence of being socially maladjusted; the smoke of a neighbor's cabin was an invitation to come in, warm oneself, and talk. In the native Irish language, one of the words for hospitality was the same as the word for honor. Hospitality was not just accommodative; it was obligatory because it was holy. Those to whom it was extended brought messages from God. In industrializing America, however, and the "fatal western environment" it required and so invented, these Irish values were illogical and disqualifying.[12]

Note the nature of the American western advance, in both its real and imagined forms, and note, too, the character of those who led it. Tocqueville called the western movement a "plunge" and those who took it "adventurers impatient of any sort of yoke, greedy for wealth. . . . There is nothing of tradition, family feeling or example to restrain them." Tradition, family feeling, and example not only restrained the Irish, they were about all they had left. But these unyoked American plungers did not simply move west and accommodate themselves to it; they "conquered," "subdued," "tamed," and "won" it. And when they had thoroughly whipped it and those who lived on it, they occupied it, much as a national army might occupy a defeated capital. "To be 'American,'" one historian has argued, came to involve locating "oneself on a map whose coordinates [were] determined by a national narrative . . . [of] conquering wilderness, subduing savages . . . and extending borders. . . . This pride in the legacy of conquest [was] integral to American nationalism and national belonging." The Irish had never conquered, subdued, or extended anything. The Irish poet Nuala Ní Dhomhnaill puts it wonderfully: the Irish were content "working out [their] psychodramas and 'walking the land,' living [their] lives, and dying. It's what the aborigines do in their homelands. They spend so much time with their wonderful rituals and their dance. . . . They don't have the urge to be conquering all they see."[13]

This is where I am in partial disagreement with Kerby Miller. I think it entirely possible that these character traits were not the disabilities that he describes. They were, to be sure, variables—they separated the Irish from the host society. If judged by the criteria of the mythical West, there is no doubt that they left the Irish all but bereft of resources and helpless. But that is the point. The mythical West was precisely that; it never existed except in the drawing rooms of an American ascendency, mostly eastern. It served useful purposes, but social control, not accuracy of description, was the central one among them. The West of contrivance and imagination was a place for self-reliant and self-made men who jousted with one another and with the environment, winnowing the former and conquering the latter. These were the most fit, made such by the radical self-containment of their lives. The western hero did not need society; he did not need anything. The Irish did not live that way and did not understand a society that apotheosized those who did—or, and more accurately, those who pretended they did. The West of reality rather than imagination was not a place to be won but a place to be negotiated with; it parceled out its rewards to those who approached it, as the Irish did everything, passively and fatalistically, which is also to say patiently and respectfully. Far from disadvantaging the Irish in the West, the variables may well have been a source of strength.[14]

James Manahan, later a prominent lawyer, tells a remarkably revealing story in his autobiography of growing up in Chatsfield, Minnesota, well within the borders of my constructed West. Manahan was born in 1866, only five years after the birth of Frederick Jackson Turner in nearby Portage, Wisconsin. Both of Manahan's parents were Irish immigrants. Chatsfield was an Irish Catholic rural enclave, one of many such in the American West, and although Manahan wrote in his autobiography that he "didn't know how the Irish within me . . . shaped my life," we can now safely say that its effect was profound. As important in the life-shaping was the extraordinary blend of elements in Manahan's story—as well as the total lack of self-consciousness in the telling of it. He speaks of his "dreams as a freckled country boy, going barefoot to school." Those dreams arose in part from "the reading of dime novels like *Bowie Knife Bill* and *Calamity Jane* recommended by my chum John Tuohy, and *The Lives of Irish Saints* urged by my father."[15]

Two more dissimilar hagiologies would be difficult to imagine. It is conceivable that the life of St. Brendan the Navigator could be placed within the same cultural framework as that of Bowie Knife Bill, but the lives of St. Columcille and St. Patrick could not have been made to fit with any aspect of the American secular faith. Indeed, Irish saints as a group were best known for their remarkable willingness to engage in acts of self-mortification—not the stuff of western hero-tales. Turner, quite needless to add, learned his lessons from a different reading list. Not surprisingly, this incongruous set of reading materials "stimulated" in Manahan "a mixture of fantastic ideals." Manahan never acknowledged that Brendan and Columcille were not fictional characters, however sanctified and sanitized the account of their lives. Bowie Knife Bill, on the other hand, was the product of economic markets, an invention of professional legend makers. Manahan seemed not to know, or at least not to care. "Secretly, in my dreams," he went on, "I was, in turn, an Indian fighter, a circus performer, a saint frightening myself by my own prayers." At least he did not dream of being all three at the same time.[16]

Not many Irish were able to work their way through these mismatched cultural icons as easily as Manahan did. It is possible that young Irish on the mean streets of New York read from similar lists, but without the immediate access to fantasy lands that Manahan had. But the variables were also on full display along other cultural fault lines, and these areas of difference need to be explored as well. I wish all of them had anecdotal evidence as vivid and immediate as Manahan's story, but most of these other cultural variables must be drawn not from what was said or written but from what was done by and to a people. They are revealed, in other words, in the history and behavior of quite ordinary Irish as they adjusted to the big changes of the nineteenth century. Saint Bowie Knife Bill may sound discordant, but Bill and the communion of the "holy" who came before and after him were secular saints as well as legendary heroes. The young Jim Manahan may have sensed that. Little wonder he was mixed up.[17]

In the American context, going west was a very modern thing to do: calculating, rational, progressive, uprooting, and undeviatingly linear. At issue is Irish Catholic readiness for this frontier component of America's advance into industrial capitalism. The intersection of Irish and American history involved the "modernization" of both, but it also took place in the context of Irish colonialism, which had insulated and isolated rural Ireland from many of western Europe's big changes. But colonial status, according to some observers, had done more than just isolate the Irish. It had made beggars and "secret beseechers" of them. The English colonial system had forced them to adopt what Seán O'Faoláin called that "so typically [Irish] form of silence, an affluence of volubility." They had become obsequious, betraying a "false and resentful humility" that fixed itself to them.[18]

The imbalances of power in their relationship with Britons had "worn [the Irish] down" and made them "servile," wrote an American in 1840; their poverty was spiritual as well as material. John Gamble, an English visitor to South Tyrone, said the same thing without knowing it when he remarked that he could tell when he was in a Catholic's cabin because he would invariably be addressed as "'your honor.'" "A Protestant" (Anglican), Gamble explained, "never gives this appellation lightly, a Presbyterian never gives it at all." Arland Usher, one the gentlest and most fair-minded of the Protestants of Ireland, recalled with bewilderment that "even when I was a small boy I was constantly addressed as 'Your Honour.'" The Irish, Usher went on, were constantly seen as "'sunk in their servitude.'" More specifically to the point of western settlement, the Scotsman Robert Knox wrote in 1850 that the Irish have "no self-confidence, no innate courage, to meet the forest and the desert . . . and are the worst of agriculturalists." His comment, particularly coming when it did, bordered on the heartless. At the least, Knox might have thought about the sources of this Irish insecurity. He may have been casually cruel and dull-witted, but he may also have been partly right.[19]

Most of these references are from early in the nineteenth century before the post-Famine semimodernization of Irish society had fairly begun. But the differences over time, assuming there were any, would have been of degree not kind. Ignatius Donnelly of Minnesota, self-consciously Irish and western American,

wrote (probably in the 1860s) that "Ireland has lost its dignity by being conquered by the dominant race, . . . and ever since been under the great disadvantage
of their continual mockery, ridicule, falsehood, and injustice." John Ireland, the
Irish-born bishop of St. Paul, agreed, telling a St. Patrick's Day audience that the
Irish were "'dispirited and broken-hearted' by persecution, some . . . have been
almost necessarily unmanned." That was a peculiar comment, and one wonders
even now if Ireland knew what he was saying. Was this an elliptical, even unconscious, acknowledgment that organized Irish resistance against those who persecuted them was frequently betrayed by informers? In fact, informers constituted
a kind of subculture in Irish society—as they did in those of all the dispirited and
broken-hearted, including black slaves and American Indians. The persecutors
could count on it. I would pose the same question to Sinn Féin founder Arthur
Griffith, who as late as 1919 was still complaining of what he called the Irish
"slave mentality." It had "destroyed our moral courage," Griffith said, "and made
us shifty, mean, evasive in speech and argument." It "impelled us to mumble 'yes'
when we mean 'No.'" It had created, in other words, an Irish Sambo. Griffith was
quick to add that England had done this to its Irish subjects, that these were
environmental not "racial" deformities. The legacies of conquest were accompanied by their diametric, the legacies of being conquered. It was not the fault of
the Irish that they were feeble.[20]

Americans did not care. They lived by Patrick Henry's code. "The battle,"
Henry had told the Virginia Convention, "is not to the strong alone; it is to the
vigilant, the active, the brave," concluding with his famous "liberty or death"
reference, which became the refrain of America's patriotic chorus. Terence McSwiney,
lord mayor of Cork, sought Irish liberty or a martyr's death; but when he died
in 1920, it was from a hunger strike in a British prison. His anthem was anything
but a call to arms. "It is not those who inflict the most," McSwiney had written,
"but those who suffer the most who will conquer." Manahan might have read
something like that in his books on Irish saints. He would not have found any
such comments coming from Calamity Jane or Bowie Knife Bill. McSwiney was
also choosing between liberty and death, but his was not a warrior's death—or
at least did not seem so to Americans. He died *not* fighting. He was submissive,
passive, and pacifist. It would be difficult to imagine two more dissimilar expressions of human will.[21]

It is at this point that Irish ethnic/national consciousness and Irish devotional
Catholicism as fundamental to that consciousness become central. The Devotional
Revolution in Irish Catholicism had consequences that were theological, litur-
gical, and ecclesiastical—and all put even more distance between the Irish and
the Anglo-Americans. The Devotional Revolution was intensely communitarian
and collective, and these "corporatist foundations" produced in the Irish a tendency
"to fear the excesses rather than celebrate the possibilities of individualism in

the context of a burgeoning capitalist, industrial, and 'materialist' economy."
The Devotional Revolution may have been partly an act of political and cultural
defiance, and/or desperation. But regardless of what occasioned it, it would be
difficult to find—or even imagine—a cultural ethos less suited to the emerging
American spirit. The social consequences of that corporatist mentality were huge,
enduring, and impossible to reconcile with American individualism.[22]

But even this was not the full extent of its irrationality. The Devotional Revolution also involved the Romanization of the Irish Catholic Church, eliminating—
or at least trying to eliminate—all vestiges of what may be called Irish folk Catholicism. The ancient practices of the Elder Faiths, from holy wells to "stations," gave
way to a grimmer, almost Jansenist Catholicism. Mass attendance soared, as did
vocations and lay involvement in sodalities, societies, and every form of official
Catholic spirituality. None of this commended the Irish to Protestant America,
but added now to the continuing sectarian quarrels over abstractions was an Irish
sacramental Catholicism as intensely communal as any belief system could be.
Paul Cardinal Cullen, Ireland's highest-ranking prelate and the spiritual and ecclesiastical leader of nineteenth-century Irish devotional Catholicism, was a very
important man in American history. The fact that he never set foot on American
soil is of no moment; millions of Irish, lay and cleric alike, did. They brought
with them a mentality that bore Cullen's unmistakable stamp.[23]

This was not the only deterrent to the social integration of Irish Catholics
or to their full participation in America's western adventure. There were "structural" problems as well. Unlike most Protestant denominations, Catholics could
not simply establish their own churches and staff them with lay ministers hired
by majority vote of the congregations. Being Catholic required receiving the
sacraments; those sacraments required a priest. This was always the case, but the
Devotional Revolution vastly increased both the power of the priests and the
syndetic relationship between being Irish and being Catholic. The Catholic Irish
could not outrun their priests without sacrificing some part of themselves; they
had to hang back and wait patiently while various hierarchies far removed from
the West gave them the signal to move out.

It was the effects of the heightened devotionalism on the basic theological
underpinnings of the Irish church that were of greatest significance, however,
because Irish Catholicism was about more than just novenas, pilgrimages, scapulars,
rosaries, stations, and sacramentalities. It was concerned with what was heard at
Mass as well as attendance at Mass. The texts of individual homilies are in very
short supply, but it is safe to assume that the essence of Irish devotionalism informed
them, meaning that what was heard was doleful and celebratory at the same
time. The Irish were poor and powerless; that was their reality. And the greater
glory to them for their weakness, for that sad reality was the source of their
redemption. It would be hard to improve on the words of Father Thomas Burke,

a well-known Irish Dominican priest, who put the matter this way in 1872: Ireland's "crown of thorns and . . . time-worn chains of slavery" revealed "the light of faith, of purity, and of God." Ireland, Burke continued, could have become like England and Scotland, "canny and cunning, fruitful and rich," but chose not to because such would make "her commonplace, and vulgar, and impure, and forgetful of herself and of God." There are two points to Burke's Irish bull, both of questionable validity. The first is that the Irish chose their role; it was not imposed upon them. They were poor because they wanted to be. The second is that they chose wisely; the poor and the powerless enjoyed God's favor—if no one else's.[24]

For the devotional Irish, particularly those like Burke for whom weakness was strength, St. Paul as surely as St. Patrick was Ireland's patron. Archbishop John Ireland was convinced that "since creation, no one suffered so much as the Irish Catholic . . . the law says: you are a slave—apostatize and you will be free; you die from starvation—apostatize and you will be rich. What a temptation!" But "fear not," the bishop continued; the Irish responded to the temptress in the words of "St. Paul: 'Who shall separate me from the love of Christ?'" Father Michael Hannan in Butte, Montana, Irish-born like Bishop Ireland, made the same point. The Irish, said Hannan, were a "people . . . of bondage, sufferings, and death. . . . enslaved, persecuted, and strangled." The English had tried to bribe them to abandon their faith; and when bribery did not work, they used "perfidy and threats." But the Irish would never "renounce their faith." Bishop Ireland and Hannan were clearly likening the Irish to Christ; they were God's new chosen people and would have to suffer as the true chosen one had suffered. This might be soul-saving, but no one would confuse it with the western ideal.[25]

But Christ, St. Paul reminded the Corinthians (and the Irish), was made "perfect through suffering." In his second letter to the church in Corinth, Paul was even more specific, and more immediately relevant to the Irish condition. In a passage that much influenced St. Patrick, Paul wrote that "if I must boast, I will boast of the things that show my weakness." He had much to boast of, listing "insults, hardships, persecutions, and constraints." The Irish did as Paul had done and Patrick had taught them, convinced, in Paul's words, that "power is made perfect in weakness . . . when I am weak, then I am strong." Here was the psalm of the powerless, the core values of a national theology. By Paul's reckoning, the Irish would have been the most nearly perfect and the most powerful people on earth. Their weakness would have made them such.[26]

Acknowledging powerlessness, even describing it as strength, did not mean accepting it as a permanent condition—even Paul was more aggressive in his evangelization than his letter to the Corinthians might have suggested—and the Irish continued to agitate against British authority. The nature and form of that agitation, however, took on a distinctly Irish cast. Like all "sunk in servitude," this involved finding and manipulating the gaps in the system more than it did open revolt.

According to Robert Scally, the "well of bitterness" among the Irish that threatened "to overflow into violence" was hidden behind "bowing submissiveness and obsequious speech." There was nothing heroic in Irish defiance; it was camouflaged and stealthy. It might have been all that St. Paul and St. Patrick—not to mention their history—had left them, but it was not the American style. Little of St. Paul's confession would have made much sense to Americans, particularly if applied to the grand national epic of westering. Skulking rebelliousness as well as deferential foot-shuffling and an "affluence of volubility" were not parts of the West of the American imagination. The frontiersman would have understood St. Paul's reference to "hardships," but "constraints" would not have sat well with him, and he would never have brooked "insults."[27]

The westerner was neither an affable babbler nor one who contrived to turn losing into winning. He (and the westerner was always a he) was laconic, grim visaged, and dominant. He was also fully civilized and brimming with "moral courage." His "mentality" was that of a free man, resolute and defiant, as far removed from slavery as he was from savagery. If he had a grievance, he stated it openly. He did not dissemble or hide behind a feigned submissiveness. Violence was never far from him; but, unlike the Irish form, it was cool, measured, and deadly. Irish violence resembled nothing so much as the temper tantrum of a child. Griffith's reference to the "slave mentality" of the Irish would never have described the white American.

It might, however, have described the black American. Griffith's remark about the Irish's "slave mentality" recalls Edward Everett Hale's comment that when he spoke of the Irish as "slaves" he was not speaking metaphorically. Hale can be interpreted in two ways. As intriguing as his direct analogy is, it is impossible to know with certainty if Hale was comparing the Irish to slaves or to Africans, whether the weakness he described was one of circumstance, and hence remediable, or of race, and hence beyond any power to change. Hale was writing from Boston in 1855, but, as noted, his construction and defense of the Irish worker as freeing up superior races for more rewarding labor would have resonated on the planter verandas of the South. At another place in his *Letters on Irish Emigration,* he commented on the capture of "fugitive" slaves—in fact, he also used the word "fugitive" to describe the Irish. The context would suggest that Hale was making a "racial" as well as a psychological or even social-class comparison.[28]

Hale would not have been alone. It is striking how many British and American observers likened the Irish to African slaves. As with Robert Knox's comment above, it would be easy to dismiss the association as simple prejudice, but there was more to it than that. Scally has described British impressions of the Irish before the Famine. "In British eyes, the men and women of Ireland were a paradigm of the barbarian, . . . brute creatures . . . [whose] features marked the

Irish peasantry more than any other European peoples of the time as born slaves."
George Templeton Strong believed that "England . . . treats Irishmen as they treat
niggers," adding that the Irish deserved no better, given how "cruel and merciless"
they were "toward their inferiors," another charge frequently brought against African American slaves. Charles Kingsley called the Irish "white chimpanzees," and
both designations were important. One of Daniel O'Connell's political opponents,
commenting on O'Connell's sexual appetites, said he was apelike, as "capricious
as the ouran outang," the same point that Jefferson had made about Africans. The
two peoples even looked alike to some: one Englishman commented on the "striking
similarities between the inhabitants of Connaught and Africa"; another placed
the Irish as the "creature manifestly between the Gorilla and the Negro."[29]

This Celtic missing link was no more likely a frontiersman than the "secret
beseecher." But it was the character of the Irish rather than their "racial" deformities
that was disqualifying. Compare these descriptions of the Irish by Daniel Mackintosh and C. H. Bretherton with the standard model of the American westerner.
The Irish, said Mackintosh in 1865, are "extremely social, with a propensity for
crowding together . . . with a veneration for authority." Bretherton extended
the list in 1925. The "Hibernian . . . has the slave mentality. . . . He is a mixture
of childishness and ferocity. He is basely superstitious, callous to suffering, . . .
thriftless, untruthful, dirty, pettily dishonest, . . . devoid of moral courage and
intensely vain. [These] are the outstanding qualities of a slave race and a slave
mentality." It is startling that something like this could have been written as late
as 1925, but that is not all that makes Bretherton's bigotry revealing. Like Hale's
seventy years earlier, his list recalls nothing so much as a Southern racialist defense
of slavery and segregation: the mix of childishness and bestiality, the obliviousness
to pain, the mendacity, cravenness, and vaingloriousness.[30]

These were the general convictions of the British regarding the Irish. It is inconceivable that they were not known to Americans, although Americans hardly
needed instructions from the British on the nature of blackness, or Irishness, or the
cultural differences between both and the rest of American society. Africans and
Irish were the first of America's "imported natives," alien types who would do the
heavy lifting. William Lloyd Garrison wrote before the Civil War that to be Irish
in America "is next to being of African extraction." Even after the war, Charles
Dudley Warner could suggest that the Irish in America, those "patriots from the
Green Isle . . . in knee britches, flourishing a shillalah," be used as the Nubians
were used in Cairo to clear the way before carriages. Garrison and Warner and all
the others who used similar language were not saying that the Irish were black,
only that they both were used and behaved like Africans. That was demeaning
enough in their eyes.[31]

Neither the Irish nor the Africans, nor—to complete the portrait—the American Indians knew the value of land or even how to make a proper use of it. In

Ireland, the Irish were told they could have access to land ownership; they had only to convert to Protestantism and otherwise internalize the values of the superior and conquering British. They refused, preferring, it seemed, to whine and issue impotent protests. That was bad enough, but it was better than what happened when they got to America. John Fiske, although he made no direct reference to blacks, used language that was clearly inspired by white images of black slaves. "Paddy at home," Fiske wrote in 1873, ". . . appears far better than his degenerate brother who comes to America." The immigrant Irishman had become "democratic and sassy"; he had lost that "reverence in manners which greatly becomes him." In other words, he had become "uppity" and forgotten his place. But sassiness was not to be confused with "manliness" any more than an "affluence of volubility" was to be confused with straight talk. For Fiske, as for the rest, the Irish, wherever found, remained the "secret beseechers," the heirs of St. Paul.[32]

The best that could be said for such a people was that they might meliorate some of the harder edges of the American character. Orestes Brownson saw this as an unexpected benefit of the Irish immigration. Their Irishness and their Catholicism—and Brownson implied that he understood they were the same thing—gave them an "influence in softening the hardness, and in relaxing the rigidity of our puritan manners, so hostile to all real virtue." It gave them the "power of infusing into our national life a freer, a more hospitable, genial and cheerful tone and spirit." In the interests of both the Irish and the Americans, Brownson hoped that the Irish would not become American but that Americans would become, if not Irish, at least more nearly so.[33]

Fifty years after Brownson's comments, the Anglo-Irishman Douglas Hyde congratulated an overwhelmingly Irish American audience that America had, in fact, fused the two cultures. The English had "an intense business faculty, perseverance and steadiness in details." These were valued and useful qualities, but they could also be cramped and crabby. Fortunately, the Irish had come to America and joined to these English features their "lightness, brightness, wit, fluency, and artistic temperament." Woodrow Wilson was grateful for his partial descent from (Scotch) Irish; from them, he was sure, came his gaiety and devil-may-care sense of humor. America had "elicited a magnificent blend of both qualities" in a new "and noble race." Brownson would have been pleased. What made Brownson's and Hyde's and Wilson's feelings doubly remarkable was how closely they duplicated what George Fredrickson has called the "romantic racialism in the North," the tendency of antislavery Northerners to find in the black slave personality an antidote to the excesses of Anglo-Americans. Blacks were "natural Christians," "gentle," "meek," and "submissive." They were "soft," "sweet," and "mellow," with an innate "light-heartedness" and a "natural talent for music."[34]

Fredrickson also notes how irreducibly feminine all this was and how at variance with images of virile Americanism. On this point, too, the parallels with Irish

Catholics were striking. Protestant Anglo-Saxons were "manly," a word with an astonishing array of meanings. But however defined, only the manly could conquer the West. Indeed, to Josiah Strong, the American variant of the race clearly had to have been created by a God of "infinite wisdom" for expressly that purpose. As for the British version, the aptly named John Bull, he was as surely, and with equal wisdom, created for imperial purposes. The Irish, however, like all Catholics, although to a greater extent, were "paradigms" not just of the barbarian but of the feminine, the maiden "backed to a tree," as the poet Seamus Heaney put it. The best that could be expected of them—in addition, of course, to providing industrial fodder—was that they might furnish a "false narrative" to the American epic, softening some of its coarser edges.[35]

All of these were debilitating weaknesses in the Irish character. But Irish deformities, their unfitness as westerners, went beyond servile obsequiousness and cultural femininity. The English and Americans had one set of ideas about the West as a place and westward as a direction; the Irish had an entirely different and opposite set of ideas. From at least the sixteenth century forward, Britons had convinced themselves that their destiny was to be found by moving out toward the west. Part of this was of necessity; the compass was boxed in every other direction. Part of it may have been owing to Ireland's location off Britain's near western shore and its potential as a rehearsing and staging ground for British imperialism. Whatever its source, the idea that the areas to the west were places of hope and profit was an established part of Britain's ideology of empire. Walter Raleigh and John Hakluyt believed it, as did William Shakespeare. Bishop George Berkeley immortalized it—and America—when he wrote: "Westward the course of empire takes its way. Time's noblest offspring is the last." Charles Kingsley—whose description of the Irish as white chimpanzees would have excluded them from time's noble, or even civilized, offspring—agreed with the first part of Berkeley's comment, sallying forth with his famous "Westward Ho!"[36]

Americans were not disposed to challenge notions of their nobility. Jonathan Edwards preached that God faced west and that "when the time comes of the church's deliverance from her enemies"—in the ranks of which God undoubtedly included papists—"the sun shall *rise in the west,* contrary to the course of this world." Henry David Thoreau was less interested in which way God was looking, but no less in love with the cosmic significance of the New World in the west. "Eastward," he said in a much quoted passage, "I go only by force; but westward I go free." He never went very far, but it was the sentiment that counted. And the sentiment was spread-eagle expansionist. "I must say," he went on, "that mankind progresses from east to west. Westward the star of empire takes its way." Thoreau, however, did not really mean the whole of "mankind." The star of empire belonged only to a segment of the whole. "Aryans followed the sun." Westward they went free. The rest could stand helplessly in their way or follow in their wake, but westering was a grand adventure reserved for the few.[37]

Other nineteenth-century political and racial expansionists agreed. Thomas Hart Benton spoke in 1819 of "the disposition which 'the children of Adam' have always shown 'to follow the sun.' All obey the same impulse—*that of going to the West;* which, from the beginning of time has been the course of heavenly bodies, of the human race, and of . . . civilization, and national power." Jedediah Morse, every bit as anti-Catholic as his better-known son, wrote simply that "it is well known that empire has been traveling from east to west." Congressman Presley Ewing increased the stakes, claiming that "the march of civilization, like the march of christianity [*sic*], has been, from the days of the wise men . . . to the present from East to West. You might as well attempt to turn back the natural sun in its course, as to revert the sun of civilization in its westward way." William Gilpin put the finishing touches on the idea when he wrote that "it is the stream of the human race flowing from the east to the west, impelled by the same divine instinct that pervades creation. By this track comes the sun diurnally to cheer the world."[38]

The Irish were not so sure. In pre-Christian Ireland, to the west was Tír na nÓg, the Land of the Young, an essentially positive image but one with more than a few ominous implications. It was the place where the fairies and the little people lived, and their playfulness could take a decidedly malevolent turn. Tír na nÓg was a land from "whence no traveler returned except to wither and die." As for America specifically, the Irish also called it *oilean ur,* the new island. But they had another word, *nua,* that meant "new" as in fresh and modern. *Ur* could signify the same, but the Irish also used it to mean "novel" as in strange and unusual. And "new," although it can mean better, can also mean worse—or have no meaning at all. The Irish might have seen America as all three. What they knew was that this new island stole their children as it seemed to steal and bury the sun. It returned only the worst of their weather. Walt Whitman tried to comfort them, assuring the "ancient mother" whose son had emigrated: "You need crouch there no longer on the cold ground with forehead between your knees, / For know you the one you mourn is not in that grave, / It was an illusion, the son you love is not really dead, / The Lord is not dead, he is risen again young and strong in another country." The Irish were well-practiced illusionists, but Whitman was asking for more than they could give.[39]

The West, for the Irish, was also Tír Tairngire, the Land of Prophecy, occasionally—and mistakenly—translated as the Land of Promise. But the Land of the Young also had a temporal aspect; it was the land of the future—which was all very well for optimists. There is a revealing passage in *The Tailor and Ansty,* Eric Cross's wonderful account of the lives of Tim and Anastasia Buckley of "the townland of Garrynapeaka near Inchigeela in West Cork," when Tim reveals that the tcst of a man's "true intelligence" is "if he has any news of the people in Tir na nOg, or if he knows what is going to happen tomorrow." This implied that if he knew the one he would also know the other. For the Irish, as for Americans, the West was a place in time as well as in space; it was tomorrow's country. For both people, tomorrow was prefigured in the past.[40]

Americans, however, expected the future to make as much sense as the past. Their tomorrows were always forecast to be times and places of promise. The American future did not even require very careful preparation. The past had been so triumphant, so providential, that Americans did not need to recall its specifics. Moving into the future made the past vanish; it could, in fact, safely be forgotten. The Irish, however, were not good at doing that. In the graphic language of Oliver MacDonagh, "a past seen in terms of subjection and struggle, seen as a pageant or tournament of heroic defeat, is one of the roads towards a fundamental distrust of or even disbelief in achievement." The Irish had played in that tournament. Unlike Americans, their past did not make sense and for that reason could never be forgotten. Recalling it made them wary of the future, not lathering to jump into it. In the Irish context, there were many more "prophets" of damnation and sorrow than of exaltation. Prophecy based on what had happened was a painful exercise. For that reason among others, it was not central to Irish cosmology.[41]

The Irish reversed the American model of facing west and turned their collective back on the past, not as a way of ignoring it—they kept a watchful eye over their shoulder—but as a means of protecting themselves from it. In Irish the word for east, *soir,* meant also the "bright place," and they directed their gaze toward it. Eden, after all, was in the East. Their word for south was *deas,* or "right hand"; for north it was *thuaidh,* or "left hand," also meaning "surly." But the West was *iar* or *siar,* which was also their word for "back," whether going back in time or a person's back side. *Tharla se sin i bhfad siar* was an idiomatic way of saying "that happened long ago." In an Irish context, then, the West was their melancholic past and did not bode well for a hopeful future. Given its malevolent nature, merely facing it was a rash and foolish act. Entering it was an act of madness. The West was the home of Ireland's "unappeasable host."[42]

It was also their unprotected flank. The Irish have a phrase *thainig me aniar aduidh air,* meaning "I sneak up on him" or "I catch him by surprise" but literally translated "I come on him from the west." The western point of the compass was the unlucky one. In certain counties, the Irish had no windows on the west side of their cabins; in others, the west room was reserved as a clean and comfortable place for the old people to go to die. There were even some who, when stacking potatoes, "refused to add any sacks on the west side of an existing stack." There was an old saying on the northwest coast of County Mayo that "only a man stronger than God would put a western extension on his house." Their church, moreover, did nothing to embolden the Irish and turn them toward the West.

In Catholic theology, the West signified "the seat of darkness and the abode of demons." Catholics, in their renunciation of sin, are asked by their priests to "turn and face west, the direction of darkness"; in their profession of faith, they are invited to "enter into these waters facing the east, the direction of the rising sun and the morning star." It was Anglo-American Protestants who went west in a straight line. They were active, eager, and full of anticipation, restless and impatient, chasing the sun. Irish Catholics were passive and hesitant; they stayed put and waited for the sun to complete its circle and come back around to them.[43]

Maybe this was because, in the language of the Irish poet Seamus Heaney, Ireland had no "empty amphitheatre / Of the west," "no prairies / To slice a big sun at evening." "The Irish don't move out and away" at all. "Our pioneers keep striking / Inwards and downwards, / Every layer they strip / Seems camped on before." America had its trackless West, but there were tracks everywhere in Ireland; it had no virgin lands, no second gardens, no new worlds—only exceedingly old ones. The very idea of America was contrary to the Irish understanding of the world. As Heaney once said in making the distinction between Irish and American ideas even more vivid, "We have archeology rather than exploration as our dominant art." But Heaney meant archaeology used not in the interest of science or even history but as a means of finding and preserving Irish mysteries. In explaining why she wrote in Irish, Nuala Ní Dhomhnaill said that only in Irish could the concept of *saol eile,* the Otherworld, be fully articulated. This Otherworld is not just a "joyful afterlife; it is also—even *primarily—an alternative to reality,"* part of the deep Irish sense "that something exists beyond the ego-envelope." The Otherworld did not require wandering; it required staying put and digging. It would be found by moving down into the past, not moving out into the future.[44]

No one can prove that the Irish were aware of these warnings that going west was a heedless and prideful thing to be doing, rather like challenging God (or the gods) to a duel. The notion that their conscious lives were spent fearfully guarding their western backsides is even more fanciful. But then, no one can prove that Anglo-Americans shouted "Westward Ho!" as they charged off into their sunsets. It is enough to say that historians take seriously—as they should—the buried and encoded parts of a people's culture. And it is altogether reasonable to assume that when the Irish looked out across the Atlantic Ocean toward the "new island," or when they looked out across the prairies toward the "lands of the young" in the American interior, they were less robustly confident and sure of themselves than those westward leaning Anglo-Americans. They did not charge into their sunsets.

The Irish idea of the West as a mildly frightening "alternative to reality" was not the only cultural obstacle to their westering. Even when the signals were given to proceed westward, or the choice not to proceed was stripped by necessity,

Irish cultural habits counseled caution. For them, in the words of E. Estyn Evans, "there is neither evolution nor devolution. The realities both of geography and history are ignored." By "geography" and "history," Evans meant space and time and the irrational—or at least quite un-American—way in which the Irish kept track of both. Some Irish wanted to escape that past, others—the more advanced of the patriots—wanted to keep it perpetually alive. But, in either instance, the hold the past had on the Irish was fierce and tenacious. As MacDonagh has put it, "while the English [and, he might have added, the Americans] do not remember any history, the Irish forget none."[45]

The Irish were much like Southerners in this regard—as in others—and quite unlike Northerners and westerners. Arnold Toynbee once described his reaction as a young boy in 1897 watching the Diamond Jubilee of Queen Victoria. He recalled the atmosphere of the occasion:

> It was: Well, here we are on the top of the world, and we have arrived at this peak to stay there—forever. There is, of course, a thing called history, but history is something unpleasant that happens to other people. . . . I am sure, if I had been a small boy in New York in 1897 I should have felt the same. Of course, if I had been a small boy in 1897 in the Southern part of the United States, I should not have felt the same; I should then have known from my parents that history had happened to my people in my part of the world.

Toynbee was only partly right. There were hundreds of thousands of small Irish boys in New York in 1897, and in scores of other places in northern and western America, who would have agreed only with his assertion that history was something unpleasant. As for the rest of his comment, they would have known very well that they did not share in New York's exemption from history. They knew that history had happened to their people in their parts of the world, and with effects every bit as calamitous as anything experienced in the South. The "irony" of American history would not have escaped these Irish; they had had some quite "un-American" experiences with defeat and poverty and other forms of unpleasantness. The past had not treated them kindly.[46]

It had been no gentler on Southerners. In *The Sound and the Fury,* William Faulkner's Quentin Compson is given a watch as a present from his father. But he is also made to understand that anything that keeps track of time is the "mausoleum of all hope and desire" and that he was given the watch not that "you may remember time, but that you might forget it now and then." Clocks marked the passage of time, recorded the tragic history of the nonenduring white Southerner. "Only when the clock stops does time come to life." Tim Buckley, the Irish tailor in *The Tailor and Ansty,* was considerably less morose, but no less "outside of time." He had a clock and maintained it perfectly, winding it every day. He just never set it. Knowing what time it was was not necessarily tragic; it simply did not matter. Those in the entirely Irish agricultural village of Melrose, Iowa, were of the same mind. When Woodrow Wilson "asked us all to move our clocks ahead so as to save daylight and win the War," the "Stump Man . . . said he had never lost any daylight. The wife, however, wanted to be patriotic, and offered to move the clock up half an hour—as the priest actually had done with the church clock trying to please all parties." The Stump Man described someone who told him that "our time is up; another asked 'what time is it?' . . . I sit here on a rainy day, and think of losing time and making it up. We pay by time and wear out in time. But what in the world is it?"[47]

The Irishman, said an Irish American who studied the Irish closely, had "a congenital disbelief in time . . . he disbelieves in what most men call time. Better still, it never occurs to him to believe or to disbelieve in it. . . . the Irishman seems to exist like God in an eternal now." Measuring time by clock ticks made no more sense than measuring land in acres rather than in how many cows the land would feed. The "old style of reckoning," whether of time or space, made "the digging" easier. It was all right to have a clock, but only if it did not keep time. Time was something the Irish passed. Like Southerners—and often for the same reason: that it had treated them so shabbily—they were acutely conscious of the past. But turning time into a commodity, the modern and American idea that one could spend, waste, lose, or save it, did not come readily or naturally to them. Being on time, like wasting it and losing it, had no meaning. Neither did gaining time or making up for any they might have lost. There may have been moments when the Irish wished they could make up for lost time, for that would mean escaping it. But it was never that easy. The Irish knew two things about time: they could not escape it and they would never run out of it.[48]

In America, however, the mythical West was the place where people went to escape time by starting over. The West cleaned the slate and obliterated the past. This was a part of the "Puritan Covenant," the deal between God and God's chosen American people. The West was a "virgin" land, a New World "garden," "Eden" restored for the "American Adam." The "frontier theory," according to one historian, "allowed Americans to escape history and its threat of social decay." Those who recorded the effects of this conscious act of forgetting, including Turner, have been quite rightly called "historians against history." They more nearly obliterated the past than preserved it; even their celebration of Anglo-Saxonism stressed change rather than continuity. But these chroniclers of a people without a past to chronicle did not limit their histories to the first generation of "new men." The West was a movable feast. It extended in time and space, and those immigrants who came later were also parties to the covenant. Their deliverance from the past was no less certain than the redemption of those who had entered the enchanted kingdom before them.[49]

There was nothing even remotely true in this self-congratulatory history of America as the second Eden. It was the stuff of the legend makers and prophets. But it had no applicability to the Irish at all, regardless of where in America their boats took them. Indeed, had they known about this covenant, they would likely have rejected it, not simply because it was absurd but because the past determined who they were. Erasing it undid them. Leaving Ireland did not make them forgetful. As Herman Melville wrote of them in 1849, "they bring all Ireland and her miseries with them." They did not just bring them; they incorporated them into their essence, constantly referring to themselves as Exiles (and poor ones, at that) of Erin. The theme of exile configured them and their American experience. It was the emblem of their identity.[50]

This theory of exile as an Irish motif is the particular and controversial contribution of Kerby Miller, whose book *Emigrants and Exiles* continues to define the field of Irish American studies. Miller has read thousands of letters from Irish in America; he has read as many speeches, newspaper accounts, and resolutions of Irish American organizations. The word "exile" appears constantly, with all of the bitterness, resentment, and hatred—and a full measure of self-pity—that figured to accompany it. As with everything in Miller's book, I am not going to deal with the theme of exile in any detail. A few points, however, need to be made. First, exile did not describe the reality of the Irish emigrant experience; it was a *motif* and a consciously manufactured one at that. As surely as the safety-valve theory benefited American industrial capitalists, so the "myth of exile" advanced the interests of Irish bourgeois nationalists, who needed the support of an impoverished and hence rebellious peasantry—as long as that rebelliousness was directed at the British and not at them. Miller argues, in Gramscian terms, that the "spontaneous philosophy" of that peasantry was the creation of middle-class Irish and that it included—was, in fact, based on—the belief that British perfidy first beggared them and then drove them from their ancestral homes. Exile, in other words, was a "hegemonic" device. Like all such devices, it was cynically used to advance a political agenda. This does not, however, diminish its cultural importance or its staying power.[51]

Second, like everything else in Irish history, exile was not a static concept. There were more self-styled exiles in the 1850s than in the 1890s.

Third, it fit perfectly the general fatalism and passivity of the Catholic Irish. Emigrants *leave* their home places; they may not want to leave; they may even be frightened of leaving. But "to leave" is an active verb and emigrants are active agents. Exiles, on the other hand, are *driven out* of their home places. They are the victims of treachery or cruelty. "To be driven out" is a passive verb form requiring a noun/agent as well as a passive object. The British system in all its multitudinous forms served as agent; the Irish were the passive objects. Miller even points out that the Irish language (which he defines as "static–active") had, in its far more common static mode, no word for "emigrate." The Irish could not suggest or signify leave-taking as a dynamic or even a willful action. I think this linguistic argument stretches the point, but the theme of emigration as exile can manage well enough without it.[52]

There was, however, another aspect of the theme of exile that Miller discusses, but too briefly. The Devotional Revolution in Irish Catholicism displayed itself in a variety of ways. As Miller has clearly shown, the exile motif antedated it by many decades, but one feature of the revolution gave new force and meaning to the theme of exile. According to Emmet Larkin, the "single most important factor in making and consolidating the Devotional Revolution" was the parish-mission movement. But the missioners who participated in this movement did more than just tidy up Irish parish life; many embraced what has been called "the cult of the Virgin Mary." They strongly encouraged membership in confraternities and sodalities with Mary as their principal spiritual focus. Stories of Mary filled Irish prayers, hymns, songs, invocations, and poetry; she was becoming Ireland's patron and protector in a manner that even St. Paul and St. Patrick had never been, and Marian devotions in all their particulars fixed themselves on the Irish church in ways and to an extent that were unique to Ireland.[53]

The clearest expression of this came with the apparition of Mary at Knock in County Mayo. The vision at Knock did not occur until 1879, but clearly the ground had been prepared well before then. The events at Knock had to have had special significance to a people with exile as part of their spontaneous philosophy. Mayo in the late 1870s, like most of the counties of the west of Ireland, was the scene of considerable tension between Catholic tenants and Protestant landlords. Tenant evictions were frequent and catastrophic in their consequences. In 1882 Archbishop John J. Lynch of Toronto, on pilgrimage to Knock, made the connection between evictions and Mary's appearance. He used interesting language. Lynch "thought that it was a most merciful condescension on the part of Our Immaculate Mother to appear in the neighbourhood of such a place" as Knock. There were many such places in Ireland, and clearly Mary's appearance at one of them was purposeful; the Virgin had come "to give the patience and courage of saints and martyrs to these poor people who . . . [had been] *driven from their homes.*"[54]

The Irish asked Mary to provide special intercessions for them, and among their favorite devotional prayers was the Fourth Breviary of the Salve Regina, the church's ancient and fervent appeal to the "Holy Queen" of Heaven, the "mother of mercy, of life, of sweetness, and of hope." To her did the Irish cry, "poor *banished* children of Eve." The banishment, of course, had been from Eden—but who among the Irish would have described Ireland in other than Edenic terms? No one was banished from hellish places. And so to Mary they sent "up their sighs, mourning and weeping in this valley of tears." That certainly cast it in Pauline terms. The Virgin was their "most gracious advocate," and they needed one. The Irish prayed that she would turn "her eyes of mercy toward" them and that "after this, *our exile*," would deliver them and "make them worthy of the promises of Christ."

As noted, this was a Catholic supplication, but it was prayed with more fervor in Ireland than in, say, France or Italy. But unless one is prepared to argue that it, too, was part of the hegemonic apparatus of the Irish bourgeoisie—an argument too cynical by half—its inclusion in the spontaneous philosophy of the Irish must be assigned to different sources. Emigration as exile had a kind of purgatorial aspect to it. The American wake, that literally outlandish ritual by which the Irish marked the emigration of friend or family member, implied that emigration was death, but the ritual also involved the hope that America was purgatory and not hell and that Mary, who had a special role as intercessor for souls in purgatory, would once again serve as gracious advocate. The Irish were still exiles, but not just political ones and not just of Erin. There was a strong Catholic as well as Irish aspect to the motif.[55]

The motif also had a strong American aspect. No one is exiled from hell or to heaven, and emigration as exile was partly a function of the conditions in the places to which the Irish had emigrated. In this sense, Catholic Irish became exiles only after they got to America and discovered that Americans were no more favorably disposed toward them than the English had been. Finally, there is that part of Irish self-identification that all but required them to suffer. Being Irish *meant* being oppressed by Britain. Emigrants, in escaping British rule, were also removing British oppression as a source of their identity. Emigration as exile restored the sense of victimization and its usefulness as a cultural marker. Indeed, it added exile to the list of Britain's sins against the Irish; the victimization of the exile exceeded that of those who were able—and lucky enough—to stay at home.[56]

These are only suggestions. The important point here is that exiles—real or invented, material or spiritual, as emigrants or immigrants—were poor excuses for westerners. Going west was an act of forgetting, of starting over and moving on. Exiles, particularly of the Catholic Irish variety, forgot nothing. Starting over was like being born again; they did not know how to do that either, and they had no desire to learn. But it must also be kept in mind that it was a mythical West that rejected these exiles and that the theme of exile was itself largely mythical. To intersecting historical lines must be added intersecting myths, the self-serving inventions of the ascendant classes of both Ireland and America: the myth of exile meets the constructed province.

This is as far as theory should ever be taken, but what gives some traction to this brief exercise are the comments of two Minnesota Irishmen who gave new and expanded meaning to static-active, not as a linguistic definition but as a cultural phenomenon, and to the idea of exile as a specific expression of that phenomenon. One of the two was Ignatius Donnelly. Sometime in the 1860s, Donnelly offered up his own version of Miller's contention that exile was a hegemonic device as well as of Slotkin's argument that the mythical West was no less so. Donnelly's charge that Ireland had lost "its dignity" has been cited. The specifics of that charge also need to be introduced. Exiles—real or imagined—had no dignity. The Donnellys, however, were not exiles. Donnelly was pleased to note that his "enterprising . . . family . . . had not been driven" from Ireland. Indeed, "if all Irishmen had fought with similar desperation, Ireland would never have been conquered." He went on to observe that "men of the name of Donnelly are settled far out on the frontier." Like all of those on far frontiers, they had "something of hazard and venture in [their] blood." In Ireland, these "men of my blood were soldiers, heroes, leaders of men, kings and conquerors." And the traits revealed in Ireland "will continue to reappear in their posterity, generation after generation, for hundreds, yes for thousands of years." No poor exiles of Erin, these.[57]

Here Donnelly seems confused. Ireland produced too few Donnellys, and this one was uncertain what to make of the shortage. He clearly took considerable pride in the fact that the Donnellys were exceptional, but what must that have meant for Ireland? The Irish, he insisted, were "unsubjected" but they were "conquered." Ireland had no memories of victory. Donnelly knew instinctively what the Irish writer Conor Cruise O'Brien meant when he wrote years after Donnelly that "those who can, gloat; those who can't, brood. Englishmen [and Americans] are born gloaters; Irishmen born brooders." And brooders select their heroes from the book of martyrs because no others are available to them. And so, Donnelly continued, Ireland, "in the midst of her gloom and desolation . . . selects as her idol one who, like herself, went down in disaster—one whose life, like her own, was a life of suffering and sacrifice." Donnelly's Catholicism was shaky at best, and it is hard to know whether he is applauding or condemning the Irish "selection" of Christ as "one like herself" and "her idol." More important, however, is that he made the same connection that Bishop John Ireland and Father Michael Hannan, among many, would also make: Christ on the cross was, if not Irish, unmistakably Irish-like. Donnelly may have understood the sources of the exile's gloom, but that understanding led more to gloating self-congratulation than to brooding sympathy. Even his well-chronicled populist rebelliousness was heroic in style. The self-pity of the exiles not only made them defective and substandard westerners but shamed and embarrassed those Irish with something of "venture in [their] blood."[58]

The other Minnesotan with something to say on this matter was James Manahan. Predictably for one with a "mixture of fantastic ideals" and a nagging uncertainty about how the Irish within him had formed his life, Manahan's description of the Irish in America was itself a fantastic mixture. In a St. Patrick's Day speech, probably delivered about 1905, he used every image and lesson he might have taken from Bowie Knife Bill, the Irish saints, and the sheer Irishness of his experiences. This is a speech worth listening to again. He asked his audience to follow the emigrant ship as it leaves Ireland:

> [S]ilently and slowly the green isle seems to sink until at last to the exile's tearful eye no answer comes save from the dark blue waters of the sea. To the west the old ship sails; farther and farther and westward still are the exiles borne from Erin. . . . Let us go with these exiles in all their journeying . . . by land and water, by city and by sea. . . . let us go with them and see whether or not they prove their manhood; let us go with them and see whether or not these exiles of Erin deserved their exile.[59]

But Manahan was not finished mixing his images. These two-boat Irish were "sad—poor—friendless": the lot of the exile and of more than a few Irish saints. But these were not disabled exiles, unfit for the American grand adventure. There was a lot of Bowie Knife Bill in Manahan's Irish.

> We see them . . . encountering the dangers of the pioneer; struggling among rocks and trees and savage men; building homes . . . in the very heart of the wilderness. We see them pushing across and developing a wild wide land; toiling over rugged hills and broad prairies; over vast plains and mighty rivers; away over the rugged mountains. . . . Everywhere in the new land . . . we see our exiles. . . . And when war comes . . . and the nation's life is threatened, we go with these Irish exiles to bloody fields of battle. . . . Brave men—these Irish exiles. . . . But there is a brighter side to this picture. Homes of happiness and wealth and honor we see . . . Irish exiles yesterday—standing by the sea shore sobbing— American citizens to-day—smiling in the sunshine. . . . I appeal to history that my picture of the Irish exile . . . has not been overdrawn. He was driven from home across the sea.

Manahan's portrait was not just overdrawn, it was overwrought. But his rhetorical sunburstery makes Miller's point. Indeed, it extends it: exile as motif has become exile as obsession.

The modern project, modernity in general, meant change, the purposeful losing of the past. So did going west, or going anywhere, when the going was voluntary and willful. All emigrants bring memories with them; the Irish brought Ireland with them. They were in two places at the same time. Some of this doubleness was simply a game "archaeologists" play. Some of it was a definitional part of being an exile. So too was the Irish ability to compress time, to treat the distant past as if it were both immediate and relevant, what Heaney refers to as "a two-timing going on in the one place." It was this other form of Irish doubleness, being in two times, that prevented them from synchronizing with Americans. American time was linear. It was based on three fundamental premises: the earth belonged to the living; the future would be better than the past; and the West was the place where the future would be found and made. Irish time was cyclical. It was based on one simple premise: the past was not dead, it was not even past.[60]

The birth documents of the two peoples, American and Irish, made these differences graphic. America's declaration referred to "self-evident truths" and "unalienable rights." The truth needed no historical validation. Those unalienable rights were part of "the creator's" endowment. Dividends continued to be paid on the principal, but there was no need to invoke the donor's name. Those rights had been violated in the past; but since they were natural and could not be forfeited, those violations represented self-evident tyranny. The colonies had shown "patient sufferance" as their natural rights were usurped by the crown, but a point had been reached when "necessity . . . constrains them to alter their former Systems of Government." The newly declared independent states did so in "the Name, and by the Authority of the good People of these Colonies," by which was meant those good people still alive. The Americans did not take this step for "light and transient causes," but neither did they take any note of or make any appeal to their past. The Declaration was written in the present tense. As Tocqueville explained, in America "the woof of time is ever being broken and the track of past generations lost. Those who have gone before are easily forgotten," not out of cruelty, but because they were not needed.[61]

They were not forgotten in Ireland. The Proclamation of the Irish Republic—not quite a birth document but close enough—was a declaration of a strikingly different sort from the American. The Proclamation was part of the 1916 Easter Rising—the timing of which in itself spoke to the intersection between Catholicism and Irish nationalism. It was written and read by the poet Padraic Pearse, who made his appeal to and for Irish freedom in "the name of God," but also in the name "of the dead generations from which *she* receives her *old traditions* of nationhood." Irish nationhood arose from *received* traditions, not self-evident truths. And these Irish traditions were *old*. Pearse made reference to Irish risings of the sixteenth century, but he also sounded that peculiarly Irish theme, implying that the origins of an independent Ireland dated back to the beginning of time, or at least to the "people who wept in Gethsemane, who trod the sorrowful way, who died naked on a cross." Such thoughts would never have reached Jefferson's conscious mind, and not simply because Pearse's proclamation came 140 years after his. Pearse had archaeology as his dominant art; he looked to ultimate origins, paying little heed to destinations. Jefferson had exploration as his art; his interest was in where America was going, not where it had been.[62]

It should be noted that Pearse acknowledged the vital role played by Ireland's "exiled children in America," and in recognizing that contribution, he was doing more than just being polite. Irish Americans paid for the Rising. But Pearse also said that Ireland was "relying in the first on her own strength" and that "she strikes in full confidence of victory." That sounded a proper heroic chord. No one, however, knew better than Pearse that the Rising was a doomed enterprise, that the rebels could not win in any rational sense of the word, that, in fact, "from the viewpoint of what was rational, . . . the revolutionaries . . . were absurd." Ireland could be made free only by blood sacrifice; Pearse and his revolutionary colleagues were martyrs, not patriots. His was not a call for liberty or death; it was more a plaintive hope that death might one day inspire liberty. It was on these grounds that "Ireland . . . summons her children to her flag." This was a summons that would have resonated only with a people with long and lively memories, the banished children of Eve, all of whose ground had been camped on before.[63]

Among the hundreds of other examples of these different concepts of time, place, and the proper ways to move through both, I will give only one more. It involves Michael MacGowan—in the Irish, Micí Mac Gabhann. MacGowan was born in 1865 in Cloghaneely, County Donegal. He immigrated in 1883, coming first to Bethlehem, Pennsylvania. He then made his way to Montana's industrial mines and finally to the gold strikes in the Yukon and the Klondike. In 1903 he returned to Cloghaneely, bought a farm, married, and had seven children. In 1948, in his native Irish, the old man told his story to an Irish folklorist; it was published in Irish as *Rotha Mór an tSaoil*. The translation is simple and straightforward: *Great Wheel of Life*. MacGowan rode the wheel. Sometimes he was at the top, at other times at the bottom; but regardless of where he was on the wheel, it always circled toward home. In 1962 his book was translated into English. For reasons never explained but easy enough to guess, its translator and English publishing house gave Michael MacGowan's book a new title. They called it *Hard Road to Klondike*. Wheels turn and circle back home; roads line up and go straight. And this road, the publisher wanted known, was a *hard* one; it ran *to* the *Klondike*, a rough and western place. There was no hint that it ever circled back. English and Americans took hard roads to nowhere—or to the Klondike, which was as close as one could come. Irish rode the great wheels of life. It was probably just as well that Micí Mac Gabhann died before the translation appeared.[64]

Nineteenth-century American history, both literally and figuratively, ran on rails, "with iron interlaced," said Whitman. This was history that could be tracked, in case anyone was interested in uncovering it. It ran toward the future, toward greater freedom, and always toward the west. In his poem "Westerning," Heaney writes from California of "Roads unreeled, unreeled / Falling light as casts / Laid down / On shining waters." The countless expressions of this American dynamic have been well and frequently chronicled. No one, however, captured this forceful and linear movement like William Gilpin. Gilpin sometimes reads like a bad parody of the western boomer, but his sentiments were widely shared and his images were striking: "The pioneer army perpetually advances, reconnoitres, strikes *to the front.*" The front, obviously, was to the west and toward the future. For the Irish, the west was to the rear and back to the "long ago." The American "recognizes and accepts the continental mission of his country and his people. His faith is impregnably fortified by this vision of power, unity, and forward motion." Needless to say, Gilpin's faith was quite secular. As he concluded his paean to linearity: "The American realizes that 'Progress is God.'" No part of this American notion of a history "unreeled and laid down" would have made the slightest sense to an Irish Catholic. Worlds in perpetual motion, constantly in the process of becoming, were not a congenial idea to a people who received their traditions from their dead generations.[65]

For Gilpin, as for all those others of similar if more moderately expressed ideas, the permanent settlement of the West was the "untransacted destiny" of the American people. The Irish did not understand untransacted destinies. They had only their transacted past. That was disqualifying enough. But there was also the fact that the untransacted had a tendency to remain such; the West and America would never be finished, America's Anglo-Saxon destiny never fully transacted. Americans were untroubled by this. The Irish were confounded by it. Charles Driscoll's book *Country Jake* contains a revealing passage about growing up Irish and Catholic in nineteenth-century Kansas. The Driscolls were surrounded by Protestants who "said wicked things about . . . the Pope." But that did not distinguish or condemn them for the Driscolls. What marked these Protestants was their fidgetiness. The Driscolls were compelled to pray for them. It was an edgy prayer. "Lord Jesus," these country Irish implored, "please do not send them all to hell. *They sing so hopefully of a land that is fairer than this.*"[66]

As was frequently the case, the Irish American Finley Peter Dunne spoke to the Irish notions of past/future, east/west—and to the outlandishness of them. Dunne was a Chicago- and New York–based journalist writing at the turn of the nineteenth century. Martin Dooley, Dunne's fictional Irish barman, was his voice, and Mr. Dooley wanted nothing to do with chasing western dreams that would always outrun him. "Me experyence with goold minin'," he told his patron, Hennessy, who was thinking of joining the Alaskan gold rush, "is it's always in th' nex' county. If I was to go to Alaska, they'd tell me iv th' finds in Seeberya. So I think I'll stay here." Besides, if Hennessy were to become rich, it would ruin him. Martin Dooley explained: "Ye'd come back here an' sthrut up an down th' sthreet

with yc'cr thumbs in ye'er armpits . . . ye'd hire a coachman that'd laugh at
ye. . . . Ye'd rackrint ye'er tinants an' lie about ye'er taxes. Ye'd go back to Ireland
on a visit, an' put on airs with ye'er cousin Mike . . . an' whin ye'd die, it'd take
half ye'er fortune f'r rayqueems to put ye r-right." Anglo-Saxons might behave
that way, Dooley told Hennessy on another occasion, but no one else in his
range of acquaintances.[67]

That, however, was the problem. Everyone in America, it seemed, was either
a bold Anglo-Saxon frontiersman or in the process of becoming one, and Dunne
took a satirical jab at this conceit as well. An Anglo-Saxon, Mr. Dooley explained,
"is a German that's forgot who was his parents. They're a lot iv thim in this coun-
thry. . . . Teddy Rosenfelt is . . . Anglo-Saxon. Schwartzmeister is an Anglo-
Saxon, but he doesn't know it, an' won't till some wan tells him." Indeed, the
country was filling with Anglo-Saxons: Bohemians and Poles, "Rooshian Jews
. . . the Dago Anglo-Saxons . . . the Sons iv Sweden an' th' Banana Club an' th'
Circle Francaize . . . an' th' Afro-Americans an' th' other Anglo-Saxons." Even
Dooley himself was "an Anglo-Saxon. I'm wan iv th' hottest Anglo-Saxons that
iver come out iv Anglo-Saxony. Th' name iv Dooley has been th' proudest
Anglo-Saxon name in th' County Roscommon f'r many years." And when all
these volk came together "f'r to raise their Anglo-Saxon battle-cry, it'll be all
day with th' eight or nine people in th' wurruld that has th' misfortune iv not
bein' brought up Anglo-Saxons."[68]

Obviously, not all the Irish would have agreed. Tens of thousands went to the next
county and the next after that, looking for gold, acting like Anglo-Saxons, and
willing to take their chances on the coachman laughing at them. William O'Brien,
Seán Ruiséal, and Séamas Ó Muircheartaigh come specifically to mind. But so
too does the notion that the three of them would have been better off had they
stopped at Martin Dooley's bar and listened to what he had to say. Or done what
Mící Mac Gabhann did and allowed *an rotha mór an tSaoil* to bring them home
again—not to Anglo-Saxony and never with the intent of putting on airs with
their cousin Mike. Progress, Gilpin's American god, meant *change*. In the tailor's
and Dooley's telling of it, the old ways of reckoning would have to give way to more
modern methods. A world based on the exchange of favors would be replaced
by one based on the exchange of money. Many of the Irish, whether in Ireland or
America, either scarcely knew what that meant or were unnerved at its prospect.
There was enough insecurity in their lives without purposefully adding more.
For all that they were genuinely funny commentaries on American westering and
Anglo-Saxon posturing, Finley Peter Dunne's pieces were as dark and night-
marish as anything Ruiséal or Ó Muircheartaigh might have written during
their time in Butte.

In the American context, Gilpin's god demanded movement from place to
place on roads that led both forward and westward. In traveling them, the Irish

risked detaching themselves from their homes and severing themselves from their pasts. Each generation of immigrants felt a little less anxious about relocating from Ireland to America, less anxious still about moving deeper into the American interior. But at that, the hard calculations that were part of both immigration and internal migration did not come easily for them. As a New York Irish emigrant aid society warned in 1849, "when you emigrate, you leave home." That was not as silly a statement as it might now appear. You leave Ireland, or, more precisely, that nook in Ireland that had nourished and preserved you. And that, according to Thomas Cahill, was the "hardest thing an Irishman could do, a much harder thing than giving up his life." Americans, on the other hand, as the Driscolls had learned, were always leaving home, which meant they had no home. They moved constantly, seeking, as they often put it, land for the landless.[69]

The Irish offered a remarkably revealing variation on that theme: they wanted "land for the friendless," a strange construction except that for the Irish to be "friendless" was to be detached from community—and that was the cultural equivalent of falling off the edge of the earth. The Irish word for community was *muintir;* there is no adequate English translation. *Na muintirí* were held together by bonds of family, tradition, and shared and intensely local values. The Irish were a "friendly" people, which had nothing to do with being hale and well met, everything to do with being part of a *muintir* and the "silent economy of friends" that held it together. A "friendly" place was not one where the people were merely affable and obliging. It may have been that, too, but to the Irish it meant full of friends—which necessarily involved a few they did not like. To be friendless was to be literally homeless, without relations—both dead and alive. That was far worse than simply not having any land. England gave the Irish the option of converting to Protestantism and keeping their land, not realizing that the conversion left the Irish friendless and as a consequence left the land barren and lifeless. In the America of the modern project, those Irish values, attenuated as they may have been, were as irrational as, say, starving oneself to death.[70]

There is more than a little irony in all this. The same spirit of enterprise that sparked an economic takeoff required the importation of the least enterprising to sustain it. Although it can still provoke heated debate, the notion that this spirit and the work ethic that accompanied it came easier to Protestants than it did to Catholics retains its credibility. Certainly it came easier to Americans than it did to the Irish who emigrated to the land of the Yankees in their unwashed and papist thousands in the 1840s and after. In the myth world of the constructed province, the West, both as a place and as a geographical ideogram, was the natal ground for self-reliance, mastery, and conquest. As noted, of all the rational, calculating, capitalistic, optimistic, linear, acquisitive, ambitious, and throughly modern things that nineteenth-century Americans could do, none could match going west to grow up with the country. Based on this standard, the self-styled Irish exiles—

those east-facing, hand-wringing, effeminate, intensely communal white Sambos with self-contradicting notions of weakness and strength and no notions at all of time—did not cut much of a figure as pioneers and frontiersmen.[71]

The Irish, however, would go west with the Americans, Irish disabilities not-withstanding. But they were always less cocksure and full of themselves than westerners were supposed to be. The progressive, almost utopian, notion that the present would give way to a more glorious future and that the West would be the new Eden made little sense to "archaeologists" for whom the West was part purgatory, part the mysterious and unsettling Otherworld. High stepping between fantasy and reality was not good preparation for the great American adventure of westering. The point is not that the Irish were unprepared for a mythical West; their myth life was richer by far than Americans'. It is that they were unprepared for *this* mythical west. It was too bumptious. It lacked subtlety and left no room for sorrow.

CHAPTER 5

Savage Twins

Indians and Irish on the Border

"Hoary priest! Thy dream is done
Of a hundred red tribes won
to the pale of Holy Church."

—*John Greenleaf Whittier, "Mogg Megone"*

There is a much-quoted exchange in a scene from *The Commitments,* the 1991 movie based on Roddy Doyle's novel of the same title. Jimmy, the manager of an Irish rock band, is attempting to persuade the group to play soul music. Specifically, he wants the group to sound like the African American artist James Brown. It should not be difficult, Jimmy reminds the working-class members of the band. After all, "the Irish are the niggers of Europe, lads. . . . Say it loud, I'm black and I'm proud." I wish Jimmy had said that the Irish were "the Indians of Europe." That would have been closer to the truth—not to mention more useful to this book. Jimmy's point that the Irish were Europe's—or at least Britain's—"Occidental others" could have been made with Blackfeet drummers substituting for James Brown. The Irish were as outlandish as either; they knew lyrics that all the Others, whether of Britain or of America, might have sung. Like the Indians, the Irish were natives of a settler society; the English settlers encountered them in the context of colonial warfare, of Native resistance to the imperial ambitions of invading Strangers.[1]

For more than three hundred years, from the sixteenth until well into the twentieth century, Ireland was England's practice field, where the English rehearsed their role as imperial lords. It was a rehearsal in full dress, involving every aspect of empire from the administrative to the ideological. At its core were the English descriptions of the Irish as savages. To be sure, those descriptions of Irish savagery were self-serving—the "cant of conquest" in the language of the historian Francis Jennings. Were the Irish not savage, the English could never have justified what they were doing to them, could never have behaved as if they were "absolved of all normal ethical restraints." The English were not striving for accuracy of description when they called the Irish savages; rather, they were looking for a moral justification for a policy of imperial aggression, including the violent suppression of colonial rebellions. As Sir Peter Carew wrote in 1569, when he was actively involved in trying to establish a colony in the Irish province of Leinster, one of the purposes of his imperial enterprise was "the suppressing and reforming of the loose, barbarous and most wicked life of [a] savage nation." It was Carew's ostensible object to bring the Irish out of savagery; he saw himself as a crusader for justice, bringing the "'gentle government'" of the English to backward Ireland.[2]

In 1596 Edmund Spenser brought Carew's and others' justification for conquest together in his *A View of the Present State of Ireland.* Spenser's account was filled with references to Irish barbarism, childish petulance, and utter irrationality. It established what would remain the moral underpinnings of the British conquest of Ireland. The Irish alternated between bowing and scraping and wild outbursts of violence, which gave even more force and credibility to the cant of conquest. But even pious platitudes in the service of policy, although they say more about English insecurities than about Irish inadequacies, when repeated often enough, can come to approach revealed truth. Spenser and the others had provided England with an "ethic of conquest" based on the moral shortcomings of the conquered. Whether the English truly believed what they were saying about the Irish is less important than the enduring hold these defining ideas had on English public consciousness.[3]

Within a generation after they had become the "guests of the Irish nation," the English encountered people as outlandish even as the Irish. Some were black Africans, others were the native peoples of England's emerging New World empire. Their moral justifications were well practiced, and the English were well prepared for both. When an Englishman familiar with "savagery" in both old worlds and new wrote in 1646 that "the wild *Irish* and the *Indian* doe not much differ and therefore . . . should be handled alike," he was expressing what had become a commonplace. "So it was," writes Patrick O'Farrell, "that the colonies of Virginia and Ulster were born under the same aegis, with Indians and Irishmen occupying equivalent roles." The bloody colonization of Ireland provided the "template for English understanding of North American savages."[4]

It is in this imperial context that what the literary critic Leo Marx called "Shakespeare's American Fable" should be read. The fable was Shakespeare's play *The Tempest,* written in 1610 or 1611 after the English had established their first colonies in Virginia. There is a clear connection between the play, set in an unidentified island once ruled by the "blue-ey'd hag" Sycorax, and still the home of her son, the anthropoidal Caliban, and England's developing interest in Western Hemisphere settlement. But 1610 was only seven years after the English had routed the Irish and their Spanish allies at the Battle of Kinsale and only a decade before the forcible dispossession and removal of the native Irish from the Province of Ulster and the "plantation" of the province by British Protestants. In other words, it is quite possible to make a clear connection between Shakespeare's play and the conquest and settlement of Ireland.[5]

It would not be going too far to say that *The Tempest* was Shakespeare's "Irish fable." There are suggestive hints that it was precisely that. Caliban is described as a "freckled whelp, hag-born"—and a fair, blue-eyed hag at that—and once is made to scream out in words that would have come easily to Ulster chieftains of Shakespeare's day: "This island's mine, by Sycorax my mother, Which thou tak'st from me." The island could easily have been in the Caribbean, but why a "*freckled whelp*"? And why "*hag*-born"? The myth world of the Irish was filled with ugly, evil-looking old women—some, doubtless, with blue eyes. Did Shakespeare know that? Had he read Spenser? Ultimately, it makes no difference which "settler society" Shakespeare had in mind—Virginia, Ireland, or both. James Joyce certainly got the point when one of the characters in *Ulysses* refers to "Patsy Caliban, our American cousin." The historian L. Perry Curtis makes the same argument less subtly when he writes repeatedly of the English caricature of the Irish as a "Celtic Caliban" or, as depicted in one cartoon, "O'Caliban." Perhaps the simplest characterization of *The Tempest* is that it was Shakespeare's fable of empire, that England had imperial interests in both Ireland and the New World, and that, in defense of those interests, he described the native peoples of both places as savages outside the pale.[6]

Whether Shakespeare had the Irish even partly in mind or not, the idea of Paddy Caliban retained its currency. To cite only one of scores of references, in 1797 John Pinkerton, a Scottish antiquarian, wrote that the Irish were "savages, have been savages since the world began, and will be forever savages; mere radical savages, not yet advanced even to a state of barbarism." Little changed between then and the caricature of simian Irish Catholics that dominated English perceptions in the nineteenth century and well into the twentieth century. The point here, however, is that I can discern no meaningful distinctions between those portraits of the Irish and William Bradford's seventeenth-century description of American Indians as a "savage people, who are cruel, barbarous, and most treacherous, being most furious in their rage and merciless where they overcome" or the 1868 Nebraska newspaper account of Indians as "savage . . . heartless creatures, destitute of all the promptings of human nature, having no respect for word or honor." They were "barbarian monster[s] . . . blood-washed animal[s]." And, like the Irish, they were irredeemably so. George Custer made the point directly:

"The Indian cannot be himself and be civilized." Like Catholicism and slavery, Irish and Indian were becoming analogies for one another. Charles Kingsley had dismissed the Irish as "white chimpanzees." In America, where the "savage over the border" provided the moral "compass" of the nation, they were more nearly white Indians.[7]

Americans were not just Britons living in a forest, as Tocqueville had described them. They were new creations still in the process of deciding who and what they were. That might have been said of them at any time in their history. As it happened, however, most of the Irish arrived during the transformative years of the great takeoff and the reconstruction of American self-identity that accompanied it. Walt Whitman believed—or at least wrote—that there was no "them who do not belong: . . . the nonkith, the nonkin . . . who demarcate what we are." Whitman was being wishful; few others were of his mind. Americans needed to validate— or, more accurately, revalidate—themselves and find what they were not in order to know what they were. Americans could assure themselves that they were still civilized by testing their well-ordered society against the barbarism of the Natives. This was as true in the nineteenth century as the seventeenth, although the nature of Indian "savagery" had changed over time. But the real difference between being American in 1680 and in 1880 was the vastly increased number and kind of savage oppositional figures available.[8]

My reference is not just to all of those "probationary whites" and "inbetween people" that historians have been finding over the last decade or so. We have learned a great deal from these historians of whiteness. But religion also counted. The Irish could not escape Catholicism by becoming white; Catholicism was not a construct. In the American search for Others, not all roads led to Rome, but some did. As the literary critic Jenny Franchot contends, it was "Romanism" that was the "force that threatened to disrupt the forming of the American self." Orestes Brownson is not a perfect source for anything, but he had it right when he wrote that "to pass from Protestantism to Catholicity is [to] . . . break with the whole world in which we have hitherto lived . . . [and to] enter into what is a new and untried region." Taking the road to Rome was culturally as well as theologically apostate.[9]

But it was not just Romanism that augmented the supply of nonkith and non-kin. Franchot links two images to produce what she calls the "twinned trials of 'savagery' and 'popery.'" "Twinned" is an apt description. Franchot acknowledges that there were "pervasive similarities between Old and New World anti-Catholicism," but there were also some important differences. French Jesuits, particularly along the New England frontier, had both converted and allied themselves with the Native peoples. This French Catholic threat to the Americans' emerging sense of themselves was graver and more culturally threatening than any the British faced. But the cultural threat was also the cultural opportunity. "Rome and her Indians," as Franchot calls the Jesuit-Native alliance, presented New Englanders with an inverse mirror of luminous clarity. Catholicism became the "foreign faith"; Catholics were literally "outsiders."[10]

More was at work, however, than reflexive anti-Catholicism. When the Jesuits converted the Indians and made them a present to Rome, they made the New World old and left the Protestant colonists as the only true Natives, the only New People. The Old World, however, did not give up easily, and the twinned terrors struck back by capturing the most innocent of the New World's New People. Franchot gives a whole new reading to the captivity tales of the seventeenth and eighteenth centuries. These tales of colonial New England become part of a developing regional and finally national consciousness. "America's long and absorbed engagement with the threat and thematics of captivity . . . shadowed the country's official vision of itself as the land of liberty."[11]

The horror and the fascination of the captivity tales arose not just because white colonists had been taken away by Indians but because Protestant colonists had been taken away by Catholics. Here was a truly menacing frontier, "a terrain disabled [both] by its primitivism and [by its] tainted affiliation with Catholic Europe." To be captured by savages was only part of it; the "worst captivity of all [was] conversion to Catholicism." According to one narrative, the Catholic Eucharist represented "capture and cannibalism." In this context, Maria Monk's "awful disclosures" in 1834 were only a slightly updated restatement of the older captivity myth; Monk's account of her capture and forced residence in a Catholic convent was not a frontier narrative, but her mention of the "squaw-nuns" in the convent gave the disclosures a kind of borderland aspect. The Reformation—and the settlement of the American forests as a continuing aspect of it—represented not just purification but escape from captivity.[12]

But after escape came counterattack. Franchot terms it "Protestant imperialism" and refers to an "expansionist Protestant United States." Even here, however, the powerful influence of Protestant Britain could be felt. Americans learned much about conquering "frontiers" by paying close attention as Britain conquered and extended its empire. Commerce and prosperity were not the only motives. John Foxe, whose anti-Catholicism was excessive even by the standards of the sixteenth century, was "conscious of England's failure in . . . permitting Antichristians to monopolize the Americas." John Hakluyt agreed, claiming biblical authority when he prophesied that the "virtuous" English would replace the "brutal Spanish" in the New Worlds. Predictably, Edmund Spenser saw the conquest and settlement of Ireland as a "testing-ground for the religious motive in colonization." But it remained for Thomas Cooper in 1615 to give the fullest statement of the British mission: "'Can you do God better service,' he asked rhetorically, 'than in promoting his kingdom and demolishing daily the power of Satan' by furthering 'this great and glorious work of the gathering in of the Gentiles by colonizing Ireland and Virginia?'" By gentiles Cooper meant, of course, Natives and papists and, where it applied, papist natives. The New World did not become truly new until it became entirely Protestant. Westward the course of true Christianity also took its way.[13]

Thus were the Catholic Irish and Indians associated in their savagery, and when the Irish began to arrive in America in numbers there was a sense that the New World was being recaptured by the forces of barbarism. Religion was a part of this. But so, too, were the real and perceived similarities in the Irish Catholic and American Indian cultures. Some of those similarities were contrived—another part of the cant of two conquests. Others, however, were real enough, and readily acknowledged by the Irish themselves. Real or imagined, the Irish found themselves leagued with Indians as they had previously been leagued with slaves, slaveholders, and Africans. The difference was that the Irish who went west placed themselves in the company of their barbaric twin: O'Caliban among the Calibans.[14]

The shared savagery of the Indians and the Irish took on a number of interesting forms. One of the similarities—the Irish, Indian, and Catholic (and black slave) as feminine—has only recently been uncovered by scholars trained in gender theory. Theories should be used with restraint, but we learn something from Franchot when she writes of "the masculine logic of Protestantism" and the "masculine world of the text." As for Catholicism, it "played the fiction to Protestantism's truth, the failure to its progress, the weaker femininity to its superior masculinity"; she identifies "Catholic and Indian cultures . . . as unfolding paradigms of the feminine, indulg[ing] in beautiful forms that disguise corrupt contents." The voice of Protestantism, Franchot goes on to say, was "objective, self-consciously masculine, and committed to disclosure; that of Catholicism . . . [was] subjective, effeminate, and bent on deception." Add to that Kirwin Klein's contention that in the American master narrative "the frontiersman was not a woman, not a black, not a Mexican, not an Asian, not an Indian"—and not, by the rules of logic, an Irish Catholic.[15]

This shared femininity arose from multiple sources. For the Irish, being Catholic was the first and most important. Anglo-American Protestants saw the Roman church as sensual, if not erotic; morbid; hopelessly sentimental; irrational; conspiratorial; stealthy; indirect; submissive and demanding of submissiveness; opulent; superstitious; interior; overly cultivated; theatrical; nostalgic; and vaporous to the point of neurasthenia. That was quite a list, and not all of the items on it comported well with notions of Irish brutishness. But so long as the Irish continued to give their spiritual allegiance to this feminized church, just so long would they be described on that basis. As was frequently the case, Theodore Parker gave religious bigotry its most graphic expression, but this time it was in the context of the association of Irish and Indian. "The Roman church," he wrote, "is the master fetish, the 'big thunder.' So the Catholic mother uses an image of the 'Virgin Mother of God,' and the Rocky Mountain savage a bundle of grass; it is a fetish." It was when the Indian mother laid down the bundle of grass and took up the image of the Virgin that the big thunder became the source of real anxiety.[16]

Religion, however, was only part of the story. Anglo-Americans were people of reasoned fact; they wrote histories. The Irish and the Indians were people of myth; they told stories. The ethnologist E. Estyn Evans wrote of a "marked Irish addiction to story telling—for hunters and fishermen are notorious story tellers." He did not say anything about American Indian hunters and fishers, but he did not need to. Their notoriety as storytellers equaled that of the Irish. Both peoples had "a wealth of folk tales and a host of legends, highly imaginative stories, and strange beliefs touching every native plant and animal." Nothing was excluded. For the Irish, every cave, rock, inlet, cove, headland, hillock, hill, drumlin, rill, pond, and bog and all who lived in, on, over, and under them had a name. For American Indians, the names would have been different, but not the insistence that everything, animate and inanimate, be named. The names, however, were spoken not written, and just the orality of Irish and Indians worlds would have been enough for the English and Americans to find places for them beyond the pale. "Once upon a time" might do for women, children, and rustic savages, but not for grown-up and civilized men.[17]

"History" for Irish and Indians alike was essentially genealogical, an account, based on memory, of the succession of kin and friends. It was constantly renewed by being constantly retold. The Irish and American Indians, like all subordinate peoples, had little interest in formal histories. They were the written records of the cantors of conquest, those whom Conor Cruise O'Brien called gloaters, and they "forcibly told [the Irish] that they are not central but marginal, that history is elsewhere, about someone else—perhaps a place where memory and history don't coincide." And even if these histories had not marginalized them, the Irish and Indians could not afford them. Thomas O'Flaherty, Irish radical, one-time American westerner, and brother of Liam O'Flaherty, put it in language that all of the world's colonized peoples would have understood: he had just finished relating the story of "Big James the Furious, . . . the terror of the [Aran] islands and the west of Galway." It was, he said, an "honest story," although whether a "truthful" one by Anglo-American standards is uncertain. The Irish, after all, "had no money to bribe the historians." O'Flaherty then ended his lesson in methodology with a storyteller's "Good night to ye."[18]

Unfortunately, femininity and the mythic storytelling that was part of it were not the only bad habit the Irish shared with Indians. Their social worlds were also uncomfortably similar. Both peoples were "wild" and came from wild places. Worse, neither had any intention of taming those places. Both were tribal, intensely local in their allegiances, and hierarchical in social structure. In 1873 the United States commissioner of Indian affairs gave voice to a commonly held belief—one with strong if unstated religious underpinnings—when he said that "'a fundamental difference between Barbarians and a civilized people is the difference between a herd and an individual.'" The commissioner was speaking only of Indians, but herding instincts were an Irish cultural commodity as well. Both the Irish and Indians were ruled by tribal/clan chiefs or chieftains; intertribal warfare was incessant among both peoples. Irish clans stole the land and the cattle of their enemies; Indian tribes stole the land and the horses of theirs—although the word "stole" has a different meaning in cultures without title deeds. Their memory keepers—*seanchaí* in Irish—learned, composed, and retold grand stories of the daring and courage of these plundering expeditions and of what great fun they had been. The Irish poet Paul Muldoon has described it perfectly: "We heard the seanchai relearn / What he has always known, Region of heroes, gentle maidens, / Giants that war and landgrab. . . . If we play back the tape /He may take up where he left off."[19]

The important point is that Indians could also take up the tape where the Irish left it off and make perfect sense of it. For the Irish as for the Indians, wealth and prestige were counted in animals—cattle for the one, horses and control of buffalo for the other. As E. Estyn Evans once wrote, Irish "epic literature [was] loud with the bellowing of bulls." His specific reference was to the Táin Bó Cúailgne, the Bull Raid of Cooley, or, in language more familiar to American western literature, the legend of Ireland's most spectacular case of cattle rustling. The bulls bellowed loudest when they were being stolen. But Evans was also talking about the hold the ancient legend of the Táin had on the imagination of twentieth-century Ireland. American Indians told culturally synonymous stories, complete with much bellowing of animals, and with equally durable holds on the people who heard them. The traditions of the two were not mirror images, but they were close, certainly closer than those of any other of the European settlers and Indians. Similar societies produce similar traditions; though the two peoples were not cultural monoliths—there were settled agricultural Indians and Irish who lived in cities and wore store-bought shoes—the dominant images of both arose from shared values.[20]

The Irish were cattle folk as the Indians were buffalo hunters. Evans writes that they would "rather have cow dung than soil" on their hands. They burned ground to increase the land open to pasturage; Indians did likewise. The rural Irish had no towns, only clachans, and they were not even facsimiles. The same was said of Indians. Indeed, according to Evans, "the whole nature of Gaelic society was opposed to urban living," a point with obvious relevance to the assumption that the Irish settlement in America was almost exclusively urban. The Irish, in the wonderful language of Alf Mac Lochlainn, "eight million of them spread over the land in their hundreds of thousands of cabins," constituted "a self-contained community of pre-industrial proletarians in a vast rural congested slum." Moreover, to return the discussion to oral and written traditions, these "cattle folk" living in their vast rural congested slums "have less need of records than arable husbandmen." For "less need" read "no need," or at least no need greater than that of Indians, those rural slum-dwelling buffalo folk.[21]

Patrick O'Farrell put together a list of Irish cultural habits as viewed by the English in his book *Ireland's English Question*. Substituting "Indian" for "Irish" and "American" for "English" will make clear why I wish the band manager in *The Commitments* had used Native Americans as the Irish musical model. The "depravity of the [Irish] people," O'Farrell writes, "was reflected in the depravity of their usages . . . the absence of a strong central government and of a stable system of landholding and agriculture. . . . Their capital consisted of cattle. They cultivated no land. They were nomadic. They had no money system. Their relationship one to another was highly personalized. They had no town. They slept in the open, or in wretched huts. They talked in Gaelic. Their appearance, half-naked, long hair, clad in animal skins, always armed, was wild."[22]

I would again add to the list. Neither the Irish nor Indians had any developed sense of private property, particularly in land that was used communally and for which there were no titles or anything resembling them. Neither had been treated fairly by the law, and both had developed a fine disdain for it. The heroes among them were not the law makers but the law breakers. The "outlandish" were also the "outlaws." How could they not have been? Defining and treating a people as the one all but guaranteed that they would be the other, or at least that they would be more tolerant of the other. They could be forced to obey the law; but until it began to treat them fairly, they could not be made to respect or feel any attachment to it. Unfortunately but not surprisingly, the inexorable logic of outcast as outlaw never occurred to those who had cast them out.[23]

Neither people had well-established work habits, both alternating periods of idleness with periods of fierce physical exertion. Both had a certain innocence: the measurement and tracking of time meant little or nothing to them. But mindfulness of the clock was not something the modern world could ignore or leave to chance. That world *ran* and it ran *on time*. The Indians and the Irish, however, objected even to having their images captured, whether by portrait painting or by photograph, because the resulting image stopped time and in the process took the subject out of it. This distorted reality. It invited bad luck, said some in the west of Ireland. The Plains Indians were more graphic. Photography was mere "shadow catching." They existed in time and over time, but, as previously noted, that had nothing to do with calibrating it to see that they were on time.[24]

Both were materially poor beyond powers of description. Irish poverty was "so extreme that, when found in the heart of the empire, it was seen as a fall from civilization and likened to savagery." Tocqueville "def[ied] a friend to picture the misery of the [Irish] population. . . . I should have believed myself returned to the huts of . . . the Iroquois." Both populations lost a staggering number of their children to early death. Both were described as besotted; they did not simply drink too much, they drank themselves into senselessness. On a theoretical level, the historian Norman Clark has written that drinking was a "ritual of . . . sub-cultures," part of a "liturgy of protest against the cruel heat of the melting pot." It served to "validate certain non-Protestant . . . non-Anglo identities. Irish-Americans . . . had this problem." But so too, according to Clark, did "American Indians . . . who drank to morbidity . . . because they had to demonstrate that they were Indians. Getting drunk was to be an Indian." Drink, wrote the historian Robert Scally, who surely was conscious of the connection he was making, "was the Irishman's 'firewater.'"[25]

The anthropologist Margaret Hogden makes the connection between these savage twins explicit—and in heavily laden language: "All frontier antagonists looked more or less alike. . . . the epithets used to describe the folk on Britain's Celtic border were interchangeable with those applied to . . . the Indians across the Atlantic." Given this close association, it was inevitable that they would become rhetorical models for one another. In both of Albion's worlds, savagery was as savagery did. Americans were as familiar with this notion as were the British, and they used it with numbing frequency to describe the more outlandish excesses of the Irish among them.[26]

During the 1863 New York riots, the analogy became a kind of political trope. The *New York Times,* for example, in describing the Irish rioters, could scarcely "imagine that there was such a race of miscreants extant. . . . we have thousands of barbarians in our midst, every whit as ferocious . . . as the Minnesota savages, and never wanting anything but the opportunity to copy every Indian deed of horror." The reference was to the Sioux uprising in Minnesota. As a Protestant minister charged, "the cruelties of the aboriginal savages can hardly rival those of the brutal [Irish] mob." The *New York Tribune* was of similar mind. The Irish were described as a "savage mob," a "pack of savages," "savage foes," "demons and incarnate devils." Four years after the riots, an article in *Harper's Magazine* re-created the terror: "A great roaring suddenly burst upon our ears, a howling as of thousands of wild Indians set loose at once. The Irish have risen."[27]

Even when not "rising" and "howling," the Irish were a threatening crowd. Edward Everett Hale offered an interesting analogy. The Irish, he wrote, had been "ruined," driven by their conquerors to the far west of Ireland. Those western points "are to be looked upon just like the 'Indian Leap' of our own legends; they are the last resting place." Hale did not deal with what happened when the ruined Irish went from the west of Ireland to the west of America. Others were less reticent. Frederick Jackson Turner, for example, used the phrase "wild Irishmen" on one occasion, enclosing the term in quotation marks. Since he never used the word "wild" when dealing with Scots Irish, it may be presumed he meant Catholics. Turner also wrote of American pioneers who "wrested their clearing from . . . the savages who surrounded them," but, to my knowledge, he never equated wild Irish with Indians. In Butte, Montana, Irish miners were called "savages"; in Denver, the working-class Irish who dominated the Democratic Party's Fifth Ward were known as "the Fifth Ward Savages." These were playful nicknames, and the Irish wore them with a certain pugnacity and pride. Nonetheless, "savage" was an interesting choice of words for western working-class Irish Democrats. It is tempting to think that the Cheyenne chief who wrote to Terence Powderly, the Irish Catholic leader of the Noble and Holy Order of the Knights of Labor, and asked the Knights to protest the theft of Cheyenne lands had been reading accounts such as these.[28]

As the modern project accelerated after the war, images of savagery once applied only to "frontier" settings became the rhetorical device of choice in describing urban and industrial violence. Strikes and other job actions did not usually have the clear ethnic component that was evident in 1863, and the charges of working-class savagery had no particularly Irish target. The use of racially and ethnically charged language to describe class conflicts, the use of a "reversible analogy between workers and savages," has been the subject of much historical debate lately. For Richard Slotkin, ascribing racial characteristics to striking workers was metaphorical, a means of bringing the Indian Wars from the frontier periphery home to the industrial metropolises of the East. Matthew Jacobson, however, contends that there was more to these reversible analogies of urban and frontier savagery. The association was not just metaphorical; class wars were, in fact, race wars in the context of the nineteenth century's definition of race. I think Jacobson is right. But this is a time to return to a central point that Jacobson all but ignores. "Race" was not the only mark of difference; religion was never far from the minds of those who used words like "savage" and "barbarian" indiscriminately and as if they had real meaning. Jacobson, for example, cites E. L. Godkin as one of those who understood that America's new working class did not just act like savages but carried "in their very blood . . . traditions" that "menace[d]" civilization. There is no question that Godkin implicated the Irish among the menacing ones.[29]

But Jacobson identifies Godkin only as the editor of the *Nation* and, by association, one of the guardians of the traditions of nineteenth-century American liberalism. Those traditions, however, included an often rancorous hostility to both Catholicism and the Irish who embraced it. Godkin was particularly well cast for this role. He was himself born in Ireland, but of brilliant Orange hue. His father was a Presbyterian minister. Godkin himself insisted that although he was "an Irishman," he was "English in blood." What made the Irish so menacing, what they carried in their blood, was popery. They were "priest-ridden, whiskey-loving, thriftless Padd[ies], . . . half-barbarous stranger[s] for whom the priest is waiting on the shore the moment" the immigrant ship arrives. Godkin seems never to have made the point explicitly, but he clearly believed that the Irish and the Indians were equally savage. As another historian has remarked, Godkin "insulted and ridiculed Irish immigrants at every opportunity." They were white, but, in Jacobson's language, theirs was a "whiteness of a different color." That color was tinged with the royal purple of Rome as well as the green of Ireland; it was a mix of "race" and faith. The Irish, as surely as the Indians, were cradle savages.[30]

The twinned savagery of Indian and Irish has another important aspect: the Anglo-American image of Caliban—whether he be Indian or Irish—powerfully influenced policy. The assumption or assignment of savagery was, after all, part of the cant of a conquest, or, rather, two separate but related conquests. The two peoples were seen as threats to imperial and material advance. That the two would be warred against in roughly the same way is not surprising. I join the historian Richard Slotkin in finding it "interesting to note the adoption of similar policies by Puritans colonizing in Ulster" and Puritans colonizing in New England. In both places there were "systematic assaults on . . . tribalism, native bardic myth-historians were forbidden to sing, isolated clans were exterminated, and the rest of the population was ravaged." James Joyce's words applied to both peoples: "Their mud-cabins and their shielings by the roadside were laid low by the batteringram."[31]

In New England, reservations—"praying towns" as they were known—were established to hold the Indians in semicaptivity. In Ireland, Oliver Cromwell tried to set up a "'wild Irish'" reservation in the province of Connacht in the West of Ireland, offering the wild ones the same option accorded to American Indians; they could choose "Hell or Connacht/Pine Ridge." Eventually, the reservations system would become the preferred American solution to its "Indian problem." The possibility that the Americans studied what the English had done with their "Irish problem" and copied it is intriguing. Equally intriguing is the possibility that the English took a lesson from American Indian policy: from the Great Hunger forward, the avowed policy of the British was to remove the Irish from their native lands, not to Connacht this time but to America. When Scally writes of the state-sponsored relocation of people from the Irish village of Ballykilcline to America during *an Gorta Mór,* the parallels with the "Trail of Tears" and the other forced uprootings of Native American peoples are striking. That the British and the Americans who arranged for the relocations did so in the name of kindness and that both sets of Natives saw their removal as an act of unspeakable cruelty—and were condemned as ungrateful as a result—adds to the resonance. Home had different meanings for the conquering and the conquered. What England and America defined as salvation and escape, the Irish and Indians saw as eviction and exile, genocidal in purpose and effect, a "vision of oblivion."[32]

There were also parallels in the treatment accorded those who resisted eviction. In the sixteenth and seventeenth centuries Englishmen killed Irish women and children because, as it was put in 1566, "the killyng of theim by the sworde was the waie to kill the menn of warre by famine." This was a somewhat different approach from the American one, with its casual reference to "nits make lice" (itself of British origin), but the consequences were the same. So, too, Cromwell's scorched earth policy in Ireland was first inspired by his careful reading of Spanish atrocities against Indians and, in its turn, was matched "exactly [by] the policy adopted by the American Puritans in King Philip's War two decades later." John Fiske, one of the more stalwart of the Anglo-Saxon supremacists, was untroubled by the chilling nonchalance of all this. As he put it in 1900, "The blow which our forefathers struck [against the Pequots] was surely Cromwellian in its effectiveness. To use the frontiersman's cynical phrase, it made 'many good Indians.'" Cromwell would have insisted that it made many "good Irish Catholics" as well. Had the *London Times* not said nearly the same when it wrote with undisguised pleasure that the starving times in Ireland ensured that soon a Celt "will be as rare in Connemara as is the Red Indian on the shores of Manhattan"?[33]

It is the case that the extermination and forced relocation of people of tainted blood—in chromatic terms, how the Irish became red, or the Indians green— were not the only options available. Some thought that savagery was a transitional stage, that Albion and its seed had themselves once been only marginally civilized. At issue was speeding the process from one stage to the next, eradicating one set of cultural forms and replacing it with a more favored one. The instrument in both nations was the same: Britain would dispatch Protestant reformers to its wild Irish, America to its no less wild Indians. The stated purposes were almost always philanthropic, although few bothered to ask if cultural reconstruction could ever be seen as arising from a generosity of spirit.[34]

Let one example stand for many. Moreton Frewen, a well-placed English gentleman whose extensive property holdings included a cattle ranch in Wyoming, described in his autobiography the Protestant mission school in Ireland established by his father in the 1860s. Frewen was a fop—but a candid one. "My religious bias," he admitted, "was vehemently anti-Catholic." It was an inheritance from his father, who "regard[ed] the Church of Rome as the foe of knowledge and progress." The anti-Catholicism of the elder Frewen was, in fact, "the tap-root of his moral science." That moral science led him to "purchase a large area of wild land in Connemara for the purpose of founding Church of England schools." That was an interesting use of the word "wild," and Frewen admitted that it "would have been difficult to discover a soil more unproductive for such a purpose." It was the nature of the purpose, however, that is of interest. "My father," Frewen went on to write in that dissembling way of his, "did not believe the Catholic communities could safely enjoy representative institutions or fit into what was then beginning to be called 'democracy.' For him, this was the seat of mischief in Ireland. Hence the Protestant missions he established in Connemara." Later in his autobiography Frewen recalled his reaction to the ferocious American response to Custer's defeat at the Little Big Horn, in the process connecting the sources of savagery and those of civilization. "Was it not," he wrote about the renewal of open warfare against the Plains tribes, "a splendid part of 'the winning of the West' for *our common* civilization?"[35]

The Protestant missions in Ireland were total failures; the record of their Protestant counterparts for America's Indians fared only slightly better. This left Britain and America with only one institution that might effect a peaceful cultural transformation of the semicivilized and uncivilized among them. The political managers of Britain's empire—including its practice field in Ireland—and of America's frontier conquest turned to compulsory state-sponsored education, hoping that it might beat into unyielding heads some semblance of civility. British National Schools were established on the "reservations" of Ireland, boarding schools on America's frontiers. That these schools were strongly, if somewhat covertly, Protestant in pedagogy and curriculum was obvious to all, particularly to Catholics. Their stated function may have been to teach republican virtues rather than Protestant piety; but since those were so nearly synonymous, they became the last redoubts of both. The Irish language was proscribed; so were the Indians' languages, along with games, songs, stories, even the tonsorial and clothing styles of both sets of savages. The pasts of the two peoples were either ignored or "demystified." The storytellers were silenced; the historians were "bribed."[36]

The geography lessons in the Irish National Schools were prepared by the Dublin Presbyterian minister and abolitionist James Carlile. His intent was far more assimilative than instructional. Irish children were taught specifically that there were "some countries . . . inhabited by half-savage tribes . . . where land is not private property, but is all one great common on which every man turns out his cattle to feed." It followed that the half-savages would have to learn that if the land were to be "properly cultivated, it must be private property." The intent cannot have been to offer up a hypothetical example of what was practiced in "some countries." Even the densest of Irish students had to have known what country was being described. American Indians were taught from the same textbooks and to the same purpose. Chasing buffalo around the great commons was more savage even than turning out the cattle to feed on an Irish outfield.[37]

Irish students would likely not have been told that America was being translated into English, that the Indian names for places, like the Irish names in their own country, were being replaced with clumsy English equivalents or, more commonly, renamed entirely. They might have been taught that America was being mapped, that cartographic lines were being drawn in the interest of clarifying land titles and making private property more secure. They could draw their own local inferences from that. Irish children, in other words, were being taught passable geography and political economy, but not in the interest of scholarship. The abiding lessons of the National Schools, as of the Indian schools which they so much resembled, were "shame and subservience . . . powerlessness, both their own and their parents'." This was schooling "for extinction"; education for both Irish and Indian was a "catastrophe of forgetting."[38]

In 1792 Hugh Brackenridge wrote *Modern Chivalry*, which Matthew Jacobson has called an "extended meditation on republican government" in the new America. Its protagonist was the wondrous immigrant "bog-trotter" Teague O'Regan. O'Regan was one of the "aborigines of Ireland," a description that, in context, could only have meant a Catholic. Like all such, he was liable "to blunders, both in . . . words and actions." That was a polite way of putting it. O'Regan was a genetic half-wit, barely removed from swinging in trees and manifestly incapable of self-government. Jacobson ignores the religious component of the aboriginal O'Regan's unfitness; but, in this instance at least, his basic argument is not seriously damaged. O'Regan is transformed from savagery to something approaching— though never reaching—the genius of America. The nature of that transformation and the role of religion in it are less important than the manner in which it was expressed.[39]

O'Regan became semicivilized because he came to hate Indians. Speaking an embarrassingly bad and doggerel Hiberno-English, Teague tells his American acquaintances how he would deal with the Indian problem. He would "trate" with "de vile savages . . . wid a good shelelah, or tomahawk to break deir heads . . . by Saint Patrick, I would give dem a good bullet hole in deir faces." At that moment Teague O'Regan shed some of his Irishness and became an American in training. O'Regan's Indian hating was a "western" version of "blacking up," a way—perhaps the only way—for "probationary" white immigrants to gain a measure of acceptance. That has become the standard interpretation of Irish immigrant entry into American low society.[40]

That is not the only interpretation. Immigrants learned the attitudes as well as the habits of their new society, and that they sometimes adopted the less lovely of those attitudes and habits was to be expected. If that new society believed that whites were superior to people of color and acted on that belief, the immigrants, even those who had never seen a person of color, did as the Americans did. This seems to me far removed from the notion that the immigrants embraced racist attitudes in a desperate effort to "become white." O'Regan was never not white. He was not thought a good candidate for republicanism; he was never more than an apprentice American who would likely never outgrow his apprenticeship, but that was a cultural judgment based largely on religion, not a "racial" one based on shades of whiteness. The truly important part of the "translation" of Teague O'Regan, however, is that it was in the language of Indian hating. The Irish aborigine had crossed over a cultural border. O'Regan ceased to be a savage by the simple expedient of sharing in the obloquy of the invented savagery of others. Brackenridge did not even hint at whether anyone recognized the paradox.[41]

But that paradox is a part of the story, and the fictional O'Regan was not the last of the aboriginal Irish to miss the point that Americans were treating the tribal Indians in much the same way the British had treated the tribal Irish. The idea that the victims of injustice learn never to behave unjustly, that the hated never hate, is a romantic fiction. They usually have some dim awareness of the inconsistencies, however, as in the case of Irish Americans who were troubled by American Indian policy in large part because it seemed so eerily and tragically reminiscent of England's Irish policy. But there were also Irish who, O'Regan-like, joined in the part of America's untransacted destiny that required the removal of Native peoples from their natal ground. Some, in fact, joined with more enthusiasm than was altogether meet and fitting. As Fintan O'Toole has written, the Irish "played more than their shared part" in the Indian Wars.[42]

Of the latter group, the most notable would have to include John O'Sullivan, who coined the spread-eagled expansionist phrase "manifest destiny" and linked it with such unlikely Irish ideas as an America "separate[d] from the past and connecte[d] to the future only." He also made reference to "Anglo-Saxons" and their "irresistible army . . . armed with the plough and the rifle and marking its trail with schools and colleges, courts and representative halls, mills and meeting houses." That was a remarkable lineup given that the native Irish were conspicuously not Anglo-Saxon and knew next to nothing of colleges, courts, and representative halls and little enough of plows. O'Sullivan had clearly lost his Irish moorings and become American. The only problem with this too easy interpretation is that he had no Irish moorings to lose. The only thing Irish about O'Sullivan was his surname. He was born in Gibraltar, where his father, of remote Irish ancestry, was a businessman. O'Sullivan's mother was English, and he married an American, became a spiritualist, and was buried in a Moravian Cemetery. No one would have confused him with Teague O'Regan.[43]

Others, however, came closer to meeting Teague's low standard. It was an Irishman, General Phil Sheridan, who may have said that "the only good Indian was a dead Indian." There has never been a full accounting of the source of that infamous remark; but whether Sheridan said it or not, he certainly acted on it. So did General James Shields, another exiled Irish patriot and Indian fighter. So did Thomas Francis Meagher, one of the leaders of the Irish rising of 1848, condemned by the British to the penal colony at Van Dieman's Land, and, after his escape, Civil

War hero, territorial governor of Montana, and active Fenian. Meagher died at Fort Benton, Montana, in 1867. He had gone there to await and take personal possession of sufficient weaponry to wage war on the Blackfeet.[44]

This list could be extended. Cork-born John J. Healy was a Fenian rebel but also the principal supplier of whiskey to the Indians along the Whoop-Up Trail in Montana and Alberta. One of his acquaintances was Charles Collins, another master Fenian intriguer, who in 1872 lobbied successfully for the opening of the Black Hills to white settlement in violation of treaty rights accorded to the Sioux. Collins was a kind of plebeian expansionist. The Black Hills could provide homes for countless of the nation's poor, as another Irishman put it, for all of those "who would rather be scalped than remain poor," and who "saw in the vision of the Black Hills, El Dorado." But Collins had particularly in mind the Irish poor.[45]

One consequence of the white incursions into the Black Hills was, of course, Custer's so-called last stand at the Little Big Horn. This was also the last stand of the entire 7th U.S. Cavalry, but the list of dead reads like a gathering of the Irish clans: Harrington, Foley, Ryan, Golden, Hogan, McElvey, Mooney, Boyle, Connor, O'Connor, Kenney, Murphy, Brody, Coleman, Manning, Carney, Donnelly, Kelly, Considine—and those are only from the first page. Reciting the names of America's western forts makes the same point. There was Fort Keough (named after Myles Keough, whose papal medal was hanging around the neck of Sitting Bull when the great Sioux leader died) as well as Forts Phil Sheridan, Kearney, Gibbon, Casey, Cummings, Harney, McDermit, McDowell, McGarry, McKinney, and Maginnis. Needless to add, forts were always named after officers. The dispossessed had become the dispossessors.[46]

They even had their own *seanchaí* in John F. Finerty. Finerty was born in County Galway in 1846, immigrated to America in 1864, and in the 1870s became a well-known and very able Chicago journalist. In 1875 he accompanied the frontier army as it ventured into what Finerty called "the demon-peopled land" west of the Missouri. In his book *War Path and Bivouac*, Finerty wrote that a "majority" of the Army's "rank and file" were of "either Irish or German birth or parentage." Many of these soldiers were direct from "the slums of the great cities and need[ed] to be tamed a little," particularly the "never war-absent Irish." As for its enemies, of whatever tribe, they were the "pests of the plains, . . . mysterious, barbaric, unreasonable, childish, superstitious, treacherous, thievish, murderous creature[s]." They were also, unlike the Irish, untamable. In other words, they were all that the Irish were described as being, and no one would have known that better than Finerty, who grew up almost literally next door to Frewen's school in Connemara and who, from the time of his arrival in America until his death in 1908, was an ardent and rhetorically ferocious Irish nationalist.[47]

The Irishmen in the western army, however, were instruments of conquest, not conquerors. As for Finerty, he was a seller as well as a teller of western stories. He wrote as he did because largely eastern audiences wanted their frontier tales to be sanguinary and filled with heroic confrontations between the forces of civilization and savagery. Style and literary convention explain him. In that sense, Finerty was no *seanchaí* at all. He was no safe-keeper of Irish tribal memories. But neither need he be deconstructed and left as an example of the Irishman moving toward whiteness. He was part of a commercial culture, a participant in the construction of American western myths rather than the preservation of Irish ones. That does not make him an example of runaway Anglo-Saxonism or of its related and only slightly more subtle ideological consort, Caucasian supremacy. For Finerty also spoke of "white greed" and said that "the blood of Oliver Twist must be plentiful in this free land, if we are to judge by our dealings with the unfortunate aboriginal." He even praised the Indians; they "had fought bravely, in every generation, for their families" and their lands. Had not the same been said of the Irish, and would not Finerty have known it?[48]

Other Irishmen put their westering experiences—including their borderland conquests—on even fuller display. There were also "frontiersmen," including Buffalo Bill, who reversed the process and turned themselves into Irish. It is impossible to explain the motives of each of them, but a few suggestions would be in order. Matthew Jacobson argues that "the unfolding national epic" was one "of encounter, conquest, enslavement and emancipation, and immigration." He asserts further that "frontier contingencies combined with rhetorical indulgences to invest American nationalism with perpetual appeals to 'civilization' and 'savagery,' to 'white' conquests and the defeat of the (always dark) Other." I think that he overstates his case; there is too much racial blood lust in it.[49]

But my differences with Jacobson are of degree not of kind. Being and/or becoming an American did, in fact, include something very like what he has described. And some western Irish knew it and knew, too, that they had played no part in some key chapters in America's "unfolding national epic." The Irish had not come over on the *Mayflower;* they were not conspicuous participants in the Revolution or the Early National years, although Michael J. O'Brien and the American Irish Historical Association formed in 1897 strove mightily to prove otherwise. The Irish had legitimate claims on the Civil War and invoked them frequently, but those claims were tarnished if not fully discredited by the outrages in New York City in July 1863.[50]

This did not leave them much; pioneering and its bloody accompaniment, Indian fighting, were the only "American" adventures in which they had participated. But with the frontier becoming as important an icon as Plymouth Rock, that would have been more than enough to establish their American bona fides. I cannot know that western Irish were conscious of this when they did their frontier strut, that acting out their western fantasies was a function of their insecurities, an effort to prove not only that they had become American but that they were among the nation's beau ideal. Whatever their level of consciousness—or self-consciousness—many Irish worked to prove that the American master narrative included them in a starring role.

James Duval Phelan, whose father immigrated from Ireland in 1821 and made his way to California in the 1850s, was not the usual sort of Irish American. He was not only born in the West, he was born rich and became richer. Mayor of San Francisco and senator from California, Phelan was also self-consciously western, a founding member of the Sons of the Golden West and inordinately proud of his role as a western pioneer. In a memorial address on the death of his friend Dennis O'Sullivan, Phelan remarked that O'Sullivan "owed much to inheritance, springing from the sturdy stock of old Ireland." But he took "his physique and temperament from his pioneer ancestry" and the "environment which his native California afforded." The West was filled with men like Dennis O'Sullivan; because of that, Phelan contended, America's future heroes would come from "the great West." It was "turning out men all the time of the right sort for fighting, not pampered by influences which prevail . . . in the luxurious cities of the East." These westerners were "hardy youths, brought up on the farm."[51]

Phelan's West, however, like that of most Americans, was not simply the home of the brave. The "racial" element was never absent from his descriptions. Phelan was as self-consciously Irish as he was assertively western, and he bristled at the assumption that western heroes were by definition Anglo-Saxon heroes. The "Anglomaniacs," as he called them, had falsely claimed that the American frontier was an Anglo-Saxon preserve, that only they could subdue it. He agreed fully with his brother-in-law, Francis J. Sullivan, that the United States generally and the western and better parts of it in particular were not dominated by Albion's seed and that the idea that they were was an "Anglo-Saxon Conspiracy." Phelan had in his magazine collection an undated and unsigned letter indicating that the "anti-British" (not, note, the non-British) population of the West was over 70 percent, much of it from Canada, which was identified as a "sort of halfway house for thousands of . . . Irish." Phelan also wrote of his native state as a "virgin land, unhampered by tradition—a mighty field for freedom, for Caucasian courage and enterprise." To be sure—sounding a lot like a Teague O'Regan with manners—he noted that it once had "its 'Indian problem,' blood thirsty savages, and settled it in the interest of civilization," by which he meant killed the Indians. "The world is better for it." He must have been delighted when Joseph Tumulty, Woodrow Wilson's personal secretary, addressed him as a "knightly Irishman 'out of the West.'"[52]

Phelan, however, hardly counts. The western alchemy of race, like the eastern, was a working-class phenomenon; the wages of whiteness counted for little to those who did not collect wages. Phelan most assuredly was not of the wage-working class. Neither were some other Irish who claimed frontiersman status. Ignatius Donnelly insisted that the Irish, "being so oppressed for centuries . . .

should always hate injustice and tyranny." Certainly he did. He had a "strong, hereditary . . . predisposition" that explained his "intense hatred of oppression and injustice. You cannot wipe out the ingrained training of 3,173 years by transplantation across an ocean." How he calculated the 3,173 years is unknown, but the Donnellys had transplanted more than just a heightened sense of justice. They also "took naturally to this peripatetic life" of the "Great West" and became its "frontiersmen and soldiers," "conquerors," and "chiefs." They were "bold" and "warlike," and they drove "the red men" from their "ancient hunting grounds" and reclaimed "the wilderness—land still trodden by the feet of savages." It did not occur to him that the reclamation project might itself be seen as unjust and tyrannical.[53]

Donnelly's close friend and neighbor Patrick Henry Rahilly of Lake City, Minnesota, shared Donnelly's borderland instincts as well as his contradictions. Rahilly, like all Irish, "despised" England "because she is the enemy of every race or people who desire liberty." He then offered glowing tributes to the pioneers, of which he was certainly one. To them America owed the "conquest of the wilderness" and of "the savages" who resided on it. His obituary spoke of the "lure of the West," and of the courage required to "answer the pioneer call." It spoke as well, however, of the golf course and tennis courts that adorned Rahilly's farm. Like Phelan and Donnelly, Rahilly did not need to wield a shillelagh in order to fit in.[54]

A number of less well-placed Irish, both in the American West and outside it, however, refused to play the O'Regan role and instead drew the obvious parallels between British policy toward the Irish and British and American policy toward the world's other native peoples. More often than not, Irish American sympathy for the beleaguered of the settler societies arose from self-interest and a quite unreflective application of the principle that shared enemies made if not friends at least natural allies. Certainly there was no felt commitment to the cause of liberty and justice when Irish Americans supported Russia in the Crimean War, supplied arms to the Zulus in the Zulu War, assisted Louis Riel, the leader of the Métis in Alberta, in his rebellion against British Canadian and Protestant authority, or fought on the side of the Orange Free State in the Boer War. The Russians, Zulus, Métis, and Boers were fighting Britain—or its colonial surrogates. That was enough. It was also enough, however, to provide striking exceptions to the historical image of mindless gangs of O'Regans breaking the heads of savages—unless, of course, the heads were attached to Englishmen, who, to the Irish, were the most truly savage. In all of this, the Irish were behaving like Irish, not like Americans-in-waiting.

In one celebrated instance, the association was not between Irish and Indians but between Irish and Mexicans—a distinction with no real difference. The occasion was the Mexican War. An Irish American brigade, the San Patricios, as it came to be known, decided that Protestant America's War against the Catholic natives of

Mexico, complete with all the cultural bias, raw imperialism, and anti-Catholicism that marked the contest and that the Irish knew well enough, was not one they wished to fight. They did not desert; they switched sides. Irish Americans revealed similar sympathies at the time of America's imperial adventures in 1898–1901. Speaking generally, the Irish supported the American effort to "liberate" the Cubans and the Filipinos from Spain's imperial grip. Granted, they did so because they hoped that Americans were in fact in the business of liberation and not of aggrandizement and that they would feel comfortable enough in the role to take on a real imperial bully and rescue an even more deserving people. What followed should have taught them hard lessons. America decided to keep Cuba and the Philippines and waged a brutal war to suppress the Filipinos, who were no fonder of American control than they had been of the Spanish. All of this raises an interesting question: how would the Irish and Irish Americans have responded had the United States detached Ireland from Britain's empire only to add it to its own?[55]

In one sense, the Irish American response to the Strangers' wars against various of the world's Natives was entirely predictable. The Mexicans, Zulus, Boers, Cubans, and Filipinos, even the Métis, were not native to the settler society in which the Irish found themselves. They posed no threat to the Irish; indeed, they presented them with opportunities—fleeting as they proved to be. As such, they do little to counter Teague O'Regan and his Indian-hating Irish friends. Countless historians of the American West have noted that very few westerners ever said anything favorable about or showed any generosity toward the "savage red man." I suspect that most of the western Irish would be included among those. That is not the same as saying that most were noticeably crueler than anyone else, just that it is difficult to find Irish who connected their own exile from Erin and the trails of tears that were part of it with what was happening to America's Indians.

It is difficult, but it is not impossible, and here is where the story takes an interesting turn. The narratives that follow are not intended to make any grand overarching theoretical point. Neither, however, should they be dismissed as random or merely symbolic—any more than the Choctaw gift of $170.00 sent to a starving Ireland in 1847 should be. There were Irish who, *as Irish,* evinced considerably sympathy for the native peoples of the world's settler societies. That is important enough.[56]

Patrick Ford is an example. Ford's newspaper, the *Irish World and American Industrial Liberator,* supported every effort to move the Irish out of America's eastern cities and into the West, ignoring the problems that attended the removal of the prior occupants. But Ford also denied that the Indians could not be civilized and then asked who between Sitting Bull and John Bull the real savage might be: "if SITTING BULL is a savage JOHN BULL is a hundred times a greater savage." Only an Irishman could have made such a comment. Similar sentiments came from even less likely sources than Patrick Ford. General John Gibbon, one of the thousands of Irish Americans in the frontier army, wrote an article in 1876 on the Sioux Wars, which he called "the 'irrepressible conflict'"— and he must have had the Civil War in mind—"between barbarism and the invading gold-seekers" in the Black Hills. Barbarism was an ungenerous reference to say the least, and Gibbon used the word "savage" repeatedly in his article. But he also wrote that the government, "having through its agents starved many of the Indians," forced the conflict. Later in the article he called some of the army soldiers "human ghouls" and said that "in war barbarism stands upon a level only a little lower than our boasted modern civilization."[57]

As for the so-called Indian Wars, Gibbon had this advice on how to avoid them: there must be a "spirit of concession and justice, a spirit directly opposite to that which has universally characterized the treatment of the red man of this continent by the American people"—which sounded as if he did not consider himself to be one of those people. From treaty violations to the wanton slaughter of the buffalo to being "outrageously swindled by the agents of the government," the wonder was not that the United States had so many Indian wars, but that it had so few. Gibbon spoke for the Native American: "*He* argues in this way. The white man has come into *my* country and taken away everything which formerly belonged to me." He made no reference to his own ethnicity in his article, except by indirection in his selection of the journal in which it would appear. It was not simply what he said that is of interest but where he said it. He published his article in the *American Catholic Quarterly Review*, and in 1877 its subscription list would likely have been overwhelmingly Irish American. It is scarcely conceivable that Gibbon did not choose the *Quarterly* for that reason.[58]

As revealing as the sympathies of Gibbon or Ford—or the San Patricios— were the comments of more obscure western Irish whose sympathies had nothing to do with Irish nationalism and were not offered up for public consumption. Tomás Ó Bríc or Bríc (Thomas Brick) was an Irish-speaker from West Kerry who emigrated in 1902 and headed straight to the farm of his sister and brother-in-law, Mary and Tim Rohan, in far northwestern Iowa, just across the Missouri River from the Winnabago Reservation. Brick was fascinated by Indians, recalling in his memoir that as his immigrant ship approached the New York Harbor he thought: "a matter of some hours now and we will be sighting that Land of the Free and many wild Indian natives." It would be interesting to know how many immigrants from whatever nation would have defined America in terms of freedom and native (and Native) wildness. He remembered as well how "I had heard so much about them in Ireland being a very savage race of people" and wondered if they "were still hostile."[59]

On the train to Chicago, Brick had bought a copy of William F. Drannan's vainglorious *Thirty-one Years on the Plains and in the Mountains*, published in 1900. Drannan identified himself as "The Last Scout" and proceeded to tell story after story of death-defying frontier escapades, most of which required him to kill Indians:

Drannan "kills and scalps five Indians"; Drannan takes "thirty-three scalps with one knife"; Drannan counts "3,000 dead Indians"; Drannan and companions "get sixty-six scalps and seventy-eight horses" then "locate a small band of red butchers and send them to happy hunting grounds." This was dime-novel trumpery masquerading as autobiography. The point of Drannan's tall tales was that this phase of western history was past: the last of the scouts was riding off into some sanguinary sunset, and it was now safe for less swashbuckling sorts to come to the golden West.[60]

That was not the point that Brick took from it. After reading the book, "with all its Indian fighting and killing, I was getting home sick and . . . wanted to go back to . . . Ireland." Who could blame him? Brick did not return to Ireland, but he did try "to coax some information from Mr. Rohan about what kind of people the Indians were." Rohan "always changed the subject," but Brick "finally got him interested and he told me that they were not the savage people as told by some of the white people. . . and that I need not be afraid of them. In fact, he told me that they were discriminated against by the . . . Government and by the white settlers with all their good lands taken up in homesteads. . . . With only the rough and poorest lands left to be occupied by the native Indians." Brick made no explicit reference to Ireland, but it is hard to imagine that he had not made a connection in his mind. Certainly he and Rohan were not about to grab "a good shelelah, or tomahawk to break deir heads." Neither would they join the other "white people" (!) in telling stories of Indian savagery. Brick and Rohan would have agreed with the Irishman from Mayo who spoke of the English willingness "to exterminate the Irish for the purpose" of stealing Irish lands. "This has always been the policy . . . of the English, *as it . . . was of the settlers in America.* What a crime—to destroy a people by brute force." This shared policy of Native "extermination" recalls Joyce's reference to "mudcabins" and "shielings by the roadside" being "laid low" by the English and American "batteringram."[61]

This is a harsh image; it may even be an exaggerated one. That, however, is less important than the fact that, for many Irish, English and American policies were alike in their cruelty. Micí Mac Gabhann (Michael MacGowan), whose life story was told in Irish in 1948, was another who made the connection. Mac Gabhann spoke of the great wheel of life (*Rotha Mór an tSaoil*) that carried him from County Donegal to Pennsylvania to Montana to the Yukon and back to Ireland. Along the way, he experienced some of almost everything the West offered; he was like an Irish Little Big Man, Jack Crabb with a brogue. As noted, the English who translated and published Mac Gabhann's story changed its title to *Hard Road to Klondike*. Books about roads through hard country doubtless made better commercial sense.

But the translator and publisher got one part of Mac Gabhann's story right. He was relating the time in the 1890s when some landless Indians—women and children only—came to the Montana mining camp where he was working. They may have been Bannock or Shoshone or Métis; he did not say and probably did not know. But whatever their tribe, they were very poor and were there to pick up the scraps of food that the miners had thrown out. They were "red devils," to be sure—and there was no ambivalence in Mac Gabhann's Irish on this point—but (and this is in the next sentence) "it was no wonder [they] were the way they were. There was neither peace nor comfort for them anywhere." Every time the "American authorities" learned that the Indians were "improving" the land, "they'd send a large army from the civilized part of America to drive these poor people further into the remotest reaches of the hills." Some "greedy white man—someone with friends at court or a planter [an interesting choice of words] . . . would then get the land."[62]

Those sentiments were not unique; other Americans, although not working-class like Mac Gabhann and not in the West, were saying the same thing. But Mac Gabhann was not finished: "The Indians that were left here and there were in a bad way and we had a great deal of pity for them—*the same thing had happened to ourselves home in Ireland.* We knew their plight well. We understood their attachment to the land of their ancestors . . . their wish to keep their own customs and habits without interference from the white man." Mac Gabhann's sentiments are also distinguished by his understanding of his own contradictory role in all this. "We were interfering with them, I suppose, as well as everybody else *but at least some of us sensed* that if they were wild itself, it was not without cause." It may be that an old man's memory was playing tricks on him; MacGowan was in his seventies when he told his story. But he was describing how he felt, and that is not something easily forgotten—or casually invented.[63]

Moving from Mickey MacGowan to Sir Roger Casement requires a long leap across social class lines, but Casement, Anglo-Irish and knighted by the British crown, made the same connections that McGowan had. Casement was born in County Antrim in the Province of Ulster. It was said that he was secretly baptized into the Catholic Church by his mother, but he was brought up an Ulster Presbyterian and became a free-thinker before his final "conversion" to Catholicism. His knighthood came as a result of a scathing report he made on the unspeakable cruelties inflicted on the native peoples of the Congo by the Belgian government and trading companies, a report based on Casement's five-year sojourn in Africa. He met Joseph Conrad while he was in the Congo. Conrad, who was then writing *Heart of Darkness,* said of Casement that "I always thought some particle of Las Casas' soul had found refuge in his indomitable body," a reference to Father Bartolomé de Las Casas, a sixteenth-century Spanish priest who had condemned the treatment of Native American peoples.[64]

Heart of Darkness became—indeed remains—the most searing and powerful literary indictment of European imperialism ever written. Its protagonist, Henry

Kurtz, was part German, part French, part English—"all Europe contributed to the making of Kurtz." But there were Americans as well as Europeans on Kurtz's voyage into the heart of the Congo, and I have often wondered why the more ardent of the "New Western historians" have not adopted the book as a metaphor for other frontier conquests and their legacies. One group of land grabbers in *Heart of Darkness,* armed with Winchesters and acting every bit the cowboy, called themselves the El Dorado Exploring Expedition. The sole purpose of the expedition was "to tear treasure out of the bowels of the land"—a kind of African gold rush. There was horror and a dark heart at the headwaters of the Chesapeake and the Missouri too. After his African experience and his 1904 Blue Paper on conditions in the Congo, Casement went to the Putumayo region of Peru, where people he identified as "Indians" were being as ruthlessly exploited by the British-owned Peruvian Amazon Company as the Congolese had been by various Belgian-owned companies. His reports from Peru were as lurid, as filled with stories of indescribable brutality against Native American peoples, as anything he wrote about Africa.[65]

It is difficult even today, a century after they were written, to read Casement's reports. He had witnessed brutal atrocities, literally savage acts against unoffending native peoples in two widely separated parts of the imperial "periphery." The "metropolis"—base camp for the strangers—found the native peoples living, as Conrad put it, "as natural and true as the surf along their coast. They wanted no excuse for being there." Neither did the Indians of North America, and neither, as Casement came to believe, did the Irish. The English journeys up the Shannon and the Liffey contained their own full share of horrors. When Casement returned to Ireland in 1910, he entered almost immediately into one of the most advanced and radical elements of the Irish nationalist movement, the Irish Volunteers. His reputation as the "champion of persecuted natives of Africa and of South America," not to mention his knighthood, "made him a heaven-sent recruit." Heaven-sent perhaps, but it is not likely that anyone could have believed that Casement would apply the lessons of the Congo and the Putumayo to Ireland.[66]

They misjudged him. Sir Roger Casement was readying a kind of Blue Paper on Ireland. It would be every bit as recriminatory as the one he had written on the Congo. Casement never really decided whether Africa and Peru had prepared him for Ireland or Ireland had prepared him for Africa and Peru. What counted, however, was that he found no meaningful differences between the imperial policies by which all three peoples were misgoverned and exploited. On one occasion, when accused by the British of an "enthusiastic attachment to romantic Nationalism," Casement answered that "whatever good I have been the means of doing in other countries was due in the first place to the guiding light I carried from my own country, Ireland." The Irish were a "bond-serf of the meanest form of exploitation I suppose any Imperial system has ever devised"—

which, given the meanness he had seen, was saying something. "Ireland has suffered at the hands of British administrators a more prolonged series of evils, deliberately inflicted, than any other community of civilized men."[67]

That was an odd use of the word "civilized" and an odd context in which to use it. Casement seemed to be suggesting an essential cultural difference between the Irish and the native peoples of the Congo and the Putumayo. He may have intended it; he was himself, after all, Irish, a colonial subject, and civilized. But consider his 1910 comment from the Connemara district of Ireland. He called the region the "Irish Putumayo" and later wrote to a friend that the "'white Indians' of Ireland were heavier on his heart 'than all the Indians of the rest of the earth.'" Consider as well his equally revealing comments that "in those lonely Congo forests where I found [Belgian king] Leopold . . . I found also myself, the incorrigible Irishman" and that "it was only because I was an Irishman that I could understand *fully* . . . the whole scheme of wrongdoing at work on the Congo. . . . I realised that I was looking at this tragedy with the eyes of another race of people once hunted themselves." He applied this same understanding to the Indians of the United States. Once, while on a trip along Lake Champlain, he wrote of Native American peoples: "You had *life*—your white destroyers only possess *things*. That is the vital distinction, I take it, between the 'savage' and the civilized."[68]

Casement was not so much an Irish nationalist as an anti-imperialist. Ireland, for him, was not a nation in the process of becoming but, as surely as the Congo, a colony of suppressed and abused people. As Rebecca Solnit has put it—in a book deserving of far more attention from Irish historians than it has gotten— Casement identified Ireland "with other European conquests rather than other European nations." This was a "great leap of unprejudiced insight." It is, of course, entirely possible that Casement's homosexuality, his "terrible disease," as he called it, was more important than his Irish background in making him the "champion of [the] persecuted" and dispossessed. That is not, however, what he said—although he was scarcely able to say anything on his sexuality at all. He said Ireland was a colony and that the native Irish were cruelly treated and that this understanding left him acutely sensitive to the injustices suffered by native peoples wherever found. Roger Casement was a complex man; we can only guess at what drove him. The English, however, hanged him as an Irish rebel. They made no fine distinctions regarding what had made him such.[69]

No guesswork is involved with Jeremiah Curtin and James Mooney, two ethnologists whose research and writing on American Indians was clearly informed by their Irishness. Curtin was the son of Irish immigrants and a Catholic—though a wavering one. He was born in Greenfield, Wisconsin, now a Milwaukee suburb but at his birth in 1835 a sparsely settled Irish rural community where marauding wolves were a constant menace. Harvard trained and the friend of John Fiske among others of the "best men," he was closer in style to Phelan than to Thomas Brick.

Curtin commented frequently on his Irish roots, usually with pride mixed with defensiveness, but his belief in the importance of understanding "primitive" myth arose from his academic interests, not his Irish background. That belief, however, led him not just to America's Indian Territory but to the west of Ireland, to Kerry, Galway, and Mayo. He was looking for the same things in both places: native speakers who could tell him stories. Ralph Waldo Emerson once told the young Curtin that he "cared no more for the history of savage peoples than for the history of so many wolves." Curtin was of different mind.[70]

Curtin traveled widely and wrote extensively, always with the purpose of understanding the present by paying a proper and, by his reasoning, thoroughly scientific attention to humankind's origins and to the legends told to explain them. He wanted the legends pure, entirely un-self-conscious, and unadulterated by popular culture—meaning uncontaminated by the language of the conqueror. The Irish and the Indians (and they in diminishing numbers) were among the only people who could satisfy his requirements. He listened to their stories then transcribed, analyzed, collected, and published them. He found them remarkably alike in form, structure, and cast of characters. Both the Irish and Indians named everything around them, animate and inanimate alike, and in the process made everything sacred. Both had wonderfully imagined other worlds; both were at once heroic, comic, tragic, and likely doomed. As Curtin put it,

> The forces of civilized society . . . are destroying on all sides, not saving that which is precious in primitive people. Civilized society supposes that man, in an early stage of development, should be stripped of all that he owns, both material and mental, and then be refashioned to serve the society that stripped him. If he will not yield to the stripping and training, then slay him.[71]

Like Casement and many others, Curtin was a bit of a romantic antimodernist, but (as with Casement) there was no doubting his passion. In America, "the great task was . . . to destroy what the Indian had in his mind and put something there which . . . he could not understand." Curtin was referring to the Indian schools and the forced abandonment of Indian languages and the myths they contained. In Ireland, it was the same. All "mental training" was "directed by powers both foreign and hostile to everything Gaelic . . . and the ancient ideas of the people. . . . Hence the clean sweep of myth tales." For Curtin, the great loss was to the world of scholarship; those myth tales held a people's history. But he learned enough of Ireland during his visits to become something of a nationalist. He was more concerned with the poverty of the place and the theft of Irish lands than with the fact that it had no parliament, but he held Britain responsible for all of it, as he held it responsible for destroying what the Irishman "had in his mind" and putting "something there which he could not understand." The point for Curtin was whether the "he"—be he Irish or Indian—should be *made* to understand and whether the "understanding" would be worth anything, to either the teacher or the pupil.[72]

There is no question that Curtin's Irishness influenced his analysis of the myth lives of "primitive" peoples. It took his experiences in the Congo to make Casement aware that he was an Irishman, and an "incorrigible" one at that. Incorrigibility led him to open rebellion, the Easter Rising, and a British hangman. Curtin's ethnogenesis, the cultural connections between himself and his subjects, was obviously more detached and academic. He studied the myths of the Irish for the same reason he studied those of the Indians: simple people had many lessons for the world. Those lessons would have to be mediated, "translated," in a sense, and that would require a certain hermeneutic of affection. Curtin was ideally suited to provide the one because he inherited the other.

It is a bit harder to know what to say about James Mooney, one of Curtin's colleagues in the Bureau of Ethnology. Like Curtin, Mooney was the son of Irish immigrants. His parents were both from County Meath. His father was also named James; his mother was born Ellen Devlin in a cabin within sight of Tara, the home of Irish kings—or so the young James was told. Both the Mooneys and the Devlins were dirt poor; both left Ireland because to stay was to starve, spent a brief and unhappy time in Liverpool, and then left, quite separately, for New York, where James and Ellen were married in 1852. The elder James Mooney was a traditional Irish storyteller, a *seanchaí;* in Ireland, he taught Irish history and the Irish language at a time when English law proscribed both. The Mooneys' second boat took them to Richmond, Indiana, where James was born in 1861— the same year as Frederick Jackson Turner. His father died when James was only eleven; the Mooneys were barely solvent. As his biographer put it, his story is "another footnote to the 'annals of the poor,' and more specifically the Irish-American poor."[73]

Mooney's "catechism" was traditional Irish Catholic, a mixture of the sacred and the insurrectionary: devotional, uniquely Marianist, and unyieldingly hostile to Great Britain. James Manahan read the book of Irish saints; Mooney probably read the same—along with a steady dose of the songs and poetry of Thomas Moore. But also like Manahan, Mooney's reading material included western myths masquerading as American truths. In 1873 he learned something of the Modoc War in northern California and southern Oregon. The military campaign against the Modocs obviously triggered something in the twelve-year-old Mooney, and he determined to learn the names and locations of every tribe in the Americas. He did exactly that, drawing elaborate and remarkably accurate maps with both tribal and language groups neatly marked. The self-taught Mooney succeeded well enough that he managed to convince John Wesley Powell to hire him at the newly formed Bureau of Ethnology.[74]

In 1878, five years after he began his inventory of Native peoples, Mooney formed the Richmond chapter of the Land League, the Irish American branch of the Irish Land League. Mooney's name accompanied the money sent from the chapter to Patrick Ford's *Irish World*. Richmond probably had more Quakers than Irish Catholics, but this did not concern Mooney; like the Modocs and all the others whose tribal identities and languages he had cataloged, the Irish had been brutally extorted, both materially and culturally. There is no question that Mooney joined the two peoples. They had similar histories; they had similar cultural habits. It was impossible for him to study the one without reference, direct or implied, to the other. When he published *The Ghost Dance Religion and Wounded Knee*, he titled the first chapter "Paradise Lost" and introduced it with a passage from Thomas Moore. The former Land Leaguer understood perfectly what the Ghost Dance meant, writing that the Indians of America lay "crushed and groaning beneath an alien yoke. . . . How natural is the dream of a redeemer . . . who shall return from exile . . . to drive out the usurper and win back for his people what they have lost." As for Ireland, it had known only "misrule, suffering and violence. Her national life was crushed into the ground by an alien tyrant . . . when the . . . nation . . . had hardly emerged from the tribal condition."[75]

Mooney's book about the Ghost Dance remains the best account of that remarkable phenomenon and one of the most moving descriptions of the consequent tragedy at Wounded Knee. It contains a detailed accounting of dozens of tribal societies and their songs, dances, and games, including one game played with a "shinny stick and ball" that would have been immediately familiar to every Irish (and non-Irish) stick-ball player in urban America. Equally impressive was his long general account of the Cheyennes. Finished in 1900, the book included a "glossary" of the Cheyenne language, more nearly a cross-referenced dictionary. Mooney would obviously not have been familiar with whiteness studies, and "how the Irish became white" would have struck him as comical. But he adds to the discussion—or rather confounds it—in his glossary. The Cheyenne word for African Americans was *Moqtai-viho*, which meant "black white men." The Cheyennes rendered the Irish as *Ma-i-viho*, "red white men." "Whiteness of a different color" suddenly takes on a whole new meaning. Blacks were white, Irish were red.[76]

Mooney's mastery of Native songs was almost exegetical. He used European musical encryption and scale, complete with key, tempo, notes, and half-notes. Listen to just one example from the hundreds he provided. It is of an Arapaho song. First Mooney gives it in the Native language:

Ani'qu ne'chawu'nani',
Awa'wa biqana'kaye'na
Iyahu'h ni'bithi'ti,

Translation

Father, have pity on me,
I am crying for thirst,
All is gone—I have nothing to eat.

He explained that this was "the most pathetic of the Ghost-dance songs. It is sung to a plaintive tune, sometimes with tears rolling down the cheeks of the dancers as the words would bring up thoughts of their present miserable and dependent condition. It may be considered the Indian paraphrase of the Lord's prayer."[77]

The Arapahos had reason to offer plaintive song and prayer. Mooney's description of Colonel John M. Chivington's attack on Arapahos and Cheyennes at Sand Creek near Fort Lyon in Colorado in November 1865 makes that clear enough. Chivington was a former Methodist minister who, before his attack, had promised to "kill and scalp all, big and little." That sounded an appropriately Cromwellian note, and Mooney might well have had Ireland in mind when he wrote of Chivington's raid. There were 500 Cheyennes and Arapahos camped on Sand Creek, "more than two-thirds . . . women and children." Black Kettle and White Antelope, their chiefs, had signed a treaty of peace just weeks earlier, and an American flag and a smaller white flag flew over the tipi of Black Kettle. Chivington commanded a thousand mounted troops with artillery. On his orders, they charged into the camp of the sleeping Indians. Mooney described what happened:

> About 150 men, women and children . . . were there massacred under circumstances of atrocity *never exceeded by the worst savages in America.* Children were brained and hacked to pieces, pregnant women were ripped open, stiffened corpses of men, women, and little children . . . were scalped, dismembered, and . . . mutilated, and the bloody scalps and members, hung at saddle bows and hatbands, carried into Denver and there paraded in a public theater.[78]

No other contemporary account of Sand Creek that I am aware of uses language this angry and graphic. There is a qualitative difference between this and the work of the Friends of the Indians or other reform efforts led by eastern patricians. Mooney's analysis was not just informed by his Irish Catholicism; it was suffused with it. As he once wrote describing Washington Matthews, also an ethnologist and his mentor, it was "by virtue of that spiritual vision which was his Keltic inheritance, [that] he was able to look into the soul of primitive things and interpret their meanings." There seems little question that Mooney thought that he had inherited this same spiritual vision, although, as his descriptions of Sand Creek and Wounded Knee would attest, he was also able to identify true savagery when he saw it.[79]

Like Casement and Curtin, Mooney studied the Indians and Irish as if they were culturally indistinguishable. A quick look at his ethnological studies of the Irish makes that clear. In 1887 he wrote that "in Connemara it is still a common practice to wear about the person what is *exactly the equivalent* to the medicine-bag of the Indian." He observed that fishermen in Mayo and Connemara took a dog with them to sea. In case of a storm, they tied the dog's legs and threw it overboard. This is *"exactly what formerly existed* among the Indians of the Great Lakes." In this same article he noted: "Another belief which exists alike in Ireland and among the Indians, is that certain localities are the abode of invisible malignant spirits." In a later piece (which, like many others of his articles, he wrote with a radically simplified spelling) he wrote that the "funeral lament . . . among the Osage Indians, in which the words, the intonation and the motions of the walers wer *exactly similar* to what we find in the Irish caoine" (keen). "The caoine itself strikingly resembles the Indian death song." The Irish, he explained, believed that people were carried off by spirits when they died and that *"exactly the same belief* is held by the Dakota Indians."[80]

It is important to note that in Mooney's mind these beliefs were not just "exactly the same" in style and content; they were exactly the same in their primitivism. For all his suspicion that modernity was a mixed blessing at best, he was not holding up Irish and Indian practices as the cultural ideal. Mooney, in fact, was not quite at ease with the Irish. They were too much like Indians, and Mooney was American enough to be uncomfortable with that. On one occasion he pointed out that belief in the evil eye was common in Ireland but not among the Indians, adding: "It may be that the idea is too subtle and intangible for the mind of a savage." More important, he was fully convinced that Irish primitivism arose from ignorance. The Irish lacked only education or, more accurately, were offered only the education their British oppressors permitted them. Their teachers and priests had been "hunted down like wild beasts . . . for nearly 700 years, teaching was a treason and education a crime."[81]

The result was "superstition," a "religion of ignorance." With the Irish, that would be remedied when Ireland became self-governing and once again the land of saints and scholars. Self-governance was not an option for America's Indians; but even if it had been, Mooney was not confident that either saints or scholars would have emerged among any of the tribes. In the index to *The Ghost Dance Religion*, under the heading "Education," the reader was told to see "Civilization, Christianity." In a revealing passage in one of his articles, Mooney wrote that "the belief that sickness and death ar due to the evil influences of spirits is common to all savage races as wel as to the uneducated classes among civilized nations." Mooney here comes perilously close to equating the "uneducated classes" with the "savage races"—whether metaphorically, as Slotkin argues, or directly, as Jacobson counters, is impossible to say.[82]

Mooney did not make clear what he meant by "civilized nations." America pretended to be one. Ireland could again be one. Whether he included Indians in his reference or not, I choose to think that he believed them fully educable. But if education was to have real value to either people, it had to preserve something of their cultures. Like Curtin, Mooney was not optimistic. The old ways were being lost, not because the Irish and the Indians were becoming enlightened but because they were being educated by their "alien" masters. Mooney in that sense was describing the end of two frontiers: one in western Ireland, one among the Native peoples of western America. Turner, writing at the same time, would have understood none of what he said. This is what makes Mooney so important. I am not going to claim more for James Mooney than the record will permit; I am not going to allow him to speak for the Irish in America. But Mooney was Irish, Catholic, and poor, and he did not "blacken up." He did not hate Indians; neither did he "play Indian." Like Curtin, he studied them as he studied the native Irish. I think the historians of whiteness should pay more attention to both of them.

And while they are at it, they should consider Finley Peter Dunne's Chicago bartender, the Irish immigrant Martin Dooley. Dunne's lampooning of westering and of Anglo-Saxon pretensions in general has already been noted. Add to them his hilarious and sulfurous attacks on American imperialism in the late 1890s, attacks in which he was joined by other Irish Americans. Dunne was at his Irish best when he had Mr. Dooley mock American expansionism in the name of "racial" destiny and progress. But he was no less Irish and no less stinging when he wrote "On the Indian War." As always Martin Dooley was behind his bar, explaining the truth of things to his most regular patron, the genial if often confused Hennessy.[83]

Mr. Dooley began on this day by praising General William Sherman for the wisdom of two of the general's remarks: "war is hell" and "th' on'y good Indyun is a dead Indyun." Sherman may not have uttered the second, but no matter. The hellishness of war, said Mr. Dooley, is "'a fine sintiment.'" The reference to dead Indians was "'a good sayin', too.'" The inconsistency between the two was more obvious for being left unstated. As for the policy that arose from good Indians being dead ones, Mr. Dooley was full of praise. "So, be th' powers, we've started in again to improve th' race; an', if we can get in Gatlin' guns enough befure th' winter's snows, we'll tur-rn thim Chippeways into a cimitry branch iv th' Young Men's Christyan Association. We will so."[84]

Some explanation was in order so Martin Dooley went on: "Ye see, Hinnissy, th' Indyun is bound f'r to give way to th' onward march iv white civilization. You an' me, Hinnissy, is th' white civilization." And that carried with it certain privileges that Mr. Dooley was not disposed to surrender. It seems he had recently found "ol' Snakes-in-his-Gaiters livin' quite [quiet] an' dacint in a new frame house." This was clearly not right. "Thinks I, 'Tis a shame f'r to lave this savage man in possession iv this fine abode, an' him . . . without a frind on th' polis foorce. So says I: 'Snakes,' I says, 'get along. . . . I want ye'er house, an' ye best move out west iv th' thracks, an' dig a hole f'r ye'ersilf,' I says." Snakes resists, so Mr. Dooley provides him with a history lesson. Snakes has to move "'because,' says I, 'I am th' walkin' dilygate iv white civilization.'" Snakes is unimpressed. "'I'm jus' as civilized as you,' he says. 'I wear pants . . . an' a plug hat.' . . . 'Ye might wear tin pair,' says I, 'an' all at wanst . . . an' ye'd still be a savage . . . an' I'd be civilized,' I says, 'if I hadn't on so much as a bangle bracelet . . . so get out. . . f'r th' pianny movers is outside.'"

Snakes then "fires a stove lid at me" and Mr. Dooley has him arrested as "a dhrunken Indyun" who "'won't let me hang me pitchers on his wall.'" The police and a "wagon load" of officers go after the "'vile savage,'" determined to teach Snakes "to rayspict th' rule iv civilization. . . . Well, me frind Snakes gives him battle, an' knowin' th' premises well, he's able to put up a gr-reat fight; but afther a while they rip him away, an' have him in the pathrol wagon, with a man settin' on his head . . . and they sind him out west iv th' thracks; an' I move into th' house, an' tear out th' front an' start a faro bank." There was a lesson in all this. "'Th' on'y hope f'r th' Indyun,'" Mr. Dooley told Hennessey, "'is to put his house on rollers, an' keep a team hitched to it, an', whin he sees a white man, to start f'r th' settin sun. . . . If he knew annything about balloons, he'd have a chanst; but we white men, Hinnissy, has all th' balloons.'"

So they did. But there was one other aspect of Dunne's tale that gave it its special edge.

It may be that Dunne selected the name "Snakes" intending to make an "Irish" point: St. Patrick drove the snakes out of Ireland and they came to America. But there is no reason for cautious language on a related issue. When Mr. Dooley demanded that Snakes leave and "'dig a hole f'r ye'ersilf,'" the Indian told him, "'Divvle th' fut I will step out iv this house,' . . . 'I built it, an' I have th' law on me side,' he says. 'F'r why should I take Mary Ann, an' Terence, an' Honoria, an' Robert Immitt Snakes, an' all me little Snakes, an' rustle out west iv th' thracks,' he says, 'far fr'm th' bones iv me ancestors . . . an' beyond th' water-pipe extension.'" It is important to read closely the names of his children.

There was something contrapuntal, almost sleight-of-hand, about Finley Peter Dunne's "The Indian Wars." It could have been read by anyone as an effective and engaging satire on the unfairness of American Indian policy. But the subtext— and only the Irish would have gotten the point—made it far more than an extended political wisecrack. Dunne's use of four of the most common Irish baptismal names as well as Mr. Dooley's reference to Snakes-in-His-Gaiters as his "friend," while having Snakes forcibly evicted by an overwhelmingly Irish police force (the urban equivalent of the equally overwhelmingly Irish western army), established a second level of meaning. It was a kind of ethnic insider's joke. Dunne's Indian War was quite literally internecine: one savage twin plundering and laying waste the other. Also at issue is the related question of ancestral inheritance. George Templeton Strong said the English were right about the Irish: they were savages and likely irredeemably so. On this point as on others, Americans—Albion's unmutated seed—had taken their cue from Britain. Dunne managed to capture all of that and more, including Irish ambivalence about who and what they were, or—and more accurately—who and what they had been made to be.

Until fairly recently scholars have not paid much attention to the connection between Irish and Indian. That has changed. Jenny Franchot, Luke Gibbons, Fintan O'Toole, Rebecca Solnit, Elizabeth Butler Cullingford, and Katie Kane, among others, have begun to look closely at the historical characters and tensions that Dooley and Snakes represent. This new interest arose principally from postcolonial theory, and historians are much in the debt of those who employ it. But the connection is not dependent solely on theory. Other cues can be taken without any theoretical adornment. Because both Ireland and America were settler societies—with frontiers marked off by pale lines—the Indian/Irish association makes perfect sense. But it is not the nature of frontiers that is the main issue but the blending of two purportedly savage cultures—the twinning of the worlds of the "aborigines," as Nuala Ní Dhomhnaill called the Irish variant.[85]

From the American Indian side of the aboriginal border, the Indian poet Simon Ortiz writes of Irish and Indians laughing about one of their mutual friends, the wonderfully named Murphy Many Horses. The too-little studied Métis blended their music with Celtic/Gaelic melodies, producing a pentatonic sound that even an Irish rock band would have recognized. It is too bad that Jimmy and the lads in his Irish band did not know of the Métis. From the Irish side of the border, the Irish American documentary filmmaker Robert Flaherty built a career depicting the world's cultural "primitives" cinematically, a dressed-up version of James Mooney's ethnographical studies. Flaherty dealt first with *Nanook of the North* then followed that with *Man of Aran*. The American film director John Ford, born John Martin Feeney, the son of Galway immigrants, moved seemingly without effort from Ireland (*The Quiet Man, The Informer*) to the American West (*The Searchers, Stagecoach, The Man Who Shot Liberty Valance, The Grapes of Wrath*). Not all of his westerns dealt with Indians directly, although the point cannot be too often or too strongly made that the western, by definition, was about conquest. At that, the best of Ford's work remains the cinematic equivalent of Finley Peter Dunne's "The Indian War" or James Mooney's *The Ghost Dance Religion and Wounded Knee*—the ambivalent Irishman, his very Catholic redemption, and his Indian "friends."[86]

That "friendship," the brotherhood of the savage twins, has been given even more recent expression in Ireland and in powerfully evocative ways. In 1993 the Irish Museum of Modern Art in Dublin held an exhibition of photographs of Irish and Indians that Elaine Reichert had collected and juxtaposed. The exhibit was entitled simply "Home Rule," and Reichert's artistic displays vividly depict the connection between the "native warriors" of the Irish Republican Army (IRA) and America's Indians. They look, dress, talk, and act the same because they are the same, the last trace elements of a tribal people whose land and lives were stolen. The American sculptor Jeanne Silverthorne wrote an essay for the catalog that accompanied the exhibit in which she explained what the show meant to her. She mentioned "a photo of Chiricahua Apaches in ceremonial garb, and one of IRA guys in balaclavas; it's like the museum has been invaded by commandos . . . it's as if the repressed of Irish and Indian history had broken out of the schoolroom, telling us they were misrepresented back there." In other words, in both cases, too many historians had been bribed and "what we were taught when we were kids wasn't quite right."[87]

The Irish poet Paul Muldoon must have attended the same kind of school. Certainly he drew similar conclusions and comparisons. His poetry is filled with Irish Indians and Indian Irish, two peoples who "have never / Stopped riding hard / In an opposite direction, / The people of the shattered lances / Who have seemed forever going back." These were contrary and outlandish people, the both of them. There was "A Sioux," Muldoon writes, "An ugly Sioux. / An Oglala / Sioux busily tracing the family tree / of an Ulsterman who had some hand in the massacre at Wounded Knee." That an ugly Connachtman might have joined him looking for the lineage of an Ulsterman who had had some hand in Cromwell's wild and bloody rides through Ireland requires no extended comment. Muldoon writes also of the time when "we met the British in the dead of winter. / The sky was lavender / and the snow lavender-blue." That sounds Irish enough. But the narrator who recalled when "we" met the British was no Irishman. "They gave us six fishhooks / and two blankets embroidered with smallpox." Martin Dooley would have liked that poem.[88]

PART II

An Alternate Frontier

The Irish in the the West

CHAPTER 6

Border Wars

Clustered Irish across the Meridian

By 1840 America's righteous empire was coming fully to life as the cheap land frontier—the western project—was conjoined to the cheap labor frontier— the modern project. Neither frontier could have been conceived or sustained without the other. The Bonanza West fed the East and kept the empire on the path of righteousness and riches. The East invented a West and then bankrolled it. It was a very tidy system. Cheap land kept cheap labor content; cheap labor made cheap land accessible. It was also, however, a highly contingent system and one that contained a built-in contradiction. If the West were ever to be lost to a rival claimant, industrializing America would become indistinguishable from industrializing Europe, and the cheap labor frontier would become a very chaotic and dangerous place. But the blunt instruments of both frontier conquests were the Catholic Irish; the righteous empire would be won by the unrighteous. The New World could be kept new only by the hard labor of the most impoverished of the old worlds. High risk attended America's imperial enterprise.

It was a risk that had to be taken. The West prevented the Europeanization of America; it made America exceptional. Jefferson had called the area west of the Mississippi River America's "meridian of partition"—a most singular phrase. America already had a frontier "meridian" that "partitioned" civilization from Native "savagery." Jefferson's reference here was to the western regions as a barricade against those who had not shed Old World habits. The Atlantic was no longer a barrier. It was more like an open door, a standing invitation to those who would blot and mix. There were also domestic challengers, Southern slave owners and the Native peoples of the West chief among them. The Mexican and Civil Wars and the Indian Wars were fought to protect that meridian. They were border duels, monumentally bloody ones, to be sure, but at least these challengers to America's modern project had a shape, a corporeal reality, an address of sorts. Their warriors and agents wore uniforms and drew lines in the sand.[1]

Another rival claimant, however, presented a different kind of challenge. The Catholic Church, it seemed, had some "imperial" ambitions of its own. The Protestant contention that God had kept North America hidden from permanent settlement until such time as Reformed Christians of Anglo-Saxon origin were ready to claim it, then kept California's gold hidden until Protestants were ready to put it to proper Christian use, seemed to Catholics excessively prideful. They would file claims of their own. Unlike Confederates or American Indians, however, the Catholic threat was diffuse and shapeless. Beecher did write that Catholic immigrants represented an "accumulating tide . . . rolling in upon us as if they were an army of soldiers, enlisted and officered, and spreading over the land." Beecher, who was nothing if not easily aroused anyway, was here speaking metaphorically. It might have been better had he not been; it would have been easier to contest the Catholic advance if the church had sent uniformed armies and nicely tailored diplomats with letters of marque. Instead it sent women religious, hundreds of thousands of job seekers, and a smaller but still substantial class of agricultural settlers, all utterly subservient to their priests. Indeed, the priests might well be sent first. Theodore Parker wrote back from Rome in 1859 that "yesterday, a new building was dedicated for *the education of priests who are to convert America.*"[2]

Even more ominously, the church knew where in America to begin. An Englishman, John Angell James, warned in 1841 that having "felt the inward heaving of ambition. . . . Popery has directed a longing eye to [the] immense tract of land . . . in the valley of the Mississippi." James presumed to know that the valley "has been . . . mapped as well as surveyed by emissaries of the Vatican; and cardinals are exulting, in the hope of enriching the Papal See by accessions from the United States." Thus would the church "compensate . . . for her[!] losses in the old world by her conquests in the new." In 1842 worried Americans learned of a pamphlet published in Dublin describing *A Proposed Plan of General Emigration Society by a Catholic Gentleman.* This unnamed gentleman was doing more than scattering information. He intended to buy large tracts of land in the Mississippi Valley and fill them with Irish, settled, said nativist critics, "in masses" and subject to the absolute authority of their priests. The West, this gentleman went on to add, "will become the heart of the country, and ultimately determine the character of the whole." The nativist response "bordered on hysteria." This was no less than a "foreign conspiracy against our *Protestantism and liberty,*" one of them said.[3]

Four years later, *an Gorta Mór* put millions of Irish either into graves or onto emigrant ships. From this point forward, the vast majority of Rome's accumulating tide with conversion and empire on its mind would be Irish. What had been a foreign conspiracy became a Celtic one. That did not change the thinking of the popish conspirators. The West remained their special target—the presumed Irish distaste for rural life notwithstanding. As E. E. Hale pointed out, "full information as to the means of passage to (and in) America" was "scattered through the most barbarous parts of Ireland." I am quite certain that the parenthetical "and in" was duly noted. By 1850 American Catholicism had taken on the distinctly Hibernian cast it would never lose—and American anti-Catholicism the distinctly anti-Irish cast it would never lose.[4]

My reference to its anti-Irish nature is partly to the well-chronicled American nativism and to the "No Irish Need Apply" postings that were part of it. Irish Catholics faced both prejudice and discrimination; it was difficult for them to feel a kinship with those who reviled them, particularly as the basis of the revilement was Anglo-Saxon superiority and presumed Celtic "racial" defects. The Irish had been listening to that kind of talk for centuries. Hearing it in broad Yankee accents did not make it less painful. As the Reverend M. J. Spalding, Catholic archbishop of Baltimore, asked in 1875, "Are [Americans] really *independent* of England?" He answered that the "political bigots among us hate Irishmen, merely because they are Irishmen; our religious bigots hate them because they are Catholics. Both have inherited this hatred from England"; they were the fruit of Albion's seed. Jeremiah O'Donovan Rossa agreed with Spalding. "I cannot feel that America is my country . . . the English power, and the English influence and the English hate, and the English boycott against the Irishman is . . . as active in America as it is in Ireland."[5]

American prejudice and the Irish response to it need not be interpreted in terms of how the Irish became white—or red, white, and blue. Far more important is that the contests on the border included the sectarian struggle between Protestant and Catholic as well as the assault by whites and probationary whites on nonwhites. In America the superior forms by whatever name—Anglo-Saxon, Caucasian, Teuton—were not just nobler and more physically and intellectually robust than their "white" inferiors, they were also Protestant by definition. Their nobility and strength arose from their Protestantism as surely as from their "race" and their whiteness. Any effort to distinguish among "race," color, and religion was meaningless—so much so that few bothered with the issue. To be Irish was to be Catholic; that was what put them beyond the pale and gave them their "whiteness of a different color." To be Anglo-Saxon was to be Protestant. There was no need to make explicit what all knew: the master race embraced the master faith.[6]

This is what I meant by my earlier comments that the Irish never "became white," that they were always white. And they always knew it. The Irish who put on blackface were far more likely to have done so for reasons of theatrical fashion than out of racialist pathology. That they did so because they needed someone

below them in order to feel better about themselves and capture a measure of
social status is not credible. That they did so in a hapless and desperate effort to
curry favor with a white America that denied their "whiteness" is nonsensical.
Irish Catholics did not necessarily want the favor of the core society, which was
a very good thing since they would have been hard pressed to know how to go
about getting it. They were uncommonly slow to assimilate to America because
a significant share of America maligned them and their faith and because they
did not identify with it and its Protestant origins.[7]

Somehow these Irish had to be put right, their deviant cultural forms transformed
or erased. This not only recasts one admittedly small part of the "whiteness"
argument but inverts it. Americans did not sit idly by waiting for the Irish to
become "white"—meaning more nearly American. Rather, they determined that
the Irish had to be *made* "white," in other words, made over, transformed. That
transformation would begin with their conversion from popery to denominational Protestantism. For some, it would end there, too. The hope was that by
ceasing to be Catholic, the Irish would cease as well to be Irish. But whether
the sectarian makeover improved the root stock or not, the effort had to be made.
And so Protestant missionaries, most associated with Bible and tract societies,
began their hard labors, working diligently in Irish American neighborhoods to
make something of these outlandish people. The missionary effort failed. The
public schools had a similar purpose—and no greater success. Indeed, the Catholic
Church responded by constructing an entirely separate parochial school system.
The contradictory and oppositional nature of Irish Catholicism would not be
removed by urban missionaries and schoolteachers.[8]

The West was a last resort. Americans began to conceptualize their meridian
of partition differently. It was still a defensive partition; it still protected American
values, but it did so as a conjuring trick. European types could pass through it;
some even would be escorted through it, but the crossing would transform them
and settlement on the far side would utterly transfigure them. The natural West
had become supernatural. It could do what the tract societies and schools had
failed to do: bring the Irish to heel and make Americans of them. The idea that
America's righteous western empire would effect a cultural metamorphosis significantly extended the list of what empires might be expected to do. Even the
British, who claimed more for empire than anyone, never thought of theirs as
capable of this magic act. The American version of empire meant that those who
conquered the West would as well be conquered by it. The region could fuse
different cultural forms into one.[9]

No one gave more fervent expression to this notion than William Gilpin. The
emphasis of most of those who spoke to the transformative power of the West
was social; the West forged one society from the myriad forms that entered it.

Gilpin added a bizarre geographic aspect to the story. Europe, he wrote, was as "convex as the camel's back," but western North America was "a sublime amphitheatre. . . . an expanded bowl." "Amphitheatre," of course, was the same word that Heaney would later use to express what Ireland was missing. By whatever name, the newest part of the New World was a place of "gorgeous fertility and transcendent proportions," and its tendency was "to receive and fuse into harmony whatsoever enters within its rim," producing "one new race, immigrant German, English, Norwegian, Celts, and Italians, whose individualities are obliterated in a single generation." In 1868 Gilpin went so far as to tell an audience of Irish in Colorado that "the sons and daughters of the Emerald Isle" had by entering the western amphitheater become "*Teutonic men and women*" who have "united themselves to us, to our country and our mission." A "single people" had emerged from this bowl, "identical in manners, language, customs and impulses: preserving the same civilization, the same religion, imbued with the same opinions." In other words, Gilpin was explaining how the Irish were made not just white but Teutonic white.[10]

Another major spokesman for the assimilative powers of the American West was, of course, Frederick Jackson Turner. In what he called "the crucible of the frontier," Turner believed "Old World" traits simply disappeared. Crucibles, after all, were used to blend disparate elements into an amalgam. Fortunately for clarity, on at least two occasions Turner was less oblique and used the more common and unfortunate term "melting pot," linking it with the equally unfortunate safety-valve metaphor. Turner had essentially restated a fundamental American assumption: Protestant principles converged with open and abundant lands to create a kind of culture-religion, an American secular faith, and the missionary impulses necessary to extend it. This was a powerful conceptual synthesis, and Americans reified and centered themselves around it. That it was steeped in myth attests not only to Americans' powers of imagination but to the significance with which they had invested this master narrative of their lives.[11]

Turner's role was not to create the western myth world—others had already done that—but to supply the historical context in which the creation took place. He began by assuring a nervous nation that the West was "'a good mixer'"; it taught "the lessons of national cross-fertilization instead of national enmities," by which he meant the ethnic/tribal divisions left over from a receding European past. Since the western frontier was "free from the influences of European ideas and institutions," the absorption of immigrants, their cultural amalgamation, and the "steady growth . . . along American lines" could proceed without check or hindrance. That, at least, was his wish. As was common with Turner, the wish gave rise to the theory, in this instance that in some geographically indeterminate West "the immigrants were Americanized, liberated and fused into a mixed race." Americans were becoming quite literally the people of the West.[12]

Merely being placed in the West, however, was not enough to qualify. The frontier could Americanize, liberate, and fuse only if Americans-to-be were disaggregated and sown broadcast. Turner certainly thought so. The West, he argued, could absorb the alien strains but only if the "line-fences" that defined the "unmodified or isolated [of] the old component elements" were torn down. "Unmodified component elements" might seem an odd way of saying that certain immigrant groups were resistant to melting, but the construction was typical of Turner. The words offend without being offensive. The western crucible could not handle "isolated" clumps of "unmodified" immigrants.[13]

That point could be and was made about all immigrant groups, Protestant and Catholic alike, but far more urgency attached to it when applied to Catholics— particularly to Irish Catholics. They were so damnably clannish, so determined not only to live among their own but, as one Know-Nothing put it, "determined that neither themselves nor their children shall ever conform to American manners, American sentiments, or to the spirit of American Institutions." They were like ethnic constellations, "banded together" in herds both urban and rural. Relocating them would be of no value if it involved settling them "in masses" as the 1842 plan of the "Catholic gentleman" was alleged to have intended. Replacing fixed Irish enclaves with movable ones only made matters worse. If they were allowed to cluster in the West as they had clustered in the East, they would remain forever a substandard stock that could produce only substandard seed.[14]

Western settlement was "a process of mutual education" among the different ethnic groups. "The outcome . . . where different groups were *compact and isolated* from the others, was a certain persistence of inherited *morale.*" Turner had to have worked hard to find that construction, too. By "persistence of inherited morale" he can only have meant tribalism. Whatever it was called, it resulted in a "slowed assimilation." Slowed, but not stopped. The cultural line-fences would, in time, be replaced by open borders through which all of the ethnic groups would pass, transformed in the process into "American pioneers, not outlying fragments of New England, of Germany, or of Norway." America's western empire was, indeed, a good mixer, what Turner had called an enlarged "neighborhood democracy."[15]

In another part of this same essay, when he was writing of the various religious denominations that met to form the democratic neighborhood that his frontier represented, Turner noted only "Scotch-Irish Presbyterian, Baptist, [and] Methodist." The common wisdom held that democratic neighborliness required mingling; the Irish were not only unused to democracy but taught by their priests to distrust it. The only neighborhoods they understood consisted of "friends," and the only people they wanted to mingle with were those exactly like themselves. They were classic "outlying fragments." Turner, however, never dealt with them. He left it to his readers to figure out whether he meant that Irish Catholics were not in the neighborhood of democracy or were not eligible to come into the neighborhood—or that he did not know what he meant or that he meant nothing at all.[16]

Others, including some whom Turner should have read, were not so indirect about the eligibility rules for admission to the West. E. E. Hale understood precisely that this was the issue. Hale's *Letters on Irish Emigration* was an effort to make maximum use of the reserve army of labor coming to America from the Celtic fringe. There was a hardheadedness about Hale's campaign, accompanied, of course, by his implacable hostility to Catholicism. Despite his prejudices—perhaps because of them—Hale's analysis of the Irish problem contained some important truths, or at least half-truths. One was his belief that "the mass of the Irish are attached to the Roman Catholic religion [not] as a matter of faith" but as a "matter of national pride." In fact, Catholicism had become a question of personal and collective identity as well as a religious faith; Irish piety was real, but being Catholic was also a source of community and of the institutional glue that held communities together. That involved much more than just national pride; Americans never really understood that. But regardless of the source of their piety, it was clear to Hale that "the attachment with which the Irish regard their religion is an obstacle to . . . [their] absorption by the country at large."[17]

Their absorption meant breaking that attachment by getting the Irish out of America's eastern cities, where they congregated like rabbits in a warren. These cohesive enclaves could not be penetrated by the non-Irish even had they wished to and were fiercely protective of the Irish who formed and were in turn formed by them. They were held together by a variety of institutions, but their lodestone was the parish church, and its guardian at the gates was the parish priest. Irish enclaves could be moved; they were not, however, easy places to leave. Hale understood this, but he also believed that the "clannish spirit of the Irish has ruined them in one country, and does a great deal to ruin them in another." Unless they left the enclaves, the Irish would remain "a stranger," and "the stranger cannot serve the country."[18]

Neither, however, could the stranger serve himself. "He must be a part of . . . the country. He must . . . be directed by its intelligence. His children must grow up in its institutions. He must, for the purposes we seek, profit by the measure of its civilization." The purposes Hale sought were hardly selfless, but no matter. The Irishman "must be, not in a clan in a city, surrounded by his own race. That is only to try a little longer the experiment which for centuries has failed." Hale added that the priests, the heads of the clans, were fully aware of this and of the enormous benefits that this failed experiment gave to them. It was for this reason that they opposed emigration from Ireland and opposed as well the scattering of the Irish in the American West. As Hale put it, the priests could not abide "the necessary loss of power which this Celtic Exodus," both first boat and second, "brings upon them."[19]

Here, however, was a role for the United States government. The Irish, said Hale, had been pushed to the farthest reaches of Ireland, but "this westward faring is now a plunge into the sea." It had come "at just the needed moment." They were "beaten men," these Irish. "Their separate existence as a Celtic race is at an end." The next move was clear. The Irishman "must plunge, or *be plunged, into* his new home." (The Irish were to do a lot of plunging, mostly off cliffs.) The English had dumped their unwanted Irish on America's eastern cities; those cities in their turn had to be able to break their unwanted Irish into fragments and dump those cultural shards on the West. The West could then heal their deformities and put them back together again as Americans. Thus the United States government should begin "forwarding the Irish to its distant Western lands, which they are to make valuable." After all—and here Hale nicely anticipated Richard Slotkin's cheap labor and cheap land frontiers—"to the ready transfer of the emigrant population to the West, the Government owes all the worth of its Western lands." Those comments alone should have been enough to get Turner's attention.[20]

The idea that the Irish were both clannish and priest ridden was hardly new with Hale. What was new was Hale's contention that they were clannish because they were priest ridden and that breaking the one bad habit would rid them of the other. America had an obligation to them, but it was a conditional one. It was America's "duty," Hale wrote, "to receive the *scattered* [Irish] fugitives . . . and absorb them into our own society." The key words were "scattered" and "absorbed." It was not America's duty to receive those clustered around their priests. But, since Hale further believed that the priests' influence had nothing to do with genuine religious faith, the entire problem could be neatly solved by appeals to Irish intelligence or, if none could be found, unclustering them and forcing the now atomized Irish onto second boats, leaving their priests behind and letting the West work its magic on them. This was not an uncommon opinion.[21]

One of those who shared it was the Anglo-Irish barrister Philip Bagenal. In 1882 Bagenal wrote his account of the American Irish and their toxic influence on American politics. The Irish, Bagenal believed, were almost single-handedly responsible for poisoning relations between Ireland and Britain and between Britain and the United States. America was "determined to throw open [its] gates of refuge to all the nations of the earth, merely as a matter of expediency." By expediency he meant the same thing Madison Grant would mean later—to solve a labor problem. This was folly, particularly when "Irish peasants" became the dominant immigrant group. Fortunately, Albion's seeds, sown and planted, had produced a rich harvest; Bagenal was certain that Americans "had inherited from their ancestors the national English contempt" for the Irish and that the Irish had done nothing to "increase [their] popularity." They had "persisted . . . in keeping up their distinctiveness of race and religion in a manner antagonistic to the great mass of the American people." Led by "the influence of their priests and their own religious instincts," the Irish settled "near together, in neighbourhoods. . . . They thus were a separate people, and appeared to the Americans incapable of ever being absorbed into the *Protestant* life of the country," which Bagenal believed was the only life the country had or needed.[22]

There was now a "new nation" of Ireland in America, led by "firebrands and perpetuators of the animosity between England and Ireland." That this animosity might have owed something to the "national English contempt" for the Irish seems not to have occurred to him. The point was that the "base of Irish revolution" had shifted "from Ireland to America." Bagenal was uncertain about what form that revolution might take and clearly confused as to the revolution's ultimate target. At one point in his book he wrote that the Irish in America were being "transformed into reckless Socialists and Communists," but whether the object of their recklessness was the land system in Ireland or the industrial systems of the United States and Great Britain was never made clear.[23]

Adding to the confusion of Bagenal's account was the offhand comment that Irish residence in the United States was "break[ing] down the political power of the priest" and that the "primitive reverence and filial obedience" of the Irish was giving way to more informed and sophisticated sentiments. Indeed, Irish Americans were "Americans first and Catholics afterwards," which meant they were on their way to becoming bad Catholics. The Irishman was learning that "he has a right to go his own way, to worship under his own forms, to speak his own thoughts." That Catholicism *was* his own way and his own form of worship and that speaking his own thoughts was not an alien concept seems also not to have occurred to him. Bagenal noted that "the Irish in America . . . believe that the vast immigration of their race" was "owing to English rule. They believe themselves to have been 'frozen out' of their native land." That, too, was "dogma" with them.[24]

Bagenal offered up a bewildering mix. The Irish in America were variously exiles, firebrands, socialists, childishly obedient Catholics, bad Catholics, and good Americans. Since he was writing immediately after the Irish Land Wars of the late 1870s and early 1880s, he also threw in a number of references to the Irish American Land League and the rural radicalism it represented. By their "birth and religion" the Irish were "obnoxious" to Americans, who thought the Irish "religion was incompatible with republicanism, hostile to popular institutions," and who "therefore looked suspiciously on a race which was both foreign and Catholic." On the other hand, the Irish were shedding their devotional Catholicism and liberating themselves from the doctrinal and political authority of their priests. Perhaps he was describing the diversity within the Irish American world. More likely, he was simply confused.[25]

There was, however, one aspect of the Irish problem about which Bagenal spoke with authority and confidence:

> The Roman Catholic clergy have . . . persuaded and commanded . . .
> the Irish masses . . . to settle in the great cities. The *scattering* of the
> Irish over the land and their *absorption* amongst the native American
> element was from the very first discountenanced by the Catholic hier-
> archy and the present misery and poverty, squalor, and crime in the
> vast Irish population of the Eastern American citizens is directly attri-
> butable to the old policy of the Catholic Church.

But that was the point. This was an "old" policy. Both the clergy and the laity
were changing. The Irish Catholics in America were not "the priest-ridden flock
of sheep Dr. Froude represents them to be." The reference to J. A. Froude
placed Bagenal directly in a line of descent from Beecher to Josiah Strong and
Frederick Jackson Turner. All were agreed: the Irish must first be scattered then be
plunged into the frontier, where their reflexive hatred of Britain would dissipate
in the clean western air.[26]

As for those who feared that the Irish would contaminate the West, they were too
gloomy by half. Americans, according to Bagenal, had nothing to fear from Irish
Catholics moving west, so long as they dropped their "neighboring instincts"—
Bagenal's polite way of saying clannishness. By whatever name, it was the Irish
living in "the tenement houses of the great cities . . . the huts by the public
works and mines" who formed "the constituencies of the anti-English demagogues and . . . contribute[ed] their money to the various 'funds' which have
become . . . the root of all political evil in Ireland." Living in America's eastern
cities had made the Irish "wicked and revolutionary." If only they could be removed
from their huts and relocated "on the land" they would soon forget they were
Irish and be cleansed of their iniquities. Irish Americans themselves should have
been able to figure this out. In a reference to Patrick Ford's newspaper, the *Irish
World,* then busily collecting money for wicked and revolutionary purposes,
Bagenal wrote: "How much better it would be for the *Irish World* to set on foot
a gigantic fund for the transportation of some thousands of the tenement Irish
to the West." This was only ten years before Turner wrote his seminal essay.[27]

Bagenal did not consider the situation entirely hopeless. "In those bygone days
when the American-Irish nation" was first forming, "had Government directed
and assisted the tide of emigration, hundreds of thousands would have been carried
out west." Bagenal's remark implied that the American government might still
do its duty. After all, the Irish were "accustomed to agricultural pursuits"; they
might still become "quiet and prosperous citizens" by "busy[ing] themselves in
agriculture" just like the "Norwegians . . . Swedes . . . and Germans." Failing some
kind of government action, Bagenal feared that the Irish would remain unmodified and continue to "block up the channels of immigration at the entrances, and
remain like the sand which lies at the bar of a river's mouth." They needed to
be sent upstream.[28]

For Bagenal as for Hale and Turner—moving the Irish into the West transformed them. But only if they were sent one at a time. Incorrigible in the East,
in their new western homes, and surrounded by non-Irish and non-Catholic
neighbors, they would become compliant and orderly. The East would be saved,
without making a sacrifice area of the West. That was the way the cheap labor and
cheap land frontiers were expected to function—in balanced harmony. Blasting
apart the Irish enclaves and sending out the now atomized residue let Americans
have it both ways. The scattered Irish, moreover, could not lead a Catholic challenge to Americans' western empire. The potential western battlefield would
become the western conversion zone. The Catholic "enemy" could be escorted
to it. The Irish would be assimilated and rendered useful—or at least harmless.
Protestant America would win by default.

In 1854, just two years after Hale published his *Letters,* the Reverend Charles Loring
Brace formed the Children's Aid Society (CAS), a private colonization society
that was to give a whole new meaning to scattering, mingling, and absorption.
The goal of the CAS was to take the poor and orphaned children of New York, the
detritus of what Brace called "the dangerous classes," and place them in western
homes. Not all of these "little heathens and barbarians," as he called them, were
Irish, but Brace was certainly familiar with the demographics of New York's poor
in the 1850s. He was also familiar with the association of Irish and Indians. As he
put it, there was a "very considerable class of lads in New York who bore to . . .
the world about them something of the same relation which Indians bear to the
civilized Western settlers." Like those Indians, these lads faced a grim future; and,
also like the Indians, their removal from civilized settlers was a social imperative.[29]

Whether Brace meant to use the word "lad" as a code for Irish is unimportant,
although his use of Indians and the Irish in connection with barbarians and heathens
assuredly is not. Twenty percent of the almost quarter-million children moved
out by the CAS were Irish-born, and a significant number of the American-born
were the children of Irish. It does not stretch credibility to assume that more than
a hundred thousand Irish rode their own trail of tears on one of Brace's orphan
trains. His motives were different from Hale's and Bagenal's. Hale had urged the
Irish to go west because the new lands needed their labor and because going to
the West would partially civilize them. Bagenal was equally determined to see them
absorbed, but principally so that the "new nation" of Irish America might be
undone and cease to confound relations between the United States and Great
Britain. Brace wanted to send the Irish west to save them from New York and
New York from them. His was an act of charity.[30]

But Brace was also one of the scores of nineteenth-century Protestant moral
crusaders who, for all their reformist impulses, were never quite able to convince
themselves that working-class Irish Catholics were fully civilized or even fully

human. Brace was a close friend of Theodore Parker and a disciple of Horace Bushnell. The New York riots of 1863 and 1870–71, with the Irish as the most conspicuous of the rioters, horrified him. Even his descriptive language seemed subtly encoded. The poor of Five Points lived in "paternal piggeries and nasty dens." Parents "were squalid, idle, intemperate, and shiftless." I grant that these words could have been used to describe the poor of whatever race or ethnicity. But Brace was referring to the poor of a particular place, New York's Five Points, and no one needed to be told who lived there.[31]

Brace offered unambiguous evidence of which ethnic element of the dangerous classes he was talking about in his book *The Races of the Old World*. The "Kelts," he wrote in what he called a "scientific" statement of "racial" characteristics, posed "one of the knottiest questions for the ethnologist." He would untie the knots. They were "numerous and warlike, carrying terror to all organized governments . . . brave," to be sure, but also "quick to quarrel, vain and fond of display, with little pertinacity." Unlike the "Teuton," they were never "attached . . . to the soil, but preferr[ed] the association of life of large towns." They were lacking in "deep moral qualities" and "from the first . . . are credulous and easily ruled by their priesthood." He went on to add that there was a far greater difference between the skull size of English and Irish than between that of Irish and Africans. To complete the picture of this most unworthy type, many of the Celts had "open, projecting mouths, with prominent teeth and exposed gums, and their advancing cheek-bones and depressed noses, bear barbarism on their very front." No one in America would likely have trouble spotting the typical Irishmen, at least those from "Sligo and Northern Mayo." Brace described them: "'five feet two inches on an average, pot-bellied, bow-legged, and abortively featured.'"[32]

Brace took no pleasure in having to report this; honesty, however, always the better part of kindness, compelled him. So did piety. Every aspect of his plan was part of "the great design of the Creator." That design could not be altered. America could deal with Irish savagery only by placing the Irish among their "racial" superiors and praying that some of the more barbaric of their features could be reversed or at least modified. There was, however, an extremely important prerequisite. The Irish had to cast off their Catholicism and their priests, which required that their "dens," "bands," "gangs," and "fever nests" be "broken up." In his best-known book, *The Dangerous Classes of New York and Twenty Years' Work among Them* (1872), Brace explained why. The issue was the use of the King James version of the Bible in the public schools and the Catholic Church's hostility to what it perceived as state-funded sectarianism. Brace responded to the Catholic position with genuine anger. "We have . . . an immense mass of very ignorant, and, therefore, bigoted people, who suspect and hate every expression of our form of Christianity, and regard it as a teaching of heresy and a shibboleth of oppression." The faint suggestion that their bigotry was a result of their ignorance and hence could be remedied was probably the nicest thing he ever said about the Irish.[33]

Brace did not need to identify what "our form" of Christianity meant. The "shrewd and cunning leaders" of those hostile to the Protestant form, "knowing the danger to priestcraft from Free Schools, use this hostility and the pretense of our religious services to separate" the children of the dangerous classes "from the Public Schools. The priests and demagogues do not, of course, care anything about the simple prayer and the reading of a few verses of Scripture." They cared only about "separate State support for Catholic Schools," so that the gangs, dens, bands, and fever nests might be kept intact and under their "absolute tyrann[ical]" control. "Parochial," to Brace, did not mean "attached to a parish." He would have used the word in its pejorative sense, as descriptive of ideas and institutions characterized by rigidity and intolerance. The system of public schools, however, was "the life-blood of the nation . . . and the bulwark of Protestantism and civilization. If it be corrupted with priestcraft, *our vitality as a republican people is gone.* Demagogism and corruption, founded on ignorance, would wield an absolute tyranny . . . and the priests would enjoy an unlimited control over all the ignorant Catholics of the country." In the end, the Children's Aid Society and its orphan trains had much more to do with saving the children of immigrants from the priests and the Catholic schools than with saving them from lives of unrelieved poverty.[34]

Whatever his motive, Brace, like Bushnell before him, rejoiced and thanked God that the United States, alone of the industrializing nations, had the means to deal with "the difficult questions of pauperism and reform"; it possessed "a practically unlimited area of arable land." Brace's understanding of western realities could be charitably described as limited. He accepted without question every feature of the mythical West, particularly its wondrous ability to transform those who entered it. His lyricism, however, was joined with a hard practicality; the magic lands of the West "demand[ed] labor . . . beyond [the] present supply." Brace would meet that demand by dispatching children as young as eight into the West. Money was exchanged; the children were put to hard labor. But in his own mind at least, his service was always more than an employment agency and western farms were more than places of employment. The West was America's great schoolhouse and one singularly unreceptive to priestcraft. The priests, unfortunately for Brace, did not see it quite that way.[35]

One problem was that Brace did not deal only with orphans. Indeed, by 1870 the definition of the word "orphan" had been expanded to include "half-orphans and . . . destitute children having both parents living." Brace expanded the meaning even further, determining that "homeless lads and girls, . . . not legally vagrant" but unwilling to be sent to asylums even had the asylums been numerous enough to contain them were also to be placed on western farms. Obviously, these "children of the outcast poor" had parents, almost always Catholic parents, who, together with their priests, challenged Brace's right to their children. As Brace put it, the "poor were early taught, even from the altar, that the whole scheme of emigration was one of 'proselytizing,' and that every child thus taken forth was made a 'Protestant.'" Since that was, in fact, Brace's announced intention, these parental and clerical fears were not groundless—nor did he ever attempt to allay them.[36]

Brace did address and try to mollify the concerns of those who believed that sending the children of the "dangerous classes" to the West involved jeopardizing the West and the future to solve the problems of the East and the present. They feared, said Brace, that the "waifs" who made up his "little colon[ies]" might "corrupt the virtuous children around them, and thus New York would be scattering seeds of vice . . . all over the land." He admitted that these were reasonable fears but then offered a comforting assurance: even though he loaded his street waifs onto his "orphan trains" in little colonies, he unloaded them one or two at a time and distributed them broadcast. The young gangsters of New York would not be sent west in gangs.[37]

The Irish World, the same paper that Bagenal wished would raise money to send Irishmen west rather than to make agitators of them, joined the Catholic Church in condemning the CAS and its efforts to take Irish youths and send them to live in Protestant homes in the West. In 1874 Ford's newspaper carried a multipanel cartoon that showed "John O'Reilly, newsboy," being "sold off" by a dismal and morbid-looking Protestant minister and representative of the CAS to a mercenary railroad agent. O'Reilly was on his way west, having been previously lectured on the "inequities of popery" by the same CAS minister. In Ford's cartoon, the Protestant child grabber is carrying a broadside, which said that "in the last decade Fifty Thousand" of New York's "children have been rescued from Popery by the Children's Aid Society. . . . Nor have . . . kidnappers in other cities been idle" and "what England failed to effect by the sword, we, through subtler arts, are accomplishing quietly year by year."[38]

The last panel of the cartoon shows "Mr. O'Reilly, Baptist Preacher," looking every bit as supercilious and joyless as the minister who had snatched him originally. Ford knew his Irish readership well. They could imagine no more complete and horrifying a metamorphosis than that of John O'Reilly, newsboy, emerging as Mr. O'Reilly, Baptist preacher, a Protestant tract tucked under his arm as he stands proud, disdainful, and quite alone in what is clearly a western landscape. There was no reference to whether he was a prosperous western preacher; it would have made no difference. The Irish would have said and believed that it was better that he remain poor and part of a larger Catholic and Irish community than that he gain the world and lose his friends and with them his soul.[39]

America's providential mission did not require John O'Reilly to become a Baptist minister, but it did require him to adjust to American values. This was particularly the case for all of the O'Reillys who boarded second boats and rode them into the interior. Fortunately, entering the interior forced the necessary adjustment—a neat bit of reasoning that many Americans accepted without acknowledging its circularity and self-justification. But that aside, the adjustment required that those who went into and through the western crucible do so on the loose. The Irish, intensely communal and tenaciously Catholic, had somehow to be dispersed—literally disbanded—if their eventual absorption into American society was even to be possible. For the more militant, absorption meant that they would shed their Catholicism—to both their and the nation's betterment. Scrambling the Irish up and spreading them about would mean no priests, no parishes, no parochial schools, no sacraments; in other words, no superstitions, no worship of idols, no deferential and abject submission to autocrats, and no possibility that those deviant practices would ever contaminate the American future as they had contaminated the European past.

The Catholic Church's response to all this was predictable. It determined to settle the West on its own terms by pushing out its ecclesiastical boundaries and ensuring that Catholics in America's eastern cities did not have to surrender their faith in the process of moving up and moving out. This meant, among other things, that the church had to proceed as swiftly as the laity. As previously noted, Catholics were at a distinct disadvantage in this race to the West; they could not just hire a preacher, make a church, and bring it with them. A diocese and a parish had to be created by the hierarchy; priests, seminary trained and ordained, had to be appointed by a bishop and had to be on the boat or in place ready to meet it when it landed. Clerics, the hierarchy in general, had to be convinced, as did the laity, that heading into the American interior was a redemptive act. The idea that it might be such did not come easily either to Rome or to all of the bishops in the eastern United States. The priests themselves had to be pioneers, nimble and quick enough to move out in advance of their westward-wandering Irish flocks, ready to prepare and bless the ground.

Once the clergy were in place, the Irish could go or be sent to western places with an established Catholic presence, or, in the company of their priests, they could establish that presence themselves. Brace's Children's Aid Society had to be dealt with directly and aggressively. In 1863, specifically to counter the CAS, Catholics established a Society for the Protection of Destitute Roman Catholic Children in New York. Protection demanded, as it did with Brace, bundling the children off to the West. Six years later, the New York Foundling Hospital was started by the Sisters of Charity of Saint Vincent de Paul, and it too was engaged in "placing out" programs. But there were essential differences: First, and without ever saying it, the church operated on the assumption that people made places, not the other way around, and that Catholic people could form the West and not be formed or transformed by it. Second, Irish Catholics either would go west in a group or would form themselves into a group once they got there. And the group would be centered on the parish church.[40]

That was the natural order of things for the Irish. Clustering meant that John O'Reilly, newsboy, might one day become Father John O'Reilly, pastor of what would likely be St. Patrick's or St. Mary's and guardian of the community, the *muintir.* The Protestants believed that moving Irish Catholics west would transform them. The Catholics reversed the order and the logic, arguing that the West was where the Irish church and the Irish faithful would find fulfillment by transforming it. Protestants insisted that the Irish break out of their clans before heading out; the Irish thought that the clans were what made and kept them Irish. Scattered Irish was a contradiction in terms. They had family and friends who needed them and whom they needed. Fortunately, their clusters were exportable, so the Irish could move out with ecclesiastical and tribal banners flying. One can imagine them issuing a variation on Seward's challenge: "come then, gentlemen of the Protestant states, we will compete for the virgin soil of Kansas"— and the rest of the West. Protestants would not win by default.

The immediate issue for these western Irish was the practical one of bringing priests to Catholics who had moved beyond the "meridian of partition" without clerical accompaniment. That clearly was a pastoral responsibility of the hierarchy. The church, however, did not stop there. The pastoral became indistinguishable from the evangelical—which was the point at which the westward movement of gathered Irish began to take on some of the features of conflicting empires. The church was as interested in making new Catholics as it was in succoring old ones. Bishop John Hughes had said so; Theodore Parker had warned as much. This was distressing enough to self-consciously Protestant America. Making matters worse was the belief that being or becoming Catholic carried with it a set of antagonistic political principles. Evangelization and conversion was a form of political as well as sectarian insurgency. An entire generation of nativists/abolitionists had sounded precisely this alarm.

The advocates of Catholic evangelization and westward expansion did nothing to quiet these fears. They were usually polite and well-mannered enough to avoid using words like "empire" or "imperial," but "mission" and "destiny" came as easily to them as to their critics. The Catholic imperial project was animated by a spirit of Catholic mission as strong as the American mission it would contest. It would be led by the Irish. As early as 1819 an Irish immigrant wrote back to Ireland from St. Louis that "the Irish are deemed by Almighty to fill this vast wilderness with the seeds of Religion as one day the race of them will inherit this land." I am not certain that the Irish saved civilization, but there can be little doubt that they "saved" the American Catholic Church, in large part by ensuring that it grew and grew up with the country. That it might "inherit" the country raised the stakes considerably. Here assuredly was a blot, an incursion across the meridian and a direct threat to America's founding principles.[41]

The Irish were made for this imperial and missionary role—or at least so they tried to convince themselves. *An Gorta Mór* had done more than kill a million of them and set another two million to wandering. To have left matters there would have completed the cultural destruction that preceded the starving times and left more spiritual wreckage than the Irish could have endured. God did not make loved and chosen ones suffer without bestowing some proportionate measure of redeeming grace. It would not be easy to find this element of grace, particularly of a kind and in amounts that might balance and sanctify their pain and sadness, but the Irish had among them some earnest seekers. And so they did some conjuring of their own, summoning their saints and converting their exile into a quite literal Godsend.

Thomas D'Arcy McGee was not the first to consecrate Irish suffering, but he must be counted among the most zealous if not apocalyptic. In 1855, one short year after the Kansas–Nebraska Act had theoretically opened the West to slavery, he wrote that "the first Irish emigrants, or exiles rather" (by which he meant those of the eighteenth century) "had failed to implant Catholicity" in the New World, but only because they were too few in number. The starving times, however, brought the Irish out in their millions and changed everything. Now the church was omnipresent in America. "The morning sun . . . salutes it," McGee wrote, "and the noonday sun looks down and cries, 'Lo, it is here also!' and the evening sun . . . lingers a while upon its turrets, and pays a parting visit to its altars." In other words—and there seems little doubt that McGee had precisely this aphorism in mind—the sun never set on it. "Catholicity had descend[ed] into the tomb to arise again glorified and immortal. The martyr age of the Irish church . . . [came] upon it. . . . That good God, who denied our fatherland domestic peace, has consecrated her to a holy war, glorious, though sorrowful." Ireland had suffered as her "Lord has suffered." "If nations could be canonized she might well claim the institution of the process."[42]

Thus did British imperialism, having undone Catholic Ireland, become the instrument of the spread of Catholicism. There can have been few greater ironies in the entire history of the British Empire—or in the history of American western expansion. The Irish people, said Orestes Brownson, were "providential[ly] . . . called, trained, and fitted by Providence to a special work in maintaining and diffusing the true faith, hardly less so than the children of Israel." This sainted nation, according to an Irish prelate, carried "the faith into other lands." This was "the only glory she possesse[d]," and the only glory she needed. "Without a doubt," said another, the Irish "discovered and colonized" America. In 1920 a Minnesota Irishman told a St. Patrick's Day audience that the "exiles carried with them always the Tabernacle where God is enthroned. The exiles planted the cross in

Arctic Ice and tropic Sun, on the rolling prairies and pampas of this continent and on the long low plains of Australia." The Irish, wrote an Irishwoman, "were the evangelisers of the English-speaking world. A people whose persecution by England was turned into a blessing for almost the whole world. They carried the lamp of faith shining untarnished."[43]

John Lancaster Spalding, bishop of Peoria (and, except for an Irish great-grandmother, of English descent), gave this blessing a grander aspect when he wrote *The Religious Mission of the Irish Race and Catholic Colonization,* a title that nicely juxtaposed—indeed, conflated—the matching aspects of what was becoming the religious vocation of "St. Ireland." Spalding identified the "Irish race . . . [as] the providential instrument through which God has wrought this marvelous revival in England, America, and Australia." He was referring to the revival of the Catholic Church, but by 1880, when Spalding wrote, "revival" was not the right word. By then the church was fully revived; it was becoming the church militant. What Spalding really meant was its dominance, and this required that the Catholic "colonization" of which he spoke in his book become the instrument of the Catholic mission. Colonization was a "commendable" enterprise in great part because the Irish, "the most important single element in the Church in this country," could then become "Catholic apostles in Protestant America."[44]

Clearly, Ireland had a destiny as manifest as that of America itself. The historian Patrick O'Farrell uses the appropriate language, writing of the "Irish empire," "Ireland's religious mission," and, most particularly, the "religious imperialism of Ireland." Irish Catholics were not just coming into the West in massed colonies, they were marching in like legionnaires. Recall Josiah Strong's warning that Catholics had "empires in their brains." The West would not reform them; they would reform it. The shock troops of this Irish and quite Catholic empire were different from those that America and Britain employed—nuns, priests, and missionaries rather than soldiers and diplomats—but recall McGee's words: these were rival empires; they contested common ground in what McGee accurately referred to as a "holy war."[45]

Among the holiest of the church's warriors were the young priests sent from the Irish seminary of All Hallows College (AHC). All Hallows was founded in 1842. It occupied an abandoned ascendancy estate in Drumcondra, just north of Dublin. The estate was a gift to the church by Daniel O'Connell, then lord mayor of Dublin. The 999-year lease by which O'Connell transferred control of the estate required that All Hallows be committed solely to the training of Irish priests for work in the church's overseas missions, of which America, East as well as West, was the largest. There is an old story, still told, that the families "with twenty cows sent their sons to Maynooth; those with three cows sent theirs to Thurles or All Hallows." AHC-tranied priests were not drawn from the comfortable and secure gentry. Like most of those to whom they ministered, they knew what it was like to live on the edge.[46]

The timing for the founding of All Hallows was ideal. The Devotional Revolution was well started by 1842, and increasing numbers of young Irishmen from both the middling and the lower classes were being drawn to the priesthood. Five years later, a starving Ireland sent even more of its sons into the church. Ireland had found itself with more priests than the domestic market could absorb. The fraction of the surplus trained at All Hallows was part of the Irish church's export trade. People (and history) were all Ireland had in surplus. The hungry and mobile Irish laity provided industrial guano; its clergy provided devotional fervor. Both were kept busy. But the missionaries had a second responsibility that, although compatible with their pastoral, was separate and distinct: they would take up command posts in advancing the church's imperial mission, making new Catholics and extending the reach of their church. The 1,500 young Irish clergy who ministered to every part of the English-speaking world, particularly the many whose assignments took them into America's constructed western province, were among Ireland's most important pale-jumpers. They were border warriors and conscious of their role.[47]

All Hallows was thus a major part of Ireland's concealed empire within an empire. The college's first president, Father John Hand, never doubted that Ireland was manifestly destined to bring Catholicism to the farthest corners of the world—which is to say, as far as the British Empire might reach. "It was obvious to [Hand]," according to the account in the college's 1848 report, "that upon this country, the obligation devolved in a most special manner of preaching the Gospel to the many millions who acknowledge the rule or who speak the language of Great Britain." There were many more who spoke the language than who acknowledged the rule, but as Britain's and America's Protestant empires grew, so also would Ireland's Catholic empire. They would be coterminous. Whether anyone involved in establishing All Hallows, including Daniel O'Connell, had any of this in mind cannot be known. One can hope. That Irish Catholic victims of British imperial aggression would tag along after their masters, subtly subverting the imperial project and building an overlapping empire of their own, might well represent the ultimate in colonial resistance and retribution. Certainly it extends the definition of "postcolonial," "diasporic," and "transnational."[48]

Like most Irish, the priests of All Hallows had never lost the sense that their exile had meaning. In 1852 the college's *Report* noted that "our own brethren to the number of some millions, have, by the mysterious providence of God, been compelled to emigrate." By their own careful reckoning, the directors of All Hallows counted 176,554 Irish who had left for America in 1854 alone. This was followed by a brief description of the British Empire, including the United States (!). The enormity of it was almost beyond the directors' comprehension;

but huge as it was, the Irish were everywhere within this mixed empire—and they were sabotaging it everywhere. Obviously, Morse, Beecher, and later Josiah Strong and countless others had more to worry about than they knew. Emigration had become the instrument by which the faith would be spread. It had fallen to "the ancient Church of Ireland" to fulfill "the designs of Mercy," and the missionary priests had no option but to "conclude that God has given her the mission."[49]

But none of this would have mattered had Ireland not been equal to the task. The director of All Hallows had no doubts, writing in 1856 that "God has most mercifully implanted in the soul of Ireland a deep, lasting, earnest, missionary spirit. It has been the characteristic of our people . . . from Saint Patrick's day to this . . . and as far as the missions in which the English language is spoken, we are the only people on Earth who can effectively accomplish it." The "it" in question was no inconsequential matter. The "majestic hierarchy" of the American Catholic church was the direct result of wandering Irish, of priests on overseas duty serving an exiled laity. "Irish poverty" would give rise to a Catholic renascence. AHC would send priests who, as one unnamed priest put it, would be "founders of a new world." By that single comment, this anonymous Irish cleric, a representative of the oldest and most doddering of the old world, denied—or corrupted— everything that Protestant Britain and its American seed meant by both "founders" and "new world." Catholics could not be founders of any part of America; their very presence was enough to destroy its newness.[50]

The priests' reports from the field made clear that the fundamental principles of American society were as mystifying to them as they were to the entire church. An AHC missionary noted in 1851 that there was "no doctrine more favorable to [Americans] than *private judgement.*" "They are a proud people," this young Irish priest continued, "fond of liberty; so much so . . . they imagine that [Catholicism] would infringe too much on liberty to submit to the doctrines . . . of our Holy religion." Eighteen years later, another AHC priest wrote back to the president of the college that "the republican principles of universal equality which prevail throughout this country are not in any way pleasing to those coming in . . . from . . . Ireland." The nativists had made the same point from fear; Brownson and Maguire had wished it away. The AHC priests knew more than either side.[51]

Going to America, however, required more than an adjustment to new political principles. The greater menace came from the social effects of those principles, particularly private judgment. AHC was characteristically unrestrained; America was home to "the licentiousness of unrestrained immorality . . . to say nothing of sects and nonbelievers." Little wonder that the AHC reported in 1854 that "many a one of our poor people sighs for the poverty and hunger of [Ireland], rather than live the hopeless, lightless life to which his unhappy fate condemns him." It cannot be known how many of those "sighs" were invented by AHC priests and made audible in Ireland only through the priests' dreary and depressing reports back to the college's directors. In all events, the directors came to confusing and contradictory conclusions regarding those who emitted them. In Ireland, the Irishman "has been persecuted and pursued," but when "he determines to go abroad, snares are flung in his way, and force often bars his progress." The snares and the force were real enough, but "progress" was presumed to be an American and British invention in which the Irish had no interest. As for exiles, they, by definition, do not "determine" to go abroad. They do not determine anything. Clearly, the directors of All Hallows had not made up their minds whether those parishioners to whom they would send their young priests were determined emigrants or helpless exiles.[52]

They were, however, certain of what was to be found at the other end of emigration/exile and unrestrained in describing it. Sectarian holy wars are always accompanied by rhetorical extravagance. This one was no exception; All Hallows' directors were as fervent as any nativist. It is the case that their comments were supposed to have been based on reports from the priests in the field; to the extent that that was the case, the reports may have reflected the pervasiveness of American anti-Catholicism. It is also possible, however, that the directors formed their opinions in advance of and quite apart from any reports from their graduates assigned to the American missions.

As a result, it is hard to know what to make of it when the directors accused England and America of having entered into a "conspiracy against the Gospel" that extended throughout the English-speaking world. The 1854 *Report* asserted that there was no "conceal[ing] . . . the fact that a great alliance has been formed between England and America to overthrow the Church of Ages in every part of the world." The directors declared in 1856 that "we have opposed to us the wealth, wisdom, hate, and power of the two greatest nations of modern times, England and the United States of America." They reported from America that "English agents and admirers of England still slander our faith and race. There are newspapers published in New York, having a wide circulation over the country from the Atlantic to the Pacific, whose sole aim seems to be to malign the Irish people . . . and bring [them] and their faith into contempt."[53]

The idea of an alliance or conspiracy between Albion and its American seed recalls the comments of Bishop Spalding and O'Donovan Rossa, especially the latter's insistence that "the English power . . . influence and . . . hate" of the Irish found full expression in America. Regardless of the accuracy of the reports, it is obvious that the priests of All Hallows knew they were involved in something more than a sectarian skirmish. America was more than just unwelcoming; it was aggressively hostile. Immigrating to it was like marching into a combat zone. The "accounts received from America" made clear that the Irish "did not estimate the afflicting bereavements" they would encounter. It was the responsibility of the

AHC priests to protect the "many a one of our poor people" who boarded those first unfriendly boat bound for unfriendly shores.[54]

What would become equally clear was that the second boats did not always deliver the Irish to more hospitable shores. AHC priests were everywhere in the West, and their letters and reports provide unique points of entry into Irish Catholicism, the West, and the collision of the two. Enmity toward "the Church of Ages" was evident at every western outpost. But it was enmity of a slightly different kind. The 1848 *Report* bemoaned the "spiritual destitution of these vast regions"; it was "extreme and most appalling." Serving the cause of empire was still grim and demanding work, but as England and America could attest, building empires was not supposed to be easy.[55]

The Irish learned that lesson quickly enough. In its 1856 *Report,* AHC described the life of the missionaries sent into America's remote settlements, and what was said of the priest applied as well to his parishioners:

> Very frequently he is placed in the midst of a district comprehending hundreds of square miles. No railways or public vehicles place him before his church door. By unfrequented paths . . . through woods and over prairies, crossing rivers or stealing along by precipices, he travels from day to day . . . often without a bed or a meal . . . the world is lonely and miserable even when material abundance has been secured.

The world was not just lonely and miserable. The weather was unlike any the Irish had ever known. It was too hot, too cold, too snowy—though never, not surprisingly, too rainy. No part of America, with the exception of the coastal Northwest, looked or felt anything like any part of Ireland. Only San Francisco's climate came in for good notices, though getting there required riding across Panama on the backs of mules. The roads, where any could be found, were often impassable and always bone-jarringly rough. Father Eugene O'Connell, an AHC missionary in California and Nevada, wrote that the stage roads in the Sierras that traversed parts of his vicariate could not be described, "except in the words of the Regicide John Milton . . . 'dire was the tossing, deep the groans.'" For more than twenty years O'Connell traveled those roads; they led to the places where "our brethren . . . are scattered over the plains and wander on the mountains."[56]

They wandered, moreover, among some very questionable company. There were Mormons, for example. O'Connell referred to Utah as "Mormondom" and to the need for him to travel there to save impressionable Irish from the "tusks of that wily boar," by which he meant Brigham Young. At the other extreme, the West was also unrestrained and turbulent. It was "relatively easy to be good" in Ireland, one AHC priest wrote back, but in western America the Irish needed "strong will and constant prayer." Neither came easily in the "western wilderness" where the population was "so unsettled" and "floating" and there were "very few women" to bring a measure of order to society. Add to all this the "great proportion of robbers and murderers, who would not hesitate to take a man's life for his money." A "six barrel revolver" and a "knife" were part of the standard western wardrobe. Add to the list of hazards the Indian wars, described in a letter to the college by Bishop Thomas Grace as war in "a wild region" filled with "tribes of roving savages."[57]

The semilegendary frontier aside, the realities of Western life did present young Irish, lay and cleric, with some totally new challenges. Eugene O'Connell was stationed in Marysville in the heart of the gold diggings, and he had only to point out the names of the towns in his vicariate: "Whiskey Diggins, Humbug Flats, Little Humbug, Hard Scrabble, and Port Wine" were a long way, both geographically and socially, from Ballyferriter, Gweedore, Tuam, and Clonmacnois—or, for that matter, from the Bowery. O'Connell initially took some solace from the name of his headquarters until he learned that it was "call'd Marysville . . . not from our Blessed Lady as I fondly supposed" but from a Baptist woman turned Mormon "now converted to Catholicism who was married or not more than once but whose partners were 'consorts' rather than husbands." Her conversion was "the crowning and last circumstance in this matrimonial Drama." What he meant is uncertain, although another of his letters supplies a clue. "How few are the caravans," O'Connell lamented, "and how destitute the people! If they were all saints, it would not be so deplorable but alas this is a most sinful place." Meeting their pastoral responsibilities in such a region was as daunting as meeting their imperial ones.[58]

So was the correlated task of protecting the faithful from all those "wily boars" who were trying to separate the Irish from their Catholicism. Part of the challenge was organizational. As one cleric told the directors of AHC, the West had no "established ecclesiastical institutions." The results were predictable. The 1854 *Report* contained the story of one "old man who presented himself to an American missionary and asked for reconciliation." He had been twenty years in the western country without access to the sacraments and was "haunted with fears and terrors day and night." A bishop in Kansas reported to All Hallows that he knew of Catholic families in the Indian Territory "who had no opportunity of seeing a priest for 25 and 30 years." This was religious "privation" of the worst sort, and news of it figured to have a dampening effect on any more Catholic families coming into the Indian Territory or later into Oklahoma.[59]

Many of these comments could probably have come from anywhere in America, but the fact that they came from the West gives them a special relevance. Added to bad roads, bad weather, and bad company was "Protestant bigotry" and the use of "every kind of aggression and stratagem to destroy the faith of the emigrants." Hundreds of Irish had "fallen away from the faith for want of a minister and are now attached to any other or everything the most fashionable." An AHC priest reported that "a large number of Catholic families are coming in every day . . . *with the hope . . . that a priest will reside among them,* and attend them as they are accustomed to be in the old country." Attending them was not all that was at issue. They "awaited the spiritual assistance which will guard them from the obloquy of ignorant strangers" and "to counteract the great efforts made by *all the Sects.*" "The Irishman's faith is attacked by bribes," wrote another AHC priest from Leavenworth, Kansas. But he could not "be won by avarice," and so he was "assaulted by opprobrium; and if he have grace to resist obloquy, he becomes the object of vengeance."[60]

The bishop of Oregon wrote back to AHC in 1849 that the Irish were coming to Oregon in substantial numbers and he had need of Irish missionaries. Their duty would not be easy, "surrounded" as they would be "by Protestants. Calumny is always busy; how sad would be our state if these vipers could find reality, by which to make more sharp their slanders." Coming to western America also meant that Irish immigrants would have to send their children to the "godless" schools managed by these sects and nonbelievers. The "public state schools," said one AHC priest from San Francisco, "are not one bit more tolerant than . . . the National Schools in Ireland." Another All Hallows priest referred to "the national or public schools" of St. Paul where the Catholic "religion is ignor'd"; he noted that the "children . . . are in imminent danger of losing their faith or morals in Non Catholic schools." O'Connell, in fact, then in Grass Valley, wrote back to All Hallows in 1870 of the "far more urgent need . . . of teachers . . . than of Priests." Most of these children and their families were Irish, and one young priest thought it the "imperious duty" of AHC to send "pious and zealous priests" to save their "souls from infidelity and perdition." Whether he meant to write "imperial duty" cannot be known, but "imperious" is not far from the mark.[61]

But it was not some generic version of Catholicism that was at issue. It was the Irish variety, intensely devotional and with exile as its theological grounding, that was imperiled "in this immense [western] territory . . . Catholicity is represented almost exclusively by Ireland and the Irish. The children of St. Patrick, . . . our own poor exiled fellow-countrymen, . . . are the missionaries of the English-speaking population of the globe." Again and always, the poor exile. These, however, were exiles on imperial assignment, as the priests almost surely let them know every Sunday. But whether the priests of All Hallows gave figurative marching orders at Mass or not, there can be no doubt that AHC was of no use at all to the cause of accommodating Irish Americans to their new national homes. They presided over parishes that were unyieldingly and defiantly segregant and oppositional. What else could be expected? AHC priests did not go west to help the Irish become American; they went to help the West become Irish and Catholic. They had exchanged their pastoral vestments for imperial robes.[62]

Among the most important aspects of this "Irish religious empire" is how closely it paralleled in time the imperial ambitions of the southern Slave Power Conspiracy. When Americans spoke of "winning" the West, they were always talking about their victory over wild lands and the wild Natives who lived on them. This was the great national hero-tale, the master narrative for a masterful people. What was neglected in this mythical narrative was the fact that the West had first to be "won" from other white Strangers before its indigenous Natives could be "conquered" in the name of modern civilization. One of these preliminary conflicts was entirely internecine: the North blocking the expansion of the South and preventing bad roads and bad morals from contaminating the West and defacing its future. The other was only partially so: nervous evangelical Protestants and other nativists blocking the expansion of popish outlanders and the equally bad roads and bad morals they represented. These contests were preludes; they were fought to determine which of the Strangers had earned the right to conquer the Natives.

These preliminaries never made their way into the western narrative. Bleeding Kansas was not a part of the "fatal environment." Neither, for that matter, was the Mormon War in "bleeding Utah" or the various jousting matches between Catholics and Protestants. The only contested West that made its way into the story line was the final and deadly conflict between white settlers and Indians. The earlier "war" against the expansion of Catholicism was either too unbecomingly European or too uncertain of outcome to be added to the national epic. It had no Gettysburg or Appomattox; nor did it ever figure to. There were many who urged an American-style Kulturkampf, but there was too pressing a need for Catholic workers to imagine the culture war ending with a Bismarckian (or Cromwellian) expulsion of the papists.

Incidents both large and small, however, reveal something of the contentiousness at the western points of contact between the righteous empire and its popish challengers. One of those, vigilantism and the political assassination disguised as a duel of David Broderick in California, has already been noted. But add to Broderick's death those of at least a dozen others in duels, lynchings, and shootouts that were fought along either sectional or ethnic and religious lines and that were as common in San Francisco as anywhere in the Old South. There was also a kind of replay of the Know-Nothing spirit of the San Francisco violence in the actions of the Montana vigilantes in the 1860s and 1870s. Great numbers of Californians made their way to Virginia City, Montana, and to the mines in nearby Alder Gulch, and some evidence indicates that they had the same nativist agenda as California's vigilantes. Given that Montana's righteous hangmen killed more than twenty men—all Democrats, though not all Catholic—it can be said with certainty that they brought with them the same taste for partisan violence, with all of the ethnic, sectarian, and sectional rivalries that went into the partisan mix.[63]

Those rivalries were on even fuller display in New Mexico's Lincoln County War. This oft-told and retold saga of gunfights and bushwhacking centered more on clashing ethnic allegiances than on some violent code of the West. Violence there was, some of it pathological, but none of it random and indiscriminate. Dolan, Riley, Brady, Boyle, and Murphy lined up against McSween, Tunstall, Chisum, Brewer, and, of course, Henry Antrim, better known, at least later, as Billy the Kid. More than twenty men were shot dead as Irish Catholics battled Scots and English Protestants for control of most of southern New Mexico and the right to cheat the Mescalero Apaches of their government-rationed beef—the cowboy equivalent of an eastern ward-heeler's "honest graft." The violence in Lincoln County was not quite the western American version of recent Catholic-Protestant clashes in northern Ireland, but it was close enough for the comparison to be made. And the "imperial" ambitions of both sides place it comfortably within any discussion of a contested West. It was much more than a simple western shoot-out; the real Billy the Kid was representative of something far more historically important than his mythical facsimile.[64]

Clearly, however, not all of the contested western "empire" was as blood-filled as San Francisco, Alder Gulch, or Lincoln County. There was an obvious Orange versus Green element to Montana's "War of the Copper King," and the war prize was certainly imperial enough. The combatants, Marcus Daly (Irish-born and Catholic) and William Andrews Clark (descendant of Scots-Irish, a 33rd-degree Mason, and a Protestant), fought to control Butte, the "richest hill on earth," and all of its mines. Clark would pay any amount of money for a Senate seat; Daly any equal amount to see that he did not get one. They then spent extravagant sums in a remarkably entertaining battle to see which of the "king's" towns would be chosen Montana's permanent capital city. Clark spent more, and Helena emerged over Daly's Anaconda. There was no effort to disguise the sectarian nature of the contest: Helena, according to one quite mistaken nativist newspaper, was a "Protestant" town; Anaconda was the seat of "Pope Marcus's" unofficial papal empire. It was an ugly fight, but at least no one was killed in the waging of it.[65]

More common, less swaggering—and less reported—were the routine encounters between people of different and antagonistic religious faiths. In *Holding Up the Hills,* Leo Ward tells the story of growing up in Melrose, Iowa. The Catholic Irish were so numerically dominant in Melrose that nuns taught in the public high school—home of the Melrose Shamrocks—from the 1850s until 1954. The Irish called Melrose the "neighborhood," meaning the place where friends lived. The neighboring instincts that so troubled Bagenal implied feelings stronger than and totally opposite of what Turner meant when he used the same word—and applied it to the same corn-belt West. Non-Irish, Ward explained, "[didn't] belong in our neighborhood." Nor, it seems, did they want to be in it. The Protestants who had initially settled the region moved back to Indiana when the Irish arrived; they disinterred the bodies of family members, loaded them and all they owned on their outbound wagons, and fled.[66]

From that point forward, the Irish of Melrose referred to any non-Irishman as a "'Hoosier,' . . . a Gentile, an outsider." This is a most revealing use of the word "gentile," but then the "neighborhood" of Melrose had strict rules for admission. Outsiders were cultural misfits. Their codes were different and incompatible. They thought differently, talked differently, obviously prayed differently. They occupied separate worlds, not just separate neighborhoods. Ward offers an example from the 1870s when the question was important and the responses to it revealing. The immediate issue was the insistence of sabbatarians that Sundays be kept holy and uncontaminated by anything that resembled fun. The folkways of the Melrose Irish were, to say the least, nonconforming. Sunday mornings they spent at Mass; the rest of the day they spent at play. "We are Irish after all," Ward wrote, "and we know that it is right—in the sense of not wrong—to play ball on Sundays." Playing ball on Sunday was bad enough. But consider, too, the strikingly different moral code: Protestant America had a more rigorous and authoritarian definition of "right" than merely "not wrong." No wonder the "Hoosiers" left.[67]

This instance of "Protestant flight" was not uncommon. I quoted earlier from an 1863 letter from Andrew Greenlees, a Protestant Irish immigrant then living on his own farm in Illinois, to his brother in Belfast. Greenlees tried to explain the meaning of the Civil War by likening it to the suppression of Irish rebels attempting to secede from Britain in order to replace "Protestant government" with "papal tyranny." The American conflict was no different; understanding it required only the substitution of slave-owning Southern Confederates for the papist Irish variety. Fifteen years later, now living in Kansas, Greenlees wrote again to his brother, telling him that he had planted impenetrable hedge rows around his farm and that in another year they would "turn stock." "We are glad of it," he continued, "for we are penned in on every side. There is a Colony of Irish Catholics from New York has bought up all the unacquired land in their neigbhourhood 150 families all together the first squad are already here and plenty more coming."[68]

Greenlees was right about that; plenty more were coming to almost every part of the rural West. And the overwhelming majority were coming in "colonies," "squads," gangs, and clusters. Florence (Big Flurry) Driscoll farmed just west of Wichita, one of a number of Irish Catholic farmers in that part of the state. Driscoll admitted that "if a [non-Irish] neighbor needed help, you were happy to offer help," but the more important reality was that the "tradition of the region . . . was that all Catholics were undesirable citizens, dangerous to the welfare of the community and addicted to idolatry": "'poor, priest-ridden sheep,'" as one itinerant evangelist called them, and "damn ole Kafflicks," according to one of Flurry's neighbors.[69]

Ole Rolvaag introduced a group of Irishmen in the role of claim jumpers in *Giants in the Earth*, his classic and only semifictionalized account of Norwegian western settlement. When told that one of the Irishmen was named O'Hara, Beret Hansa, fresh from Norway, said, "What strange names . . . they must be Indians!" Another Norwegian was made to say that at least the Irish were "*white* folks." Perhaps so, but the Hansas moved on nonetheless. Rolvaag said nothing about the fate of the O'Haras. Claim jumpers seldom settled regions; they were there to plunder. At that, one can imagine them responding to Father Martin Mahoney of Currie, Minnesota, who pointed out in a letter to the *Boston Pilot* that much of the land the Irish were settling in western Minnesota was in regions where many farms were still owned by Americans and Scandinavians. These, however, "don't care much for the peculiar Catholic aspects of the place, and could be very advantageously bought out."[70]

Mahoney was more pragmatic and enterprising than belligerent and imperial. He would contest the West by bargain hunting. Thomas Francis Meagher's plan to colonize territorial Montana with his fellow Irish Catholics was considerably more combative. It was also totally unorganized, and no part of it was ever implemented. But Meagher's plans and the pugnacious claims he made in their name are deserving of special mention. They reveal something of every aspect of the Irish Catholic presence in the West and of Catholicism's presumed menace to the future of the region. For reasons impossible to discern, Meagher decided to challenge not just Protestant claims to the West but the specific Protestants who made them and to do so in incendiary language. No one ever gave the Irish empire such forceful and provocative expression—or the American empire such a contemptuous dismissal.

In 1866 Meagher was the acting territorial governor of Montana. Given his résumé as an Irish patriot in the rising of 1848 and the leader of a New York Irish unit in the Civil War, this was not a particularly prestigious posting, but Meagher determined to make the most of it by becoming, as he put it, "the representative and champion of the Irish Race in the wild great mountains." "I want my countrymen to place me up and beyond the sneers of these 'blackguards'—who are, ever, so ready to run down an Irishman." Being the representative of the Irish in the great mountains was a good start. Specifically, he planned to turn the entire territory into a vast Irish colony. His friend Martin Maginnis said that Meagher "sought new . . . lands, where . . . his own . . . scattered countrymen" would find "new hopes and new homes," meaning, among other benefits, that they would no longer be scattered. Meagher spoke of his plan to Bishop Thomas Grace of St. Paul, a frequent correspondent with the directors of All Hallows College, who promised to support Meagher in the enterprise.[71]

But Meagher also had in mind using these settlers as part of an extended sectarian and partisan campaign. What Montana needed, Meagher told a friend in 1866, was "a strong infusion of . . . Celtic blood to counteract the acidity and poverty" of the territory's non-Irish and non-Catholic elements. By poverty, Meagher meant what most Irish meant—spiritual poverty and parsimoniousness, the curse of Albion and its seed. If Montana was to be truly civilized it would not be through the agency of Anglo-American Protestants but by the "heart," the "genius" of the "true Irish Celt." And it was not just "the bounty of the Celtic sceptre" that Montana needed. Equally important was "the aspiring piety of the Celtic mitre." Montana, in other words, required the Irish faith as well as Irish muscle. As Meagher told his "Protestant fellow-countrymen," the spirit of St. Patrick "would convert 'every mother's sowl of them' with that miraculous crozier of his." This turned the conjuring trick on its head; the West would not be the place where the Irish were turned into Americans: it would be the place where Americans were turned into Irish. Many of these remarks were made playfully as part of Meagher's St. Patrick's Day address in Virginia City. But in the nineteenth century—in a room filled with Republicans, Union Leaguers, vigilantes, and Masons—converting Protestants to Catholicism was not something to be joked about.[72]

Neither was converting western territories from Republican to Democrat. Meagher, who had dallied with both parties, had settled upon the Democrats and had appointed himself the party's representative and champion as well. The surest sources of Democratic voting strength in post–Civil War America were Irish Catholics and Southerners. Meagher courted and recruited both. The Irish American journalist John Finerty called him "a non-sectionalist; he loved the South as well as the North." Meagher was doing a bit of reconstructing of his own when he allegedly stated that the West should be dedicated to "the consolidation of liberty with law, the crushing of the malevolence of faction, nationality against sectionalism." No Montana Republican would have needed to be reminded that, politically and socially, the vast majority of the Irish Catholics were no better than Confederate rebels and no more easily reconstructed. Montana had more than its share of both classes of sinners and renegades. That its acting governor intended to bring in thousands more was dumbfounding.[73]

Meagher cannot have been unaware of these feelings, which means that he was audacious or arrogant enough to believe that he could overwhelm them. In 1866 he told a probably astonished audience:

> It is the American who . . . has no thought beyond putting a mighty dollar out at mighty interest, who . . . hates the Irish for their generous qualities, their *infallible religion* and their inveterate democracy . . . the American who . . . has "the Ten Commandments" written on his face, and looks so virtuous that he might commit any crime, and no one believe in the possibility of his guilt.

He continued in language even more intemperate, asking if loyalty to Ireland was incompatible with "loyalty to America," as his critics had charged. The question was "an ignominious one." It came from "vicious bigots—men of small brains and smaller hearts—men of more gall than blood—who assert . . . that love of Ireland . . . invoke[s] an equivocal allegiance to the United States." And then, to "great cheering," he roared: "Out upon the bastard Americanism that spews this imputation." This type of American "regards with cod-liver eye, a nutmeg nose, a Maine-Liquor-Law howl, and a Cromwellian deprecation, the love of Ireland." They were men of "depraved and distempered natures . . . jack-rabbits . . . skunks . . . vermin . . . pimps . . . lame poltroons . . . despotic Radicals . . . palsied politicians . . . crumbling fossils" who "stood, or rather cowered, with quivering legs and palpitating heart." This was fairly heady language even for that time and place.[74]

These remarks were greeted by "loud and long continued cheering" from the Irish in Meagher's audience, but what truly aroused the crowd was his final peroration:

> Let the marrowless bigot . . . carp and deprecate; let the hungry Puritan with his nasal music importune the God of Blue Laws to save the Yankee nation from the witch-craft of St. Patrick's daughters and the deviltry of St. Patrick's sons . . . the Irish people in America will not, and can not, forget the land of their birth, their sufferings, their dearest memories, and proudest hopes.

This was less a declaration of cultural war than a ringing announcement that such a war had already begun and would be waged with no limits, at least on rhetoric. No other Irishman in America, in public at least, ever used language so calculated to inflame sectarian and political hatreds and over an issue—the control of a large part of the West and of the ideology of empire—of such national importance.[75]

And Meagher was not finished. Montana's Territorial Assembly, at the urging of Thomas Dimsdale, the superintendent of education, had passed a public education bill. Meagher responded by firing Dimsdale, English-born and a Republican, and replacing him with Peter Ronan, an Irish Catholic Democrat. Then he vetoed the bill appropriating money for the schools, "for the reason that [the bill] does not authorize the Superintendent . . . to exclude from the public schools of this Territory any sectarian tracts or other publications [that] . . . excite discord upon religious subjects. Nor does it empower him to prevent and suppress sectarian instruction, in which the world knows, teachers of every religious denomination are apt and prone to indulge." Recall Charles Loring Brace's comment that these schools were "the life-blood of the nation. . . . and the bulwark of Protestantism and civilization." There were very few issues in American politics from the 1840s until well into the twentieth century that were more divisive than the public schools, and Meagher certainly knew that.[76]

On July 1, 1867, Meagher drowned in the Missouri River at Fort Benton, Montana. His body was never recovered. The assumptions were that Meagher was drunk (not an unknown condition for him), careless, or suffering severely from dysentery and dehydration. His most inveterate political enemy, Wilbur Fisk Sanders, who was present in Fort Benton on the night Meagher died and present during the Irishman's earlier speech in Virginia City, said later that Meagher had committed suicide. That was, and remains, the most unlikely of explanations. There is also the possibility that Meagher's drowning was not accidental. Sanders, in fact, had written in a letter to a friend that a "quietus" had to be put on Meagher. "Quietus" was archaic even when Sanders used it, but it was a euphemism for death then as now, and Sanders did not intend it metaphorically.[77]

Father Hugh Quigley said that Montana's vigilantes—he called them "murderous banditti"—had "dogged" Meagher and, "in the dark hour of midnight, assassinated the hero by stabbing him and flinging his body into the muddy waters of the Missouri." Quigley did not add, but might have, that Sanders had been a very active vigilante. Montana's vigilance men were overwhelmingly drawn from the Masonic lodges and the Republican Party. Sanders was a member of both of those organizations. Nativism was no more alien to the western vigilantes than lynching. Meagher had to have been their worst nightmare. He was an Irish Catholic Democrat who wanted to fill the territory with those like himself. There was no room in the postwar West for anything like Thomas Francis Meagher and his dreams of making Montana a key part an Irish Catholic "empire."[78]

It is also possible that Meagher had in mind more than just mitres and sceptres. The "heart" of the true Irish Celt included a large measure of rabid Anglophobia and an equal measure of physical force militancy. He doubted that the Irish, wherever in their transnational wanderings they might be found, would turn to his brand of Irish republicanism; they were too loyal to their little platoons to be true nationalists and to the semimonarchical chieftains who led those platoons to be republicans. But that they would join an Irish army in exile was a certainty; their education in the principles of nationalism and republicanism could wait. For the moment, Ireland needed soldiers, not political theorists. Meagher made no specific public reference to it, but Montana's border with Canada might also have been part of his calculations. American Fenians saw Canada as a war prize to be traded back to Britain for the freedom of Ireland. Meagher's own involvement in American Fenian activity was almost covert, but his participation in the Irish Rising of 1848 had certainly not been. Other Montana Irish, Martin Hogan and Andrew O'Connell in particular, were clearly enlisted in the Fenian cause, and Meagher (who missed few opportunities to remind people of his Irish republicanism) was well known to both men.[79]

Less than a decade after Meagher's death (his funeral was attended by uniformed Fenians), John O'Neill began an Irish colonization movement in Nebraska. Like Meagher, but more openly, O'Neill was also playing Irish patriot games. He had been an officer—a general by his account—in the reckless Fenian raids into Canada, intended as the first salvoes in an Irish rising against Britain. Those raids had begun in western New York; they did nothing to loosen the British hold on Ireland but quite a lot to confirm nativist assumptions about the Irish grasp on reality. Nebraska was to be O'Neill's next staging area. He had "always believed in striking at England wherever we could reach her and wherever the English flag floats." It was then floating in the Red River Country, and the Irish, "particularly the Irish exiles whom her oppressive laws have driven from their native land, have a right to go there and make war." Indeed, "if we could meet England at a disadvantage at the North Pole that . . . would be the best place to strike her."[80]

The general explained in a pamphlet promoting the settlement of O'Neill, Nebraska, that he "started out with the fixed determination, with God's help, to organize one hundred colonies in different parts of the West." That was a good start, but O'Neill went on to write: "I sincerely hope that the example I have thus set will be followed by others, until there are a thousand Irish-American Colonies scattered all over the West." He assured those looking to settle in O'Neill that he did not wish "to see the Irish people leave their native land and come here to go out West," but "their tyrant oppressor" was still setting them to wandering, and O'Neill "always believed that the next best thing to giving the Irish people their freedom at home, is to assist . . . such of them as are here, or who may come here . . . in procuring homes for themselves and their children." The exiles of Erin had become the impoverished of New York. The West would make them free and ready for "the not far distant day . . . when they will be needed at home . . . to free their native land." O'Neill, Nebraska, was intended as an Irish boot camp.[81]

Charles Collins of Sioux City was a third Irish colonizer/warrior. Between 1866 and 1874 he agitated constantly for opening up the Black Hills as an Irish Fenian colony. Like the settlement of O'Neill, with which Collins was briefly associated, his colony was a barely disguised military encampment and open only to Irish with the right political instincts. The Fenians of Nebraska, organized as the Irish Confederation and including John O'Neill, would lead the enterprise. It was an ambitious one. The Fenians were to enter into an alliance with Louis Riel, the leader of the Métis Rebellion against the Anglo-Protestant government in Ottawa. The Métis were people of "mixed blood"—the true in-between people—and the mix was often between the "savage twins." Riel claimed that he was seven-eighths white and that "Riel" was a shortened version of O'Reilly. The flag of his break-away republic had a buffalo, Catholic symbols and icons, and a cloverleaf that looked very much like a shamrock. The Irish were invited by name to join Riel's "new Ireland in the North-West," his Catholic "empire" captured from

British Canada by a military assault originating on American soil. The contest for
the American West was taking on some very large foreign-policy implications.[82]

This Irish version of empire was always more rhetorical than real; the genuine
article was far beyond their reach. Still, there was a real Irish and an even more
dominant Catholic presence in the West. The Catholics, of course, were ethnically mixed; but the Irish were the lance points of an expansionist American
Catholicism, and it was they who were most often associated with the American
church. Jefferson's "meridian of partition" dividing America from Europe had
been overrun by aggregated Celtic clans, drawn like iron filings to a magnet to
their local parish and its resident and always Irish priest. The result was a crisis on
the border. The West was becoming the home of Catholic colonies and enclaves,
parochial schools, priests and croziers, and all the paraphernalia of popery. Albert
Barnes and many others had predicted in the 1840s that Catholicism was a cultural
trespasser and could never fix itself on the West. They were wrong. By the 1860s
trespass had become permanent residence.

This was not a proper legacy of the Civil War. Saving the West from Southern
slavery only to have it be captured by a European slavery scarcely less sinister and
conspiratorial profaned hallowed ground and violated sacred trusts. This was the
crisis Josiah Strong and his associates' country faced. It had arisen in large measure
because massed squadrons of Irish refused to be atomized and split off from their
community. The priests held them in thrall, said the nativists, but they also held
them together, hidden behind Turner's line-fences. If Turner was worried about
this, however, his "doomsday" colleagues—for want of anything better to call
them—were greatly despairing. They were also more direct, which is to say less
subtle in their conclusions and more overtly prejudiced in reaching and commu-
nicating them. Woodrow Wilson, John Fiske, James Russell Lowell, Francis Amasa
Walker, John Bach McMaster, Edward Channing, James Schouler, Madison
Grant, and, obviously, Josiah Strong would resurrect the Anglo-Saxon volk in
all its Protestant-inspired superiority.[83]

The Irish immigration was obviously not the sole cause of their concern; Jews
and Italians and other undesirable "new immigrants" in the East were more important in prompting this newest Anglo-Saxon counterattack. The Irish, however,
were still as far beyond the pale as they had been before the Civil War, when
Morse and Beecher and the others were issuing their alarms. Schouler referred
to Irish peasants as "unlettered and boozy foreigners, the scum of European
society." Their instincts "made them Roman Catholic," which certainly closed the
door on their conversion to something more in keeping with American institutions. But booziness aside, what most captured the attention of these quite public
intellectuals was that the Irish had crossed Jefferson's cultural divide with their
herding instincts intact.[84]

The historian Edward Channing had more to say on this point than the others, and he was unsparing in the way he said it. In accounting for and justifying the Know-Nothings, Channing wrote that they arose because of "the clannishness of the Irish Roman Catholics. They lived apart by themselves and acted on the advice of their priests." Channing later accounted for this clannishness, noting that "there was no reason for them to form themselves into colonies and communities, because their race and religion bound them together indissolubly." In sum, they were born and remained forever tribal Irish. They were of "foreign mind" and, it seemed to many, of evil intent. They had infiltrated the West, where, in the language of Jon Gjerde, "they were able to cordon themselves off from the developing American tradition." "Cordon off" is an apt phrase. Channing had implied as much. There was something covert, almost subterranean, about these thickets of Irish. In 1868 the Irish immigrant Maurice Wolfe wrote back to Ireland from the western fort to which he had been assigned. He was pleased to report that "the Irish are very Strong party, . . . and if they pulled together they would rule a good deal of the destiny of this Country." By "this Country," I think he meant the western and better half of it.[85]

That was a frightening prospect. In 1887 in Clinton, Iowa, uneasy Protestants formed the American Protective Association (APA). This was less than twenty years after an All Hallows priest had written of the West's greater religious tolerance and less than thirty miles south of where he was when he wrote it. The members of this latest of America's nativist organizations "solemnly promise[d] that [they would] always . . . labor, plead and wage a continuous warfare against ignorance and fanaticism," by which they meant that they would do their "utmost . . . to strike the shackles and chains of blind obedience to the Roman Catholic church from the . . . priest-ridden and church-oppressed people" and would "do all in [their] power to retard and break down the power of the Pope, in this country or any other." By 1896 the APA had more than two and a half million members nationwide, but they were concentrated in the West among God's sectarian warriors on the contested border between Anglo-Saxon and Celt.[86]

In 1890 Bishop Thomas O'Gorman of Iowa attempted to counter the APA's charges, particularly those that came from what O'Gorman called "the West," the region of "broad . . . minds" and "generous spirit." Anti-Catholicism arose solely from the "conceited ignorance . . . and prejudice of misfits, much of it dating back to the 16th century." Let reason replace ignorance, and the prejudice would disappear. Still, O'Gorman had no choice but to deal with the charge that Catholics did not believe in "private judgment" (the same term and the same context an All Hallows priest had used) and that the priests did have "teaching authority," by which was meant temporal or secular as well as religious authority. This was not disqualifying, however, at least to O'Gorman; Catholics could still participate in American society.[87]

O'Gorman also insisted that "Protestantism has no rational right to judge Catholic doctrines" by standards of church law "denied by us." He asked—practically begged—his Protestant "separated brethren" that they "not judge Catholic doctrines by Protestant first principles which we do not grant." O'Gorman's arguments were unassailable, but he missed two important and related aspects of the issue. Protestant first principles were also American first principles, and the West was expected to provide the surety for both. Bagenal understood this perfectly when he referred to the "Protestant life of the country" and advocated a western resettlement—and rehabilitation—program for those who had not yet figured this out. O'Gorman was upset because Protestants were unfairly judging his people. But it was America, after all, that the American Protective Association was pledged to protect, not Protestantism. "Nativism" had shared roots with "nation." The tension arose from that. Americans, but particularly western Americans, were supposed to be those who had broken loose, started over, and been made free. An ethnic enclave culture, particularly a Catholic one, was outlandish to them.[88]

For the Irish, however, that culture was all they knew. Jumping their line-fences and breaking loose did not make them free; it put them into cultural free fall and stripped them of meaning. And so they set up their parallel universe— their own schools, churches, fraternities, neighborhoods, and rookeries. I think this was when the "frontier," as Jefferson and Turner defined it, really ended. It was done in by all those pale-leapers. The quantity of people per square mile was always less important than the quality of those people. Whether as frontier or region, this vast and righteous western empire was not just supposed to *be* something; it was expected to *do* something. Turner knew that and gave it some very specific tasks. By the time he wrote, the West could not do what it was supposed to do, what, in fact, he had said it had done. That knowledge should have saddened him more than it appears to have.

Some overly excitable members of the APA in Majors, Nebraska, deserve to have the final word on this matter. In 1893 the Majors APA sent a petition to Nebraska governor Lorenzo Crounce. It was written by the Reverend O. Knepper and signed by seventy-eight others. They laid out quite a case, which would have addled even Thomas O'Gorman: "Whereas you must know the reports of the shipment of firearms and Ammunition to Catholic Priests in our County as well as to other places and whereas . . . our lives, the lives of our families are in great danger . . . we demand as American citizens" state-supplied weapons and "without a moment's delay . . . military protection. . . . We fear we will be raided upon at any moment and massacred." This was, of course, precisely the language that was used by western settlers petitioning the government for military aid against marauding Indians. The frontier/meridian had turned against and become a parody of itself.[89]

CHAPTER 7

Finding a "Fair Living"

Patterns of Irish Migration and Settlement in the West

The basic questions about the Irish immigration to western America are obvious. Where were they, and where were they not? How and from whom did they come to learn about a specific place? Why did they go where they did, and what did they do for a living when they got there? In other words, what was the social ecology of their emigration/immigration? What structures and "rules" emerge from the historical data? There are also some more theoretical issues. The Irish had not only moved geographically. The New World was not just of a kind not before seen. Socially and culturally, it was of a kind not before imagined. Add to that the exile motif: the Irish had been taught that they had no choice but to leave home. They were nearer to being victims of a kind of ethnic cleansing than to being emigrants. But even the well-used (and well-manipulated) theme of exile cannot erase the obvious: the Irish may have had to leave Ireland, but they did not have to leave it for the place they called Meiriceá; and once in America, they did not have to stay where their first boat left them. Exile was unique to them; it had a profound effect on them psychologically. But it did not materially affect their migration and settlement patterns.[1]

A discussion of what did influence those patterns must begin with another unique aspect of the Irish scattering. Before the starving times, two-thirds of the Irish immigration was male. After about 1850 more women than men left Ireland for America; the ratio by 1890 was 1,150 to 1,000. No other immigrant group sent more women than men, which says something about the nature of American immigration generally. But it suggests something even more important about the nature of Irish immigration specifically. The problem with attempting to determine what this gender imbalance might have meant in terms of western settlement patterns—or anything else, for that matter—is that there are so few records of the lives of Irish women, whether in Ireland or in America. As Kerby Miller notes, "If historians had access to the . . . documentation, . . . it is highly probable they would discover that women from different class, regional, and cultural backgrounds in Ireland had significantly different patterns of and motives for emigration and significantly different work and marital experiences in different regions of the New World."[2]

That is quite a number of significant differences. Unfortunately, tentative and hypothetical conclusions must be substituted for discovery. The first of these conclusions concerned timing. What happened in the 1840s that might have occasioned so dramatic a shift in the sex ratio of the Irish emigration? It was once argued that women chose to remain in Ireland because conditions were relatively favorable for them between 1814 and 1845 and nothing they knew about America—assuming they knew anything at all—tempted them to abandon their homeland. Then came the Devotional Revolution in Irish Catholicism together with the horrors of the Famine years. The first tightened the hold of a patriarchal church; the second further subordinated women to men, diminished their social and economic roles, and severely reduced what passed for opportunities. Irish women responded by racing to the first boats and heading for Tír na nÓg. Some historians argued that they hoped to find jobs, others that they hoped to find husbands.[3]

No part of this explanation is very persuasive. It suggests, first of all, that Irish women were rather meek and acquiescent in Ireland; that, even more than Irish men, they shuffled and cringed before authority—including that of Irish men. It is impossible to reconcile that image with what was written about and by Irish women at the time, particularly those from the west of Ireland. Ansty was not the tailor's maid servant; Peig Sayers and the other Blasket Island women were not servile fawners. Describing the women of Inishmaan in the Aran Islands, John Millington Synge wrote that they "are before conventionality, and share some of the liberal features that are thought peculiar to the women of Paris and New York." In fact, in *Grania: The Story of an Island,* Grania, one of the women of Inishmaan, is far more certain of herself and her place in the world than are the Victorian English gentlewomen who come to see her. The English objectify Grania as a subservient semisavage, totally unaware of how completely and hopelessly conventional they are. There is no reason to assume that the women who emigrated were more meek and submissive than those who stayed.[4]

The Devotional Revolution, moreover, did not diminish women's status in Ireland: it enhanced it. They became treasures of Catholicism, the guardians of the Marian tradition, and bulwarks in the church's fight to keep Ireland pure and free from secular—and Protestant British—influence. For its part, the post-Famine economy did not restrict women's economic opportunities: it improved them.

TABLE 1

Total Population of the United States and the West (in millions)
and Western Percentage of Totals: 1850, 1870, 1890, 1900

	1850	1870	1890	1900
United States	23.3	39.9	63.1	76.1
West	0.49	3.7	10.7	13.7
% West	2	9	17	18

Source: The Statistical History of the United States, 12–13.
Note: Figures for the "partial" states of Michigan, Wisconsin, Missouri, and Texas are estimates.

Granted, it began from a very low base, but the increased female emigration after the Famine is more easily explained by improving conditions and opportunities than by misery and discontent. Most of the women who left Ireland after 1850 were young, single, and self-assertive, eager to move out and move on. They left Ireland because they could afford the passage, were literate in English and could read about new worlds and new prospects, and were by then connected to family and friendly chains that guided their way. There were not many doleful exiles of Erin in this crowd of Irish immigrant women; their Irish national feelings seem to have been less defensive than those of Irish men and less filled with bellicose rhetoric. That is not, however, the same as saying that they had forgotten their homeland or that they did not still carry with them and retain cultural reminders of their role in sustaining the new Irelands to which they attached themselves. As for the presumed conflict between economic opportunities and marriage, it dissolved; one led to the other. As Mary Brown, an immigrant from County Wexford, put it in 1859, she emigrated in order to find "love and liberty"— likely in that order. Brown was writing from New York City in 1859. It is not known if she found either "marital bliss" or "economic opportunity" or if she limited her search to eastern America. Finding individual Irish is difficult; finding individual Irish women is almost impossible.[5]

As a result, western Irish settlement patterns can only be pieced together from aggregate census figures. They tell us where they were and how many there were. Sadly—and inexplicably in a nation of wanderers—the figures tell us next to nothing about where they had been. We have head counts by state or territory and country. Start with that. The first and basic point that emerges is that the geographical distribution of Irish immigrants leaves the standard version of Irish America in tatters. They were not stuck somewhere between Boston and the lower East Side with a few wayward ones in Chicago and San Francisco. Between 1850 and 1910 my admittedly idiosyncratic West was second only to New England in the percentage of Irish in both the total and the foreign-born populations. Irish America does not mean eastern America. The Irish were transnational; the Irish Americans were transcontinental (see tables 1 to 4).

TABLE 2

Irish-Born Population of Selected States, with Percentage of
Irish in Foreign-Born Population, 1900

	Irish-born	Total foreign-born	% Irish
Massachusetts	249,916	846,324	30
New York	425,553	1,900,425	22
Pennsylvania	205,909	985,250	21
Illinois	114,563	966,747	12
California	44,476	367,240	12
Colorado	10,132	91,155	11
Montana	9,436	67,067	14
Nevada	1,425	10,093	14

Source: U.S. Bureau of the Census, *Twelfth Census: 1900, Population,* clxxiii.
Note: The West had 18 percent of the nation's population and 23 percent of the nation's Irish-born.

The numbers speak for themselves, so I need only repeat some general conclusions regarding where the Irish were to be found in the West. The first is immediately apparent: the Irish, both men and women, did not flock to the West. But neither did anyone else—men or women. The second point is equally obvious: the western Irish presence in general was predominately urban, but, as with the total population, the context is important: most of the Bonanza West was urban. The Irish favored certain kinds of cities: Sioux City, Omaha, Kansas City, and others with large slaughterhouses; Denver and Anaconda, Montana, and Globe, Arizona, with their huge ore-processing facilities; San Francisco and Butte, commercial and industrial cities that already contained large numbers of Irish. All of the West's cities had streets to pave, buildings to erect, and a class of newly rich with domestic chores that needing tending. Overall, the Irish did not break any molds as they boarded their various westbound transports.[6]

The third basic point also has been made: the Irish, in wildly disproportionate numbers, were the instruments of America's western advance, what the Census Bureau called the "progress of the nation." Their numerical dominance of the western army jumps off the census pages. In 1870 Irish immigrants made up almost a quarter of the frontier army (see table 4) and more than 60 percent of its foreign-born. If second-generation Irish and the Irish from "British Canada" are factored in, it is not unreasonable to assume that half of all those blue-coated soldiers were Irish. But note, too, how few of them remained in the West after their military tours of duty were over. It was the army that attracted them, not the West's scenery or agricultural prospects. As soldiers, they were only probationary westerners to begin with, mercenaries of a kind, as they were in the British imperial army and

TABLE 3

Western Irish Population (Absolute and as Percentage of Foreign-Born) by States and Territories: 1850, 1870, 1890, 1900

	1850			1870			1890			1900		
	Foreign	Irish	% Irish	Foreign	Irish	% Irish	Foreign	Irish	% Irish	Foreign	Irish	% Irish
Michigan	—	—	—	23,263	5,775	25	54,000	3,900	7	54,200	3,200	6
Wisconsin	—	—	—	57,329	7,100	12	104,000	6,660	6	170,000	8,240	5
Minnesota	2,048	271	13	160,697	21,746	14	467,356	28,011	6	505,318	22,428	4
Iowa	21,232	4,885	23	204,692	40,124	20	324,069	37,353	12	305,920	28,321	9
Missouri	*	—	—	—	—	—	—	—	—	—	—	—
Texas	**	—	—	—	—	18	—	—	—	—	—	—
Dakota	—	—	—	4,815	888	—	—	—	—	—	—	—
N. Dakota	—	—	—	—	—	—	81,461	2,967	4	113,091	2,670	2
S. Dakota	—	—	—	—	—	—	91,055	4,774	5	88,508	3,298	4
Nebraska	—	—	—	30,748	4,982	16	202,542	15,963	8	177,347	11,127	6
Kansas	—	—	—	48,392	10,940	22	147,838	15,870	11	126,685	11,516	9
Oklahoma	**	—	—	—	—	—	—	—	—	—	—	—
Montana	—	—	—	7,979	1,635	21	43,096	6,648	15	67,067	9,436	14
Wyoming	—	—	—	3,518	1,102	31	14,913	1,900	13	17,415	1,591	9
Colorado	—	—	—	6,599	1,685	26	83,990	12,352	15	91,155	10,132	11
New Mexico	2,063	292	14	5,620	543	10	11,259	966	9	13,525	692	5
Idaho	—	—	—	7,885	986	13	17,456	1,917	11	24,604	1,638	7
Utah	1,990	106	5	30,702	502	2	53,064	2,045	4	53,777	1,516	3
Arizona	—	—	—	5,809	495	9	18,795	1,171	6	24,233	1,159	5
Washington	—	—	—	5,024	1,047	21	90,005	7,799	9	111,364	7,262	7
Oregon	1,159	196	17	11,600	1,967	17	57,317	4,891	9	65,748	4,210	6
California	22,358	2,452	11	209,831	54,358	26	366,309	63,138	17	367,240	44,476	12
Nevada	—	—	—	18,801	5,035	27	14,706	2,646	18	19,093	1,425	7

Sources: U.S. Bureau of the Census, Seventh Census: 1850, Report of the Superintendent, 16–19; Ninth Census: 1870, Compendium, 399–443; Eleventh Census: 1890, Foreign Born Population, 613–82; Twelfth Census: 1900, Statistics of Population, clxxxiii.

*Inconsequential except in some counties.

**Inconsequential.

TABLE 4
Irish Soldiers in Western Forts and Barracks, 1870

	Irish	Total	% Irish
Arizona	208	825	25
California	31	940	33
Colorado	80	231	35
Dakota	455	1,937	23
Idaho	76	278	27
Kansas	22	1,219	18
Montana	177	750	24
Nebraska	29	1,380	21
New Mexico	270	1,116	24
Washington	84	241	35
Wyoming	343	1,534	22
Totals	2,521	10,451	24

Source: U.S. Bureau of the Census, *Ninth Census: 1870, Population,* 720–65.

navy. They might have stayed in the army, but few stayed in the West, at least in the parts of it where they had been stationed. I think it is interesting that Josiah Strong had nothing to say on the topic of Irish soldiers. He worried about Catholic designs on "our country," in particular its western regions where the country's future would be determined, but he expressed no concern that that future would be secured by Catholics. The irony that "our country" would be extended by those he thought beyond its pale escaped him entirely, as it did all the other nativists.[7]

Neither did Strong have anything to say about two other aspects of western expansion and development in which the Irish played predominant roles. Great numbers of them were involved in building the transcontinental railroad system and even greater numbers spent their time in the West blasting and digging the hard rocks of western mines. Railroad construction, by definition, not only was transient labor but also presented the census enumerators with constantly moving targets. Building a railroad was not the same as working for one. Something other than quantifiable evidence will have to suffice to establish an Irish presence. Fortunately, there is some. The Union Pacific, for example, was said to have gotten its construction gangs from "a mixed crowd of . . . Federal soldiers, mule skinners, Mexicans, New York Irish, bushwhackers and ex-convicts." Except for the Mexicans, the Irish were well represented among all the other parts of the mix. Thus, if Irish not from New York are factored in, the old saying that "there was an Irishman buried under every western railroad tie" was probably at least figuratively true.[8]

TABLE 5

Irish-, American-, British-, and Chinese-Born Miners
in Western Hard-Rock Mining States and Territories, 1870

	Irish	American	British	Chinese
California	2,858	12,518	3,143	9,087
Colorado	271	1,216	462	—
Idaho	569	1,229	219	3,853
Michigan	937	233	1,521	—
Montana	824	2,691	350	1,415
Nevada	1,826	3,439	1,329	240
Total	7,285	21,326	7,024	14,595

Source: U.S. Bureau of the Census, *Ninth Census: 1870, Selected Occupations,* 722, 723, 730, 740, 744, 746.

Hard-rock mining figures are easier to get. Individual Irish may have moved from mine to mine, but the mines did not move and the Irishness of the mine work crews did not change. They were by a considerable margin the largest European immigrant group in the western mines (see table 5), and there must have been—figuratively again—at least one Irishman buried at the bottom of every shaft. Those other old sayings that the Irish only knew how to dig and that the invention of the wheelbarrow was all that got them to walk upright probably originated in the 1830s to describe Irish canal workers. But they would have applied just as well at any time from 1850 to 1910, from Hancock, Michigan, to Butte, Montana; Telluride, Colorado, to Bisbee, Arizona; Goldfield, Nevada, to Bodie, California (see table 6). Josiah Strong was strangely silent on this point, too.

But what of Irish women? The numbers tell a compelling story (see table 7). Women may have been a majority of the Irish in America, but they were a relatively small percentage of the Irish in western America. Whatever brought them to this New World, little compelled or encouraged them to move into its newest western reaches. They may have been eager to board that first boat, but the second one had negligible appeal. Again, I offer the disclaimer: few of any group moved west and still fewer women. That would change over time; but speaking very generally, the Irish West, like every other one, was male dominated. The West, particularly in its imagined and mythic form, had a greater appeal to Ireland's sons than to Ireland's daughters.[9]

Also consistent with general patterns, the Irish women who came to the West tended to concentrate in its urban centers. Most were engaged in what the Census Bureau called "personal service." The bureau counted Irish men in this same category; unfortunately, it made no distinction based on sex. Still, it is safe to say that in St. Paul, Kansas City, Denver, San Francisco, and every other western city, town, village, and hamlet with pretensions of gentility, the Irish maid was as ubiquitous

TABLE 6

Western Catholics (Totals, Selected Percentages, and Ranks) by States and Territories, 1850–1906

1850 State	1850 Catholics	1860 State	1860 Catholics	1870 State	1870 Catholics	1870 Rank	1890 State	1890 Catholics	1890 %/Rank	1906 State	1906 Catholics
California	7,300	California	39,720	Arizona	2,400	1	Arizona	19,000	70/1	Arizona	35,071
Iowa	3,990	Iowa	31,273	California	66,640	1	California	156,846	56/1	California	416,951
New Mexico	76,100	Kansas	2,250	Colorado	8,575	1	Colorado	47,111	54/1	Colorado	117,435
Oregon	1,833	Minnesota	17,475	Dakota	850	1	Idaho	4,809	20/2	Idaho	21,244
		Nebraska	700	Idaho	575	2	Iowa	164,522	30/1	Iowa	244,243
		New Mexico	78,750	Iowa	57,280	3	Kansas	67,562	20/2	Kansas	109,641
		Oregon	1,850	Kansas	14,605	3	Minnesota	271,319	51/1	Minnesota	445,045
		Washington	2,325	Minnesota	42,370	1	Montana	25,149	77/1	Montana	85,128
				Montana	1,700	1	Nebraska	51,503	26/1	Nebraska	118,545
				Nebraska	2,935	5	Nevada	3,995	68/1	Nevada	11,729
				Nevada	3,250	1	N. Dakota	26,427	44/1	N. Dakota	72,072
				Oregon	2,750	5	New Mexico	100,576	95/1	New Mexico	143,009
				Washington	1,785	2	Oregon	30,231	43/1	Oregon	41,549
				Wyoming	800	1	S. Dakota	25,720	30/1	S. Dakota	71,781
							Utah	5,958	4/2	Utah	9,831
							Washington	20,848	35/1	Washington	88,213
							Wyoming	7,185	61/1	Wyoming	12,075

Sources: U.S. Bureau of the Census, *Seventh Census: 1850, Statistics of the Churches*, 30–41; *Ninth Census: 1870*, 520–65; *Eleventh Census: 1890*, 298–304; *Report, Religious Bodies: 1926*, 2: 1257.

TABLE 7

Sex Ratios in Western States and Territories (Males to 100 Females), 1880–1910

	1880	1890	1900	1910
Arizona	230.4	135.3	140.4	138.2
California	149.5	137.6	123.5	125.5
Colorado	198.1	146.7	120.9	116.9
Idaho	202.2	151.5	136.5	132.5
Iowa	109.2	108.4	107.6	106.6
Kansas	116.8	111.4	109.5	110.0
Minnesota	115.9	114.5	113.9	114.6
Montana	256.6	187.0	160.3	152.1
Nebraska	122.7	117.8	112.5	111.2
Nevada	207.5	173.3	153.0	179.2
N. Dakota	169.1	123.8	125.3	122.4
New Mexico	117.1	116.9	114.4	115.3
Oregon	144.8	137.1	129.0	133.2
S. Dakota	150.9	119.7	116.6	118.9
Utah	107.3	113.3	104.9	111.5
Washington	157.7	163.3	142.2	136.3
Wyoming	213.2	180.5	169.4	168.8

Source: U.S. Bureau of the Census, Thirteenth Census: 1910, Population, 1:267, 270–71.

in the urban West as in New York. There is also some evidence that single Irish women were not eager to take up farm life—not because the Famine had taught them that God did not intend them to be sowers and reapers, but because single women were improbable farmers in Ireland or America. Love and liberty were more likely to be found in San Francisco than on a prairie homestead.[10]

But Irish men did more than shoulder rifles, lay track, pound spikes, dig holes, and detonate black powder and dynamite and Irish women did more than set other peoples' tables and scrub other peoples' floors. There was also a relatively large and by definition self-consciously Irish Catholic population in rural and agricultural areas. I say self-consciously Irish because this subgroup of western Irish does not show up as such in the published census returns. To find them I turned to the newspaper lists of contributors to Irish national causes in the late 1870s and early 1880s and in 1905. Giving money to the Irish Land League or to the Skirmishing or Spread the Light funds meant that Ireland was still on the minds of these Irish, including Irish women, many of whom were identified as "treasurer" of the local Irish Land League.[11]

It also meant that there were sufficient numbers of Irish in the area to form a local nationalist organization. These organizations held meetings; their members talked among themselves and talked about Ireland, almost surely about their own exile. Money was sent from many such places, including cities, small towns, and rural areas (see the appendix).

This class of western Irish has been all but ignored. Some of this neglect may be the result of some unfortunate habits of the U.S. Census Bureau. Little houses on the American prairie had women in them (farm wives and farm daughters), who shared in the work and joined in the play. That was the literary convention. But it owed nothing to the data gatherers. Married women on American farms did not count—or were at least not counted. The census did not include farm wives or daughters among those engaged in "agricultural occupations"—another instance of inadequate documentation. In 1880, for example, the census recorded 78,785 men and 611 women as "engaged in agriculture" in California. In Montana the numbers were 4,504 and 9; in Iowa, 302,171 and 1,386. That would have been news to the women in the neighborhood of Melrose. Thus it can only be assumed that the majority of western Irish farm women were the wives and daughters of western, usually Irish, farmers and that the census did not count them as being meaningfully engaged in anything.[12]

The neglect may also be owing to the incongruity of the pairing, which returns the discussion to literary convention. The women of those little prairie houses were not expected to host Irish wakes and dances, have pictures of the Sacred Heart on their walls, contribute money to the cause of Ireland free, or march as a column to Mass to receive sacramental grace and communion with saints. To understate considerably, Irish Catholics on western American farms and ranches and in the villages that served those enterprises are not a historical image that comes trippingly to mind. The western heart of America not only belonged to the palesmen, it defined them as such. They, not Irish Catholics, were the giants in the earth. German or Norwegian accents were acceptable, but Hiberno-English was not so much an accent as a discordant noise, or, as in the case of Turner, an inaudible one.

It is past time to make that voice audible. Listen to some of Minnesota's township names: Graceville, Kilkenny, Kildare, Clontarf, Tyrone, Derrynane, Cashel, Dublin, Tara, Shieldsville, Croke, Erintown, Lismore, and Parnell. Added to that list would be "disguised" Irish villages like Belle Plaine, Jessenland, Faxon, Hollywood, and Cloquet. To Minnesota's rural Irish clusters should be added Beaver Island, Michigan; Emmetsburg, Imogene, Kinross, Salix, Coggan, Garryowen, and Melrose, Iowa; Emmett, Walshtown, Egan, and Garryowen, South Dakota; Milligan, Kelly, Jackson, O'Neill, and Parnell, Nebraska; Cleveland, New Mexico; Shonkin, Helmville, Philipsburg, Garryowen, and Charlo, Montana; a variety of ranches and sheep stations in Lake, Harney, and Morrow Counties, Oregon; and dozens of other small towns scattered about the West. Some of these villages mixed commercial fishing, logging, or mining with agricultural economies—they were like rural

Ireland in that regard. The important point is that these semirural enclaves were as Irish as the Chicago of Mr. Dooley or Studs Lonigan, although both of those fictional Irishmen would have found the physical environment of Milligan, Nebraska, or Shonkin, Montana, as alien as the dark side of the moon. Unfortunately, few of these rural Irish outposts had a *seanchaí*, no storyteller like Melrose's Leo Ward, who could remember and keep memorable the Irish worlds that were made in these most unlikely places.[13]

Where the Irish were is clear enough. That brings up the next and more historically important question: why did they go to these places? The Irish did not wander aimlessly into their western neighborhoods; they were drawn to them. Knowing something of what drew them does not provide a perfect or even an imperfect understanding of these Irish. It only permits a conversation with them. This one will be about choices, about why they went to certain parts of the West, together with a few brief and random comments about why they did not go to other parts.

The directors of All Hallows College provided a proper beginning for this discussion when they identified the first principle of exile: it was one of God's more mysterious gifts to the Irish, not just that they might establish the "Irish empire" but that they might never be without friends. Though they were "dispersed over the whole globe," said an AHC priest, "*they are still united.*" They were connected to their enclaves; and their enclaves, however distant and movable, were connected to each other. The Irish were clustered even when physically remote from one another. These millions of Irish, said the directors of All Hallows, continued to look to Ireland, "and in the only, holy, catholic, and apostolic faith they had received from her do they find *a bond of union* stronger than death!" Allowing for its melodramatic excess and its more wishful than descriptive nature, that remark must be granted special status.[14]

Gathered exiles, rather than having no home, were always at home. That was particularly true of gathered Irish Catholic exiles. Physically, home was in Ireland and they did not live there, but they also lived in their Catholicity. The issue was not where they were but with whom. Home was less a geographical concept than a social one. Thus the first principle of the "Irish Catholic in exile" was that Irish Catholics went first to where the Catholics were, later—and as a result— to where the Irish Catholics were. That was a piece of the western Irish immigration pattern that, like most of the other pieces, revealed a great deal of the whole. And the Irish had plenty of western places from which to choose. In 1880 Catholicism was first in church membership in eighteen of the twenty-three states of the West, in second place in three others. The entire West was the second most Catholic region in America; parts of the West were the most Catholic in all of America. In 1886 Josiah Strong feared that papists might one day fill the West; it was too late. Catholics were not filling the West; they had already filled it.

Whether "diasporic" or "transnational," the Irish were part of a movable nation. This gave rise to the Irish bull that "the only place in Ireland where a man can make a [living] is in America." But even that fabled bit of sensible nonsense was slightly misleading, which leads to another general point regarding patterns of migration and settlement. Except in a technical sense, the Irish did not come from Ireland. They came from townlands, from all of the "little platoons" of the island they shared. Mickey MacGowan's wanderings through western America's mining country have been recounted; his "great wheel of life" had carried him from Cloghaneely in Donegal to Pennsylvania to Montana to the Yukon and Klondike and then back to Donegal. He covered almost as much ground as William O'Brien. For the moment, however, consider only the following: MacGowan knew he was Irish, but when he spoke of "my people" his reference was to his small part of a somewhat larger part of a county-sized part of Ireland. He described a time in the 1890s when he returned to the mines of Granite, Montana, "even though the chances were that there wouldn't be any work for me there." That was beside the point. Granite "was where my friends were—men from Cloghaneely. . . . It was that more than anything else that drove me back to the mines." Maybe that was why he and his friends "didn't get rich quick." They had learned well the advice of the "old people" of Cloghaneely: "'Wherever the world is heading, head the other way.'"[15]

It is the case that doing so produced mostly head-on collisions. Heading the other way was outlandish—or at least irrational. But MacGowan made clear why being among friends counted for so much. The "one gift . . . my people had . . . was [the] friendship and charity among them; they helped one another in work and in trouble, in adversity and in pain and it was that neighbourliness which, with the grace of God, was the solid stanchion of their lives." All of this was spoken in Irish; words like "friendship," "charity," "neighborliness," and "my people" take on meanings that English cannot capture. I think it likely that Thomas O'Donnell spoke only part of the truth when he said he would move west if someone would give him the money. He would also have wanted to know where all of his "friends" had gone and exactly how he might find them. That did not mean where those from Ireland were. Given his surname, O'Donnell was almost surely from somewhere in County Donegal. So would his friends have been.[16]

But that raises a question. Someone (or someones) had to have jump-started the process by getting to a place first. And exiles would seem to be unlikely pioneers; the one role contradicts the other. There is strong evidence, however, that these trail-blazing Celts traveled in the company of other Irish; their second and subsequent dockings were closer to massed gate crashings than to solitary wanderings. But what were the other selection criteria of these out-of-the-ordinary pioneers and of those who followed their lead? Among the 5,000 immigrant letters that Kerby Miller uncovered was one by an obscure Irishman by the surname of O'Callaghan who was writing back to Ireland from America in 1883. O'Callaghan had some advice for others in his Irish home village who were considering emigration. "This America is not what it used to be," he warned, and "any person who can make a fair living at home are better Stay theire."[17]

I have always been taken by that comment, to the point that I am prepared to make it say far more than O'Callaghan ever intended and despite the fact that I do not know what he meant by "*this* America" or if he had an accurate idea of what America used to be. I do not even know from what place in America he was writing. As with Mary Brown's "love and liberty" comment, it is not the practical lessons O'Callaghan's letter contained but the words he chose to express it that most interest me. The phrase "make a fair living" should be read literally, because the Irish meant it as "make a fair life." O'Callaghan did not say "get a good job." More was involved than employment. I cannot know why he used the word "fair," or whether he intended it in its multiple meanings. The Irish language has a different word for each of those meanings, but in English "fair" could mean impartial, just, passable, respectable, dignified, decent, not excessive, about average, even pleasing to the eye. He may have meant all of those things. But being around friends was a necessary part of each.

O'Callaghan's reference to America not being what it used to be is trickier to interpret—or read into. Historical context provides some clues. By 1883 America had already "taken off." The market revolution was over; to no one's great surprise, the forces of free markets won. There is no arguing with Kerby Miller's assessment. America, Miller writes, had a "generally-expanding but highly unstable, ruthlessly competitive, and even physically brutal industrial economy. Financial panics and crippling economic depressions were common, and skilled as well as unskilled emigrants suffered grievously at such times." I would add that workers were not supposed to suffer at all, at least for long, and never long enough to grow mutinous. The "myth of concern" in the service of this industrial economy held that access to the western frontier would relieve the suffering and steady and reinvigorate the economy. By 1883 that promise had been exposed as a nineteenth-century urban legend, an invention that served only "the class that produced it." But it had been exposed as such only to those paying very close attention, and their voices were seldom heard and never heeded.[18]

It is possible, however, that O'Callaghan was persuaded that the myth of concern had once been true and that this now-vanished America had been a place of magical frontiers where the chance to make a fair living was substantially improved by all that open ground to the west of almost anywhere one happened to be. He likely had not been in America very long and thus may be forgiven for not knowing that the one he thought was lost had, in fact, never been. It was entirely coincidental, but O'Callaghan's letter was written the same year that O'Donnell was explaining to a congressional committee that the only way he could take advantage of "free" land in the West would be if someone would give him the $1,500 it would cost to take him there.

For working-class Irish, the worst part of the industrial economy was its "highly unstable" aspect. History had treated them roughly, and instability was all that many of them had ever known, both in Ireland and in America. They had grown mightily weary of it. It was not a fair way to have to live. The result was Irish anxiety and self-doubt, and the consequences of both were profound. They are also impossible to measure, but at that I believe the Irish must be counted among the most insecure of America's immigrants. If they spent longer in the working class than other immigrant groups—and they did—it was because they had learned that becoming rich meant risking becoming poor; it was better to find steady work and become and stay respectably not-poor. Eugene O'Neill said that the Irish learned early "'the value of a dollar and the fear of the poorhouse.'" Particularly an American poorhouse: as an Irish immigrant recalled upon returning to Ireland, "'there was always the fear that one might lose his position and become destitute, and destitution in America made life unbearable.'"[19]

The Irish did have a few options as they dealt with economic instability. As Edward Everett Hale and countless others made clear, they were an indispensable element in the American takeoff and in the industrialization and the formation of a working class that followed it. They were also the crude instruments of what passed as frontier conquests. That did not mean that they were gratefully received into the host society. At best, it gained for them a certain grudging tolerance—which was about all unskilled laborers could expect, whatever their nation of origin. One partial exception to that rule was particularly important among Irish in the West: the many thousands who had worked in the copper mines in Avoca in County Wicklow, Knockmahon in Waterford, and Beara in Cork. These Irish were used to the pace and rhythms of working underground, usually for large corporations. Beginning in the 1850s, thousands of experienced hard-rock men, particularly from Beara, made their way to the copper mines of Michigan's Upper Peninsula and to every hard-rock gold, silver, and copper mining camp from California to Arizona to the Black Hills of South Dakota. Once in place, they established an Irish presence that served as an informal recruiting office, attracting thousands of other Irish. Most of these later arrivals were not experienced miners; they would be tutored by the "practical" Irish miners who had come before them. They learned quickly.

Their capital city was Butte—which was probably better known in West Cork than Dublin was. With the exception of the Cornish, the Irish had a greater familiarity with shaft mining than anyone on earth. They went west and took jobs in the mines because they already knew how to get rocks out of the ground or because they were Irish and were eligible for admission to the Irish "trade schools," with the "classes" in mining conducted in Hibernia Halls. It was said that a hard-rock miner aboveground was just another unskilled digger. That mattered little. Once they went underground, they became essential commodities and were in great demand. A quite finite number of men were comfortable using hammers, drills, and explosives thousands of feet below the surface. The Irish among them were part of a natural aristocracy of labor; that was not a status they had anywhere else. It was also not one that they would keep; the use of power drills turned them into unskilled diggers and haulers who happened to be underground.[20]

More than most, the Irish wanted to be depression-proof, or as close to it as they could get. That meant either government work—usually local—or jobs with the largest and most economically invulnerable corporations they could find. They did not become policemen because they had a particular fondness for guns and cudgels. They did not join fire departments because they were uncommonly adept at using hooks and ladders. They did not dig canals and build roads because they preferred or only knew how to use tools with long handles. A fair living required them to find work that was steady through good times and bad. Police and fire departments provided steady work, probably more of it in bad times than good. As for America's roads, not only were they not paved with gold, they were not paved at all and were frequently pockmarked with potholes—so named because they were of the same size and shape as the holes dug in the dirt floors of Irish cabins to hold the potato pot. Add to the presumed steadiness of these jobs the fact that so many of their friends were at the job site; Irish took jobs in the Butte mines, for example, because there were so many Irish in the Butte mines—which turns the question into a tautological one.

As for the Irish dominance of the western army, let me add at the outset that they did not enlist so that they might become white men by the simple expedient of killing those known as red men. The Irish joined because they were poor and the poor always fight a nation's wars, particularly, it would seem, wars of aggression against others poorer even than themselves. Irishmen understood that a willingness to do hard or dangerous labor was enough to guarantee that someone would always ask them to do it. They never had the fields entirely to themselves—although the 5,000-plus of them who made up half of the western army came close. The point is that the physical brutality of the work was what made it so steady—and by every accounting, western workplaces were more physically brutal than those elsewhere in America. The Irish did not go west to escape the rigors of the eastern economy. They went west hoping to escape the insecurities of the eastern economy.

The key was finding and hanging onto steady work. In 1914 Cornelius (Con) Kelley, the boss of Butte's giant Anaconda Copper Mining Company, the son of Irish immigrants, and a former hard-rock miner, told the same Industrial Commission that would later hear from William O'Brien that "when a man obtains a job underground it is a very steady position if he takes care of it." Kelley spoke also of the "very large floating population coming in and going out at Butte": "they can get employment, but they don't remain; they are floating." Kelley was not just speaking as a corporate head. This was a lesson he knew from his own experience. Kelley's assurance was not sufficient to satisfy a consummate floater like O'Brien; the Anaconda boss was talking to and about an entirely different constituency. On one occasion in his testimony Kelley even strongly suggested that Butte's miners enjoyed a special status by virtue of their willingness to take on the dangers of going underground. There was a manliness, even a certain heroism, to being a hard-rock man.[21]

Kelley made a few remarks about the dangers of the work, about serious injury and miners' consumption, but said nothing about the effects those hazards had on steady work. He knew that the work was steady precisely because it was unsafe and that it was comparatively well paid and respected for the same reason. If the dangers were to be removed, the Irish would lose their preferred position in the labor force; if the work were suddenly to become safe, anyone could do it. But Kelley also said nothing about the Anaconda Company's adoption of power drills, its increasing reliance on southern and eastern European workers, or its not so gentle reminder to grumblers in the workforce that there were "a dozen men waiting to take [their] jobs." He was not asked about the matter, but I doubt he would have had any comment on the Butte Irish miners' insistence that the "Finns drove us out of Michigan and other places. They are not going to drive us out of Butte."[22]

In 1890 the Census Bureau, in a masterful understatement, complained that "natives of the countries which have contributed the largest numbers to our foreign born population are distributed very unevenly over the United States." It was not referring only to the Irish, but the description—or complaint—certainly applied to them. Regardless of whether the bureau was unhappy about it or not, there was no mystery to this uneven distribution. The Irish avoided areas that were hostile to them or to their faith. Their experiences in the East had taught them hard lessons, including staying away from areas with "No Irish Need Apply" signs. Indeed, one wonderfully ironic and quite unintended consequence of the takeoff and the passage of the Republic was that the job notices on eastern factory walls that excluded the Irish, when added to the rhetorical excesses of the eastern nativists who would save the West from Romanism, served mostly to increase the number of Romanists in the West. Escaping prejudice is not routinely listed as one of the reasons for going west, but it should be.[23]

It was also, of course, a factor in determining where they would go once they got there. Butte provided the model—guaranteed employment in an extended Irish neighborhood. A nativist organization even complained that "No English Need Apply" signs were posted on the hiring offices of some of the largest mines. But there was only one Butte. Generally, Irish went to cities and mining camps, to the smelters and packing houses and quarries and rail yards, because they would face no job discrimination—they would not be driven out. They would, in fact, be left free to drive out the non-Irish. This was the one big reason they did not go to Oklahoma, Arkansas, or Texas or, in numbers, to Missouri. In Arkansas and Texas and to a lesser extent in Oklahoma and Missouri, a black underclass was in place. The Irish did not like anyone who might challenge their job security. In this sense, they were racist and ethnocentric—or at least intolerant, defensive, and acutely race conscious. Intolerance, however, does not explain their settlement patterns; nervousness does.

It also explains another and conspicuous empty spot on the map of the western American Irish: Mormon-dominated Utah. From 1850 to 1910 the census turned up only one county in Utah with a significant percentage of Irish. That one exception was Summit County, which contained the mining camp of Park City. In 1910 first- and second-generation Irish were 12 percent of the immigrant/ethnic population of the county. The British (English, Scots, and Welsh) made up 52 percent. Add to that the well-developed policy of Utah mine and smelter owners to work through padrones and hire contract laborers, particularly Greeks, Italians, and Japanese. It is also the case that the Irish did not like Mormons, in part because the Mormons did not like Catholics. Mormonism arose in the 1830s and 1840s out of the ferment of the Second Great Awakening and the modern project that accompanied it. Only the latter half of that mix of piety and profits, of moralism and modernity, was well disposed toward Irish Catholics. Indeed, the Book of Mormon declared the Catholic Church "the mother of harlots." To understate considerably, the Irish did not find Utah congenial. They did not go there if they could help it and did not stay there any longer than they had to.[24]

Urban or rural, industrial or agricultural, the Irish did not go west, Thoreau-like, because "westward they went free." Neither did they light out for the territories. They did not go to escape society; they went to remain connected to their narrow version of it. The West itself was not unimportant in their choice of western homes; neither was the western myth. They knew the stories, had heard of the fabled promised lands. It was impossible to live anywhere in America and not know something—whether true or not—about America's great frontier. What distinguished the Irish was their response to the stories. They had more reasons than most to want to leave the East, but taming a wild West, building nations, and making fortunes were not among them. The western Irish were simply building lives. They would leave the heroics to others. That establishes one other similarity between the urban and the rural western Irish: those in Melrose, Iowa, and those in Butte were both out of place. The West was intended for more expansive dreamers. By American standards, a fair living was a pinched and petty dream.

What the Irish knew of the West they learned from a variety of sources, all of them made available by a "gift" from the British. In 1831 the imperial government established the system of National Schools in Ireland. The Irish children who attended them began each school day by reciting the following ditty:

> I thank the goodness and the grace
> That on my birth have smiled;
> And made me in these Christian days
> A happy English child.

Happy English children did not use the Irish language—were, in fact, taught that it was a barbaric remnant. Their songs were about the English and in English. Songs were followed by lessons in which the Irish pupils learned about the Welsh— "a remarkably clean, active, industrious people; their houses and persons are very neat"; about the Scots—"a steady, industrious people, and schools . . . universal among them"; and about themselves, the Irish—"a clever, lively people; formerly, very much given to drink, and very ignorant . . . it will be their own fault if they are not . . . educated." The English had brought these three together and given them, as the school lessons had it, "one and the same language (all at least who are educated)." The rates for Irish literacy in English suggest that most of the Irish were "educated"; as they would have put it, they had the English.[25]

Ironically, forcing the Irish to reject their native language and learn that of their conquerors did not make them more likely Britons; it made them more likely Americans. They would use the English to read about America. After all, as one national schoolmaster told his pupils, "'that's where the most of ye will be going.'" That was certainly true, although apparently not important enough for the school system to spend much time on the topic. From their schoolbooks they learned only that "the United States are partly wild, full of forests, mountains, and lakes; partly flat and cultivated. The inhabitants are of British descent, and all speak English. The principal towns are New York, Boston, and Philadelphia— all in the eastern or cultivated states." They and their parents learned little more from Vere Foster's *Work and Wages, or the Penny Emigrant's Guide to the United States and Canada,* a quarter-million copies of which were distributed in Ireland by the British government. Foster wrote only of work in areas already "cultivated." He said nothing about western land, crop yields, and commodities markets; nothing about the bracing climate of the prairies and the plains; and certainly nothing of gold–paved streets in El Dorado. Had Philip Bagenal really cared about the Irish cluttering up the eastern cities and turning them into hotbeds of Irish nationalism, he should have brought his concerns to the attention of the National School Board and men like Vere Foster. The Irish were being trained to be Americans, but obviously not to be western American farmers.[26]

That same selectivity was true of the gazettes, that uniquely American contribution to early advertising campaigns. These massive volumes describing western America contained nothing overtly hostile to the Irish, but neither did they contain anything that might have encouraged an Irish land rush, even had it been possible. Many of these gazettes, moreover, were written by quite partisan Republicans; it would be naive to think that there was not also a subtext. Catholic churches dotting the landscape were not part of the West's self-image or of the image the land promoters wished to construct. The assumptions, then as later, were that the Irish did not want to farm and did not know how to farm. As noted, these were false assumptions, at least at a functional level. The Irish did want to farm and they did know how, but they wanted to farm the Irish way and only knew how to farm that way, which meant in close proximity to other Irish farmers and on a small scale on well-watered ground that had been plowed before.[27]

American land promoters targeted certain Europeans—Scandinavians and ethnic Germans in particular. They did not target Irish, partly because so few Irish had the means to buy their product but partly, too, because they were thought unfit to make productive use of it. Moreover, even the promoters' generic appeals would have had little effect on an Irish audience. Many of those appeals—to understate—stretched the truth. That in itself would not have been enough for the Irish to ignore them, but the nature of those untruths and what they implied about those who told them might have. In particular, the promoters' argument that plowing the soil was increasing the rainfall in the semiarid regions would have struck the Irish as nonsensical. The idea that "by man's mastery over nature, the clouds are dispensing copious rains" and that the plow "is the instrument which separates civilization from savagery" was a supreme arrogance, lacking all fairness, regardless of how defined. It was impossible to convince a people whose remembered pasts included watching helplessly as their potatoes rotted in the ground of "man's mastery over nature"—or over much else. The Irish were not likely readers of Josiah Strong, but they were familiar enough with his type. Had they known he was of the same moonstruck opinion regarding increasing rainfall, I suspect they would have been amused but not surprised; in Strong's country, palesmen had command over everything, even the clouds.[28]

If the Irish were going to read anything useful about the West, both its farms and its jobs, they would have to rely on accounts written by other Irish and specifically for them. They had a fair sampling from which to choose. Edward Everett Hale's *Letters on Irish Emigration* was, of course, intended for American readers, but it was known in Ireland. Any Irish who might have chanced upon it—once they had cut through Hale's overt bigotry—would at least have known a job was waiting. Thomas D'Arcy McGee's *Catholic History of North America* (1855) and *History of the Irish Settlers in North America* (1852) would have guided most of the second boats to Canadian ports, although they contained some information on the United States and considerable support for massed Irish Catholic colonies. Of the purely American guidebooks written for an Irish audience, the first was the Reverend John O'Hanlon's *The Irish Emigrant's Guide for the United States* (1851). Others followed: Jeremiah O'Donovan's *Irish Immigration in the United States* (1864), John Francis Maguire's *The Irish in America* (1868), the Reverend Thomas Butler's *The Irish on the Prairies and Other Poems* (1874), and Hugh Quigley's *The Irish Race in California and the Pacific Coast* (1878) were also intended for the Irish—or at least for a certain class of Irish.

These books were not precisely gazettes; they were more nearly extended and random observations on life in America. O'Hanlon, in fact, specifically warned potential immigrants that the gazettes were little more than "cheap tracts" filled with false promises of the "stranger find[ing] a welcome, the exile a country, . . . the laborer employment . . . the landless a farm." The Irish might well have wondered what else mattered for poor exiles than friends, jobs, and land. Despite O'Hanlon's reference to the landless finding a farm, however, he also wrote encouragingly—and falsely—of the farming prospects in western America and urged his "countrymen" who had to emigrate to "direct [their] course to the West." But for those who had a choice, O'Hanlon offered the reminder that "friendly relationships" in Ireland brought more "positive enjoyments" (read "fair living") than that "Model Republic," that "Land of Liberty" across the sea. O'Hanlon's summary was slightly mocking, but his point was strictly Irish: liberty and republicanism were no substitute for friends and fairness.[29]

O'Donovan's book was basically a primer on Irish American political insurgency. It was intended for Irish exiles, for those "millions, not thousands, of my countrymen," according to O'Donovan, who had somehow escaped being "either starved, hanged, or decapitated by remorseless villains who were sent across the channel by the most repacious [*sic*], unfeeling, ungodly and cruel government that has been established in any civilized or savage country under the canopy of Heaven." That would have gotten an Irish reader's attention. Among those countrymen he counted "constellations of scientific men, emitting the purest effulgence in the firmament of science." That raises an issue: O'Donovan's entire book is filled with language like that, and it may be fairly asked if even the National Schools had prepared the Irish for "canopy," "firmament," and "effulgence." What degree of literacy in English would have been required to understand O'Donovan, and would those Irish who could in fact make sense of his ornate prose have been interested in America, East or West?[30]

Maguire's book would have been no less a challenge to read—and was only slightly less angry and denunciatory. But from Maguire even more than from O'Hanlon, the Irish would have learned of western America, of its huge expanse of available lands and its clear superiority over the East as the ultimate immigrant destination. Maguire knew his audience well. "The first and pressing necessity . . . to the poor or the plundered Irish . . . was employment." But there had also to be "old friends . . . to . . . [meet] with" and the "'chapel [had to be] handy,' 'a Christian [shouldn't] be overtaken for want of a priest.'" All of this and more could be found among "the trees of the virgin forest . . . nodding their branches in friendly invitation, and the blooming prairie expanse" with "its fruitful bosom." Unfortunately, the trees nodded and the prairies bloomed without stirring an Irish response. The "Irish peasant," scolded Maguire, the "man of the spade, the plough, and the barrow," had this "pernicious tendency" to "rush . . . headlong into the great cities," there to "adopt a mode of livelihood for which he is not suited by previous knowledge or training, and to place himself in a position dangerous to his morals, if not fatal to his independence." Maguire's next state-ment sounds like something from Bagenal: "there is no excuse whatever for [the Irish peasant] to remain in the cities of America, crowding and blocking them up . . . when the rudest hut in the midst of a forest, the loneliest cabin on the prairie would be a palace" compared to the fetid tenements of the East.[31]

Butler's 180-page book of poetry belongs in this discussion—not, certainly, because of the worth of his poems, which were at best cloying, but because he intended them for both Irish American and Irish readers. Some of what he included in this collection had been previously published in the *Nation*, a Dublin maga-zine of advanced nationalist views. He obviously was well acquainted with the exile trope; his poems had titles like "The Friends Whom I Loved Long Ago," "My Lovely Isle, Adieu!" and "Farewell Dear Land!" But he was writing from Leavenworth, Kansas, and his collection included verses such as "Gazing Westward" and "O, Lovely Land!" as well as the title poem. Butler thought Kansas a proper Irish home, but he knew better than Maguire that lonely prairie cabins were not only not better than palaces: they were not better than the friendly cabins of Ireland. It was, Butler wrote, "far sweeter to follow old customs, and live like our fathers of old, / Than wander a stranger midst peoples, and die in the struggle for gold." "No music is heard in our shanty, no music is heard on the plain, / No music amidst the wild forests, where silence and solitude reign." The Ameri-can plains were bleak, flat, and unchanging; nobody "walketh to Mass," and Butler "miss[ed] the bright streamlets of peasants." "Mayhap in the future, beside this lone home in the West, / Some heart-broken exiles of Erin may seek for a shelter and rest." This future would see that "a New Ireland of beauty and pow'r shall have grown." Until then, until new Irish had "plant[ed] all the joys of 'the Old Land' amidst / the bright scenes of 'the New,'" the Irish should either stay home or come prepared to live without "the heart's music . . . [they] heard in the years long ago!"[32]

Quigley's eight-hundred-page volume was closer in spirit and purpose to Maguire's than to Butler's. It offered all the evidence any Irish could want of the truth of Maguire's claims—and without the rude huts and lonely cabins. An ordained priest who came to America in 1848 and spent many years in New York, Quigley was better known for his three novels than for his guidebook, but there was a natural sequence to his work; his fictionalized accounts of Protestant bigotry and Irish obsequiousness and apostasy in eastern America nicely contrasted with California's sturdy and pious defenders of what Quigley called the "Celtico-Roman" spirit. The Anglo-Saxons were no match for these Celtico-Romans—nor was Anglo-Saxonism any more foolish than Celtico-Romanism. *The Irish Race in California* contained chapters on Irish statesmen, capitalists, military men, clergymen, journalists, and doctors, all of them rich but still Irish—which was no easy thing—and all living witnesses to the "terrestrial paradise" they had found under "the Pacific skies." No wonder that the Irish "seldom or never return to the East after having pitched their tents under the glorious skies of California."[33]

It is impossible to know how many Irish trusted all or any of these sources or how many headed west expecting to find "terrestrial paradises." But raising that issue introduces another important point. The Irish just quoted were writing for and to the people in Ireland. Maguire was from Ireland and had come to America as a visitor. Butler's poetic lamentations were intended as a warning; certainly they were not likely to cheer any already exiled to Kansas. But what of those whose exile took them only to New York or Boston? Given their limited resources—both financial and psychological—it may safely be presumed that most of the immigrant Irish in the West had made previous stops in other parts of America and that what they knew of western America they had learned in America. Emigrating was adventure enough for the moment; going west would have to wait.

The *Irish Nation,* one of New York's Irish American newspapers, reported on the arrival of all of the immigrant ships carrying Irish passengers and on the ultimate destinations of those Irish. Perhaps two in a hundred said they were headed into the American interior; only slightly more indicated that they were leaving New York at all. One ship docked in early December of 1881, and some of its Irish were heading directly from New York to San Francisco; Doylestown, Wisconsin; Dubuque, Walnut, and Walton, Iowa; and Portland, Oregon. The *Irish Nation,* however, signaled the ship's arrival with a special headline; these few were not to be counted among the usual huddled Irish masses but as "Exiles of Erin Seeking a Home under the Stars and Stripes." For most, however, finding that home under western stars would have to wait. The very idea of a California, as far from New York City as Ireland itself, was not something easily grasped.[34]

But while they waited, they listened and learned—and acclimated. Wherever they were in America, there would have been talk and stories of a fabled West.

The more savvy of them would have known that there were some significant differences between the lived West and the storied one. "Becoming American," in this instance as in others, meant becoming aware that America's tall tales were often carefully crafted and that they had to be read with skepticism. That said, the Irish would have learned from these stories something of what they would have to do to get to the West, the number and type of transports, the transfer stations, and the unfathomable distances. Fortunately, they were not unused to migration. Their passages to America did not commence at the docks of Liverpool or Queenstown and did not end at Castle Garden or Ellis Island. It was door to door, often cabin door to tenement door, but the point is that all Irish-Americans were multiboat immigrants; there were a lot of middle passages, even for those who barely crossed to the west side of the East River and never saw the west side of the Hudson. They knew where the West was and knew how to get there. They even knew—or thought they knew—something of what life was like there.

None of this was unique to the Irish immigrant experience. Neither was this next point—except for the significance that they attached to it. If at all possible, the Irish were not going anywhere that did not have a resident—and Irish—Catholic priest. In their "western selection process," nothing was more important. MacGowan spoke for the vast majority—and said more than he knew—when he reminisced about "life without a priest" in the Klondike. There were "a couple of things," he explained, "that we never got used to at all. What we Irishmen found hardest to bear was the lack of a priest. . . . No matter where we were, we tried not to miss Mass, if it was at all possible. We often walked ten miles for it." Even without a priest, the Irish miners did not work on Sundays, and on those days when they could not "hear Mass, a crowd . . . would get together in one of the cabins and say the Rosary—and say it heartfully." So crowded was the cabin that latecomers knelt outside—which reminded MacGowan of "home . . . for I frequently saw people kneeling outside the door of the church in Gotahork in the same way." By the time he was about to leave the area, "a priest had come to live among us." It happened to be an Irish priest, which made this doubly good news; the miners "raised enough money . . . to build a small wooden chapel; and we built for the priest a cabin like one of our own."[35]

To repeat, Catholicism was not the sole source of Irish identity; in fact, Mac-Gowan followed the story of life without a priest with an account of St. Patrick's Day in the Klondike. It was not an event marked by a particular piety. It is also relevant that the longer they worked in America the more many of the Irish began to think of themselves as workers who were Irish rather than Irish who worked. But either way, Catholicism was part of both their ethnic and their social-class identities. The church's presence meant that the spiritual requirements of these Irish set to wandering could be met, but a Catholic church and its *sagart* (resident priest) were also evidence that the areas to which they wandered were not overrun by nativists and that those who were in the vicinity could be dealt with effectively. The priest was the defender of the oppressed and one of the few who could speak the truth to power. The point is not that the Irish had some kind of childlike and absolute faith in their clergy and followed them blindly. That was a nativist canard. Rather, they came from a place where priests were among their most important friends.[36]

The Irish needed to know if a particular place had a church, but it was an added bonus if they could hear what the church had to say about that place—which returns the discussion to the missionary priests of All Hallows College. Their letters back to Drumcondra were solemn and filled with self-righteous lamentations; the college turned out a number of young men who were almost as sepulchral as the Protestant minister who stole John O'Reilly. That earnestness, however, made them particularly effective chroniclers of Irish life anywhere in America. When they took up their posts in western America, their piety—that uniquely Irish mixture of expatriation, martyrdom, and devotional Catholic gloominess—created a historian's dream: their task was to bring Ireland to the exiles, not themselves to be exiled. Neither were they emigrants; they were always going to return home. Who better to describe the Irish world beyond the American pale? They were like friends on call—somewhat melancholy friends, to be sure, but the Irish were used to that.

The annual reports of the college were themselves gazettes of a sort, although far more believable even than those published by the Irish for the Irish. The letters from the priestly field officers doing the heavy work of advancing the "Irish Catholic empire" made up most of those reports, and they were filled with information about America's prospects and America's dangers. I grant that the letters back to Ireland were published only in the *Annals* of the college and read by few. Those few, however, would have included priests in both Ireland and eastern America, and it is reasonable to assume that the reports found their way into everything from homilies to casual conversations, from speeches to newspaper accounts. Those reports from the borderlands come as close as anything we have to forming a kind of composite Irish portrait of western America. For all of these reasons and doubtless others, the college's priests were key players in determining the migration and settlement patterns of the diasporic Irish, wherever found. AHC had more to do with the uneven distribution of those Irish than anyone could have known.

It was the job of these "pious and zealous priests" to save Irish "souls from infidelity and perdition." Infidelity, however, had a dual meaning. Irish Catholics were at least as interested in the Irishness of their clergy as they were in their denominational robes. The exiled flocks were Irish as well as Catholic; shepherding them had an ethnic and national aspect as well as a doctrinal one. All Hallows understood the distinction. By way of obvious example, the Hispanic Catholic presence was established in California and the entire American Southwest; ecclesiastical institutions were in place, as they were in other sections of the West. There were too few of them to meet the needs of all the Catholics (of whatever ethnic origin) who were chasing after gold, but that was not the only problem. Trouble arose because these institutions were run by non-Irish ecclesiastics.[37]

This is not an issue of Irish ethnic intolerance. The matter is less laden with sinister meaning. Part of the problem for the Irish was that the French, Spanish, Italian, German, Belgian, and particularly Mexican priests already resident in the West spoke a highly accented English—if they spoke any English at all. The Irish could not understand what they were saying, and that was not unimportant. I am not arguing that language barriers were all that divided Irish Catholics from their non-Irish co-religionists. That would suggest a measure of Irish tolerance that never existed. Tribalism was never far from the Irish response to anything in America—East or West. Non-English-speaking priests could still provide the sacraments. They were Catholic enough. But they were not Irish at all, which meant, at one level, that they were not sufficiently devotional and knew nothing of exile, nothing of "perfidious Albion" and of Brits behaving badly. But at a more important level, they were simply not the right people. The word *muintir* would have to be explained to them—as would their ineligibility for admission to it. The Irish, as the St. Patrick's Benefit Society of Marysville told Father Eugene O'Connell, wanted AHC to send "priests [and nuns] of our race and kindred, acquainted with our manners and habits."[38]

Principal among those manners and habits was the Irish insistence that they were the exiled sons and daughters of Erin. This idea, whether an artificially contrived "motif" or a reasonable explanation of what had happened to them, significantly increased the importance of having Irish clergy to serve Irish immigrants. Exile as constructed motif required constant reinforcement. The Irish needed to be reminded that they had not emigrated but rather had been set to wandering, and not just from Ireland to America but within America. As noted, the directors of All Hallows were as confused and contradictory as the Irish in general when it came to fixing responsibility for Irish leave-taking. Were the Irish driven into exile or did they emigrate? More than semantics is involved. But whether emigrants or exiles, the overwhelming majority of Irish did not disassociate themselves from Ireland; they remained affiliated—displaced and misplaced Irish.

It is in this context that I interpret the significant number of letters from missions in the American West noting—quite disapprovingly, it should be added—that the Irish wanted their priests to be orators, not theologians. Eugene O'Connell complained that "every . . . swagger[ing] . . . talker and spouter, whether of sense or nonsense, is look'd upon as a luminary all thru this country." If they "hadn't the gift of the gab they wouldn't be thought anything about in this 'land of the free.'"

O'Connell's remarks could be interpreted in a variety of ways, but swaggering, spouting, and gabbing about what? Those references plus his semisarcastic allusion to America as the land of the free suggest that he thought the Irish wanted patriotic and Anglophobic priests rather than thoughtful and doctrinally sound ones. Theologically sophisticated homilies on redemptive suffering might do in Ireland; they would not do among the exiles of Erin or even among Irish immigrants determined to progress.[39]

That did not change even after the "exile motif" became a less important part of the Irish and Irish American patriot games. All Hallows trained non-Irish priests for the foreign missions, but it sent only Irish priests to serve Irish communities. The college's *Annals* for 1862 contained the following passage that even the most ardent of Gallicans in France or elsewhere would have had difficulty matching: "It is from the midst of . . . spiritual destitution . . . that the Irish emigrant looks back on Ireland 'as the common centre and emporium of the faith.' . . . To this appeal . . . we cannot remain insensible. God forbid that our exiled countrymen should ever have to say of us: 'My kinsmen had forsaken me, and they that knew me have forgotten me.'" Ireland, not Rome, was the center of the faith; the exiles looked to their "kinsmen" not their co-religionists to remember them and provide them with spiritual direction. This was not a very catholic Catholicism, but the Irish were not a very catholic people.[40]

American churchmen knew this and seldom reproached them for their ethnic provincialism—probably because the other components of American Catholicism were only slightly less provincial. In 1853, almost a decade before AHC's emphasis on "kinsmen," Father Frederick Baraga, the non-Irish vicar apostolate of the Upper Peninsula of Michigan, wrote to All Hallows that he had been working among the "Chippewa . . . but in the year 1845, the copper-mines . . . began to be discovered" and workmen, "amongst whom there was always a good proportion from Ireland," began to arrive in numbers. On his last visit to the new settlements near Lake Superior, Baraga noted that he had "baptised no less than fifty-six new-born babes . . . chiefly Irish." His request was simple. "I wish very much . . . to find some good and zealous Irish Priests who would . . . labour for the salvation of thousands of abandoned souls of their own dear countrymen."[41]

Because abandonment could lead to apostasy, a real sense of urgency attached to requests like Baraga's. All Hallows reported that in the "wilds of Texas and the vast prairies of the Western States . . . were thousands of persons, descendants of Irish Catholics, who now belong to some of the innumerable sects which are found in America." That was bad enough. What made the situation worse was that these thousands would still be "Catholics, had their forefathers been followed to the land of their adoption by priests *from Ireland.*" Irish priests, and they alone, could have ensured "the propagation and preservation of the *faith of Ireland* among Ireland's children." The only question was which came first and attracted the other, the priests or the children.[42]

All Hallows priests stationed in western America understood that what brought the "large number of Irish Catholic families coming in every day was the hope . . . that a priest will reside among them and attend them as well as they are accustomed to be in the old country." "Many an exile," the directors reported, "was encouraged to emigrate by the knowledge" that "those who were still at home would send them priests; and shall we disappoint them?" Obviously they would not, but that raises a number of questions. What of all those discouraging reports of blighted landscapes, bone-jarring roads, sinful people, and rotten weather? Western lands without a Catholic church bred only John O'Reilly, Baptist minister, and that was a profanation. But a church on unproductive land bred only Catholic poverty and—though an improvement over Pastor O'Reilly—that was not something that rested easily on AHC's conscience. And what of the "Catholic empire," in the cause of which the emigrants—quite unknown to themselves— had been conscripted? This sectarian border war was being fought out on tough and unyielding terrain, and All Hallows meant that in both a physical and a spiritual sense. The myth of exile held that the Irish had no choice; they had to leave Ireland. But did they have to come to Marysville or any of its many western equivalents?[43]

Fortunately, by the 1860s and 1870s either the American West had begun to take on a more benign aspect or AHC had invented a more benign West. Father J. B. Miege, for example, a non-Irish AHC missionary in Kansas, noted as early as 1855 that keeping Irish as well as Catholic souls intact was "a great blessing," but he offered that commonplace in a letter asking that more Irish priests be sent out to help him then adding with undisguised pleasure that more Irish were bound for "our rich lands. . . . You can hardly find elsewhere a better and fairer field than Kansas and Nebraska." I think he used "fairer" for exactly the same reasons O'Callaghan and Cornelius Kelley would later use "fair" and "steady." As the West became more settled and "modern" and as good crop yields, particularly from the areas east of the semiarid zone, made their way to growing markets, some of the missionaries began to see and describe the West differently. They never quite became admen, never practiced the artful deceptions of the western land agents, but some did write letters back to Ireland informing the directors of the opportunities available in the areas to which they had been assigned. Some of their descriptions were overly sanguine.[44]

Eugene O'Connell may have complained of the near presence of Mormondom, the wickedness of the population, and the origins of the name "Marysville," but he also wrote that "the climate of this country is an excellent antidote against consumption" and "far superior" to Ireland's. "In fact, Doctors have been oblig'd to give up their profession and betake themselves to grazing or farming or mining." Given the Irish predisposition to tuberculosis (consumption) that report had to have had a particular appeal. O'Connell appears to have been the only All Hallows priest to contend that a climate might be superior to Ireland's, but he described

Oregon's climate as "similar"; and Iowa, Minnesota, and Nebraska, though admittedly cold and snowy, were also reported to be "most congenial to health" and to have "pleasanter weather than in any part of the U.S."[45]

More to the point of economic stability, Father John Curtis, writing from Omaha, specifically denied the existence of any "'Great American Desert,'" insisting that "this 'desert' is richer in fertility—undoubtedly—than many of the best cultivated lands of this great Continent." In another letter, Curtis, sounding a bit like William Gilpin, insisted that America's "boundless prairies" could "grow almost anything except tropical or semitropical fruits" and would "be sufficient to support all the people in Europe"—comments that might explain why the Union Pacific railroad gave him a free pass to travel anywhere along its line. Iowa formed another part of that boundless prairie and was at least as productive as Nebraska according to an 1867 report from John Hennessey, bishop of Dubuque. "In soil and climate," he wrote, "[it] is not surpassed by any state in the Union."[46]

Iowa's commercial prospects were no less encouraging. Chicago may have been "nature's metropolis," but Iowa was the most favored of Chicago's natural periphery areas and would in time come to have a few metropolises of its own. As Hennessey explained, Iowa was situated between the Mississippi and Missouri Rivers and "in a direct line between the great Territories of the West, such as Montana, Idaho, . . . whose mineral wealth is fabulous, and the Eastern markets." It already had "four lines of Railroads running east and west" and new lines would soon connect it to "the Gulf of Mexico. . . . The West being confessedly the best part of the country to make a fortune, some of the most enterprising and talented Americans and Europeans are to be met with in our towns and cities." Hennessey then told his superiors: "I send you this information for the benefit of any who may in future apply to you about [Iowa's] resources."[47]

It is hard to imagine that many of Ireland's poor would have been particularly taken by Curtis's promotion of Nebraska, but there is no question that the young graduate seminarians from All Hallows were among the forces drawing Irish into the West. Their reports worked a subtle change not in the definition of a "fair living" but in where and how one might be made. To return to a point made earlier, most of the Irish who made their way west had made intermediate stops in other parts of America. Their western dreaming was unconventional by American standards. It was less expansive and less filled with visions of conquest, more insistent on the primacy of friends and a fair living. But they did not totally ignore the Bonanza West and its outsized promises. Western fables were as much a part of the American culture code as exile was of their own. The hundreds of AHC priests wandering through the West were a part of the Irish adjustment to America—if not of America's adjustment to the Irish.

The same could be said of the directors and agents of the scores of Irish American colonization societies formed to bring the Catholic Irish out of captivity:

out of the cities and into America's great open western lands. All of the Irish gazetteers, particularly Thomas D'Arcy McGee, believed strongly in formally sponsored colonization; so did a diverse set of Irishmen from William Onahan in Chicago to Dillon O'Brien, John Sweetman, and James Shields in Minnesota to John O'Neill and Jeremiah Trecy in Nebraska, Thomas Francis Meagher in Montana, and Charles Collins in South Dakota. Their attempts to direct rather than merely influence the distribution of America's Irish have received a great deal of historical attention, and little needs to be added here. But a few aspects of these efforts at directed migration should be noted. The first is the primacy of the church in all of them; the second is the faintly Turnerian concepts of the role that western settlement was supposed to play as America took off into market capitalism—and then came down with a bad case of the postindustrializing blues.[48]

For an understanding of the first point, recall the plight of the unfortunate if fictitious John O'Reilly or the frequent complaints of the All Hallows priests that moving west meant moving beyond the influence of the church, with the loss of faith that occasionally followed. Colony organizers, many of whom were themselves Catholic clergymen, understood this perfectly. The most active of those prelates was Bishop John Ireland of St. Paul, Irish-born and determined to rescue his fellow Irish in America from their urban impoundment but with their Catholicism intact and well tended. Father Martin Mahoney's description of Bishop Ireland's blueprints for the construction of Irish colonies makes it clear that the bishop knew his potential recruits well. Mahoney was writing in 1885 from one of the many organized colonies in Minnesota, the Sweetman Catholic Colony in Murray County. His account of how the colonies were organized spoke to each of the friendly services that the priests could provide; it is an instructive list.

> In every colony which he founded Bishop Ireland invariably began by placing on the spot a priest whose duty it was to advise and help the colonists as well as to minister to their spiritual needs. Next he arranged for the erection of a church around which the life of the colony would center, and also for the building of an immigration house which would afford temporary accommodations for the families of settlers while they were selecting their farms.

The great fear of the priests and the colony developers was what Mahoney called the lure of "worldly inducement." A few worldly rewards would have been welcomed by most of the laity, but they also shared Mahoney's and Bishop Ireland's concern about "the total lack of provision for [the colonists'] spiritual wants."[49]

Fortunately, "the wonderful development of Catholicity in the West" had stilled those very real anxieties. Now it was possible for Catholics to have land "without loss, even with gain, to their religious interests." They could "get themselves homes among Catholic neighbors, and near and around a church with Mass . . . every Sunday and holyday, and indeed throughout the week . . . four miles from the colony . . . there is a fine convent . . . with a school and an academy." The reference to the convent, school, and academy was appropriate. It would be hard to imagine a better or more complete definition of a fair living and of the role of friends in the making of one. It would also be hard to imagine a prospect more frightening to nativists—or to the merely suspicious: a clustered and solely Catholic (and Irish) neighborhood, holy days, daily Mass, a convent, and most particularly a Catholic school and academy.[50]

It was not just the sponsored colonies that occasioned nativist anxieties. Irish "colonies" or enclaves arose almost organically. Gathered Irish attracted more Irish. No chartered and incorporated colonization company was required for the Irish to find one another and form a community. In the early 1880s, for example, "the undersigned resident Catholics of Summit Precinct, Dakota Co., Nebraska, respectfully ask[ed] your Lordship [by which they meant the vicar apostolic] for permission to build a Catholic Church . . . for our spiritual wants." Those wants included more than the solace of the sacraments. Patrick Twohig, who wrote the letter, explained that the petitioners, overwhelmingly Irish, had been in the area for more than twenty years and numbered more than 250 "souls," with "not 12 protestants in the whole district." This was the Irish Catholic version of the western paradise, a completely insular world inhabited only by friends.[51]

Put simply, the Irish collected and defined themselves around their parish. It drew them in and drew them close. The priests and nuns, and the church and school over which they presided, were the surest evidence that this was a fair and friendly place. The Irish could not make a church, but the absence of a church could unmake them. And so, to cite from the promotional literature for the Sweet-man colony, "Wherever . . . there is a clustering of Catholic settlement, there you will find a clustering of Catholic churches." Ed O'Hanlon spoke for many thousands of others when he wrote back to Ireland from his new home in Wisconsin. He had first emigrated to the "upper province in Canada" then made his way to the United States. A number of factors had influenced his move but "the great disadvantage of all was the want of the catholic clergyman there was none within fifty miles of this place. this above all resolved me to leave this place and seek some where that I might at least have the advantage of hearing mass on Sunday."[52]

The second feature of these colony plans that deserves mention is the orga-nizers' assumption that the Irish had been farmers in Ireland and wanted to be farmers in America. The colonizers were as convinced as Beecher or Strong—or Turner—that the West was where the American story and theirs should be played out. Thomas D'Arcy McGee put it succinctly: "The great salvation for the Irish," he wrote in 1852, "lay in taking them out of the cities and back to the

land. The root of all their misfortune sprang from their stopping in the cities."
The shanties had to come down. The Irish had to go west "to win respect for a
fallen race." Fortunately, the "fallen race," as surely as the "chosen," was also a pioneering one. Maguire said that the Irish were "specially suited" to settle in the
West because in "no country have the peasantry exhibited a stronger or more
passionate attachment to the land . . . than in Ireland. Quitting the town would
come easily for them." And those "*who settle on the land*, and devote themselves
to its cultivation, do well, . . . surround themselves with solid comforts, and bring
up their families respectably."[53]

Martin Mahoney was scarcely less effusive in his descriptions of the Sweetman
Colony. The "bushwhackers and roughs" were gone, he explained, which must
have been a comfort even in the absence of any evidence that they were ever
very plentiful in that part of Minnesota to begin with. Murray County's population was "sober, peaceful and . . . neighborly." That last characteristic was synonymous with friendly and would have been especially important. Mahoney then
made references to the climate, calling it "most healthful . . . seldom is catarrh
caught, or chest or lung diseases." As to the land, it was "gently rolling prairie;
the soil a dark rich loam about two feet deep. . . . No clearing needed, or
manure, or drains, or irrigation; no stumps, or stones, or swamps." With induce-
ments like this, it was obviously "not too late to give to Irish emigration that same
healthy westward course, which has changed the agricultural laborer . . . into a
landed proprietor."[54]

And landed proprietors were what the Irish were quite manifestly destined
to be. After all, as an earlier Minnesota Irish colonization brochure had put it, "the
great mass of the Irish immigrants" had been farmers in Ireland and were "peculiarly fitted for the same pursuits here." However well fitted, far too many had
"settle[d] down in some obscure alley, there to compete . . . with thousands of his
countrymen, for that doleful pittance which [by] whim" he gets for his labor.
While the "poor misguided immigrant languishes in . . . our great cities, a field
larger than the whole of Europe stretches out temptingly before him, an expanse
in which riches, happiness and all the sources of human comfort lie concealed
within its folds." That was quite a lot more than just a fair living. "Irishmen!
Will you continue this order of things?" The "laboring men in a city never can
rise. . . . Working for yourself on your own land, where is the man above you?
working for another in New York, where is the man below you?"[55]

In this context, it was not only unfortunate but profoundly embarrassing when
Bishop Ireland brought over 300 impoverished Irish from the Connemara district
of County Galway in 1880–81 and sent them directly to Graceville, Minnesota.
After one winter, the unprepared immigrants were huddled in St. Paul's "Connemara Patch." There were none below them. This was obviously not the only
sad story from the Irish West, but it was certainly the most publicized failure from

the rural Irish West. It was also "completely demoralizing [to] many [other Irish] who were contemplating emigrating to the West" and an object lesson on the folly of bringing the Irish poor to the West without some intermediate stops. Bishop Ireland called "the incident the greatest grief of his life."[56]

That brings up a final general point on sponsored Irish colonization schemes. Some of them, in the language of Irish-born archbishop John Hughes of New York, were based on "gilded and exaggerated report[s] of theoretical blessings . . . this idea is dangerous, just so far as any Catholic emigrant is liable to be misled and deceived thereby." Hughes made his remarks in the 1840s, but they apply with equal force to the colony plans forty and fifty years later. The West that appeared so grandly bedecked in the literature of the Irish immigration and colonization agents was often as misleading, deceptive, and mythical as anything coming out of railroad company's land office. It was also frequently as self-serving. Those Irish who were socially well placed had learned that lace curtains on the windows and a piano in the parlor were not enough to gain entry into the pale. The status of all Irish was adversely affected by the often lawless and boisterous actions of the most wretched of them. It was better for all concerned—was in fact an act of self-protection for those with lace curtains—if Pat and Bridget went west to grow up with the country or at least to grow up.[57]

Clearly, the Irish had plenty of sources of information about the western parts of America. Reliability was suspect in some instances, but the settlement patterns that emerged were not the results of random selection or accident. The Irish went west with a purpose. The most important guide to life in new worlds, however, was not a gazette or a colony pamphlet. The image of western America that was most credible was contained in the spontaneous writings of Irish who had settled there, what the historian Robert Scally calls the "Irish townlands' American library." These libraries consisted of letters sent back to Ireland from specific parts of America, both those that historians have seen and those that they may—with proper care—invent. They also contained songs about America as well as stories told in conversations and speeches, including homilies delivered at Sunday Mass. All went into the mix; the stories that their families and their friends had passed down to them—whether directly or not, whether true or not—were the play scripts, what might also be called the Irish chronicles of America.[58]

The Irish immigrants made their door-to-door journeys tied by long, stout chains that connected those doors. Chains are both integrated and integrative. These chains, however, encouraged and paid for emigration, and emigration would appear to have been disintegrative. It divided families and friends. It was "uprooting," which seems a strange way of unifying and sustaining community. But in the Irish world of exile and "surplus" children, dividing communities was the only way to keep them whole. This, too, was an Irish bull; but like most such, it was irrational and internally contradictory only to those who did not think of emigration as exile. Letters from America were the most obvious signal that old bonds still held and that friendliness was still taking the Irish outside themselves. Whether retold in Ireland or in Irish America, these stories, the images they contained, and the constant stream of new immigrants of which they were both cause and effect were the carriers of Hibernia's seed.[59]

The letters of Irish immigrants were a form of Irish sociability and friendliness as well as a means of transferring information. They were chatty, full of gossip, what the Irish call good *craíc*. Even the topics were the same as those that had once dominated around the turf fire: friends, family, the weather, crops, animals, children being born, old people dying, the sacred and the profane. Letters home extended the meaning and the range of the neighborhood. They were not just welcome ties with those who had left; they were indispensable ties. They contained the stories and the formed images of America. And it was those images that allowed the Irish to be in two places at the same time; to be, as Rebecca Solnit has put it, "polylocal." "Transnational" and "diasporic" are the terms more commonly applied to them; by whatever name they are known, the ties between Ireland and Irish America were reinforced by thousands of stories of life in Meiriceá.[60]

But people who love to talk must also love to listen—and not just to the cheerful hum of Irish background noises now being sounded in America. *Craíc*, to be good, also had to be useful. The chatter in their letters was precisely that. The "townlands' American library" was very public and very well used. Letters were read aloud and passed around. The writers/talkers had eager and multiple readers/listeners. That was true of stories from anywhere in America to Ireland, but I suspect it was even more true of those from outside New York City or Boston. America had an almost unlimited number of potential ports of call. The Irish, whether in Sligo or New York, needed to know which of those ports offered the greatest promise.

So what stories were told of western America? What did the letters, songs, fifth-hand stories, conversations, and speeches of various sorts say? Generalizations about them are difficult—except that the indifferent spelling and grammar of the letters may indicate that the writers were not paying a lot of attention during their classes at the National School. In important ways, the chronicles from western America reveal the same divided opinion that characterized the letters from the All Hallows priests. Some praised the West, saying that it offered special opportunities, which always included the presence of friends, the proximity of a local Catholic church, and economic opportunities, whether from steady jobs or from available and productive lands. Others condemned the West, complaining of the absence of all of the above, with a few asides about the weather and the strange mix of people who lived there. Unlike the "myth of concern," which depicted a West that was unvaryingly heroic and full of promise, the stories in the Irish chronicles were not of a kind; they were contradictory—as the lived West was contradictory. Some were written to pull Irish in; others to warn them away. The key issues, however, were the same in both instances. Could a fair living be made, could friends be found? If the answers were yes, then the writer was describing a likely Irish home on the western range—or, as often as not, in one of its mines or factories. Other matters were almost incidental.

There could be no better example than the section of the Irish chronicles that dealt with Butte. To say that the reports from there were mixed is an understatement. I know of only one set of letters from Butte; they were written by an Irish-born priest, Father Patrick Brosnan, back to his parents in County Limerick. All were written in 1917 and 1918, but the information contained within them would have applied at any time between 1890 and 1920. Although Brosnan was not attempting to persuade his parents to join him, it is likely that the elder Brosnans shared their son's letters and added them to the "American library."

Father Brosnan was either a man of most peculiar tastes when it came to judging where the Irish should make their American homes or a mass of contradictions. Merely juxtaposing his comments creates a bewildering mix of images. "Butte is a great city," but "there is not a tree nor a shrub nor a blade of grass up here." "Poor men are killed every day in one or another mine. . . . The men die like gods down here in the mines," but "Marcus Daly was the man that made Butte an Irish town. . . . He did not care for any man but an Irishman and . . . did not give a job to anyone else." Some of the city's Irish "clear out either to a ranch or to the old country. But a good many get married and don't have enough to leave," and "they all remained in the city where they are near their friends and where they can have weddings, wakes, etc." "The Irish run all the saloons and themselves and their friends are the best customers," and "hundreds who were raised decent now stand and beg for ten cents to get a drink," but "we have seven fine Catholic parishes, all Irish." In context, however, there is nothing contradictory or confused in any of Brosnan's comments and no reason to assume that his parents were surprised when he also wrote that "some 2,000 Irish boys had come to Butte in the last month." Brosnan knew what mattered.[61]

Butte was as totally removed from the myth of concern as any place in the West. It did not pull the Irish in so much as it called them home. Butte was an important part of the extended Irish nation. It would be useful to have more letters from the place. But if immigrant letters reveal something of the history of when and where they were written, then those roles may be safely, albeit very carefully, reversed. History may be made to reveal something of what letters from Butte might have contained and what they might have contributed to the chronicles. Father Brosnan nicely summarized some of that history. His letters home contain images echoed in a song heard frequently in the west of Ireland: the coda called Butte the town "where the streets were paved with Irish bones." Brosnan's letters contain some of the poetic imagery of Seán Ruiséal and Séamus Ó Muir-cheartaigh—without their anger. They even bear traces of all that was implied by the testimony before the 1914 Industrial Commission by witnesses as diverse as William O'Brien, Joe Shannon, and Con Kelley.[62]

The Butte section of the Irish townlands' libraries would have included as well the "letters" of Father Michael Hannan, pastor at St. Mary's and like Brosnan a native of County Limerick. Hannan's thoughts survive only in his diary, but diary entries, in an important sense, are letters to oneself. Although diaries are not to be shared, diarists also write letters to others—probably more of them than most people. Hannan was also known in Ireland, where he was dubbed Butte's patriot priest for his unwavering support of radical Irish republicanism. His best friend in Butte was Sean O'Sullivan—from whom Hannan was taking Irish language lessons. O'Sullivan hosted Eamonn de Valera whenever the Irish leader visited Butte. In other words, it is inconceivable that Hannan did not share what he placed in his diary with other Irish, both in America and in Ireland. He presided over Butte's "Irish Miners' Church"—the name he gave St. Mary's. He was a member of all of Butte's Irish nationalist organizations; he delivered speeches, wrote an Irish patriotic book, delivered hundreds of homilies, heard thousands of confessions. I said earlier that even in cases where none have been found, letters and their contents may be presumed, even invented. This is such a case.[63]

Hannan's diary entries were for the years 1922 and 1923; but as surely as Brosnan's letters, they could have been written twenty or thirty years earlier. The difference was that Hannan had nothing good to say about Butte, the West, or America. His were gloomy chronicles and no Irish who knew of them, however indirect the knowledge, would ever have been tugged toward any part of Meiriceá. His entries were closer to supplications than descriptions: "God help these poor Irish people! They have no stability . . . in this country." He did not mean economic stability. The Irish who had been born or spent any length of time in America had been "raised and brought up in a country that is in every fibre of it materialistic and sensual." It was "no wonder [that] the green-house faith that [the Irish] brought abroad soon perished before the withering blasts of atheism and materialism. God, if things are as we see them and we have been taught to believe them, there is a fearful loss among the souls of the Irish."[64]

As for their new associates, Americans were "a rotten tribe . . . a bunch of pagans." It is impossible to know exactly to whom Hannan was referring. By 1922 Butte had a large Italian and Croat population. These "new" immigrants were Catholic, and Hannan was a professed priest of their church. Remarkably, there was not a single diary reference to any of Butte's other Catholics. Brosnan also spoke only of the Irish, but he was writing back to parents in Ireland. Hannan was writing a diary. I grant that 498 of St. Mary's 500 families were Irish, but Butte by then had eight Catholic churches, all of them parts of a diocesan system with dozens more, most of them not Irish and none of them even remotely as Irish as St. Mary's. Hannan ignored all of these others. He was not a priest of the Catholic Church; he was a priest of the Irish church. And when he spoke of "rotten pagan" Americans in a place as ethnically diverse and overwhelmingly Catholic as Butte, he cannot have been referring only to native-born Protestants. In other words, Hannan was as determined (and bigoted) a champion of Celtic superiority as Madison Grant or countless others were of Anglo-Saxon superiority. He never used Quigley's "Celtico-Roman" construction, but he clearly believed it. "The full-blooded bulldog at home in England," he wrote, "is a far superior class of animal to the Hybrid-breed in this country." Given the intensely Anglophobic Hannan's feelings toward English "bulldogs," no judgment could have been harsher. Unfortunately, in some instances the children of immigrant Irish crossed over the lines and mixed with these mongrel Americans. This was miscegenation; Hannan was describing how in America the Irish *ceased* to be white.[65]

Completing this portrait of and from hell, Butte's and Montana's weather beggared description. "I hear people trying to make out . . . that this is a fine climate," Hannan recorded in his diary. "A fine climate indeed, where the cattle freeze to death on the hoof. . . . No humans should live in this climate." It had been 24 degrees below zero in Helena, colder than that in Butte. He added, interestingly, that "it certainly is not a suitable climate for white men." "Cold! Cold!" he complained on another occasion. "This is a climate of never ending winter." As for the projects to move the Irish out of America's cities and onto western farms, "Farming in Montana! Lord, deliver *our poor people* from it." Deliver them, in fact, from all of America. This pagan land had stolen the friendliness of the Irish and left them with no chance to make a fair living.[66]

For Michael Hannan, the Irish in western America were not simply beyond the pale, they were beyond the reach of civilization and grace. The historical lines of Irish and Americans had collided, and the Irish had been nearly demolished. By all that was right—and, Hannan would have added, holy—the two peoples should have occupied separate constellations. Exile had placed the Irish in Butte, and they had lost their way. It was Hannan's role to make them Irish again, which meant that St. Mary's, under his pastoral care, not only slowed assimilation but stopped it in its tracks—or tried to. His was an exiled parish for an exiled people, and the holier for being such. Hannan spoke of the "millions of *his race* who were destined to travel . . . a via dolorosa": the definition of exile cannot be stretched any further than that.[67]

As for Hannan personally, he was "fearfully blue and depressed. . . . How lonely the life of the priest." That was a not uncommon clerical lament, but Hannan made it on the Fourth of July, a day Butte celebrated with a massive and rambunctious parade in which the Irish took full part. Only one so far beyond the pale that the holiday had absolutely no meaning could have been lonely on that day. But it is his repeated and totally un-self-conscious references to "his race" and "our poor people" that command attention. As I noted, the Irish were not very catholic Catholics. Hannan is my star witness. Butte's Irish priests are buried in a tidy, well-kept row in the city's St. Patrick's Cemetery. Conspicuous by its absence is the headstone of Michael Hannan. He insisted that he be buried in Ireland. If his letters were an indication—and I think they were—it is obvious that the Butte section of Ireland's American chronicles held some interesting, diverse, and conflicting "volumes."[68]

So, however, did the entire western collection—this time of real rather than imagined letters. The only consistent references in the correspondence dealt with the fact that living on the border presented special challenges. Some of these were expressed in exaggerated form and could easily have been taken from the richly stocked storehouse of western legends. They may have been used to present the writer as a heroic and fearless sort; they may also have been believed if not necessarily experienced, attesting to the reach and power of the western myth world. Some of them may even have been partially true. No more certainty attaches to how they were received at the Irish end and what effect they might have had on immigrant destinations. They may have made the West seem an unlikely permanent home but just the place for dashing boyo types to test themselves. It is not the accuracy of these accounts, however, that is important. What counts is that many western Irish Americans said that the West was not the East, that it took some getting used to, and that their friends in Ireland should know that.

There were numerous comments regarding the wildness of the frontier and the restlessness of its people. Jeremiah Cahill described Montana in 1889 (the year of its statehood) as "far wilder than the parts of Africa or India that I have been in. We have plenty of work keeping back the Indians and hunting Horse thieves which are very plentiful here. We have also 9 months of Winter here we have to wear Buffalou robes." Hugh Daly (later O'Daly) was told the same thing, though not in a letter, by an acquaintance in Chicago; when he heard Daly was going to Montana, he warned that "it was only inhabited by wild Indians, gun men. And highway robbers." Maurice Wolfe, then serving in the western army, wrote back to Ireland that in the West "a Man is always in danger of loseing his life by Indians and other bad persons, who infest this place. . . . This is a wild reckless Country . . . a man will Shoot another man upon the Slightest provocations, every man here Carries his brace of Revolvers and Bowie Knife in his waist belt." There was a Wild West show aspect to Wolfe's remarks, but the image may explain why Mike Hurley, then in Cedar Pass, Nevada, wrote to his mother in 1871 that the time he spent in the West had left him no "better civilized than an indian."[69]

These discouraging words, however, were matched by reports of all-day cloudless skies, fish in the rivers and game in the woods, and no landed aristocrats to

keep the Irish from taking them. The Irish were not unaware of the advantages
the West afforded them—or at least afforded some of them. But equally important, the letters back to Ireland from the Irish American West were always in
the context of Irish memory and culture. Wolfe, for example, told his uncle that
"a [western] man [would] walk up to the President and Speak to him without
takeing his hat off." Ed Hanlon wrote back to his brother that "I have many
times seen one Chief Justice of this Judicial districk take his pail and go into his
Barn yard and milk two or three of his Cows between 5 & 6 oclock in the
morning and work on the roads with the sweat pouring off him . . . this is the
general rule rather than the Exception." William Lalor complained of all the
"yankee middle men" who took their exorbitant share of his crop as it made its
way to "John Bull" but then pointed out that "we own the land." He followed that
with the obligatory Irish finale: "And I have high heavenly hopes that the Irish
people will before many years own the land robbed from their ancestors."[70]

   J. F. Costello, writing in 1883 from the "far and distant shores of Paget Sound"
in Washington Territory, made the best and most complete case for the Irish
American West, telling his family that he was in "as good a country as there is
in the world to day for a poor man." That might or might not have had meaning
to them. What followed certainly did. "There are no Gentlemen here. If a farmer
in Ireland made 3 or 4 thousand dollars in a Year you couldnt walk the road with
them You would have to go inside the fence or they would ride over you." The
overwhelming majority of "farmers" making that kind of money and riding the
countryside in Ireland in 1883 were English landlords of the squireen class—
"Protestants with a horse," the Irish playwright Brendan Behan called them. Costello almost surely had them in mind, as he did when he offered his next observation from western America. "When Sunday comes," he would take "a rifle or
shotgun, go out to hunting Wild animals of all description abound here. And as
for wild ducks they are as thick as the cows to home. Also pheasants & grouse
& you can take your gun, or four if you want to, and nobody will ask where is
your license. All you want is money enough to buy a gun."[71]

   In an Irish world of game wardens and constables, this was an unimaginable
privilege. News of it gave substance to Costello's final comment: "to sum all up
this is a free Country. If they see such men . . . here they would tie them and
drown them in the river." By "such men" he likely meant ascendancy Protestant
dandies, by "here" he definitely meant western America. He could not have written
as he did from anywhere else in the country. And his remarks would not have
had the same resonance anywhere else than in Ireland. Not doffing one's hat to
the ascendancy lords of Ireland was unthinkable; so was seeing one of those lords
sweating—except perhaps from overindulgence. As for owning the land, that
meant never doffing your hat to anyone; it might even come to mean the right to
"evict" in the most forceful way possible all of those Protestants and their horses.[72]

Not only that, but the wild edge was being taken off the West. By 1891, for example, Hurley could write from Spokane that the "wilds of America are becoming civilized rapidly," an unsurprising commentary given the date. He said nothing about other Irish coming west as a result of this slow progress toward civilization and civility, but he really did not need to; his remark would have been received as encouraging. The same can be said of other letters. Some strongly urged friends and family in Ireland to board as many boats as necessary and become part of the new Irelands in the American West, often promising remittances to pay for both passages. Ed Hanlon, then living in Nebraska City, wrote to his brother Bernard in Ballymote, County Down, that the sooner Bernard's children got to America, the sooner they would be "launched on the manners and habits of this country under parents eye . . . and the less risk of a division of the family." The important thing was that the members of the family come "out here *by degrees*"; that way they would not have "to form [new] associates"—another Irishman mindful of the importance of clustering and of friends.[73]

Lewis Doyle, writing from Kilkenny, Minnesota, also encouraged his family to leave Ireland, telling his cousin John in County Carlow that "the people here are not rich, but they are independent," and he promised to "do all I can to help you." It was time for John and "all other good honest and faithful Irishmen" to "Just Shake the dust from your feet and leave your curse upon the system that Exiled you . . . from [your] native land. . . . Now John I advise you . . . to come as far west as you can." And, while you are about it, "please Send Some good young widows or old maids. . . . I want to get one from my own County . . . because I know her and I could get along very well together." I like that Doyle said "I know her"—although literally he did not—and "my own County," implying that he would not have gotten along very well with any Irish woman. He needed one drawn from his little platoon. Beyond that, he expressed no preferences. His letter concluded with a singularly unromantic "pick out one for me and tell her I will take her on your reccomend and pay her passage into the Bargain. . . . I have two good Horses 4 cows 8 sheep 20 hogs and . . . will give her all the tea and coffee and pork She can possibly get. . . . I have remained Single long enough, and now I want to take Comfort, Good Bye and write soon."[74]

In 1852 Michael Callahan wrote from St. Paul to his brother in New York City advising that his brother and as many of his friends as he could collect should come and join him in Minnesota. Michael admitted that "Som peoppel finds fault with the winters being so long," but "there is purty good wages . . . a dollar and a quarter a day." Doing what, Callahan did not say. He did not need to; the Irish would do almost anything for pretty good wages. Besides, as Callahan also noted, "there is plenty of whiskey." That last comment was offered half-jokingly. Maurice Wolfe's correspondence was similar to Callahan's. Wolfe's only reference to whiskey was to note that the Irish drank too much of it, but his emphasis on steady work at decent pay matched Callahan's. Wolfe, however, was quite specific about the nature of his employment. Despite being "always in danger of losing his life" to Indians or other desperadoes, he wrote back to Limerick that "for my part I would live & die in the U.S. Army before I would be the Slave of any Landlord." "Uncle Sam is the best Boss. he never refused a Man for a Job or Board and Clothing and very good pay for a small share of work."[75]

There was nothing subtle about the political implications of Wolfe's comments. Being a slave to landlords was a reference to Ireland and to an unfair land system and the unfair living that resulted from it. Being refused a job would indicate that Wolfe spent some time in eastern America and encountered a few "No Irish Need Apply" notices. As for Uncle Sam, he was not only the best boss but, by Irish reckoning, a good and loyal friend who offered steady and undemanding work at a good wage. Besides, Wolfe was "not lonesome in the Army, as a man who Conducts himself has always plenty of friends and as much Sport as he wants, and I have always easy times of it, plenty to eat and Sleep and not much to do." Recall that it was Wolfe who also wrote that if they "pulled together," the western Irish "would rule a good deal of the destiny of this Country." Little wonder that four years later Wolfe had the same boss: "I am Still under the Government . . . its far better to work for the Govt. Than for any private individual or Corporation, as a mans pay is always Sure, no matter whether it be great or small. I get 20 Dollars a month, Board, Washing and Lodgings included." Maurice Wolfe's definition of a fair living fit the formula perfectly: never being lonesome, decent pay, steady work, plenty of friends, plenty to eat, and all the sport a man could want.[76]

There can be no definitive explanation for why the westering Irish settled where they did, but the evidence is strong that migration chains, the frequent use made of the "townlands' library," and dog-eared copies of the Irish chronicles had a great deal to do with it. All lead to the same general conclusion: the Irish went to where the Irish were. In general, it is safe to work backward and let where they went in the West explain what they were seeking from the West. The standard explanations—upward mobility, land, wanderlust, the romance of the frontier— seem to have had negligible traction with most of them. I do not think they had much of an influence even for William O'Brien or Mickey MacGowan. The Irish about whom Maguire and the colony agents had written—those with that primal Irish instinct to grab a plow and break sod—were plentiful enough, but instincts were one thing, opportunities quite another. The Bonanza West was littered with people, Irish and non-Irish, who had learned that free land was not free. The goal of the westward movement of the Irish in America appears not to have been appreciably different from that of the western movement that had brought them to America: steady work in the company of people of like mind and heart, including prominently those who presided over the local Catholic church. That was home. At least some of them found it.[77]

CHAPTER 8

The Worlds the Irish Made

Transplanting the Townlands to Western America

In 1850, in a colossal misreading of Americans' habits, the Bureau of the Census expressed its belief that one day "when the fertile plains of the West shall have been filled up, and men of scanty means cannot by a mere change of location acquire a homestead," the American people would give up their "roving tendenc[ies] . . . become comparatively stationary, and . . . exhibit [some] attachment to the homes of their childhood." This was a matter of no small importance, because the bureau was convinced that the "want of" that attachment was "an unfavorable trait in our national character." Not only did this plea for stability fly in the face of America's history, but it came just as the market revolution and the rush to California and its gold were changing the meaning of everything the bureau had named. "Scanty means," "mere change of location," "fertile plains," and the idea of "home" no longer evoked the same images or elicited the same set of responses. Even before the passage of the Republic to market capitalism, however, the far more commonly held belief had been that Americans were born new, a westward-dreaming and westward-tilting people. Rambling was not an unfavorable trait. It was a birthright; it not only antedated the Republic: it was midwife to it.[1]

Immigrants shared only part of this birthright. They were well-practiced rovers, many of them westbound rovers. At issue was the other half of the formula; would their migration advance the cause of republicanism? Immigrants were old and bore old and worn-out ideas. Coming to America was supposed to make time run backward and make them young. It was a movement through time as well as space. That, at least, was the dream. Moving west, however, also untethered them from American culture and institutions. Americans hoped that the West would change people, but into what? Making the West the schoolhouse of

American principles would work only if the guardians of those principles, in Turner's carefully modulated phase, "checked and guided" the lesson plans and somehow prevented the "students" from congregating in tribal gangs. As the historian Jon Gjerde puts it, the West was both a promise and a threat, an opportunity and a "symbol of fear," particularly, he goes on to say, when the "migrants" were from "Catholic Europe." Left untended, their westering could easily become aimless vagabondage—or worse. It would not advance republicanism; it would retard it.[2]

The Irish, the newest Americans in the 1840s, were the first cases in point. They seemed not to grasp any part of the American dream world. They were certainly dreamy enough, but their visions were seldom of heading out in mixed company and learning to be American. By the logic of exile, the Catholic Irish did not even want to go west *to* America; detaching oneself from the community and then going west *in* America bordered on lunacy. Leaving it and heading off to the wilderness might do for those who either did not have a home or did not define it on the basis of the friendly company they kept, but by Irish standards these types were social misfits. As for the Census Bureau's hopes that Americans might develop some affection for the "homes of their childhood," Irish childhood homes were in Ireland; the physical attachment had been severed, but the psychological bonds were still "stronger than death." Of all the old, outdated, and outlandish habits the Irish brought to America, this one might have been the worst and the most disqualifying. The Irish had committed the unpardonable sin: they had left Ireland without ever leaving it behind or displacing it in their affections. Indeed, it grew miraculously fairer the further, both in time and space, they were from it.

But the Irish were not just polylocal. They were also, to invent a term, polychronic. Irish community life included exiled generations long removed; it also included past generations long dead. They were not simply people who left one place and went to another. They were "nomads," but they were not "drifters." In Irish folk belief, those who drifted from home could never be holy. If home was transferable, then holiness remained within reach, so they brought home with them. That included (obviously symbolically) the interred dead, who were as much a part of home as anyone or anything. Americans could not possibly understand this. Their earth, they had been told and believed, belonged to those then living on it. The Irish came near to turning this on its head. The earth belonged to the dead. Americans could not figure out how the geographically disconnected could remain so spiritually attached to one another, how the Irish could disassociate home and community from physical proximity or even location, including whether one was above or below ground.[3]

Irish immigrants were parts of transnational road shows. They were like repertory companies with carefully screened ensembles and very limited play lists. Exile was their semiliterary trope, a catchword that captured the profound alienation of these lost and wandering tribes. It was one of the shared values around which Irish friendships formed, and it must be placed with its kindred notion of neighborliness as part of the explanation for the Irish tendency to congregate. Exiles huddle. Clustered Irish established distinct and impermeable ethnic communities, which, in the American context, was outlandish enough. Worse was that these immigrant and ethnic settlements—both urban and rural—tended to be replicas or at least rough facsimiles of homeland cultures. The source of holiness for the Irish was their *muintir*—a word derived from *monasterium*—so they bundled it up, shedding none of it on the way, and followed circuits that maintained their attachment to movable and multiple *muintirí*.[4]

This story, however, had another and hugely ironic aspect. As Gjerde has pointed out, for all that the American host society distrusted and feared these huddled clans of Irish, it was never in a position to contest them or to break them up and scatter the players. This was true partly because America needed workers— a point made earlier. But it was also true because America and Americanization contained an inherent contradiction, particularly when the Western myth was inserted into the discussion. America's gift to those who immigrated to it was freedom, but "'freedom,'" as Gjerde writes, "was used [and defined] in multifarious ways." However used and however defined, if it was to have any real meaning, it had to include the freedom to reject the culture, the "civil religion," of America. "Becoming American" in the political sense had to include the right not to become American in the cultural sense, the freedom, in other words, to remain Irish Catholic and hence unfree.[5]

Making matters worse, the West "best exemplified" this freedom that had turned on itself. Irish identities were resilient and adaptive, and they did travel well. But that would have availed them little if the West had not been rich and fertile ground for them. Gjerde's language applies to every immigrant and ethnic group, but I am taken by its specific applicability to the Irish:

> The settlement of the rural Middle West was powerfully influenced by the presence of communities formed from dense migration networks. . . . The fact that people with similar pasts possessed the freedom to colonize . . . also enabled them to live in a new environment apart from others with differing worldviews. . . . These conditions promoted a renewal of localized traditional societies. . . . Paradoxically, they valorized their allegiance to . . . the broader "invented community" of American citizenship as they reified their ethnic affiliations.[6]

The rural West, the schoolhouse of last resort for the teaching of what American freedom meant, permitted the greatest degree of ethnic seclusion and separation.

Those vaunted wide-open spaces not only allowed ethnic enclaves to exist, they encouraged them to exist. "Foreign citizens"—and Gjerde uses "foreign" in all of its meanings—could separate themselves "from the developing American tradition. . . . Practioners of the foreign mind—*Roman Catholics in particular*—could ultimately use the landed wealth and the republican tradition of the United States, ironically two of the linchpins of American greatness, to threaten the American state and society." Gjerde is writing only of the corn-belt West, but his argument can be applied to the whole of the constructed province, from the prairies to the plains, the mountains to the coasts.[7]

The West was essentially a "structurally segregated society, an ethno-cultural patchwork quilt." The pieces of the quilt were "clannish" and "clustered, . . . secluded" behind meridians of partition that negated everything Jefferson—and Turner—had meant by that term and its various equivalents. In Gjerde's words, the West "did not create 'the American, this new man,' so much as provide the liberty to retain . . . old beliefs" and "reestablish and embellish upon former patterns of life . . . in a new context." Old and new—"foreign" and "American"—could even "be mutually supportive and self-reinforcing." The patches in the quilt created an ethnic pluralism based on "the power of place," on local as well as ethnic identities. The pluralism, the ethnic and religious segregation, was not as rigid as black/white (of whatever color of whiteness); it was not encoded in law, but the borders of the American pale were still starkly visible.[8]

Physically the West was so vast, empty, and socially disconnected that the Irish within it could develop a dual but "'complementary identity' that pledged allegiance to both American *citizenship* and ethnic adherence." It was simply too easy to hide out in western America. Besides, and this is a related point, it was difficult to Americanize anybody in a place that had so few Americans—or anybody else—in it. The West was a society in the process of becoming; it was unbuilt and empty. It needed builders and needed to fill its emptiness, even if that meant that the Catholic Irish, among the most irrational of old Europe's artifacts, had to be given a place within it. The pattern was not that different from what existed in Ireland. An Irish cultural world could "coexist"—the word is Gjerde's—with the American as surely as it did with that of the British Ascendancy in Ireland.[9]

To use other theoretical language, the Irish confronted fewer countervailing powers in the West. Theirs were not the first boats to Boston, New York, Philadelphia, or even Chicago; those places were settled and set. They contained a "host society," though its members were not very hospitable hosts. The Irish were unruly intruders on cultural worlds already defined and well defended. They encountered not just countervailing powers but scowling and disapproving ones. That was not the case in the West, where their second boats were often the first to have landed. They were among the "charter groups"; they had earned "entrance status." In the West, the wayward Irish were huddled together in ethnic fortresses to which the non-Irish were denied entrance and from which the Irish themselves seldom ventured. Their outlandish conduct was not quite hidden from view, but neither was it easily subject to reproval or correction. Contrary to a standard image, westerners were not more tolerant than easterners, but there were a lot fewer of them. It was easier to transplant on empty ground.[10]

This was an enormous improvement over what the Irish had known in the East and leads—rather more easily than it should—to the "immigrant upraised" or "ethnic Turnerian" argument that the farther west they went, the better they did. "Better" refers to the less overt prejudice they encountered and becoming more upwardly mobile, prosperous, and contented. A list of all of the western Irish Americans who grew rich usually follows. The issue is more complicated than that. First of all, there was the obvious fact, which the Irish could not have hidden had they wanted to, that being Catholic had as much to do with Irish traditions and "former patterns of life" as being the exiled victims of the British Empire. Being Irish Catholic had not suddenly become an acceptable strain or variant. Gjerde's "complementary" identities were still adversarial identities. Irish identity was based "on common ancestry, nation, [and] religion"; so was American identity. The problem arose from their different ancestries, nations, and religions. The Irish were not the only "cordoned off" patches in the ethno-cultural quilt, but their presence did nothing to improve the look of it or make it more harmonious with "American lines." The western Irish were not so much upraised as they were ignored and left alone to be as clannish as they wished—which was as clannish as only they could be.[11]

That in itself, however, was no inconsequential "gift." The Irish in the West had more self-determination than those in the East; they could be more patriotic—though the *patria* was Ireland; they could speak their minds more freely—but their minds had been made up in Ireland. Not having to bow and scrape, however, did not make them content, it only made them more likely to express their discontent. That was upraising enough. Many who spoke for or from the West were still hostile to them, but their critics could do little or nothing to convert the Irish or to exchange them for more acceptable types. That was a heady kind of freedom; the Irish had known little of it in America's eastern cities, little enough of it in parts of Ireland. The ability to establish a complementary identity was itself empowering. They "could use apparent American freedoms to reestablish" their traditions and keep them "segregated from the impurities of other cultural groups." Among all of those "cultural impurities," however, were those that defined America. This would include "private judgment" and a host of other Protestant-inspired "errors." But it would also include the democratic republicanism and free-market capitalism that those errors produced and sustained. Uprising the Catholic Irish was risky. It could lead to big trouble.[12]

In one of his previously cited comments, Gjerde used an important and perhaps unexpected word to make his point: the West allowed immigrants to "reestablish and *embellish* upon former patterns of life." I am struck by Gjerde's use of the word "embellish," and persuaded by its applicability to the Irish. The Irish did not simply restore the townland worlds they had left; they strengthened them and gave them fuller play than was possible in Ireland. To apply the conventional metaphors, they may have been "uprooted," but they "transplanted" themselves and became more sturdily Irish in the process. For westering Irish, however, that process of uprooting and replanting was a twice (or more)–told tale. They had uprooted themselves from Ireland and then from the Irish American worlds of the eastern United States. That second trip at times must have been as disorienting as the first one. But whether heading west was done fearfully or with wonder and eager anticipation, there is absolutely no indication that the Irishness of the stock was diminished by their being twice removed.[13]

The opposite was in fact the case. They did not shed their Irishness in moving west: they increased their supplies of it. In other words, and directly contrary to the conventional view, the farther west they went, the *more* Old World they became. I have to be very careful here. There was no *essential* Irishness in the sense of some ethnic culture code that was immutable and unvarying. A quick look at the differences among the Irish Catholic experience in America, Australia, and Canada is enough to show that. The Irish in Australia did not behave like the Irish in America because Australia was not America. We need to be reminded of that commonplace from time to time. That does not, however, change the fact that settling new and unfamiliar ground made the old and customary more important, not less so. In reestablishing and embellishing their old townland cultural systems, the Irish constructed an "alternate frontier." In the process, they changed the West from what it would have been had they not come to it. As noted, the Western master narrative is in error. People make places, places do not make people.[14]

In the case of the western American Irish, the places made resembled the communities they had known. There is no great mystery in this. Americans believed—or at least hoped—that immigrant peoples would throw their cultural baggage overboard and reinvent themselves. This metamorphosis would occur somewhere mid-ocean, and by the time their boats docked they would be fully formed "new men." Unhappily for these hot-house assimilationists, immigrants did not transform themselves but rather transplanted themselves. They built social worlds using the only cultural materials they had at hand. Leaving their Old World communities did not mean they did not like the form and function of them; it often meant they liked them more than they had when they lived in them. The metamorphosis did not happen. Common sense would dictate that it could not have happened.

But before a discussion of what did happen can even begin, a previously noted feature of the movement of Irish into western America must be reintroduced into the conversation. This feature would seem to controvert the very idea that an Irish community, of whatever sort and style, was even possible. The point is this: more Irish women than men immigrated to America, but that female majority was only in the eastern Irish America. The worlds the Irish built in the West, particularly in the early years, were so overwhelmingly male as to be socially defective if not socially deformed. Indeed, the gender imbalance in all of the Wests, and by whomever built, was one of the region's most striking characteristics. In 1850, for example, men made up 93 percent of California's population— or at least 93 percent of those the census counted. Other western territories and states had figures comparable to those of California in their early settlement years and in some cases for a significant time after that early sorting-out period. For Americans, this was a dangerous imbalance. Communities and the cultural continuities that sustain them are not thought to come easily in misshapen "settler societies" like the American West. Women were thought to be the gentle tamers of male societies that tended to be anarchic, violent, and brutish. The case could be made that the absence of women and children, joined by extremely high rates of transiency, meant that no community of any sort was even possible.[15]

This is not a case I care to make. In the first place, transiency itself usually took place in groups: witness Michael MacGowan, who followed the great wheel of his life in the company of Donegal Irishmen he had known since his youth and a few other stray Irishmen he and his friends had picked up along the way and adopted. Communities can wander and remain intact. Indeed, the wandering may become part of their culture and strengthen them. As for gender imbalance as disqualifying, consider that "32 percent of households sampled in Grass Valley . . . contained male kinsmen." Overwhelmingly male groupings in the California gold fields might have seemed unlikely candidates for community, except that the men "worked beside and fought beside those of similar origins; they fought against and segregated themselves from those of different origins."[16]

Often those "origins" were American regional. But in the case of the Irish, though they could be Irish regional, they were ethnic and/or tribal. That did not make them less cohesive or less fierce; it made them more so. It is obviously the case that these enclaves as war parties could not reproduce themselves; there would be no rookeries in the mining camps or army barracks, but the communal Irishness of these movable enclaves was palpable nonetheless. The anarchy and outlawry were in the external relations of the Irish. Internally, a strong discipline was imposed. In fact, the internal discipline was necessary if the Irish were to cope with the external anarchy. The *muintir* had been channeled and adjusted. They had not been undone. "No Non-Irish Need Apply" was still posted on the clubhouse doors. The presence of Irish women did not change that pattern very much, if at all.

I do not dispute the requisiteness of women to the Irish *muintir*. As Scally writes, "the culture of which the townland was a part had always depended on some women of strong character despite their lack of prescriptive status or rights." He was describing Irish society, however, not Irish American society. If the culture depended on women, then the transplanted version would depend on what part of that culture the women brought with them. And women, as Kerby Miller put it, were far more likely than men "to make realistic assessments of America's comparative advantages" and far less likely "to cling to old customs or romanticize the society left behind." Their accommodation to American society was accompanied by fewer complaints and less resistance. The "society left behind" was based solidly on the local townlands. It was not Ireland that had been romanticized but the hundreds of little platoons that made it up. Irish women felt these local allegiances, but they did not feel them in the same way. They were not so tribal. They were not as quick to divide themselves on the basis of chieftains and clansmen, and they were less likely to cling to the little platoons. That being so, there is a possibility that a growing female presence, though it more nearly fixed the enclaves in place, may have *weakened* the "bonds stronger than death" that held those enclaves together.[17]

Women were also a lot less eager to head west to break up prairie sod, chase after big rock candy mountains, or "tame the frontier." They encountered the West later and in its more "civilized" and "urban" stage. Few Irish women were in a position to replicate rural Ireland, even had they wanted to, and most did not. But they had no prejudice against western cities. The mere assembling of a certain number of people—as in the aptly named mining *camps*—did not make a city; but once urban amenities (such as they might be) were in place, Irish women, most unmarried, headed west as willingly as anyone else. They married, had children, and attached themselves to the church; in sum, they restored the townland culture they had known, adjusted slightly to meet their new circumstances.[18]

But consider those new circumstances and that living in cities meant living among or near non-Irish. These non-Irish were not enemy combatants; they were not rivals for jobs and had no effect on making a fair living. The evidence is sketchy at best, but I believe a case could be made that Irish women were less ethnically exclusive in their associations than Irish men, that women knew more non-Irish than did the men. Irish men worked, drank, fraternized, played, and fought with other Irish men. The women were less ethnically isolated, whether working as unmarried maids in the homes of Yankees and learning the ways of those homes or as married women and mothers in an ethnically mixed working class or even as farm women shopping at the rural crossroads store. As Margaret Lynch-Brennan writes, women had a "kind of constant contact and interaction that [was] . . . rare in hired employment of men."[19]

I would propose a quite hypothetical but nonrhetorical question: if the Irish had not known English, would women have been more or less likely than men to have been the first to learn English? I have no answer, but the possibility that Irish women were less prickly and defensive, less in thrall to the exile motif, happier to be in America, and more in contact with it must be a part of the analysis. Lynch-Brennan argues further that Irish women "pushed their children to Americanize, *but not at the expense of their Catholic religion or by wholly abandoning their Irishness.*" Indeed, "they pioneered" (interesting choice of words) a new way to be American: "they showed that one could be at the same time both ethnic Irish and American." In other words, they pioneered the Irish immigrant road; in Jon Gjerde's terms, "they valorized their allegiance to . . . the broader 'invented community' of American citizenship as they reified their ethnic affiliations" and preserved "particular Irish cultural notions." This, says Lynch-Brennan, "was the legacy of Bridget," wherever in America she found herself. The world of Irish America ran from Irish graves to an Irish heaven. It did not, however, extend outward to take in "Hoosiers" and "gentiles." Western Irish women did not broaden this world, but they changed it internally and, in so doing, made it less irritable and argumentative. They were not less clannish than the men, but they belonged to slightly larger clans.[20]

So what kind of a West did the Irish build? What did this alternate frontier of theirs look like? A few preliminary points are in order. First, this is a very large topic, and I can only deal with aspects of it. Most of my examples will be taken from three places, Melrose, Iowa; Butte, Montana; and San Francisco. The material realities of these three were as diverse as western America was diverse. Melrose was a small agricultural community on the West's eastern edge; Butte was a middle-sized industrial mining city in the Rocky Mountains; and San Francisco was a commercial metropolis on the Pacific Coast. The three do not represent all that westerners did for a living or all the subregions where they did it, but they come very close. Second, the sheer Irishness of the three means that the Irish can be observed in their "natural" condition—clannish and clustered. They did not negotiate with the host society. They were the host society, and they kept a tight grip on important features of civil life. Melrose was almost entirely Irish and Catholic; Butte was the most Irish city in America in terms of percentage of the population; and San Francisco had the largest Irish population in the West and one of the largest in the country. But that leads to a third general point: despite the various forms, shapes, and sizes of their worlds, culturally these three Irish American enclaves looked much like each other, much like the Ireland their builders had left—and not much like the Irish American communities of eastern America.[21]

That last point means that the transplanted and embellished cultural traditions arose not from the nation, even had the Irish had one, but from the well-hidden "little platoons," the *muintirí* of the local Irish townlands. *Muintir* is a versatile word; it also means "the people" in much the same way "Cheyenne" means "the people." Its extension, *muintearas,* means neighborliness. To be sure, it was an exclusive and exclusionary neighborhood, but for those within it, the *muintir* pro-vided a sense of belonging that no social or political or national affiliation ever could have. It is instructive that when the agricultural cooperative movement began in Ireland in the 1930s the local co-ops were known formally as Muintir na Tire, the "people of the country," in this instance, "the parish working together for the common good of all." The name represented a bit of political expediency but also a great deal of historical truth. Robert Scally says of the townland that it "was a realm in which [a man's] place and identity was clear and secure." I think his use of the singular verb is intentional and important. Place and identity were one and the same thing; to lose your place was to lose all of the relationships that made up yourself.[22]

That was Leo Ward's belief as well, which makes his *Holding Up the Hills* a good place to begin any discussion of the townlands of western Irish America. Ward was a rural sociologist with a professional's eye for description. But he also grew up among the hills surrounding Melrose, Iowa. He was not observing its people from the outside perspective of disinterested social science. His was a description from the inside. *Holding Up the Hills* is oral literature; the writing of the stories seems almost an accident—which is the case with much Irish writing. Ward's book sounds Irish. In places, it almost begs to be memorized and said aloud, not only because it is so well written—though it assuredly is—but because the stories and the words that tell them seem chosen to be told rather than read. The fact that Ward was born in Melrose speaks to the durability of an Irish oral tradition and to the ease with which it was passed down. He did not learn these stylistic tricks in school. He may not even have been conscious of them. They were a part of the townland culture transplanted to the prairies, and so part of his inheritance. That Ward would use them to tell the story of a prairie townland is entirely fitting.

Ward's accounts of Melrose may have been wishful and idealized. Such accounts tend to the panegyric. It is also possible that Melrose was not that different from non-Irish rural settlements and quite different from other Irish American enclaves—particularly those in urban areas. Growing corn and raising pigs in southern Iowa from 1850 to 1930 made similar demands on Irish and non-Irish alike. It required mostly "main strength and awkwardness," as Melrose's John Nolan described it. *Holding Up the Hills* is an Iowa story and a farming story as well as an Irish one. But it is as an Irish story that I consult it. The issue of its applicability to the rest of western Irish America is answered by Ward's offhanded and deceptively simple statement that Melrose was a place for "Irish refugees looking for a way to live"—in other words, exiles looking for fairness. But that could be said of most of the western Irish regardless of where they were found, from the mining camps to the tumbled neighborhoods of western cities.[23]

Ward subtitled his book *The Biography of a Neighborhood*. "Biography" was an apt word. He was telling a life story. "Neighborhood," however, revealed little of what he meant—except to other Irish. In Irish, the root prefix for neighborhood is *comh,* meaning joint or equal. That was the root for a great number of words, including advice, reciprocation, fellowship, alliance, agreement, cooperation, congregation, sympathy, combination, harmony, correspondence, compromise, coalition, and making the sign of the cross. It was also used to form the word that in English means to conspire. However the word was used, the only thing that distinguished this Irish neighborhood from those of Butte or San Francisco was its rural setting. In everything else that counted, Melrose was like every other part of western Irish America.

Ironically, the first point about Melrose is not one that Ward made. He included a fair number of surnames in his book; Evelyn Tierney in her story of Melrose, *But of Course They Were Irish,* supplied some more. Using both sources, I found eighty-one Irish surnames. More than seventy of them were most commonly found in only six of Ireland's thirty-two counties, and those six—Donegal, Galway, Roscommon, Fermanagh, Sligo, and Mayo—were all in the northwest and all adjoining. There were a few strays—a couple from Cork, one from Kerry, another from Tipperary—but in general a small piece of linen would have covered the map area from which Melrose's Irish came. They did not form a little platoon; they were closer to a small squadron, but it was centered in Galway and its adjacent counties. I suspect it never occurred to Ward to mention the obvious, that Irish neighborhoods were transplanted from small patches of Ireland. Why would his neighborhood have been different? What he did not say makes the case as well as what he might have said.[24]

This implies that it was far easier to remain Irish, in that peculiarly local way of theirs, in Melrose than it would have been had the Wards and all their friends gone to Dublin or Cork City—or to farm land in Tipperary. Melrose was more "Irish" than those places because it was friendlier. The splendid isolation of Melrose obviously helped. As Ward put it, "three generations" of Irish "in Iowa" had been "left largely to themselves." They were free to hold up their hills in their own way and to keep themselves once removed from the "impurities of other cultural groups." (That would have pleased Michael Hannan—assuming that anything would have.) The townland world of Melrose was so self-contained that one can imagine the Irish of West Cork being counted among those "other cultural groups." In time, of course, Melrose became more Irish-inclusive; countyism, the modern version of faction fighting, gave way to a kind of pan-Irish movement. Ward took notice of it, writing that the "Connaughtmen used to stand against Corkmen, but the era of that feeling has past." Melrose was becoming a more extended Irish neighborhood.[25]

But not too extended; Ward was acutely aware that he was describing a people of what might charitably be called narrow vision. He wrote of one of his neighbors: "Well, there she is, a big massive woman, Irish of course, yet also Iowan."

He did not identify her as "yet also American," because she would not have identified herself in that way. This was not a political issue. Iowa had meaning. She sought her fair living there. America was an abstraction, an idea detached from anything specific. So, however, was Ireland. Ward said "Irish" not "from Ireland," and the chances are better than even that she was Irish from or near Galway and that it was from there, too, that she took her identity. Maurice O'Sullivan said the same thing when he wrote that he had Irish blood in him but that he was from the Blasket Islands, adding that "it would be more to my liking to go among my companions beyond [the sea] than to set out for the capital city of Ireland . . . if you go to Dublin you will never see any of your kinfolk again." O'Sullivan wrote in Irish; he used *muintir* for kinfolk, *cara* for companion, making no rigid distinctions between the two because there were none that counted for much.[26]

There are moments when it seems as if Ward felt he had no way to make Melrose comprehensible to non-Irish. He searched for a word that could make sense of his intensely communal world, writing at one point in his book that "our community is literally a 'church.'" It was "a group of people conscious of the neighbor's need . . . ready to give for each other, and all of them with like beliefs about God and man." He did not say that the Irish alone felt that way, only that theirs was one of Gjerde's "minds of the West" and that the folkways of transplanted Irish townlands deserved to be discussed on their own without the clutter of explicit pale lines. He *implied* that the lines were there, but he was far too gentle and uncomplaining a man to say that directly or to offer the "Irish mind" as superior to the other minds. He wanted only to make the point that his people were not the same as other people. That meant something. Different people make different places.[27]

Because their mind was different from the others, the Irish occupied a different West and an alternate frontier. This one was entirely relational; it was full of individuals with no self-consciousness of their individualism who would never have described themselves as ruggedly individualistic. In addition, "almost everybody was poor. Poverty was the thing we commonly saw and understood." Here was another endurable "bond of union," what in the Irish townlands Scally called "a unifying banner of resistance." Ward put it more simply: "No one has ever known our people when they were not close together." They all belonged to "the Rookery," so named because of the "prolific people" and the "rough land," the "kind that has to be made, and to be kept well made." Janet Finn, a social anthropologist, calls this the "crafting of the everyday." It is an appropriate phrase. Melrose's Irish did it collectively. "Neighboring has always taken our people outside themselves"; given the range of meanings of the Irish root of "neighbor," that could mean everything from conspiracy to fellowship. In a community as cohesive as this one, there was some of both.[28]

The Rookery had strict rules of eligibility. It was remarkably tolerant of those who met those rules, as remarkably intolerant of those who did not—the "gentiles" or "Hoosiers" as they were called. Those who married outside this community *qua* church were essentially expelled as apostates; they no longer "belonged." The people of the Rookery had "great feeling for their neighbors" but little enough for anyone else. They had "almost a weakness for sociability," but only with their neighbors. After a visit to Mayo, where many of Melrose's Irish families were from, Ward reported that "all the people like to mix, to visit the friends [and he meant friends as the Irish did], to sit before the open fires and talk, or to listen. They deeply love company and society; it is almost a fatal weakness with them"—which sounded a lot like a "weakness for sociability."[29]

Ward's comment that his "people were Irish farmers and they sometimes drank whiskey" was heavily and probably unconsciously encoded, but the code is not difficult to break. There were weddings, funerals, "threshings and fairs, and dances." Even the games they played were Irish. Ward described a night when "three of us played cut-throat"—the three-man form of the ancient Irish game of handball—"till eleven." "Hard times and all, . . . the neighbors kept playing; they are ready nearly any night for a hand." There were also kitchen conversations at all hours, trips to town, meetings at the Hibernian Hall, and wakes. He described the last as "mild carousal[s], a man called the jigger-boss was put in charge; he was really the bar tender." All of these were "within the neighborhood and belong[ed] to everybody."[30]

But these were not just Irish farmers who needed their society. All of this neighborliness took place in a profoundly religious context. They wore their Catholicism lightly in Melrose, but they felt it deeply. "They went into the town especially on Sundays and on holy days; that was a point taken for granted, because the people were Irish and Catholic; it was as ordinary and as expected as getting up in the morning or going to bed at night." Families helped one another make molasses; it was one of the many occasions for gathering. But it was also "a communal act, an act of devotion to each other." I think Ward meant "communal" in a sacramental sense. Society was sacred; it was never God forsaken. The church was the social and spiritual center of their lives. "All of them went to Mass every Sunday if they could. If they could not because they had to work the fields, other members of the family went for them." Those working stopped and knelt when the church bells were rung at the consecration, a scene closer to the medieval French or Italian—or contemporary Irish—countryside than to Iowa's.[31]

There was another strong Irish element in the mix: the shared work experiences. These were, after all, Irish Catholic Iowa farmers. As with the ethnic, religious, and regional aspects of the neighborhood, the occupational aspect knit the Rookery together. Most worked hard. Not all worked efficiently—main strength and awkwardness would not qualify as efficient—but, as Ward made clear, efficiency was not particularly treasured. It was not just the work they did, however; it was the attitude they brought to their work. Ward said this about one of them: "He had good judgment on men, none at all on cattle . . . he had very little interest in bargains: that was not his line. It is true that he had to make a living, but he did it not by trade but by knocking it out of a stubborn patch of earth. Then with the living more or less secured he was no longer interested even in that, but only in life and in people. . . . He was a country gentleman who worked hard and never had money." That did not matter in the transplanted townlands. E. Estyn Evans wrote that the West Irish were "poor in material resources but rich in spiritual values, resisting change and worshiping other things than progress." Ward would have known what he meant. "After all," he wrote of Melrose, "trade was not the top thing in the world. People were above trade, and in a vague yet assured way, God and a man's soul had first place."[32]

Of another man, Ward wrote that he "called his cattle 'the lads.' But what he really loved were horses." If one of his mares got sick, the neighbors knew he would "send for the priest." "The neighbors will always know him as a man who trod humble on our Iowa soil, who thought highly of good horses and looked on people with reverence." As for John Nolan, he of main strength and awkwardness, he had "worked for other people whom he never hated, helped build the railroad, got a hold of rough land and . . . peopled it with children and cattle." Leo Ward described his own father simply: he "was twenty-one years in paying for a poor rough place; at best it was not a place greatly enviable . . . but the neighbors were so kind as to say he had made his farm into one of the best improved small farms around: he had a house built largely by himself, his own two little orchards, his own fences . . . a log stable roofed with straw, and eventually a barn built by himself and the boys, sheds and cattle barn of native lumber logged in the winter. . . . All in all, a home-made farm." Everything in Melrose was homemade.[33]

Leo Ward's "biography of a neighborhood" depicted an entirely vertical world. The Rookery did not extend outward. The dances, wakes, games, even the cadence of speech were distinct and distinctly Irish. Melrose was like a small confraternity, complete with all the recondite rituals of such, the unconscious equivalents of passwords and secret handshakes. Its members had special names—partly because so many surnames were held in common, partly as badges of membership. "It won't do to say 'Bill McGraw,' because there are (at least) Bill and Billy and Bill's Billy and Billy's Billy." Some names were "so common that we had to say: Long John, Little John, Johnny, J.C., and Yellow Hammer; also Big Jim, Little Jim, Broken Nose, Red Jimmy, and Sorrel." In *Holding Up the Hills,* Ward writes of the Granger, the Lean Man, the Stump Man, the Big Man, the Bog Man, and the Humanist. These nicknames and "titles" were not merely descriptive; they signified that the ones to whom they were affixed were in full communion with their neighbors, that their "place and identity was clear and secure."[34]

Everything that Ward recorded had something of the sacred about it because everything that the people of Melrose did expressed "our respect for the living, and also for the dead and for the whole community and for God." The earth of Melrose did not belong only to the living; it had multiple owners, including some buried underneath it in the Irish northwest. To Americans, these were wildly idiosyncratic habits, but to the men and women of the Rookery, they were contained within the well-knit and "thick web" of Irish culture and thus part of themselves. There was an old man in Gweedore, County Donegal, near where many of the Rookery families were from, who lamented that his neighbors had all gone "into strange and distant lands and never returned since." He was only half right. Distant those lands were, but, as Leo Ward made clear, strange they were not—at least not at their origin and for some time after that.[35]

The Irish were not left so "largely to themselves" in many other places in America, East or West. But there were plenty of western farms where the combination of place, occupation, ethnicity, and religion, in varying and shifting order of importance, defined the Irish. Melrose was special, but it was not sui generis. The problem is that these other farmlands had no *seanchaí,* not to mention one as clear-eyed and gifted as Leo Ward. Points of entry into their lives must be inferred from a very few scattered and random records. There were a lot of strong and, in many instances, awkward Irish farmers in western America. I believe Ward told the story of all of them. It is easier to believe that because these next accounts align themselves so perfectly with Ward's neighborhood biography.

Among these other farming Irish were the families of Tom and Patrick Laverty, who, along with many from their part of County Donegal, were tenants on Iowa farmland outside Laurel in Marshall County owned by the Protestant Ulsterman S. A. Paul. We know nothing of the Lavertys' life except what Paul tells us in his diary/day book. Paul kept track of his tenants. He seems not to have been an evil or officious landlord, but he was certainly an interested one. He may even have been a caring one. His entries record the carefully crafted everydays of an Irish farmer in central Iowa in the early twentieth century. They were entirely unremarkable days, which is why they deserve to be retold; they provide entry into thousands of historically neglected lives. We learn that Paul had paid the passage fare from the Irish port of Moville and that, on occasion, he personally escorted his tenants to the land. He mentions—whether with disapproval cannot be told—that Pat Laverty "went to a democrat cacus to night" and that later he was the "vice presedant" of the Laurel Farmers' Elevator Company (a producers' cooperative, most of whose other officers also bore Irish surnames). He notes— with obvious pleasure, even pride—that "Old Tom" had paid off the terms of his tenancy and was on his way to the Marshall County seat to secure the title deed to what was now his farm. Pat Connolly seemed to be just starting on his way to the same hoped-for and happy conclusion to his tenancy; in November 1908 he paid $180, "first payment of rent . . . which leaves fifty dollars yet to pay."[36]

But note, too, the following entries for 1908 to 1911: "Hog sale netted Tom $1755.89." S. A. Paul, it would seem, cared about his tenants down to the last nickel. "Young Tom Laverty was hauling manure"; "the Lavertys planted potatoes today"; "the Lavertys dehorned 14 calvs"; "Old Tom Laverty castrated eight calvs and a boar today"; Pat and Tom "layd tile in a ditch." He also refers to the Daughertys, the Ryans, the Garvins, and the Carrolls (the last two families on Paul's land near Concord and Dixon, Nebraska). During one stretch of hard times, Paul notes that farmers "around O'Neill" (Nebraska) provided his tenants with potatoes. Paul even hinted that the Lavertys farmed by the rules and customs in *Old Moore's*, the Irish farmers' almanac and required reading in every Irish farmer's home since the 1840s, and that they and their Irish neighbors planted and harvested on the basis of the seasonal and festal rhythms of Donegal.[37]

John Kernan Mullen, later a very prominent Denver businessman and civic leader, left a brief record of his childhood in tiny Troy, Kansas. Troy was not Melrose; the Mullens, in fact, according to him, were the only Catholic family in the area. That was not true; Troy was only about ten miles from St. Joseph, Missouri, fewer than fifty from Leavenworth, Kansas, both with sizable Irish Catholic populations. Mullen, however, wanted to make a point. Living in Troy taught him something that the Rookery could not have; something, in fact, that the vertical world of Melrose would not even have understood. Growing up in Troy, he wrote, taught him "liberality." Leo Ward would have understood his point, but he would also have known that it came at a cost.[38]

Mullen would have thought the same of Big Flurry (Florence) Driscoll. Like the Irish of Melrose, Driscoll had a farm that needed to be made and kept well made. And Big Flurry showed the same strength in making it as the Granger or the Stump Man or any of the other patriarchs of the Rookery had shown. Flurry's place, however, was near Wichita, where "damn ole Kafflicks," as one Protestant critic called them, were relatively plentiful—but not overwhelmingly Irish and a long way from dominant. At that Big Flurry never lost his Irishness. If he skipped Mass, and he regularly did, it was because he disliked the priest—he actually disliked all priests—not because he was being assimilated or had learned liberality. Given where he lived, however, his stock of Irishness had to be replenished from external sources, so Big Flurry went to the wellspring, returning to Ireland and "Long Island in the Bay of Roaring Water," where he was born.[39]

Flurry stayed for a year and a half. He did not so much describe his visit as sing of it in the Irish epic style: "'Big Flurry,' the son of Con, that went to America and got rich, has come back." He could once again "gather to drink the barrel of ale . . . speak Irish and fish in the open sea." Sadly, he could not stay "in this paradise" but had to return to "the active, surging, prosperous land beyond the water." But, in a neat reversal of America turning time backward and making people young, his time in Ireland "renewed his youth." Ireland had become Tír na nÓg. He "moved back to Wichita and got a farm. He prospered and worked prodigiously," the essential western American Irishman except that he shared his West with numerous strangers.[40]

That brings us to more of the story of Thomas Brick. In 1970, then almost ninety years old, he wrote his fifty-page "Memoirs of an Irish Emigrant [sic] to USA, 1902." I introduce him as he introduced himself: Thomas Brick was from the clachan of "Gortadoo, West Kerry, by Smerwick Harbour, a famous mackeral snapping" townland. In other words, he was from a small cluster of fishermen's cabins at the far end of the Dingle Peninsula in west County Kerry. It was Brick's class that the English schoolteacher advised to study about America for "that's where the most of ye are going." Brick recalled looking west off the Kerry coast and wondering "how Columbus ever got the courage to discover America in those three little galleys that Queen Isabella . . . furnished him." In 1900, with no prospects of acquiring land and no money to apprentice himself and learn a trade, Brick decided "why not take the chance Columbus did." He went by train from near Gortadoo to the Queenstown harbor just south of Cork City and from there to Southampton, England, where he boarded the liner *Oceanic* to New York. He and the other immigrants were told that when passing the Statue of Liberty they were "supposed to remove our caps and hats . . . and salute that sizeable lady, . . . which we all did."[41]

Brick had a migration chain in place; he left New York by train to join his married sister, Mary Rohan, and her family on their "ranch three miles south of Salix" in far northwestern Iowa near the South Dakota border. After attending Mass, Mary and her husband, Tim Rohan, picked Brick up at the Salix train station. He worked for the Rohans for a few years, learning the hard way how it was to farm in America. In language the Granger or the Lean Man would have understood perfectly, he described a working day prior to planting. His "first field work job" was "stalk cutting, that is cutting up the old corn stalks remaining . . . since last year." The cutting machine was pulled by a "two horse team with the driver riding on [the] seat between both wheels"; to Brick it "was a dangerous outfit on account of those revolving sharp blades. In case the driver would happen to fall off his seat." Once cut, the stalks were "raked up into wind rows" and burned. The burning was "usually . . . done evenings and provided an interesting sight with so many of the neighboring farmers doing likewise."[42]

Brick had no complaints about his wage: $1.00 plus room and board for a twelve-hour day of cultivating corn, milking cows, currying horses, and cleaning out the barn—and escorting his nieces and nephews to the "Sisters' school in Salix." In general, he was well pleased with northwest Iowa. He could not get used to perfervid accounts of whites killing Indians, but the only really troubling aspect of life on an Iowa farm was the isolation. Those were "very lonesome days for me out in the cornfield. Some days it was hard for me to keep from crying." He particularly missed the "crossroad dancing at Bally Ferriter, . . . rowing about in [a] Curra . . . to Bally David, to take in the dancing on that side of the harbor . . . two drinks at Peg Carty's bar." All were part of a fair living.[43]

Later, after he had moved just across the Missouri River to the Irish-speaking township of Garryowen in Union County, South Dakota, Brick went to picnics and played baseball—American equivalents of Irish sociability and neighborly enough. His "assimilation" to American culture, however, was only partial. Garryowen was as Irish as Gortadoo or, in context, as Irish as the little platoons around Galway. Brick remembered eleven names from his baseball team; of the nine of them that can be placed, eight were most commonly encountered in Counties Roscommon, Fermanaugh, Galway, and Donegal. Brick and the Sullivans were the outsiders, a Kerryman and Corkman standing against the Connaughtmen and some Far Downs—the name given those from the province of Ulster, where Fermanagh and Donegal were.[44]

There was one other important aspect to an Irish life in southeastern South Dakota. The township maps for Spink in Union County and Bethel in neighboring Clay County—both very near Garryowen—show about two hundred farms; fifty-one of those were owned by Irish, the rest by Americans, Germans, and Scandinavians. These were, from all outward appearances, ethnically blended townships. If the numbers alone were used, they would show the frontier working its expected magic and producing one of Turner's mixed neighborhood democracies. The numbers, however, mislead. All of the Irish-owned farms were tightly clustered on the western edge of Spink township, the northern edge of Bethel, and all were adjacent to one another. From south to north in Spink, the farms were owned by one or more families named Merrigan, O'Connor, Manning, Sullivan, Connolly, Mahan, Doohen, Casey, Donahue, Walsh, Lynch, and Kavanaugh. There were no other Irish in the township. Tom Brick worked for the Merrigans, the O'Connors, and the Doohens. From east to west in Bethel, the farms belonged to one or more of the McKillips, McMunigals, Morrisons, Dwyers, Slatterys, Morrisseys, Devines, Keelys, Reardons, Donahues, Collinses, and Donovans. As in Spink, the Irish farms formed an almost solid ethnic phalanx. To the south of it were the farms of Jens Jensen, Magnus Johnson, Ole Bervin, Nels Nelson, Lena Kluckholm, "et al." The borders of these rural Irish neighborhoods were as clearly marked as those of any Irish section in urban America.[45]

The Melrose story has historical significance on three levels. First, it and the other accounts that align with it, including Tom Brick's, have an intrinsic value; the accounts of ordinary people living everyday lives always do. In this case, they were farming people living farming lives. Second, it establishes that Irish women and men were among those farming people, that among the various and diverse "minds of the West" was the one brought from Ireland. But what gives the Melrose and the other stories their greatest historical traction exists at the third level: the fact that there were so few cultural differences between the Rookeries and industrial Irish redoubts like Butte. Butte may have occupied an entirely different material and physical universe from Iowa and South Dakota corn country, but its dominant Irish transplanted a version of a townland that was remarkably like that of Melrose.

Leo Ward would have recognized Butte immediately—although a few things would have surprised him. He would have been unprepared for the level of social class tensions in Butte; not every Irish family was poor, and some were poor beyond anything that he had seen in Melrose. He likely would not have known what to make of the fact that all of Ireland's thirty-two counties were represented in Butte, though the numerical dominance of West Cork and the self-conscious countyism of the place, particularly in its early years, would have been familiar to him. The rivalry would have been reversed; in Butte he would have found Corkmen standing against Connaughtmen—and everyone else from other tribal areas. The transiency of this and every other mining city in the West would also have been strange to him. The Irish of Melrose were fixed in place; few left, fewer entered. But if he concentrated on telling the story of only the stable and settled Irish—many thousands of whom lived in Butte—I think he would have told of Irish holding up (or digging up) their hills as Ward's Irish held up the significantly smaller ones of Melrose. He would have found Irish miners who defined themselves partly on what they did for a living, who sometimes drank whiskey, waked their dead, helped their neighbors, went to Mass, loved their society, and lived homemade lives.

Some of the well-crafted everyday would also have been familiar to him. Everyone who stayed long enough in Butte had a nickname, partly because surnames were so commonly shared, in greater part as a rite of passage into a closed order. Butte's names tended to be less affectionate than Melrose's—Callahan the Bum, Con the Horse, Filthy McNabb, Mickey the Bird Sullivan, Crooked Ass Healy, Mike the Mule, Tommy the Man Eater—but they served the same function. Ward would have recognized the handball courts at McCarthy's gym and at Jack Crowley's Up Kerry Saloon, named to celebrate Crowley's little platoon and with a court in the back. Butte even had an active Gaelic Football League; in 1910 the Wolfe Tones defeated the Emeralds, who had upset the Shamrocks in the semifinals, for the championship. All sides then adjourned to Harrington and Sullivan's Bar in Hibernia Hall, where they could smoke Douglas Hyde cigars and drink Guinness stout. There can have been few meaningful differences between that day in Butte and game-day in any of dozens of towns and villages in both Ireland

and Irish America. Melrose was too small for events this grand, but handball and a beer in Melrose was only a scaled-down version of the same friendliness.[46]

Robert Scally writes that there was no "indication that any townland . . . abandoned their handicapped dependents." In Irish, dependents were known as *duine le día*, the people God takes special care of. A town like Butte had many *duine le día*. To abandon them was to abandon God. Injured and stricken miners in Butte were paid sick and death benefits by their Irish fraternal societies. In Melrose, Ward writes that taking care of sick neighbors "was the custom . . . it was the common thing to watch all night with sick people." It was the custom in Butte, too, where the Irish societies sent willing members as "nurses" to sit with dying friends. The caretakers were always from the same parts of Ireland, often from the same village, and had probably known those whose needs they attended for decades. Miners who were blinded were routinely elected to judge-ships. Even more revealing is that the true characters of the Irish enclave (and Butte had some legendary characters)—the ones who told the best stories, whose lives were the most open and revealing of other lives—were given special atten-tion; they had easier jobs in cooler drifts, soft jobs when they grew too old to do the hard ones. These characters were the ones who gave the enclave its character. They had more friends than most, largely because they brought and kept the Irish world together, never consciously but simply by being who they were.[47]

All of these western Irish enclaves grew more porous over time; regional and local American ideas and attitudes—themselves in constant flux—infiltrated and changed them. And from Hancock, Michigan, to St. Paul, Melrose to Butte, Denver to San Francisco, Irish Americans were themselves changing. "Strangers," given enough time, became "Natives." But always Natives with a difference. Ward put it gently: "We get more native as we go, and yet any outsider would notice at once our accent, our noses and our chins." Irish-born Father Peter Yorke of San Francisco was more pugnacious—and concerned with more than noses and accents. He insisted that "men will remain what they were in the beginning." The Irish-man "who poses as an American" is like "the hippopotamus, which, at the fancy dress ball, got itself up like a swallow, or like the ostrich which put its legs into the sleeves of the keeper's overcoat and pretended to be an elephant." Being friendly was part of being a hippopotamus. It was a means, often the only means, for the Irish to share the instabilities and "socialize the uncertainties" that went with being blunt instruments in the midst of a takeoff into industrial capitalism. But they were also well practiced at it; Scally refers to it as the Irish "culture of hospitality." It came naturally to a people who had always been taken outside themselves by neighboring.[48]

The question of whether these Irish American worlds synchronized with Ameri-can society, whether their transplanted townland cultures were compatible with western American values, or even with capitalism's values, does not permit an easy answer. As noted, Ward implied that they were not compatible, that if the culture of capitalism included the maximization of advantage and profit, the neighborhood was literally irrational. If the sovereignty of the self was a part of the culture of republicanism, it became doubly so. In the West, however, Irish townland values could coexist with America's regnant values, including those that were applied to the mythic frontier, "the fatal environment." That does not mean that these Irish were not still beyond the pale. It meant that they were tolerated. Thus did the West become a menagerie rather than a melting pot, a place where hippopotamuses lived near swallows, ostriches near elephants, none trying to be like the others. Indeed, in those parts of the West where their numbers and power permitted it, the Irish converted the swallows to hippos, assimilating America to them.

No social order is fully egalitarian, and the transplanted Irish townlands of western America, for all of their neighborliness, were no exception. The nativists' argument that the Irish were born Catholics was a cloak for prejudice; they knew next to nothing about either the Irish or Catholicism. At that, however, they had a point. Every tier of Irish society, from the local to the provincial, was hierarchical. The little platoons had to have commanders-in-chief who were skilled in both diplomacy and war. Those adept at both were paladins, the protectors of the *muintirí;* their praises were literally sung. If their control was regional, these clan leaders called themselves *rí* (king); a few even became *ard rí* (high king). At the local level, however, their proper title was *an ceann fine* (chieftain, literally, the head of the family and of all the friends who were part of it). Whatever their rank, these leaders commanded loyalty and were treated with the respect their royal status deserved. The Irish liked kings, but only so long as they were Irish and their "realms" remained local; they had no use at all for British kings who pretended to the kingship of all Ireland.

The Ireland of the *ceann fine* was well hidden from the ascendant Anglo-Irish, which was just as well; they would have disapproved of every feature of the chieftains' rule. Transplanting the townlands to America made the chieftains' rule visible again—although the American ascendancy was as disapproving of it as the British would have been. Irish American chieftains behaved as if they had read the owner's manual on how to conduct a proper chieftainship. And there was a manual, an instructional guide to the fine art of being a wise king. It was written in the third century by Cormac MacAirt under the title *The Counsels of Cormac.* It is highly unlikely that any of the American Irish ever read it. But it is impossible to read it now and not be struck by how closely the boss Irishmen of the nineteenth and twentieth centuries adhered to Cormac's counsel. They did not have to read it to know its lessons; Cormac's counsels were part of their cultural inheritance.

When asked "what is best for a king," Cormac replied, "that's easy. . . . Geniality rather than arrogance, attention to tradition, true reciprocity, . . . goodwill to tribes, just judgments. . . . Attention to every unfortunate, many charities." "Let him visit the ailing. . . . Let him quell fear." The good chieftain was "affable, humble, . . . firm, . . . a poet, a traditionalist." He was "generous, genial, compassionate." He would "feed every orphan." Two vital considerations were the "protection of amity . . . [and] consolidating relationship"—the essence, in other words, of a neighborhood. The chieftains were like oracles; they knew what to do, knew the difference between wisdom and folly. In Melrose, the Granger was such a one. "What he said stuck in our minds," wrote Leo Ward; "it counted . . . it was The Granger said it." The Granger and his sister were "a byword in the community and looked upon in many ways as the model; what they did and as they did— that was the way to succeed." The Granger's was "the place to go . . . for a sense of power and sufficiency and order."[49]

In urban areas, the chiefs were surrounded by a semiregal entourage of bosses, sachems, cronies, and ward heelers. These, as the historian Mary Wingerd writes about those of St. Paul, were the ones who could "deliver the goods," and the goods were "power, sufficiency, and order." If nothing else—and there was a great deal else—they provided the jobs that sustained the enclaves. Even as late as 1900 most of those jobs were unskilled or semiskilled, but control of them gave the chieftains enormous power locally. They could be used to reward loyal friends and punish those friends who were enemies. They were also bargaining chips in what passed for negotiations with non- and anti-Irish. The priests could speak the truth to power, particularly when palesmen had most of it. The chieftains, however, were the power. The jobs they commanded allowed the neighborhood to form; once formed, the power of the chieftains defended it. The palesmen's rules, even their laws, did not apply in the realm of *na ceann fine*.[50]

The best-known and most frequently chronicled of those urban chieftains were the bosses of the local Democratic Party, with emphasis on local. They were also among the most important of the established Irish who could deliver the goods— for the simple reason that they had more than the usual supply of goods at their disposal. Patronage jobs, particularly in public works and in police and fire depart- ments, belonged to the ward bosses, and they dealt them out like a faro dealer distributing cards. One story can stand for tens of thousands: in 1887 Patrick Browne wrote back from San Francisco to his brother in Ireland that he was going to try to "get a job in the street cars it is a nice clean job and easy work . . . it is very easy for a steady person to get a good place when he is known in the city." By "the city" he meant the Democratic ward bosses who ran it; "being known" meant enjoying the chieftain's favor.[51]

A story is told of the evening in the 1880s at the consecration of St. Patrick's Cathedral in New York City when "Honest John" Kelly, the first Irish boss of

Tammany Hall, gave one of the toasts. "God bless the two greatest organizations in the world," said Honest John, "the Catholic Church and Tammany Hall." After a momentary silence, someone shouted, "What's the second one?" The story rings truer, I suppose, in the East than in the West. But it need not and should not. From Minnesota and Iowa's Irish Catholic farm towns to the so-called Daly-crats in Butte, to Edward Keating and the Fifth Ward Savages in Denver, to the St. Paul, Omaha, Los Angeles, Burlington, Duluth, Pueblo, Spokane, and Kansas City "machines," to David Broderick, Christopher Buckley, James Phelan, Father Peter Yorke, Patrick McCarthy—politicians, a priest, and the "baron" of San Francisco labor—and the rest of the fractious San Francisco Irish Democrats, it was never easy and seldom necessary to differentiate between the two. The "conquest" of America's cities by Irish Catholic Democrats extended from ocean to ocean.[52]

Like Tammany, the Irish bosses/chieftains demanded loyalty, not political fastidiousness. Predictably, "good government" reformers—dismissed by Irish Democrats as goo-goos—identified this "system" as corrupt. Most of these reformers were Republicans and the heirs of antislavery and the anti-Catholicism that went with it. They were a recognizable social type. To these reformers, working-class Irish were culprits not victims, co-conspirators not constituents. That was the point; chieftains did not have constituents, they had friends. As one historian put it, "Irish Catholics in America voted Democratic . . . because they wanted supremacy over those who poured scorn upon them." That included prominently the goo-goos. "Who held power, their friends or their enemies? That was the key question. The emotional facts of the nineteenth century . . . fueled its politics fully as much as did its economic facts." For "emotional" read ethnic, religious, cultural. And recall that the Irish never forgot their history.[53]

San Francisco offers a perfect example. Democratic politics in San Francisco from the 1850s until the 1930s was dominated by the Irish. David Broderick, the son of Irish immigrants, was the first of its bosses. Broderick's control of San Francisco's Irish was described in language that might have been taken from an English or American nativist primer on the management of the ungovernable Irish. One of Broderick's critics could not "distinguish . . . between the serf of Nicholas and the slave of Broderick. . . . From the mass of debased and down-trodden exiles, . . . thousands prove unworthy of the privileges which our law extends to them." They become "dangerous elements in our government." Scores of others had said the same, but this critic of Irish politics saw not the hand of the church, as the nativists had, but the hand of the tribal chieftain—although, as the response to "Honest John" Kelly indicated, that might have been a distinction without a difference. "Where one man emerges from this mass," the Irish "band themselves together in . . . coteries, and vote in solid phalanx. . . . They follow their ringleader, and as he jumps so precisely do they all jump."[54]

Broderick was succeeded as ringleader/chieftain by another son of Irish immigrants, Christopher Buckley, the so-called blind boss. I acknowledge at the outset that Buckley's reign was more complicated than the brief discussion that follows would indicate. The important point here is the indisputably "Irish" aspects of the blind boss's rule. The historians William Issel and Robert Cherny describe Buckley this way: "His power derived . . . from his stance in the center of a complex set of personal relationships," many of them forged at Buckley's Alhambra Saloon. Issel and Cherny doubtless intended what came next metaphorically. I do not. I quote them because, in a strictly Irish context, their language would have fit perfectly the patterns and images in countless Irish myths and hero-tales, including the *Counsels of Cormac*. Buckley's "organization always had a feudal quality about it—Buckley might be king, but he ruled because of the loyalty of several great nobles who had power bases of their own." Those other great nobles, needless to add, were also Irish, allies of Buckley, the *ard rí*. What follows also aligns well with Irish lore: "At times, some of these other leaders rose in revolt and tried to seize the reins of power from Buckley, but throughout the 1880s he quashed such rebellions."[55]

San Francisco, said one critic of its Democratic machine, was organized and governed on the "village system." It was, in other words, government based on friendship and loyalty. That critic did not say "Irish" village, but he was speaking of "many of our large cities," he offered his opinion in the same year John Paul Bocock was describing "the Irish conquest of our cities," and his specific reference was to San Francisco. He did not need to say "Irish village system." San Francisco was run like a vastly enlarged Melrose—or Gortadoo. For all of its size and cosmopolitanism, it may as well have been an Irish townland clachan with Irish politicians, labor leaders, Catholic clergy, and other elders playing the roles of kings and nobles. As one resident of Los Angeles said about San Francisco, "I don't like this railroad-ridden boss-ruled city at all; there is no enterprise. It is Ireland over again, owned by foreign landlords." He was very nearly right. It was railroad ridden and boss ruled, and its village system of government was something like Ireland all over again. The blind boss even had to deal with "foreigners," strangers like Leland Stanford, close enough to a Protestant with a horse and certainly rich enough to qualify as ascendant. The whole point of his friendly government was to take care of a triune cultural phenomenon, the Irish Catholic Worker—three separate identities in one—and to protect it from the ascendant.[56]

The only way this system could change was for the chieftains to gather in council. The first such gathering took place in 1896. Civic reformers, the vast majority of them not Irish, not Catholic, and not in the working class, proposed a reform charter and brought it to a popular vote. Father Peter Yorke—Irish-born, Irish patriot, protector of the Irish against the nativists, Catholic priest, and champion of labor—said loudly that the new charter did not take care of those he was pledged to defend. The charter was defeated. The neighborhood elders had spoken. Two years later, in 1898, there was another council and another reform charter. The chieftains were better represented this time and made sure that it addressed the needs of Father Yorke's constituency. The key player was James Duval Phelan, the extraordinarily wealthy son of Irish immigrants.[57]

It is difficult to include Phelan among the chieftains, in part because it is impossible to imagine him in Buckley's Alhambra Saloon, lifting a pint to anyone or anything on Yorke's list. Phelan was a life member of the Audubon Society, a patron of the San Francisco Opera, president of San Francisco's exclusive Bohemian Club, chair of both the city's McKinley Monument Committee and the Junipero Serra Monument Fund, an active member of both the Hibernian Social and Literary Society and the Society of California Pioneers, vice president of the Anti–Capital Punishment League of California, and a founding member of the Native Sons of the Golden West and the San Francisco Art Club. In sum, he was a proper gentleman, what Yorke—whose later feud with Phelan could also have been fitted into an Irish hero-tale—would have called an Irishman trying to be a peacock.[58]

Phelan may have been every bit of what Yorke charged. Certainly he was closer in both style and political substance to the "best men" of progressivism than to the ward heelers at Buckley's saloon. Phelan lived on both sides of the pale, and that required some truly fancy high stepping. He not only was a member of the Bohemian Club, which billed itself as "an association of gentlemen connected professionally with art, music, and drama, and . . . having appreciation of same," but also owned 800 shares in Amalgamated Copper and was invited by John Hays Hammond to join the National Civic Federation. Hammond was a mining engineer, a friend of Cecil Rhodes, and a champion of British imperialism and American capitalism. Phelan was also a member—again at Hammond's invitation—of the Rocky Mountain Club of New York, know as the "Eastern Home of Western Men." In addition to the well-heeled Hammond, his club mates included Louis Hill, owner of the Great Northern Railroad, and John D. Ryan, president of Amalgamated. That he managed to stay on the right side of the Irish, the church, and labor while simultaneously socializing with Anglo-American Protestant high society was a tribute to his political agility and/or exceptional Irish luck.[59]

Whatever its source, Phelan's position in both worlds made him the ideal mediator between Irish Catholics and progressive reformers, an important role for any chieftain. His negotiating skills were on full display during the heated debate over the reform charter of 1898. Mayor Phelan brokered and marketed the charter, even arguing that it "would give the city what the people of Ireland have been fighting for . . . home rule." What sense that made to the non-Irish cannot be known; the comment likely enraged the more radical Irish republicans, including

Father Yorke, who by 1898 were demanding a lot more for Ireland than home rule. Pat McCarthy, however, San Francisco's labor baron and by then a Phelan appointee to the Civil Service Commission, knew what home rule meant in both the Irish and the San Francisco contexts. He supported the charter, as did the mostly non-Irish members of the conservative Merchants' Association. It would never have succeeded, however, had Phelan not assured San Francisco's Catholics that the APA was not behind the reform movement, had it not been endorsed by only slightly lesser nobles like McCarthy, and had it not received the imprimatur of Father Peter Yorke, who may well have outranked them all. As Phelan learned, Irish village politics demanded a great deal of its chieftains.[60]

The new charter was advertised as the urban government equivalent of scientific management—modern, progressive, and businesslike. It was, but only to a limited extent. Some "village" aspects survived the reform almost intact. Phelan, whether as mayor or U.S. senator, continued to play the Irish Catholic Worker card, even when dining with friends who would neither have understood nor have supported any part of the complex whole. As for all those well-established Irish/Catholic/Workers, they continued to divide up the goods that an only partially modified village system delivered to them. S. H. Kent, president of the San Francisco Building Exchange and no friend of either labor or San Francisco's Irish, said in 1905: "We have no labor troubles. We give the men what they want," meaning they gave Pat McCarthy what he told them his men wanted. Nine years and a major earthquake and fire later, the writer Gertrude Atherton, a daughter of San Francisco's elite, asked Phelan what "ails" San Francisco; is "it the rivalry of Los Angeles and Seattle . . . or is it the dominance of the labor unions?" Her question involved more than she could have known. Answering it would have required an Irish history lesson, which was more than Phelan was prepared to give.[61]

Atherton wrote a number of novels about San Francisco and the golden West, including *The Californians* (1898), *Rezánov* (1906), and *The Ancestors* (1907). But she also wrote a little-known and underappreciated novel about Butte, *Perch of the Devil*. In the book she described the "appalling surface barrenness of the place," "the sulphur and arsenic fumes of ore roasted in the open or belching from the smelters." The town looked like a "giant ship wreck." But it was the devil himself, not where he was perched, that most interested her. And the devil was the same one she had encountered in her native San Francisco, a closed and, by good-government standards, corrupt political system based on that peculiar Irish sense of fealty and friendliness.[62]

The pattern in Butte was different from that in San Francisco. It had no political bosses like Broderick, Buckley, and Phelan and no priest with the power of Father Yorke; Michael Hannan was far too crabbed and ill-tempered to play that role. The Democratic Party and the labor unions dominated Butte politically, and the Irish dominated both the party and the unions. But the party and the unions did not run the town in the sense of controlling the steady jobs or deciding who got them. Jobs in the public sector were not Butte's stock-in-trade. The chieftains who mattered were the Irishmen in charge of the giant Anaconda (or Amalgamated) Copper Company and the handful of lesser nobles with power bases of their own who served these chieftains. Anaconda employed many thousands of people. It paid them well and rewarded their loyalty with steady work. Those jobs also killed men at a rate exceeded only by the military in the midst of siege warfare; but in a population of less than 70,000, 15,000 ACM jobs (10,000 of them underground in the "war" zone) were the goods that counted.[63]

The only slightly inferior nobility that assisted in getting those jobs for Butte's Irish was drawn from the leadership of the Butte Miners Union and from the two Irish fraternal organizations, the three divisions of the Ancient Order of Hibernians (AOH) and the Robert Emmet Literary Association (RELA) or Clan na Gael. The AOH and the RELA were professed Irish nationalist organizations, formed to free the motherland from the hated *sassenach*. And they did in fact work for the cause of Ireland. In some ways, they were a part of the invention of Ireland. But they were far more active in the cause of the Irish, the people rather than the nation. They were friendly societies, Celtic brotherhoods, and were central to the maintenance and social vibrancy of Butte's Irish world.[64]

But their most important responsibility was getting the jobs that allowed that world to exist in the first place. Both associations had job committees consisting of well-placed merchants and professionals—the Irish nobility—who lobbied corporate leaders in the "employment interests" of the RELA or the various divisions of the AOH. They were job offices or employment agencies and, like all such, they collected a fee for their services. The fee was in the form of membership dues in Irish nationalist societies. Most of the members were sufficiently committed to the cause to pay it willingly; others paid it because, as one of them said, it gave them the chance "to know those who are in a position to give employment." As one AOH (and union) officer said when a "few grumblers" complained about the dues, "let them join the 'Birds and Animals' organizations and see how many jobs they will secure for them." Those dues or fees, however, meant that only those "patriots" who could afford to join and/or had work skills valuable enough to stay employed had the protection of the chieftain and his noble court. This was a fragile base. Each of its three elements—Irish nationalism, solvency, and work skills—depended on what was happening in Ireland and in corporate boardrooms. Still, Butte's Irish understood well that secret handshakes had occupational as well as ritualistic and patriotic significance.[65]

What made Butte unique was that these two Irish friendly societies negotiated from within the brotherhoods. The Anaconda Copper Company's corporate and hiring officers were also members of one or both of them. Indeed, John D. Ryan,

the third head of Anaconda, outdid even James Phelan in juggling his allegiances. Like Phelan, Ryan was a member of the Rocky Mountain Club of New
York. But he was also a member of the RELA, which openly advocated the use
of physical force to drive the British from Ireland and form a fully independent
and united Irish republic. It is altogether safe to say that Ryan was far more
interested in the social affairs of the Rocky Mountain Club than in the radical
republicanism of the RELA, particularly as that radicalism moved toward a
Marxist workers' republic. His membership in the RELA was a ceremonial gesture;
he could not pretend to a chieftainship without it. It gave him an organizational
affiliation that allowed him to act out his assigned role, and Ryan knew it.[66]

There is every reason to believe that Ryan was following the example set by
ACM's founder, Marcus Daly of Ballyjamesduff, County Cavan. Daly's support
for Ireland and the Irish was on full display as he built ACM into the fifth
largest corporation in America. I think Daly's Irishness was more genuine than
Ryan's, but that is not the same as saying that Daly did not know exactly what
his affiliation with Irish organizations was worth to him in gaining and keeping
the loyalty of an Irish-dominated workforce. Paying for the building of Catholic
churches and sponsoring Irish patriotic displays was a tool in labor-management relations; it was also good for business and Daly knew it as surely as the
more calculating Ryan. One of his political rivals called him Butte's "boss Irishman,"
an interesting title and one altogether consonant with "chief." Daly counted his
money in the millions and controlled tens of thousands of jobs. There was no
Irishman like him anywhere in the East and not many of comparable power in
the West. Western Irish got to choose their chieftains differently than in the
East and to select them from a wider pool of those-who-would-be-king. Daly
is the perfect example. Whether he genuinely cared for the thousands of Irish
who worked for him—not to mention the Ireland from which he and they had
come—cannot be known. He acted as if he did, and the Irish were not easily
fooled on matters that affected them so directly.[67]

Daly also defied Butte's other and non-Irish copper barons by refusing to cut
wages and he welcomed, or at least tolerated, the formation of the Butte Miners
Union in 1878, in time the largest local union in the world. His hand-picked
successors who carried the dynastic line to 1956 were William Scallon, John D.
Ryan, and Cornelius Kelley, each of them as self-consciously Irish and Catholic
as Daly himself. But Daly, far more than the other three, also seemed at least to
be the protector of labor. Under his leadership, ACM granted the Butte Miners
Union a closed shop; paid the highest wages in America; and, years before
American unions secured an official Labor Day, gave all of Butte's miners the day
off on St. Patrick's Day, Robert Emmet's birthday, the day of the all Irish Societies
picnic, and Miners Union Day. Daly, who loved racehorses and who owned the
fastest one in America, even gave his miners a shift off, with pay, during race

meets. ACM also paid off some widows' mortgages and gave everyone who worked for it a Christmas turkey. These were unimaginable privileges, and dismissing them as meaningless paternalism or worse misses the point. This was what Irish chieftains did. This was how they were expected to behave.[68]

Cormac MacAirt had no explicit counsel for those whom the chieftains commanded and cared for, but it was obvious that they were expected to be loyal. Tens of thousands of Irish who found jobs in Daly's mines were aware of what Butte provided them and at whose hand. Loyalty and cooperation came easily to them. They likely were not aware that Daly also used spies and union infiltrators and that he threatened to close his mines for two or three days rather than submit to wage demands by the company's railroad workers. But even had they known all of this, I doubt it would have lessened their affection for him by much. Daly had a right to protect what was his—and, as was true of all good chieftains, what was his was also theirs. One Irishman called him the "noblest Roman" of them all. It was a nice compliment, but it also meant that they were all Romans.[69]

In 1906, five years after Daly's death, Butte's miners raised more than $5,000 toward building a bronze statue to Marcus Daly. It was sculpted by the Dublin-born Augustus Saint-Gaudens and was placed on a hill across the street from the post office in uptown Butte. The simple fact that workers helped pay for the statue makes it a document of sorts, a text in the language of contemporary historians. Its inscription gives it added interest. Daly was identified as "a pioneer miner who first developed the famous properties on the hill. . . . This memorial . . . is erected by his fellow citizens in tribute to his noble traits of character, in grateful remembrance of his good deeds and in commemoration of [his] splendid services" to his city and state. It made no reference to his Irishness; in Butte, that would have been the ultimate redundancy. His fellow citizens who gave their money did so because they wanted to honor their chief. There may have been other working-class towns where workers joined in building monuments to capitalists, but I am not aware of them.[70]

Matty Kiely, a native of Waterford and one of Butte's genuine characters, may be considered a proxy for thousands of others. He never passed the memorial without doffing his cap and saying a prayer. Daly had personally given Kiely the first of his many jobs, shoveling copper ore at the giant Anaconda Mine. Kiely never forgot either the job or all the days off that came with it. Indeed, it worried him that the statue was placed in such a way that Daly faced the town, his back to the hill and its mines and miners. "'Tis no luck will ever come of it," Kiely was reported to have said. "In life Marcus Daly never turned his arse on the mines of Butte or the miners who dug them." The statue has been moved since it was built; it now commands a site with Daly's back to the Montana School of Mines. But he is at least facing the mines, now all closed, standing guard over a deindustrialized Butte and the ghosts of its hard-rock miners.[71]

It could be that Matty Kiely and all the others were foolish men who did not understand their class interests; confused men who thought their ethnic interests were more important than their class; or corrupt men who bartered away their real interests and their working-class comrades along with them. Each of these explanations is possible and has been proffered; the statue has been deconstructed. It is more likely, however, that Matty Kiely and his friends were not foolish or confused or corrupt. They may have been preindustrial cultural left-overs, but the history of industrial America generally had its full share of those. They were aware of what was true to them: Marcus Daly gave them jobs at a time when others told them not even to apply, and he did not turn his arse on them. How, they would have asked, could that be considered a false premise from which to commemorate Daly—and themselves?

Melrose, San Francisco, and Butte each revealed different specific aspects of the transplanted Irish townlands: localism, neighborliness, village politics, and the importance of the chieftains central among them. But taken together, the three present in clear relief some of the more general features of the Irish migrations as well. The Irish transferred more than just a "weakness for sociability" and a dependence on patrons in the form of chieftains. They brought their fatalism and passivity and their stubborn traditionalism. They did not need to read *The Counsels of Cormac;* they literally knew it by heart. And, of course, they brought their sense of community, made more powerful by being so narrow. Hidden Ireland and its secret economy of friends was first exposed then modified, packed up, and moved to America.[72]

The values of the Irish townlands supplied the cultural base on which Western Irish American worlds were constructed; the jobs arranged and protected by friends, local Democratic Party bosses, fraternal societies, and other chieftains provided the economic base. But building those enclaves was one thing, holding them together was quite another. That required shared points of reference, cling-stones of a sort, that connected individuals and made them a community. The most important of these was the Catholic Church. Irish immigrants, many of them desperately poor, spent a significant percentage of their incomes on building and maintaining the church and the separate system of education that went with it. To their critics, these expenditures were utterly mindless. These critics missed the point, as they so frequently did. When the Irish put up a church, they were building something more—and, I suppose, something less—than a place where they went to pray. The social structure of the enclave was built around the parish. Whether a cathedral or a small chapel, the church was both a hideout and a fortress. It was a social center, a place from which the parades and picnics could begin, where the dances could be held and the parties hosted. The opening of a new church building, and the parochial school attached to it, was also a formal announcement that the Irish had arrived and that they were not going to be driven off or ignored. It was a sign of their presence, and the grander the church, the grander—the more certain and inescapable—the Irish influence.

Another centripetal force was Irish nationalism. The Irish had been dispossessed. They wanted Ireland back. They wanted it to be free—though there was considerable disagreement within the Irish ranks regarding the precise meaning of freedom—and they wanted the British, of whatever sort, to be put out of it. So, at least, they told themselves endlessly as they sent money back to Ireland to forward the national cause. Their critics said the same thing about the irrationality of this as they had said about money "wasted" on the church and its duplicate system of education. They missed the point here, too. The national home of the Irish had been stolen and they had been banished from it. They were the sons and daughters of a British colonial appendage, a fictive nation. As the church served more than just the spiritual needs of the faithful, so Irish American nationalism served more than just the causes of Ireland.

Exile was the starting point of this defensive nationalism. Even after 1856, when, in Kerby Miller's words, most of "the Irish emigrated voluntarily . . . [even] eagerly . . . in order to better themselves . . . economically," the sense that they were being forced from home was powerful; leave-takings were still accompanied by much wailing and gnashing of teeth. Some of this was entirely for effect, an effort by willing emigrants to evade the charge that family, friends, and even nation were being abandoned and that they were "selfish," "ungrateful," and "disloyal." In Scally's language, "what would later become 'the myth of exile' was an emigrant nationalism, suffused with bitter hindsight." Only this can explain the almost compulsive need of those from Ireland's townlands to display their Irishness by forming organizations attesting to their banishment and then building a hall where others banished could gather, commiserate, and plot their revenge. Indeed, part of the hold of these associations was due to their ability to reify exile by their near constant invocation of the Irish past. As Father Hugh Quigley wrote from San Francisco, Irish Americans showed they were "patriots by [their] love of country and advocacy of the independence of [their] native land." And whatever else may be said about them, these Irish fraternities in the guise of nationalist and patriot clubs slowed the Irish mutation from a hippopotamus to a swallow.[73]

These organizations of exiled patriots ranged from the militantly nationalist to the purely social, with everything else imaginable in between. Some were only for Catholics and others were ostensibly nonsectarian. The Ancient Order of Hibernians had a "ladies' auxiliary," the Daughters of Erin. The Clan na Gael was self-consciously manly and heroic; the Irish Volunteers was openly militaristic. Many of these Irish clubs were formed within weeks of the immigrants' arrival, sometimes before a Catholic church was chartered and built. The Clan na Gael camp in San Francisco was known as the Knights of the Red Branch (KRB); but before its formation, San Francisco's Irish had a Fenian Brotherhood and another slightly less rebellious association, the Sons of the Emerald Isle. Father Eugene O'Connell of All Hallows wrote that the Sons of the Emerald Isle had "turned out . . . on St. Patrick's Day" in 1854 "mounted on prancing steeds and decorated with the insignia of the Green Isle . . . they contributed the sum of 21 pounds"—toward what, he did not say.[74]

Some of these nationalist organizations raised money and bought guns; some prayed, or relearned and spoke Irish, or played Gaelic games. Each of them was given to sunburstery, rhetorical excess in the exaltation of Ireland and the damnation of Britain. Each gave tens of thousands of dollars to advance its various causes. Some of this patriotic fervor was of the barroom variety; some of it was thought good for business or political advancement. One unhappy—and uncommonly articulate—Irishman wrote back to Ireland that the nationalist clubs' only purpose was taking an Irishman's money: "I've had nothing but my salary to live on, and when it is taken into account that every Irishman out of employment who has ever had anything to do with the national movement has always almost invariably made a demand on my purse." Another immigrant complained of some of the San Francisco Irish who "strove to [gain] prominence as . . . suffering professional exiles and patriots," but whose main purpose was to win political office and sell liquor. Regardless of how easily patriotism may have come to those 4,000 miles from Ireland, however, the commitment to Irish republicanism was genuine, even if blended with other needs.[75]

Add to that blend the fact that some of these organizations, particularly the Clan na Gael, were clandestine and—in their own minds, at least—mysterious, even slightly menacing. They did their work in whispers and had secret handshakes, passwords, and other ritualistic practices. In other words, they met many of the same psychological needs as the Masons, Odd Fellows, and Knights of Pythias, including the reinforcement of manhood as the Victorians defined it. Each also had what can only be called a full social agenda, from gala New Year's balls to countless picnics, parades, concerts, fairs, and speeches. These social events had two distinct functions. The stated one was to raise money to liberate Ireland. The other was to assemble the exiles so that they might re-create something of the townland cultures, the camaraderie and good *craíc,* that still sustained them. It is hard to tell which of the two was the more important, and unnecessary to try.[76]

The Irish had the widest possible range of clubs making demands on their purses, seeking their votes, filling out their social calendar, confirming their manhood—and womanhood—and selling them liquor. Denver and the mining camps immediately to its west may serve as an ideal first example. Between the 1860s and the 1920s the Irish had the following from which to chose, offered up in no particular order: the Irish American Literary and Benevolent Association;

the Fenian Brotherhood; the Clan na Gael; the Ancient Order of Hibernians, with Ladies' Auxiliary; the Irish National League; the Irish American Progressive Society; the Irish American League; the Irish Military Company, known as the Mitchell Guards; the Irish-American Land League; the Irish National Land League; the Irish Agitation Society; the St. Patrick's Mutual Benefit Society; the Gaelic League; the Friends of Irish Freedom; and the American Association for the Recognition of the Irish Republic. Some of these clubs were replicas of Irish societies; others arose to meet the special demands that America placed on the Irish. All of them, however, were based on Irish townland notions of sociability and friendliness.[77]

This tendency to gather up the exiles and draft a charter of one sort or another affected the Irish wherever they landed in America. Every Irish city in the West revealed a pattern like that of Denver and the Colorado mining towns. Sacramento had a Fenian Circle; the curiously named Sacramento Irish Sufferers Relief Committee; the Dillon Branch of the Land League; the Robert Emmet Club; the Emmet Guards; the Sarsfield Grenadier Guards; two divisions of the AOH; the Hibernian Benevolent Association; and the Father Matthew Total Abstinence Benevolent Association. Portland had an AOH as early as 1878 as well as a Hibernian Savings and Commercial Bank. St. Paul had an Irish American Club whose "fundamental principle" was the "immutable belief in Ireland's right to be governed by and for her own people as an independent Nation." That may have been its fundamental principle, but it was "organized for social, literary [and] artistic purposes" as well as "the propagation of national sentiment." When M. J. Boyle reached St. Paul from his native Donegal in 1876, he found its Irish enclave already anchored to the place. He joined the Emmet Light Artillery, taught catechism, read and reread "Father Egan's 'Exiles of Erin,'" attended speeches by Bishop John Ireland and Ignatius Donnelly as well as Charles Stewart Parnell and Michael Davitt, and went to meetings "to sympathize with the peasantry of Ireland."[78]

The small Irish settlements in the West were no less active. Marysville, California, had a Hibernian Benevolent Society—which may have been partial compensation for the scandalous origins of the city's name. There were AOH divisions in Crockett, California; Scammon and West Mineral, Kansas; and Washougal, Washington. By 1912 there were eighty-two AOH divisions in Minnesota, including ones in such comparatively small towns as Graceville, Anoka, Madison Lake, Hastings, Montgomery, Ellsworth, Belle Plaine, and Clontarf; and each of these had its own Hibernia Hall. An 1893 promotional gazette describing Dakota County, Nebraska, spoke glowingly of the hamlet of Jackson, the "best town in Dakota County," with its new St. Patrick's church and the St. Patrick's Benevolent Society, formed in 1888 and consisting of the "best men of the community, industrious, honest, temperate." If more were needed, Jackson also had an AOH with its own Hibernia Hall and "a fife and drum band" to play in it.[79]

Iowa's rural and small-town Irish were equally engaged—and equally self-absorbed. As might be expected, there were AOH divisions in Melrose and Emmetsburg. But Albia, Georgetown, Creston, Keokuk, Massena, Imogene, Williamsburg, and doubtless many others also had active chapters. One of those was in Kinross, and the Minute Books of its bimonthly meetings survive. The Kinross Hibernians were as militantly nationalistic as their brothers in Butte or anywhere else in the New Irelands. They missed meetings for different reasons; in Butte having to work the late shift was a frequently cited excuse. In Kinross, calving or lambing or bad weather prevented attendance—most of the members were farmers who lived miles from the town. But the meetings in both places began and ended with prayer—probably the same prayer—and the discussions were likewise similar, ranging from the importance of sobriety to fervent and angry denunciations of British misrule in Ireland.[80]

Like the Butte AOH divisions, the one in Kinross supported a chair in the Irish language at Catholic University; the Iowans also donated one "addoring Angell to St. Patrick's Church" in Keokuk, sent money to their "suffering brothers in Spring Valley, Illinois," loaned money to "Jimmy Barrett," canceled that loan, and then raised money to wake and bury him. Members sent money to the orphan's home in Killarney, as well as to "brother Hibernians" among San Francisco's earthquake victims, and considered building a hall. Mostly, however, they discussed the upcoming dance (Kinross's Hibernians sponsored six or seven yearly) and the next scheduled picnic. Both functions were expected to raise money to free Ireland but, as noted and without questioning motives, both served to bring an extraordinarily clannish people together for the sheer joy the companionship of other Irish gave them. When the exiles were not at a dance or on parade, they were at a picnic. Finley Peter Dunne's fictional Chicago barkeep, Mr. Dooley, was not talking about Kinross—or even Butte—when he remarked that "be hivens, if Ireland cud be freed be a picnic, it'd not on'y be free to-day, but an impire, begorra," but his comment applied to Iowa's Irish farm towns as well as to Chicago's Irish neighborhoods.[81]

Dunne was not being entirely fair. Immigrant and ethnic celebrations were one thing, but there was something inherently radical about any gathering of exiles, even if only to picnic. This is one of the fundamental differences between the Irish and other major American immigrant groups. The Irish were not the only immigrants who came from a colony, a subordinate part of another nation's empire. But the level of hate was much deeper among the Irish than among any other immigrant or ethnic group. And the Irish were the only immigrants committed to violent wars of liberation. Similarly, the Irish were not the only immigrants to pay close attention to political developments in their home lands, but the American Irish did more than track events in Ireland; they tried to direct them. They had left Ireland without surrendering even a shred of their Irishness.

That was the way of exiles. They remained soldiers. They were simply temporarily displaced and held together by their shared displacement—exiles picnicking.

Other sources of enclave solidarity deserve brief mention. "Digger O'Dell,"
the Irish undertaker, was indispensable and ubiquitous; the Irish, after all, as James
Mooney had written, had a "horror of burial at the hands of the stranger."
Thomas O'Flaherty was quite wrong when, upon returning to Ireland from
Montana, he told his friends that in America the Irish paid "no more attention
to the dead than . . . to the living." The death ways of the Irish were the same in
both old and new Ireland and included extended wakes that only other Irish could
plan 'and superintend. Digger O'Dell knew how to put on a proper wake; the
stranger did not. The commemoration and consecration of a well-lived Irish life
required a well-conducted Irish death ritual. This was not something the Irish
could leave to the Hoosiers—even Catholic Hoosiers.[82]

At least as important as the Digger O'Dells were the thousands of Irish American saloon keepers, western versions of Mr. Dooley. Working-class Irish saloons
like Martin Dooley's establishment on Chicago's Archey Road were the American equivalent of the Irish *shebeen,* the unlicensed cross-roads drinking station.
In small communities like Melrose they may have been precisely that; Leo Ward
did not say where the Rookery got its whiskey, only that the neighbors were
known to drink it. In western industrial towns, the saloons were closer to way-
stations between dirty and dangerous Irish jobs and small and sometimes even dirtier
rooms in Irish boardinghouses. There was a Martin Dooley in every Irish town,
even the smallest and whatever its character. As with the Chicago original, he
did more than just draw beers.[83]

The saloon keeper told stories and arbitrated disputes, loaned money, and
counted and miscounted votes. Nothing in the neighborhood was unknown to
him. In some instances, he was a petty nobleman; but in all instances, he was the
resident sage and prophet. His place was where friends gathered. The townland
clans needed chieftains; they also needed a clubhouse, apart from the one in the
church and presided over by a resident "doctor of philosophy," Finley Peter Dunne's
honorific title for Martin Dooley. It was they who kept the "barbarians around
them . . . moderately but firmly governed, encouraged to passionate votings for
the ruling race, but restrained from the immoral pursuit of office." These barbarians, all "friends of Mr. Dooley," were the "most generous, thoughtful, honest,
and chaste people in the world . . . knowing and innocent; moral, but giving no
heed at all to patented political moralities"—or, I think Mr. Dooley would have
agreed, to the casual cruelties they contained. It was the job of the barman to
keep track of the sham platitudes of the myth makers. Mr. Dooley did. He "reads
the newspapers with solemn care" and "heartily hates them."[84]

Dunne never said if any of the numerous Irish American papers were among
those Mr. Dooley read and hated. Western Irish doctors of philosophy had the

Leader in San Francisco; the *Irish Standard* and the *Celtic World* in Minneapolis; the *Northwestern Chronicle* and the *Western Times* (a self-proclaimed "Irish and Catholic Household Journal") in St. Paul; the *Butte Independent* (identified by Patrick Pearse as a "binding force among the Irish in the West"); the *Rocky Mountain Celt* in Denver; and countless others. Each of these papers had sections containing news from Ireland, organized county by county. The publications that spoke for all Irish America—the *Gaelic American, Irish World,* and *Freeman's Journal*— did the same, filling entire pages with nothing but news from the townlands. The news was always of the most routine sort: marriages, children, deaths, arrests (though seldom for anything serious), parties, visits between families, good crop yields and bad. Like immigrant letters, they were filled with the quotidian realities of rural Ireland, the "jarring noises of crickets and cows," as Dunne put it. Transplanting townlands involved seeing that the transplanted had a steady supply of news about the root stock.[85]

All of this—from the handball courts to the fraternities, newspapers, saloons, and funeral parlors—helped the Irish to stay together and stay Irish. That meant, of course, to retain their strong local attachments. There were "Little Italys" and "Kleine Deutschlands" in America, but there were no "Little Irelands." The townlands had been transplanted, not the nation-in-waiting. And the townlands of America were only partially confederating; the pan-Irish movement was slow to start and halting in development. For example, John Devoy, the head of the U.S.-based Clan na Gael, speaking for both Ireland and America's new Irelands, wrote in the *Gaelic American* as late as 1904 that "localism is still a stronger trait in the Irish character than nationalism. . . . [It] is our national malady and until we overcome this weakness there is not hope for independence at home or respect abroad." Devoy was writing from New York not Ireland, but "home" and "abroad" were reversed from his location.[86]

This was not a sentiment universally shared, even by Irish American nationalists. Two years before Devoy's comment, Father Peter Yorke, certainly as fervent an Irish nationalist as Devoy, scored those "mild and gentle folk who deprecate the county idea" as well as "some vinegar degenerates who sneer about faction fights and rivalries." Yorke clearly had a deep affection for Irish localism. It meant that the people were still townland Irish, ignoring the irony: if there were ever to be an Ireland there would be Irish to live in it, but few of them with any sense of it being their national home. Transplanting the townland meant living with a residual form of it. Eliminating the faction fights and rivalries was only for vinegar degenerates and hippos pretending to be swallows. The Irish would love this new nation of theirs because it did not insist upon their love.[87]

Oscar Handlin once wrote that European "peasants" who immigrated to America, including presumably the Irish, "found nowhere an equivalent of the village, nowhere the basis for reestablishing the solidarity of the old communal life." He was mistaken. Irish enclaves, both urban and rural, were as friendly, meaning as intensely tribal, as the Irish townlands that were their models. That meant, of course, that they were also as "boss-ruled" and as intensely fractious and unruly.[88]

There is a joke that Butte's Irish like to tell on themselves. In some ways it is a uniquely Butte story, but it has a relevance to other Irish American towns and villages, particularly, I think, in the West.[88]

It was early in the morning of the day after an election, and Nora Lynch and her daughter Mary Pat went up to the polling place near St. Mary's Church in an almost entirely Irish precinct. Nora was Irish-born, Mary Pat was the savvy American. They were checking to see how Nora's brother Mike, a Democrat needless to add, had done in his contest for assistant city building inspector. The vote was posted on the outside door, and the two noted with pleasure that Mike had defeated his Republican opponent by a vote of 393 to 2. Nora, however, was puzzled. "And who," she asked Mary Pat, "might the two votes against Mike have been?" Her daughter pointed out some of the realities of American politics. "Well, you know, Ma, there's the Nelsons; they live on the edge of the gulch but in this precinct." "Ah yes," nodded Nora, "the Nelsons. But who might the other have been?" "Well," said Mary Pat, "remember the family just moved in at the north end, the Thompsons, I think they are." "Sure, and you're probably right," said Nora, "the Thompsons." And then the older woman paused. "Clannish bastards, aren't they?" Yes, they were.[89]

CHAPTER 9

An Alternate Frontier

The Irish Strain in Labor's Western American Heartland

In 1853 Jedediah Vincent Huntington, a convert to Catholicism, wrote *The Forest,* a fictionalized account of the settlement of western America. In it he made some interesting points about what the Catholic presence in the western hinterlands implied. He acknowledged that America was the end product of Protestantism but insisted that "beyond the limits of . . . Protestant settlement the Catholic influence can be depicted in a setting entirely free of the influence of American institutions." Here in the forests, Huntington wrote, "one finds order, stability, peace, a quality of life that can only be called pastoral, where passivity and humility are the cardinal virtues." Almost a half-century after Huntington, Harold Frederick extended the argument. His 1896 novel *The Damnation of Theron Ware* was an account of a Methodist minister of orthodox American beliefs, a palesman but an imperfect one. His spiritual roads would not run straight. They kept circling back, and he found himself drawn inexplicably to Catholicism and its alternative visions. When his fascination with the Irish Catholic Celia Madden, the "earth mother" of this tale, was not requited, he sought out that other avenue to redemption: he headed west to make his fortune in real estate.[1]

The West of Huntington and Frederick was too idyllic and their Catholics too comfortable to serve as anything more than regional and cultural cartoon characters. For the moment, however, it is not the look and shape of the Irish Catholic West that is important, but the assumption that Catholic "influences" were different from "American influences," that Catholics and Protestants did not see the world in the same way. Those differences did not manifest themselves by Catholics escaping into the forest to live in splendid isolation, far from the progressive pathfinders and builders of cities. Neither was it a matter of Catholics

287

invoking sacred tradition while Protestants sold real estate. That vastly oversimplified both peoples and the western regions in which they fought their cultural duels. The two peoples lived alongside one another; their lives ran parallel, occasionally even intersected. But only rarely did the meaningful parts of those lives touch. Putting a people beyond the pale also put them out of reach.

Some years later, the English Catholic G. K. Chesterton challenged the contentions of both Huntington and Fredrick—without, I am quite certain, ever having heard of either. Chesterton said that in America "even the Catholics are Protestants." He was not speaking only of the Irish and he was certainly not making a theological point. Assuming that he was making any point at all, it was sociological: American Catholics, Irish included, had been thoroughly assimilated. They were as progressive and acquisitive and fitted for modern American culture as any member of a Protestant charter group. Chesterton never said when exactly American Catholics began to act and think like Protestants, but it had to have been after 1896 and Frederick's book, which meant after the "spirit of capitalism" had been enshrined and the Catholic alternative to reality that Frederick had found had ceased to have relevance.[2]

Although Chesterton's remark is funnier, I think the comments of Evelyn Waugh—another English Catholic—are nearer the truth. Waugh's assessment of the collective personality of the Irish was in the context of what they had brought with them to America; it was a discouraging assessment, particularly for those non- and anti-Irish who had always placed them beyond the pale. Waugh was favorably taken by their "hard, ancient wisdom," but wisdom of the Irish sort was not what America wanted or needed from them. "Alone of the newcomers," Waugh went on, they "are never for a moment taken in by the *multifarious frauds of modernity.*" Those frauds were part of the "spontaneous philosophy" that the ascendant classes used to establish their cultural hegemony. But Waugh was not done. Hard, ancient wisdom put to bad use was not all the Irish brought with them to America. They also brought "all their ancient grudges and the melancholy of the bogs." The mood of the bogs had mysterious sources, but "ancient grudges" is a clear reference to a tragic history. History had made them—and made them, as Waugh phrased it, "at heart . . . [an]. . . adroit and joyless race." Irish "wisdom" came at considerable cost—to them and to America.[3]

The Irish looked at the world through their own cultural prism, the result of their own collective history. Whether this explains their resistance to the modern project may be debated, as, for that matter, might the very assumption that they resisted. It is time to move the discussion to safer ground and restate the obvious: the Irish did not think and act like Americans thought and acted. There were four essential reasons for this: first, their devotional Catholicism as both a faith tradition and a cultural marker; second, their intense hatred of Britain and its empire and a practiced ability to express their feelings through organizations that were at least quasi-political; third, an unshakable belief—or at least a recurring insistence— that they were exiles; fourth, an interdependence and sense of mutuality and "friendliness" that beggared description. All four of these pieces of Irish culture are important in understanding the alternate frontier that the western American Irish made.[4]

I have occasionally called these western Irish "pioneers," but I do so only hesitantly. "Pioneer" is a heavily laden word; it is better simply to note that they were among the earliest arrivals. But being early meant they could and did inscribe unsettled areas with their own values. And, being less careful than I am, the Irish called themselves pioneers all the time. They established their place in the hierarchy of American heroes by laying claim to a part in America's great and defining adventure, the settlement of the West, or, for the more self-congratulatory, the winning of it. This gave them certain privileges. A story from Montana makes the point. In 1914 a critic of Irish influence in Butte was told by an Irish woman: "75 per cent of the Butte people are Irish, why shouldn't we have 75 per cent" of the power? "And we were pioneers in Butte, so we should have the first say so." This called for the not so gentle rebuke that there "were pioneer Americans long before there were pioneer Butteites and even if 75 percent of the Butte people are Irish, that does not accord them the privilege of establishing Irish standards in any American city."[5]

That was a remarkable comment. Like Huntington's "Catholic influences" and "American influences" it acknowledged that there were in fact Irish standards and that they were not the same as American standards, which were passed down through a kind of impartible inheritance based on ancestry rather than age, on being the right-born rather than the first-born. Claiming to be a "pioneer Butteite" did not count for much in determining a legitimate line of descent. One had to be a pioneer American, a successor of one of the original and founding charter groups. Butte's Irish did not see it that way. They would have agreed that Irish values were not the same as American values, that in America the Catholics were not Protestants. They would not, however, have accepted or even have understood the ceremonial investiture that followed from being Protestant. America might not belong to them but Butte did, and so did other large parts of the western landscape.

This brings the story briefly to an admittedly curious mingling of Irish and Mormon. Had a critic of Mormonism made the same charge that was brought against the Irish in Butte, the Mormon response would have been identical: we got here first and in numbers. Brigham Young said "this is the place" and it remains *our* place. Gentiles and Hoosiers need not apply. But there is something far more essential in the comparison than having founders' rights. The important issue is determining what it was these unorthodox pioneers founded. At its beginnings, according to one historian, the "culture of the Mormons rested on a communal way of life that furnished a critical perspective on capitalism." That communal way of life, however, did more than just misalign them with capitalism. "Their record," according to Wallace Stegner, "is a record of group living, completely at variance with the normal history of the West." Compare that with Kerby Miller's and Oliver MacDonagh's "Irish Catholic variables" or with the historian John Duffy Ibsen's argument that the Catholic Irish were "fundamentally at odds with the commercially inspired progress faith of the United States." The Irish were as communal as the Mormons and as out of touch with many of the assumptive features of both capitalism and the grand Western narrative that was so central to it. To have been discrepant with both capitalism and the "normal" history of the West was to be in special company.[6]

What gives historical traction to what might be called the "Irish critique" of the gilded industrial age and of the fables that sustained it was Irish dominance of America's labor unions. Their "complete variance with the normal history of the West" was in the group record of their lives, but their "critical perspective on capitalism" was read in labor union halls. David Montgomery made a count of Irish union officers. It yielded such an impressive number that he found a "distinctly Irish strain" in the American labor movement, adding that "they were everywhere and into everything." Sean Wilentz went even further, writing that "an American labor history minus a thorough account of the Irish cannot even pretend to the name." It is not just the Irishness of the labor movement that is of concern here. Both Montgomery and Wilentz were speaking in terms of the entire nation, but, as Tony Lukas learned, the American labor movement had not only an Irish strain but a distinct westward tilt. Montgomery wrote that "the heartland of labor's electoral strength had been the West—from Wisconsin to Washington." I have extended that argument: the heartland of American labor generally had been the West. That is where Tony Lukas found the biggest trouble. He also found a great number of Irish big troublemakers.[7]

Both the strain and the heartland need to be accounted for. I am persuaded that the western labor movement was strong in part because the West had been trumpeted as a region of unlimited promise—or at least a place better by far than where one was and wherever one was. Those unhappy in the East were told to go to the West. But no one had any advice for unhappy westerners. Where were they to go? If the West's "lemonade springs where the bluebirds sing" ran dry and still, what was left? And they routinely ran dry. The economy of western America, to quote Kerby Miller again, was more "highly unstable, ruthlessly competitive, and physically brutal" than the national economy. And because it was that, it also violated and mocked everything the West was supposed to be. Learning that provided a lesson in disillusionment. Consider just one example: William Z. Foster was one of America's most militant Communists. That much is well known.

Less so is that Foster's working-class parents were born in Ireland and that his christening as William Edward took place in a Catholic church in New Jersey. He grew up in one of Philadelphia's toughest Irish neighborhoods, the aptly named Skittereen. By any accounting, William Z. Foster (the "Z." was given to him by the Communist Party) was a part of the Irish strain in American labor.[8]

But Foster was also part of labor's western heartland. He spent most of his working life in the West and learned his hardest lessons there. One of them is directly relevant to the issue of what happened when the West did not work its expected magic. In 1903 Foster homesteaded on Mosier Creek in north-central Oregon, exactly the sort of thing that the poor in the East had been told to do. Oregon was the antithesis of and the antidote to Skittereen. Foster was going to grow apples on his farm. He never expected to get rich; but in reading his account of the experience in his *Pages from a Worker's Life*, one senses the eagerness with which he began his great and redemptive western adventure. Unfortunately, he lost his claim when an unnamed corporation bought up everything around him; he and the other homesteaders in the region had their hopes "wrecked on the rocks of inhospitable economic conditions." Mosier Creek was a long way from Skittereen, but the only real difference between Oregon and Philadelphia was the scenery. William Edward Foster never specifically states it in his *Pages*, but it is inconceivable that his Oregon experience was not a part of the making of William Z.[9]

I do not offer Foster up as typical of anything. The Irish did not always push American labor leftward; neither did learning western lessons the hard way. The Irish strain produced an assortment of ideologies and policies from the pragmatic and accommodationist to the doctrinaire and militant; it cannot be typecast. But if that were all that could be said about it, why identify the Irish as a "strain," a breed, a variant of the larger whole? Montgomery and Wilentz would not have chosen the language they did if Irishness within the American labor movement had not meant something. What did it mean? Since the issue cannot and should not be dodged, did it provide even a partial answer to the question posed in 1906 by the German socialist Werner Sombart? "Why," he asked with a clear note of frustration, "is there no socialism in the United States?" In addition to the false premise—there *was* socialism in the United States—Sombart's question is based on the a priori assumption that there *should have been* a revolutionary class-conscious socialist movement in America. Something quite exceptional, almost unnatural, must have happened that prevented it.[10]

It is easy enough to reject all of Sombart's premises and the theoretical notions behind them. The answers to Sombart are simple, beginning with "Why should there have been?" and ending with "American workers thought about revolutionary socialism but rejected it, and for reasons that were neither unnatural nor exceptional." All of that said, however, if Sombart's question is taken without its philosophical suppositions and seen only as an expression of a healthy curiosity, it was not an illegitimate thing to ask. What follows, in other words, is not intended as my entry in the American exceptionalism debate. I am interested in what did happen, not what an ideological theory said should have happened. And those who ran the working-class organizations had a lot to do with what happened, which returns the discussion to where it should be: to the effect of the Irish strain on American labor's response to industrial capitalism. That, not the futile search for revolutionary class consciousness, is the context. And in that quite sufficient context it exaggerates only slightly to say that the Irish, particularly the western Irish, would determine if there was even to be an American working class, never mind a socialist one.[11]

It once seemed that nothing could be written dealing with this issue without a bow in the direction of E. P. Thompson's *The Making of the English Working Class*. That time has passed. American historians have come to understand that there was no real American working class but rather a wild and unruly mix of American working classes. A case can be made that in terms of theory—and not just Marxist theory—a society with more than one proletariat has no proletariat. Thompson would have had a hard time with that feature of American working-class formation. That does not mean, however, that he has nothing left to say to historians of American working people and of their alternative ideologies.[12]

Thompson is especially useful when it comes to the Irish. In writing of Irish workers in England in the early nineteenth century, he notes that the "Irish influence is most felt in a rebellious disposition in the communities and places of work; in a disposition to challenge authority, to resort to the threat of 'physical force,' and to refuse to be intimidated by the inhibitions of constitutionalism," a polite way of saying they were thought to be, and to an extent were, lawless urban bandits. They were a people of "rebellious dispositions," and it made no difference what the object of their rebelliousness might have been. These types, he concludes, were more likely to take part in "trades unions, combinations, and secret societies." They were also more likely to bring to those associations "their revolutionary inheritance." All of that sounds about right.[13]

So do other of Thompson's observations. It was true that the "most enduring cultural tradition which the Irish peasantry brought . . . was that of a semi-feudal nationalist Church," but that free and easy way the Irish had with the law ran it a close second. Thompson includes some interesting specific examples of that latter tradition, writing of the "rapid movement of men with blackened faces at night, the robbery of arms, the houghing of horses and cattle—these were methods in which many Irishmen had served an apprenticeship." He writes also of their "sometimes violent, sometimes good-humoured contempt of English authority. Not only were the rulers' laws and religion alien, but there were no community sanctions which found prosecution in the English law courts a cause of shame." By Irish reckoning, English law was neither blind nor disinterested: it was either ruthlessly calculating or maddeningly capricious. It made little difference to the Irish which; they suffered from its enforcement in either case. As memory was more reliable than history, so, and for similar reasons, was custom fairer than law. The historians could be bribed; the judges clearly had been. Thompson, of course, is discussing the early nineteenth century; but, as he puts it, all of these traditions endured "to the third and fourth generation." Each was at play in the making of an Irish American working class. They were part of what Thompson calls, in a marvelous turn of phrase, "the natural freemasonry of the disinherited."[14]

Eric Hobsbawm is another Marxist historian of British labor who has something to say on the Irish in the British working class and, by extension, in the American working class. It was the unskilled Irish, Hobsbawm notes, who formed the "revolutionary" element in the British working class, but for reasons that had little to do with their work lives. They "almost certainly sympathized with revolution," Hobsbawm writes, "*not because they were labourers, but because they were Irish,* . . . a tradition of armed rebellion formed part of the political experience of their country." The Irish were angry and disinherited at the start of the industrial process and before they were directly involved in it, and they remained that way. That also rings true. John Millington Synge said this about the Aran Islanders of the west of Ireland: "The impulse to protect the criminal is universal in the west. It seems partly due to the association between justice and the hated English jurisdiction, but more directly to the primitive feeling of these people, who are never criminals yet are capable of crime." John Commons, the American economist who presided over the Industrial Commission when it met in Butte, later wrote of Irish who, "in their own country, had lived through . . . storm and stress"; the experience "had made them lawless." That might also be a lesson he brought from Butte. In other words, the outlanders were outlaws—or at least more interested in equity than in the strict observance of a code of laws.[15]

Thompson and Hobsbawm were writing about style and tactics. The Irish were very good at hating; the source of that hatred or at whom it was directed was less important than the mere fact of it. They also knew how to target their hostility. But neither Thompson nor Hobsbawm saw any direct—or even indirect—association between being angry at Britain and being angry at capital. I want to add the association of imperialism and capitalism to the discussion and to talk about the substance of the Irish protest, not just the fact that they were well practiced at protesting. There was a coalescence of causes. The Irish did not redirect their hatred from one target to another. Many of them saw only one target; others either saw no meaningful differences between the targets or believed that the sins of the one made possible the sins of the other. Whether the British imperialists empowered capitalism or the other way around was of no moment; the two strode in lockstep as they ravaged Ireland and disinherited the Irish.

Big Flurry Driscoll once admitted that "possibly there is an element of self-pity in the behavior patterns of all persecuted people." He then quoted the poem of "The Poor Exile of Erin," with its mawkish and quite self-pitying refrain, "'There came to the beach a poor exile of Erin . . . / Sad is my fate! Said the heart broken stranger. I have no refuge from famine and danger. / A home and a country remain not to me.'" Flurry admitted that this was "the clamor of a beaten, persecuted, homeless, sentimental, home-loving people, adrift in a foreign land," and that "your neighbors seldom know what you are crying about, and they wouldn't care if they did know." That would not be enough to keep the Irish from crying.[16]

But what exactly were they crying about? Elizabeth Gurley Flynn was best known as an American radical, but she spoke in her autobiography of being raised on the fierce Anglophobia of the Irish nationalist movement as well as the rhetoric of working-class protest; her father never said the word "'England'" without then muttering "'God damn her.'" As previously noted, she added the important codicil: "when one understood British imperialism, it was an open window to all imperialism." William Z. Foster's experiences were similar. His father was a Fenian, driven out of his native Ireland by the crown's colonial government. Foster described him as a "refugee from Queen Victoria's vengeance . . . he fed us hatred for the oppressor England. It was the intellectual meat and drink of our early lives. I was raised with the burning ambition of one day taking an active part in the liberation of Ireland." But Foster was thousands of miles from Ireland. He needed an enemy closer at hand. And so he made a connection between the two: "It seemed as natural to hate capitalistic tyranny in the United States as English tyranny in Ireland."[17]

All of this was part of the "historically transmitted pattern of meanings" that went into the making of ethnic identity. In the case of the Irish, both in Ireland and in America, poverty and insecurity were joined by the atmosphere in which they were raised. Even when their target was not England, the simple, well-practiced ability to be angry and the almost innate suspicion of and contempt for codes of law gave them a running start in the search for other targets. America provided them with a multitude. I think that Foster's and Flynn's comments included a fair bit of reading back, what William Wordsworth called "after meditation." There is no evidence that they ever thought about Ireland or the Irish again after their leftward turn. The meat and potatoes of their youth had become thin gruel—although, interestingly, Foster asked to see a Catholic priest as he was dying. They came to hate injustice because they understood that Ireland had been treated unjustly. Foster was not inventing something in 1939 that was not there in the 1890s but inferring a connection because the association of the two causes made such perfect sense—particularly after Foster, the son of a working-class Irish American father, went broke on a western homestead.[18]

The causes were joined at a seam line. On the one side were demands to relieve the poverty of the Irish people; on the other, equally insistent demands for an independent Irish nation. In Ireland, to cite a radical example, James Connolly argued that the communalism, the sheer clannishness of the Irish, made them natural Communists. An Ireland freed from Britain and decontaminated from its influence would, by definition, be a workers' republic organized along Marxist lines. It could not be anything else without surrendering its Irish soul. In Connolly's reading of Irish history and culture, an Irish capitalist was either a contradiction in terms or someone who had internalized the culture of the oppressors.[19]

Granted, Connolly's was an extreme formulation, but aligning oneself on both sides of the seam required some very fancy footwork, regardless of how the sides were defined. Nationalism could mean only home rule or it could mean a republic; the republic could be modeled on the American, the French, or, later, the Russian model—which Connolly argued was prefigured by the ancient Irish. Whatever its ultimate form, this republic could be secured through peaceful persuasion, parliamentary obstruction, or physical force. As for reform, it could be concentrated on the land system, the labor system, or both. It might mean anything from peasant proprietorship to land nationalization, from syndicalism to the dictatorship of Ireland's still nascent industrial proletariat. Throw in the church, which insisted that the movement be kept within well-established ecclesiastical and doctrinal lines; add finally the cultural nationalists, who insisted that the entire nationalist agenda be publicized and carried out in the Irish language—no wonder the Irish were confused and conflicted.[20]

Whether in Ireland or in America, they had to choose on which side of the seam line they would make their stand. Many Irish Americans, particularly in the East, ended up as simple Catholic nationalists, in part because a liberated Ireland meant they no longer had to live with the shame and diminished status that came with being the descendant of a slave nation—or non-nation. What counted was seeing Ireland (Éire) added to the roster of nations, its flag unfurled over an all-Irish parliament (Dáil). These types were perfectly content with an Ireland that was America writ small. The eastern Irish were more affected by this, as seen in the disproportionate amount of money sent from the East to John Devoy's Irish National League. Thomas Brown called Devoy "Lenin-like" in his single-minded commitment to an independent Irish state—and his hostility to any intra-Irish feuding over the nature of that state.[21]

Those who were less captivated by America or less optimistic about their future prospects—which amounts to the same thing—continued to operate on both sides of the seam, frequently on the radical edge of both. That does not mean that they came down on the side of Connolly and his primitive Irish communism, only that they did not compartmentalize or alternate their protests. Many of these were in and of the working class. They veered leftward in their American as well as their Irish politics. For them, the last thing the Irish needed—the last thing the world needed—was another modern, market-driven, and acquisitive capitalist republic sustained by what Waugh called "multifarious frauds," whether of American or Irish origin. Building a miniature America—or Britain—was not a shortcut to an Irish Ireland. For those of this mind, moving from side to side across the seam came naturally. An independent Ireland was important; but so were the rights of the Irish people, wherever found. It was the importance of the rights of the *non-Irish* people that was problematic.

I think a disproportionate number of these seam-jumpers lived in the American West, which opens up an interesting line of historical inquiry. Did labor's western heart produce a more radical brand of Irish American nationalism that matched *and accompanied* it? I have already mentioned the part of the western narrative that was peopled by social bandits and outlaws rather than conquerors and trailblazers. As Thompson's and Hobsbawm's accounts make clear, the Irish liked outlaws. But apart from the Irish appreciation of creative criminality and outlawry's close association with wild wests, simply read again the title of Patrick Ford's newspaper: the *Irish World and American Industrial Liberator*. There were no means of worker liberation that did not involve the West, very few that did not require some direct challenges to existing law. Did the West witness more and more intense involvement on both sides of Ford's two-front campaign and did the alternate frontier of the Irish arise in part from the volatile mix of the two? The effort to liberate the American industrial worker occasioned more big trouble in the West than in the East. Could the same be said regarding the commitment to the liberation of the Irish world?

History is never this formulaic, but consider the correlation between Irish nationalism and the labor movement as well as the Irish strain in the labor movement and the western heart of that movement. Formulas aside, consider that the western Irish all but ignored John Devoy's brand of nationalism in favor of Patrick Ford's. Devoy's insistence that an independent Irish nation counted for more than the relief of the suffering of the Irish people—wherever found—did not play nearly as well in the West as in the East. California, for example, gave a grand total of $50 to Devoy in 1882. Massachusetts gave almost $20,000; Connecticut almost $8,000. By way of comparison, California's and Colorado's 85,000 Irish-born gave as much to Ford's Land League Fund as did the 400,000 Irish-born in Massachusetts and Connecticut. In February 1882 twenty-three new branches of Ford's Land League were formed; twelve of those were in the West. Add the formula to the dollars and a strong case can be made that western Irish America was far more likely than eastern Irish America to battle on both sides of the twinned banners of Patrick Ford's masthead (see the appendix).[22]

In his article on the reformist American Land League and the money sent by its branches to Ireland via the good offices of Ford's *Irish World,* Eric Foner pointed out that much of the money came from working-class areas. He offered a table taken from an 1881 issue of Ford's newspaper listing the contributions from various industrial cities. This table was quite intentionally incomplete. Its purpose was to reinforce the working-class sources of the funds and what Foner identified as the "symbiotic relationship between class conscious unionism and Irish nationalism," what Philip Bagenal called an "alliance" between the "Fenian brotherhood" and "what is known in America as the Labour party." I agree that the relationship existed. But studying the complete list tells another and equally important story; this nationalist crusade had a regional as well as a social-class and occupational dimension. A significant number of Irish living in the West—and not just in its industrial cities—gave money through Ford's paper. To borrow Foner's language, there was a relationship, varying between symbiotic and merely of convenience, between the Irish in the West and Ford's brand of Irish nationalism.[23]

It manifested itself in a variety of ways, many of them minor but all of them telling. In Leadville, Colorado, in the early 1880s the Wolfe Tone Guards were officially a part of the Knights of Labor–affiliated miners' union. Labor-union gatherings all through the West were occasionally described as "monster meetings," a term previously used to describe the huge crowds that had come to hear Daniel O'Connell in Ireland. Those same unions adopted the Irish Land League tactic of boycotting, adjusted slightly to meet industrial conditions, as one of their favored tactics. Bagenal's reported "alliance" was predictable of him; he worried about everything the working-class Irish were doing. The formal affiliation of an Irish nationalist organization with a Knights of Labor assembly suggests that the Irish were hopelessly confused, remarkably prescient, or careful readers of Patrick Ford. Nothing of great importance was implied by the use of "monster meeting"—except that it was a tag line brought over from the nationalist movement in Ireland and applied to the labor movement in American.[24]

Boycotting was a different matter. It involved direct action and, as an Irish Land League veteran then mining in Colorado put it, "no more effective weapon . . . could possibly be used by a labor organization." That use, moreover, occasioned some vehement protests from the APA and from other non-Irish, one of whom called it "a foreign importation only a little less obnoxious to decent American citizens than nihilism, communism, and kindred tenets of foreign cut throats and robbers, . . . the lowest, meanest, most despicable instrument of malice and revenge that was ever imported, . . . an un-American principle." That was a bit hyperbolic—which might also be why the Irish liked it so much. During World War I, when Montana's xenophobic Council of Defense proposed to prohibit "strikes and boycotts," an Irish American representing the State Federation of Labor pointed out that "that word boycott would probably reach farther than the labor organizations." It certainly would have.[25]

In 1876 Ford published an extremely revealing letter from a reader who called himself "Ballaghaslane Beara." The pseudonym was pure West Cork and straight from the exile motif. Ballaghaslane roughly translated meant "evacuated [expelled] from home," and the largest copper mines in Ireland were on the Beara peninsula. Beara read Ford's masthead literally. "We are slaves in the United States, and . . . the reason is plain." At this point in his letter, most Americans would have assumed that the plain reason was that capital had made slaves of them. That was not where Beara was taking this argument. By the "we" who were slaves he meant only the Irish, and the reason for their enslavement was not capital, at least not directly. It was "because we haven't an Irish nation. England defrauded us of the means by which we could afford to settle down on a western farm; and we are therefore chained down to live in the mire of the cities."[26]

Note two things about Beara's lament, other than its uniquely Irish assignment of responsibility. First, he was not writing from eastern America, where most of the wage slaves were presumed to live, but from Virginia City, Nevada, in the Great West, where slaves went to be free. Second, study the language: "slaves," theft of nationhood, settling down on western farms, "chained" to the cities. If Ballaghaslane Beara omitted any of the intersecting lines, I cannot find them. He had taken separate issues, joined them at the seam, and made them one. It is unfortunate that no committee ever called Ballaghaslane Beara and asked him how exactly he would address the mix of issues he had raised: England had defrauded them of their nation, which made them industrial slaves, which left them mired in the cities, which prevented them from settling on a western farm, which kept them perpetually poor. This was the Irish master narrative, and it was the absolute antithesis of America's national saga.

The Irish turned that mixture of causes into an art form. "General" John O'Neill's effort to establish "a thousand Irish-American Colonies scattered all over the West" has been noted. What needs to be emphasized is the multiple responsibilities those colonies would have. Each would be in strict "conformity with Church discipline." Each would "be devoted to the cause of Ireland," would be, in fact, a staging area for an Irish American attack on Canada. And each would provide an escape for Irish trapped in eastern cities, pauperized by economic depressions, and exploited by capitalists who "count[ed]" their "dollars by the thousand . . . and fatten[ed] on the . . . laborer [who] receives 50 cents for a dollar's worth of work." O'Neill at one and the same time was a devout if somewhat defensive Catholic; a physical-force Irish nationalist; and a rather radical participant in the class wars. His colonies would serve the same interests, which was asking a lot of small western towns.[27]

Sometimes these connections came so naturally to western Irish Americans that the seam line entirely disappeared. Strikes in 1886 against the railroads and for the eight-hour day were linked to the Irish "No Rent Manifesto" of 1882. So, remarkably, was the Pullman strike in 1894, long after the manifesto had lost its currency in Ireland—but not its hold on the consciousness of Irish Americans. Denis Hurley wrote back from Carson City, Nevada, to his mother in Ireland with news that his brother Michael had been involved "in the 'No Rent Manifesto' or *sympathetic Pullman strike movement.*" Sympathy strikes were important, but they were also by definition secondary to the cause with which they were in sympathy. Denis Hurley's mind was still fixed on Ireland and its grievances, not on America and its challenges. Financial panics, marching armies of the unemployed, and wage reductions were not the issues in 1894. Ireland was the issue—and Ireland in 1882. Hurley had mastered that remarkable Irish ability to be in two places at the same time, two times in the same place, and done so completely without self-awareness.[28]

Even more revealing evidence of this Irish magic act came when Dan Sullivan of Butte testified before a Montana state committee investigating labor unrest in 1911. I first read Sullivan's testimony twenty years ago; I was puzzled by it then. I think that I understand it now and that it makes sense of the seam and much else in the western Irish experience. Sullivan was being questioned about the occupational hazards of working in the Butte mines. The committee called him because he had worked underground in Butte for fifteen years and had recently been elected the president of the Butte Miners Union. His militancy was not yet on full display, but in 1911 the BMU was turning sharply leftward and Sullivan's election was a part of that radical tilt. As for Sullivan's other associations, the committee would neither have known nor have cared that he was also an active member of the Robert Emmet Literary Association (RELA), the Butte chapter of the Clan na Gael. His Irishness had nothing to do with why he was called or with the questions the committee asked of him.[29]

It had everything to do with his answers. Sullivan was asked about the sanitary conditions in the Butte mines, specifically whether he thought Butte miners would use toilet cars if the companies were to provide them. He answered, "I think some of them would probably; it may be like some of the men in the South; for instance, Habana. They had a very insanitary condition there, and there was a law that was passed over there. Since then they have a pretty sanitary city, so I am told." His questioner then offered a gratuitous remark: "I take it that the civilized conditions existing among the miners in Butte are a little better than what they had down there?" The inference was clear: Butte miners were civilized white men; Cubans were of an inferior sort. Sullivan would have none of it. "I don't know anything about that," he said, "but I know the Cubans are free; that they got their freedom." Sullivan did not say that Americans had helped them get it; neither did he say that in a fairer and friendlier world America would help Ireland get its freedom. But that is what he meant. There was not an Irish American worker, East or West, who would have needed to have Sullivan's comment interpreted.[30]

To most Americans, however, including those in the working class, his answer would have been a non sequitur. Questions regarding labor were thought to require answers drawn from the experience of labor. "Irish" answers to working-class questions seemed unintelligible and confusing at best, indicative of a false consciousness at worst. Sullivan switched roles from union president to radical Irish nationalist almost mid-sentence, and he did it so spontaneously, so seam-lessly. He was not trying to change the subject. There was only one subject with two heads: Britain exploited Ireland, which allowed capital to exploit Irish workers. Connolly had said it. "The cause of labour is the cause of Ireland; the cause of Ireland is the cause of labour. They cannot be dessevered." Connolly was wrong, but he was certainly not the only one to make the case. Karl Marx had said the same thing, without knowing exactly what it was he was saying. So had Patrick Ford when he wrote of the cause of the poor in Donegal being the cause of the factory slave in Fall River.[31]

One of those Donegal poor was Ed Boyce, but he made his case from the American West, not from Fall River. Boyce was born in Deenystown, Donegal, in 1862, immigrated to Boston in 1882, and then began his westward trek: first to Wisconsin, where he worked on the railroad, then to the hard-rock mines of Leadville, the Coeur d'Alenes, and Butte. His union career began in Leadville, where he joined the local miners' union, probably through the Wolfe Tone Guards. In 1892 Boyce was one of the leaders of the miners striking against the Bunker Hill and Sullivan mines in the Coeur d'Alenes. By 1895 he was the president of the Western Federation of Miners, headquartered in Butte, a position he held until 1902. Had historical events aligned themselves somewhat differently, the WFM under Boyce might have had a genuinely radical impact on American labor history. As it was, Boyce pushed the WFM as far left as it ever went. His speeches and articles contained blistering attacks on the insolence of "brutal corporations" that "have no souls." Workers were left to "pine in chains." The industrial order had made America "a strangers' land," nowhere more so than in the West.[32]

I think those last references should be taken as written. Boyce understood better than most that soulless corporations had a particular fondness for border-lands and frontiers. He also was aware of the contradictions in this; like Beara (or Jefferson), Boyce wanted the American worker to have the chance to "settle down on a western farm" and not be "chained down to live in the mire of the cities." This agrarian dream was frustrated not just because England had "defrauded" the Irish of their nation but because western American corporations were so uncommonly rapacious. And so Boyce determined that the western labor movement had to become uncommonly militant. Labor would unmake and remake the West that capital had made. For Boyce, western unions were far more relevant than eastern ones because to change the West was to change the future by preserving the agrarian dream. But Boyce did more; he also inverted the meaning of the American pale by identifying the strangers, the outlandish ones, as home-born, home-grown, and westward moving.[33]

The western shoot-out that Boyce prophesied was going to be truly epic. "There can be no harmony between organized capitalists and organized labor. . . . There is nothing in common. . . . There can be no harmony between employer and employee . . . nothing short of the complete abolishment of the present wage system will ever adjust it. Our present wage system is slavery in its worst form." About a year later he wrote that "all the natural resources of the nation are controlled by a few corporations that dictate to their white slaves how much they shall receive for their labor and where they shall spend what they do receive." Boyce urged workers to demand "the overthrow of the whole profit-making system, the extinction of monopolies, and the land for the people." This was to be "a glorious fight for the emancipation of the wage slave. I can see the dawn of a new era of co-operation." In other words, he could see the Irish's alternate frontier, agrarian and neighborly.[34]

Ed Boyce was a major part of the Irish strain, but that means a place in that strain must be found for his belief that among the settler societies being cruelly treated was Ireland. His scribbled notebook and diary entries are filled with quotations, such as "But where is my father's low cottage of clay / Where I've spent many a long happy day? / Alas! Has his lordship contrived it away? / Yes, 'tis gone. I shall ne'er see it more." "Accurst be the dastards, the slaves that have sold thee, / And doomed thee, lost Eire, to bondage and shame!" No one can know whose bondage and shame, worker or Irish, was more important to Boyce. It depended partly on the circumstances. But he was Irish before he was a worker. Indeed, he was the one because he was the other, and it is likely that his Irish nationalism gave rise to his worker militancy, not the other way around. He was an active and vocal member of the Butte Clan na Gael, for example, and at one meeting in 1899 condemned "our Enemy, the British tyrannical Government." All knew what he meant by "our." *Miners Magazine,* the official organ of the WFM and edited by Boyce until 1900, carried column after column dealing with Irish resistance to British imperialism—as well as Finley Peter Dunne's "Mr. Dooley" columns. Boyce did not carry Irish nationalist news simply as a means of keeping his working-class readership happy. For Boyce, splitting the two causes left both devoid of meaning.[35]

If only it had been that easy. Unfortunately, sometimes workers' rights and the cause of the Irish nation either could not be pursued simultaneously or were mutually exclusive, as when an Irish worker nationalist confronted an Irish capitalist nationalist in what were only slightly updated versions of medieval faction fights. Occasionally the fighting was on full public display. Those who tracked the Irish resistance knew of the hostility of some prelates of the Catholic Church toward the more radical of the nationalists' schemes, particularly those that called for the use of physical force, and the factional disputes between and among Land Leaguers, National Leaguers, Gaelic Leaguers, Plan of Campaigners, Parnellites, anti-Parnellites, and republicans. At the tactical level, working-class Irish Americans openly condemned wealthier Irish for not paying a fair share of the costs of Irish revolutions—something that happened with greater frequency as the Irish national movement veered away from a bourgeois state and toward a workers' republic.[36]

Many of these battles of green versus green, however, occurred behind the closed and guarded doors of Hibernia Hall, which is why the rest of this must be a Butte story. First, the records of its nationalist associations survive. Those records indicate that Irish of every social class were involved in Ireland's various and at times contradictory patriot games. Second, in all the Irish world, only in Butte was "Irish Catholic captain of industry" not an internally contradictory phrase. It described a recognizable social type: the chieftain from the Anaconda Copper Mining Company (ACM), which produced from one-quarter to two-fifths of the world's copper and, at its peak, was the world's fifth largest corporation. As befitted an ACM official, the boss wore well-tailored suits, was surrounded by a cortege of lesser nobles, and was well represented on Catholic parish rosters and on the membership lists of Butte's three divisions of the Ancient Order of Hibernians and the more radical RELA. The same things, including the quality of their tailoring, could have been said of all the officers of the BMU. Butte was the "Gibraltar of American Unionism" because of the BMU. With a membership of 8,000 to 18,000 men, it was the largest local organization of workers in the world and the richest. More important than that, 145 of its 180 officers between 1885 and 1914 were Irish, and 64 of the 94 men who held those 145 positions were members of one or both of Butte's Irish nationalist associations.[37]

The Anaconda Copper Mining Company and the Butte Miners Union were the most powerful Irish-run organizations in the entire transnational Irish world. Nothing in Ireland, including Parnell's Irish Parliamentary Party, had the same influence. Their only rivals in America would have been the Catholic Church and the Democratic Party, and the Irish had to share power with non-Irish in both. The Irish of ACM and the BMU shared power with no one. California had its share of Irish millionaires—James Fair, John Mackay, William O'Brien, and James Flood (the "Irish Four" silver kings), James Duval Phelan, Garrett McEnerney, and John Francis Neylan prominent among them—but combined they did not control a tiny fraction of the tens of thousands of paychecks drawn on Anaconda accounts. San Francisco's Hibernians and clansmen included both capitalists and laborers—but the latter did not work for the former. On labor's side of the social-class divide, Patrick McCarthy was the acknowledged "baron" of San Francisco's powerful building trades unions, but no single component of that workforce ever approached the 15,000 men organized by the BMU, which had a closed-shop contract with ACM that lasted for thirty-six years and which essentially joined the union and corporation at their Irish hip.[38]

All of this creates a fascinating and important object lesson in postcolonialism. In Ireland Strangers were still in control; the Irish still confronted English and Anglo-Irish Protestants with horses. In the eastern United States Irish Americans were still warring with a hostile host society. But in the West they frequently were the host society, and in Butte they ran everything. Butte was what every Irish town would be if only it could afford it. And that includes Irish towns in Ireland. It was a place where the strangers were gone or had been routed and all of the enemies were friends. As such, it provides an exceptionally "clean laboratory" for the study of direct intratribal conflict. The divided loyalties to ethnicity and social class were fully revealed and the strength of each frequently tested. The working-class Irish felt the strain of divided loyalties more than did the corporate managers, which says something about whether workers or capitalists were more class conscious. But for both sides of the class divide, being Irish in Butte was not something that could simply be declared. It had to be negotiated.

Also at issue is whether the corporation and the union were somehow each responsible for the influence of the other and whether that reciprocity not only produced Irish power but arose from a shared Irishness. Marcus Daly had a lot of reasons to hire the Irish: they knew how to mine, he liked and sympathized with them, and he shared many of his workers' anti-British attitudes; he had himself been "exiled." But did he also hire Irish workers because he knew they hated the British far more than they could ever hate capitalists, particularly Irish capitalists? Daly was the ultimate chief, a western American high king. He was counting on the Irish staying loyal to him. To suggest, however, that Daly created a carefully crafted public image designed to pacify those Irish less favored than himself is too cynical. I return to a point made earlier: a number of statues in America honor conspicuously wealthy capitalists. But the statue of Daly is the only one built with money subscribed by the working class. It may be that the statue was built by money subscribed by the Irish "class," but that is the point: only in "clean laboratories" can such issues be tested.[39]

The laboratory evidence strongly suggests a mutual dependence between union and company. It was charged that compliant Irish BMU officers were given leases by grateful Irish ACM officers; many used the money from the leases to abandon the American labor movement and move back to Ireland. When the enormously wealthy merchant Dan Hennessey died, the AOH commissioned a portrait of him to be hung in Hibernia Hall. The portrait was painted by John D. Ryan, the chief of ACM. When Ryan was made president of the holding company that owned Anaconda, the Hibernians, whose officer list was predominantly working class, sent him a letter of "appreciation" rather than the more natural "congratulation." Ryan's promotion benefited them all, and they appreciated it. When Bill Haywood, the IWW officer, told Butte's miners to "nail the red flag to the mast of #1 [the Butte Miners Union Hall]" and have Anaconda "officials . . . get down on their knees to it," the Irish-led BMU was derisive. But when it was suggested that the RELA get its hands on an airship, float it over the British Houses of Parliament, and drop explosives down the stacks, the worker-led RELA enthusiastically voted to look into the idea.[40]

On balance, far more Irish workers in Butte cooperated with the more powerful Irish than contested them. More important than portraits and airships was the fact that for thirty-six years, from its founding in 1878 until its self-destruction in 1914, the Irish-run Butte Miners Union engaged in not a single job action against the Irish-run Anaconda Company. An IWW organizer excoriated the Butte miners for those "thirty-six years of peace and prosperity," insisting that they should be "ashamed" of themselves for not making some "big trouble." The reality of the BMU's "submissiveness" has always been difficult for historians to explain; for that matter, it was difficult for non-Irish contemporaries to explain. I propose a hypothesis: the BMU did not confront ACM because any job action, especially a strike, would interfere with wages, a significant percentage of which went back to Ireland to drive out the British Strangers and help out friends. In the long run, a strike might benefit working miners, but the costs in the short run would be borne by Ireland and the Irish. Since those working miners included a sizable number of non-Irish, this was not a deal the Irishmen who ran the BMU were willing to make.[41]

None of this was a formula for labor militancy. In the clean laboratory of Butte, the Irish strain tended toward an accommodation with capital rather than assaults on it. Radical challenges to capital were for class warriors, which, for the ultranationalists, meant those who had nothing better to do. Cooperation with capital, on the other hand, was central to the Irish national struggle, for the simple reason that getting along with the bosses, even if they were non- or anti-Irish, meant steady wages that could be used to finance a warrior's return from exile or shared with Ireland and used to buy guns to arm the home guard. When the bosses were themselves Irish, cooperation meant interclass ethnic solidarity and even more guns. In either case, cooperation with the more powerful in matters affecting labor did not mean that the Irish had grown timid and soft. It often meant just the opposite.[42]

It also hopelessly complicated the Irish strain. As William Foster's deathbed request for a Catholic priest would attest, it was tricky being an Irish Catholic Communist. James Connolly provides another example. To oversimplify only slightly, the cause of labor needed Connolly alive; the cause of Ireland needed him dead. He would have to sever the two causes by choosing one or the other. He chose Ireland, and England obliged him by shooting him—something it would never have done had he been a mere Communist. The night before he was executed, he also called for a priest and gave an answer to all his incredulous non-Irish working-class comrades who were alternately astonished, furious, and grief-stricken. "The socialists will not understand why I am here," Connolly said. "They forget I am an Irishman." He did not even say "I am *also* an Irishman."[43]

Ed Boyce navigated along the seam a bit differently. His fervent Irish nationalism, his unwavering Catholicism, even his fondness for bathetic Irish poetry in no way diminished or conflicted with the genuineness of his worker radicalism. He tried to juggle all three. Butte would not let him. Or, rather, Daly's influence would not let him. Boyce never mentioned this in his letters, never hinted at it in his diary, and certainly never commented on it in his speeches or in the pages of the *Miners Magazine*, but it seems obvious that the Irishness of Butte was what drove him and the Western Federation of Miners Executive Committee to move WFM headquarters to Denver. Butte's world was too pervaded with Irishness to serve the working-class purposes that Boyce envisioned for the WFM. Boyce moved the WFM just as money was being raised for the Daly statue; this cannot have been pure coincidence. The Irish, he was saying in effect, forget I am also a worker. The "also" is important.[44]

In *The Counsels of Cormac,* Cormac is asked: "What is best for a king?" Among his answers: "True reciprocity." When asked "What is best for the interest of a tribe?" he answers: "Not oppressing the wretched. . . . Sternness toward enemies, innocence toward kin." There were many ways of "acquiring incapacity"; Cormac identifies the first among them as "wronging friends." As for "who is the worst protector," Cormac answers directly: "A protector of little dignity who sells his honor, his support, his hand, his breast, his heart, the right of his clan, his people, and his prowess." The Irish did not have to have read Cormac to live by the same rules. In fact, a people disinherited, exiled, and beleaguered may have needed Cormac's counsels more even than those who had read him. But consider carefully the various social nexuses around which the chieftains' identities formed: "tribe, kin, friends, clan"—no one else. That would not change. The Irish would have no false gods and no false bonds. They, too, were a covenanted people, but the covenant was not just with God; it was with themselves. Americans could exploit other Americans and still be American. The British could do the same to other British and still be Britons. In fact, some—particularly the Irish—would contend that exploiting one another was what proved that they were still the genuine article. The Irish could exploit other Irish, too; but if and when they did, they lost their identity and became recreant.[45]

In James Moriarty's poetic lament, both sides of the seam—both Ireland and the Irish poor—are represented. "When I bade farewell to my poor sad mother; /

I never saw gold on the street corners— / Alas, I was a poor aimless person cast adrift . . . / It's far far better to be in Ireland where there's cheer, / Listening to the melodious bird songs, / Than looking for work from a crooked little miser / Who thinks you're only an ass to be beaten with a stick." I think the Irish poor are given more emphasis than the cause of Ireland; I also think Moriarty would not have cared one way or the other. What he would have cared about was who was doing the beating. He was not writing in or about Fall River and its Yankee mill owners. He was writing about Butte and its Irish mine owners. It is clear that the crooked little misers he reviled were the self-consciously Irish officers of the ACM. He certainly had John D. Ryan in mind and perhaps Marcus Daly as well. But notice one other thing about Moriarty's poem: he was not working *for* the crooked little Irish miser; he had not reached that stage. He was looking for a job *from* him so that he might be beaten—and beaten down. Obviously, members of the tribe would disagree on whether Cormac's rules had in fact been broken, whether the ACM chieftains were crooked little misers or patrons. Witness again the Daly statue. For that matter, witness Daly and all of Butte.[46]

Predictably, the Irish placed the misers and others among them who wronged their friends in two special categories, two uniquely Irish circles of hell reserved for those who "sold" their honor and their prowess by selling out the rights of their people. These categories were reserved only for the other Irish; the non-Irish who exploited them were evil, to be sure, but allowances had to be made: they were not Irish and so knew no better. Irish perfidy was an entirely different matter. The first category was that of *na gaimbíni*, the gombeens. *Gaimbin* was the Irish word for usurer; when the Irish charged each other an excessive interest, when the fee in the form of loyalty for services rendered was unfair or undeserved, they were literally guilty of usury. But they were guilty of stealing far more than just money. Stealing money was a silly charge. The Irish did not have any money. The gombeens broke the covenant; they stole from the storehouse of the Irish soul. The second category was an extension of the gombeens. *Na seoniní,* the shoneens (Little John Bulls, Irish flunkeys trying to be English bulldogs or, more graphically, Irish "ass-lickers"), joined the gombeens on the Irish roster of ignominy. In one sense, all gombeens were shoneens. Since the Irish word for the English was the same as their word for being begrudging, acting English was an act of cultural apostasy. Brendan Behan's description of the Anglo-Irish as "Protestants with [and usually on] a horse" has been cited. The gombeen was a variant: a Catholic with a horse—likely stolen. The shoneens were Catholics who *posed* with a horse.[47]

By the 1870s, in both Ireland and Irish America, the Irish were discovering that their worlds were filled with gombeens and shoneens. I think that they learned that hard lesson in America before they did in Ireland and that they learned it in western America before they learned it anywhere else. The result was another of the many Irish bulls: the fighting Irish were more often than not fighting among themselves, accompanied by much shouting and general disorder. As Thompson pointed out, in addition to being "quick to come to each other's aid," they were also intensely factional, "quick to quarrel," and "constantly fighting among themselves." Gjerde made exactly the same point and extended its application to the Irish mind of the West: "Because boundaries *between* communities were often strictly defended, conflict *within* the communities was common." The conflicts within the western Irish American communities were assuredly that.[48]

In sum, the Irish were border warriors fighting the nativists and Hoosiers and protecting the clan; they were also and at the same time faction fighters engaged in intraethnic battles over who ran or even was still in the tribe. In the latter role, their natural freemasonry went a long way toward making Irish life interesting. In their role as border warrior, and in the context of American labor, the split allegiance of the disinherited Irish confounded any effort to build a coherent worker ideology. The important issue is that both were "Irish roles." Playing them made for more history—or more memories—than the Irish domestic market could consume. So they exported the playbook, often disguising it as "hard, ancient wisdom." The United States became the largest and among the least enthusiastic of their trading partners. They were ill-tempered, semilawless, and extraordinarily clannish. They built bonds among themselves, borders to protect themselves; they did not build bridges.

This raises some important issues. Did Moriarty leave any room for the non-Irish "asses" who were also being "beaten with a stick"? Could Beara have explained the enslavement of America's non-Irish workers who were not defrauded of their nation, forced into exile, and mired in the cities? Did they matter to him? Do the banners and labels need to be changed? There is no doubt that Father Michael Hannan was a priest of an "Irish" church that was only loosely affiliated with the Catholic Church. But what of the other associations with which the Irish were confederated? Were they in fact if not in name the *American* (Irish) *Industrial Liberator,* the Western Federation of (Irish) Miners, the Butte (Irish) Miners Union, and the (Irish) *Miners Magazine*? But the tribal qualifier must itself be qualified by words that identify the kind of Irish in question—the side of the seam in which they placed themselves. The only things not subject to debate were that the Irish were papists, they were Paddies, and they were poor. They would occasionally have to decide which of those they were at given moments in time, but that did not require that they throw off the others or that they stop choosing their friends only from those like themselves.

No other feature of the Irish strain had a greater influence on the American labor movement than this conjunction and occasional confusion of issues. It had the effect of making American labor policy a subordinate aspect of Irish nationalism. British imperialism became a target of the American labor movement as surely as the gross excesses of American capitalism. American working-class issues were interpreted and decided in the context of how they might impact both the cause of Ireland's freedom and the freedom of Irish labor. In *Why Is There No Socialism in the United States?* Werner Sombart not only asked a question, he supplied answers to it. Interestingly, the Irish strain was not among those answers. It should have been. The Irish strain in American labor arose from detached Irish social outliers. The Irish were not on the side of the working class; they were on the side of the Irish working class. The disinherited did not have the resources to fight the world's battles, even if they had wanted to.[49]

The American land reformer Henry George learned this the hard way. George had moved to San Francisco as a very young man. Growing to adulthood there provided him with firsthand knowledge of both the most golden part of the Golden West and the Irish who lived in it in great numbers and in varying degrees of comfort. In 1879 George wrote *Progress and Poverty,* one of the most eloquent pleas for an alternative to the Gilded Age and its multifarious frauds. That he wrote it from the West and in great measure about the West says volumes about the disparity between the image of the region and the reality and about the profound disillusionment that accompanied learning that the West as imagined bore no meaningful resemblance to the West as found. Some thought that Ireland should become America writ small; George was arguing the unthinkable: America had become Ireland writ large.[50]

Poverty, George argued, was the organic accompaniment of progress. This malfunction in industrial capitalism, East and West, arose from an inherent defect. The open lands upon which progress and industrial capitalism were dependent had either been bought up by or given to speculators. George's solution to the problem was less impressive than his discussion of the nature of it. He wanted the federal government to impose a single tax on ground rents, ensuring what he called the "communal ownership of land." It was not land nationalization—George had too deep a distrust of the government to push for it to own much of anything—but it was close enough that his critics, with some justice, accused him of being in favor of abolishing private property in land. The single tax would appropriate all rents to the government; it was "the taking by the community, for the use of the community, of that value which is the creation of the community."[51]

George's whole scheme was hopelessly utopian, but what makes his book so important to the discussion here is that he made Ireland the "great stock example" of a land system gone horribly wrong. *Progress and Poverty* was a passionate book, filled with apocalyptic visions. George had a far better command of the evangelical Protestant tradition with all of its millennialist dreams than he did of political economy. But whatever inspired him, nothing inflamed him as Ireland did. He wrote of the people's "misery," of "merciless . . . horde[s] of landlords," and of their "remorseless rapacity." He knew "of nothing better calculated to make the blood boil than the cold accounts of the grasping, grinding tyranny to which the Irish people have been subjected." He made references to the "native population" being "driven off to emigration, to become paupers, or to starve," but not because Ireland could not feed them. Ireland produced food enough and more, but that food went "as a tribute—to pay the rent of absentee landlords; a levy wrung from producers by those who in no wise contributed to production."[52]

This kind of hot-blooded language was bound to attract the attention of the Irish and Irish Americans, particularly those who cared less about Ireland free than about the Irish fed. George had made his case for American land reform by comparing American land policies with those in Ireland; he then connected the Irish and American land question both with Irish nationalism and, more emphatically, with American labor. This was Ballaghaslane Beara's formula translated and expanded. Predictably, Patrick Ford was one of the first to realize that Henry George might be one successor to the antebellum reform movements who would give Catholic Ireland a fair hearing. He was not entirely wrong, at least initially. George's other Irish sponsor was Michael Davitt, the leader of the Irish Land Leagues, then on a fund-raising tour of the United States. In 1881, at Davitt's urging, George wrote a pamphlet on the "Irish Land Question," and it may well have been Davitt who prompted Ford to ask George to go to Ireland to cover the Land Leagues for the *Irish World*. George accepted the assignment eagerly.[53]

This was not an auspicious pairing of reporter and subject. George wanted to remake Ireland, not merely to report on it. It would be his testing ground for what have been called his "alternative social arrangements." The ultimate sources of those "arrangements" were to be found in his evangelical Protestantism, his deep sympathy for American workers, his agrarianism, his Westernness, and his belief in the global applicability of the single tax. For him, the Irish land question was not a "mere local" issue, "arising out of conditions peculiar to Ireland." It was "nothing less than . . . the great social problem of modern civilization, that question of transcendent importance which is everywhere beginning to convulse the civilized world." It is true that he said that "the land of Ireland belongs of right to the whole people of Ireland." "Ireland," however, could have been replaced by a blank line that readers could fill in with their people and nation—or nation to be—of choice.[54]

The sunburst of Irish nationalism was eclipsed; it stood no chance against anything so grand as the single tax. As George wrote prior to sailing for Ireland, "let [the Irish] be Land Leaguers first, and Irishmen afterwards. . . . Let them arouse to a higher love than the mere love of country." Actually, the Irish had a barely formed and indistinct sense of country; what George should have said is love of place, and he learned quickly enough that, for the Irish, there was no higher love—for some of them, no other love. They were no more interested in George's plans to convert the world than George was in Irish nationalism. Indeed, George told them that their incessant attacks on all things English were "the very madness of folly . . . political blunders worse than crimes." Like Marx and Engels before him, he believed that "the natural allies of the Irish agitation are the English working-classes" and that the wise course was for the Irish leaders to "avail themselves of the rising tide of British democracy." He was wrong on all counts. The English working class despised the Irish. And the rising tide of British democracy did not figure to raise many Irish boats.[55]

Scolding the Irish for being harshly critical of British policy and urging them to be conciliatory ignored both history and reality and doomed George's mission. The Irish world was the only one they knew or understood. Everything else was either distinctly subordinate to it or a part of it. But George's education in the recondite realities of the Irish world was only beginning. He also learned to his despair that the Irish liked the idea of owning and controlling their land. Having the state assume the role of landlord had no appeal for them. The fact that the state was Britain made the idea absolutely unthinkable. It was not good land-lords they wanted, but no landlords at all. The land defined them. It was "their world—their identity." "Without land no one could acquire anything"—and this from the Irish Communist Thomas O'Flaherty. The Irish writer George Russell (AE) wrote in 1911 that "an Irish farmer would pour down boiling lead on the emissaries of the State who tried to nationalise his land, the land he sweated sixty years to pay for."[56]

George returned to America chastened and confused. He could only hope that the American Irish were less tribal and more cosmopolitan than those backward sorts left in Ireland. He urged "the Land League of the United States to announce this great principle [of the single tax] as of universal application; making it a movement for the regeneration of the world." This required a "wider patriotism than that which exhausts itself on one little sub-division of the human race, one little spot on the great earth's surface." Subdivisions and spots they may have been—and little ones at that—but for Irish Americans, as for the Irish, they were what counted. The little spots defined the little human subdivision. The American state was no more welcome to their fields than the British had been. Leo Ward spoke for more than just the Irish of Melrose when he wrote that "to own something, even to hope to own something—that has always been the blood and bone of our community; *that is what the grandfathers came to Iowa for.*" Owning part of Iowa completed them; renting land from the state completed nothing, a point that was unfathomable to George.[57]

Irish nationalists in America were no more impressed with George's ideas than those in Ireland had been. The *Boston Pilot* was harshly critical of "Mr. Henry George and his school." They "care nothing for Irish nationality. They only want to see their communistic ideas put into practical operation." For militant nationalists

George's social reforms divided the Irish along class lines rather than uniting them around shared national goals. The nation came first. Let the Irish get that and they could be as fractious as they liked; they could go after one another hammer and tong. In George's eyes, the entire transnational Irish world was hopelessly parochial. Irish nationalist politics were a "great blind groping forward." Toward what, he did not say, but he knew it would not be toward his single tax. George had nothing left to learn from Ireland or the Irish. He would leave them to grope blindly.[58]

Henry George was not a part of the Irish stain in American labor, although he certainly made Ireland and its land issues a part of the cause of labor reform. *Progress and Poverty* was a plea for the working classes. *The Land Question,* his "Irish" book, had as one of its co-titles *The Condition of Labor.* In 1881, just before he left for Ireland, he joined the Knights of Labor, headed by the Irish Catholic Terence Powderly, who had only recently joined the Irish-American Land League. All of the connections were in place; all except the one between George and the Irish would hold, and even it held for a time. David Montgomery has written that Henry George was one of those who embedded "the causes of Irish nationalism and land reform deeply within the American labor movement." To the extent that he did so, he did it unintentionally. He worked on the seam without understanding either side of it.[59]

The same could not quite be said of Powderly. He did understand one side of it. Powderly was a conspicuous Irish nationalist, at one time serving as the senior guardian of the Scranton, Pennsylvania, Clan na Gael. He would not have stumbled through Ireland as George had. That said, he was every bit as committed as George and Ford were to the idea that the monopolization of land was the only meaningful obstacle to America's industrial liberation. Powderly and Ford sounded like the labor reformers of the 1830s and 1840s: if only western lands could be made available to the eastern proletariat, class tensions would evaporate and poverty would no longer be a constituent part of progress.

There was an element of nostalgia and more than a little naiveté in this. Jeffersonian agrarianism and Jacksonian democracy were apotheosized again. The official name of the association—the Holy and Noble Order, Knights of Labor—sounded almost quaint, more like a federation of medieval artisan guilds than of labor unions. "In my opinion," Powderly said in 1882, "the main, all-absorbing question of the hour is the land question." The eight-hour day was important; so were child labor laws and the "currency question." These were all of "weighty moment to the toiler." But even if all of these reforms were secured, capital could frustrate the effects of each because capital owned the land, and not just in America. As was the case with George, Ireland provided Powderly with his model. "The people of Ireland are driven by enforced emigration from their native land; they flee from the landlord . . . only to face him in a still worse form on this continent."

Landlordism in Ireland was preventing a nation from forming, driving a people from their cottages and farms and depositing them in America's industrial cities; landlordism in the West of America was keeping them in those cities, threatening the peace of the nation and preventing it from being true to itself.[60]

The important point is the connectedness of the issues—the poor tenant in Donegal has been disinherited by imperial landlords. He is driven from Ireland and becomes a wage slave in Fall River; there he languishes, unable to "go west on a farm"—to cite again the advice to the uncomprehending Thomas O'Donnell—because the West and its farmlands have been alienated. He has again been disinherited, this time by capitalist landlords. In 1881 Ford pleaded again with America's "Workingmen!" not to "lose sight of the significance of the present movement *in Ireland. . . .* Destroy the occupation of the landlord and you" save the poor of Donegal and "sound the doom of . . . factory slave[ry] in Fall River." O'Donnell was a surname associated almost exclusively with County Donegal and he slaved away in Fall River, which added a nice, if entirely coincidental, symmetry to Ford's comment. O'Donnell, however, could not go west. How he was going to benefit directly from the destruction of Irish landlords would also have required some explanation.[61]

That returns the discussion to Sombart and why there was no socialism in America. It is hard to quarrel with Montgomery's contention: the preoccupation with the landlord—specifically the Protestants on horses in Ireland—as the bane of the American working class may have "helped keep labor organizations alive with political agitation." But it also "provided a major stumbling block in the path of socialist efforts within the movement." I would object only to the implication that "socialist efforts" would otherwise have been made, might have succeeded, and would have helped liberate industrial America—or Ireland. I make a different but related claim. Conditions in Ireland affected American labor because most working-class Irish Americans saw building bridges to the non-Irish as an act of Irish national disloyalty. It broke tribal bonds. To speak of Irish worlds and *American* industrial liberation as if they were parts of one whole prevented a true understanding of either.[62]

To this point the Irish strain was angry, lawless, antimodern, internecine, focused on Ireland and/or landlords, working on a seam that at times resembled a tightrope, and astonishingly parochial and clannish. That clannishness, however, not only meant that the Irish would build no bridges: it also meant that they would claim jobs by ethnic inheritance where and when they could. They got steady work not because they had the skills or the experience to perform it, not even because they were themselves steady, but by cooperating with friends. This necessarily involved the exclusion from those jobs of people with whom they were not friends. In the Irish world, non-Irish were nonfriends. They were, in fact, "the *indispensable* enemies"; their status as "strangers" gave the Irish, in Hobsbawm's language, "the ability to exclude" them from the workforce, "*never mind how.*" More often than not, the "enemies" list was drawn on racial and ethnic lines. The result was an Irish aristocracy of labor. It was not, however, a natural aristocracy but a contrived one, and the instrument of contrivance was race/ethnicity.[63]

Asking the Irish, as George did, to turn Ireland into a laboratory for a global reform movement was at best unrealistic; at worst, it revealed an insensitivity to the real sufferings of the Irish people as well as to the intensity of their friendly attachments, including those to their own "little spots on the great earth's surface." As for asking them to become more ethnically and racially tolerant, the hard fact is that—with the exception of those like George—few of their contemporaries asked them to be or even brought up the topic. American society generally was not notably broad minded; intolerant societies do not question or rebuke intolerance. Indeed, George was himself at least as anti-Asian as anyone in California. Historians are in a different position. It is altogether legitimate that they ask why Americans were so ethnocentric and racist. It is not legitimate when they press only the Irish to answer, but that is irrelevant to the larger issue: is it possible that the Irish strain specifically and *because it was Irish* brought to western American labor history a greater intolerance than it would otherwise have shown?[64]

The answer must begin with the obvious: the Irish would only take care of themselves. But consider something at least as obvious: if they had no non-Irish friends, it was because history had not provided them with any. The possibility that they might have spurned such friends if it had must also be weighed. If they sought and claimed jobs because they were Irish, to the exclusion of those who were not, it was not because they were trying to ingratiate themselves with the host society by becoming white. They did not even like the host society; why would they flatter it by imitation? The host society, moreover, did not dislike the Catholic Irish any less because they were whitening. In fact, of all the strategies for immigrant acceptance, "becoming white" has to rank as among the least effective. The Irish excluded because, by definition, that is what anxious and clannish people do, because they had come into a system that was based on exclusion, and because so few of them had the job skills necessary to a natural worker aristocracy. They may have been misanthropic, but they were equal-opportunity misanthropes. The historian Thomas Archdeacon, who knows the Irish well, once said that he "half-seriously" believed that "the Irish are not prejudiced against particular groups; they do not like anyone except other Irish and they are not too sure about them." Call it the Archdeacon Principle.[65]

In 1892 James McFadden, an Irish immigrant, wrote back to Ireland from Mapleton, Iowa, complaining that the place was overrun with "Indians, negros, chinese, Germans, Sweeds & Norwegans." Five years later, he again commented on the mix of people, but this time he made it clear that Mapleton's polyglot population was not just exotic. "They all hate an Irishman," McFadden said, adding, "but . . . an Irish man does not care much for them" either. That last pugnacious line could have been the title of the anthem of Irish America. The lyrics, however, would have had a particular resonance for those in western America. The West was more brightly multihued than the East; it had more strangers who could be excluded. This racial and ethnic diversity was a major part of labor's western heartland. Other western Irish would have added Finns, Slavs, Italians, Greeks, Poles, Jews, Croats, Serbs, Bohemians, Slovenes, Montenegrins, Hispanics of various sorts, an ethnic miscellany of "Yankees," and countless others to McFadden's list. The Irish did not care for any of them, including those with whom they shared a Catholic faith. There was even considerable tension between older, established Irish and younger and more recent Irish immigrants. As surely as any of the others, they were a threat to jobs hard earned and tenaciously held. Archdeacon meant it when he remarked that the Irish liked only other Irish and were not too sure about them either.[66]

By the 1890s the economy of western America had become increasingly dependent on a transient and disposable workforce drawn from a vastly extended labor market and a comparably expanded labor pool. Every culture, every religion (including the aggressive denial of religion), every manner of thought and habit and tradition could be found in the West that industrial capitalism made. The Wobblies alone tried to organize this piebald proletariat. It is enough to make one wonder if they took the name Industrial Workers of the World intending also to signal that they were the industrial workers *from* the world. What made the "new immigration" new was not so much that it consisted of new people but that so many of those who were part of it were not immigrants in any meaningful sense of the word. They were transient sojourners; many of them "immigrated" multiple times between return visits home. The pattern was closer to a panhemispheric bracero program than to immigration. Hiring in this labor system was a zero-sum game, a cutthroat version of ethnic and racial musical chairs.[67]

In 1894 the Bunker Hill and Sullivan Mining Company in Shoshone County, Idaho, reported that its workforce consisted of "84 Americans (many of these of Irish descent); 76 Irish; 34 Germans; 25 Italians; 18 Swedes; 15 Englishmen; 15 Welshmen; 13 Scotchmen; 11 Austrians; 8 Finlanders; 6 Frenchmen; 5 Danes; 5 Norwegians; 2 Swiss; 1 Icelander; 1 Portuguese." Note that this list of mine workers did not include any of the more than a hundred Chinese in the county in 1890. The Irish clearly dominated (as evidenced by the parenthetical reference to "Irish descent"), but it was quite a cosmopolitan assemblage. This was the common pattern throughout the western economy. These "new immigrants," moreover, did not just show up. They were ordered up—often from padrones and labor contractors. Like every other imported raw material, they were put to very specific purposes. Those included breaking both strikes and the Irish hold on jobs and unions. Powderly put it this way: employers would "import human beings to America to take the places of others who would not submit to reductions in wages . . . or had become so restless and dissatisfied as to strike." That was a very subtly loaded use of the words "human beings."[68]

That leads to another reason why the Irish strain involved a fondness for ethnic preferment over class solidarity. The employing class knew of the deep and abiding rivalries between and among the various ethnic components of this new American working class. Playing on those rivalries was as much a part of scientific management as time and motion studies were. Montgomery writes in a chapter on the "superior intelligence" of those wearing "white shirts" that "it was necessary . . . to select workers of the right nationality, race, and sex for each position." One anonymous labor leader called the practice "a worse form of slavery than the one abolished by the Civil War." It cannot be known if the man who said this knew all that his statement implied. I suspect that he did, that he understood fully that racial slavery divided the working class into white and black and that playing on ethnic and religious suspicions and hatreds was similarly divisive.[69]

Patrick Ford insisted that "divide and conquer" was the "motto Labor's enemies have always acted upon . . . the keeping asunder of Catholic and Protestant workingmen." Powderly also insisted that a racially and ethnically divided workforce was purposeful; it provided capital with an essential instrument of social control. When he first entered the Knights of Labor he "found men arrayed against each other in hostile camps, on religious lines, on political lines and on race lines." A worker, he added, "should not be obliged to go to a clergyman, a politician or some big man of his own race to tell him how much he weighed in the industrial scale." Ed Keating, the acknowledged and conspicuously Irish Catholic leader of the Denver labor movement, went further, arguing that employer efforts to divide workers on religious and ethnic lines were based on what Britain had done in Ireland. Elizabeth Gurley Flynn tried constantly to show workers "how all differences are used by the bosses to keep [them] divided and pitted against each other," mentioning specifically "traditional enemies . . . in hostile European countries, . . . English and Irish." Ed Boyce was of the same mind, telling labor that it must "banish forever that miserable, contemptible, religious bigotry that has proved the ruination of the laboring people for centuries."[70]

Boyce's comment is particularly important. He knew from hard personal experience how capital had used that miserable bigotry to try to ruin labor movements. Boyce had been directly involved in the violent 1892 strike in the Bunker Hill and Sullivan mines in Idaho, which had been called by overwhelmingly Irish-led unions. Bunker Hill attempted to deal with the threat of renewed labor militancy in two related ways. It made neither public, but it is inconceivable that Boyce was unaware of the company's tactics. First, it closed its mines and imported hundreds of what F. W. Bradley, its resident manager, called "Dagos," of the "most intense dago type," to take the places of the Irish who had once worked the mines and were then threatening another strike. When the company learned that these Italians were no less willing to strike than the Irish, it tried to "weed" them out along with the Irish and to continue its search for a more docile cohort of workers.[71]

It also adopted a second tactic, one that Patrick Ford had anticipated. The company actively encouraged the formation of chapters of the American Protective Association, turning the APA into a kind of Bunker Hill Protective Association. The company's great fear was that the labor force in the Coeur d'Alene district would begin to resemble Butte's, which is to say that it would become more Irish than was good for non-Irish mine owners. One mining company officer told a Bunker Hill official that Butte "ought to be made a reservation and those kind of people be required to live there and never be allowed to step outside the line." The kind of people he meant were the Irish, and he intended "reservation" to be taken quite literally. As I have argued, Butte already was that, a cordoned-off outland run by tribal chieftains. But the best comment came from another mine owner, who told Bradley that he was "very sorry to hear of your strike; it is an outrage upon you and your Company and I sincerely hope you will find it in your power to teach *the Irish* a lesson which they will not soon forget." Every now and again, a historian is handed a remark that simply cannot be improved upon; this is such a time.[72]

The nativists would be the instrument of instruction. By the spring of 1895 Bradley was told that the local APA "numbers 120, is growing rapidly and will soon be strong enough to guarantee us our rights." Those rights were basic. They included absolute control of hiring, a "reduction of wages," and "guarantee[d] protection to all those who choose to work for wages that we can afford to pay." One company officer was so encouraged that he wrote that "there are many signs that the Union has weakened very much lately, and as a fighting organization I believe it to be quite played out. The APA has, no doubt, had much to do with this result . . . the Union is in fear of that order." Bradley even wanted "to have the Company make a good contribution to the next 4th of July . . . celebration. . . . It is going to be an A.P.A and B.H. &S day. These affairs tend to make the relations closer between employers and employee and I am satisfied that whatever we contribute to the coming celebration will be repaid us many times over."[73]

Bradley admitted that he did not personally agree with the APA "movement generally," but the stakes were high and the situation called for extraordinary measures. As he told company headquarters in San Francisco, in the Coeur d'Alene district, "The Poorman is the only . . . mine that . . . has no friction with the Union." Given the friction Bunker Hill was having, this would seem a happy state of affairs with some important lessons to teach. Anyone reading Bradley's letter would expect him to suggest that Bunker Hill do as the Poorman had done. The problem for Bradley was that labor peace came at an unacceptable cost. It prevailed at the Poorman "because each member of the whole crew from the manager down is an Irish Catholic and the Union has anything and everything it asks for." He then quite unwittingly contradicted himself in the next sentence, but the contradiction was telling. "Were we to accept Coeur d'Alene Union conditions, I am of the opinion that we would have as much trouble as ever unless we were officered, manned and managed as the Poorman is."[74]

This new western world of workers from strange places was not an Irishman's dream environment. The Irish were not more racist or ethnocentric than anyone else, although neither were they less so. And they did not issue many pleas for worker solidarity. They were too tribal in their allegiances for that and too insecure and terrified at the thought of being far from home, out of work, and broke. Life in industrial western America was hard on the nerves of all who worked for wages, but harder, I think, on already badly frayed Irish nerves than on most. James Duval Phelan was a quite untypical western Irishman: rich, powerful, and something of a social dandy. But he spoke an important Irish truth when he wrote that "for a man with a family, the 'bondage' of regular employment, rather than the pickings of sporadic freedom, looks rather attractive."[75]

The Irish boarded their second boats because they wanted to find places where they could have steady jobs and make the "fair living" that had been denied them in Ireland. Phelan's bondage of regular employment was the idea behind the aptly named Poorman Mine. It was why the Irish came to dominate so many city halls. Control of local politics gave them control of the appointment of police and firemen, of jobs on public works, even of the appointment of teachers in the public schools. In 1889 a member of the Montana legislature complained that it was "a matter of common report that the laborers of [the] Anaconda [mines] were almost exclusively Irish." He acknowledged that "clannishness was characteristic of the human race," but questioned the fairness of a system—and it was a system—where if "two men [were] equally competent to fill a position, the Irishman invariably got it." That was the whole idea: call it the wages of Irishness.[76]

If the matter could be left there, the Irish would be guilty of nothing more odious than trying to hang onto steady work and to live fairly. I grant that many were unable or unwilling to shed their ethnic identities and put on a new working-class one, which disappointed certain of their contemporaries as well as a fair number of historians. James Barrett has argued that immigrant assimilation was often from "the bottom up," that there were at least two Americas from which immigrants could choose—middle-class and working-class—and that many chose the latter. Barrett makes a sound point, but he also misses a third option. Some Irish chose neither the bottom-up nor the top-down approach. They clung instead to Irish standards that were beyond the pales of both Americas. The American working class, always something of an abstraction, was undone by this, as Ed Boyce knew it would be. In Thompsonian language, it was unmade as a self-aware social class with a distinct cultural identity.[77]

But Barrett's point—and Thompson's and Montgomery's—is based on the assumption that class was the "appropriate" identity of workers, Irish American workers included. The argument suffers from what might be called the Sombartian flaw. Appropriateness should be neither presumed nor assigned. Besides, the ultimate source for hiring practices was to be found in the offices of industrial capitalists who cynically manipulated ethnicity and race; the fault should not rest solely with those being manipulated. A writer from the *Butte Bystander,* one of the city's labor newspapers, put the matter succinctly: "Corporations . . . delight in religious strife." That they did. Working-class Irish were not the only ones for whom ethnic clannishness was "characteristic." The mine manager who said "Irish" rather than "union" when complaining of an impending strike and, most dramatically, Bunker Hill's mobilization of the APA as a means of combating a labor threat did as much to rearrange and confuse the relationship of class and ethnicity as anything Irish workers ever did.[78]

It is in this context that the Irish involvement in the anti-Chinese agitation and violence of the 1870s and 1880s should be interpreted. In many ways that involvement was a culmination of all that went into that western Irish experience, particularly Irish disinheritance and exile joined to the American "cant of conquest" and the rest of the "multifarious frauds" of western expansionism. The anti-Chinese sentiments of western Irish Americans can be seen as evidence that the Irish not only had been instrumental in extending America's borders but had incorporated the racialist ideas that served to justify that extension. The Chinese were the most conspicuous of the "barbarian races" whom the Americans were determined to keep from their western gates. And by "Americans" I mean those with their Anglo-Saxon bona fides intact as well as those still on probationary status. For these reasons, anti-Chinese prejudice has become for historians the western and equally ugly offspring of antiblack prejudice and discrimination elsewhere in America, the contextual reference point for what Jacobson calls "the alchemy of race." Specific to the discussion here is the question of whether the Irish among those western alchemists used the presence of the Others from China to turn themselves into white people—which, upon reflection, was the same as turning base metals into gold.[79]

It is impossible to know what percentage of those who participated in the "Chinese must go!" agitation were Irish. It is clear that most of the agitators were immigrants; a story in the *Argonaut,* a San Francisco newspaper sympathetic to the Chinese, called the anti-Chinese gangs "the refuse and sweeping of Europe, the ignorant, brutal, idle off-scourings of civilization . . . [an] idle and worthless foreign gang." That kind of language was used to describe many of western America's "whites of a different color"; but these were San Francisco's idle off-scourings, and no one can have wondered which of Europe's brutal and ignorant the *Argonaut* was talking about. Besides, the story specifically referred to the "Sand Lot" where Cork-born Denis Kearney gave countless speeches on labor reform, ending each with the refrain the "Chinese must go." Jacobson is certainly right when he argues that Kearney was "one of the movement's most vocal leaders" and that "many anti-Chinese agitators in California and elsewhere were Irish."[80]

The drive to rid California of Chinese, however, was a working-class movement, not an Irish one, and Jacobson is ambiguous about what that meant: it was clearly "racially based," but its "driving force . . . was economic." It was, in fact, "vigorously prolabor"; although there were "misgivings about the Chinese presence on the grounds of their religion or 'civilization,' . . . the laborite strain of the movement was predominant." Kearney, by way of obvious example, founded the Working-man's Party of California (WPC), identified by Jacobson as the "first Marxist political party in the United States." But then comes the confusion. What point was Jacobson making when he said that many of the agitators were Irish? So what? Jacobson sees the anti-Chinese movement in much the same way that he and others see the New York riots of 1863—or Teague O'Regan's threat to use a "good shelelah . . . to break deir [Indian] heads." This was the western Irish way of whitening themselves. Jacobson puts it this way: "An Irish immigrant in 1877 could be a despised Celt in Boston . . . and yet a solid member of the Order of Caucasians . . . in San Francisco." In other words, the Irish were "racial" probationers trying to reach the promised land of whiteness.[81]

For those who make this argument, becoming white eased insecurities and gave the persecuted someone to persecute. But it also made them eligible for the whiteness wage scale, in part by extending to the newly whitened the privilege of excluding the nonwhite from the labor market. Moving from "despised Celt" to "gallant Caucasian" was heady enough; getting a pay raise to accompany the "racial" promotion was a bonus. And thus "many anti-Chinese agitators in California and elsewhere were Irish," involved in the "predominate laborite strain" of what was a "racially based" movement. Jacobson mixes and stirs these three aspects of the one movement and comes up with a pack of western Irish racial alchemists.

I am troubled, however, by the absence of any clear explanation of the timing of this Irish-led crusade to defend white civilization and make the higher wages that went to the civilized white workers. Why did those many Irish laborers wait twenty-five years before undertaking it? There was a sizable Irish and Chinese presence in California as early as 1850. Ironically, but significantly, the organizations of both, in the words of Alexander Saxton, "were vertical rather than horizontal." There was also some anti-Chinese "agitation" in these early years, but it did not feature the Irish and never took on an Irish aspect. That leads to my question: if the Irish had simply been trying to "pass" as white or get beyond the in-between stage—if racism, whatever its source, had been all that moved them—would they not have singled out the Chinese immediately upon confronting them in the West? Why did these racially insecure Irish not play the Teague O'Regan role and break some Chinese heads?[82]

One answer might be that California's working-class Irish were making a very fair living in California in the 1850s and 1860s. Wages were high not because of the "whiteness" of those who made them but because there was more work to be done than men, of whatever color, to do it. Those palmy days were long past by the time Denis Kearney and the many Irish who listened to him started to demand that the Chinese must go. Kearney began his agitation in 1877, in the middle of nationwide strikes against the railroads and at the end of a devastating depression: nerves were stretched tight and tensions—economic, social, and racial—were high. The completion of the transcontinental railroad in 1869 had made available to California all of the world's new technologies—and all of the world's people. The Irish "monopoly" on jobs was broken by a railroad built largely by Irish and Chinese workers—which must count as one of the West's most malevolent practical jokes. Finally, land monopolies, always a feature of the California economy, meant that no easy escape from the hard times was readily at hand.[83]

In 1879 Patrick Ford combined these developments and turned the package, as only he could, into a kind of Irish requiem for a once Golden West. Ford wrote that the land was unavailable to the poor who needed it and that the new machines were not easing the labor of the unskilled, as the prophets of progress had said they would, but rendering skills economically irrelevant. That was bad enough. Then came the final indignity: "the Chinaman ready to work for 50 or 40 or 30 cents a day, or less! That is the third destructive power that is bearing down upon us. . . . 'Machinery and Mongols' will do all the work under the corporations." Ford next offered a bow to Henry George, arguing that making "the lands available to the people [was] the means of escape from impending destructions." But he did not dispute Kearney's refrain that the "Chinese must go." Three weeks after Ford had summarized the labor problem in California, the *Irish World and American Industrial Liberator* carried a drawing of Denis Kearney. To say that he appeared upright and brave is an understatement. He was majestic, a chieftain. His portrait was as far from the cartoon caricatures of Irish apes as could possibly be imagined.[84]

Kearney's crusade was unimaginable in the 1850s or any time prior to the crises of the 1870s. The reason is simple. His campaign was not about race—although race was part of it. It was not about the "wages of whiteness"—although wages were certainly part of it. It was about the "ability to exclude, never mind how" in order to have a chance at the bondage of regular employment. It appeared to western workers that capital was using Chinese labor to drive down wages.

They were only partly right; capital would use anything and anyone to drive down wages, including importing antiunion miners from the dazzlingly white, non-Irish, and non- if not anti-Catholic workforce in the lead and zinc mines around Joplin, Missouri. There is no doubt that the Chinese would work for less money than anyone else; this certainly caught the attention of western capitalists, which in turn gave rise to organized labor's association of Chinese "coolie" labor and African slave labor. The Chinese, said Henry George, were "long-tailed barbarians"—the racial element—and "ignorant tools in the hands of oppressive capitalists"—the "laborite" complaint. The same mix of race and social-class insecurity had been a part of Northern labor's response to the slavery issue before the Civil War. The slaves had been ignorant tools in the hands of oppressive slave owners, as well. This is not to argue that the Irish felt any sympathy for Chinese or black workers, only that the oppressors were so nearly unassailable—at least by the Irish. The attack would be made on the ignorant tools.[85]

The Irish routinely couched their demand for Chinese exclusion in racialist terms, but that was the discourse of choice for America, especially multiracial western America. Establishing Otherness required the use of some heavily loaded deprecatory language. The Chinese, moreover, were visibly Other. They could not "pass," could not escape their "tribal" identity and all that went with it. In addition, the Federal Immigration Act of 1790 restricted immigration to "free white persons"; that plus the fact that they had no 14th Amendment rights left the Chinese without legal protection. I am not arguing that race was not the issue. It was. Race alone gave western workers the ability to exclude without having to mind how. To use their word of art, the Irish "boycotted" the Chinese because they could boycott them; it did not require that they build bridges to the Caucasian brotherhoods and apply for membership.

A half-serious case could be made that if the act of 1790 had not said "free white persons" the Irish would have insisted upon the exclusion of all but themselves. It was nothing personal—or racial. William Hogan, for example, one of Butte's Irish, explained rather matter-of-factly that there was nothing specifically racial in the anti-Chinese feelings in his city and that "the Chinese in this matter [working for lesser wages] would be the same as any other person[s]." They were "Eastern [Asian] scabs." Another western Irishman, George Hickey, risked his life during Denver's anti-Chinese riots in 1880, trying—unsuccessfully—to prevent a mob from lynching a recent Chinese immigrant. Yet another, Frank Roney, opposed Kearney and the Chinese exclusion, arguing that the "boycott" should be directed against the nonproducing classes. Alexander Saxton calls the Roney-Kearney conflict a "factional fight," contending further that "the power struggle between" the two Irishmen was "the opening round in a cycle of conflict which has characterized both radicalism and labor organization in the West."[86]

It is not my contention that Hogan, Hickey, and Roney were more representative Irishmen than Kearney or that they spoke to some innate Irish sense of racial fairness that has somehow escaped historical detection. Indeed, Saxton's use of "factional fight" may have been an intentional effort to establish that the Irish were not just present at the creation of the western labor movement but brought "the melancholy of the bogs," their "ancient grudges," and—to extend Waugh's list—their ancient narrowness of vision to the event. "Hard, ancient wisdom"—theirs or anyone else's—was less conspicuous. Given the WPC's close association with Greenbackers, Irish Land Leaguers, and other western insurgents, these marks of the Irish strain were also a major part of the western core of the working-class reform movement generally. This was true not just in Irish numbers but in the seamlessness with which being and remaining Irish was insinuated into this and later labor battles. I agree that driving the Chinese out was an Irish as well as a workers' fight. I disagree only with the assignment of motives and with the implication that only Irish motives need to be studied and assigned.[87]

Whatever Kearney and his friends were doing, or may have thought they were doing, they had plenty of help in their fight against the "Eastern scabs." Joseph Buchanan, a major player in Denver's labor movement, was born in Hannibal, Missouri; his parents were Scots Methodists. He complained bitterly that workers were "all very clannish, and each clan must have its own club or society to keep us from identifying with the people among whom we have come to live." Some of those, however, were not worth living with—may not, in fact, have been people at all. In 1883 Buchanan called on workmen of "all countries" to unite against the Chinese, whom he described as "vermin, like so many leeches sucking our blood." "[I] feel like going forth and inciting people to butcher every thieving infernal Chinaman in the country."[88]

Two years later, railroad and coal mine workers in and around Rock Springs in Sweetwater County, Wyoming, massacred twenty-eight Chinese in a paroxysm of racial violence. Except for the fact that women and children were not among those killed, Rock Springs begs comparison with the slaughter of unoffending Indians at Sand Creek and Wounded Knee. The working-class origins of the Rock Springs atrocity were obvious; the Irishness of it was questionable. In 1890 the county's more than 2,500 foreign-born included 178 Irish, along with 1,200 Britons, more than 400 Germans and Scandinavians, and 250 Russians (most of them almost certainly ethnic Germans). There were 350 Chinese, down from 500 in 1880. This would be a good time to recall McFadden's list: "Indians, negros, chinese, Germans, Sweeds & Norwegans." Was the outrage in Rock Springs a violent display of "Germans, Sweeds & Norwegans" becoming white? What of those born in England, Scotland, and Wales? These northern Europeans, moreover, did not care for the Irish, according to McFadden. Was hostility to in-between people, probationary whites like the Irish, as useful in establishing whiteness as hostility to those who were clearly not white? Is it not at least curious that the only people who had to "become white" were non-Protestants?[89]

Racism was not the issue; tribalism was. Calling the Chinese "scabs" says more about what set the Irish off on their anti-Chinese crusade than any solely racist reference ever could. It coalesces Jacobson's categories: the campaign against the Chinese was Irish, exclusionist, racially based, and economically motivated. The last three aspects followed predictably from the first. As such, trying to divide those who were yelling "The Chinese must go!" into Irish *qua* Irish and Irish *qua* worker categories is futile. It is also unnecessary, even deceptive. To repeat another theme, the Irish strain was guided by a subtle variation on Connolly's formula: the cause of labor was the cause of Irish American laborers. In a revealing moment in his response to Lord Bryce's highly critical account of "Kearneyism in Califor- nia," Kearney said that the authorities, "finding their efforts to break up the [anti- Chinese] movement of no avail, decided to proclaim the meetings *à la* Balfour in Ireland." It is possible that Kearney used an Irish example only because he was from Ireland, that he meant nothing by his reference to Balfour and was not suggesting that breaking up labor meetings in California was the *ideological* equi- valent of breaking up nationalist meetings in Ireland, but it is not very likely.[90]

This was true, to a greater or lesser extent, of the entire labor history of the West, not just of Kearney and the WPC. I invoke again the Archdeacon Principle of Irish misanthropy. The "contested West" was not simply a place where the Blackfeet fought the Sioux and then a bunch of undifferentiated "Euro-Ameri- cans" fought "Native Americans." Patricia Limerick says more than she knows when she writes that "Western history has been an ongoing competition for legitimacy—for the right to claim for . . . one's group the status of legitimate beneficiary of Western resources." Tribal warfare did not just involve the Natives; the tribal Strangers were also engaged in group competition for resources—none more so or more ferociously than the Irish. In this, they were quintessentially western; their war parties were as at home on the range as those of any of the other tribes. The West the Irish built was outlandish only in the context of the western myth. Indeed, there is something of that myth in the notion that they were trying to shed their savage selves and become white. The Irish were behaving like the diggers they were: ensuring the friendliness of their world. This does not make them more tolerant than the whiteness scholars would have them; it may, in fact, make them less so.[91]

In this context, Limerick's idea of "western conquest" can be given an Irish reading. Limerick writes that "conquest basically involved the drawing of lines on a map." Map lines are used to distinguish between and among peoples; in this instance they were used as a means of determining "the definition and allocation of ownership." They were visual representations of some deeply held and highly racialized ideas about which people were destined to own all those contested western resources. The tribes of Irish were among the line-drawers. Doing so was part of the Irish strain—both the part of it that was inherent and the part that was historically derived. Those lines established borders, frontiers, and meridians of partition. They marked off an ideological and geographical territory; those who were outside it were outlanders, Hoosiers beyond the Irish pale.[92]

None of this is intended to diminish the genuine cruelty that Chinese exclusion represented. In 1882 the federal government passed the aptly named Chinese Exclusion Act, formally barring their entry into the United States. The Chinese were excluded from the American economy—and from America. But if indignation over the racism inherent in that exclusion can be temporarily set aside, there was also genuine radicalism in it. I doubt that this is what Jacobson had in mind when he called the WPC "Marxist," but look at what labor's demand that hundreds of thousands of competing workers be taken out of the labor pool meant. The implications of this were at least as far reaching as the simultaneous demand for an eight-hour day. Finding and hiring workers were management prerogatives as surely as determining the length of the working day; both affected production, costs, and profits. Restricting this cherished right of capital might have been American labor's one major victory during the entire industrial era. The WPC persuaded the federal government that "the Chinese must go" and in the process told management it could not hire an entire group of potential workers. Capital would simply have to adjust its ledger books.

Here the discussion can be profitably returned to Sombart and his simplistic question—and Thompson and Hobsbawm and their thoughtful, if only implied, answers. Both Thompson and Hobsbawm, as noted, wrote from a Marxist perspective, a more intellectually sophisticated one than that of Marx himself but Marxist nonetheless. Yet their previously quoted comments about the Irish contain some rather strikingly non-Marxist or at least nonmaterialist aspects. Thompson's "natural freemasonry of the disinherited" is another way of saying the Irish were part of a community of exiles that was based on a shared history, not on a relationship to the means of production or any other material standard. History counts.

But so—to go back to an even earlier theme—does religion. The Irish were also distinguished by their church. Thompson called it a "nationalist Church," the most conspicuous feature of Irish national identity. He also called it "semi-feudal" (preindustrial), which had some clear implications for its ability to deal effectively with modern industrial economies, not to mention for what that Irish national identity would be like. Hobsbawm said the same thing. The Irish were sympathizers with revolution, "not because they were laborers, but because they were Irish." But Hobsbawm extends the point. To be Irish was to be or to have been Catholic. Whether they were Irish because they were Catholic or Catholic because they were Irish may be left to others to ponder. The Catholic influence on the American labor movement was the same in either case. The Irish strain was also a Catholic strain.[93]

The specifically Catholic effect on the American labor movement is an important and contentious topic, but not one that requires a full discussion here. It is important for the same reasons the Irish strain is important; it is contentious because so much of what was written about the church's role came from those who either did not read or were never disposed to take seriously what it had to say on labor questions. The fact that the church in America, like the Irish who ran it, was given to some determined faction fighting does not ease matters. One point, however, is clear: the Catholic Church had no tolerance for any form of socialism or collectivization. In that sense, the Catholic strain supplied a partial answer to Sombart's question; and even if Sombart did not comment on that fact, others did.

Less frequently noted was that the church also had very little tolerance for market capitalism. The church saw socialism and capitalism as co-equal parts of a modernity with many abhorrent features—including its anti-Catholicism. Both were materialistic, inherently selfish, and typical of an era that Catholicism condemned as one of "covetous greed." But it was even more important that one gave rise to the other, was dependent on the presence of the other and on the dialectic that paired them. The church would war on both. Granted, it usually only wagged ecclesiastical fingers, but in fairness that was all it could do; physical force and militancy were not a part of its arsenal of weapons. Its support for reform was almost entirely exhortative and symbolic. Leading cheers, however, was significant. So were symbols. The church cheered for the poor; it used its moral authority to insist on "the special consideration due to the poor." There was nothing particularly new in any of this. As Ed Keating, the Irish Catholic leader of Denver labor, put it with commendable simplicity in 1932, "the Church did not suddenly 'go liberal' 41 years ago."[94]

Keating was referring specifically to the 1891 encyclical of Pope Leo XIII, *Rerum Novarum: On the Condition of Labor*, which Keating called an effort to "impress on us that in our dealings with our fellow human beings we should act like Christians and not like barbarians outside the pale"—a nice reversal of the usual assigned roles. It contained "a platform . . . as liberal, if not more so, than the declaration of principles of any labor union in this or any other country." That statement took in a lot of labor unions, including those based on socialist, Communist, or syndicalist principles. *Rerum Novarum* was the "Catholic Manifesto on Labor," the most forceful expression of the church's critical perspective on free market capitalism. That it was based in part on the language and ideas of some American bishops is significant.[95]

By any accounting, *On the Condition of Labor* is a remarkable document. It was—and is—easy enough to be critical of any statement of principles that strikes for a middle ground, particularly when the contest is as explosive as the condition of labor. Leo XIII had some interesting things to say on the issue. He began by establishing that Catholic middle ground, what Monsignor John A. Ryan called a "system of cooperation, and not either Socialism or present-day capitalism, that is in harmony with Catholic traditions and Catholic social principles." The pope then offered his and the church's strong support to unions, "mutual combinations of the working classes." Under the heading "The State Must Protect the Laborers' Rights" came the words "when work-people have recourse to a strike." Later he wrote that the laboring classes were "free to work *or not*," which some of his more venturesome readers, including many Catholic clergy, interpreted to mean the right to strike.[96]

It may have. *Rerum Novarum* was no tepid endorsement of the principle of collective organization and bargaining. Class warfare was not on the church's agenda, but fairness clearly was. Wages, the pope went on to say, had to be sufficient for the worker to live in "reasonable and frugal comfort," a phrase easily mocked by radicals but reminiscent of that anonymous Irishman who wanted the right to make "a fair living" and the basis of Monsignor Ryan's notion that guaranteeing a "living wage" by law was a moral imperative of the just state. It is worthy of note that Ryan was Irish, a Minnesotan, and the son of a Fenian.[97]

The problem was that the pope—although not Ryan—stripped American workers, and especially western American workers, of the only means to get fairness and living wages and to live reasonable lives. "Christian workmen," the pope wrote, could "either join associations in which their religion will be exposed to peril, or form associations among themselves—unite their forces and courageously shake off the yoke of unjust and intolerable oppression." By "Christian" he meant, of course, "Catholic." The English bishop Henry Manning once wrote that *Rerum Novarum* was a document in which "surely the New World overshadow[ed] the old." It was not that, particularly on this issue. New Worlds were settler societies, and the settlers were from everywhere and of every belief. The pope issued no clarion call to Catholic workers to don the mantle of a multinational, multicultural proletariat; if anything he did the opposite. He was not only not influenced by Manning's New World: he either studiously ignored it or was ignorant of its realities. In multiracial, multicultural workforces, the only way open to a recognition of labor's rights was for workers to reach out across ethnic, national, and, most particularly, religious divides; in sum, to build bridges and join associations in which "their religion would be exposed to peril."[98]

The pope's encyclical took away that option. That was not what E. P. Thompson meant when he said the church was semifeudal, but the description fit well enough—and it did not even require an Irish influence. In this sense *Rerum Novarum* was an encyclical *On the Condition of* (Catholic) *Labor.* It represented a return to Christendom, in which church, state, and private associations—unions in this instance—were governed under a single set of rules. To say that this was of negligible relevance to the polyglot working population of western America is an understatement. The West that capital made consisted of workers from every corner of the globe; if the only associations open to them were those formed among themselves, there would be literally scores of associations. That was not a shortcut to shaking off the yoke of oppression. If anything, it validated the exclusionist tendencies, the clannishness, of Irish Catholics and led to some very big trouble indeed.

Perhaps Manning meant Pope Leo's next statement when he claimed New World inspiration for this decidedly Old World document. It is possible that Leo had the newest sections of New Worlds in mind when he wrote that the industrial working class also had to be given access to the land. He did not explain how that was to happen or consider whether it would have made any real difference. Leo was describing what should be; he would leave the specifics and the implementation to others. As he put it, "God has given the earth to the use and enjoyment of the universal human race." Clearly, the pope knew that in the industrial nations the earth was firmly in private hands and being put to private use. The encyclical insisted, however, that governments do whatever was in their power to "favor multiplication of property owners." He wrote that line in 1891, one year after the U.S. Census Bureau said the American new world had suddenly aged, two years before Frederick Jackson Turner explained what that premature aging might mean, what might happen when new worlds grow old.[99]

The context adds interest, but Leo was not reading U.S. Census Bureau reports when he composed his letter. Still, his remarks are on topic. "Working people," he said, should "be encouraged to look forward to obtaining a share in the land" and to bringing "it into cultivation and lavish[ing] upon it [their] care and skill." This was a fundamental human right. Denying it would leave laborers in "galling slavery," a comment that sounded an almost Turnerian note. What came next was so squarely on the seam line that Patrick Ford (or Ballaghaslane Beara) could have written it. This was Leo's bow in the direction of the Irish. If given access to land, the pope said, "men would cling to the country in which they were born; for no one would exchange his country for a foreign land if his own afforded him the means of living a tolerable and happy life." Unlike Marx and Henry George, both of whose manifestos beg comparison with *Rerum Novarum,* Leo said nothing specifically about Ireland and the effects of British policy on the conditions of the working classes. But given the near synonymity of "tolerable and happy life" with "a fair living," it is certain that he believed that modest dreams enjoyed God's favor. Just as certainly he knew well that the Irish for generations had been exchanging their country for "foreign lands."[100]

None was more literally foreign than the United States, in no small part because none was more "reformational" and "protestant." Four years before the pope issued *Rerum Novarum* he received the following history lesson from James Cardinal Gibbons, one of his American "advisors." Gibbons spoke of the "democratic and co-operative institutions of medieval Europe" then on "their death bed." "Trade and business" was once conducted "on the principles of mutual help and assistance. . . . But with the breaking down of the corporate feeling of united Christendom, methods of business were introduced which [were] deeply immoral." Gibbons had "unlimited competition" specifically in mind, concluding that the "discovery of the New World . . . greatly increased the evil." As for American expansion across that New World, it "dispossessed" the "mass of the working people," "large numbers" of whom were Catholic, and left them in "economic slavery."[101]

In this context, *Rerum Novarum* reads like Leo XIII's analytical gloss on Max Weber. Since sequence does not permit this reading, let me reverse it: perhaps Weber's *The Protestant Ethic and the Spirit of Capitalism* was his gloss on *Rerum Novarum*. Whatever his feelings about America, Leo's insistence on a preferential option for the poor struck a chord, at least among Catholics. The fictional French priest in Georges Bernanos's *Diary of a Country Priest* (1937) said that "'Rerum Novarum' . . . was like an earthquake. The enthusiasm! The simple notion that a man's work is not a commodity, subject to the law of supply and demand, set people's consciences upside-down!" Whether *Rerum Novarum* did all of that can, I suppose, be debated. But Bernanos's priest was in a "mining district" and preaching to "mining fellows." Had he been in the Coeur d'Alenes among that wild mix of mining fellows working for Bunker Hill or in Butte, or anywhere in the heart of western America's mining district, he would probably have found a similar enthusiasm for the sentiments—accompanied by incredulity at the solution. Ed Boyce undoubtedly read *Rerum Novarum*. I wonder only if Marcus Daly did.[102]

Leo's letter, obviously, was a Catholic statement, not an Irish one. It belongs in the Irish strain only because the Irish put it there. Unfortunately, American anti-Catholicism was such that the encyclical, along with everything else that was part of this "Catholic critique of the Gilded Age," was all but ignored. As noted, Eric Foner has tried to show that "the alienation between Irish-Americans and the mostly Protestant native-born reformers" was largely overcome; that the Irish Land League forged a "symbiotic relationship" between the two. Obviously, I disagree. The alienation was not even put on hold. Native-born Protestant reformers never got past their inherited and strongly held anti-Catholicism; they never forgave the Irish Catholics for being Irish and Catholic. The Irish may have built few bridges, but the Left built none at all. Nothing had changed from before the Civil War.[103]

The Populist movement and the People's Party offer a perfect example. There were some connecting links. Mary Elizabeth Lease began her political career giving Land League speeches for the Irish Land League; Ignatius Donnelly's eccentricities make him difficult to categorize, but his Irish and Populist credentials were certainly in place, as were those of Minnesota friends like James Manahan and Patrick Rahilly. But the only thing the Populists and the Irish workers had in common was a commitment to free silver and reform of some sort, which was not nearly enough to conjoin them. Both were movement cultures, but the cultures were so different that the movements could not even make contact. The historian Lawrence Goodwyn has asked: "What could a Protestant, Anglo-Saxon [Populist] organizer say to the largely Catholic, largely immigrant working classes of the North" and West? Actually, he could have said quite a lot, but only if some ancient prejudices could have been suppressed. I grant that Tom Watson was among the most virulent anti-Catholics in America and that his comments may have reflected only his own psychopathic delusions rather than the general feelings of the Populism he represented. But how could the Irish make common cause with someone who called Catholicism a "stupid, degrading . . . jackassical faith"?[104]

Liberals and radicals of every stripe, East and West, urban patricians and rustic plebeians, were as venomous in their attacks on the Catholic Church as Watson. Max Eastman wrote in the *Masses* that Catholicism was "the most tragically stupendous swindle that human and animal nature ever combined to produce." Upton Sinclair said of Leo XIII that he was "as wise and kind and gentle-souled a Pope as ever roasted a heretic." As for the "new radicals, the intellectuals as social types," they were no kinder, just less crude. Sixteen years after *Rerum Novarum,* the Protestant minister and social gospeler Walter Rauschenbusch could write that "the Catholic Church tends to keep alive and active the despotic spirit of decadent Roman civilization. . . . If we ask why . . . society . . . failed to reorganize . . . on a basis of liberty and equality, we have here one of the most important answers." The antebellum "conjunction" between liberal reform and nativism that David Potter correctly diagnosed was fully restored by the 1890s and as fully incapable of "ecumenical" cooperation. Everyone, it seemed, demanded the ability to exclude.[105]

Conjunctions are possible only if the things being conjoined are from the same taxonomic group or at least occupy the same plane of existence. *Rerum Novarum,* among other Catholic manifestos, does not meet that rule. It was a compromise between capitalism and any of a variety of reforms, but the middle ground it staked out represented an entirely separate and discrete way of looking at social and economic reality. It cannot be measured on the same scale or by the same theoretical criteria that apply to capitalism or liberalism or progressivism or socialism or any of the other movements and movement cultures of the era. Those were the coins of the realm within the pale. The Catholic critique, by whatever ideological accounting, was beyond that pale. Liberals dreamt of freeing men and women from external shackles, including the received religious and cultural belief system that held ethnic enclaves together. Liberalism was radically individualistic; unbound by community, including most particularly those other worlds of dead saints and friends. American liberals answered only to the minimal rules of pragmatism. Their sole objective truth was that there were no objective truths. Their earth belonged to the living. The past was dead.

Irish Catholicism was a lot of things, but pragmatic was not one of them. The only form of individualism the church countenanced was mystical and contemplative, not political and economic. Catholics shared their earth with those who had come before them. As for a received belief system, the Irish might well have asked what other sort there might have been. Certainly, it was the only one they knew. It did not shackle them. Its sacraments were not ideological leg irons and the clergy who administered those sacraments were not jailers. In sum, the conjuncture between Irish Catholic workers and liberals of sundry sorts foundered not because the Irish were so conservative and against reform. It failed because a common purpose is not enough in the absence of a common ideological denominator; some things simply do not mix. Separate worlds can be bridged; separate worldviews cannot. And it failed because the reformers were so nativist and anti-Catholic. Secular and Protestant liberals, progressives, and radicals of various kinds assaulted the Catholic Church then retired to their salons wondering aloud why working-class Irish Catholics had not followed them into their brave new worlds. America's history might well have been happier had they worked harder at their own bridge building. Certainly it would have been different. It avails nothing, however, to wish conjunctures into existence.

By whatever name it is called—even something as detached and impersonal as "pursuit of common goals"—any political cooperation between American reformers and Irish Catholic workers would have erased the distinction between those within and those beyond the pale. The line marking the meridian of partition would be erased from the cultural maps. The palesmen could not bring themselves to do it. Effacing the meridian effaced them. Catholics had not earned the right to enter into the pale; indeed it was not a right they could earn. Their alternative world—including most particularly their alternative frontier—was not something that could simply be adjusted and made to harmonize. Teague O'Regan was invented by and for palesmen; he had no objective existence. Ostriches were not elephants. But that leaves unanswered the question of whether Irish American Catholics would have accepted an invitation to join in a "symbiotic relationship" with those within the pale, even had one been extended. I think the clerical jousting match within the Catholic Church known as the Americanist controversy should be interpreted in this same context.

The controversy began in 1884 at the Third Plenary Council of American bishops. It involved myriad issues from the appropriate response of Catholic workmen to the Knights of Labor to Catholic children in public schools. The fundamental quarrel, however, was over the proper place and role of Catholicism in

American society. The two sides have been starkly drawn. Liberal or Americanist bishops believed that Catholic and American values were entirely compatible but that this would be easier to prove if the church shed some of its more autocratic and foreign habits and behaved in accordance with the democratic values and the cultural pluralism of the United States—in short, if it built bridges and then crossed them into the pale. They were opposed by anti-Americanists who were no less certain than their opponents that Catholicism had a place in America but contended that Catholics were not required to close the distance between themselves and the crassness and godlessness of secular American society in order to hold their place. The proper role of Catholics in America was to remain separate, beyond the pale and beyond reach. Let America build the bridges and come to them if it wished; the church was not budging.[106]

Both sides were captained by Irish; given the Irish dominance of the American clergy it could hardly have been otherwise. The Americanists were led by John Ireland of St. Paul. They determined to chart an ecclesiastical course that would protect Catholics and Catholic values in a society not always friendly to either. That hostility, however, would disappear once America understood how Catholic it was—or should be. As Ireland put it in 1901, "the teachings and spirit of the Catholic Church . . . beget and nurture the cherished ideals of the American Republic." Those who saw a conflict between Catholicism and republicanism were "given sore disappointment." There was no conflict; Americanism and Catholicism were perfectly paired. Ireland was realist enough to understand that Catholics would also have to work to make what Ireland's biographer calls "this marriage contracted in heaven." Specifically, they would have to concede and yield up their ethnic distinctiveness and move in from the cultural outlands. They would need to "mingle far more than their fathers did with their non-Catholic fellow citizens." The Americanists did not like being outside the pale, clustered and huddled in ethnic enclaves. Since American values were not going to change to suit Catholics, it would be necessary for Catholics to change and at least act like palesmen. Catholic immigrants did not have to shed their faith, but they did have to polish their manners and catch up with the times.[107]

Conservatives, led by New York bishops Michael Corrigan and Bernard McQuaid, were not so sure of either argument, partly because they were not convinced that time was something that one caught up with. After all, as the pope told them in *Rerum Novarum*—ironically, a document the liberals claimed as validation of their position—the events of one century were wonderfully like those of another. For the conservatives, keeping a respectful distance between themselves and their "hosts" was where Catholics should be. It was also where Pope Leo XIII's 1899 letter *Testem Benevolentiae,* which condemned "Americanism," put them and told them to stay. That letter, some historians have insisted, marooned two more generations of American Catholics outside mainstream America. It did so only if they wanted to be in the mainstream, and there is not a lot of evidence that they did. Besides, they had been placed outside the mainstream. They did not put themselves there.[108]

For my purposes, however, the most important point is that the Americanist controversy was over tactics and strategy, not fundamental doctrine. I agree entirely with the historian R. Laurence Moore when he writes that the Americanist conflict was never "over the question of whether immigrant Catholics should become American. The quarrels were about how. Indeed they were about what it meant to be an American." At stake was not just religion but the entire panoply of ethnic habits that literally made Catholic immigrants who they were. To have abandoned ethnicity, which is what the Americanists were urging, would have left them cultural nullities. In other words, the conservatives understood instinctively what historians like Jon Gjerde, Kathleen Conzen, Frederick Luebke, Thomas Archdeacon, and Moore himself have come to understand: immigrants could and did become American by remaining ethnic. The West made this easy. Gjerde could write of the "minds of the West." Vertical worlds were still possible there. The "minds of the East" would be an altogether different and more fractious story, assuming that it could even be written.[109]

No wonder, then, that most of the Americanists were westerners of a sort. "Assimilation" had less meaning there. I am tempted to say it had no meaning at all. "Isolated settlements"—that "patchwork quilt" of Gjerde's—meant that immigrants did not have to "forsake their cultural pasts. Rather than competing, the dual loyalties to nation and [ethnic community] . . . could be complementary," which makes the old labels meaningless. The liberals were "assimilationists"; the conservatives were "separatists." But if, as Gjerde in particular has argued, immigrants assimilated by remaining separate, if the two positions were not only compatible but paths to one another, the conflict disappears and is replaced by tolerance if not amity. Seen in that way, Irish-born Father Peter Yorke of San Francisco becomes more representative than either John Ireland or Michael Corrigan. Yorke was an Irish nationalist; an American, or at least a western, patriot; a reformer in the mold of European Christian Democrats; a man who delighted in mocking America's economic elite—Catholic and non-Catholic alike; a vigorous and outspoken opponent of APA nativism; and an equally vigorous champion of the rights of labor. He worked indefatigably for his church, his city, and the advancement of his Irish friends—which, he sincerely believed, would work to advance the non-Irish with whom he had a cordial relationship. He was neither liberal nor conservative. Indeed, he often confounded and controverted both labels by being a little of each and in the process rendering each irrelevant.[110]

Here is Father Yorke at the 1902 San Francisco Irish Fair: a celebration "of the People . . . the everyday life, the pastimes and amusements of the plain . . . Irish people." Many of them had been gone from Ireland for half a century. No matter;

they were still what they had always been and would always be. Yorke admitted with undisguised disdain that "there be a class of Irish who are always apologizing for their race"—and that Hiberno-English "there be" was undoubtedly intentional. These types point to Irish "notables . . . as proof . . . that we are not utter savages." Yorke knew, however, that "the Irishman . . . doesn't need the prestige of a few great names to hold his own." And he did not need to apologize for being plain and Irish. That was what made him an American. Once Peter Yorke begins to make sense, the entire Americanist "controversy" takes on a new and different meaning.[111]

A related point: the assimilationists consistently and mistakenly equated Americanness with Anglo-Americanism. The only seeds belonged to Albion. James Barrett was cited earlier arguing that immigrants could assimilate from the bottom up, adopting working-class rather than middle-class values. Laurence Moore switches the axis. The "American experience," he writes, "was the experience of immigrants, and the claim of Protestant evangelicals that American culture and their culture were synonymous was open to challenge." In fact, the claim was absurd on its face—and the Americanists should have known it. This is where the West, or rather the myth of the West, enters the discussion. There was little that distinguished John Ireland from Frederick Jackson Turner or Theodore Roosevelt other than his vestments. Yorke would have included Ireland, who was a staunch Republican, among the ostriches pretending to be elephants. Finley Peter Dunne would have called him a champion of Anglo-Saxon superiority; certainly Ireland counted the conquest of the frontier—and Spain in the Spanish-American War—as evidence of American greatness, as he counted his frontier experience as evidence of his own.[112]

Moore is right when he argues that Irish American Catholics, from diocesan offices to the pews, wanted "something more than a merger with the status quo of American life." They molded what he calls an "outgroup mentality," not for reasons of piety—although those were not irrelevant—but as a badge of social identification. Social identification, however, meant more than just folkways and physical appearance. In the case of the Irish, odd speech patterns, the waking of the dead, and even clannishness were not enough. It had to mean something to be Irish and Catholic. It did. Thick webs of culture always do. It meant different ways of tracking time, archaeology rather than exploration as the dominant art, a certain suspicion of the casual meliorism of America. In the process of living out these folkways, as Moore writes, the Irish "profoundly affected the *myth* of what American Protestant culture was supposed to be." For "myth" read "multifarious frauds."[113]

The liberal clergy argued that a merger would have hastened immigrant Catholic social mobility. They were probably right. The problem was that the type of merger they favored represented cultural self-immolation. The conservatives knew that, and they knew as well its corollary. Social mobility was not a part of the culture code of many of their immigrant parishioners. This is a tough issue. Irish Catholics did stay longer in the working class than other immigrants. Various explanations have been offered: Gaelic Catholic disabilities, including the exile motif; American anti-Catholicism; the baleful effects of conservative and antimodernist priests; Catholic anti-intellectualism; the waste of too much money on the cause of Irish nationalism; the waste of even more money on churches and the separate school system that went along with them.

Each of these explanations, however, was external to the Irish American world. Each was based on a social template taken from the guidebook on how to succeed in America. Irish Catholics did not read that book and would not have understood or necessarily agreed with the definition of success if they had. As James Henretta has written, "like their peasant relations in Ireland, [Irish] laborers wanted security in their old age, a rent-free house to which they could retire." That was not exactly the American dream. But Henretta was also right when he added that "the point of departure for the study of any cultural group must be its own values and aspirations." It is the case that those values isolated the Irish and left them isolated—left them, in other words, precisely where they wanted to be.[114]

What, then, was the Irish Catholic relationship with western America? A large and quite alliterative choice of descriptive words is available. They assimilated, accommodated, acculturated, Americanized. I would like to extend the list— and without affecting the alliteration. In a recent article on the "articulation" of the worlds of slaves and masters, the historian Christopher Morris writes about black slave culture in language that, if used with proper caution, might easily describe both Irish and Irish American worlds. Morris speaks of the slaves' cultural "autonomy," of their "extra-economic priorities," their "precapitalist sense of community not unlike that . . . of free white farming settlements . . . isolated from the market." Slaves did not assimilate to the culture of their white owners. How could they have, and would they have wanted to had they been able?[115]

The connection between slave and master was an articulated link that allowed those on both sides of it to move, to live separate yet co-dependent lives. Articulation resolved ambiguities. It permitted capitalism to coexist with peasantry; black to coexist with white. Slavery was capitalistic; the slaves were not. The free market in the North was capitalistic; those who labored in it were not. Morris writes of "parallel [white and black] belief systems," of the "internal economy" of the slaves, and of their "alternative perspectives toward time, work and status." This is strikingly similar to "hidden Ireland" and the "silent economy of friends" that sustained it and kept it hidden and also very close to the notion that the Catholic Irish were "fundamentally at odds with the commercially inspired progress faith of the United States." It is, in other words, what would be expected of a people who transplanted the culture of once hidden townlands. Articulation was how the Irish stayed green.[116]

But articulation is a highly suggestive and elastic theory. It also permits the speculative point that ethnicity was as much a part of social class identity as the relationship to the means of production or any other material standard. I have already noted that the Irish lived in ethno-occupational enclaves, but "ethno-occupational" is a hybrid. Articulation leaves open the possibility that ethnicity and social class formed roughly equal parts of a single identity. To move away from theory and be specific, it supports the argument that to be Irish American, regardless of what one did for a living, was to be in a discrete "class," conscious of itself, aware of its interests, and acutely aware that those interests were not solely economic. The binary world of labor versus capital will not survive this new definition of class as culturally rather than socially and economically derived. But the old binary system, particularly if accompanied by the assumption that revolutionary class consciousness was built into the capitalist system, did not explain anything very accurately anyway.[117]

Obviously, "Irish American class" is intended descriptively rather than analytically. I mean only to suggest that the Irish often behaved like social classes were expected to behave. They placed themselves in history and had their own arcane consciousness and habits of thought, which frequently had an antagonistic relationship with those of the dominant non-Irish. Out of this came a movement culture that was frankly countercultural. This sense of themselves was both the cause and the effect of their disinheritance. In America, all of them—rich, poor, and middling—were in one sense disinherited. They had been told that they had no legitimate claims on the West, which meant no legitimate claims on the American future. So they built their own West and their own future. Only Irish needed to apply.

Epilogue

A Different Kind of West

"The Past and the Other," writes Greg Dening, "are two of humanity's main preoccupations." Remembering the past in order to determine who has a legitimate claim on it is how people live the present. When historians study people who lived before them, they are studying people who are the products of their pasts. The Others in the Irish cultural cosmology consisted of everyone who was not Irish—and a few who were. As for the past, they had what may safely be called very busy memories—not "accurate" in the sense of "truthful" memories, just busy ones. The Irish forgot nothing and—since much of what happened to them was hard and cruel—forgave little, which partly accounts for that long list of Others. Not only were the Irish the products of their past, but they still lived there. Verb tenses do not have the same meanings to a people the Irish Australian historian Patrick O'Farrell once called "constant anachronisms." Americans' preoccupations assumed a different form because the American past was so much happier and more triumphant.[1]

The past and the symbolic codes in which it was recorded, stored, and related made the Irish different from the Americans. Like the explorers they were, Americans looked outward toward where they were going. Americans had little confidence in memory. They remembered the past and told stories of it, but they insisted on distinguishing between what they remembered and what they called history. When they were being mature and serious—and they usually were—they wrote the past rather than told it. Their language had to be clear and unambiguous, but it did not need to be particularly memorable because it did not need to be remembered. Readers could always unshelve the book and read it again. The American language was good for researching the past and writing down what happened. Or at least so they told themselves.

That was not the way with the Irish. Like the archaeologists they were, the Irish looked downward to where they had been. The Irish in America was a story of the shovelers amid the conquistadors. The Irish told their stories, expecting that they would be remembered and retold. The language of the telling had to be memorable, as in easily remembered. The Irish used different literary tropes and more wildly imaginative words than did Americans. The "truth" of a story was in its ability to tether one generation to those that came before it, to keep the past alive and lively. Writing the past may not kill it, but it does entomb it. It seems to me a conceit that this American way of keeping the past was "truer" than the Irish way. That it made the past—whatever the level of the "truthfulness" of its telling—less immediately available for use seems to me indisputable. The Irish were anachronistic; the Americans were amnesiacs.

These distinctions between American and Irish storytelling and time- and score-keeping were part of what placed the Irish beyond the American pale. But they were only part. These were not just Irish people who found themselves misplaced to and in America. They were Catholic people, and the vast majority were in the American working classes. Fitting Irish Catholic workers into American society was difficult—witness the culture wars in eastern America. Fitting them into western American society presented a different set of issues, but it was scarcely less difficult. Put simply, Americans had one vision of the world and of the West and of their place in both; Irish had an alternative if not antithetical vision. These different visions created different Wests.

It is fitting to conclude this account of Irish Catholics and Protestant western America with a couple of stories or sets of stories. Both of them are "true" accounts as historians define truth. No bribery, even well concealed, is involved in the telling of them. But, like most good stories and all good Irish stories, the facts of the simple unadorned text are only part of the truth of them. Both, but particularly the second one, are offered up as allegories. They speak to truths larger than their particulars; in these instances much larger. The Irish *seanchaí* would have told them for the lessons they taught and for those larger truths. They would not even have had to embellish them to make them sing. I am not permitted that freedom, even were I capable of putting it to use. At that, I happily concede that once again history has handed me a story; I could not have made up characters, content, and settings that serve the interpretive purposes of this book better than these two tales of late nineteenth-century America, the West of its fanciful imagination, and its westering Irish.

The first story is directly to the point of the overlapping Irish and Western strains in American labor. As noted, David Montgomery not only singled out an Irish strain but also wrote of labor's western "heartland." The two references came in different articles, and he never explicitly connected them. He never needed to. I did. I need now to offer another example, and a perfect one is at hand. It connects not just the Irish and the West but the mythic West with the real one. Even its narrator is ideally cast. In 1886 Karl Marx's daughter Eleanor, accompanied by Dr. Edward Aveling, went to America to raise money for the socialist cause in Europe. They traveled from New York to Kansas City, giving lectures and attempting to make sense of *The Working-Class Movement in America,* as they titled the book that recounted their visit.[2]

They would have been well advised to go beyond Kansas City if they were really to learn something about the American working-class movement, but fortunately they had a chance encounter in Cincinnati that advanced their education. Friends had taken them to a "dime museum," where the featured attraction was "a group of cowboys . . . clad in their picturesque garb." A "spruce gentleman, in ordinary . . . garments, began to make stereotyped speeches about them." These were cowpokes on display, stage cowboys no less unreal—though more attractive—than the stage Irish of the same time. Americans were fascinated by them. They represented the best of a nation. The very fact that they were in a traveling museum in Cincinnati rather than riding the lone prairie suggested that they were of doubtful and diminishing relevance, but this point was too painful to contemplate and thus was frequently ignored.[3]

After a time, and "mercifully" for Marx and Aveling, the "spruce gentleman" stepped aside and gave the stage to "a cowboy of singularly handsome face and figure, with the frankest of blue eyes." His name was "Mr. John Sullivan, alias Broncho John," and it was expected that he "would take up the parable." Marx's reference to the cowboy tales as "parables" is of more than passing interest; that Broncho John was an Irishman—and of regal bearing, no less—is of surpassing interest. So was what he had to say. Sullivan clearly departed from the prepared text. He recited no parables, gave no stereotypical speech. As Marx put it, "to our"—and, I would guess, everyone else's—"great astonishment," Broncho John "plunged at once into a denunciation of capitalists in general and of the ranch-owners in particular." Contrary to stories in the eastern press, the 8,000 to 10,000 cowboys in the West were not the free-ranging paladins of myth but a brutally exploited class of workers. As Marx and Aveling wrote, the "cowboys themselves have made plain to us . . . that they are distinctly members of the non-possessing, yet producing, and distributing class; that they are as much at the mercy of the capitalist as a New or Old England cotton-worker; . . . their supposed 'freedom' is no more of a reality than his."[4]

Broncho John and his "pards" did what exploited workers were doing everywhere; they tried to "connect themselves with the laboring masses and with the general movement of that class," probably through the Knights of Labor. Sullivan spoke for all the herders. "No class is harder worked, . . . none so poorly paid." The reasons were simple: the cowboys had no union and the ranch owners had "one of the strongest and most systematic and . . . despotic unions that was ever formed." Sullivan was referring to the stock growers' associations that were inescapable parts of the politics of every western state where ranching was economically important. The employers in the association paid the best of their riders twenty-five dollars a month; they provided their "boys" with a horse but nothing in the way of equipment. The work was dirty, exhausting, and dangerous and included dealing with "marauders" and "Indians." The "cowboys have a serious struggle with actual want." They were told to fatten the cattle as they drove them but were not provided with enough food to keep themselves adequately fed. The cattle arrived at the market towns sleek and plump; the cowboys who brought them there arrived exhausted and gaunt. Sullivan concluded his remarks by telling his audience that the election of James Blaine in the presidential contest of 1886 would mean that "all the thieving would go on," while the election of Henry George as mayor of New York would "'make a change.'" And something had to change. As matters stood, "such is the system," we "dare not protest."[5]

They may have dared after the IWW formed a "broncho busters" local—in itself an important indication of the "western strain" at its most radical—but cowboys remained too scattered and transient a workforce to put up an effective challenge. Besides, no protest could have been enough to beat the stock growers' associations. Sullivan offered an example from Wyoming. The "Association of Ranchers" (the politically powerful Wyoming Stock Growers' Association) had secured the passage of a Maverick Law that allowed them to claim or "repleve" all unbranded cattle. Marx explained that "repleve" was "wild-western for seizing." It was, in other words, legalized theft. The Maverick Law and the legal challenges to it brought by small ranchers and cowboys—the association called them rustlers— "never [got] into Eastern papers. Meanwhile, 'repleving' goes on merrily, and the small settlers, robbed of their little stock, become cowboys and the wage-slaves [that word again] of the ranchers, who are all staunch upholders of the sacred rights of property." The western parables were filled with mavericks and dogies (a slang word derived from the Irish language). The myth had little room for what repleving really meant and no room at all for cowboy Wobblies.[6]

A bit of historical reconstruction is in order. Marx did not say if Sullivan was an immigrant Irishman. Assuming he was—and that seems a safe assumption—and that he was about forty years of age when he began his "stage" career, he would have been born during the worst of the Great Hunger. Given his surname, he was almost surely from either West Cork or Kerry, and it does not stretch credibility to imagine that he had been active as a younger man in the Irish Land War of the late 1870s and "houghing" English horses, as E. P. Thompson put it. If he emigrated as a young child or was born in the United States, his memories and experiences would not have been more pleasant or less intensely political. He had learned difficult lessons in western America. His reference to Henry George is especially revealing. Broncho John was no frontier primitive. He was aware of the New York City mayoral race, almost surely from his reading of Patrick Ford's *Irish World*. He would also have known of George's coverage of Irish affairs, of the single-tax theory, and of George's and many others' efforts to effect an alliance between labor and agricultural interests, between the Knights of Labor, for example, and the Populists—in language Eleanor Marx would have recognized, between those with hammers and those with sickles. There is a great deal of speculation and assumption here, but one thing appears certain: John Sullivan's songs around the cowpunchers' campfires would have been of a most unconventional sort.

In Eleanor Marx's account, John Sullivan rose and "spoke a piece," a familiar western idiom. The difference was that in his case being or even playing western had some countercultural features that would challenge the master narrative rather than embody it. Something close to this happened every time radicals adopted western poses and styles, as they routinely did. The image was no less heroic; western chivalry was still at the service of the helpless. But the black-guards and scoundrels were captains of industry, and the fighting spirit of the West was not enlisted in their cause but in that of labor militancy. That a cattle herder—and an Irish one at that—would speak lines commonly assigned to an eastern and urban proletariat is compelling evidence of this. Broncho John was a cowboy, the single most powerful iconic symbol of the mythic West. His speech would have sounded wildly discordant notes, had anyone been paying attention.[7]

Six years after Eleanor Marx had listened in wonder to John Sullivan, what was called a war was fought between large ranchers and small farmers and cattle-men in Wyoming's Johnson County. At the heart of the conflict was the Maverick Law and the charges brought by the cattle kings—often absentee—that the small holders were stock thieves. The conflict had no direct Irish connection, though the novel and movie based on it feature a wandering and disconnected hero with the certain Irish name of Shane. He could have been Broncho John. Sullivan identified the true thieves and smugglers as the rich using the Maverick Law to plunder the poor—a familiar enough theme among exiled Irish. The Johnson County War also involved, however indirectly, Moreton Frewen and Sir Horace Curzon Plunkett, Anglo-Irish lords acting out their cowboy dreams on their Wyoming ranches. Both were active members of the Wyoming Stock Growers' Association and charter members of the exclusive Cheyenne Club, a combination hunting-lodge and gentlemen's drinking club—Pall Mall moved to southern Wyoming. Both were determined to protect their cattle from those who came to be called "the banditti of the plains," the western American equivalent of the Irish rapparees and Whiteboys during the various Irish land wars.[8]

Considerable attention was paid to this western range war, and not just in the context of the Wild West, where boyos will be boyos. This was class war. Certainly Broncho John Sullivan, cowboy wage slaves, and Wobblies on horseback were

not what the bitterly antiunion Owen Wister intended when he had his Virginian
amble into Medicine Bow, Wyoming. That Wister would take the side of the
large cattlemen in *The Virginian* was entirely predictable. So was the fact that
Theodore Roosevelt, never entirely rational when dealing with western issues and
with more than a little of the counterfeit cowboy about him, would write that
in *The Virginian* Wister had captured the true "note of manliness . . . the great
virile virtues . . . of courage, energy, and daring: the virtues which beseem a
masterful race—a race fit to . . . conquer continents."[9]

Others saw the matter differently. The 1892 Omaha Platform of the People's
Party, much of it written by Ignatius Donnelly, the party's vice-presidential candidate, made specific reference to the Johnson County War, condemning "the recent
invasion of the Territory of Wyoming by the hired assassins of plutocracy, assisted
by federal officials." This was in the same document in which Donnelly and the
party warned that a "vast conspiracy against mankind has been organized on two
continents, and it is rapidly taking possession of the world." Labor was "impoverished; . . . the land concentrating in the hands of capitalists." Farmers and
small ranchers had to join with industrial labor in a coalition of the producing
classes if America was not to "degenerate into European conditions." The inclusion of a western range war in that Populist and working-class indictment must
have been doubly disheartening to advocates of American exceptionalism. The
newest parts of the New World had been subverted.[10]

In Ireland, Broncho John Sullivan would have ranked with Big James the
Furious as a figure of heroic proportions. His story would have been told and
retold. James Manahan would have been reading about him rather than about the
entirely fictional Bowie Knife Bill. In America, however, even in western America,
there was no room in the histories for Broncho John. I would like to think that
the Irish in Butte or San Francisco or Melrose knew of him and told their children
and friends the story of Sullivan's speech in Cincinnati, as incendiary in its way as
anything from the storehouse of Irish legends. The anthology of American legends,
however, was a different matter. The myth of the West was pervasive. Most of it
was also in service to overwhelmingly powerful economic forces who would not
have hesitated to "bribe" both the storytellers and the historians. It had no room
for Broncho John Sullivan. He was big trouble, not in the sense that he and all
of his leftist cowboy comrades combined could have overthrown the system but
only because—like William Foster on his Mosier Creek homestead—they gave
the lie to the myths that propped the system up.

The second, more allegorical story is really a collection of related stories, all of
them represented in one fashion or another at the 1893 World's Fair and Columbian Exposition in Chicago. Chicago was like a grand dramatic presentation—all
of modern America on parade. The fair provided the principal players in the

modern project with an opportunity to make curtain calls. They did so with a flourish. The Irish were not principal players and made no curtain calls. Some of them were stage props; but for most, their role was that of the chorus at a Greek comedy, except that they were outlanders, non-Greeks. Call them the barbarian chorus. Laurence Moore has written that the Irish affected the myth of what Protestant America was supposed to be. But the Irish did more than affect the myth; they exposed it and evinced a clear aversion to sharing in it. The chorus was their proper role. They were positioned off to the side, and the fair looked very different from their observation point. The exposition was a Native ritual; the Irish were the Strangers busily taking ethnographic notes and singing their lamentations.[11]

Yeats, in one of his more passionately Irish stages, personified Ireland as an old woman, Cathleen Ní Houlihan. Her words as she seeks shelter from the "hard wind" could easily have been sung by my imaginary Irish chorus. "Have you traveled far to-day?" she is asked. "I have traveled far, very far," Ireland answers; "there are few have traveled so far as myself, and there's many a one that doesn't make me welcome." "It's a wonder you are not worn out with so much wandering," adds another character. Old woman Ireland answers: "Sometimes my feet are tired and my hands are quiet, but there is no quiet in my heart. When the trouble is on me I must be talking to my friends." She is then asked by one of those friends: "What was it put you wandering?"—in historical language, who sent you into exile? "Too many strangers in the house," says Cathleen Ní Houlihan, and "my land . . . was taken from me." Later, in the poem "The Indian to His Love," Yeats commented on the distances Cathleen Ní Houlihan would come to cover and what she would find when her wanderings ended: "Here we will moor our lonely ship. . . . / How far away are the unquiet lands."[12]

Chicago made clear to the Irish just how far, and in the process gave the barbarian chorus much on which to comment. Quite unintentionally, the managers of the fair provided the Irish—and historians—with examples and metaphors for all of the times and places the American and Irish historical lines had intersected. Consider first the occasion for the fair, the 400th anniversary of Columbus's "discovery" of the Americas. That sounds innocent enough, except when it is recalled that Catholic bishop James Gibbons, an Irish American, had told the pope that the "discovery of the New World" along with the Reformation was when all that Catholicism held dear was placed on "death-bed" alert. And Gibbons was one of the Americanists. Then scan the program. Ignatius Donnelly's sister Eleanor gave a speech in which she told her audience that the "purified literature" of the past was giving way to the "putrid carcasses tossed upon the rocks by the preceding deluge of human passion," a lurid and typically Irish and Catholic indictment of modernity and its multiple errors and frauds.[13]

Buffalo Bill Cody was also there with his Wild West show. The deadly strikes of the previous summer in the Coeur d'Alenes and the nearly simultaneous war in Johnson County, Wyoming, told far more representative western stories than did Buffalo Bill, but that Wild West had no attraction. The young historian Frederick Jackson Turner was also at the exposition. He presented his paper on the "significance of the frontier in American history" and then proceeded to his funeral dirge: the frontier was gone; America would have to do without its magic lands. The entire national economy was in free fall from 1893 to 1897, which gave an added poignancy to what postfrontier America would have to contend with. The essay's less elegiac themes, however, complemented Cody's show nicely. Both offered up inflated symbols of vanishing frontiers and legacies of conflict.[14]

A year after Turner talked about the frontier movement from east to west as an act of self-liberation and then warned that the frontier was gone, the Northwest Industrial Army, part of Jacob Coxey's army of unemployed, reversed the process; the workers sought relief by marching from west to east. Just a month before Turner spoke, rebellious western miners, many if not most of them Irish, had met in Butte and formed the Western Federation of Miners, then and for years after the most radical of American labor organizations. One can imagine the chorus keening. The Irish language had it right: America snuck up on and came after the Irish from the west. They had no choice but to contest the assault on native grounds.[15]

For a closer look at the new West, fair-goers could visit the Montana exhibit, which featured an uncommonly ugly six-foot statue of Lady Liberty. It was made of solid silver, recovered from hard rocks dug out of thousand-foot-deep holes in Butte. The unyielding and refractory ores were then pounded to pebbles in giant steam-powered stamp mills and processed and refined chemically by using mercury. This was not the West of Buffalo Bill. The muscle for this heaviest of industries was provided by an Irish-dominated western working class, members of the Butte Miners Union, local #1 of the WFM. The statue was direct evidence of the work they did. The chorus would have reminded the fair-goers of that, as it would have reminded them that the electricity that powered the 7,000 arc lamps and 120,000 incandescent lamps that lit up the fair's buildings was carried by copper wire made from Butte rocks and dug by those same miners. Meanwhile, scattered throughout the White City of the fairgrounds were sculptures by Augustus Saint-Gaudens, who less than a decade later would create the ultimate monument to Marcus Daly, Butte's—and to a great extent the West's—boss Irishman.[16]

In another building on the grounds were the dynamos. Henry Adams, the politically unanointed son of founding Americans, was much taken by them, believing that people prayed to those great steam engines. It was not until 1900 at the Paris World's Fair that Adams made a direct comparison between the nineteenth century's worship of the dynamo and the twelfth century's worship of the Cross and the Virgin, but the source of that comparison was Chicago. "Chicago," he wrote, "asked in 1893 for the first time the question whether the American people knew where they were driving." Adams was uncertain, but it was obviously not toward a restored medieval faith. Neither, however, was it toward the simplicity of the mythical West; the world of William Gilpin was as dead as the world of St. Thomas Aquinas—or George Washington, for that matter. The dynamo hummed. It possessed explosive energy. No wonder people prayed before it; this was a powerful and unfathomable god. Chicago represented a new world of capitalism and its machines. It was the "first expression of American thought as a unity," Adams said. "One must start there."[17]

Close by the dynamo room was the Parliament of Religions, where Catholic priests, whose day probably included a prayer to the Virgin, were sitting next to Protestant ministers, who thought the prayer idolatrous, and Jewish rabbis, who thought it meaningless. The entire parliament was a source of consternation for the anti-Americanists, elation for the Americanists, which added to the occasion. So did the remarkable speech to the parliament by Bishop John Ireland, who declaimed against the "popular literature of the day." Sounding every bit as censorious as Eleanor Donnelly, he warned of "novels exhaling [the] stygian stench . . . of impurity," of "papers teeming with salaciousness," of "theatrical posters [that give] our young people . . . object lessons in lasciviousness." But note that each of Ireland's catalog of sins was distinctly urban and, by inference, eastern. Rural western America was not guilty of such godlessness. Ireland's speech was at least in part an effort to appeal to the evangelical Protestants at the parliament and build a rickety bridge that would provide Catholics with access to the pale. Not many in the chorus would have been interested or even have taken him seriously.[18]

But the managers of the Chicago fair were not finished with their parade of images and icons, all the more wondrous because so inadvertent. This last example is my favorite, because the irony and connectedness that came first to my mind would never have occurred to those who put this exhibit together. In a building close to the arena in which Buffalo Bill staged his show was a display of non-whites put on by the Smithsonian Institution. These human exhibits offered graphic evidence of what the racial wars on American's western border had meant as well as all the scientific proof of the superiority of the victorious side that anyone could need. Unnoted was that the Irish American ethnologist James Mooney, recently back from Ireland, had collected most of the artifacts that were being worn and shown. It is not likely that any of those viewing this ethnological carnival made the connection with England and Ireland. But Mooney did. In my imagination, I like to think that Martin Dooley left his bar on the Archey Road, not far from the fairgrounds, to spend a day in the chorus. It pleases me even more to imagine that Dooley's friend Snakes-in-His-Gaiters was there with him. They would have been an interesting pair, those two from beyond the pale. Dooley and Snakes would have made Mooney's connection and a few more of their own. But the Smithsonian put no savage Irish on display, and the point was muted. The members of the chorus would have sung of Caliban and O'Caliban, but they would have sung only to themselves.[19]

All of these displays and shows have been given considerable attention by historians. But one other exhibit deserves inclusion in this summary of intersecting lines. Lady Aberdeen, a member of the English Committee of the fair's Board of Lady Managers, had commissioned the construction of a "typical Irish village," complete with thatched roofs, dirt-floored cabins, Celtic crosses in the cemetery, and a modest stone church. Lady Aberdeen was, to understate, well placed. Her husband was Britain's lord lieutenant or viceroy for Ireland and as such the personal representative of the British monarch to the Irish people. Lady Aberdeen's village, in other words, was a distinctly non-Irish project. This was a case of English Strangers presenting Irish Natives to the world.[20]

The massive thousand-page *Book of the Fair* described the exhibit, informing fair-goers that "we find here a turf fire above which a potato pot is boiling." In another part of the Irish show, "dairymaids, rosy and buxom, are showing what their deft fingers can accomplish with the aid of modern utensils." Interestingly, the flag of this mock-up (and mockery) of an Irish clachan was "Ireland's banner of green." That was likely a concession to Chicago's large Irish population, which doubtless would have found the Union Jack objectionable. Banner of green notwithstanding, the members of the Irish chorus would have considered the village contrived and wondered why it was there. They would have been right to wonder. The Irish village was in the curiously named Midway Plaisance, where, according to the fair's managers, visitors could see examples of the customs and folk art of "the civilized, semi-civilized, and barbarous," from "Caucasians" to "African blacks," with heads shaped "like coco-nuts." It made no specific reference to where the Irish should be placed in this hierarchical ranking; but their village was very near those of "South Sea Islanders, Javanese and Bedouins," implying that they were somewhere in the middle of the ethnographic pack, literally "in-between people."[21]

Lady Aberdeen may have thought she was doing the Irish a favor by displaying their weavers and dairymaids before the world. In this historical circumstance, however, it would seem that her village served the same purpose as did the Indian or Javanese villages or, more directly, the Smithsonian's Indian exhibit that Mooney had so carefully collected and organized. Parading one's "civilization" and "modernity" required a simultaneous display of "semicivilization" and "barbarism"—or at least premodernity. The fair had an assortment of peoples from whom to choose the negative referent. The fairgrounds had no "typical Southern plantation," but only because such a display would have been in bad taste politically. It would be quite possible, however, to imagine a "typical New England whaling town" or artisan's shop or a "typical western cow camp." An Irish village in the middle of the Midway Plaisance of the White City of the World's Columbian Exposition provided fair-goers with the ultimate in cultural contrasts.

There was, however, one terribly confusing aspect to all this. What of those highly civilized sorts who were offended by the results of the modern project and who saw that gleaming White City as a symbol of what had gone terribly wrong? This is no place for a full discussion of the antimodernist movement, but irony alone commends some mention of it. For those who had wearied of—or been offended by—the direction of industrial society, the Irish and the other villages were sad reminders of all that had been lost, not some kind of cultural baseline by which to judge all that had been gained. For the Irish, of course, both sides of this debate were unfathomable. Thatched roofs, dirt floors, potato pots, and dairymaids with primitive utensils were part of the day-to-day reality of their lives, not symbols to be used to judge the advance or decline of society or to inventory what had been abandoned in the rush to build more and better dynamos.

In both America and Ireland, "the men of the West"—and in America that meant all of the men, regardless of color or culture—were becoming antimodernist antidotes to the fops and "dudes" (interestingly, another slang word taken from the Irish) of New York in the one, Dublin and London in the other. The Catholic peasantry of the west of Ireland was given prominent mention in the catalog of alternatives to urban, industrial, and market-driven societies. So were American Indians, the Irish's savage twins, as well as cowboys. The primitivism that had made them obstacles to progress was now seen as a necessary counterfoil to the more unlovely features of that progress.[22]

The western stretches of both Ireland and America were beginning to take on aspects of a theme park. Anglo-Irish non-Catholics like William Butler Yeats, John Millington Synge, and Douglas Hyde rediscovered—or reinvented—the Irish peasants. They were no longer the hopelessly retrograde and outlandish half-wits the British and the Americans had once described, but the repository of traditional virtues. Yeats railed against the "filthy modern tide" and contrasted it with parts of the west of Ireland where "people live according to a tradition of life that existed before commercialism, and the vulgarity founded upon it." Unlike James Gibbons, Yeats did not state explicitly that the vulgar world of commerce came skulking in with the Protestant Reformation, but he was aware of—and troubled by—that possibility. Certainly he knew that had the Irish "become Britons," as the English, Scots, and Welsh did, they would have been uninteresting and useless. To speak of an Irish tradition of life without the Catholicism that formed and animated that tradition was a dodge.[23]

A few antimodernists faced up to this reality, however, and found in the "semi-feudal" church of the Irish another way of combating modernity and its discontents. But they were in the minority; most antimodernists ducked the issue by concentrating on the thatched-roofed cottages to the exclusion of the steepled and croziered chapels. Old habits and religious sensibilities aside, the inclusion of Catholicism—popery in an earlier incarnation—among the forces holding back the tide pushed irony to its limits. But these were tough times. What, for only one example, were Americans to make of it when they heard that William Tecumseh Sherman's son had not only converted to Catholicism but become a Jesuit priest? The elder Sherman had conquered Southern slavery and western savagery; the younger was attacking the APA as the tool of Protestant Orangemen who did not understand America. That hopeless muddle of images pushed irony perilously close to farce.[24]

There had to be some place where modernity's vulgarity and the crassness could be confronted and repelled. The fishermen and peasants of Ireland's wild west would be leagued with American Indians, with Roosevelt's cow-punchers and reckless riders, and, for some, with proud ex-slaveholding Southrons. These heroic sorts would not be asked if they wanted the role; nor would many of them participate in the fashioning of it. The Irish were invented by Anglo-Irish, the Indians by white Americans, the western cowboys by easterners, the Southerners by Northerners. All of these symbols of innocence even shared a primitive aesthetic. Westerners (both cowboys and Indians), the Irish, and Southerners alike could not pave their roads without imperiling their souls. This was inherently unfair: primitives had to remain primitive lest they lose their usefulness. It was far better that they be extinguished than that their material circumstances be improved.[25]

The cultural norms of these semicivilized peoples were not just distinct, they were irrational. That was what made them so appealing. What Yeats wrote of the Irish Catholic peasantry could have been ascribed to all of these primordial folk. A few alterations would have been needed to make the descriptions fit; pre-modernity, obviously, came in different styles. But with a few nips and tucks, Yeats's language would have covered them all: "Once every people in the world believed that trees were divine . . . and all the poets of races who have not lost this way of looking at things could have said of themselves . . . 'I have learned my songs from the music of many birds, and from the music of many waters.'" There is something terribly—almost embarrassingly—contrived in that, but Yeats was not alone in thinking that "this way of looking at things" was far the best way. "Ireland and England," he once told an American audience, "represent two different principles of human life." "When one talks to the people of the West of Ireland," he wrote, "and wins their confidence, one soon finds that they live in a very ancient world." That world was one of "open air, the hunt, changing seasons, love, animals, food, and drink." That had a certain nobility, as did the duplicate worlds of noble semisavagery, wherever found. It was the modern world that was base and filthy.[26]

And so Yeats and the others in Ireland devised a "cult of the peasant"; it matched in language if not always in purpose the nearly simultaneous American cult of the primitive. Occasionally the archetypes blended. James Manahan, for example, portrayed the Irish farmers of his part of Minnesota in language that sounded like a passage from Irish legend—or a mix of Bowie Knife Bill and Red Cloud, with a few of the cultural leftovers of Southern cavaliers. They were "strong and courageous. Their spiritual temperament was superb, even knightly . . . but their thinking was very elementary, they were as a class unsuspecting and childish. I almost wrote 'stupid.'" He did not mean that unkindly. Better to be stupid than like the "railroad builders, . . . lumber barons and bankers." Those types were "united and organizing for self protection and mutual advantage." Manahan's heroes had other and better things to do than count money. They were "grubbing, planting, harvesting, drinking, sleeping and love-making." Manahan omitted only the bellowing of the bulls. Theirs, too, was a very ancient world. The cult of the west Irish peasant, matched in rhetorical excess by various American cults, produced a kind of transatlantic antimodernist chant. When the American chanters turned toward Indians and cowboys—as they frequently did—the result was a "Western critique" of the Gilded Age.[27]

One of the good books on the Irish component of the antimodernist movement is Deborah Fleming's *"A Man Who Does Not Exist": The Irish Peasant in the Work of W. B. Yeats and J. M. Synge.* That title could be applied to many aspects of American antimodernism as well, including the "typical Irish village" at the Chicago World's Fair and Columbian Exposition. What was ignored by the antimodernists was that looking with sad longing upon facsimiles of an Irish village, enclosing and encasing it within the White City, was the quintessence of modernity. So was playing cowboy or playing Indian. Most of the critics of the Gilded Age were writers and intellectuals. Their celebration—uncomprehending as much of it was—of the preindustrial virtues of Irish Catholic, Western, or American Indian society and culture was that of outsiders peeking in. They could not have participated in these alien worlds even had they wanted to—and they most assuredly did not want to. Playing a cowboy was safer and less wearying than becoming one. Studying Catholic cathedrals, as the undeviatingly antimodern Henry Adams did, was respectable and intellectually satisfying; praying in them would have been outlandish. Collecting Indian and Irish folktales and offering them up as antidotes to modernity was better than spending a lifetime of cold nights in floorless tepees and cabins telling and listening to them. The frontier of the antimodernists was a result of cultural voyeurism; it consisted of people who did not exist.[28]

The people who manifestly did exist were lost sight of. The western Irish American Catholics—the real objects this time, not the invented heroes of breathless antimodernists or the invented enemies of unhinged nativists—did not need to invent their differences with modern society. They were Hibernia's seed and so born to the task. They did have to "revise" some of their own history, bribing a few storytellers in the process, but that involved only minor adjustments. They did not have to hold back the filthy modern tide; they needed only to be what they had always been: outlanders, "constant anachronisms," ill-suited or only fractionally suited to English or American values. Being beyond the pale came naturally to them. It was a defining part of who they were.[29]

It remained that. Being out of time and out of place made them more resistant to the multifarious frauds of modernity. Perhaps diggers are harder to fool. Certainly the victims of conquest are less easily taken in by the self-congratulatory legends of conquerors. Whatever the reason, this account of the intersecting lines of Irish and western American history cannot end without mention of a few occasions when the lines not only intersected but were plaited. In 1992 the Irish writer John B. Keane wrote a novel called *Durango,* about an Irish cattle drive from the village of Tubberlick to the great fair and cattle sale at the market town of Trallock. This is not one of Keane's best works, but it is one of his funniest: a comic parody of every bad American western, whether novel or film. One of the characters asks in a perfect western drawl, "What's this I hear about a cattle drive?" —followed immediately by the equally perfect Hiberno-English "Is it in Texas or Tubberlick you think you are?" Trallock's movie theater is showing Gene Autry and a number of sanitized Indians in *Springtime in the Rockies.* The town's biggest saloon is the Durango, and "you can have anything you want in Durango," including Bessie LieDown, whose name certainly suggests American Indians. The story line has evil cattle barons and honest cowboys, a stampede, a shoot-out, a bully firing his pistol at the feet of Bollicky Bill Gobberley to make him dance, and a character named Danny Dooley (I imagine him as Martin's Irish cousin) who says with a perfectly straight face that "wronging a horse is as bad as wronging a woman. A good woman or a good horse will never let you down." Of non-Americans, only an Irishman could have written *Durango.* No other could have exposed the mythic American West as Keane did.[30]

Keane was not the only one who put the mythical American West in Ireland or an often mythical Ireland in the American West. F. Scott Fitzgerald (who was all three) used Irish, Catholic, and Western themes in both *The Great Gatsby* and *The Love of the Last Tycoon: A Western.* Gatsby behaved like a twentieth-century Benjamin Franklin, chasing the constantly receding American dream of finding a second-chance country; the dream ran away faster than Gatsby could run chasing it, and there were no second chances. It is the case that Gatsby pursued from west to east, reversing the conventional course, but West Egg and East Egg were a lot like Tír na nÓg. Martin Dooley, among other Irish, would have gotten the point and used it to warn Hennessy of the perils of chasing after gold mines. The Irish poet Eamonn Wall, now living in the United States, writes movingly and consciously of Ireland and the American West in his collection of poems *From the Sin-é Café to the Black Hills*. The Irish band U2—the name may have been taken from the spy plane or be a simple play on words, but it also reads like a cattle brand—uses Irish and western themes in its album *The Joshua Tree*. The Irish painter Sean Keating, probably unconsciously, depicts three figures in his painting *Men of the West* who look like well-armed characters from a Randolph Scott or John Wayne movie.[31]

Recall, too, that when James Brown proved too black and soulful for the Irish band in *The Commitments* the band's manager put them in western outfits and gave the band members names like Tex Wallace. They may have recorded "The Streets of Laredo" (set to an old Irish tune) or "Two Shillelagh O'Sullivan," a song from the album *Green Fields of America,* played by Mick Maloney, Robbie O'Connell, and Jimmy Keane. The lyrics would have fit: "There's many a man who rode a horse across the Western Plains / There's never been one like the Irishman, / O'Sullivan was his name. / He never carried a shootin' iron, the need he never felt. / With two shillelaghs always there, / a hanging from his belt. / Yippee cay yae, oh me buckoo, begorra and yippee cay yo. / Two Shillelagh O'Sullivan, he'd give any man a go." All of this might have been simply funny: the Irish burlesquing Americans' claims to have conquered the frontier. The problem— and the tragedy—is that the presumed conquest of wild lands always involved, whether stated directly or not, the conquest of the wild people who lived on them. O'Sullivan's ride across the western plains would not have gone uncontested.[32]

In that context, a case can be made for an essential Irishness joined to an equally essential and shared Indian/Irish savagery in Cormac McCarthy's novels, particularly *Blood Meridian,* his gory burlesque of the heroic western myth. McCarthy took the name Cormac (he was not born with it), which certainly suggests that he was conscious of his Irishness and wanted his readers to be as well. Renegade Irish, including an ex-priest by the name of Tobin, play prominent and murder- ous roles. But consider, too, another of McCarthy's novels. The American West was, he said, borrowing a line from Yeats, "no country for old men," a sentiment that begs comparison with Julia O'Faolain's novel of Ireland, *No Country for Young Men*. I can imagine the Irish choristers, in their lighter moods, singing of Two Shillelagh O'Sullivan as they wandered by the Smithsonian Exhibit set up by James Mooney. I can as easily imagine them, in their more frequent darker moods, chanting the titles of McCarthy's and O'Faolain's novels as they wandered through Lady Aberdeen's Irish village. The fair-goers, however, would not have been listening and would not have understood the lyrics even if they had been.

Western Communities That Sent Contributions to Support Irish Nationalism (1880–1882, 1905)

CITIES (22)

Clinton, Iowa
Council Bluffs, Iowa
Davenport, Iowa
Denver, Colorado
Dubuque, Iowa
Duluth, Minnesota
Iowa City, Iowa
Lincoln, Nebraska
Minneapolis, Minnesota
Omaha, Nebraska
Portland, Oregon

Pueblo, Colorado
Reno, Nevada
Rochester, Minnesota
Sacramento, California
San Bernardino, California
San Francisco, California
Seattle, Washington
South Omaha, Nebraska
Spokane, Washington
St. Paul, Minnesota
Topeka, Kansas

MEDIUM-SIZED AND SMALL TOWNS (188)

Minnesota (31)

Assumption
Avoca
Carimona
Chatfield
Corcorantown
Crookston

Dayton
De Graff
Fergus Falls
Forestville
Fountain
Freeburg

Hassan
Hokah
Jamesville
Kilkenny
Lanesboro
LaSueur County

Minnesota (cont.)

Leroy
Litchfield
Mankato
Marysburg
Meeker County

Preston
Sauk Center
Shakopee
Sibley

Spring Lake
Stillwater
Waseca
Wilton

Iowa (70)

Ackley
Anamosa
Beaver
Bevington
Boone
Briscoe
Brush Creek
Burlington
Butler
Cascade
Cedar City
Cedar Creek
Center Grove
Charles City
Claremont
Clarinda
Council City
Cresco
Delhi
DeWitt
Dougherty
Dunlap
Dyersville
Elkader

Emmetsburg
Farley (100 members in
    Land League, Jan. 21, 1882)
Fonda
Garner
Gary Owen [sic]
Georgetown
Grand Junction
Guthrie Center
High Lake
Highland
Iconium
Independence
Keokuk
Lamont
Lansing
Latty
Lothrop
Lyons
Mason City
McGregor
Melrose (James and Malachy
    Ward)
Middlefield

Modale
Monona
Morengo
Muscatine
New Albion
Newton
Osage
Otter Creek
Otto
Ottumwa
Panora
Pee Dee
Red Oak
Riverside
Sailex
St. Ansgar
Stewart
Tivoli
Toronto
Vernon Township
Volga City
Washington Township
Waucoma
Westerville

Kansas (31)

Atchison
Beattie
Bellevue
Carbondale

Centralia
Concordia
Council Grove
Edgerton

Ellinwood
Emerald
Emporia
Gardner

Kansas, cont.

Geary City	McPherson	Reno County
Girard	Olathe	Ridgeway Ford
Grant	Osage City	Scammonville
Idell	Osage Mission	Scranton
Independence	Ottawa	Strong City
Little Elmsdale	Pierceville	Wyandotte
Longford		

Dakota Territory (6)

Bismarck	Mandan
Fargo	Olivet
Huron	Redwater Valley

Colorado (8)

Alamosa	Middle Kiowa
Ft. Collins	S. Pueblo
Greeley	Trinidad
Hugo	Walsenburg

Nebraska (21)

Atkinson	Forest City	Ponca
Battle Creek	Friendville	Sand Creek
Beachamville	Greeley	Shelton
Blair	Jackson	Summit
David City	Oakdale	Tecumseh
Exeter	Oakland	Vernon Township
Fairmont	O'Neill	Wahoo City

California (7)

Anaheim	Paso Robles
Arcata	San Miguel
Hayward	Santa Rosa
Menlo	

Oregon (4)

Harrisburg   The Dalles
St. Paul   Umatilla

Montana (6)

Choteau   Miles City
Hamilton   Shonkin
Helmville   Sun River

Washington (3)

Cheney
Deep Creek
Walla Walla

New Mexico (1)

Farmington

Military (14)

Camp Thomas, Arizona   Ft. Lander, Wyoming
Ft. Abraham Lincoln, Dakota   Ft. Laramie, Wyoming
Ft. Bidwell, California   Ft. Leavenworth, Kansas
Ft. Buford, Dakota   Ft. Sanders, Wyoming
Ft. Ellis, Montana   Ft. Scott, Kansas
Ft. Garland, Colorado   Ft. Stevens, Oregon
Ft. Keough, Montana   Vancouver Barracks, Washington

MINING TOWNS (82)

Idaho (7)

Bonanza City   Leesburg
Castle Creek   Salmon City
Florence   Silver City (gave $500.00)
Idaho City

Colorado (22)

Alma
Ashcroft
Bijou
Breckenridge
Central City
Coal Creek
Del Norte
Divide
El Moro
Georgetown
Golden
Kokomo

Lake City ("enclosed find $120.00, the proceeds of a meeting of Irish exiles in Lake City, Colorado" [32 of them])
Las Animas
Leadville (gave $2,000.00)
Ouray
Red Cliff
Red Elephant Mountain
Rico
San Antonio
St. Elmo
Telluride

Montana (8)

Bear Mouth
Beartown
Butte City
Canton

Helena
Hughesville
Lyon City
Race Track

California (20)

Alcatraz
Bodie
Castroville
Colfax
Covelo
Downeyville
El Monte
Eureka
Folsom
Forrest City

Howland Flat
Madison
Marysville
Mojara
North Tennehal
Ravenna
Salmon Creek
Tipton
Williams
York's Creek

Arizona (7)

Benson
Bisbee
Harsboro
Harshaw

Prescott
Tombstone
Winslow

Nevada (9)

Austin
Candelaria
Carson City
Cherry Creek
Empire City

Eureka
Silver City
Virginia City
Ward

New Mexico (4)

Cubero
Daly
Elizabeth Town
Georgetown

Dakota (3)

Central City (meeting in Miners Union Hall)
Deadwood
Lead City

Utah (2)

Park City
Silver Reef

Railroad Towns (10)

Black Canyon, Colorado
    ("RR camp")
Evanston, Wyoming
Granger, Wyoming
Laramie, Wyoming
    ("Union Pacific RR crew")

Lone Tree, Wyoming
Pen D'Oreille [*sic*], Idaho
Rawlins, Wyoming
Rock Springs, Wyoming
Ruhns Crossing, Colorado
Sheep Ranch, Colorado

Sources: Irish World, Apr. 17, Apr. 24, and May 1, 1880, Land League; *Irish World,* Jan. 24, 1880, Anti-Rent War; *Irish World,* Jan. 29, 1881; *Irish Nation,* Feb. 25, 1882; *Irish Nation,* Apr. 1, 1882, State Land League Anti-Monopoly; *Irish World,* Jan. 7, 1882, No Rent Fund; *Irish World,* Jan. 14, 1882, Spread the Light Fund; *Irish World,* Jan. 21, Jan. 28, Feb. 4, Feb. 11, Feb. 18, Feb. 25, Mar. 4, Mar. 11, Mar. 18, Mar. 25, Apr. 11, Apr. 15, Apr. 22, May 13, May 20, May 27, June 3, June 17, Aug. 12, and Oct. 7, 1882; *Irish Nation,* Sept. 1, 1883, Parnell Testimonial Fund (vast majority of money from East); *Gaelic American,* Mar. 11 and Mar. 18, 1905; *Gaelic American,* Mar. 14, 21, 1908.

Notes

INTRODUCTION

1. For general studies, see Lee and Casey (eds.), *Making the Irish American;* Wittke, *Irish in America;* Shannon, *American Irish;* McCaffrey, *Irish Diaspora in America;* Clark, *Hibernia America;* Potter, *To the Golden Door;* Kenny, *American Irish;* Kenny (ed.), *New Directions*; and Glazier (ed.), *Encyclopedia;* on industrial skills, see Ferrie, *Yankeys Now,* 71–100; as much about Ireland as Irish America, and in a class by itself, is Miller, *Emigrants and Exiles.* I use the term "large differences" because I disagree with Akenson, *Small Differences.*

2. To trace the paths of Irish immigrants, see Glazier (ed.), *Encyclopedia.* See also Burchell, *San Francisco Irish;* Brundage, *Making of Western Labor Radicalism,* 25–52; Emmons, *Butte Irish;* Blessing, "West among Strangers"; Shannon, *Catholic Colonization;* O'Connell, *John Ireland;* Ridge, *Ignatius Donnelly;* Sarbaugh and Walsh (eds.), *Irish in the West;* Dungan, *How the Irish Won the West;* Doyle, "Irish as Urban Pioneers"; Akenson, *Small Differences,* 18–19, 86–107; idem, *Irish Diaspora;* and Ferrie, *Yankeys Now,* 39–70.

3. Shannon, *American Irish,* 27; Anbinder, *Nativism,* 8. See also McCaffrey, *Irish Diaspora,* 63–66; MacDonagh, "Irish Famine Emigration," 417, 436; and Fuchs, *John F. Kennedy,* 43–45.

4. For Australia, see Campbell, *Ireland's New Worlds;* for Canada, see Akenson, *Irish Diaspora;* Yeats, "Remorse for Intemperate Speech," in *Poems,* 32 ("great hatred"); Miller, *Emigrants and Exiles,* 193–279.

5. Nugent, *Into the West;* Robbins, "Western History"; Emmons, "Social Myth"; Igler, "Industrial Far West"; Malone, "'New Western History'"; Abbott, "Urban West"; Ferrie, *Yankeys Now,* 130–55.

6. "Strangers" and "Natives" in Dening, *Death of William Gooch.* Dening capitalizes "Stranger" and "Native" because they define rather than merely describe.

7. Colley, *Britons.* It was an invention in that Britons consisted of separate peoples: English, Scots, and Welsh.

8. Ibid., 5, 8, 18, 31.

9. Jennings, *Invasion of America.*

10. Marty, *Righteous Empire.*

11. Dickson, *Ulster Emigration;* Doyle, *Ireland, Irishmen, and Revolutionary America;* idem, "Scots Irish or Scotch-Irish," and Miller, "Ulster Presbyterians," both in Lee and Casey (eds.), *Making the Irish American;* Wilson, *United Irishmen.*

12. For provocative accounts of the Irish and whiteness, see Jacobson, *Whiteness;* Roediger, *Wages of Whiteness;* and Allen, *Invention of the White Race* (vols. 1 and 2).

13. Jacobson, *Whiteness,* 158–61.

14. Sellers, *Market Revolution;* Rostow, *Economics of Take-off;* idem, *Stages of Economic Growth;* Barney, *Passage of the Republic;* Marty, *Righteous Empire.* See also North, *Economic Growth;* Tilly, "Retrieving European Lives"; Nugent, "Frontiers and Empires"; Wilentz, *Chants Democratic;* Foner, *Free Soil;* and Laurie, *Artisans into Workers.*

15. Johnson, *Shopkeepers' Millennium;* Slotkin, *Fatal Environment,* 1–47.

16. White, *"It's Your Misfortune,"* 613; Richardson, *West from Appomattox,* 143.

17. Miller, *Emigrants and Exiles,* 107. The exile motif runs through Miller's entire book.

18. Miller, *Emigrants and Exiles,* 569–82 (quotation on 412; see also 363–64); Diner, *Erin's Daughters,* 30–42; Ó Gráda, *Ireland,* esp. 151–71; Ó Gráda, "Irish Emigration"; Golab, *Immigrant Destinations,* 134, 141; Blessing, "West among Strangers"; for Irish emigration statistics, see Vaughan and Fitzpatrick (eds.), *Irish Historical Statistics,* 259–353; and Miller, *Emigrants and Exiles,* 569–82 (see also 363–64). Miller's critic is Akenson, *Irish Diaspora,* 237.

19. Woodham-Smith, *Great Hunger;* Donnelly, *Great Irish Potato Famine;* Ó Gráda, *Black '47;* Scally, *End of Hidden Ireland,* esp. 3–8.

20. Limerick, *Legacy of Conquest;* Licht, *Working for the Railroad,* 221–25, 295–300; Stanton, "Fighting Irish."

21. Gordon argues that the Irish assimilated easily. See *Assimilation,* 92, 97, 133–35, 197–202, 217. I disagree. So does Ibsen, *Will the World Break Your Heart?*

22. Stone, *Past and the Present,* 80; Marsden, *Outrageous Idea;* Geertz, "Religion as a Cultural System."

23. Bodnar et al., *Lives of Their Own;* Genovese, *Roll, Jordan, Roll* (subtitled *Worlds That Slaves Made),* esp. 161. See also Gilley, "Roman Catholic Church," 206–207.

CHAPTER 1. FROM IRELAND TO AMERICA'S MYTHIC WEST

1. Adams, *Age of Industrial Violence,* 30–67; U.S. Senate Commission on Industrial Relations, *Final Report and Testimony* (hereinafter cited as Commission, *Report*).

2. Emmons, *Butte Irish.*

3. Commission, *Report,* 3778–79; on the election of McDonald, see the *Butte Miner,* Aug. 11, 1914.

4. Commission, *Report,* 3778–79; Polk, *Butte City Directory, 1901,* 506; idem, *Butte City Directory, 1902,* 511; Derickson, *Workers' Health,* 28–56; Emmons, *Butte Irish,* 148–53; idem, "Immigrant Workers and Industrial Hazards."

5. Commission, *Report,* 3779.

6. See Dening, *Death of William Gooch,* 56; idem, *Performances;* Donnelly, "Construction of the Memory."

7. Dening, *Death of William Gooch*.

8. The literature on the American West is so vast that it would be impossible even to begin to cite it. The studies I used most are White, *"It's Your Misfortune"*; Gjerde, *Minds of the West;* Nugent, *Into the West;* Cronon et al., *Under a Western Sky;* Slotkin *Regeneration;* idem, *Fatal Environment;* idem, *Gunfighter Nation;* and Milner, O'Connor, and Sandweiss (eds.), *Oxford History.* For accounts of America's mission in the West, see Jacobson, *Whiteness,* 39–90, 201–22; Horsman, *Race and Manifest Destiny,* 79–185; Klein, *Frontiers;* Nugent, "Frontiers and Empires"; Robbins, "Western History"; Limerick, *Legacy of Conquest;* Lamar, "From Bondage to Contract"; Schwantes, "Protest in a Promised Land"; idem, "Concept of the Wageworkers' Frontier"; and Emmons, "Constructed Province." On Ireland as a conquered province, see Miller, *Emigrants and Exiles;* O'Farrell, *Ireland's English Question;* Kiberd, *Inventing Ireland;* Gibbons, *Transformations;* Cullingford, *Ireland's Others;* O'Toole, *Lie of the Land;* idem, *Ex-Isle of Erin,* esp. 67; MacDonagh, *States of Mind;* and Solnit, *Book of Migrations.*

9. Jacobson, *Whiteness,* 204. See also Roediger, *Wages of Whiteness;* and Allen, *Invention of the White Race.*

10. Welter, *Mind of America,* 298–330; Gjerde, *Minds of the West,* 1–50; Lamar, "From Bondage to Contract"; Barrett, "Americanization from the Bottom Up."

11. Jacobson, *Whiteness,* 41; on Irish mobility, see Scally, *End of Hidden Ireland,* 3–8.

12. On name/place association, see McLysaght, *Irish Families,* 16–17, 28–37; Commission, *Report,* 3779. Emmons, *Butte Irish,* 15, 19–21; and O'Dwyer, *Who Were My Ancestors?*

13. Bagenal, *American Irish,* 126 ("the very capital"); McLysaght, *Irish Families,* 38, 41; Perl and Wiggins, "Don't Call Me Ishmael."

14. Commission, *Report,* 3778; on chain migration, see Emmons, *Butte Irish,* 1–34.

15. Commission, *Report,* 3778; Vaughan and Fitzpatrick (eds.), *Irish Historical Statistics,* 300; Donnelly, *Land and the People,* esp. 219–50; Mageean, "Emigration from Irish Ports"; Derickson, "Industrial Refugees"; for the Antipodes, see Kearns, *Broken Hill;* O'Farrell, *Irish in Australia,* 214; and Idriess, *Silver City.*

16. Commission, *Report,* 3778; on the extent of Irish speaking, see Miller, *Emigrants and Exiles,* 70–71, 119–28; and Mulligan, "Irish Miners"; on speaking in one language and thinking in another, see Palmer, *Descent into Discourse,* 8–9.

17. Commission, *Report,* 3779; Scally, *End of Hidden Ireland,* 160 ("profoundly localized mentality"); on the exile motif, see Miller, *Emigrants and Exiles.* See also Hannan, *"An Ball Uaigneach Seo."*

18. McLysaght, *Irish Families,* 85.

19. Commission, *Report,* 3778.

20. Yeats, *Poems,* 32; see Polk, *Butte City Directory, 1914.* See also Silver Bow County Board of Health, "Report."

21. Commission, *Report,* 3779 and passim.

22. Ibid., 3855.

23. Emmons, "'Spleene'"; Deverell, "To Loosen the Safety Valve"; Commons, "Bringing about Industrial Peace," 14.

24. Commission, *Report,* 3856. See also Adams, *Age of Industrial Violence,* 60.

25. Vaughan and Fitzpatrick (eds.), *Irish Historical Statistics,* 52; Larkin, "Devotional Revolution in Ireland."

26. Colley, *Britons;* Hill, *English Bible;* Akenson, *Small Differences;* on Catholic versus Protestant imagination, see Greeley, *Catholic Myth,* 34–64; Bellah, "Religion and the Shape of National Culture"; Jenkins, *New Anti-Catholicism;* and Massa, *Anti-Catholicism,* 51–58.

27. For the statistics, see Kleppner, *Cross of Culture,* 55–56 and passim; and Jensen, *Winning of the Midwest,* 58–88; Kenny, *American Irish,* 3 (quotation), 4, 8–14, 23–44; for anti-Catholicism, see Billington, *Protestant Crusade;* Higham, *Strangers in the Land.* See also McGreevy, *Catholicism and American Freedom;* Massa, *Anti-Catholicism;* Jenkins, *New Anti-Catholicism;* Schultz, *Fire and Roses;* Jensen, "'No Irish Need Apply'"; Miller and Boling with Kennedy, "Famine's Scars" (on the Scotch-Irish); Miller et al., *Irish Immigrants;* and all of Akenson's books cited above.

28. On "Irishness" as problematic, see Foster, *Paddy and Mr. Punch,* 281; Campbell, *Ireland's New Worlds;* and Fitzpatrick, *Oceans of Consolation.*

29. O'Sullivan, *Twenty Years A-Growing,* 249–50; for "countyism" as a term of reproach, see Emmons, *Butte Irish,* 305; Burke, *Reflections on the Revolution in France,* 44. See also Kiberd, *Inventing Ireland,* 287–89.

30. Glazier (ed.) *Encyclopedia.* Local studies include Wingerd, *Claiming the City;* O'Connor, *Boston Irish;* Bayor and Meagher (eds.), *New York Irish;* Brundage, *Making of Western Labor Radicalism;* Burchell, *San Francisco Irish;* Clark, *Irish in Philadelphia;* Walsh (ed.), *San Francisco Irish;* Gleeson, *Irish in the South;* Meagher, *Inventing Irish America;* idem, "The Fireman on the Stairs," in Lee and Casey (eds.), *Making the Irish American;* Kelly, *Shamrock and the Lily;* McCaffrey, *Irish Diaspora;* and Kenny, *Making Sense.*

31. On the stages of American industrialization, see Gutman, "Work, Culture, and Society"; and Bodnar, *Transplanted.*

32. Donnelly, *Great Irish Potato Famine;* Woodham-Smith, *Great Hunger;* Mokyr, *Why Ireland Starved;* Ó Gráda, *Black '47;* on revisionism, see Donnelly, "Great Famine and Its Interpreters"; idem, "Construction of the Memory"; and Daly, "Revisionism and Irish History."

33. Marx and Engels, *Ireland,* 24.

34. Slotkin, *Fatal Environment,* 281; Gutman, "Work, Culture, and Society"; Beatty, *Age of Betrayal.* See also Cochran, *Frontiers of Change;* Gerschenkron, *Economic Backwardness;* Barney, *Passage of the Republic;* Berthoff, *Unsettled People;* idem, "Peasants and Artisans"; and Kasson, *Civilizing the Machine,* 1–106.

35. Slotkin, *Fatal Environment;* Richardson, *West from Appomattox,* 113–14 ("romantic view").

36. Roosevelt, *Autobiography,* 103–104. See also Richardson, *West from Appomattox,* 219.

37. Bryce, *American Commonwealth,* 2:830–31.

38. The discussion of western borders is taken from Emmons, "Constructed Province."

39. Fischer, *Albion's Seed,* 792; White, *"It's Your Misfortune,"* 3.

40. Nugent, "Where Is the American West?"; idem, *Into the West,* 3–7.

41. Schumpeter quoted in Beatty, *Age of Betrayal,* 27 (my emphasis); Worster, "Beyond the Agrarian Myth," 19.

42. Flynn, *Rebel Girl,* 84; Lankton, *Cradle to Grave;* idem, *Beyond the Boundaries.* See also Robbins, *Hard Times;* Kluger, *Clifton-Morenci Strike;* and Schwantes, *Radical Heritage.*

43. Schwantes, "Concept of the Wageworkers' Frontier"; Limerick, *Legacy of Conquest,* 27.

44. See Gjerde, *Minds of the West.*

45. Slotkin, *Fatal Environment,* 30, 33.

46. White, "Outlaw Gangs"; on Ned Kelly, see Carey, *True History*; and Clune, *Ned Kelly*. There is a pub in West Kerry, Ireland, named the "Jesse James." Letter from Richard White, October 12, 2008.

47. Moore, *Social Origins*; Foner, *Free Soil*; Montgomery, *Beyond Equality*; Beatty, *Age of Betrayal*, 14–24, 88 (quotation); Slotkin, *Fatal Environment*, 33.

48. U.S. Senate Committee on Education and Labor, *Report*, 3:453; Greeley quoted in Beatty, *Age of Betrayal*, 94.

49. Scally, *End of Hidden Ireland*, 156. See also Richardson, *West from Appomattox*, 116–18; and Beatty, *Age of Betrayal*, 88–89.

50. Slotkin, *Fatal Environment*, 23, 26, 35 ("myth of concern"); Emmons, *Garden in the Grasslands*. See also Richardson, *West from Appomattox*, 5.

51. Slotkin, *Regeneration*, 3–180; Morse, *Foreign Conspiracy*, 148.

52. Gjerde, *Minds of the West*, is a compelling account of a diverse West of many "minds."

53. Nugent, *Into the West*, 56.

54. Dungan, *How the Irish Won the West*.

55. White, *Eastern Establishment*.

56. Kerby Miller shared with me his copies of these poems in Irish. They were originally in Ó Dubdha (ed.), *Duanaire Duibhneach*, 127–29, 132–33 (translated by Bruce Boling).

57. See also Schwantes, "Concept of the Wageworkers' Frontier."

58. My conversation with Lukas took place at a private dinner after a session of the American Studies Association conference in Kansas City, Missouri, November 2, 1996.

59. The main books and articles that I read in my own search for "big trouble" in the West are Gregory, "West and Workers"; Schwantes, "Concept of the Wageworkers' Frontier"; Cornford (ed.), *Working People*; Tygiel, *Workingmen in San Francisco*; Dubofsky, *We Shall Be All*; idem, "Origins of Western Working-Class Radicalism"; Robbins, *Hard Times*; Jensen, *Heritage of Conflict*; Lingenfelter, *Hardrock Miners*; Wyman, *Hardrock Epic*; Brown, *Hard-Rock Miners*; Jameson, *All That Glitters*; Derickson, *Workers' Health*; and Suggs, *Colorado's War*.

60. See, among many titles, Gieske, *Minnesota Farmer-Laborism*; Green, *Grass-Roots Socialism*; Goodwyn, *Democratic Promise*; Ostler, *Prairie Populism*; McMath, *American Populism*; and Clinch, *Urban Populism*.

61. Dubofsky, *We Shall Be All*, 314–17, 321–22, 343–45; Flynn, *Rebel Girl*, 200.

62. See Welter, *Mind of America*, 298, 371.

63. Emmons, "Constructed Province." See also Murdoch, *American West*; and Wrobel, *Promised Lands*.

64. The Harvard professor is quoted in Welter, *Mind of America*, 315.

65. On history and memory, see Solnit, *Book of Migrations*, 75; White, *Remembering Ahanagran*; and idem, "Comments."

CHAPTER 2. IRREPRESIBLE CONFLICTS

1. Tilly, "Retrieving European Lives."

2. Anderson, *Imagined Communities*. See also Wiebe, "*Imagined Communities*, Nationalist Experiences."

3. Colley, *Britons*, 5, 8, 18, 31.

4. Ibid., 23.

5. On this point, see Kiberd, *Inventing Ireland;* and O'Farrell, *Ireland's English Question;* Said, "Yeats and Decolonization."

6. Scott, *Weapons of the Weak;* Hawkins, "'We Must Learn,'" 23 ("linguistic imperialism"); Kiberd, *Inventing Ireland;* 2, 618. See also Higgins and Kiberd, "Culture and Exile"; Larkin, "Myth," 68; and Friel, "Translations."

7. O'Toole, *The Ex-Isle of Erin,* 15; O'Farrell, *Ireland's English Question,* 57–66, 77–80, 92; Donnelly, "Marian Shrine"; Tocqueville, *Journeys,* esp. 121–28. See also Delay, "Devotional Revolution."

8. Fischer, *Albion's Seed;* Colley, *Britons,* 137; Phillips, *Cousins' Wars;* Burke quoted in Fuchs, *John F. Kennedy,* xii. See also Gould, *Persistence of Empire;* and Archdeacon, *Becoming American,* 20–21.

9. Hill, *English Bible,* 8; Kelley, *Transatlantic Persuasion,* 62n6; Arieli, *Individualism and Nationalism,* 265–68; Beecher, *Plea,* 10–11. See also Billington, *Protestant Crusade,* 1–31; Elson, *Guardians of Tradition,* 45–47, 52–62, 245–62; Shain, *Myth of American Individualism;* Niebuhr, "Protestant Movement"; Noble, *Eternal Adam,* 59; Ahlstrom, *Religious History,* 555–58; and Breen, "Ideology and Nationalism," esp. 21–26.

10. Quebec Act in Commager (ed.), *Documents,* 74–76; Foner, *Tom Paine,* 12, 72, 81 (quotation), 113; Bailyn, "Religion and Revolution," 85–86 (quotations); Billington, *Protestant Crusade,* 17–19. See also Fuchs, *American Kaleidoscope,* 36–37.

11. Commager (ed.), *Documents,* 84, 93, 101.

12. "Resolution of Congress on Public Lands," Oct. 10, 1780, in ibid., 120; "Virginia's Cession of Western Lands to the United States," Dec. 20, 1783, in ibid., 121; "Report of Government for the Western Territory," Apr. 23, 1784, in ibid., 122; "Memorial of the Presbytery of Hanover," Oct. 24, 1776, in ibid., 125; "Virginia's Statute of Religious Liberty," Jan. 16, 1786, in ibid., 125; Pole, *Pursuit of Equality,* 87–88 ("permeated with Protestant assumptions"); Gjerde, *Minds of the West,* 13 ("American Protestantism and American republicanism"); on the rejection of England, see Fuchs, *John F. Kennedy,* 30; on Catholics as "outsiders," see Higham, "Integrating America," 15; Wiebe, *Opening of American Society,* 255. Many historians seem loath to admit the anti-Catholic origins of American identity. For examples, see the articles by Carol Smith-Rosenberg, Patricia Limerick, and Ronald Takaki in Thelen and Hoxie (eds.), *Discovering America,* 7–39, 58–78, 187–215.

13. Tocqueville, *Democracy in America,* 2:37. See also ibid., 1:301; Crèvecoeur, *Letters,* 60–99; and Carey, "Republicanism within American Catholicism."

14. Larkin (ed. and trans.), *Tocqueville's Journey in Ireland.* See also Zeitlin, *Liberty, Equality and Revolution,* 83–87.

15. Brownson quoted in Stephanson, *Manifest Destiny,* 30; on Brownson, see Schlesinger, *Pilgrim's Progress,* 252–53; and Knobel, *Paddy and the Republic,* 5; for Hughes, see Gorn, "Introduction," 12–13; and Brownson's "Archbishop Hughes on Slavery"; for a dismissal of Brownson's ideas, see Parker, "The Letter from Santa Cruz" (1859), in Parker, *Life and Correspondence,* 2:461.

16. Chevalier, *Society, Manners, and Politics,* 355–56.

17. Ibid.

18. Ibid., 408, 411.

19. Billington, *Protestant Crusade;* Hofstadter, *Paranoid Style;* Pope Gregory quoted in Morris, *American Catholic,* 69; McGreevy, *Catholicism and American Freedom,* 43–67.

20. See Fuchs, *John F. Kennedy,* 92–96; and McGreevy, *Catholicism and American Freedom,* 43–90.

21. Pole, *Pursuit of Equality,* 91–92; Welter, "From Maria Monk to Paul Blanshard"; on the "whiteness" question, see Jacobson, *Whiteness,* 8–9, 38, 147–48; on Catholicism as the largest denomination, see Ahlstrom, *Religious History,* 527. See also Gjerde, *Minds of the West,* 38.

22. Burlingame quoted in Anbinder, *Nativism,* 45; Whitney quoted in Gjerde, *Minds of the West,* 36. See also Morrison, *Slavery and the American West,* 56–62, 151; Knobel, *Paddy and the Republic,* 134; Phillips, *Cousins' Wars,* 357; and Slotkin, *Fatal Environment,* 230–32.

23. Parker to Dr. Cabot, February 3, 1850, in Parker, *Life and Correspondence,* 1:417; Parker to W. R. Alger, July 7, 1857, in ibid., 2:219; "Letter from Santa Cruz," in ibid., 2:496; Busey quoted in Welter, *Mind of America,* 342.

24. Beecher quoted in Davis, "Some Themes of Countersubversion," 14–15; Seward quoted in Foner, *Free Soil,* 69–70.

25. Parker to Sumner, Jan. 14, 1856, in Parker, *Life and Correspondence,* 2:159; Anbinder, *Nativism,* 190. See also Morrison, *Slavery and the American West,* 151.

26. Jenny Franchot is an exception. She deals with the St. Clares in *Roads to Rome,* 103. Anbinder, *Nativism,* 211; Ibsen, *Will the World Break Your Heart?* 4–7; Bean: "Aspect of Know-Nothingism"; idem, "Puritan versus Celt."

27. Boynton quoted in Gjerde, *Minds of the West,* 335–36n49. See also Anbinder, *Nativism,* 149; and Walker, *Moral Choices,* 161.

28. *Strong, Diary,* Oct. 4, 1865, 4:8; May 20, 1856, 2:275–76; Oct. 17, 1867, 4:154, Jan. 15, 1868, 4:180; Feb. 9, 1871, 4:345; July 19, 1863, 3:343.

29. Garrison quoted in Anbinder, *Nativism,* 45–46; antislavery spokesman quoted in Phillips, *Cousins' Wars,* 359–60; Morrison, *Slavery and the American West,* 57. See also Holt, *Political Crisis,* 159–64, 176–80, 215–16; and idem, "Politics of Impatience."

30. Parker to Gov. Fletcher, Nov. 11, 1856, in Parker, *Life and Correspondence,* 2:205; to Miss Cobbe, Dec. 4, 1857, in ibid., 1:463; to John Manley, Dec. 12, 1859, in ibid., 2:382; to Rev. J. T. Sargent, Sept. 18, 1859, in ibid., 2:354–55; Fellman, "Theodore Parker"; Roney, *Irish Rebel,* 93–94, 140, 173–74, 178–79; Rice, *American Catholic Opinion;* for O'Connell, see Osofsky, "Abolitionists, Irish Immigrants"; for Mitchell, see Gleeson, *Irish in the South,* 132, 137, 140, 154–56; idem, "Parallel Struggles"; McGovern, "John Mitchell"; Miller, *Emigrants and Exiles,* 338–39; Helper, *The Impending Crisis,* 214; Anbinder, *Nativism,* 49 ("Slavery, Romanism, and Rum"). See also Gerteis, *Morality and Utility,* 136; and idem, "Slavery and Hard Times."

31. Strong, *Diary,* Nov. 12, 1863, 3:371; *Harper's* quoted in Jacobson, *Whiteness,* 48; Godkin quoted in ibid., 167; Godkin, *Life and Letters;* Sproat, *Best Men,* 18–19, 145–46, 230–32, 250–51, 273–74.

32. Bernstein, *New York City Draft Riots;* Jacobson, *Whiteness,* 52, 56 ("The mob!" and "whooping"); Strong, *Diary,* Nov. 12, 1863, 3:371; Knobel, *Paddy and the Republic,* 68–103. See also the semifictionalized account in Quinn, *Banished Children of Eve.*

33. Sept. 7, 1863, Miller Collection (original spelling, punctuation, and capitalization in all quotations from letters in this collection).

34. Ibid. (my emphasis).

35. Morrison, *Slavery and the American West,* 57; Parker quoted in Thomas (ed.), *Slavery Attacked,* 152. See also Walters, *American Reformers,* ix.

36. Phillips, *Cousins' Wars,* 317–456; Walters (ed.), *Slavery Attacked;* Jacobson, *Whiteness,* 48 (see also 52–56).

37. Carey, "Republicanism within Catholicism," 437; Potter, *Impending Crisis,* 251–52.

38. Bagenal, *American Irish,* 41, 59; Anbinder, *Nativism,* 246–78; Moore, *Religious Outsiders,* 70; Scally, *End of Hidden Ireland,* 227. See also Gjerde, *Minds of the West,* 37; and Morrison, *Slavery and the American West,* 233, 237.

39. Quoted in Knobel, *Paddy and the Republic,* 57.

40. Gjerde, *Minds of the West,* 39; Nott quoted in Jacobson, *Whiteness,* 45–46; Bodo, *Protestant Clergy,* 80 ("marvelous defection"; Bodo's book, originally published by Princeton University Press, is itself more than a little anti-Catholic). See also Horsman, *Race and Manifest Destiny,* 87, 170; and Knobel, *Paddy and the Republic,* 57, 65, 109–16.

41. Parker to Rev. J. T. Sargent, Sept. 18, 1859, in Parker, *Life and Correspondence,* 2:355. See also Parker to Charles Ellis, Jan. 29, 1860, in ibid., 417; and Bagenal, *American Irish,* 67–68.

42. Maguire, *Irish in America,* 345–48, 490–91 (quotation).

43. On the "volk," see Jacobson, *Whiteness,* 48–52, 70–72, 138, 204–206; and Horsman, *Race and Manifest Destiny,* 162, 170 ("few Celts"), 170 178–80, 226, 249–56, 285–90, 301–302; Knobel, *Paddy and the Republic,* 12, 22 (Parker quotations), 42, 70, 82–89, 100, 109–10; Parker to Gov. Fletcher, Nov. 27, 1856; Parker to John Manley, Dec. 1859, in Parker, *Life and Correspondence,* 2:204, 382; Anbinder, *Nativism,* xiii; Elson, *Guardians of Tradition,* 47, 53, 147; Welter, *Mind of America,* 281; Strong, *Diary,* Oct. 26, 1840, 1:150. See also Fuchs, *John F. Kennedy,* 30.

44. Knobel, *Paddy and the Republic,* 57; Berg quoted in Franchot, *Roads to Rome,* 171.

45. Pole, *Pursuit of Equality,* 89; Phillips, *Cousins' Wars,* 431; Foner, *Free Soil.* Slotkin develops these same ideas in his *Fatal Environment,* 378–79. See also Welter, *Mind of America,* 318; Johnson, *Shopkeepers' Millennium;* Noll (ed.), *God and Mammon;* and idem, *Civil War as a Theological Crisis.*

46. See Foner, *Free Soil,* 40–72; and Wiebe, *Opening of American Society,* 335–37. See also Daly, *When Slavery Was Called Freedom.*

47. Foner, *Free Soil;* Adams, *Education,* 47. See also Slotkin, *Fatal Environment,* 378–79.

48. Seward quoted in Foner, *Free Soil,* 41; Adams, *Education,* 44, 47.

49. Slotkin, *Fatal Environment;* Gladstone, *Englishman in Kansas,* 216–29; Fischer, *Albion's Seed,* 605–32.

50. Parker to Rev. J. F. Clarke, n.d., in Parker, *Life and Correspondence,* 2:337; Know-Nothing publication quoted in Anbinder, *Nativism,* 114; on Mexico, see Horsman, *Race and Manifest Destiny,* 229–48; and Pinheiro, "'Religion without Restriction.'" See also Wiebe, *Opening of American Society,* 336; and Fuchs, *John F. Kennedy,* 30.

51. Bede quoted in Roy, "Celtic Soul," 27; Ewing quoted in Taylor, *Occasions of Faith,* 55. See also Coleman, *Going to America,* 231.

52. Evans, *Personality of Ireland,* 37–38; on Protestants, see Curtis, *Apes and Angels,* 79, 137; Barnum, *Romanism as It Is,* 617 ("intelligence and thrift"); for John Bunyan, see Hill, *English Bible,* 371–91. See also Bertelson, *Lazy South,* 9–12, 63–66, 72–80.

53. Scally, *End of Hidden Ireland,* 194, 233. See also Thompson, *Making of the English Working Class,* 432–33.

54. Coleman, *Going to America,* 89–90, 134, 231–34; Foster in Abbott (ed.), *Historical Aspects,* 299–301. See also Miller, *Emigrants and Exiles,* 356, 401, 478.

55. Scally, *End of Hidden Ireland,* 233; Miller, *Emigrants and Exiles,* 344–46; idem, "Assimilation and Alienation," 93–94; Miller and Boling, "Golden Streets, Bitter Tears," 17–18, 25–27; newspaperman quoted in Shannon, *American Irish,* 29; Brownson, "Father Thébaud's Irish Race," 562. See also Welter, *Mind of America,* 62; Knobel, *Paddy and the Republic,* 163; Gerteis, *Morality and Utility,* 146; Montgomery, *Fall of the House of Labor,* 70–81; Potter, *To the Golden Door,* 113–60; and Gjerde, *Minds of the West,* 29.

56. Abbott (ed.), *Historical Aspects,* 110.

57. Hale, *Letters,* 52.

58. Ibid., 56, 54; for Hale, see Glickstein, *Concepts of Free Labor,* 99–104; Edwards, "American Image of Ireland," 277–80; Lee, *Modernization of Irish Society,* 144, 154–56; Solnit, *Book of Migrations,* 53; O'Farrell, *Ireland's English Question,* [1]; Elson, *Guardians of Tradition,* 122–28.

59. Brownson, "Father Thébaud's Irish Race," 561–62; Hale, *Letters,* 52.

60. Hale, *Letters,* 52–53 (Emerson "guano" quotation); Parker to John Manley, Feb. 17, 1859, in Parker, *Life and Correspondence,* 2:274; Engels, *Condition of the Working Class,* 102; Emerson quoted in Smith, *Chaplain's Sermons,* 72 ("black vomit"); Knobel, *Paddy and the Republic,* 120 ("deteriorated in size"). Henry David Thoreau was also anti-Irish. See Myers, "'Till their . . . bog-trotting feet'"; Buckley, "Thoreau and the Irish"; and Ryan, "Shanties and Shiftlessness."

61. Strong, *Diary,* Apr. 28, 1848, 1:318; Carlyle quoted in Engels, *Condition of the Working Class,* 102; Knobel, *Paddy and the Republic,* 124, 77.

62. Genovese, *Political Economy;* idem, *The World the Slaveholders Made;* Adams, *Education,* 44.

63. —— to Parker, Feb. 11, 1855, in Parker, *Life and Correspondence,* 2:86; Grayson, "Hireling and the Slave," 67–68.

64. Fitzhugh, "Selections from *A Sociology for the South,*" 42, 47.

65. Ibid., 68; idem, *Cannibals All!* 111, 119, 142, 145, 150, 258; Pole, *Pursuit of Equality,* 164–65; O'Farrell, *Ireland's English Question,* 117. See also Genovese, *World the Slaveholders Made.*

66. Bagenal, *American Irish,* 41, 59; Anbinder, *Nativism,* 212–19, 225, 228 (quotation), 229, 273–74.

67. Foner, *Free Soil,* 151 (quotation), 242–60; *Irish World,* Nov. 13, 1880 (my emphasis).

68. Foner, "Class, Ethnicity, and Radicalism"; Montgomery, *Beyond Equality.*

69. Cunliffe, *Chattel Slavery,* 1–31; Roediger, *Wages of Whiteness,* 13, 47, 50, 53, 66–87, 149–50; Morrison, *Slavery and the American West,* 233, 237.

70. *Irish World,* Jan. 7, 1882.

71. Brownson quoted in Browne, *Catholic Church,* 6; Powderly, *Thirty Years of Labor,* 31–32; Pope Leo XIII, *Rerum Novarum,* 58.

72. Powderly, *Thirty Years of Labor,* 31; Clark, *Deliver Us from Evil,* 79–81; Sproat, *Best Men,* 257–71.

73. For Phillips, see Foner, "Class, Ethnicity, and Radicalism," 150–51, 162, 181, 195; Edwards, "American Image of Ireland," 259–69; Ashworth, *Slavery, Capitalism, and Politics,* 161–62; on Phillips's distrust of Catholics, see Bartlett, *Wendell Phillips,* 91–92; for Redpath, see McKivigan, *War against Proslavery Religion;* Redpath, *Talks about Ireland.*

74. Bagenal, *American Irish,* 135–36. See also Hernon, *Celts, Catholics, and Copperheads.*

75. Foner, *Reconstruction; Irish World,* Jan. 7, 1882.

76. Noll, "The Bible and Slavery," 56, 60. See also Genovese, "Religion in the Collapse of the American Union"; and Fredrickson, "The Coming of the Lord."

77. Disraeli quoted in O'Farrell, *Ireland's English Question,* 153.

CHAPTER 3. SLAVERY, THE IRISH, AND WESTERN AMERICA

1. See Marty, *Righteous Empire;* Jefferson quoted in Arieli, *Individualism and Nationalism,* 129–30.

2. Jefferson quoted in Pole, *Pursuit of Equality,* 87–88.

3. Johnson, *Shopkeeper's Millennium;* Ryan, *Cradle of the Middle Class.* See also Smith, *Civic Ideals,* 197–242.

4. Morrison, *Slavery and the American West,* 13; Smith, *Civic Ideals,* 202 ("ascriptive civic myths").

5. George Fitzhugh quoted in Horsman, *Race and Manifest Destiny,* 273 (see also 75, 85, 162, 170, 177–78); Jacobson, *Whiteness,* 48–52, 138, 205–206; Welter, *Mind of America,* 322; Knobel, *Paddy and the Republic,* 87–89; Klein, *Frontiers,* esp. 78–92; Slotkin, *Fatal Environment,* 203 (Kit Carson story), 227–34, 490, 512–15. See also Steckmesser, *Western Hero.*

6. Bushnell quoted in Pole, *Pursuit of Equality,* 89; Howe, "Social Science of Horace Bushnell."

7. Crèvecoeur, *Letters from an American Farmer,* 60–99; Chevalier, *Society, Manners, and Politics,* 71–77, 194–201, 213–16; 405–18. See also Rischin, "Creating Crevecoeur's 'New Man.'"

8. Morse, *Foreign Conspiracy,* 95–97; Le Beau, "'Saving the West.'"

9. Beecher, *Plea,* 11–13, 39, 71–72; Le Beau, "'Saving the West,'" 106. See also Robert Dunne, "A Plea for a *Protestant* American Dream."

10. Beecher, *Plea,* 91–92.

11. Barnes quoted in Gjerde, *Minds of the West,* 45.

12. Webster quoted in Potter, *Impending Crisis,* 102; Fehrenbacher, *Dred Scott Case,* 164; Holt, *Political Crisis,* 84. Morrison, *Slavery and the American West,* 6–7.

13. *Congressional Globe,* May 25, 1854 appendix, 769 (Seward quotation); Barney, *Road to Secession,* 10–12; Genovese, *Political Economy;* Wilson, "Controversy over Slavery Expansion."

14. Meade quoted in Richards, *California Gold Rush,* 95–96; Freehling, *Prelude to Civil War,* 53–69 ("servile revolt").

15. Meade quoted in Richards, *California Gold Rush,* 95–96; Lowndes quoted in Morrison, *Slavery and the American West,* 118. See also Richardson, *West from Appomattox,* 33.

16. Foner, *Free Soil,* 57; Strong, *Diary,* August 11, 1863, 3:347.

17. Chase quoted in Foner, *Free Soil,* 56–57.

18. Parker quoted in Thomas (ed.), *Slavery Attacked,* 148–52; and Davis (ed.), *Fear of Conspiracy,* 129.

19. Know-Nothing quoted in Anbinder, *Nativism,* 210–11; Godkin, *Life and Letters,* 1: 117–18.

20. For John Brown, see Potter, *Impending Crisis,* 121–328.

21. Home Missionary Society quoted in Gjerde, *Minds of the West,* 44 (my emphasis). See also Morrison, *Slavery and the American West,* 157–87; Griffin, *Their Brothers' Keepers,* 198–218; Goodykoontz, *Home Missions;* and Billington, *Protestant Crusade,* 269–88.

22. Hurlburt quoted in Griffin, *Their Brothers' Keepers,* 209; Parker to John Ayres, Immaculate Conception Day (December 8), 1859, in Parker, *Life and Correspondence,* 2:394.

23. Pierce, *Letter,* 4; nativist quoted in Anbinder, *Nativism,* 121.

24. For the California vigilante movement, see Issel and Cherny, *San Francisco,* 20–22; Burchell, *San Francisco Irish,* 120–32; Decker, *Fortunes and Failures,* 125–41; Starr, *Americans and the California Dream,* 92–97; Blessing, "West among Strangers"; idem, "Culture, Religion"; Senkewicz, *Vigilantes,* 135–65; Brown, *Strain of Violence;* idem, *No Duty to Retreat,* 87–128; and idem, "Pivot of American Vigilantism."

25. Richards, *California Gold Rush,* 5–6, 26–32, 129–31, 176–95, 198–210, 212–18.

26. Ibid., 33, 91–92, 184–89, 219–22 (quotations on 189 and 222). See also Burchell, *San Francisco Irish,* 120–31; and Starr, *Americans and the California Dream,* 121–22.

27. Richards, *California Gold Rush;* on western antiblack feelings, see Berwanger, *Frontier against Slavery;* and Rawley, *Race and Politics.*

28. Helper, *Land of Gold,* 214; Gay quoted in Issel and Cherny, *San Francisco,* 19.

29. Senkewicz, *Vigilantes,* 136 (quotations); Starr, *Americans and the California Dream,* 94–95.

30. Starr, *Americans and the California Dream;* Dana, *Two Years before the Mast* (1859), quoted in Jacobson, *Whiteness,* 41.

31. Nathan Beman quoted in Abzug, *Cosmos Crumbling,* 63; see chapter 3, "The War in the West."

32. Gilpin, *Mission of the North American People,* 124.

33. Slotkin, *Fatal Environment,* 46.

34. Welter, *Mind of America,* 315–16 (quotation); Deverell, "To Loosen the Safety Valve"; Ashworth, *Slavery, Capitalism, and Politics,* 1:143.

35. Allen quoted in Welter, *Mind of America,* 304.

36. Marx, *Capital,* 2:856–58; Beatty, *Age of Betrayal,* 88; Fitzhugh, "Selections from *A Sociology for the South,*" 34–50; idem, *Cannibals All!*

37. Rhett quoted in Welter, *Mind of America,* 304; Marx, *Capital,* 2:857; *Hansard's Parliamentary Debates,* in Abbott (ed.), *Historical Aspects,* 172.

38. Coleman, *Going to America,* 35, 36, 39; Zahler, *Eastern Workingmen,* 109–26; Gilpin, *Mission of the North American People,* 97. See also Ford, "Frontier Democracy"; Spence, "Landless Man"; and Fraysse, *Lincoln, Land, and Labor.*

39. Fitzhugh, *Cannibals All!* 40.

40. Hammond, "'Mud-Sill' Speech," 123–24.

41. Ibid., 124.

42. See, for example, West, "Chattel Slavery," 432.

43. Foner, *Free Soil,* 57; see also Berwanger, *Frontier against Slavery.*

44. Pierce, "Letter," 10–11.

45. For Scandinavian voting patterns, see Kleppner, *Cross of Culture,* 51–53, 84–88.

46. On the conflation of capitalism and republicanism/democracy, see Beatty, *Age of Betrayal;* and McCloskey, *American Conservatism.*

47. Richardson, *West from Appomattox,* 4, 5.

48. Richardson, *Greatest Nation.*

49. Slotkin, *Fatal Environment;* Saveth, *American Historians,* 14 ("Plymouth Rock"); Richardson, *West from Appomattox;* Gjerde, *Minds of the West,* 56–64, 111–12, 236–55.

50. D'Arcy, *Fenian Movement;* O'Broin, *Fenian Fever;* on the 1867 riots, see Archdeacon, *Becoming American,* 98; for the Molly Maguires, see Broehl, *Molly Maguires;* and Kenny, *Making Sense.*

51. Gordon, *Orange Riots.*

52. Strong, *Diary,* Feb. 9, 1871, July 15, 1871, and Sept. 16, 1874, 4:345, 373, 538; *New York Times* quoted in Gordon, *Orange Riots,* 165.

53. Godkin quoted in the *Nation,* Apr. 27, 1871; Sproat, *Best Men;* Slotkin, *Fatal Environment,* 495; Grant quoted in Gjerde, *Minds of the West,* 29; and in Avella and McKeown (eds.) *Public Voices,* 73.

54. Engels quoted in Scally, *End of Hidden Ireland,* 208; *New York Tribune* (1877) quoted in Slotkin, *Fatal Environment,* 483 ("incendiaries"); British press quoted in Bagenal, *American Irish,* 129–30 ("boiling over"). See also Jacobson, *Whiteness,* 20, 72.

55. Grant, *Passing of the Great Race,* 203.

56. Froude, "Romanism and the Irish Race," 523, 527–28. See also part II of Froude's essay in the next issue of the *Review,* 31–50.

57. Strong, *Our Country,* 225.

58. Ibid., 89–91, 199. See also chapter 5: "Perils: Romanism."

59. Ibid., 10–11; Fredrickson, "Coming of the Lord," 120*n*45 (see also 124–25).

60. Strong, *Our Country,* 203–204, [11].

61. For Turner, see the two biographies: Billington, *Frederick Jackson Turner;* and Bogue, *Frederick Jackson Turner;* as well as biographies by Howard Lamar in Cunliffe and Winks, *Pastmasters,* 74–109; and White, "Howard Lamar." See also Hofstadter and Lipset (eds.), *Turner;* "Centennial Symposium on the Significance of Frederick Jackson Turner"; Hofstadter, *Progressive Historians;* Ridge, "Introduction"; and Faragher, "'Nation Thrown Back on Itself.'" For an account of pre-Turner "Turnerians," see Hauptman, "Mythologizing Westward Expansion."

62. Turner, "Contributions of the West," 86, 92, 98.

63. Jacobson, *Whiteness,* 88; Roosevelt quoted in Richardson, *West from Appomattox,* 221.

64. Billington, *Frederick Jackson Turner,* 110; Mulder, *Woodrow Wilson;* Gorn (ed.), *McGuffey Readers,* 1–4, 7, 8–9, 16, 21, 22; Hauptman, "Mythologizing Westward Expansion," 277–80.

65. Turner, "Significance of the Frontier," 34, 47, 59; idem, "Problem of the West." See also Klein, *Frontiers,* 16–17; and Fischer, *Albion's Seed,* 5–8, 642, 870.

66. Fuchs, *John F. Kennedy,* 5; Billington, *Frederick Jackson Turner,* 31–32, 51, 67, 424–25; Bogue, *Frederick Jackson Turner,* 22–23, 153; Riley, "Frederick Jackson Turner," 59–72; Turner, "Significance of History," 27 ("Presbyterians"). See also Klein, *Frontiers,* 17, 83–84, 87, 142–43; and Saveth, *American Historians,* 129.

67. Turner, "Significance of History," 22; population figures from *Thirteenth Census: 1910, Population,* 1084; Statistics of Churches, in U.S. Bureau of the Census, *Ninth Census of the United States: 1870,* 559. See also Luebke, "Turnerism"; and idem, "Introduction," in *European Immigrants in the American West.*

68. Turner, "Significance of the Frontier," 54, 55 (my emphasis); Jacobson, *Whiteness;* Gjerde, *Minds of the West;* Baldwin "Centre of the Republic," 412, 418.

69. Turner, "Significance of the Frontier," 55, 57.

70. Ibid., 57.

71. Ibid., 49.

72. On the APA, see Kinzer, *Episode in Anti-Catholicism;* and Higham, *Strangers in the Land,* 62–63, 80–87, 108.

73. Bellah, "Religion and the Shape of National Culture," 10; Novick, *That Noble Dream,* 68; see also Saveth, *American Historians,* 13–14.

74. Limerick, *Legacy of Conquest,* 20–23, 49, 253–54; Riley, "Frederick Jackson Turner"; Pascoe, "Western Women"; Johnson, "'Memory Sweet to Soldiers'"; Jacobson, *Whiteness,* 88; Luebke, "Turnerism."

75. Roosevelt quoted in Fuchs, *John F. Kennedy,* 62; and Bogue, *Frederick Jackson Turner,* 113; see also Gerstle, "Theodore Roosevelt"; Wilson in Baker (ed.), *Woodrow Wilson,* 125; Wilson, *History of the American People,* 4:132–33, 162–64; Saveth, *American Historians,* 141–42; Mulder, *Woodrow Wilson,* 70, 231.

76. On Turner and civil rights, see Bogue, *Frederick Jackson Turner* (subtitled *Strange Roads Going Down*), 237; and Billington, *Frederick Jackson Turner,* 436.

CHAPTER 4. MOST UNLIKELY WESTERNERS

1. Colley, *Britons;* Fischer, *Albion's Seed.*

2. Fischer, *Albion's Seed* (the twenty-four folkways are listed and defined on 7–11); MacDonagh, *States of Mind,* 6 (quotation), 99–103; on the various folkways, see also O'Faoláin, *Story of the Irish People,* 32; Dangerfield, *Damnable Question,* 36–37, 43, 98, 163, 263, 295; Kee, *Green Flag,* 426–29, 440; Kiberd, *Inventing Ireland,* 25, 44, 151, 350.

3. Fischer, *Albion's Seed,* 8–11.

4. Miller, *Emigrants and Exiles,* 107.

5. MacDonagh, "Irish Famine Emigration," 107, 445; Akenson, *Irish Diaspora,* 237–38; idem, "Historiography of the Irish"; Kenny, "Diaspora and Comparison." See also Evans, *Personality of Ireland,* 67; Ibsen, *Will the World Break Your Heart?* 19–21; and Rodgers, *Work Ethic.*

6. Archdeacon, *Becoming American;* Gleason, *Speaking of Diversity,* 47–90; idem, "Trouble in the Colonial Melting Pot"; idem, "Crevecoeur's Question"; Gordon, *Assimilation,* 60–83; see also Miller, *Emigrants and Exiles,* 7–11, 145–46, 268–70, 552–54; for *sassenach,* see Scally, *End of Hidden Ireland,* 33.

7. On the exile motif as hegemonic, see Miller, *Emigrants and Exiles,* 3–10, 427–91; and idem, "Class, Culture, and Immigrant Group Identity."

8. On Irish communal culture, see Glassie, *Passing the Time;* Taylor, *Occasions of Faith;* Evans, *Personality of Ireland;* Corkery, *Hidden Ireland;* Scally, *End of Hidden Ireland;* Arensberg, *Irish Countryman;* Cross, *Tailor and Ansty;* Arensberg and Kimball, *Family and Community;* Casey and Rhodes (eds.), *Views of the Irish Peasantry.*

9. Scally, *End of Hidden Ireland,* 87.

10. O'Connor, *Guests of the Nation;* Beresford, *Ten Men Dead;* Yeats, "The King's Threshold," quoted in O'Malley, *Biting at the Grave,* 3; Sweeney, "Irish Hunger Strikes."

11. Friel, "Translations."

12. Evans, *Personality of Ireland,* 59–61, 95; Scally, *End of Hidden Ireland,* 33, 87; Cross, *Tailor and Ansty,* 37; Arensberg and Kimball, *Family and Community,* 75, 315; Slotkin, *Fatal Environment.*

13. Tocqueville quoted in Kammen, *Season of Youth,* 4; Jacobson, *Whiteness,* 204 ("To be American"), 215 ("This pride"); Ní Dhomhnaill quoted in McDiarmid and Durkan, *Writing Irish,* 107.

14. See White, *Eastern Establishment.*

15. Manahan, *Trials,* 10, 11, 30 (see also 47–50).

16. O'Faoláin, *Story of the Irish People,* 45–52; Manahan, *Trials,* 48; Wohl, "'The Country Boy' Myth."

17. See also Denning, *Mechanic Accents,* esp. 157–66.

18. Scally, *End of Hidden Ireland,* 133, 5, 160; O'Faoláin, *King of the Beggars,* 41.

19. Knobel, *Paddy and the Republic,* 53, 109 (Knox quotation); Gamble quoted in Nolan, Review, 30; Usher, *Face and Mind,* 11, 19; See also Miller, *Emigrants and Exiles,* 362.

20. Donnelly, "Miscellaneous Notes on Ireland and the Irish People," handwritten, n.d., in the Ignatius Donnelly Papers, vol. 134; Ireland quoted in O'Connell, *John Ireland,* 104; Griffith quoted in the *Butte Bulletin,* May 24, 1919; Lee, *Modernization.* See also Blessing, "West among Strangers," 103–48; idem, "Irish Emigration," 18, 21; Miller, *Emigrants and Exiles,* 358–66, 407; and idem, "Assimilation and Alienation," 93–94, 100. On informers, see Scally, *End of Hidden Ireland,* 32, 37, 69–74; O'Flaherty, *Informer;* Miller, *Shingwauk's Vision;* Joyce, *Portrait of the Artist,* 233; Knox, *Rebels and Informers;* Morgan, *Slave Counterpoint,* 470–75; and Genovese, *Roll, Jordan, Roll,* 588–97.

21. Henry quoted in Gorn (ed.), *McGuffey Readers,* 158; McSwiney quoted in O'Malley, *Biting at the Grave,* 26–27.

22. Gjerde, *Minds of the West,* 261, 11; Larkin, "Devotional Revolution."

23. Larkin, "Devotional Revolution"; Gjerde *Minds of the West;* Taylor, *Occasions of Faith;* Fuchs, *John F. Kennedy,* 82; Larkin, *Roman Catholic Church and the Creation;* idem, *Roman Catholic Church and the Plan;* idem, *Roman Catholic Church and the Fall.* See also Guilfoyle, "Religious Development" (I and II).

24. Burke quoted in O'Farrell, *England and Ireland,* 150–51.

25. Ireland, *De Fide Hernorum,* Mar. 17, 1869, quoted in O'Fahey, "Reflections," 248; Hannan quoted in the *Butte Independent,* Sept. 24, 1910; and Hannan, "Father English," 2, 6–7.

26. 2 Corinthians 2.9–11, 11.30. 12.1–11. St. Patrick was powerfully influenced by St. Paul. See de Paor, *Patrick,* 63, 108; and St. Patrick, *Works,* 9. See also Larkin, "Devotional Revolution"; and Kiberd, *Inventing Ireland,* 430–31.

27. Scally, *End of Hidden Ireland,* 59, 84, 85.

28. Josiah Nott, one of the South's leading "scientific racist" defenders of slavery, referred to "dark skinned Celts" who were "fading away before the superior race." Quoted in Horsman, *Race and Manifest Destiny,* 131. For more on Nott, see his comments on the "Types of Mankind" (1854).

29. Scally, *End of Hidden Ireland,* 8; Strong, *Diary,* Oct. 7, 1865, 4:40; Genovese, *Roll, Jordan, Roll,* 327–65; Kingsley quoted in O'Farrell, *Ireland's English Question,* 147; Horsman, *Race and Manifest Destiny,* 75–77; comment on O'Connell from Curtis, *Apes and Angels,* 100 ("capricious"), 102 ("striking similarities"), 17 ("creature"); Lebow, "British Images"; Jefferson reference from Jordan, *White over Black,* 458–60. See also Miller, "Black and the Green."

30. Mackintosh and Bretherton quoted in Curtis, *Apes and Angels,* 18, 115; see also Jacobson, *Whiteness,* 123. White Americans often commented on black people's "ability" to tolerate pain. See Fredrickson, *Black Image,* 117–21.

31. Scally, *End of Hidden Ireland,* 6, 186, 202; Garrison quoted in Gerteis, *Morality and Utility,* 146; and Osofsky, "Abolitionists," 907; Warner quoted in Jacobson, *Whiteness,* 146. See also Curcan, "Foreword," ix.

32. Knobel, *Paddy and the Republic*, 86; Fiske quoted in Saveth, *American Historians*, 39–40. See also Elson, *Guardians of Tradition*, 122–28; Furnas, *Road to Harpers Ferry*, 232; Potter, *Impending Crisis*, 373; and Theodore Parker to Francis Jackson, Nov. 24, 1859, in Parker, *Life and Correspondence*, 2:174–76.

33. Brownson, "Father Thébaud's Irish Race," 562–63. See also Parker, "Letter from Santa Cruz," Apr. 19, 1859, in Parker, *Life and Correspondence*, 2:461; and Spalding, *Miscellanea*, 512.

34. Hyde quoted in the *Butte Miner*, Apr. 6, 1906; Mulder, *Woodrow Wilson*, 66; Fredrickson, *Black Image*, 97–129.

35. Strong, *Our Country*, 222; Welter, *Mind of America*, 312; Jacobson, *Whiteness*, 48; Heaney, "From Ocean's Love to Ireland," 46; Franchot, *Roads to Rome*, 55; Klein, *Frontiers*, 238–45; Curtis, "Four Erins"; on manliness and masculinity, see Bederman, *Manliness and Civilization*.

36. Berkeley, "Verses on the Prospect of Planting Arts and Learning in America," line 21; Hill, *English Bible*, 135–40; Baritz, "Idea of the West," 633–37; Horseman, *Race and Manifest Destiny*, 75, 83; Klein, *Frontiers*, 73; Gjerde, *Minds of the West*, 31.

37. Edwards and Thoreau quoted in Baritz, "Idea of the West," 637, 639; Horsman, *Race and Manifest Destiny*, 25–42.

38. Benton quoted in Horsman, *Race and Manifest Destiny*, 90; Morse and Ewing quoted in Hauptman, "Mythologizing," 277, 278; Gilpin, *Central Gold Region*, 170.

39. On the Land of the Young: Miller, *Emigrants and Exiles*, 558 (quotation); Yeats, *Fairy and Folk Tales*, 185–89; and Jockers, "In Search of Tir-na-Nog"; Baritz, "Idea of the West," 624; Solnit, *Book of Migrations*, 621; Scally, *End of Hidden Ireland*, 133–34; Whitman quoted in Evans, "American Motif," 4; Trachtenberg, *Incorporation of America*, 19.

40. Cross, *Tailor and Ansty*, 51.

41. MacDonagh, *States of Mind*, 13.

42. Yeats, "The Unappeasable Host," in *Poems*, 58.

43. Evans, *Personality of Ireland*, 34, 64–65 ("refused to add" and "only a man"); Arensberg, *Irish Countryman*, 39–43; Scally, *End of Hidden Ireland*, 134; Mooney, "Holiday Customs," 391, 426; idem, "Funeral Customs," 266; Ferguson, *Signs and Symbols*, 46 ("seat of darkness"); Morris, *Rights of Catholic Initiation*, 129 ("turn" and "enter"). See also Miller, *Emigrants and Exiles*, 557.

44. "Westering" and "Bogland" in Heaney, *Selected Poems*, 48, 22–23; Heaney quoted in the *Missoula Independent*, Mar. 24, 1994; Ní Dhomhnaill, "Why I Choose" (my emphasis); idem, "Cé Leis Tú?"

45. Evans, *Personality of Ireland*, 14; Heaney, "Correspondences," 23; Solnit, *Book of Migrations*, 55, 75, 125; White, *Remembering Ahanagran*; MacDonagh, *States of Mind*, 1.

46. Toynbee quoted in Woodward, *Origins of the New South*, facing ix. See also idem, "Irony of Southern History"; idem, "Second Look"; and Leslie, *Irish Issue*, 121.

47. Faulkner, *Sound and the Fury*, 76, 85; Cross, *Tailor and Ansty*, 20, 37–38; Ward, *Holding Up the Hills*, 74. See also Glassie, *Passing the Time*.

48. Ward, *All Over God's Irish Heaven*, 193, 231; see also idem, *Irish Portraits*.

49. Smith, *Virgin Land*; Marx, *Machine in the Garden*; Sanford, *Quest for Paradise*; Noble, *Eternal Adam*; Lewis, *American Adam*; Noble, *Historians against History*. See also Saveth, *American Historians*; Klein, *Frontiers*, 293; Slotkin, *Fatal Environment*, 227–34, 512–15; Novick, *That Noble Dream*, 23, 61, 80–81, 112; Elson, *Guardians of Tradition*, 53, 180–84; and Susman, "Frontier Thesis."

50. Scally, *End of Hidden Ireland,* 217; Melville quoted in Coleman, *Going to America,* 223.

51. Gramsci quoted in Miller, "Class, Culture," 98. See also idem, "Emigration, Capitalism, and Ideology"; Solnit, *Book of Migrations,* 52–53; and Foster, *Paddy and Mr. Punch,* 281–305.

52. Miller, *Emigrants and Exiles,* 119–22.

53. Ibid., 117; Larkin quoted in Donnelly, "Marian Shrine of Knock," 63.

54. Lynch quoted in Donnelly, "Marian Shrine of Knock," 59 (my emphasis).

55. On wakes, see Miller, *Emigrants and Exiles,* 556–61.

56. Fitzpatrick, *Oceans of Consolation;* idem, "'That beloved country.'" See also Gerber, "Epistolary Ethics"; O'Farrell, *Irish in Australia;* MacDonagh and Mandle (eds.), *Ireland and Irish-Australia;* Campbell, *Kingdom of the Ryans;* idem, *Ireland's New Worlds;* and O'Brien and Travers (eds.), *Irish Emigrant Experience.* Miller is keenly aware that conditions in America might have had as much to do with the exile motif as conditions in Ireland did. See Miller and Boling, "Golden Streets," 31–32; and Miller, "Assimilation and Alienation," 102–107.

57. Donnelly, Speech in St. Paul, Birthday of Robert Emmet, n.d.; on Ireland not being conquered, see "Donnelliana, an Incomplete MS, of *Donnelliana: An Appendix to Caesar's Column, 1892";* both in Donnelly Papers, vol. 134.

58. Donnelly, "Ireland and the Irish People," typed manuscript, n.d., n.p., vol. 134, Donnelly Papers; O'Brien quoted in Novick, *That Noble Dream,* 478; Miller, *Emigrants and Exiles,* 11–25.

59. Manahan, Speech in St. Paul, n.d. (ca. 1905), Manahan Papers.

60. Heaney, "Correspondences," 23; Hughes, "Tradition and Modernity," 21; James Madison's the "earth belongs to the living" quoted in Kammen, *Season of Youth,* 5.

61. Declaration of Independence, in Commager, *Documents,* 1, 100–103; Tocqueville quoted in Kammen, *Season of Youth,* 4.

62. C. G. Chesterton said that traditional societies give "votes to that obscurest of classes, our ancestors. It is the democracy of the dead"; quoted in Kammen, *Season of Youth,* xxxiii; Pearse quoted in Edwards, *Patrick Pearse,* 258, 280–81 (my emphasis). See also Krause, "Connolly and Pearse."

63. "Proclamation of the Irish Republic" in Edwards, *Patrick Pearse,* 280–81; O'Farrell, *Ireland's English Question,* 264; O'Toole, *Ex-Isle of Erin,* 172 ("from the viewpoint").

64. MacGowan, *Hard Road to Klondike (Rotha Mór an tSaoil).*

65. Whitman, *Leaves of Grass,* quoted in Countryman, *Americans,* 129; Heaney, "Westering," in *Selected Poems,* 49; Gilpin, *Mission of the North American People,* 99.

66. Slotkin, *Fatal Environment,* 33; Driscoll, *Country Jake,* 106 (my emphasis).

67. "On Gold-Seeking," in Dunne, *Mr. Dooley in Peace and War,* 104; Fanning, *Irish Voice,* 198–237.

68. "On the Anglo-Saxon," in Dunne, *Mr. Dooley in Peace and War,* 55–56. Ignatius Donnelly was equally contemptuous of "the Anglomaniacs," suggesting that they "be put in petticoats, if it were not for the injustice it would do . . . women." From his Journal (1890) in Donnelliana, vol. 134, Donnelly Papers.

69. Scally, *End of Hidden Ireland,* 218; Coleman, *Going to America,* 29 ("when you emigrate"); Cahill, *How the Irish Saved Civilization,* 183.

70. Coleman, *Going to America,* 35 ("land for the friendless"); for friendliness, see Arensberg and Kimball, *Family and Community,* 70–83.

71. See Weber, *Protestant Ethic;* Tawney, *Religion;* McClelland, *Achieving Society;* and Landes, *Unbound Prometheus.* See also Welter, *Mind of America,* 369.

CHAPTER 5. SAVAGE TWINS

1. Doyle, *Commitments* (1991 film adaptation); Onkey, "Celtic Soul Brothers," 147; idem, "'Not Quite White'?"; Gibbons, "Race against Time"; Cullingford, *Ireland's Others,* 132, 158–59, 168–69; O'Toole, *Lie of the Land,* 19; Kiberd, "White Skin, Brown Masks." Both Colley and MacDonagh use the word "Other" in connection with the Irish: Colley, *Britons,* 5, 6; MacDonagh, *States of Mind,* 107. See also Doan, "How the Irish and Scots Became Indians"; and Dening, *Death of William Gooch.*

2. Jennings, *Invasion of America;* Canny, "Ideology," 583, 584, 588 (quotations).

3. Canny, *Kingdom and Colony,* esp. 2, 6–8, 15, 18–19, 28–29, 31, 35–39, 46, 103–107, 111–14; O'Farrell, *Ireland's English Question,* 25 ("ethic of conquest"); Quinn, *Elizabethans.* See also Smyth, "Western Isle of Ireland"; Muldoon, "Indian as Irishman"; Takaki, "*Tempest*"; Brady, "Spenser's Irish Crisis"; Hooper, "Unsound Plots"; and Herron, "Spanish Armada."

4. O'Connor, "Guests of the Nation"; Jacobson, *Whiteness,* 38 (1646 and "template" quotations); O'Farrell, *Ireland's English Question,* 36. See also Phillips, *Cousins' Wars,* 483.

5. Marx, *Machine in the Garden,* 34–74; Takaki, "*Tempest,*" 29–30.

6. Takaki, "*Tempest,*" 27–28, 31, 45; Joyce quoted in Kiberd, *Inventing Ireland,* 280; Curtis, *Apes and Angels,* 2, 4–5, 20, 22, 29, 45 ("O'Caliban"), 68, 88–89, 101, 107, 143, 167–68. See also Foster, *Paddy and Mr. Punch,* 171–72, 191–93; Williams, *'Twas Only an Irishman's Dream,* 57–77; and Fredrickson, *White Supremacy,* 74–75.

7. Pinkerton quoted in Curtis, *Apes and Angels,* 95; Bradford quoted in Slotkin, *Regeneration,* 38; Slotkin, *Fatal Environment,* 410 (1868 quotation), 392 (Custer quotation); Kingsley quoted in Curtis, *Apes and Angels,* 160; Jacobson, *Whiteness,* 73, 156–59 ("savage over the border" on 156), 204. See also MacLeod, "Celt and Indian"; and Palmer, "Borderlands and Colonies."

8. Whitman quoted in Countryman, *Americans,* 129 (for a discussion of Indians, see 234–35); Jacobson, *Whiteness,* 16–66, 141–58, 204–22; Slotkin, *Regeneration;* idem, *Fatal Environment.* See also Deloria, *Playing Indian,* 3; Horsman, *Race and Manifest Destiny,* 1–77.

9. Jacobson, *Whiteness,* 42; Barrett and Roediger, "Inbetween Peoples"; Franchot, *Roads to Rome,* 88; Brownson quoted in Dolan, *In Search of an American Catholicism,* 62.

10. Franchot, *Roads to Rome,* xx, 5, 88, 95. See also Kennedy, *Jesuit and Savage;* and Billington, *Protestant Crusade,* 1–31.

11. Franchot, *Roads to Rome,* 67–68, 72–81, 87 (quotation), 106, 135–36; Demos, *Unredeemed Captive,* 34–36, 57–58, 69–70, 114–23, 130–34, 151–53; Billington, *Land of Savagery,* 25–28.

12. Franchot, *Roads to Rome,* 88, 151 ("terrain"), 97 ("worst captivity" and "capture and cannibalism"); *Awful Disclosures of Maria Monk,* 47–48; Slotkin, *Regeneration,* 58, 124, 444.

13. Franchot, *Roads to Rome,* 40; Slotkin, *Regeneration,* 40, 67–68; Foxe, Hakluyt, Spenser, and Cooper quoted in Hill, *English Bible,* 35, 135, 269 (see also 139–40, 249–50, 323); Herron, "Spanish Armada."

14. Slotkin, *Regeneration,* 384–88.

15. Franchot, *Roads to Rome,* 14, 55, 49; Klein, *Frontiers,* 99. See also Johnson, "'A Memory Sweet to Soldiers.'"

16. Parker, "Letter from Santa Cruz," in Parker, *Life and Correspondence,* 2:462–63.

17. Solnit, *Book of Migrations,* 51; Evans, *Personality of Ireland,* 52, 71. See also Klein, *Frontiers,* 129; and O'Sullivan, *Twenty Years A-Growing,* 99.

18. Davitt, *Jottings,* 18; Friel, "Translations," 373; Klein, *Frontiers,* 293 (see also 239, 259); Nabokov, *Forest of Time;* Franchot, *Roads to Rome,* 120–21, 79; Solnit, *Book of Migrations,* 4, 55; O'Flaherty, *Cliffmen,* 244, 261.

19. Evans, *Personality of Ireland,* 57; on Indian intertribal warfare, see White, "Winning of the West"; Muldoon, "Seanchas," 20.

20. Evans, "Peasant Beliefs," 39; idem, *Personality of Ireland,* 48, 53, 85; Solnit, *Book of Migrations,* 98–99; Arensberg and Kimball, *Family and Community,* 24, 292, 300; Cross, *Tailor and Ansty,* 120–21; Glassie, *Passing the Time,* 50, 270–71, 536, 663–64, 740; Bull Raid of Cooley in Dunn, *Ancient Irish Epic Tale;* Mooney, "Myths of the Cherokee"; idem, *Ghost Dance Religion.*

21. Evans, "Peasant Beliefs," 38 ("rather have cow dung"), 13 ("cattle folk"); on clachans: idem, *Personality of Ireland,* 55, 62, 63, 86 ("whole nature"); Lochlainn, "Gael and Peasant," 31.

22. O'Farrell, *Ireland's English Question,* 26.

23. Tocqueville reported that the Irish poor "have not the least confidence in justice" and "believe themselves . . . outside the law." Larkin (ed. and trans.), *Tocqueville's Journey in Ireland,* 43; White, "Outlaw Gangs."

24. Cross, *Tailor and Ansty,* 135; Kammen, *Season of Youth,* 14; Heski, *Little Shadow Catcher.*

25. Scally, *End of Hidden Ireland,* 212 ("so extreme"), 209 ("firewater") (see also 29); *Tocqueville's Journey to Ireland,* 7; Clark, *Deliver Us from Evil,* 17–18, 215.

26. Hogden quoted in O'Farrell, *Ireland's English Question,* 25.

27. Jacobson, *Whiteness,* 54, 41, 52, 56.

28. Hale, *Letters,* 51; Turner, "Middle Western Pioneer Democracy," 171, 167; on Butte, see Emmons, *Butte Irish,* 145; Keating, *Gentleman from Colorado,* 79–83; Fink, *Workingmen's Democracy,* xiii (Cheyenne chief).

29. Slotkin, *Fatal Environment,* 311, 305 (see also 139ff.); Jacobson, *Whiteness,* 166–67. The Molly Maguires are an example: see Kenny, *Making Sense;* and Slotkin, *Fatal Environment,* 293, 480–85, 497.

30. Godkin, *Life and Letters,* 1:1–11, 182–83 (quotations); Sproat, *Best Men,* 231; Jacobson, *Whiteness,* 166.

31. Slotkin, *Regeneration,* 42; Joyce, *Ulysses,* 329; Evans, "American Motif," 7.

32. Kane, "To Hell or Pine Ridge"; Scally, *End of Hidden Ireland,* 64 ("vision of oblivion"), 89–90, 111, 121; on Indian removal, see White, *"It's Your Misfortune,"* 85–118, esp. 87–91; Trennert, *Alternative to Extinction;* on definitions of home, see O'Toole, *Lie of the Land,* 165–69. See also Hill, *English Bible,* 398; O'Farrell, *Ireland's English Question,* 108–109, 177–79; and Donnelly, "Construction of the Memory."

33. Slotkin, *Regeneration,* 42; Canny, "Ideology," 582 ("the killyng"); Kane, "Nits Make Lice"; Phillips, *Cousins' Wars,* 210; Fiske quoted in Drinan, *Facing West,* 241; *London Times* quoted in Miller, *Emigrants and Exiles,* 307; Joyce made specific reference to the *Times* comment in *Ulysses,* 329. See also Solnit, *Book of Migrations,* 101; and Evans, "American Motif," 7.

34. Canny, "Ideology," 588–92.

35. Frewen, *Melton Mowbray,* 22–24, 132 (my emphasis); Richardson, "Moreton Frewen"; Brayer, "76 Ranch." See also Beck, "Journeys."

36. Scally, *End of Hidden Ireland,* 144, 154.

37. Ibid., 153–54, 157 (quotations), 251n42.

38. Ibid., 158; Adams, *Education for Extinction;* Solnit, *Book of Migrations,* 52 ("catastrophe of forgetting"). See also Friel, "Translations"; and Coleman, "Responses."

39. Jacobson, *Whiteness,* 15.

40. Ibid., 16, 118; Archdeacon, *Becoming American,* esp. 220–32; Gordon, *Assimilation;* Gleason, *Speaking of Diversity,* 3–90.

41. Jacobson, *Whiteness,* 15–17.

42. O'Toole, *Lie of the Land,* 67.

43. O'Sullivan, "Divine Destiny"; idem, "Annexation"; Sampson, *O'Sullivan and His Times.*

44. Slotkin, *Fatal Environment,* 398–404; Horsman, *Race and Manifest Destiny,* 249, 262; Hays, *Race at Bay,* 136–38, 238, 260–61, 313–15; Athearn, *Thomas Francis Meagher,* 149–65; Keneally, *Great Shame,* 429–37, 446–57. See also Maurice Wolfe to Uncle Maurice, May 12, 1867, Miller Collection.

45. For Healy, see Dungan, *How the Irish Won the West,* 170–81; Hunt, *Whiskey Peddler;* Finerty, *War Path,* 17. Slotkin, *Fatal Environment,* 330–31 (quotation); Conrad, "Charles Collins"; D'Arcy, *Fenian Movement,* 159–61; 303–11, 334–68, 377–82.

46. Casualty list from Finerty, *War Path,* 348–52; for Keough's papal medal, see O'Toole, *Ex-Isle of Erin,* 67. See also Saum, "Private John F. Donohue's Reflections"; Utley, *Frontier Regulars,* 23; and Adams, *Class and Race.*

47. Finerty, *War Path,* xi–xii, 165, 75, 306, 185, 68–69. See also Jacobson, *Whiteness,* 218–19.

48. Finerty, *War Path,* 235.

49. Jacobson, *Whiteness,* 158, 160–61; O'Toole, *Lie of the Land,* 26–27. See also White, "Frederick Jackson Turner"; and Warren, "Buffalo Bill Meets Dracula."

50. Jacobson, *Whiteness,* 158; O'Brien, *Irish Settlers;* idem, *Hidden Phase;* idem, *Pioneer Irish;* Fitzgerald and King, *Uncounted Irish,* 147–78; on the New York riots, see Bernstein, *New York City Draft Riots;* Archdeacon, *Becoming American,* 82–84.

51. Phelan, "Dennis O'Sullivan"; see also "The Pioneers of California"; Phelan to Archbishop Patrick O'Riordan, September 11, 1907; Speech of Honorable James D. Phelan in the Senate of the United States, July 13, 1916, 4–5; all in Phelan Papers.

52. F. J. Sullivan, "Oration," Robert Emmet's Birthday, March 7, 1904; copy in Orations; "An American Democrat," Magazine Collection, Sullivan Papers; Phelan, *Travel and Comment,* 129–30; Douglas Hyde to Phelan, Dec. 20, 1929, Box 62; Tumulty to Phelan, April 24, 1924, Box 109. Phelan was also very active in the American Irish Historical Society. See Phelan to Thomas Lee, Mar. 7, 1910, Box 25; John Lenehan to Phelan, Mar. 21, 1912; Joseph Clarke to Phelan, Nov. 24, 1914; Edward Daly to Phelan, June 1, 1915; and John J. Splain to Phelan, June 4, 1927; all in Box 25, Phelan Papers.

53. Donnelly, "Miscellaneous Notes on Ireland and the Irish People," typed MS, n.d., vol. 134; "Donnelliana, an Incomplete MS, of *Donnelliana: An Appendix to Caesar's Column, 1892,*" vol. 134; Memoriam to Katherine McCaffrey Donnelly, July 1895, vol. 134; see also Diary, July 26 and Nov. 11, 1888, vols. 54–57, microfilm roll 147; all in Donnelly Papers.

54. Rahilly, undated clipping of a speech in 1902, Box 1; *Wabasha Herald,* n.d., clipping, Box 1; Rahilly Speech to the "Old Settlers of Wabasha County," Feb. 22, 1901, Box 4; Obituary, Jan. 15, 1931, clipping in Box 4; see also his speech to the Knights of Columbus, Feb. 11, 1906, which was filled with references to American conquests: typescript copy, Box 4,

all in Rahilly Papers. Keating, born in Kansas of Irish immigrant parents and raised in Denver, also spoke of his father coming west to "conquer the wilderness, redeem the desert, and bring the continent to the service of God." Speech to Tammany Hall, July 4 [no year], Box 4, Keating Papers.

55. On the San Patricios, see Hogan, *Irish Soldiers;* Stevens, *Rogues' March;* Miller, *Shamrock and Sword;* Pinheiro, "'Religion without Restriction'"; on Irish-American anti-imperialism, see Jacobson, *Special Sorrows,* 177–216; idem, *Barbarian Virtues,* 213–15, 254–56; Doyle, *Irish Americans.* See also Slotkin, *Fatal Environment,* 187–90; Jacobson, *Whiteness,* 157–58; Klein, *Frontiers,* 249–56; Gibbons, "Unapproved Roads"; and Stephanson, *Manifest Destiny,* 37.

56. There were also Irish who treated the Indians fairly but left no evidence that this had anything to do with being Irish, such as Thomas Fitzpatrick, an early fur trader. See Hafen, *Broken Hand;* Potter, *To the Golden Door,* 490–95; Parker, *Singing an Indian Song;* and Purdy (ed.), *Legacy of D'Arcy McNickle.* The Choctaw story is from Kane, unpublished lecture on Irish and Indians, University of Montana, Feb. 27, 2009.

57. Ford quoted in Slotkin, *Fatal Environment,* 475; Gibbon, "Last Summer's Expedition," 3, 42.

58. Gibbon, "Last Summer's Expedition," 60–61; on Gibbon and Catholicism, see Casper, *Church on the Fading Frontier,* 45–48.

59. Bríc (Brick), "Memoirs," 23, 28, 30–31.

60. Drannan, *Thirty-one Years on the Plains,* chaps. 10, 23, 25, 31, 33, 41.

61. Bríc (Brick) "Memoirs," 28; Ward, *God in an Irish Kitchen,* 181 (my emphasis); Joyce, *Ulysses,* 329. See also West, "Reconstructing Race."

62. MacGowan, *Hard Road to Klondike,* 64.

63. Ibid., 65 (my emphasis).

64. Conrad to R. B. Cunninghame Graham, Dec. 26, 1903, in Singleton-Gates and Girodias, *Black Diaries,* 93. In that letter Conrad refers to Casement as a "Protestant Irishman, pious too." Conrad's letter is frequently cited, but the reference to Las Casas is almost always elided. See, for example, Gwynn, *Traitor or Patriot,* 29; Inglis, *Roger Casement,* 31–32; and Hochschild, *King Leopold's Ghost,* 196–97, 203. An exception is Solnit, *Book of Migrations,* 31, where the Las Casas reference is included.

65. Conrad, *Heart of Darkness,* 273, 261, 250, 232–33, 237; Hochschild, *King Leopold's Ghost,* 196; Inglis, *Roger Casement,* 217; Casement quoted in Singleton-Gates and Girodias, *Black Diaries,* 234. See also Ó Siocháin, "Roger Casement." The movie *Apocalypse Now,* based on Conrad's novella, certainly finds a heart of darkness on the Mekong.

66. Conrad, *Heart of Darkness,* 266; Gwynn, *Traitor or Patriot,* 188.

67. Solnit, *Book of Migrations,* 32; Gwynn, *Traitor or Patriot,* 208, 219; Singleton-Gates and Girodias, *Black Diaries,* 358.

68. Inglis, *Roger Casement,* 225; Casement quoted in Hochschild, *King Leopold's Ghost,* 267–68 (on the Irish); Casement quoted in Inglis, *Roger Casement,* 263 (on Indians); Solnit, *Book of Migrations,* 96.

69. Solnit, *Book of Migrations,* 32; Singleton-Gates and Girodias, *Black Diaries,* 18 (on Casement's homosexuality); Hochschild, *King Leopold's Ghost,* 199–200, 286; Inglis, *Roger Casement,* 14–15, 63–65, 163–65, 179–81, 193–94.

70. Curtin, *Memoirs,* 31–51, 52–53 (on Fiske), 60–64 (Emerson quotation on 62), 181, 242–46, 408–409.

71. Curtin, *Myths*, 12 (quotation); and idem, *Hero-Tales*, xlvii. He was also interested in West Slavs. See his *Memoirs*, 129–74, 232–42, 662–83, 876–94.

72. Curtin, *Memoirs*, 502; idem, *Myths*, 10.

73. Moses, *Indian Man*, 1–7 (quotation on 3). See also Elliott, "Ethnography."

74. Moses, *Indian Man*, 1–9. One of Mooney's sisters became a nun.

75. On the Land League, see Moses, *Indian Man*, 5–7; Mooney, *Ghost Dance Religion*, 657; idem, "Holiday Customs," 378–79; idem, "Medical Mythology," 136. See also idem, "Gaelic Factor."

76. Mooney, *Ghost Dance Religion*, 964; idem, "Cheyenne Indians," 427–28.

77. Mooney, *Ghost Dance Religion*, 977.

78. Mooney, "Cheyenne Indians," 385–86 (my emphasis).

79. Mooney, "In Memoriam: Washington Matthews," 520.

80. Mooney, "Medical Mythology," 147, 150–51, 145, 146; idem, "Funeral Customs," 271, 273, 263, 249–50, 256–57 (all emphases mine; original spelling). Mooney used the phrase "exactly alike" or its equivalent every time he was comparing Indian and Irish practices.

81. Mooney, "Funeral Customs," 274–75; idem, "Medical Mythology," 146, 136.

82. Mooney, "Medical Mythology," 136; idem, *Ghost Dance Religion*, 1117; idem, "Funeral Customs," 263 (original spelling).

83. For Dunne on the Spanish-American War, see *Mr. Dooley in Peace and War*, 1–13, 30–52, 58–94.

84. "On the Indian War," in ibid., 245–48.

85. Franchot, *Roads to Rome*; Gibbons, *Transformations*; O'Toole, *Ex-Isle of Erin*; idem, *Lie of the Land*; Solnit, *Book of Migrations*; Cullingford, *Ireland's Others*; Kane, "Nits Make Lice"; idem, "To Hell or Pine Ridge"; idem, "'Will Come Forth'"; Ní Dhomhnaill quoted in McDiarmid and Durkan, *Writing Irish*, 99.

86. On the Métis, see Foster, *We Know Who We Are*; on Flaherty, see Hubendorf, *Going Native*; on John Ford, see Eyman, *Print the Legend*; Davis, *John Ford*; Gallagher, *John Ford*; Ellis, "On the Warpath"; and Dowling, "John Ford's Festive Comedy." Add to this list the Irish writer Brian Moore, whose "frontier" novel *Black Robe* is joined seamlessly with his Irish novels.

87. Silverthorne quoted in Reichek, *Home Rule*, 9. Silverthorne also mentions that Indians gave money to the Irish during the starving times and that Eamonn de Valera was given an Indian name by the Blackfeet on his 1919 visit to Montana (ibid., 18). My thanks to Desmond Bell for bringing the Reichek exhibit to my attention and sending me a copy of the catalog. On the IRA's use of Indian symbols and language, see Beresford, *Ten Men Dead*, 46; and Rolston, "From King Billy to Cú Chulainn."

88. "The Indians on Alcatraz," "The More a Man Has the More a Man Wants," "Meeting the British," in Muldoon, *Poems*, 24, 134, 160–61. The whole of Muldoon's long poem "Madoc: A Mystery" is concerned with Indians, Irish, imperialism, colonialism, "frontiers," and utopias. See also Cosgrove, "Paul Muldoon's Explorer Myth"; McCurry, "'S'crap'"; idem, "A Land 'Not Borrowed' But 'Purloined.'" Seamus Heaney also deals with Indians in some of his writings. See Parker, "Gleanings, Leavings."

CHAPTER 6. BORDER WARS

1. Jefferson quoted in Arieli, *Individualism*, 129–31. The irony is that Ireland was "partitioned" in 1921 for similar reasons.

2. Beecher, *Plea*, 56; Parker to John Ayres, Dec. 8, 1859, in Parker, *Life and Correspondence,* 2:394 (his emphasis); Marty, *Righteous Empire,* 47. See also Hansen, "Millennium"; Billington, *Protestant Crusade,* 1–31, 280, 290–9; and Le Beau, "'Saving the West,'" 112.

3. Gjerde, *Minds of the West,* 44 (James quotations), 42 (other quotations). See also McGreevy, *Catholicism,* 34–40, 46–56, 72, 73, 79–81.

4. Hale, *Letters,* 6.

5. Spalding, *Miscellanea,* 509, 510 (my emphasis); Rossa quoted in Jacobson, *Whiteness,* 51. See also *Irish World,* Jan. 28, 1871, Jan. 3, 1874, and Mar. 20, 1875; Strong, *Diary,* July 19, 1863, 3:342. Jensen argues, not convincingly, against the "No Irish Need Apply" signs. See "'No Irish Need Apply.'"

6. West, "Reconstructing Race"; Barrett and Roediger, "Inbetween Peoples"; Eagan, "White, If 'Not Quite'"; Foley, *White Scourge;* Roediger, *Wages of Whiteness;* and Gordon, *Great Arizona Orphan Abduction;* Jacobson, *Whiteness.* The association of the Irish with racism is challenged in Arnesen, "Whiteness"; Curtis, "Comment"; and Kolchin, "Whiteness Studies."

7. On blackface, see Roediger, *Wages of Whiteness,* 115–32 and notes; Ibsen, *Will the World Break Your Heart?*

8. Knobel, *Paddy and the Republic,* 109–11; Van Dussen, "American Methodism's *Christian Advocate*"; for the school issue, see McGreevy, *Catholicism,* 19–42.

9. Welter, *Mind of America,* 305; Horsman, *Race and Manifest Destiny,* 87.

10. Gilpin, *Mission of the North American People,* 104, 216–17; idem, *Central Gold Region,* 20, 119 (my emphasis). See also idem, *Notes on Colorado;* Slotkin, *Fatal Environment,* 219–26.

11. Turner, "Significance of the Frontier," 47; idem, *Frontier in American History,* 23, 349; Billington, *Frederick Jackson Turner,* 372 ("melting pot"); Turner, "Middle Western Pioneer Democracy," 171. See also Saveth, *American Historians,* 132–38; Jacobs, *On Turner's Trail,* 23, 25, 52–53; and Richardson, *West from Appomattox,* 270–71.

12. Turner, "Middle Western Pioneer Democracy," 172, 173 ("good mixer" and "lessons"); idem, "Contributions of the West," 86 ("free from the influences"); idem, "Significance of the Frontier," 34 ("steady growth"), 47 ("immigrants").

13. Turner, "Middle Western Pioneer Democracy," 173.

14. Anbinder, *Nativism,* 107. See also the Letter to Lord John Russell in Abbott (ed.), *Historical Aspects,* 109–11; Socolofsky, *Landlord William Scully;* idem, "William Scully's Irish and American Lands"; Miller, *Emigrants and Exiles,* 356, 400–401, 472, 478, 507, 537; and Harris, "'Where the Poor Man Is Not Crushed Down.'"

15. Turner, "Middle Western Pioneer Democracy," 171 (my emphasis).

16. Ibid., 168.

17. Hale, *Letters,* 36, 37.

18. Ibid., 33, 56; see Handlin, *Boston's Immigrants,* 55.

19. Hale, *Letters,* 56–57, 23.

20. Ibid., 48–49, 52, 57 (my emphasis). See also Bagenal, *American Irish,* 86–88; "State Aid Condemned, 1847," in Abbott (ed.), *Historical Aspects,* 100–15; and McGee, *Catholic History,* 105–107, 130–33.

21. Hale, *Letters,* 52 (my emphasis).

22. Bagenal, *American Irish,* 38, 47–48 (my emphasis).

23. Ibid., 73–75, 111.

24. Ibid., 135, 67–68, 218.

25. Ibid., 37–38, 47–48, 157–75 (on the land question).

26. Ibid., 64–68.

27. Ibid., 36, 87; on *The Irish World,* see Rodechko, "Patrick Ford."

28. Ibid., 73–75.

29. Brace, *Dangerous Classes,* 97; O'Connor, *Orphan Trains;* Holt, *Orphan Trains,* 41–79, 98–102, 120–55; Gordon, *Great Arizona Orphan Abduction,* 8–12.

30. The resemblance of Brace's schemes to the Indian Removal policies is noted by Slotkin, *Fatal Environment,* 310–11; O'Connor, *Orphan Trains,* 73, 168.

31. Brace, *Dangerous Classes,* 30–31, 158; O'Connor, *Orphan Trains,* 18–28, 73, 76, 81–82, 166–68.

32. Brace, *Races,* 88–89, 465–66, 473, 477, 512.

33. Brace, *Dangerous Classes,* 26, 27, 425.

34. Ibid., 426 (my emphasis).

35. Ibid., 225; Holt, *Orphan Trains,* 44.

36. Holt, *Orphan Trains,* 23–24 (on the changing definition of "orphan"); Brace, *Dangerous Classes,* 225.

37. Brace, *Dangerous Classes,* 224–27, 234; Holt, *Orphan Trains,* 55 ("little colonies").

38. Cartoon in O'Connor, *Orphan Trains,* facing 168.

39. Ibid.

40. Ibid., 168–75; Holt, *Orphan Trains,* 107–109, 114; Gordon, *Great Arizona Orphan Abduction,* 3–5, 14–18, 65–75, 276–88.

41. Andrew Doyle, St. Louis, to Brother and Friends, May 31, 1819, Miller Collection; Cahill, *How the Irish Saved Civilization.*

42. McGee, *Catholic History,* 103, 150; idem, *History of the Attempt* (1853) quoted in O'Farrell, *Ireland's English Question,* 86.

43. Brownson, "Father Thébaud's Irish Race," 547; the clergyman and the Irishwoman are quoted in O'Farrell, *Ireland's English Question,* 215, 236; Quigley, *Irish Race,* 105; Robert E. O'Donnell, Speech to the Minnesota Ancient Order of Hibernians, Mar. 17, 1920, M. D. O'Donnell and Family Papers, Box 1. See also Michael Hurley, Cedar Pass, Nevada, to Parents, Aug. 26, 1871, Miller Collection.

44. Spalding, *Religious Mission of the Irish Race,* 63; Shannon, *Catholic Colonization,* 76; Morris, *American Catholic,* 53; Bagenal, *American Irish,* 63–64.

45. O'Farrell, *Ireland's English Question,* 13, 235, 215; MacDonagh also uses the term "Irish 'empire'" in "Irish Famine Emigration," 379; Strong, *Our Country,* 90. See also Miller, *Emigrants and Exiles,* chap. 8; Maguire, *Irish in America,* 253–61, 345–46, 423–25; and Irene Whelan, "Religious Rivalry," in Lee and Casey (eds.), *Making the Irish American.*

46. AHC also inspired the formation of a number of Irish women's religious orders, and thousands of young Irish nuns and sisters also did missionary work overseas. See Hoy, *Good Hearts;* and idem, "Journey Out." The story about the twenty-cow and three-cow families was told to me by Father Sarsfield O'Sullivan of Butte, Montana.

47. Murray, "Calendar of the Overseas Missionary Correspondence of All Hallows College," microfilm copies made available through the generosity of Professor Jay Dolan at Notre Dame

(hereinafter cited by place and letter number, with the Calendar Serial Number abbreviated CSN). All the *Reports* and *Annals* were published in Dublin by John F. Fowler. For All Hallows, see Morris, *American Catholic,* 48–49; Schrier, *Ireland and the American Emigration,* 67; Dwyer, *Condemned to the Mines;* and Glazier, *Encyclopedia,* 791; London, *Missionary College of All Hollows.*

48. *1st Report, 1848,* 2; *Annals, 1862,* 31. See also Kenny, "Diaspora and Comparison"; Barkan, "America in the Hand"; Gabaccia, "Is Everywhere Nowhere?"; and Van der Linden, "Transnationalizing."

49. *9th Report, 1858,* 13; *5th Report, 1852–53,* 3 ("our own brethren" and "conclude"); *6th Report, 1854,* 11 ("designs of mercy").

50. *Annals, 1861,* 27–28 (quotations); *8th Report, 1856,* 10–11 ("Irish poverty").

51. Fr. Michael Sheehan to Fr. John Kavanaugh, June 28, 1851, Galveston.1, CSN362 ("private judgment"; my emphasis); Fr. John Curtis to Fr. Thomas Fortune, Oct. 29, 1869, Omaha.15, CSN710 ("republican principles").

52. *6th Report, 1854,* 7–8, 10–12 (quotations); Fr. Martin Murphy to Fr. William Fortune, June 16, 1873, Pittsburgh, CSN835.

53. *6th Report, 1854,* 12–13, 16; *7th Report, 1856,* 10–11; Murphy to Fortune, in ibid.

54. *6th Report, 1854,* 10–11. See also *Annals, 1863,* 24–25.

55. *1st Report, 1848,* 2. See also Fr. Pierre de Smet's comments re AHC in Fr. John Curtis to All Hallows College, April 30, 1867, Omaha.8, CSN703.

56. *8th Report, 1856,* 6–7, 8; Fr. Con Delahunty to Fr. Eugene O'Connell, Mar. 13, 1862, in *Annals, 1862,* 57; a letter from B. P. Loras to Fr. Bartholomew Woodlock, Feb. 21, 1848, Dubuque.3; CSN288 (Iowa and Minnesota weather); John Curtis to William Fortune, Apr. 25, 1867, Omaha.7, CSN702 (Nebraska); O'Connell to Fr. John Mullally, Aug. 12, 1861, Marysville.6, CSN513 (California); O'Connell to Thomas Fortune, June 22, 1866, Marysville.28, CSN534 (Milton quotation); Pastoral Letter of Jose Sadoc Allemany, archbishop of San Francisco, n.d., in *Annals, 1863,* 30–31 ("our brethren"). See also the reports from women religious in Hoy, "Journey Out," 68.

57. O'Connell to Bennett, Sept 16, 1861, Marysville.7, CSN514 ("Mormondom"); O'Connell to Bennett, Apr. 23, 1862, Marysville.12, CSN518 ("wily boar"); Fr. J. O'Grady in Omaha to Fr. John Sheehy, Apr. 1, 1910, Ireland ("easy to be good in Ireland"); B. P. Loras to Woodlock, Aug. 16, 1856, Dubuque.1, CSN301; O'Connell to Fortune, Oct., 2, 1872, Marysville.60, CSN566 (see also O'Connell to Mullally, Aug. 12, 1861, Marysville.6, CSN513); F. P. Machebeuf to Bennett, Sept. 3, 1869, Denver.1, CSN814; Allemany to Woodlock, Dec. 4, 1856, San Francisco.34, CSN997; in All Hallows College (Dublin, Ireland) Records, University of Notre Dame Archives; *6th Report, 1854,* 24–25 ("western wilderness" and "so unsettled"); Fr. William Byrne to Fortune, Dec. 11, 1874, Omaha.32, CSN726 ("floating"); O'Connell to Fr. David Moriarty, July 10, 1851, San Francisco.2, CSN963 ("very few women"); Fr. Thomas Curtis to Fortune, Sept. 2, 1869, Omaha.14, CSN709 ("great proportion" and "six barrel revolver"); *6th Report, 1854,* 25 ("knife"); Grace to Woodlock, Aug. 20, 1860, St. Paul.1, CSN940 ("wild region"). On Indians, see also Fr. Patrick Martin to Moriarty, in *6th Report, 1854,* 31–32; and Fr. Patrick O'Reilly to Bennett, *Annals, 1863,* 92–98.

58. O'Connell to Bennett, Sept. 16, 1861, Marysville.7, CSN14 (names of camps); O'Connell to Woodlock, May 27, 1861, Marysville.4, CSN511 (Marysville name story); O'Connell to Bennett, Jan. 28, 1862, Marysville.10, CSN517 ("How few are the caravans"). Some AHC

priests thought that Britain might set up another Botany Bay on Vancouver Island; see J. R. Demers to Woodlock, Mar. 9, 1855, Vancouver.17, CSN1429; *2nd Report, 1849,* 21–23; *4th Report, 1851,* 4. See also Johnson, *Roaring Camp;* and Holliday, *World Rushed In.*

59. Pastoral Letter of Jose Sadoc Allemany, in *Annals, 1863,* 30–31; *6th Report, 1854,* 9–10; *8th Report, 1856,* 8.

60. J. B. Miege to Hand, Oct. 19, 1854, Leavenworth.12, CSN477; J. B. Miege to Woodlock, June 3, 1855, Leavenworth.1; CSN468 (my emphasis); *9th Report, 1858,* 9; *1st Annual Report, 1848,* 10 (quotations); *5th Report, 1852–53,* 4–5; Maguire, *Irish in America,* 253–61, 345–46, 423–24.

61. F. N. Blanchet, archbishop of Oregon City, to Woodlock, June 18, 1849, in *2nd Report, 1849,* 20 ("surrounded"); Blanchet to Fortune, Oct. 19, 1866, Oregon.12, CSN799; Bishop J. S. Allemany to Fr. Bartholomew Woodlock, June 15, 1858, San Francisco.41, CSN1004 ("godless"); *1st Report, 1848,* 10; Fr. William Riordan to Fr. William Fortune, Feb. 18, 1870, San Francisco.12, CSN949 ("public state schools"); Fr. Eugene O'Connell to Fr. Thomas Bennett, Sept. 26, 1862, St. Paul.18, CSN524 ("national or public schools"); O'Connell to Fortune, May 25, 1870, Marysville.51, CSN557 ("losing their faith or morals"); O'Connell quoted in Hoy, *Good Hearts,* 26 ("far more urgent"); *6th Report, 1854,* 7–8 ("imperious duty"). See also *Annals, 1862,* 33; and *Annals, 1863,* 24–25.

62. *1st Annual Report, 1848,* 2, 10; John Curtis to William Fortune, Jan. 30, 1867, Dubuque.26, CSN315. See also Curtis to Fortune, June 5, 1874, Omaha.30, CSN724.

63. On the Montana vigilantes, see Wylie, *Irish General,* 229–36, 264–65; and Allen, *Decent, Orderly Lynching.*

64. Utley, *Billy the Kid;* Dungan, *How the Irish Won the West,* 206–54; Nolan, *West of Billy the Kid;* idem (ed.), *Billy the Kid Reader;* Tatum, *Inventing Billy the Kid.* See also Quintelli-Neary, *Irish American Myth.*

65. Malone, *Battle for Butte;* Emmons, "Orange and the Green," 232.

66. Ward, *Holding Up the Hills,* 50; Tierney, *But of Course They Were Irish,* 22.

67. Ward, *Holding Up the Hills,* 57–58, 173, 189. See also Lauck, "'You can't mix wheat and potatoes.'"

68. Andrew Greenlees, Glensharrold, Kansas, to his brother in Ireland, Sept. 7, 1863, and Oct. 24, 1878, Greenlees Family Letters, Miller Collection (original spelling).

69. Driscoll, *Country Jake,* 235, 115, 69.

70. Rolvaag, *Giants in the Earth,* 115, 122–24, 134–40, 146–49; Reverend Martin Mahoney, Currie, Minnesota, to the Editor of the *Boston Pilot,* Feb. 6, 1884, in Sweetman Catholic Colony, "Letters from the Pastor," 7, 9.

71. For Meagher's life, see Wylie, *Irish General;* Athearn, *Thomas Francis Meagher;* Cavanaugh, *Memoirs;* Keneally, *Great Shame;* Meagher to Cornelius C. O'Keefe, Sept. 26, 1866, Meagher Papers (quotations); and Maginnis, "Thomas Francis Meagher," 102–103, 117; for Meagher's colonization plans, see Carroll, "Ecclesiastical Jurisdiction," Feb. 17, 1910, typescript; and Palladino, "Origins," typescript; both in Brondel Papers.

72. Meagher to the Rev. George Pepper, Jan. 20, 1866, quoted in Spence, *Territorial Politics,* 36; Meagher, "Recollections of Ireland," 35 ("bounty" and "aspiring piety"); "St. Patrick's Day speech in Virginia City," Mar. 17, 1866, in "Recollections of Ireland," 22. See also "Priestly Recollections," 130–35.

73. Finerty, "Oration by Col. Finerty," 139; Meagher quoted in Maginnis, "Thomas Francis Meagher," 105; on Meagher's Catholicism, see Athearn, *Thomas Francis Meagher*, 144–46; Wylie, *Irish General*, 92–93, 223–24, 308–309.

74. Meagher, "Recollections of Ireland," 28–30; from idem, "Address," Aug. 5, 1866 ("depraved and distempered natures"), in ibid., 50–55.

75. Meagher, "Recollections of Ireland," 29–30.

76. Executive Office, Territory of Montana, Apr. 1866, in Meagher Papers; Ronan is listed as superintendent in Montana, *House Journal*, 2nd sess., 1866.

77. Sanders to James Fergus, Feb. 14, 1866, Fergus Papers.

78. Emmons, "Strange Death"; Quigley, *Irish Race*, 167–68, 543; Emmons, *Butte Irish*, 118–20.

79. Meagher to O'Keefe, Sept. 26, 1866, Meagher Papers; Martin Hogan to Andrew O'Connell, July 21, Aug. 25, and Sept. 17, 1866, and Jan. 6, 1867; in Hogan Collection; on O'Connell as a close friend of Meagher's, see Ronan, *Frontier Woman*, 44; Cavanaugh, *Memoirs*, appendix, 1–2.

80. O'Neill, "To My Fellow Countrymen," Dec. 8, 1876.

81. Ibid.

82. Slotkin, *Fatal Environment*, 330–31; Riel, *Collected Writings*, 556 (quotations); idem, *Queen v. Louis Riel*, 166–70; *Omaha Daily Herald*, July 18, 19, and 23, 1871; Dan Lyne to James C. Olson, Jan. 2, 1866; and J. P. Sutton to Addison Sheldon, Sept. 29, 1926; copies in Sutton Papers. See also Howard, *Strange Empire*.

83. For Turner's concerns, see "Problem of the West," 68. Turner did look farther West; he simply never incorporated what he saw into his grand narrative. See "Contributions of the West," 90–91.

84. On the end of the frontier, see Wrobel, *End of American Exceptionalism;* Schouler, *History of the United States*, 4:177, 180, 203, 5:304–306; Saveth, *American Historians*, 159–63, 184–92.

85. Channing quoted in Saveth, *American Historians*, 197; Gjerde, *Minds of the West*, 7; Wolfe to Cousin Maurice, Apr. 12, 1868, Miller Collection.

86. APA oath quoted in Burns et al. (eds.), *Keeping Faith*, 85; Gjerde, *Minds of the West*, 284–89; Higham, *Strangers in the Land*, 80–87; Kinzer, *Episode in Anti-Catholicism*. See also Oregon APA Records, 1894–98.

87. O'Gorman, *How Catholics Come to Be Misunderstood*, 4.

88. Ibid., 12–15.

89. May 24, 1893, Lorenzo Crounce Papers, Box 7. The Irish in Lincoln had begun a newspaper, *Irish American Weekly*, expressly to meet the APA threat. It published only one issue, on May 15, 1892.

CHAPTER 7. FINDING A "FAIR LIVING"

1. The literature on these topics is vast. The starting point but not the ending point would be Handlin, *Uprooted*. Some more recent and better accounts would include Archdeacon, *Becoming American;* Bodnar, *Transplanted;* idem, "Remembering"; Nugent, *Crossings;* Yans-McLaughlin (ed.), *Immigration Reconsidered;* Gjerde (ed.), *Major Problems;* idem, *Minds of the West;* Kazal, "Revisiting Assimilation"; Barkan, "Race, Religion and Nationality"; idem, "Introduction"; idem, *From All Points;* Conzen et al., "Invention of Ethnicity"; Luebke (ed.), *European Immigrants;* and Taylor, *Distant Magnet*.

2. Guinnane, *Vanishing Irish,* 104–107; Campbell, *Ireland's New Worlds,* 133; Miller, "For 'Love and Liberty,'" 304–305.

3. Diner, *Erin's Daughters;* Nolan, *Ourselves Alone;* Miller, "For 'Love and Liberty.'"

4. Cross, *Tailor and Ansty;* Synge quoted in Edwards, "Irish New Woman"; Sayers, *Peig;* O'Sullivan, *Twenty Years A-Growing;* O'Crohan, *Day in Our Life;* idem, *Island Cross-Talk;* T. O'Crohan, *Islandman.*

5. Miller, "For 'Love and Liberty,'" 315.

6. See Doyle, "Irish as Urban Pioneers."

7. Quoted in Meinig, *Transcontinental America,* 33; see Adams, *Class and Race.*

8. Larson, *History of Wyoming,* 40. See also Shannon, *American Irish,* 28; Clark, *Hibernia America,* 23–33; Licht, *Working for the Railroad,* 221–39; Ambrose, *Nothing Like It,* 18, 21, 177, 217–18, 327, 378; and Blessing, "Irish," 531.

9. Miller, *Emigrants and Exiles,* 488.

10. U.S. Bureau of the Census, *Tenth Census, 1880, Population,* 1394.

11. States and territories from which funds were sent to the Land League between 1881 and 1882 included Arizona ($1,091), California ($4,109), Colorado ($4,200), Dakota Territory ($449), Idaho ($138—no Land Leagues), Iowa ($2,400), Kansas ($1,700), Massachusetts ($7,401), Minnesota ($1,800), Montana ($2,048), Nebraska ($1,500), Nevada ($1,500), New Mexico ($537—no Land Leagues), Oregon ($1,500), Pennsylvania ($16,750, mostly from Molly Maguire country), Utah ($2.50—Mormon deterrence?), Washington ($432), Wisconsin ($1,400), and Wyoming ($210). From *Irish World,* Sept. 24, 1881.

12. *Tenth Census: 1880, Population,* 1360.

13. Glazier, *Encyclopedia;* Ryan, *Civic Wars,* 79–85; Jameson, *All That Glitters,* 25–29, 60–61, 89–90, 105–108, 142–59, 164–72, 189–93; Emmons, *Butte Irish;* Lankton, *Cradle to Grave;* idem, *Beyond the Boundaries;* Brundage, *Making of Western Labor Radicalism,* 40–52; Burchell, *San Francisco Irish;* Wingerd, *Claiming the City;* Fitzgerald and King, *Uncounted Irish;* Walsh (ed.), *San Francisco Irish;* Sarbaugh, "Exiles of Confidence"; Prendergast, *Forgotten Pioneers;* Blessing, "West among Strangers"; Saxton, *Indispensable Enemy,* 28–40; Delury, "Irish Nationalism"; Walsh, "Irish in the New America"; Price, *Trails I Rode;* Sarbaugh and Walsh (eds.,) *Irish in the West;* and, Jordan and O'Keefe (eds.), *Irish in the San Francisco Bay Area;* Quigley, *Irish Race.* The following works are a few of the sources consulted to find rural and small-town Irish. For Iowa: Laughlin and Laughlin, *Century of Memories;* WPA, "Graves Registration Project." For the Dakotas: Rees, *Farewell to Famine;* Kemp, *Irish in Dakota; Atlas of Clay and Union Counties, South Dakota;* Duratschek, *Builders.* For Minnesota: Butler, "Lynch Family Chronicles"; O'Meara, *Cloquet;* idem, *We Made It;* Manahan, *Trials;* Regan, "Irish"; Johnston, *Minnesota's Irish;* AOH, "Minnesota Irish." For New Mexico: Woods, "Cleveland." For Oregon: Kilkenny, *Shamrocks and Shepherds;* O'Hara, *Pioneer Catholic History.* For Montana: O'Daly, "Life History"; Butler, "They invented whiskey"; Sullivan, *Our Yesterdays;* Coughlin, "History of Helmville." For Nebraska: Casper, *Church on the Northern Plains.* For Colorado: Gibbons, *In the San Juans;* Keating, *Gentleman from Colorado.* For California: Roney, *Irish Rebel.*

14. *1st Report, 1848,* 3; *5th Report, 1852–53,* 3; *Annals, 1862,* 26–27 (my emphasis).

15. Schrier, *Ireland and the American Emigration,* 19–20; MacGowan, *Hard Road,* 60, 132.

16. Scally, *End of Hidden Ireland,* 87; MacGowan, *Hard Road,* 2–3 (see also 121).

17. Miller, *Emigrants and Exiles,* 358–59; idem, "Assimilation," 93 (original spelling).

18. Miller, "Assimilation," 93–94; Slotkin, *Fatal Environment,* 30 ("myth of concern").

19. Miller, "Assimilation," 94 ("highly unstable"); idem, *Emigrants and Exiles,* 498 (O'Neill quotation and "always the fear").

20. On labor aristocracies, see Hobsbawm, *Workers,* 214–72.

21. U.S. Senate Commission on Industrial Relations, *Final Report and Testimony,* 3700–3701.

22. *Montana Socialist* (Butte), Oct. 23, 1915 ("a dozen men waiting"); U.S. Senate Commission on Industrial Relations, Final *Report and Testimony,* 3786 ("Finns drove us out"). See also Peck, *Reinventing Free Labor.*

23. U.S. Bureau of the Census, *Twelfth Census, 1900,* clxxii; Browne, "Archbishop Hughes," 260, 276.

24. *Thirteenth Census, 1910,* 886–87; Book of Mormon, I Nephi 13:5, 14:16, quoted in Madsen, *Glory Hunter,* 66.

25. Doggerel quoted in Kiberd, *Inventing Ireland,* 268; Scally, *End of Hidden Ireland,* 151, 149 (on the Welsh, Scots, and Irish); Bríc (Brick), "Memoirs"; Miller, *Emigrants and Exiles,* 418; idem, "From the Gaeltacht."

26. Bríc (Brick), "Memoirs"; Scally, *End of Hidden Ireland,* 153; Foster quoted in Abbott (ed.), *Historical Aspects,* 299. See also Moran, *Sending Out Ireland's Poor;* and Harris, "'Where the Poor Man Is Not Crushed Down.'"

27. Emmons, "Influence of Ideology."

28. Emmons, *Garden in the Grasslands,* 127–43 (quotation on 139), 146–64, 180–96; Strong, *Our Country,* 37.

29. O'Hanlon, *Irish Emigrant's Guide,* 10–11, 140 (see also 144, 165).

30. O'Donovan, *Irish Immigration,* 5.

31. Maguire, *Irish in America,* 216–17, 260–61, 227–28.

32. Butler, *Irish on the Prairies,* 24, 17, 29, 40.

33. Quigley, *Irish Race,* 81–104; Starr, *Americans and the California Dream,* 191; Matthew Jockers, "Literature," in Jordan and O'Keefe (eds.), *Irish in the San Francisco Bay Area;* Fanning (ed.), *Exiles,* 123–29; idem, *Irish Voice,* 141–52. See also Burchell, *San Francisco Irish,* 184–85; and Rodechko, "Patrick Ford."

34. *Irish Nation* (New York), Dec. 3, 1881; see also Nov. 23, 1881.

35. MacGowan, *Hard Road,* 124–25.

36. On the authority of Irish priests, see Taylor, *Occasions of Faith.*

37. *6th Report, 1854,* 7–8. On Hispanic Catholicism, see Maffly-Kipp, *Religion and Society;* and Engh, *Frontier Faiths.* Horgan's *Lamy of Santa Fe* and Cather's *Death Comes for the Archbishop* remain classics.

38. St. Patrick's Benefit Society to O'Connell, Dec. 12, 1862, in *Annals, 1863,* 32–33. I found no hostile comments about the Hispanic church in the reports and correspondence of AHC. F. P. Machebeuf praised Hispanics in a letter to Bennett, Sept. 3, 1869, Denver.1, CSN814; on the language issue, see Casper, *Church on the Northern Plains,* 138; on the preference for Irish priests, see Bishop Grace to AHC, June 27, 1867, St. Paul.6, CSN945; O'Connell to Bennett, Mar 28, 1862, Marysville.37, CSN518; O'Connell to Fortune, Dec. 17, 1867, Marysville.37, CSN543; Curtis to Fortune, Jan. 19, 1869, Omaha.10, CSN705; and B. P. Loras to Moriarty, Nov. 11, 1847, Dubuque.3, CSN287.

39. O'Connell to Fortune, Dec. 17, 1867, Marysville.37, CSN543. See also O'Connell to Bennett, Mar. 28, 1862, Marysville.11, CSN518, and Jan. 9, 1863, Marysville.22, CSN528; Grace to Fortune, Aug. 11, 1871, St. Paul.14, CSN951, and Aug. 25, 1874, St. Paul.18, CSN955, and Sept. 10, 1877, St. Paul.23, CSN960; Demers to Woodlock, Nov. 24, 1860, Vancouver Island.12, CSN1434, and May 22, 1866, Vancouver Island.13, CSN1435; O'Connell to Bennett, Jan. 9, 1863, Marysville.22, CSN528; and "A Catholic Late of Ireland" to Woodlock, Mar. 17, 1857, in *Annals, 1860,* 21.

40. *Annals, 1862,* 28; *6th Report, 1854,* 8–9. Fr. J. Largan, Napa City, California to Fr. John Forde, Nov. 1, 1858, in *Annals, 1859,* 40; Bishop J. Amat to Fr. Dan Dowley, June 23, 1860, Monterey and Los Angeles.3, CSN599; and Amat to Fortune, Nov. 18, 1868, Monterey and Los Angeles.11, CSN607.

41. Fr. Frederick Baraga, Dec. 9, 1853, in *5th Report, 1852–53,* 21; *1st Report, 1848,* 20.

42. Fr. T. Brosnahan to Sheehy, Dec. 19, 1910 (my emphasis), All Hallows College Records. Bishop John Brondel of Montana went to Ireland to recruit priests: Brondel to the *Helena Independent,* Sept. 6, 1890.

43. *Annals, 1861,* 29.

44. J. B. Miege to Woodlock, June 3, 1855, Leavenworth.1, CSN468.

45. O'Connell to Bennett, Apr. 23, 1862, Marysville12, CSN518; O'Connell to Moriarty, May 23, San Francisco.11, CSN974; see also Allemany to Woodlock, May 17, 1858, San Francisco.40, CSN1003; on the Irish and tuberculosis, see Dubos and Dubos, *White Plague,* 192–93; Emmons, *Butte Irish,* 72–75; and McGrath, *Charnel House;* O'Connell to Moriarty, May 23, 1853, San Francisco.11, CSN974 (on Oregon); Blanchet to Woodlock, June 18, 1849, in *2nd Report, 1849,* 20; Loras to Woodlock, Feb. 21, 1848, Dubuque.3, CSN288 (on Iowa); "A Catholic Late of Ireland" to Woodlock, Mar. 17, 1857, in *Annals, 1860,* 21 (on Minnesota and Iowa); Fr. William Riordan to Fortune, Feb. 18, 1870, St. Paul.12, CSN949; Fr. Patrick McCabe to Woodlock, Aug. 9, 1856, in *8th Report, 1856,* 48–49.

46. Curtis to Fr. Tom Molloy, June 11, 1873, Omaha.28, CSN722; Curtis to Fortune, June 5, 1874, Omaha.30, CSN724; McCabe to Woodlock, Aug. 9, 1856, in *8th Report, 1856,* 48–49; Curtis to Fortune, May 17, 1866, Dubuque.26, CSN315; Riordan to Fortune, Feb. 18, 1870, St. Paul.12, CSN949; on the railroad pass, see Curtis to Fortune, May 10, 1871, Omaha.19, CSN714; Hennessey to Fortune, Jan. 30, 1867, Dubuque.26, CSN315. See also McCabe to Fr. James Clarke, Mar. 1, 1853, in *5th Report, 1852–53,* 15–17.

47. Hennessey to Fortune, Jan. 30, 1867, Dubuque.26, CSN315; for a brilliant discussion of the true metropolis, see Cronon, *Nature's Metropolis;* Curtis to Fortune, Mar. 22, 1871, Omaha.18, CSN713.

48. Shannon, *Catholic Colonization;* O'Connell, *John Ireland,* 136–60; Moynihan, "Archbishop Ireland's Colonies"; Regan, "Irish"; Browne, "Archbishop Hughes"; Campbell, "Immigrants on the Land"; idem, "Other Immigrants"; idem, "Ireland's Furthest Shores"; Moran, "'In Search of the Promised Land'"; Casper, *Church on the Northern Plains,* 35–54, 66–77, 82–85, 94, 95; Slotkin, *Fatal Environment,* 327–31; Wylie, *Irish General;* Emmons, "Strange Death"; letter to Meagher from Jackson City, Michigan, Feb. 12, 1866, Meagher Papers; Nugent, *Into the West,* 52; Fox, "Revisiting Eugene Macnamara's Irish Colony Scheme"; on Ignatius Donnelly as an active recruiter, see Donnelly, "Chronology," Donnelly Papers; Ridge, *Ignatius*

Donnelly, 18; on Irish Catholic prospects in the West, see A. F. Mace to John Ireland, Mar. 5, 1897, Ireland Papers.

49. Mahoney quoted in Moynihan, "Archbishop Ireland's Colonies," 217–18.

50. Mahoney to the *Boston Pilot,* Feb. 6, 1884, in Sweetman Catholic Colony, "Letters from the Pastor," 7, 9; Hoy, *Good Hearts;* idem, "Journey Out."

51. Petition quoted in Casper, *Church on the Northern Plains,* 159.

52. Sweetman Catholic Colony, "Letters from the Pastor," 8; Ed Hanlon or O'Hanlon to his father, Sept. 20, 1843, Miller Collection (original spelling and capitalization); Golab, *Immigrant Destinations,* 120–22.

53. McGee, *History of the Irish Settlers,* 24–25; Maguire, *Irish in America,* 76–77, 243–44; Gjerde, *Minds of the West,* 52; Shannon, *Catholic Colonization,* 17–22; Browne, "Archbishop Hughes," 262; Kelly, *Catholic Immigrant Colonization Projects,* 231.

54. Mahoney to the *Boston Pilot,* Feb. 6, 1884, in Sweetman Catholic Colony, "Letters from the Pastor," 9.

55. *Address of the Minnesota Irish Emigration Convention . . . to the People of Ireland,* Jan. 20, 1869, 1, 2; and *Address of the Irish Immigration Society for the Year 1870,* 1; in the Minnesota Historical Society.

56. Moran, "'In Search of the Promised Land'"; Shannon, "Bishop Ireland's Connemara Experiment," 212, 213 (quotations); Sweetman, Sweetman Catholic Colony, "Letters from the Pastor," Apr. 9, 1911, 65; Connelly, *Forgetting Ireland.*

57. Hughes quoted in Browne, "Archbishop Hughes," 271.

58. Scally, *End of Hidden Ireland,* 134.

59. Emmons, *Butte Irish,* 3–19; Gjerde, *Minds of the West,* 89–100; idem, "New Growth"; idem, "Following the Chain."

60. Miller, *Emigrants and Exiles;* Miller et al., *Irish Immigrants;* Schrier, *Ireland and the American Emigration;* Fitzpatrick, *Oceans of Consolation;* idem, "'That beloved country'"; Kamphoefner et al. (eds.), *News;* Gerber, "Immigrant Letter"; Solnit, *Book of Migrations,* 132.

61. Scally, *End of Hidden Ireland,* 134; Brosnan to Mother, Nov. 20, 1917; to Father, Feb. 18, 1917; to Father, Sept. 1, 1918; to Mother, April 11, 1917; to Mother, n.d., 1917, Brosnan Papers.

62. The song about paving the streets with Irish bones comes from Kara Kelly (personal communication, 1987), whose Irish-born grandmother remembered hearing it.

63. Emmons, *Butte Irish,* 328, 360, The patriotic book was *Irish Leaders of 1916.*

64. Hannan Diary, Feb. 12, Feb. 14, Feb. 19, and June 6, 1922.

65. Ibid., Feb. 14 and Mar. 31, 1922.

66. Ibid., June 6, 1922.

67. Hannan, "Father English," 6–7.

68. Hannan Diary, Mar. 23, Oct. 17 (quotation), Feb. 24, Mar. 22, and Feb. 25, 1922.

69. Jeremiah Cahill to Brother Patrick, June 23, 1889; O'Daly, "Life History," [7]; Wolfe to Cousin Maurice, Oct. 14, 1867, Apr. 12, 1868, and Mar. 6, 1879; Hurley from Cedar Pass, Nevada, to Parents, Aug. 26, 1871; all in Miller Collection (original spelling and capitalization).

70. Maurice Wolfe to Uncle, Sept. 25, 1863; Ed Hanlon, Nebraska City to bro. Bernard, Co. Down, Mar. 4, 1871; Hanlon, to father, Jan 8, 1860; Lalor to bro. Richard, Feb. 10, 1868; all in Miller Collection (original spelling and capitalization).

71. J. F. Costello to family, Jan. 11, 1883, Miller Collection (original spelling, capitalization, and punctuation); Behan, *Hostage,* 143.

72. Costello to family, Jan. 11, 1883.

73. Hurley to Mother, Jan. 13, 1891, and Dec. 3, 1897, Miller Collection; Ward, *Holding Up the Hills,* 80–81; Miller, *Emigrants and Exiles,* 353–58; Schrier, *Ireland and the American Emigration,* 111–16; Edward Hanlon, Nebraska City, to brother, Dec. 11 and 26, 1870, Mar. 4, 1871 (my emphasis; original spelling); Hurley to Mother, Dec. 3, 1897; all in Miller Collection.

74. Lewis Doyle to John Doyle, Jan. 23, 1873, Aug. 17, 1873, July 15, 1877, Jan. 27, 1880, Miller Collection (original spelling and capitalization).

75. Michael Callahan to brother, Sept. 20, 1852; Maurice Wolfe, Ft. Steele, Wyoming Territory, to brother Batt, Dec. 5, 1868; Maurice Wolfe, Ft. Russell, Wyoming Territory, to uncle Maurice Woulfe, Mar. 6, 1870; all in Miller Collection (original spelling and capitalization).

76. Maurice Wolfe, Washington, D.C., to uncle Michael, Limerick, Nov. 9, 1874, Miller Collection (original spelling, capitalization, and punctuation).

77. See, for example, Thomas Higgins, Mosinee, Wisconsin, to Nuala O'Malley, care of Celia Keefe, Co. Longford, May 16, 1916, Miller Collection.

CHAPTER 8. THE WORLDS THE IRISH MADE

1. U.S. Bureau of the Census, *Seventh Census: 1850,* 15.

2. Turner, "Significance of the Frontier," 54, 55; Gjerde, *Minds of the West,* 25–49 (quotation on 27). See also Jacobson, *Whiteness,* 215–22; and Baldwin, "Centre of the Republic," 412, 418.

3. Yeats, "Introduction," in *Fairy and Folk Tales,* 6.

4. For *muintir* and *monasterium,* see Evans, *Personality of Ireland,* 81.

5. Gjerde, *Minds of the West,* 7.

6. Ibid., 7, 226.

7. Ibid., 7 (my emphasis).

8. Ibid., 102, 8; Wingerd, *Claiming the City.*

9. Gjerde, *Minds of the West,* 8 (quotations; my emphasis), 40. See also Luebke (ed.), *European Immigrants;* Van Nuys, *Americanizing the West;* Hine, *Community;* Morris, "Articulation of Two Worlds"; Luebke, "Ethnic Group Settlement"; Conzen, "Historical Approaches"; idem, "Mainstreams"; Gerstle, "Liberty"; Gjerde, "New Growth"; and Kazal, "Revisiting Assimilation."

10. Porter, *Vertical Mosaic,* 61–73 (quotations); Klein, *Frontiers,* 208.

11. Gjerde, *Minds of the West,* 7; Rolle, *Immigrant Upraised.* The "immigrant upraised" thesis is most closely associated with James Walsh, the late Tim Sarbaugh, and Robert Burchell. See Walsh, "Irish in the New America"; Sarbaugh, "Ireland of the West"; idem, "Exiles of Confidence"; and Burchell, *San Francisco Irish.* See also Emmons, "Faction Fights."

12. Gjerde, *Minds of the West,* 7–8.

13. On transplanting, see Bodnar, *Transplanted;* and Tilly, "Transplanted Networks."

14. Gjerde, *Minds of the West,* 7–8; Gitlin, "On the Boundaries of Empire," 86 ("alternate frontier").

15. White, *"It's Your Misfortune,"* 303; Nugent, "Frontiers and Empires"; see also Courtwright, *Violent Land;* and Brinley, *Migration,* table 82, 270. Thirty-nine percent of the children on the Orphan Trains were girls. O'Connor, *Orphan Trains,* 216.

16. White, *"It's Your Misfortune,"* 303.

17. Scally, *End of Hidden Ireland,* 125–27; Miller, *Emigrants and Exiles,* 507.

18. Diner, *Erin's Daughters;* Nolan, *Ourselves Alone;* Miller, "For 'Love and Liberty.'"

19. Lynch-Brennan, "Ubiquitous Bridget," 332; Driscoll, *Country Jake,* 91; Manahan, *Trials,* 11–12, 23; Ward, *Holding Up the Hills,* 120–21, 130; Francis Foley, Interview, July 14, 1978, Oral History Project, State Historical Society of Iowa.

20. Lynch-Brennan, "Ubiquitous Bridget," 346 (my emphasis); Gjerde, *Minds of the West,* 228–29. See also Fitzgerald, *Habits of Compassion;* Diner, *Erin's Daughters,* 33–36, 39–45, 72–76, 120–26; Golab, *Immigrant Destinations,* 148–53; Nolan, *Ourselves Alone;* idem, "Education"; Peterson, "Religious Communities"; Coburn and Smith, "'Pray for Your Wanderers'"; idem, *Spirited Lives,* esp. 97–128; Wiemers, "Rural Irish Women"; Cummings, "'Not the New Woman?'"; McClymer, "Gender"; Hotten-Somers, "Relinquishing and Reclaiming Independence"; *Women and Irish Migration;* and Ronan, *Frontier Woman.*

21. Meagher, *Inventing Irish America;* Bayor and Meagher (eds.), *New York Irish;* Kelly, *Shamrock and the Lily;* Tierney, *But of Course They Were Irish,* 204–206.

22. Ward, *All Over God's Irish Heaven,* 168, 175; Scally, *End of Hidden Ireland,* 159. The cooperative movement was led by Horace Plunkett, an Anglo-Irishman who had lived for a time on his Wyoming ranch. See Plunkett, *Ireland in the New Century;* Woods, *British Gentlemen;* and West, *Horace Plunkett.*

23. Ward, *Holding Up the Hills,* 79, 158.

24. Tierney, *But of Course They Were Irish;* McLysaght, *Irish Families.*

25. Ward, *Holding Up the Hills,* 22, 151.

26. Ibid., 33 (see also 84, 151); O'Sullivan, *Twenty Years A-Growing,* 239–40. See also Gjerde, *From Peasants to Farmers,* 1–11.

27. Ward, *Holding Up the Hills,* 158.

28. Ibid., 139, 74 (see also 151–54); Scally, *End of Hidden Ireland,* 35; Finn, *Tracing the Veins,* 147–76.

29. Ward, *Holding Up the Hills,* 162; idem, *God in an Irish Kitchen,* 140.

30. Ward, *Holding Up the Hills,* 72, 151.

31. Ibid., 188–89, 107 (see also 52, 121, 139, 146–47). See also Bellah, "Religion and the Shape of National Culture."

32. Ward, *Holding Up the Hills,* 11, 16, 75; Evans, *Personality of Ireland,* 57 (quotation), 58–62, 96, 109; Scally, *End of Hidden Ireland,* 33–35.

33. Ward, *Holding Up the Hills,* 42, 43, 82, 140.

34. Ibid., 39, 112.

35. Ward, *Holding Up the Hills,* 151, 74, 63, 18–19, 147, 82; Gweedore man quoted in Miller, *Emigrants and Exiles,* 365.

36. Paul Diary, Nov. 11, 1908; vol. 1 (original spelling). See also Apr. 8, 1911, vol. 3.

37. Ibid., vol. 2, May 4 and 5, Oct. 14, 1910; vol. 3, Mar. 17, 1911; vol. 1, Mar. 22 and 25, 1909; vol. 3, Mar. 2, 1911; vol. 1, Feb. 3, 1908 (original spelling); Arensberg and Kimball, *Family and Community,* 285 (*Old Moore's;* see also 3–30, 46–60, 298); Mooney, "Holiday Customs."

38. Mullen to John J. Mullen, June 8, 1926, Mullen Papers.

39. Driscoll, *Country Jake,* 233, 115, 69.

40. Ibid., 82, 186; idem, *Kansas Irish;* see also Jockers, "Window Facing West."

41. Bríc (Brick), "Memoirs," 1, 14, 18–23. See also Miller, "From the Gaeltacht."

42. Bríc (Brick), "Memoirs," 35–36.

43. Ibid., 43–44, 37–38.

44. Ibid., 44.

45. *Atlas of Clay and Union Counties, South Dakota;* Bríc (Brick), "Memoirs," 39–44.

46. Hand, "Nicknames"; WPA, *Copper Camp; Butte Independent,* Feb. 5, 1910, June 6, 1914; Ward, *Holding Up the Hills,* 72; 22nd Annual Picnic and Athletic Games of Co. A. Irish Volunteers, 9/20/14, Irish Collection, Butte/Silver Bow Archives.

47. Scally, *End of Hidden Ireland,* 159; Hoy, *Good Hearts*; Fitzgerald, *Habits of Compassion;* Ward, *Holding Up the Hills,* 139, 152; Emmons, *Butte Irish;* Kevin Shannon, interview in *Sceal ar Butte, Montana.*

48. Ward, *Holding Up the Hills,* 84; Yorke quoted in *All Ireland,* May 1, 1902; Denis Hurley to his brother John, Dec. 11, 1913; Mink, *Old Labor,* 186; Scally, *End of Hidden Ireland,* 159.

49. MacAirt, *Counsels of Cormac,* viii, 3, 4, 8, 13–15, 24, 31; Ward, *Holding Up the Hills,* 7, 5, 131.

50. Wingerd, *Claiming the City,* 68, 81.

51. Patrick Browne to parents, Aug. 16, 1887, Miller Collection (original punctuation); Levine, *Irish and Irish Politicians;* Erie, *Rainbow's End;* Buenker, *Urban Liberalism;* McCaffrey, *Textures,* 89–124; idem, "Irish-American Politics"; Doyle, "Catholicism, Politics and Irish America"; O'Connor, *Last Hurrah;* Curley, *I'd Do It Again;* Califano, "Who's a Catholic to Vote For?" 11 (quotation).

52. Manahan, *Trials,* 61, 95, 97, 99, 111, 113; Chambers, "Social Welfare Policies"; for San Francisco, see, among many sources, Roney, *Irish Rebel,* 94–95, 173–74, 198–99, 302–303, 419–20; Issel and Cherny, *San Francisco;* Bullough, "Charles Buckley"; Kazin, *Barons of Labor;* Keating, *Gentleman from Colorado;* Kleppner, "Voters and Parties." In 1960 in Minnesota's rural Irish neighborhoods, Kennedy defeated Nixon in the township of Derrynane by a count of 285–45; in Graceville, 307–109; in Clontarf, 138–11; in Dublin, 113–21; in Kildare, 116–17; and in Tara, 94–24. Hallberg (ed.), *Legislative Manual;* Schmahl (comp.), *Legislative Manual;* Donovan (comp.), *Legislative Manual.*

53. Bocock, "Irish Conquest"; Kelley, *Transatlantic Persuasion,* 48 (quotation); Walsh, "Introduction," [3]. See also Doyle, "Irish as Urban Pioneers"; and Erie, *Rainbow's End.*

54. Quoted in Burchell, *San Francisco Irish,* 127–28.

55. Issel and Cherney, *San Francisco,* 131; see also Bullough, "Christopher Buckley."

56. Issel and Cherney, *San Francisco,* 140, 148; Bocock, "Irish Conquest." See also Steffens, *Shame of the Cities;* Williams, *Democratic Party,* 5; Erie, *Rainbow's End;* idem, "Politics"; Levine, *Irish and Irish Politicians;* Issel, "Class and Ethnic Conflict"; and Tygiel, "Where Unionism Holds Undisputed Sway."

57. Issel and Cherny, *San Francisco,* 140–52, 193–94; Bean, *Boss Ruef's San Francisco;* Bullough, *Blind Boss;* Decker, *Fortunes and Failures;* Walsh (ed.), *San Francisco Irish;* and Williams, *Democratic Party.*

58. *In Memoriam, James Phelan.* See also James D. Phelan to Mary Phelan, Sept. 18, 1906; and Phelan to Matthew Carroll, Feb. 29, 1908, Phelan Papers, Box 1. For Phelan's affiliations with the Audubon Society, see Charles Bryant to Phelan, Nov. 17, 1927; for opera, see Phelan to "My dear Firenze, n.d. 189[9]"; for the Bohemian Club, see Phelan to Hibernian Social and

Literary Society, Apr. 10, 1907; for the McKinley and Serra organizations, see Phelan to James McDonald, Sept. 5, 1906, and to Edgar Matthews, Nov. 14, 1906; for the Hibernian Social and Literary Society, see Phelan to the Society, Nov. 12, 1906; all in Box 1, Phelan Papers; for the anti–capital punishment campaign, see Annie Bear to Phelan, Sept. 16, 1912, Box 12, Phelan Papers; for the San Francisco Art Club and the Native Sons of the Golden West, see Kazin, *Barons of Labor*, 40; and Hennings, "James D. Phelan" (Noel Sullivan, Phelan's nephew, was equally refined: see his Correspondence and Papers); on Yorke, see Phelan to Lincoln Steffens, Dec. 16, 1907, Box 1, Phelan Papers.

59. Address of Phelan at Complimentary Banquet, Dec. 12, 1901, in Phelan Magazine Collection, vol. 6, no. 6; see also Phelan to Dr. C. M. Lathrop, June 5, 1908, Box 1, Phelan Papers; Bohemian Club description quoted in Bean, *Boss Ruef's San Francisco*, 262; Phelan to the National Bank of Commerce, Apr. 25 and May 2, 1907; Hammond to Phelan, Mar. 24, 1909, Sept. 13, 1915; both in Box 58, Phelan Papers; on Hammond's career, see his *Autobiography;* on the National Civic Federation, see Montgomery, *Fall of the House of Labor*, 259–306.

60. Issel and Cherny, *San Francisco*, 140–52 (quotation on 149); Walsh, "Peter Yorke and Progressivism"; idem, "Father Peter Yorke"; idem, "Peter C. Yorke." See also Riordan, "Garret McEnerney."

61. Issel and Cherny, *San Francisco*, 80 (quotation), 140–61; Atherton to Phelan, June 17, 1914; see also Atherton's letter to Phelan, Oct. 18 [1907], Box 26, Phelan Papers.

62. Atherton, *Perch of the Devil*, 57; Starr, "Gertrude Atherton, Daughter of the Elite," chapter 11 of *Americans and the California Dream*, 345–64.

63. Emmons, *Butte Irish*, 97–103.

64. Ibid.

65. Quoted in ibid., 140–41.

66. Ibid., 96, 107, 140, 233, 240–44, 257, 269, 319–25, 384–85, 399, 405.

67. Ibid., 19–21, 37, 145–47, 191 ("boss Irishman"), 195 (see also 99–102, 113–15).

68. Ibid., 107–108, 140–46, 229–33, 241–42, 268–69; WPA, *Copper Camp*, 230–33.

69. Emmons, *Butte Irish*, 191 ("noblest Roman"); Bodnar, *Workers' World*, 4–9, 65, 165–85; for spies and the threat to close the mines, see Daly to M. J. Donahoe, Feb. 13, 1890; C. M. Weber to Donahoe, Aug. 19, 1896; Daly to Donahoe, Dec. 22, 1898, Anaconda Company Records, Boxes 1, 3, and 9.

70. WPA, *Copper Camp*, 8–9, 124, 291, 294. The inscription on the statue is no longer legible. See the photograph in James, *Butte's Memory Book*, 58.

71. WPA, *Copper Camp*, 204 (quotation); on Kiely, see also Green, *Wobblies*, 192–95.

72. Scally, *End of Hidden Ireland*, 128; Miller, *Emigrants and Exiles;* Lee, *Modernization;* Evans, *Personality of Ireland;* Taylor, *Occasions of Faith.*

73. Miller, *Emigrants and Exiles*, 133, 6, 488; Scally, *End of Hidden Ireland*, 160; Quigley, *Irish Race*, iii.

74. O'Connell to David Moriarty, May 2, 1854, Marysville.2; Brown, *Irish-American Nationalism;* Funchion (ed.), *Irish-American Voluntary Organizations,* See also O'Dea, *History of the Ancient Order of Hibernians.*

75. Thomas J. Kelly to mother, Mar. 24, 1876, Miller Collection; Roney, *Irish Rebel*, 202–203 (see also 183–84).

76. Carnes, *Secret Ritual;* Dumenil, *Freemasonry.* See also Bederman, *Manliness and Civilization;* Emmons, *Butte Irish,* 94–132; *Celtic Union,* Aug. 20–Sept. 10, 1898; and *All Ireland,* May 1–May 24, 1902.

77. Woodbury, *Tourist Guide to Denver; Daily Miners' Register,* pamphlet file, Colorado Historical Society; *Daily Central City Register,* Jan. 21, 1871, Sept. 12, 1871; *Rocky Mountain News,* Apr. 25, May 8 and 29, and June 21, 1866; July 7, 1872; Feb. 13 and 15, 1876; Dec. 10, 1879; Jan. 9, Apr. 29, and Oct. 7, 1880; Apr. 1 and 13, Oct. 24 and 29, and Nov. 23 and 28, 1881; Jan. 12, 23, and 30, 1882; Jan. 14, Feb. 4, 10, and 27, Apr. 9, May 10, and July 27, 1884; Mar. 6 and 12, Oct. 31, and Dec. 15, 1885; Mar. 18, 1892; June 24, 1906; Apr. 12, 1920; *Denver Times,* Jan. 10 and 17, 1874; Mar. 15–18, 1899; Mar. 17 and May 21, 24, and 25, 1900; Oct. 27, 1901; May 13, June 12, July 24, Aug. 8, and Nov. 24, 1902; June 12, 1903; Oct. 30, 1919; *Denver Tribune-Republican,* Feb. 8, 1886; *Rocky Mountain Herald,* Oct. 25, 1873; *Denver Post,* Aug. 15, 1910; Jan. 8 and July 16, 1913. See also Denver city directories from 1902 to 1915, which list the various Irish organizations.

78. Ancient Order of Hibernians of Portland, Oregon Historical Society; on the Savings and Commercial Bank, see Andrew Smith to Edward Boyce, Feb. 27, 1920, Boyce Papers; see also F. Leo Smith's account of why his Irish family came to Portland: "Smith Family History, 1762–1987"; Irish American Club of St. Paul, *Constitution, By-Laws, House Rules,* 5–6; Diaries of M. J. Boyle, entries of Jan. 3 and Aug. 13, 1876, Feb. 25 and Mar. 7, 1877, Feb. 7, Mar. 3, and Nov. 7, 1878, Dec. 18, 1879, Feb. 26, 1880, and June 7, 1883.

79. The Irish marched on St. Patrick's Day in Weaverville, California; see Fr. Pat O'Reilly to Bishop O'Connell, Mar. 18, 1862, reprinted in AHC, *Annals, 1862,* 55; O'Connell to Fr. Thomas Bennett, Jan. 9, 1863, Marysville.22, CSN 528; for the California, Kansas, and Washington AOH divisions, see a list in the "Addendum," Keokuk County, Iowa, AOH, June 14, 1909; AOH, "Minnesota Irish"; *Irish Standard* (Minneapolis), Jan. 20 and Sept. 28, 1912; Warner, *History of Dakota Co., Nebraska,* 80 (quotations). See also the "Roll Book of the Ancient Order of Hibernians," Lincoln, Nebraska, 1885–89.

80. Minute Books of the Kinross AOH, Dec. 14, 1889, Mar. 6, 1892, July 7, 1895, Feb. 7, 1897, Apr. 24, Sept. 3, and Dec. 10, 1899, Oct. 5, 1902, May 6, 1906, and Dec. 14, 1910.

81. Ibid., Aug. 14, 1888, Feb. 16, 1889, Oct. 5, 1902, Feb. 1, 1903, Apr. 5, 1903, May 1, 1898, June 5, 1898, June 1, 1902, and July 6, 1906; "Freedom Picnic," in Dunne, *Mr. Dooley in the Hearts of His Countrymen,* 92.

82. Digger O'Dell was the name given to the Irish undertaker in the 1950s radio program *The Dennis Day Show;* Mooney, "Funeral Customs," 290; O'Flaherty, *Cliffmen,* 126–27; Emmons, *Butte Irish,* 149; on wakes, see Ward, *Holding Up the Hills,* 8, 42, 80; Cross, *Tailor and Ansty,* 173–76.

83. For saloons, see West, *Saloon;* Burke, *Rhymes of the Mines,* 65–75.

84. Dunne, *Mr. Dooley in Peace and War,* ix–x.

85. Ibid.; the *Irish Standard* claimed that it "circulated in Minnesota, Wisconsin, Michigan, Iowa, North Dakota, South Dakota, Montana, Oregon, and Washington," May 30, 1914; *Western Times* (masthead); *Butte Independent,* 1910–37 (Pearse's remark from Oct. 8, 1910); *Rocky Mountain Celt* from *Rocky Mountain News,* Apr. 30, 1887.

86. *Gaelic American,* Feb. 6, 1904.

87. *All Ireland,* official paper of the Irish Fair, May 1, 1902.

88. Handlin, *Uprooted,* 165, 83–88, 105.

89. Father Sarsfield O'Sullivan, interview, Nov. 19, 1984.

CHAPTER 9. AN ALTERNATE FRONTIER

1. Huntington quoted in Messbarger, *Fiction,* 41–45; on Huntington's conversion, see Kenrick and Frenaye, *Kenrick-Frenaye Correspondence,* 485; Frederick, *Damnation of Theron Ware;* Drewniany, "Not Marionettes." See also Lears, *No Place of Grace,* 196–97; and Lasch, *True and Only Heaven.*

2. Chesterton quoted in Dionne, "We're All Liberals Now"; Weber, *Protestant Ethic.* See also Kleppner, *Cross of Culture;* Jensen, *Winning of the Midwest;* Greeley, *Catholic Imagination;* and Tracy, *Analogical Imagination.*

3. Waugh quoted in Shannon, "Irish Catholic Immigration," 204–205 (my emphasis); on the exile motif as a hegemonic device, see Miller, "Class, Culture." See also Slotkin, *Fatal Environment,* 13–226; and Lawner, "Introduction," 42–45, 49–55.

4. Shannon, "Irish Catholic Immigration," 205.

5. For the Irish as pioneers, see the *Butte Independent,* Aug. 13, 1910; the Butte story is from Mrs. John C. Adams, "In Honor of Three Men," pamphlet, n.d., 1914, Box 1, McGlynn Collection. The APA denied that Catholics were western pioneers. See Kinzer, *Episode in Anti-Catholicism.* The KKK made the same point. George Estes, Oregon KKK to Empire Publishing Co., Feb. 7, 1923, Estes Papers. But see Hara, *Pioneer Catholic History.*

6. Mark Leone quoted in Moore, *Religious Outsiders,* 42 ("culture of the Mormons"); Stegner, *Mormon Country,* 62; Ibsen, *Will the World Break Your Heart?* 8. Ironically, Mormons and Irish Catholics are now counted among the politically orthodox or conservative/reactionary.

7. Montgomery, "Irish Influence," 12; idem, "Irish and the American Labor Movement," 205; Wilentz, "Industrializing America," 586; Montgomery, *Fall of the House of Labor,* 486. Montgomery would not extend the argument as I have. Montgomery to author, Sept. 22, 2009.

8. Stegner, *Where the Bluebird Sings;* Miller, "Assimilation and Alienation," 93–94; Foster, *Pages,* 15–19; Johanningsmeier, *Forging American Communism,* 10–30, 158.

9. Foster, *Pages,* 30–33.

10. Sombart, *Why Is There No Socialism?* See also C. T. Husband's "Introductory Essay" in this edition.

11. On the futile search for revolutionary class consciousness, see Tilly, "Review"; Kraditor, *Radical Persuasion;* Laslett and Lipset (eds.), *Failure of a Dream?;* and Lipset and Marks, *It Didn't Happen Here;* on American exceptionalism, see Voss, *Making of American Exceptionalism;* Wilentz, "Against Exceptionalism"; Salvatore, "Response"; Montgomery, "Why Is There No Socialism?"; Diggins, "Comrades and Citizens"; Oestreicher, "Industrialization"; and idem, "Urban Working-Class Political Behavior."

12. Thompson, *Making of the English Working Class;* Oestreicher, "Industrialization"; idem, "Urban Working-Class Political Behavior"; idem, *Solidarity and Fragmentation.*

13. Thompson, *Making of the English Working Class,* 442–43.

14. Ibid., 436, 442.

15. Hobsbawm, *Workers,* 222 (my emphasis); Synge, *Guide,* 38; Commons quoted in Walkowitz, *Worker City,* 168–69. See also Kelley, *Transatlantic Persuasion,* 214.

16. Driscoll, *Country Jake,* 198.

17. Flynn, *Rebel Girl,* 35; Foster quoted in Zipser, *Working-Class Giant,* 9–10.

18. Geertz, "Religion as a Cultural System," 89; Wordsworth's "after meditation" quoted in Dening, *Death of William Gooch,* 83; Johanningsmeier, *Forging American Communism,* 353.

19. Connolly, "Irish History," in *Words of James Connolly,* 58–88. The seam is a basic theme in Emmons, *Butte Irish.*

20. On Irish nationalism, see O'Farrell, *Ireland's English Question;* Mansergh, *Irish Question;* Kee, *Green Flag;* Feeney, *Sinn Féin;* Rumpf and Hepburn, *Nationalism and Socialism;* Kiberd, *Inventing Ireland;* and Dangerfield, *Damnable Question.*

21. Brown, *Irish-American Nationalism,* 123; for contributions by regions, see *Gaelic American,* Feb. 22, 1882.

22. U.S. Bureau of the Census, *Eleventh Census, 1890,* 600–601; *Irish World,* Sept. 24, 1881, and Feb. 11, 1882.

23. Foner, "Class, Ethnicity, and Radicalism," 176, table on 171; Bagenal, *American Irish,* 174–75.

24. On the Wolfe Tone Guards, see Buchanan, *Story of a Labor Agitator,* 33; Kee, *Green Flag,* 201–10; Emmons, *Butte Irish; Irish World,* Feb. 6, 1879. See also Dorrity, "'Monkeys in a Menagerie.'"

25. Quoted in Emmons, *Butte Irish,* 204, 207, 372.

26. Beara quoted in Brown, *Irish-American Nationalism,* 64. See also Rodechko, "Patrick Ford."

27. O'Neill, "Preface" to "O'Neill's Northern Nebraska," 3–4.

28. Brown, *Irish-American Nationalism,* 147; Denis Hurley, Carson City, Nevada, to mother, Oct. 15, 1894; Hurley to parents, Aug. 22, 1879, Miller Collection; Salvatore, *Eugene V. Debs,* 126–136.

29. RELA, Membership and Dues Ledger, 1902–25, Irish Collection.

30. U.S. Commission on Industrial Relations, *Mining Conditions,* 3928; Emmons, *Butte Irish,* 52, 117–18.

31. Connolly quoted in Rumpf and Hepburn, *Nationalism and Socialism,* 12; Emmons, *Butte Irish,* 52, 349–50; on Marx, see Mansergh, *Irish Question,* 103–32.

32. Labor Day letter in *Miners Magazine,* Sept. 6, 1897; WFM, 11th Annual Convention, Denver, May 26, 1903, 17–18, WFM Papers.

33. Boyce speech of May 26, 1902, reprinted in WFM, *Proceedings, 1910,* 13, WFM Papers.

34. Boyce speech to WFM, Sept. 6, 1897, in Boyce Papers. Boyce speech on Miners' Union Day, June 15, 1899, in *Miners Magazine* (Butte), Mar. 1900, vol. 1, no. 1; see also speech to WFM, 10th Annual Convention, Denver, May 26, 1902; *Miners Magazine* (by that time published in Denver), June 1901, vol. 2, no. 4, and Apr. and May 1900.

35. Boyce Notebooks, July 20, 1886; Emmons, *Butte Irish,* 234 (quotation).

36. Brown, *Irish-American Nationalism;* Ward, *Ireland and Anglo-American Relations;* Tansill, *America and the Fight for Irish Freedom;* Miller, *Emigrants and Exiles,* particularly 277–79, 328–46, 440–47, 532–56. See also Emmons, *Butte Irish,* esp. 292–339, 350–51.

37. For the ACM, see Malone, *Battle for Butte;* Marcosson, *Anaconda;* for the BMU, see Emmons, *Butte Irish,* 186–87, 200–203, 230–36.

38. Lewis, *Silver Kings;* Walsh, *San Francisco Irish;* Kazin, *Barons of Labor.*

39. Emmons, *Butte Irish,* 20–21, 52–53, 96–101, 140–46, 190–94.

40. Ibid., 194 ("appreciation"), 264 ("nail the red flag"); 310 (dropping dynamite). Kenny, *American Irish,* 190, writes that Haywood was Irish, but he was not. Haywood, *Bill Haywood's Book,* 7, 14.

41. Emmons, *Butte Irish,* 282 (quotation), 357–83.

42. Bodnar, *Workers' World.*

43. Connolly quoted in Rumpf and Hepburn, *Nationalism and Socialism,* 19.

44. Boyce Diary and Notebooks, 1885–1941, Boyce Papers; unidentified newspaper clipping in Scrapbooks, Box 1 and scrapbook 3, Kenehan Papers; Haywood, *Autobiography,* 91. See also Boyce, "WFM Travels, 1896–97"; Diary, May 24 and June 7, and 11, 1897, Nov. 13, 1900, Boyce Papers; *Miners Magazine,* Dec. 1902.

45. MacAirt, *Counsels of Cormac,* 3, 8–9, 24–25, 47, 29.

46. Ó Dubhda, *Duanaire Duibhneach,* 132–33. See also Robert Murphy to brother Davy in Belfast, Nov. 29, 1875, Dec. 12, 1878, Oct. 16, 1879; Denis Hurley to mother, July 3, 1896, and Dec. 1, 1896; Hurley to brother Tim, Feb. 11, 1897; all in Miller Collection.

47. Scally, *End of Hidden Ireland,* 37; Behan, *Hostage,* 143.

48. Thompson, *Making of the English Working Class,* 436, 442; Gjerde, *Minds of the West,* 19. See also Evans, *Personality of Ireland,* 81.

49. See Emmons, *Butte Irish,* 255–92.

50. George, *Progress and Poverty.* The percentage of tenantry by state in 1910 and 1925 was Minnesota, 21, 27; Iowa, 38, 45; North Dakota, 14, 34; South Dakota, 25, 42; Nebraska, 38, 46; Kansas, 37, 42; Montana, 9, 22; Wyoming, 8, 18; Idaho, 10, 24; Colorado, 18, 31; New Mexico, 5, 17; Arizona, 9, 22; Utah, 8, 11; Nevada, 12, 8. In neighboring Arkansas, Louisiana, Oklahoma, and Texas the percentages were 50, 57; 55, 60; 55, 59; and 52, 60, respectively; statistics from *Producers' News* (Plentywood, Montana), Nov. 23, 1928. See also Gates, *Landlords and Tenants;* Bogue, *From Prairie to Cornbelt,* 56–66, 286–87; Ostler, *Prairie Populism,* 13; *Irish Nation,* July 8, 1882; and *Irish World,* Jan. 3, 1880.

51. George, *Land Question* (originally *The Irish Land Question*), 10; idem, "Condition of Labor"; idem, *Progress and Poverty,* 127 ("communal ownership"), 306, 346 ("taking by the community"); single tax on 6–11, 282–96; for Irish influence on George, see Barker, *Henry George,* 126 (see also 431–38). See also Thomas, *Alternative America,* 118–24, 198–200.

52. George, *Progress and Poverty,* 123–28.

53. Ibid., 125, 57. See also Davitt, *Jottings,* 43–44, 168–72; and Montgomery, "Irish and the American Labor Movement," 216–17.

54. George, *Land Question,* 21; Thomas, *Alternative America,* 178; Rodgers, *Atlantic Crossings,* 70; Lasch, *True and Only Heaven,* 64–72; Foner, "Class, Ethnicity, and Radicalism," 184–99. See also Roney, *Irish Rebel,* 298.

55. Thomas, *Alternative America,* 176–83; George, *Land Question,* 62, 61, 60, 8–9, 31–34, 54; Brown, *Irish-American Nationalism,* facing 117.

56. George, *Land Question,* 21–22; O'Flaherty, *Cliffmen,* 118; AE quoted in O'Farrell, *Ireland's English Question,* 209. See also Davitt, *Fall of Feudalism;* and Scally, *End of Hidden Ireland,* 95.

57. Ward, *Holding Up the Hills,* 107 and 62 (George quotations), 202 (my emphasis).

58. *Boston Pilot,* July 1, 1882; George, *Land Question,* 107, 62, preface, 6.

59. Montgomery, "Irish and the American Labor Movement," 216; *Irish World,* July 8, 1882.

60. Powderly, *Thirty Years of Labor,* 175.

61. Ford quoted in Bagenal, *American Irish,* 203–204 (my emphasis). See also Palmer, *Irish Land League Crisis,* 125; Mansergh, *Irish Question,* 122–29, 142–44, 243–56; Miller, *Emigrants and Exiles,* 388–400, 43–45, 464–65; and Donnelly, "Land Question."

62. Montgomery, "Irish and the American Labor Movement," 216.

63. Saxton, *Indispensable Enemy* (my emphasis); Hobsbawm, *Workers,* 234 (my emphasis).

64. Barker, *Henry George,* 122–23.

65. Archdeacon to the author, Sept. 25, 2006.

66. James McFadden, Mapleton, Iowa, to Michael McFadden, Donegal, Jan. 30, 1892, and Oct. 17, 1897, Miller Collection (original spelling). See also Gutman, "Work, Culture, and Society"; Robertson, *Capital, Labor, and State;* Powderly, *Thirty Years of Labor,* 210; for Irish against Irish, see Ryan, *On the Drumhead;* and idem, *Dangerous Thoughts.*

67. Dubofsky, *We Shall Be All.*

68. F. W. Bradley to N. H. Harris, Feb. 13, 1894, and Jan. 8, 1895, Bunker Hill and Sullivan Mining Company Papers; Peck, *Reinventing Free Labor;* idem, "Divided Loyalties"; idem, "Mobilizing Community"; Powderly, *Thirty Years of Labor,* 210. See also Pinkerton, *His Personal Record,* 12, 24; Foster, *Pages,* 40; Boyce to James McGrade, May 3, 1901; and Boyce Diary, March 12 and 13, 1901, Boyce Papers.

69. Montgomery, *Fall of the House of Labor,* 242–44; labor leader's remarks in a letter to Phelan, 1915 [no specific date], Box 67, Phelan Papers. See also Donnelly, undated issue of the *Anti-Monopolist,* Donnelliana MSS, vol. 134, Donnelly Papers.

70. Ford quoted in *Irish World,* May 12, 1894; Powderly quoted in Montgomery, "Irish and the American Labor Movement," 210–11; Keating, *Gentleman from Colorado,* 59–72; Flynn, *Rebel Girl,* 133–34; Boyce quoted in *Miners Magazine,* Apr. 1900.

71. "Driving out the Dagoes," typescript of newspaper story, 1894 (quotation); F. W. Bradley to N. H. Harris, Feb. 13, 1894, and Jan. 8, 1895, Bunker Hill and Sullivan Mining Company Records and Papers. See also Aiken, "'It May Be Too Soon to Crow.'"

72. *Irish World,* May 12, 1894; W. S. Haskins to Bradley, Nov. 28, 1894 ("ought to be made a reservation"); Charles G. Griffith of United Smelting and Refining Co., Helena, to Bradley, Dec. 3, 1894 (my emphasis); Bradley to William J. McConnell, Dec. 17, 1894.

73. Frank Burbridge to Bradley, Apr. 8, 1895.

74. Bradley to Harris, Mar. 8 and Jan. 22, 1895.

75. Miller, *Emigrants and Exiles,* 498; Phelan, *Travel and Comment,* 132.

76. Quoted in Emmons, *Butte Irish,* 145.

77. Barrett, "'Americanization from the Bottom Up.'"

78. *Butte Bystander,* June 25, 1895.

79. Jacobson, *Whiteness,* 204–205.

80. Ibid., 159. See also Meagher, *Columbia Guide,* 214–33, 272; and Cross, *History of the Labor Movement,* 88–129.

81. Jacobson, *Barbarian Virtues,* 76, 78, 79; idem, *Whiteness,* 5, 159.

82. Saxton, *Indispensable Enemy,* 29.

83. Ira Cross, "Editor's Introduction," in Roney, *Irish Rebel,* vii.

84. *Irish World,* Aug. 23, 1879; Kearney illustration in *Irish World,* Sept. 13, 1879; see also May 13, 1882.

85. On Joplin area miners, see Foster, *Pages,* 40; Haywood, *Bill Haywood's Book,* 91; George quoted in Jacobson, *Barbarian Virtues,* 76; on slavery in the western territories, see Rawley, *Race and Politics;* and Berwanger, *Frontier against Slavery.*

86. Hogan quoted in Flaherty, "Boycott," 38, 44; Brundage, *Making of Western Labor Radicalism,* 35; Saxton, *Indispensable Enemy,* 120–26.

87. Jacobson, *Whiteness,* 159; Cornford, "To Save the Republic," 295, 297.

88. Buchanan, *Story of a Labor Agitator;* Buchanan quoted in Brundage, *Making of Western Labor Radicalism,* 39; and Saxton, *Rise and Fall of the White Republic,* 299.

89. U.S. Bureau of the *Census, Eleventh Census: 1890, Foreign Born,* Sweetwater Co., Wyoming, 682; James McFadden to Michael McFadden, Jan. 30, 1892, Miller Collection (original spelling and capitalization). In 1882 there was a Land League branch in Rock Springs. *Irish World,* Jan. 21, 1882.

90. Bryce, *American Commonwealth,* 2:879.

91. Limerick, *Legacy of Conquest,* 27.

92. Ibid., 27. See also Saxton, *Rise and Fall of the White Republic,* 303.

93. Thompson, *Making of the English Working Class,* 436, 442; Hobsbawm, *Workers,* 47, 51–52, 60–65, 315.

94. Pope Leo XIII, *Rerum Novarum,* 79 ("covetous greed"), 78 ("special consideration"); Keating, "The Encyclicals of Pope Leo XIII and Pope Pius XI," Address of Edward Keating, Catholic University of America, May 16, 1932, Keating Papers. See also Suggs, "Religion and Labor."

95. Keating, "Remarks," Mar. 28, 1943, Keating Papers; idem, *Gentleman from Colorado;* idem, *Story of "Labor."*

96. Ryan, "Introduction," xi, xiii; Pope Leo XIII, *Rerum Novarum,* 83, 88; Manning, "Review," 170; Browne, *Catholic Church,* 114.

97. Ryan, "Introduction," xvii; Pope Leo XIII, *Rerum Novarum,* 57, 79, 83–84 (quotation), 88; Broderick, *Right Reverend New Dealer;* Ryan, *Social Doctrine,* 8–9. Ryan's other books include *The Catholic Church and the Citizen* and *Distributive Justice.* See also Harrington, *Catholicism, Capitalism, or Communism;* and Glickman, *Living Wage,* 62–63, 152–59.

98. Pope Leo XIII, *Rerum Novarum,* 83; Manning quoted in Browne, *Catholic Church,* 340. See also Manning, "Review."

99. Pope Leo XIII, *Rerum Novarum,* 61. See also the 1889 "St. Louis Demands" of the Southern Farmers' Alliance and the Knights of Labor and the 1890 "Ocala Demands" of the National Alliance and Industrial Union in Hicks, *Populist Revolt,* 427–32.

100. Pope Leo XIII, *Rerum Novarum,* 84–85, 92.

101. Ibid., 91; Gibbons, "Memorial," 145–46.

102. Bernanos, *The Diary of a Country Priest,* 54. Weber's book was written in 1904.

103. Foner, "Class, Ethnicity, and Radicalism," 179; on anti-Catholicism as the cause for the neglect of the encyclical, see Rodgers, *Atlantic Crossings,* 524n67; for general discussions, see Abell, *American Catholicism,* 73–80; idem, "Reception"; May, *Protestant Churches,* 153; Browne, *Catholic Church,* 232–33; Karson, "Catholic Church"; Saposs, "Catholic Church and the Labor Movement," 298; George, "Condition of Labor," particularly 70–71, 77–80; Barker, *Henry George,* 465, 486–90. See also *Irish World,* Oct. 22, 1887, scrap in John McGauran Papers; Rodechko, "Patrick Ford," v, 42, 45, 47, 73–79, 83–90; Messbarger, *Fiction,* 73; and Browne, *Catholic Church,* 304–308.

104. Goodwyn, *Democratic Promise,* 309–10; Watson quoted in Woodward, *Tom Watson,* 349–50; for Lease, see McMath, *American Populism,* 136; Manahan, *Trials;* the Rahilly Collection is filled with references and clippings on his Populism.

105. Eastman quoted in the *Irish Standard,* Jan. 10, 1914, copy in McGauran Papers; Sinclair, *Profits of Religion,* 116; Rauschenbusch, *Christianity and the Social Crisis,* 192; Woodward, *Origins of the New South;* idem, *Tom Watson;* Ayers, *Promise of the New South;* Green, *Grass-Roots Socialism;* Lasch, *New Radicalism* ("new radicals"); idem, *True and Only Heaven;* Lears, *No Place of Grace;* and Menand, *Metaphysical Club;* for anti-Catholic intellectuals, see Ross, *Changing America.* See also O'Neill (ed.), *Echoes of Revolt;* Graham (ed.), *"Yours for the Revolution."*

106. Moore, *Religious Outsiders,* 48–71; Abell, *American Catholicism,* esp. 16–17, 65–70, 79–80, 92–97, 288; O'Connell, *John Ireland;* Curran, *Michael Augustine Corrigan;* Fogarty, *Vatican;* Cross, *Emergence of Liberal Catholicism;* Morris, *American Catholic,* 86–112; Hennessey, *American Catholics,* 196–205.

107. Ireland, "Church in America," 240, 234, 239; O'Connell, *John Ireland,* 193. See also idem, "Fifty Years of Catholicity," 251–78. The second of these addresses was included in the promotional literature of the Irish American Colonization Association.

108. Moore, *Religious Outsiders,* 57; Fuchs, *John F. Kennedy,* 107–116; Messbarger, *Fiction,* 1–4; O'Connell, *John Ireland,* 462–64, 468, 477–78; Hennessey, *American Catholics,* 202–203, 215–17; Morris, *American Catholic,* 108–10; Ireland, "Leo XIII"; on Americanism, see also D'Agostino, *Rome in America.*

109. Moore, *Religious Outsiders,* 51.

110. Gjerde, *Minds of the West,* 52, 53, 59.

111. *All Ireland,* May 1, 1902 ("of the People"); Peter Yorke, "The Spirit of the Great West," *Butte Independent,* July 23, 1910 ("there be a class," "notables," "the Irishman"). See also Weber (ed.), *Documents,* 205–206; Walsh and Foley, "Father Peter C. Yorke"; Cronin, *Father Yorke;* and Gribble, "Advocate for Immigrants."

112. Moore, *Religious Outsiders,* 67–68, 49. See also Fuchs, *John F. Kennedy,* 72, 98–108; Messbarger, *Fiction,* 12, 78–79, 88; Maguire, *Irish in America,* 262–63, 273–80; Wangler, "Birth of Americanism"; O'Connell, *John Ireland;* Moynihan, *Life of Archbishop John Ireland;* O'Fahey, "John Ireland's Rhetorical Vision"; *Irish Standard,* July 22, 1916; Farrell, "Archbishop Ireland and Manifest Destiny"; Crislock, *Progressive Era,* 99–100; Ireland, "Personal Liberty and Labor Strikes"; idem, "Labor and Capital"; and O'Neill, "Development of an American Priesthood."

113. Moore, *Religious Outsiders,* 71, 50, 53 (my emphasis).

114. Miller, *Emigrants and Exiles,* 346–53, 492–555; idem, "Class, Culture, and Immigrant Group Identity"; idem, "Assimilation and Alienation," 87–98. Henretta, "Study of Social Mobility," 39, 40. See also Moore, *Religious Outsiders,* 67.

115. Morris, "Articulation," 998, 999, 1004.

116. Ibid., 1003–1004; Scally, *End of Hidden Ireland,* 87 ("silent economy"); Ibsen, *Will the World Break Your Heart?* vii, 8 ("fundamentally at odds"). See also Joyner, *Down by the Riverside.*

117. "Ethno-occupational" from Bodnar, *Workers' World,* 63.

EPILOGUE

1. Dening, *Death of William Gooch,* 16, 13l; idem, *Performances,* xiv; O'Farrell, *Ireland's English Question,* 3. See also White, *Remembering Ahanagran.*

2. Marx, "Working-Class Movement in America."

3. Ibid., 84. For a provocative look at the Wild West shows generally, see Warren, *Buffalo Bill's America.*

4. Ibid., 83–84.

5. Ibid.

6. Ibid., 88; for the broncho busters union, see Flynn, *Rebel Girl,* 77; on "dogies" as inspired by the Irish language, see Cassidy, *How the Irish Invented Slang,* 33, 133.

7. "Spoke a piece" was Sullivan's term; Marx, "Working-Class Movement in America," 84.

8. Schaefer, *Shane;* for Frewen and Plunkett, see Woods, *British Gentlemen;* West, *Horace Plunkett,* esp. 7–11, 257; Mercer, *Banditti of the Plains.*

9. Wister, *Virginian;* Roosevelt quoted in White, *Eastern Establishment,* 197.

10. Omaha Platform quoted in Hicks, *Populist Revolt,* appendix F, 439–44; on Donnelly's involvement in writing the Omaha Platform, see ibid., 227; and Ridge, *Ignatius Donnelly,* 311, 345.

11. For solid accounts of the fair, see Rydell, *All the World's a Fair;* Bolotin and Laing, *World's Columbian Exposition;* and Cronon, *Nature's Metropolis,* 341–73.

12. Yeats, *Cathleen Ní Houlihan,* in *Modern Irish Drama,* ed. Harrington, 6; Yeats, *Poems,* 14.

13. Gibbons, "Memorial," 145; Donnelly quoted in Messbarger, *Fiction,* 67.

14. White, "Frederick Jackson Turner and Buffalo Bill."

15. Schwantes, *Coxey's Army.*

16. Montana Board of World's Fair Managers, *Montana Exhibit;* Cronon, *Nature's Metropolis,* 341 (see also 367); on St. Gaudens, see Adams, *Education,* 341.

17. Adams, *Education,* 343–45, 379–90.

18. Barrow, *World's Parliament of Religions;* Ireland quoted in O'Connell, *John Ireland,* 386–88. See also Larson, *Devil in the White City.*

19. On Mooney, see Moses, *Indian Man,* 74–75, 110, 182. See also Rydell, *All the World's a Fair,* chap. 2.

20. Photo caption in Bancroft, *Book of the Fair.*

21. Ibid., 73–74, 836–38.

22. Lears, *No Place of Grace;* Lasch, *True and Only Heaven;* on "dudes," see Cassidy, *How the Irish Invented Slang,* 55–58, 136.

23. Yeats, "The Statues" (1938), in *Poems,* 337. See also Kiberd, *Inventing Ireland,* 139, 135–54; Glassie (ed.), *Irish Folk Tales,* 24–25; and Unterecker, "Countryman, Peasant, and Servant."

24. On Sherman, see *Irish World,* May 24, 1893.

25. See, among many sources, White, *Eastern Establishment;* Boris, *Art and Labor,* 180–85; and Wister (ed.), *Owen Wister Out West.*

26. Yeats quoted in Fleming, *"A Man Who Does Not Exist,"* 79–81; Yeats's remarks to Americans reported in *Gaelic American,* Jan. 9, 1904.

27. For the "cult of the peasant," see O'Farrell, *Ireland's English Question,* 170, 229–35; Manahan, *Trials,* 45–47.

28. England and America were beginning to celebrate what they were destroying. Rebecca Solnit makes this point in *Book of Migrations,* 102–105.

29. O'Farrell, *Ireland's English Question,* 3 ("constant anachronisms").

30. Keane, *Durango,* 53, 101, 142.

31. Fitzgerald, *Love of the Last Tycoon;* idem, *Great Gatsby;* Meyers, *Scott Fitzgerald;* Fessenden, "F. Scott Fitzgerald's Catholic Closet"; Gingrich, "Introduction," ix–xxii; Bewley, "Scott Fitzgerald's Criticism"; Jasper, *Restless Nation;* Wall, *From the Sin-é Café to the Black Hills;* idem, "Black Hills"; on U2, see Solnit, *Book of Migrations,* 123; on Keating, see Gibbons, *Transformations,* 25.

32. "Two Shillelagh O'Sullivan," in *Green Fields of America.* Also listen to the lyrics of "Kilkelly" on the same disc. For the "Streets of Laredo" connection, see Hand, "Cowboy's Lament"; and Wilgus, "*Aisling* and the Cowboy."

Bibliography

PUBLIC ARCHIVAL COLLECTIONS

All Hallows College (Dublin, Ireland) Records, University of Notre Dame Archives, Notre
    Dame, Indiana
    Reports and *Annals*. Dublin: John F. Fowler, by year. Microfilm.
Bancroft Library, University of California, Berkeley
    All Ireland (Official Paper of the San Francisco Irish Fair), Mechanics' Pavilion, May 1–
    May 24, 1902.
    Delmas, D. M. "Oration Delivered at the Request of the Fenian Brotherhood, July 4,
    1867." Corcoran Circle, Fenian Brotherhood. San Jose: C. L. Yates, 1867.
    Farley, Hugh. "Celebration of St. Patrick's Day, 1863, by the Sons of the Emerald
    Isle." San Francisco: Irish Nationalist Office, 1863.
    Francis Sullivan Papers.
    "Irish Fair Programme." San Francisco: The Fair, 1902.
    James Duval Phelan Papers.
    Noel Sullivan Correspondence and Papers, 1911–56.
    Pamphlet File, The Irish in California.
Butte/Silver Bow Archives, Butte, Montana
    Diary of Fr. Michael Hannan (1922–23).
    Irish Collection. Records and Papers of Butte Ancient Order of Hibernians; Robert
    Emmet Literary Association; and Irish Volunteers.
    Terrence McGlynn Collection.
Colorado Historical Society, Denver, Colorado
    John McGauran Papers.
    John Mullen Papers.

Diocese of Helena, Helena, Montana

   Bishop John Brondel Papers.

   Hannan, M. J. "Father English and St. Mary's Parish, Butte, Montana: The Miners Catholic Church and Parish." 1917.

Eastern Washington Historical Society, Spokane, Washington

   Edward Boyce Papers.

Kerby Miller Collection, University of Missouri

   Bartholomew Colgan Letter, June 13, 1862, Carson City, Nev.

   Bríc (Brick), Tom. "Memoirs of an Irish Emigrant to USA, Spring, 1902." Typescript, 1970.

   Denis Hurley Letters, 1873–1937, Carson City, Nev.

   Edward Commins Letter, April 1, 1874. San Francisco.

   Father Patrick Brosnan Papers. Copies also in Butte/Silver Bow Public Archives, Butte, Montana.

   Flanagan Family Letters, 1873–99, Napa, Calif.

   George Dillon Letter, December 24, 1869, Tomales, Calif.

   Greenlees Family Letters, 1863–80, Kansas.

   Hanlon (or O'Hanlon) Family Letters, 1843–1932, Nebraska City.

   James McFadden Letter, January 30, 1892, Middleton, Iowa.

   Jeremiah Cahill Letter, June 23, 1889, Ft. Assiniboine.

   J. F. Costello Letter, January 11, 1883, Kings Co., Wash.

   John Fitzgerald Letter, January 23, 1888, Lincoln, Neb.

   Katie O'Sullivan Letter, December 5, 1906. San Jose, Calif.

   Lewis Doyle Letters, 1873–80, Kilkenny, Minn.

   Mary Ryan Diary, 1887–88, Denver.

   Maurice Wolfe Letters, 1863–77, Forts Steele, Bridger, Bedford, Sedgwick, and Russell, Wyoming Territory.

   Michael Hurley Letters, 1871, Carson City, Nev.

   O'Daly, Hugh. "Life History of Hugh O'Daly." Typescript, 1945.

   Patrick Kearney Letter, December 21, 1890, Whatcom Co., Wash.

   Patrick O'Callaghan Letters, 188[?]–83. Ft. Snelling, Minn.

   P. Brown Letter, August 16, 1887, San Francisco.

   P—— C—— to Mr. Tuke, March 14, 1884, St. Paul.

   Robert and William Murphy Letters, 1875–81, San Francisco.

   Stephen Owens Letters, 1899–1903, Clontarf, Minn.

   Thomas Higgins Letter, May 16, 1916, Mosinee, Wisc.

   Tim Leahy Letter, April 12, 1914, San Francisco.

   William Lalor Letters, February 10, 1868, and March 31, 1872, Dunn, Wisc.

   Wolfe Papers.

Minnesota Historical Society, St. Paul, Minnesota

   Ancient Order of Hibernians. "Minnesota Irish." n.d. Typescript

   Diaries of M. J. Boyle.

   Ignatius Donnelly Papers.

   Irish American Colonization Association (IACC) Papers.

   James Manahan Papers.

John Ireland Papers.

M. D. O'Donnell and Family Papers.

Patrick Henry Rahilly Collection.

P. J. O'Donnell Papers.

Quigley, Walter. "Out Where the West Begins." Typescript, St. Paul, 1932.

Sweetman Catholic Colony. "Letters from the Pastor and Others" (1885).

Montana Historical Society, Helena, Montana

Anaconda Company Records.

Andrew O'Connell Collection.

Finerty, John F. "Oration by Col. Finerty: Dedication of the Meagher Memorial, July 4, 1905." *Contributions to the Historical Society of Montana* 6 (1907): 125–28.

Maginnis, Martin. "Thomas Francis Meagher." *Contributions to the Historical Society of Montana* 6 (1907): 98–123.

Martin Hogan Collection.

Thomas Francis Meagher Papers.

Nebraska State Historical Society, Lincoln, Nebraska

Governor Lorenzo Crounce Papers.

John P. Sutton Papers.

O'Neill, John. "O'Neill's Northern Nebraska." Pamphlet. Sioux City, 1875.

———. "To My Fellow Countrymen." Pamphlet. December 8, 1876.

"Roll Book of the Ancient Order of Hibernians." Lincoln, Nebraska, 1885–89.

Oregon Historical Society, Portland, Oregon

Ancient Order of Hibernians of Portland.

George Estes Papers.

Oregon American Protective Association (APA) Records, 1894–98.

Smith, F. Leo. "The Smith Family History, 1762–1987."

South Dakota Historical Society, Pierre, South Dakota

Anderson Map and Atlas Publishing Co. *Atlas of Clay and Union Counties, South Dakota. Map of Bethel Township, Clay County, Spink Township, Union County.* Des Moines: Anderson Map and Atlas Pub., 1924.

History and Manual, St. Mary's Catholic Church, Sioux Falls, South Dakota. Sioux Falls: Brown and Saenges, 1900.

Works Progress Administration (WPA) "Graves Registration Project, Cemetery Information. St. Mary's Catholic." Union Co., Beresford, S.D., January 29, 1940.

State Historical Society of Iowa, Iowa City, Iowa

Diary of S. A. Paul, 1907–10. 3 vols.

Iowa Oral History Project.

Keokuk County, Iowa, Ancient Order of Hibernians (AOH), 1909.

Kinross Ancient Order of Hibernians (AOH), Minute Books.

University of Colorado Western History Collection, Norlin Library, Boulder, Colorado

Edward Keating Papers.

Roady Kenehan Papers.

Western Federation of Miners (WFM) Papers.

University of Idaho Archives, Moscow, Idaho

Bunker Hill and Sullivan Mining Company Records and Papers.

University of Montana Archives, Missoula, Montana
    James Fergus Papers.

GOVERNMENT RECORDS AND PUBLICATIONS

Federal

Congressional Globe, May 25, 1854, 33 Cong., 1st sess., Appendix.

U.S. Bureau of the Census. *Seventh Census of the United States: 1850.* Washington, D.C.:
    GPO, 1850.

————. *Ninth Census of the United States: 1870.* Washington, D.C.: GPO, 1870.

————. *Tenth Census of the United States: 1880.* Washington, D.C.: GPO, 1880.

————. *Eleventh Census of the United States: 1890.* Washington, D.C.: GPO, 1890.

————. *Twelfth Census of the United States: 1900.* Washington, D.C.: GPO, 1900.

————. *Manuscript Census, Population Schedule: 1900, Marshall, Marion, and Polk Counties,
    Iowa.* Microfilm copy.

————. *Thirteenth Census of the United States: 1910.* Washington, D.C.: GPO, 1910.

————. *Manuscript Census, Population Schedule: 1910, Marshall, Marion, and Polk Counties,
    Iowa.* Microfilm copy.

————. *Fourteenth Census of the United States: 1920, Population.* Washington, D.C.: GPO, 1920.

————. *Census of Religious Bodies, 1926.* 2 vols. Washington, D.C.: GPO, 1929.

U.S. Bureau of Labor. *Report on Labor Disturbances in the State of Colorado from 1880–1904.*
    Washington, D.C.: GPO, 1905. Printed as Senate Document #122, 58th Cong., 3rd sess.

U.S. Commission on Industrial Relations. *Mining Conditions and Industrial Relations in Butte,
    Montana: Final Report.* Washington, D.C.: GPO, 1916.

U.S. Senate Commission on Industrial Relations, 64th Cong., 1st sess. *Final Report and Testi-
    mony,* 1915, Senate Document 415, vol. 22.

U.S. Senate Committee on Education and Labor, 48th Cong., 2nd sess. *Report upon Relations
    Between Labor and Capital,* 1883, vol. 3. Washington, D.C.: GPO, 1885.

State

Donovan, Joseph, comp. *Legislative Manual of the State of Minnesota, 1961–62.* St. Paul: the
    State, 1962.

————, comp. *Legislative Manual: Statistics of Minnesota, 1961–62.* St. Paul: the State, 1963.

Hallberg, George, ed. and comp. *The Legislative Manual of the State of Minnesota, 1897.* St. Paul:
    Harrison and Smith, 1897.

Montana. *House Journal,* 2nd sess., 1866.

Schmahl, Julius, comp. *The Legislative Manual of the State of Minnesota, 1913.* St. Paul: Harrison
    and Smith, 1913.

Local

Silver Bow County Board of Health. "Report on Sanitary Conditions in the Mines and
    Community, Silver Bow County, December, 1908–April, 1912." Typescript. Copy
    also available in the Montana Historical Society, Helena.

———. "Report Showing Results of Inspection of Dwellings, Hotels, Rooming Houses, and Boarding Houses and Their Surroundings." 1912. Typescript. Copy also available in the Montana Historical Society, Helena.

NEWSPAPERS

All Ireland (San Francisco)
Boston Pilot
Butte Bulletin
Butte Bystander
Butte Independent
Butte Miner
Catholic Bulletin (St. Paul)
Celtic World (Minneapolis)
Daily Central City Register
Daily Miners' Register (Denver)
Denver Post
Denver Times
Denver Tribune-Republican
Freeman's Journal (New York)
Gaelic American (New York)
Irish American Weekly (New York)
Irish Nation (New York)
Irish Standard (Minneapolis)
Irish World and American Industrial Liberator (New York)
Leader (San Francisco)
Miners Magazine (Butte, 1899–1902; Denver, 1902–)
Missoula Independent
Montana Catholic (Helena)
Nation (New York)
Northwestern Chronicle (St. Paul)
Omaha Daily Herald
Producers' News (Plentywood, Montana)
Rocky Mountain Celt (Denver)
Rocky Mountain Herald (Denver)
Rocky Mountain News (Denver)

PUBLISHED PRIMARY SOURCES

Abbott, Edith, ed. *Historical Aspects of the Immigration Problem: Select Documents.* Chicago: University of Chicago Press, 1926.
Adams, Henry. *The Education of Henry Adams* (1907). Boston: Houghton Mifflin Co., 1973.
Atherton, Gertrude. *Perch of the Devil.* New York: A. L. Burt, 1914.
The Awful Disclosures of Maria Monk: The Hidden Secrets of Convent Life (1834). London: Senate, 1997.
Bagenal, Philip H. The *American Irish and Their Influence on Irish Politics.* London: Kegan Paul, Trench and Co., 1882.

Baker, Ray Stannard. ed. *Woodrow Wilson: Life and Letters, Princeton, 1890–1910.* New York: Doubleday, 1927.

Baldwin, James. "The Centre of the Republic." *Scribner's Magazine* 3 (January–June 1888): 408–19.

Bancroft, Hubert Howe. *The Book of the Fair: An Historical and Descriptive Presentation.* Chicago and San Francisco: Bancroft Company, 1893.

Barnum, Rev. Samuel W. *Romanism as It Is: An Exposition of the Roman Catholic System, for the Use of the American People.* Hartford: Connecticut Pub. Co. 1872.

Barrow, John Henry. *World's Parliament of Religions.* 2 vols. Chicago: Parliament Publishing Co., 1893.

Beecher, Lyman. *A Plea for the West.* Cincinnati: Truman and Smith; New York: Leavitt and Lord, 1835.

Bocock, John Paul. "The Irish Conquest of Our Cities." *Forum* 17 (April 1894): 186–95.

Brace, Charles Loring. *The Best Method of Disposing of Pauper and Vagrant Children.* New York: Wynkoop and Hallenbeck, 1859.

———. *The Races of the Old World: A Manual of Ethnology.* New York: Charles Scribner, 1864.

———. *The Dangerous Classes of New York and Twenty Years' Work among Them.* New York: Wynkoop and Hallenbeck, 1872.

Brownson, Orestes A. "Archbishop Hughes on Slavery" (1862). In *The Works of Orestes A. Brownson,* collected by Henry F. Brownsonm 17:179–210. 18 vols. Detroit: Thorndike Nourse, 1885.

———. "Father Thébaud's Irish Race" (1873). In *The Works of Orestes A. Brownson,* collected by Henry F. Brownson, 13:547–66. 18 vols. Detroit: Thorndike Nourse, 1885.

Bryce, James. *The American Commonwealth.* 2 vols. New York: Macmillan, 1897.

Buchanan, Joseph. *The Story of a Labor Agitator.* New York: Outlook Co., 1903.

Burke, Edmund. *Reflections on the Revolution in France* (1790). London: J. M. Dent, 1955.

Butler, Rev. Thomas Ambrose. *The Irish on the Prairies and Other Poems.* New York: D. and J. Sadlier, 1874.

Carroll, H. K. *The Religious Forces of the United States . . . Returns from 1900 and 1910 Compared with the Census of 1890.* New York: Chas. Scribner's Sons, 1912.

Cavanaugh, Michael. *Memoirs of General Thomas F. Meagher.* Worcester: Messenger Press, 1892.

The Celtic Union (official program of the San Francisco Irish Fair and Industrial Exposition, August 20–September 10, 1898). San Francisco: H. S. Crocker Co., 1898. Copy in Bancroft Library.

Chevalier, Michel. *Society, Manners, and Politics in the United States* (1836). Gloucester, Mass.: Peter Smith, 1967.

Commager, Henry Steele, ed. *Documents of American History.* 2 vols. in 1. New York: Appleton-Century-Crofts, 1958.

Commons, John. "Bringing about Industrial Peace." Presented to the National Association of Employment Managers, December 13, 1919. Reprinted as "Industrial Relations" in *Trade Unionism and Labor Problems,* edited by John Rogers Commons, 1–16. Boston: Ginn and Co., 1921.

Connolly, James. *The Words of James Connolly.* Edited by James Connolly Heron. Dublin: Mercier Press, 1986.

Conrad, Joseph. *Heart of Darkness* (1899). In *Three Great Tales,* 217–307. New York: Vintage, 1961.

Crèvecoeur, J. Hector St. John de. *Letters from an American Farmer and Sketches of Eighteenth-Century America* (1782). New York: Signet, 1963.

Curtin, Jeremiah. *Myths and Folk-Lore of Ireland* (1890). New York: Weathervane Books, 1975.

———. *Hero-Tales of Ireland.* Boston: Little, Brown and Co., 1894.

———. *Memoirs of Jeremiah Curtin.* Edited by Joseph Schafer. Madison: State Historical Society of Wisconsin, 1940.

Davitt, Michael. *Jottings in Solitary* (1881). Edited with introduction by Carla King. Dublin: UCD Press, 2004.

———. *The Fall of Feudalism in Ireland* (1904). Dublin: Irish University Press, 1972.

Devoy, John. *Recollections of an Irish Rebel* (1929). Shannon: Irish University Press, 1969.

———. *Devoy's Post Bag.* 2 vols. Edited by William O'Brien and Desmond Ryan. Dublin: C. J. Fallon, 1948, 1953.

Douglass, Frederick. *My Bondage and My Freedom* (1855). New York: Dover Publications, 1969.

Drannan, William F. *Thirty-one Years on the Plains and in the Mountains; or, the Last Voice from the Plains: An Authentic Record of a Life Time Hunting, Trapping, Scouting, and Indian Fighting in the Far West—by Capt. Wm. E. Drannan, Who Went West on to the Plains When Fifteen Years Old.* Chicago: McClure Pub. Co., 1900.

Driscoll, Charles. *Kansas Irish.* New York: Macmillan, 1943.

———. *Country Jake.* New York: Macmillan, 1946.

———. *Foclóir Póca: English-Irish/Irish-English Dictionary.* Baile átha Cliath (Dublin): An Gúm, 2001.

Dunn, Joseph. *The Ancient Irish Epic Tale, Táin Bó Cúailnge.* London: David Nutt, 1914.

Dunne, Finley Peter. *Mr. Dooley in Peace and War.* Boston: Small, Maynard and Co., 1898.

———. *Mr. Dooley in the Hearts of His Countrymen.* Boston: Small, Maynard, 1899.

Engels, Frederick. *The Condition of the Working Class in England* (1844). New York: Oxford University Press, 1993.

Farms for Sale in Minnesota by the I-American Colonization Co., Currie, Murray County. Chicago: Rand McNally, 1881.

Finerty, John F. *War Path and Bivouac, or the Conquest of the Sioux* (1890). Norman: University of Oklahoma Press, 1994.

Fitzhugh, George. *Cannibals All! or Slaves without Masters* (1856). Edited by C. Vann Woodward. Cambridge, Mass.: Harvard University Press, 1960.

——— "Selections from *A Sociology for the South*" (1854). In *Slavery Defended: The Views of the Old South,* edited by Eric McKitrick, 34–50. Englewood Cliffs: Prentice-Hall, 1963.

Flynn, Elizabeth G. *Rebel Girl: An Autobiography, My First Life.* New York: International Publishers, 1955.

Ford, Patrick. *Criminal History of the British Empire.* New York: Irish World, 1881.

Foster, Vere. *Work and Wages, or the Penny Emigrant's Guide to the United States and Canada* (1855). In *Historical Aspects of the Immigration Problem,* edited by Edith Abbott, 299–301. Chicago: University of Chicago Press, 1926.

Foster, William Z. *Pages from a Worker's Life.* New York: International Publishers, 1939.

———. *American Trade Unionism: Principles, Organization, Strategy, Tactics: Selected Writings by William Z. Foster.* New York: International Publishers, 1947.

Frederick, Harold. *The Damnation of Theron Ware* (1896). New York: Rinehart, 1961.

Frewen, Moreton. *Melton Mowbray and Other Memories.* London: H. Jenkins, 1924.

Froude, J. A. "Romanism and the Irish Race in the United States, Part I." *North American Review* 129 (December 1879): 519–36.

———. "Romanism and the Irish Race in the United States, Part II." *North American Review* 130 (January 1880): 31–50.

George, Henry. *Progress and Poverty: An Inquiry Into the Cause of Industrial Depression* (1879). New York: Robert Schalkenbach, 1942.

———. "The Condition of Labor: An Open Letter to Pope Leo XIII." In George, *The Land Question: Property in Land and The Condition of Labor* (1891), 3–105. New York: Robert Schalkenbach, 1945.

———. *The Land Question: Property in Land and The Condition of Labor* (1891). New York: Robert Schalkenbach, 1945.

Gibbon, General John. "Last Summer's Expedition against the Sioux and Its Great Catastrophe." *American Catholic Quarterly Review* (April and October 1877). Republished in facsimile as *Gibbon on Sioux Campaign of 1876.* Bellevue, Neb.: Old Army Press, 1969.

Gibbons, James Cardinal. "Memorial Presented to the Holy See on the Knights of Labor." In *The Church and Labor,* edited by John A. Ryan and Joseph Husslein, 145–58. New York: Macmillan, 1924.

Gibbons, Rev. J. J. *In the San Juans* (1898). Telluride: St. Patricks, 1986.

Gilpin, William. *The Central Gold Region: The Grain, Pastoral, and Gold Regions of North America.* Philadelphia: Sower, Barnes and Co., 1860.

———. *Notes on Colorado and Its Inscription in the Physical Geography of the North American Continent.* London: Witherby and Co., 1870.

———. *Mission of the North American People: Geographical, Social, and Political.* Philadelphia: J. B. Lippincott and Co., 1873.

———. *Mission of the North American People: Geographical, Social, and Political.* 2nd ed. Philadelphia: J. B. Lippincott and Co., 1874.

Gladstone, T. H. *The Englishman in Kansas, or Squatter Life and Border Warfare.* New York: Miller and Co., 1857.

Gleeson, William. *History of the Catholic Church in California.* San Francisco: A. L. Bancroft, 1872.

Godkin, Edwin Lawrence. *Life and Letters of Edwin Lawrence Godkin.* Edited by Ogden Rollo. 2 vols. New York: Macmillan Co., 1907.

Gorn, Elliott, ed. *The McGuffey Readers: Selections from the 1879 Edition.* Boston: Bedford/St. Martin's, 1998.

Graham, John, ed. *"Yours for the Revolution": The Appeal to Reason, 1895–1922.* Lincoln: University of Nebraska Press, 1990.

Grant, Madison. *The Passing of the Great Race, or the Racial Basis of European History.* New York: Charles Scribner's Sons, 1916.

———. *The Conquest of a Continent, or The Expansion of Races in America.* New York: Charles Scribner's Sons, 1933.

Grayson, William. "The Hireling and the Slave." In *Slavery Defended: The Views of the Old South,* ed. Eric McKitrick, 57–68. Englewood Cliffs: Prentice-Hall, 1963.

Hale, E. E. *Letters on Irish Emigration, First Published in the Boston Daily Advertiser* (1852). Freeport, N.Y.: Books for Libraries Press, 1972.

Hammond, James Henry. "'Mud-Sill' Speech" (1858). In *Slavery Defended: The Views of the Old South,* ed. Eric McKitrick, 120–24. Englewood Cliffs: Prentice-Hall, 1963.

Hammond, John Hays. *Autobiography of John Hays Hammond.* New York: Farrar and Rinehart, 1935.

Harrington, Jeremiah. *Catholicism, Capitalism, or Communism.* St. Paul: E. M. Lohmann Co., 1926.

Haywood, William. *Bill Haywood's Book: The Autobiography of William H. Haywood.* New York: International Publishers, 1929.

Helper, Hinton Rowan. *The Land of Gold: Reality versus Fiction* (1855). Ann Arbor: University of Michigan Book Store, 2006.

———. *The Impending Crisis* (1857). In *Ante-Bellum: Writings of George Fitzhugh and Hinton Rowan Helper on Slavery,* edited by Harvey Wish, 157–256. New York: Capricorn, 1960.

In Memoriam, James Phelan. Read at a Meeting of the Society of California Pioneers, San Francisco, April 3, 1893. San Francisco: The Society, 1893. Copy in Bancroft Library.

"In Memoriam: Washington Matthews." *American Anthropologist,* n.s. 7 (1905): 514–23.

Ireland, John. "The Church in America." In *The Church and Modern Society: Lectures and Addresses by John Ireland,* 2:219–50. 2 vols. St. Paul: The Pioneer Press, 1905.

———. "Fifty Years of Catholicity in the Northwest." In *The Church and Modern Society: Lectures and Addresses by John Ireland,* 2:279–302. 2 vols. St. Paul: Pioneer Press, 1905.

———. "Labor and Capital." In *The Church and Modern Society: Lectures and Addresses by John Ireland,* 2:341–76. 2 vols. St. Paul: Pioneer Press, 1905.

———. "Leo XIII." In *The Church and Modern Society: Lectures and Addresses by John Ireland,* 2:163–92. 2 vols. St. Paul: Pioneer Press, 1905.

———. "Personal Liberty and Labor Strikes." In *The Church and Modern Society: Lectures and Addresses by John Ireland,* 2:326–40. 2 vols. St. Paul: Pioneer Press, 1905.

Irish-American Benevolent Society. "Articles of Incorporation, Constitution, By-laws, and Rules of Order . . . May, 1860." Copy in Bancroft Library. San Francisco: J. M. Crane and Co., 1871.

Irish American Club of St. Paul. *Constitution, By-Laws, House Rules . . . of the Irish American Club of St. Paul.* St. Paul: Brown, Treacy and Co., 1887. Copy available in Minnesota Historical Society, St. Paul.

Keating, Edward. *The Story of "Labor": Thirty-Three Years on Rail Workers' Fighting Front.* Washington, D.C.: the author, 1953.

———. *The Gentleman from Colorado: A Memoir.* Denver: Sage Books, 1964.

Kenrick, Francis Patrick, and Marc Antony Frenaye. *The Kenrick-Frenaye Correspondence: Letters . . . of Francis Patrick Kenrick and Marc Antony Frenaye, 1830–1862.* Philadelphia: Wickersham Printing Co., 1920.

Kingsbury, George. *History of Dakota Territory;* and *South Dakota.* Edited by George M. Smith. Chicago: S. J. Clarke, 1915.

Leo XIII, Pope. *Rerum Novarum: Encyclical on the Condition of Labor* (May 15, 1891). In *The Church and Labor,* edited by John A. Ryan and Joseph Husslein, 57–94. New York: Macmillan, 1924.

Leslie, Shane. *The Irish Issue in Its American Aspect.* New York: Chas. Scribner's Sons, 1917.

MacAirt, Cormac, King of Ireland. *The Counsels of Cormac: An Ancient Irish Guide to Leadership.* Translated by Thomas Cleary. New York: Doubleday, 2004.

MacGowan, Michael. *The Hard Road to Klondike* (*Rotha Mór an tSaoil*) (1948). Translated from the Irish by Valentin Iremonger. London: Routledge and Kegan Paul, 1962.

Maguire, John Francis. *The Irish in America* (1868). New York: Arno Press, 1969.

Manahan, James. *Trials of a Lawyer.* St. Paul: the author, 1933.

Manning, John Cardinal. "Review of the Encyclical of Pope Leo XIII on the Condition of Labor." In *The Church and Labor,* edited by John A. Ryan and Joseph Husslein, 159–76. New York: Macmillan, 1924.

Marx, Eleanor. "The Working-Class Movement in America" (1888). In *Broken Image: Foreign Critiques of America,* ed. Gerald Emanuel Stearn, 81–88. New York: Random House, 1972.

Marx, Karl. *Capital* (1867). Translated by Eden Paul and Cedar Paul. 2 vols. New York: E. P. Dutton, 1930.

Marx, Karl, and Frederick Engels. *Ireland and the Irish Question* (1853–70). Moscow: Progress Publishers, 1971.

McGee, Thomas D'Arcy. *A History of the Irish Settlers in North America from the Earliest Period to the Census of 1850.* Boston: Patrick Donahue, 1852.

———. *The Catholic History of North America.* Boston: Patrick-Donahoe, 1855.

Meagher, Thomas Francis. "Recollections of Ireland." Address at the Fenian Library, December 30, 1865. In *Lectures of Governor Thomas Francis Meagher in Montana,* compiled by John P. Bruce, 32–38. Helena: Bruce and Wright, 1867.

Mercer, A. S. *The Banditti of the Plains or the Cattlemen's Invasion of Wyoming in 1892* (1894). Norman: University of Oklahoma Press, 1975.

Montana Board of World's Fair Managers. *Montana Exhibit at the World's Fair and a Description of the Various Resources of the State, Mining, Agriculture, and Stock Raising.* Butte: Butte Intermountain, 1893.

Mooney, James. "Medical Mythology of Ireland." *Proceedings of the American Philosophical Society* 24 (1887): 136–66.

———. "Funeral Customs of Ireland." *Proceedings of the American Philosophical Society* 25 (1888): 243–96.

———. "Holiday Customs of Ireland." *Proceedings of the American Philosophical Society* 26 (1889): 377–427.

———. *The Ghost Dance Religion and Wounded Knee* (1896). New York: Dover, 1973.

———. "Myths of the Cherokee." In *Nineteenth Annual Report of the Bureau of American Ethnology, 1897–98,* part 1, 506–48. Washington, D.C.: GPO, 1900.

———. "The Cheyenne Indians." *Memoirs of the American Anthropological Association,* vol. 1, part 6. Lancaster: New Era Printing Co., 1907.

———. "The Gaelic Factor in the World's Population." *American Anthropologist,* n.s. 16 (1914): 117–19.

Morse, Samuel, F. B. *Foreign Conspiracy against the Liberties of the United States.* New York: Leavitt, Lord, and Co., 1835.

Nott, Josiah. "Types of Mankind" (1854). In *Slavery Defended: The Views of the Old South,* edited by Eric McKitrick, 126–38. Englewood Cliffs: Prentice-Hall, 1963.

O'Brien, Michael. *A Hidden Phase of American History: Ireland's Part in America's Struggle for Liberty.* New York: American Irish Historical Society, 1919.

O'Connor, Frank. *Guests of the Nation.* New York: Macmillan, 1931.

O'Crohan, Sean. *Island Cross-Talk: Pages from a Blasket Island Diary* (1928). Translated by Tim Enright. New York: Oxford University Press, 1986.

————. *A Day in Our Life: The Last of the Blasket Islanders* (1969). Translated by Tim Enright. New York: Oxford University Press, 1992.

O'Crohan, Tomas. *The Islandman* (1937). Translated by Robin Flower. New York: Oxford University Press, 1985.

O'Donovan, Jeremiah. *Irish Immigration in the United States: Immigrant Interviews* (1864). New York: Arno Press, 1969.

Ó Dubdha, S. O., ed. *Duanaire Duibhneac.* Translated by Bruce Boling. Dublin: Foilseacháin, 1933.

O'Farrell, P. A. *Butte: Its Copper Mines and Copper Kings.* New York: J. A. Rogers, 1899.

O'Flaherty, Liam. *The Informer* (1925). Harvest Books, 1980.

O'Flaherty, Thomas. *Cliffmen of the West.* London: Gollancz, 1935.

O'Gorman, Thomas. *How Catholics Come to Be Misunderstood.* St. Paul: Catholic Truth Society, 1890. Copy available in the Minnesota Historical Society, St. Paul.

O'Hanlon, John. *The Irish Emigrant's Guide for the United States* (1851). New York: Arno Press, 1976.

O'Hara, Rev. Edwin V. *Pioneer Catholic History of Oregon.* Portland: Glass and Prudhomme, 1911.

O'Neill, John. *O'Neill's Northern Nebraska as Home for Immigrants.* Sioux City, Iowa: Sioux City Times Printing, 1875. Copy available in the Nebraska Historical Society.

O'Sullivan, John L. "A Divine Destiny for America." *United States Democratic Review* 6 (1839): 426–30.

————. "Annexation." *Democratic Review* 17 (July–August 1845): 5–10.

O'Sullivan, Maurice. *Twenty Years A-Growing.* Translated from the Irish by Moya Llewelyn Davies and George Thomson. New York: Viking Press, 1933.

Parker, Carleton. *The Casual Laborer and Other Essays* (1920). Seattle: University of Washington Press, 1972.

Parker, Theodore. *Life and Correspondence of Theodore Parker.* Edited by John Weiss. 2 vols. New York: Arno Press, 1969.

Patrick, Saint. *The Works of St. Patrick.* Translated by Ludwig Bieler. London: Longmans, Green, 1953.

Phelan, James Duval. *Travel and Comment.* San Francisco: A. M. Robertson, 1923.

Pierce, Edward L. *Letter of Edward L. Pierce . . . in Regard to the Foreign Vote, Jan. 26, 1857.* Boston: Commercial Printing House, 1857.

Pinkerton, William John. *His Personal Record: Stories of Railroad Life.* Kansas City: Pinkerton Publishing Co., 1904.

Plunkett, Horace. *Ireland in the New Century.* New York: E. P. Dutton, 1904.

Polk, R. L. *Butte City Directory, 1901.* St. Paul and Butte: R. L. Polk, 1901.

————. *Butte City Directory, 1902.* St. Paul and Butte: R. L. Polk, 1902.

————. *Butte City Directory, 1914.* St. Paul and Butte: R. L. Polk, 1915.

Porter, Kirk, and Donald Johnson, eds. *National Party Platforms, 1840–1956.* Urbana: University of Illinois Press, 1973.

Powderly, Terence. *Thirty Years of Labor, 1859–1889* (1890). Reprint, New York: Augustus M. Kelley, 1967.

Price, Con. *Trails I Rode: Memories of Old Cowboy Days and Charlie Russell.* Pasadena: Trail's End Pub. Co., 1947.

Quigley, Hugh. *The Cross and the Shamrock, or How to Defend the Faith: An Irish-American Catholic Tale of Real Life* (1853). Tehachapi, Calif.: Kevin Coleman, 2002.

———. *The Irish Race in California and the Pacific Coast.* San Francisco: A. Roman, 1878.

Rauschenbusch, Walter. *Christianity and the Social Crisis.* New York: Hodder and Stoughton, 1907.

Redpath, James. *Talks about Ireland.* New York: P. J. Kennedy, 1881.

Riel, Louis. *The Queen v. Louis Riel.* Toronto: University of Toronto Press, 1974.

———. *The Collected Writings of Louis Riel.* Edmonton: University of Alberta Press, 1985.

Roney, Frank. *Irish Rebel and California Labor Leader: An Autobiography.* Edited by Ira Cross. Berkeley: University of California Press, 1931.

Roosevelt, Theodore. *An Autobiography.* New York: Macmillan, 1913.

Ross, Edward. *Changing America.* New York: Century Co., 1919.

Ryan, John A. "Introduction." In John A Ryan and Joseph Husslein, S.J., *The Church and Labor,* v–xvii. New York: Macmillan, 1924.

———. "A Living Wage." In *The Church and Labor,* edited by John A. Ryan and Joseph Husslein, 259–71. New York: Macmillan, 1924.

———. "The Reconciliation of Labor and Capital." In *The Church and Labor,* edited by John A. Ryan and Joseph Husslein, 272–90. New York: Macmillan, 1924.

———. *The Catholic Church and the Citizen.* New York: Macmillan, 1928.

———. *Distributive Justice: The Right and Wrong of Our Present Distribution of Wealth.* New York: Macmillan, 1935.

———. *Social Doctrine in Action: A Personal History.* New York: Harper and Bros., 1941.

Schouler, James. *History of the United States under the Constitution.* 5 vols. New York: Dodd Mead, 1895.

Sinclair, Upton. *The Profits of Religion* (1918). Amherst, N.Y.: Prometheus Books, 2000.

Smith, John Talbot. *The Chaplain's Sermons.* New York: William H. Young and Co., 1899.

Sombart, Werner. *Why Is There No Socialism in the United States?* (1906). New York: M. E. Sharpe, 1976.

Spalding, John Lancaster. *The Religious Mission of the Irish Race and Catholic Colonization.* New York: Catholic Publication Society, 1880.

Spalding, M. J. *Miscellanea: . . . Reviews, Lectures, and Essays.* Baltimore: John Murphy and Co., 1875.

Steffens, Lincoln. *The Shame of the Cities* (1904). New York: Hill and Wang, 1963.

Strong, George Templeton. *Diary of George Templeton Strong.* Edited by Allan Nevins and M. H. Thomas. 4 vols. New York: Macmillan, 1952.

Strong, Josiah. *Our Country: Its Possible Future and Its Present Crisis.* New York: Baker and Taylor Co., published for the Home Missionary Society, 1890.

Sullivan, Francis J. *Fourth of July Oration* (1903). San Francisco: James H. Barry Co., 1905.

Synge, John Millington. *Guide to the Aran Islands* (1898). Edited by Ruth Wills Shaw. Old Greenwich, Conn.: Devin-Adair, 1975.

Tocqueville, Alexis de. *Democracy in America* (1835). 2 vols. New York: Vintage Books, 1945.

———. *Journeys to England and Ireland* (1835). New York: Anchor Books, 1968.

Turner, Frederick Jackson. "The Significance of History" (1891). In *Rereading Frederick Jackson Turner: "The Significance of the Frontier in American History" and Other Essays,* edited by John Mack Faragher, 11–30. New York: Henry Holt, 1994.

————. *The Frontier in American History* (1893). New York: Henry Holt, 1947.

————. "The Significance of the Frontier in American History" (1893). In *Rereading Frederick Jackson Turner: "The Significance of the Frontier in American History" and Other Essays,* edited by John Mack Faragher, 31–60. New York: Henry Holt, 1994.

————. "The Problem of the West" (1896). In *Rereading Frederick Jackson Turner: "The Significance of the Frontier in American History" and Other Essays,* edited by John Mack Faragher, 61–76. New York: Henry Holt, 1994.

————. "Contributions of the West to American Democracy" (1903). In *Rereading Frederick Jackson Turner: "The Significance of the Frontier in American History" and Other Essays,* edited by John Mack Faragher, 77–100. New York: Henry Holt, 1994.

————. "Middle Western Pioneer Democracy" (1918). In *Rereading Frederick Jackson Turner: "The Significance of the Frontier in American History" and Other Essays,* edited by John Mack Faragher, 159–80. New York: Henry Holt, 1994.

Usher, Arnold. *The Face and Mind of Ireland.* Old Greenwich, Conn.: Devin-Adair, 1950.

Warner, M. M. *History of Dakota Co., Nebraska.* Lyons, Neb.: Mirror Job Office, 1893.

Weber, Max. *The Protestant Ethic and the Spirit of Capitalism* (1904). London: Unwin, 1930.

Wilson, Woodrow. *History of the American People.* 5 vols. New York: Macmillan, 1902.

Wister, Owen. *The Virginian: A Horseman of the Plains* (1902). New York: Dover, 2006.

Woodbury, Frank. *Tourist Guide Book to Denver, 1882.* Denver: Times Steam Printing House, 1882.

Yeats, William Butler. *Fairy and Folk Tales of Ireland* (1888, 1892). New York: Macmillan, 1983.

SECONDARY SOURCES

Books

Abell, Aaron. *American Catholicism and Social Action: A Search for Social Justice.* Notre Dame: University of Notre Dame Press, 1963.

Abzug, Robert H. *Cosmos Crumbling: American Reform and the Religious Imagination.* New York: Oxford University Press, 1994.

Adams, David. *Education for Extinction: American Indians and the Boarding School Experience.* Lawrence: University Press of Kansas, 1997.

Adams, Graham. *Age of Industrial Violence, 1910–1915: The Activities and Findings of the United States Commission on Industrial Relations.* New York: Columbia University Press, 1966.

Adams, Kevin. *Class and Race in the Frontier Army: Military Life in the West, 1870–1890.* Norman: University of Oklahoma Press, 2009.

Ahlstrom, Sydney E. *A Religious History of the American People.* New Haven: Yale University Press, 1973.

Akenson, Donald Harman. *Small Differences: Irish Catholics and Irish Protestants, 1815–1922: An International Perspective.* Kingston and Montreal: McGill–Queens University Press, 1988.

————. *The Irish Diaspora: A Primer.* Toronto: P. D. Meany Co., 1996.

————. *An Irish History of Civilization.* 2 vols. Toronto: McGill–Queens University Press, 2006.

Allen, Frederick. *A Decent, Orderly Lynching: The Montana Vigilantes.* Norman: University of Oklahoma Press, 2004.

Allen, Theodore. *The Invention of the White Race.* Vol. 1: *Racial Oppression and Social Control.* London: Verso, 1994.

————. *The Invention of the White Race.* Vol. 2: *The Origins of Racial Oppression in Anglo-America.* London: Verso, 1997.

Ambrose, Stephen. *Nothing Like It in the World: The Men Who Built the Transcontinental Railroad, 1863–1869.* New York: Simon and Schuster, 2001.

Anbinder, Tyler. *Nativism and Slavery: The Northern Know Nothings and the Politics of the 1850s.* New York: Oxford University Press, 1992.

Anderson, Benedict. *Imagined Communities: Reflections on the Origin and Spread of Nationalism.* Rev. ed. London: Verso, 1991.

Archdeacon, Thomas. *Becoming American: An Ethnic History.* New York: Free Press, 1983.

Arensberg, Conrad. *The Irish Countryman: An Anthropological Study* (1937). Garden City: Natural History Press, 1968.

Arensberg, Conrad, and Solon T. Kimball. *Family and Community in Ireland.* Cambridge, Mass.: Harvard University Press, 1940.

Arieli, Yehoshua. *Individualism and Nationalism in American Ideology.* Cambridge, Mass.: Harvard University Press, 1964.

Ashworth, John. *Slavery, Capitalism, and Politics in the Antebellum Republic.* Vol. 1: *Commerce and Compromise, 1820–1850.* Cambridge, Mass.: Cambridge University Press, 1995.

Athearn, Robert. *Thomas Francis Meagher: An Irish Revolutionary in America.* Boulder: University of Colorado Press, 1949.

Avella, Steven, and Elizabeth McKeown, eds. *Public Voices: Catholics in the American Context.* Maryknoll, N.Y.: Orbis, 1999.

Ayers, Edward. *The Promise of the New South: Life after Reconstruction.* New York: Oxford University Press, 1992.

Barkan, Elliott. *From All Points: America's Immigrant West, 1870s–1952.* Bloomington: Indiana University Press, 2007.

Barker, Charles. *Henry George.* New York: Oxford University Press, 1955.

Barney, William. *The Road to Secession: A New Perspective on the Old South.* Westport, Conn.: Praeger, 1976.

————. *The Passage of the Republic: An Interdisciplinary History of Nineteenth-Century America.* Lexington: D. C. Heath, 1987.

Barrett, James. *William Z. Foster and the Tragedy of American Radicalism.* Urbana: University of Illinois Press, 2001.

Barth, Gunther. *Instant Cities: Urbanization and the Rise of San Francisco and Denver.* New York: Oxford University Press, 1975.

Bartlett, Irving. *Wendell Phillips: Brahmin Radical.* Boston: Beacon Press, 1961.

Bayor, Ronald, and Timothy Meagher, eds. *New York Irish.* Baltimore: Johns Hopkins University Press, 1996.

Bean, Walton. *Boss Ruef's San Francisco: The Story of the Union Labor Party, Big Business, and the Graft Prosecution.* Berkeley: University of California Press, 1952.

Beatty, Jack. *The Age of Betrayal: The Triumph of Money in America, 1865–1900.* New York: Knopf, 2007.

Bederman, Gail. *Manliness and Civilization: A Cultural History of Gender and Race in the United States, 1880–1917.* Chicago: University of Chicago Press, 1995.

Beer, Thomas. *The Mauve Decade: American Life at the End of the Nineteenth Century* (1926) New York: Vintage, 1960.

Behan, Brendan. *The Hostage.* In *The Complete Plays.* Introduction by Alan Simpson (1958). New York: Grove, 1978.

Beresford, David. *Ten Men Dead: The Story of the 1981 Irish Hunger Strike.* New York: Atlantic Monthly Press, 1987.

Bernanos, Georges. *The Diary of a Country Priest.* Translated by Pamela Morris. New York: Macmillan, 1937.

Bernstein, Iver. *The New York City Draft Riots: Their Significance for American Society and Politics in the Age of the Civil War.* New York: Oxford University Press, 1990.

Berry, James. *Tales of the West of Ireland.* Edited by Gertrude Hogan. Buckingham: Colin Smythe, 1988.

Bertelson, David. *The Lazy South.* New York: Oxford University Press, 1968.

Berthoff, Rowland. *An Unsettled People: Social Order and Disorder in American History.* New York: Vintage, 1971.

Berwanger, Eugene. *The Frontier against Slavery: Western Anti-Negro Prejudice and the Slavery Extension Controversy* (1967). Rev. ed. Urbana: University of Illinois Press, 2002.

Billington, Ray Allen. *The Protestant Crusade: A Study of the Origins of American Nativism* (1938). New York: Rinehart and Company, 1952.

———. *Frederick Jackson Turner: Historian, Scholar, Teacher.* New York: Oxford University Press, 1973.

———. *Land of Savagery, Land of Promise: The European Image of the American Frontier in the Nineteenth Century.* New York: W. W. Norton, 1981.

Bodnar, John. *Workers' World: Kinship, Community and Protest in an Industrial Society, 1900–1940.* Baltimore: Johns Hopkins University Press, 1982.

———. *The Transplanted: A History of Immigrants in Urban America.* Bloomington: Indiana University Press, 1985.

Bodnar, John, Roger Simon, and Michael P. Weber. *Lives of Their Own.* Champaign: University of Illinois Press, 1981.

Bodo, John. *The Protestant Clergy and Public Issues, 1812–1848* (1954). Philadelphia: Porcupine Press, 1980.

Bogue, Allan. *From Prairie to Cornbelt: Farming on the Illinois and Iowa Prairies in the Nineteenth Century.* Chicago: Quadrangle, 1968.

———. *Frederick Jackson Turner: Strange Roads Going Down.* Norman: University of Oklahoma Press, 1998.

Bolotin, Norman, and Christine Laing. *The World's Columbian Exposition: The Chicago World's Fair of 1893.* Urbana: University of Illinois Press, 2002.

Boris, Eileen. *Art and Labor: Ruskin, Morris, and the Craftsman Ideal in America.* Philadelphia: Temple University Press, 1986.

Brinley, Thomas. *Migration and Economic Growth: A Study of Great Britain and the Atlantic Economy.* Cambridge: Cambridge University Press, 1954.

Brissenden, Paul. *The IWW: A Study of American Syndicalism.* New York: Columbia University Press, 1920.

Broderick, Francis. *Right Reverend New Dealer: John A. Ryan.* New York: Macmillan, 1963.

Broehl, Wayne G., Jr. *The Molly Maguires* (1964). New York: Chelsea House, 1983.

Brown, Richard M. *Strain of Violence: Historical Studies of American Violence and Vigilantes.* New York: Oxford University Press, 1975.

————. *No Duty to Retreat: Violence and Values in American History and Society.* New York: Oxford University Press, 1991.

Brown, Ronald. *Hard-Rock Miners: The Intermountain West, 1860–1920.* College Station: Texas A&M University Press, 1979.

Brown, Thomas. *Irish-American Nationalism, 1870–1890.* Philadelphia and New York: J. B. Lippincott, 1966.

Browne, Henry, S.J. *The Catholic Church and the Knights of Labor.* Washington, D.C.: Catholic · University of America Press, 1949.

Brundage, David. *The Making of Western Labor Radicalism: Denver's Organized Workers, 1878–1905.* Urbana: University of Illinois Press, 1994.

Buenker, John. *Urban Liberalism and Progressive Reform.* New York: Chas. Scribner's Sons, 1973.

Bullough, William. *The Blind Boss and His City: Christopher Augustine Buckley and Nineteenth-Century San Francisco.* Berkeley: University of California Press, 1979.

Burchell, R. A. *The San Francisco Irish, 1848–1880.* Berkeley: University of California Press, 1980.

Burke, Bill. *Rhymes of the Mines.* Vancouver: Bill Burke, 1964.

Burns, Jeffrey M., Ellen Skerrett, and Joseph M. White, eds. *Keeping Faith: European and Asian Catholic Immigrants.* A volume in *American Catholic Identities.* Maryknoll, N.Y.: Orbis, 2000.

Burns, Robert E., S.J. *Jesuits and the Indian Wars of the Northwest.* New Haven: Yale University Press, 1966.

Byrkit, James. *Forging the Copper Collar: Arizona's Labor-Management War of 1901–1921.* Tucson: University of Arizona Press, 1982.

Cahill, Thomas. *How the Irish Saved Civilization: The Untold Story of Ireland's Heroic Role from the Fall of Rome to the Rise of Medieval Europe.* New York: Anchor Books, 1995.

Campbell, Malcolm. *The Kingdom of the Ryans: The Irish in Southwest New South Wales, 1816–1890.* Sydney: New South Wales University Press, 1997.

————. *Ireland's New Worlds: Immigrants, Politics, and Society in the United States and Australia, 1815–1922.* Madison: University of Wisconsin Press, 2007.

Canny, Nicholas. *Kingdom and Colony: Ireland in the Atlantic World, 1560–1800.* Baltimore: Johns Hopkins University Press, 1988.

Carey, Peter. *True History of the Kelly Gang.* Brisbane: University of Queensland Press, 1998.

Carnes, Mark, *Secret Ritual and Manhood in Victorian America.* New Haven: Yale University Press, 1989.

Casey, Daniel, and Robert E. Rhodes, eds. *Views of the Irish Peasantry, 1800–1916.* Hamden, Conn.: Archon Books, 1977.

Casper, Henry W., S.J. *The Church on the Northern Plains, 1838–1874.* Milwaukee: Bruce Publishing, 1960.

————. *The Church on the Fading Frontier, 1864–1910.* Milwaukee: Bruce Publishing, 1964.

Cassidy, Daniel. *How the Irish Invented Slang: The Secret Language of the Crossroads.* Petrolia, Calif.: CounterPunch, 2007.

Cather, Willa. *Death Comes for the Archbishop* (1927). New York: Vintage, 1999.

Chaplin, Ralph. T*he Centralia Case: Three Views on the Armistice Day Tragedy* (1920). New York: Da Capo, 1971.

———. *Wobblie: The Rough and Tumble Story of an American Radical.* Chicago: University of Chicago Press, 1948.

Chrislock, Carl. *The Progressive Era in Minnesota, 1899–1918.* St. Paul: Minnesota Historical Society Press, 1971.

Clark, Dennis. *The Irish in Philadelphia: Ten Generations of Urban Experience.* Philadelphia: Temple University Press, 1973.

———. *Hibernia America: The Irish and Regional Cultures.* New York: Greenwood, 1986.

Clark, Norman. *Deliver Us from Evil: An Interpretation of American Prohibition.* New York: W. W. Norton, 1976.

Clinch, Thomas. *Urban Populism and Free Silver in Montana.* Missoula: University of Montana Press, 1970.

Clune, Frank, *Ned Kelly.* Sydney: Angus and Robertson, 1954.

Coburn, Carol, and Martha Smith. *Spirited Lives: How Nuns Shaped Catholic Culture and American Life, 1836–1920.* Chapel Hill: University of North Carolina Press, 1999.

Cochran, Thomas C. *Frontiers of Change: Early Industrialism in America.* New York: Oxford University Press, 1981.

Coleman, Michael. *American Indians, the Irish, and Government Schooling: A Comparative Study.* Lincoln: University of Nebraska Press, 2007.

Coleman, Terry. *Going to America.* Garden City: Anchor Press, 1973.

Colley, Linda. *Britons: Forging the Nation, 1707–1837.* New Haven: Yale University Press, 1992.

Collins, Michael L. *That Damned Cowboy: Theodore Roosevelt and the American West, 1883–1898.* New York: Peter Lang, 1990.

Condon, Kevin. *The Missionary College of All Hallows: 1842–1891.* Dublin: All Hallows College, 1986.

Connelly, Bridget. *Forgetting Ireland.* St. Paul: Borealis Books, 2003.

Corkery, Daniel. *Hidden Ireland: A Study of Gaelic Munster in the Eighteenth Century.* Dublin: M. H. Gill and Son, 1925.

Cornford, Daniel, ed. *Working People of California.* Berkeley: University of California Press, 1995.

Countryman, Edward. *Americans: A Collision of Histories.* New York: Hill and Wang, 1996.

Courtwright, David T. *Violent Land: Single Men and Social Disorder from the Frontier to the Inner City.* Cambridge, Mass.: Harvard University Press, 1996.

Crislock, Charles. *The Progressive Era in Minnesota, 1899–1918.* St. Paul: Minnesota Historical Society Press, 1971.

Cronin, Bernard. *Father Yorke and the Labor Movement in San Francisco, 1900–1910.* Washington, D.C.: Catholic University Press, 1943.

Cronon, William. *Nature's Metropolis: Chicago and the Great West.* New York: W. W. Norton, 1991.

Cronon, William, George Miles, and Jay Gitlin, eds. *Under a Western Sky: Rethinking America's Western Past.* New York: W. W. Norton, 1992.

Cross, Eric. *The Tailor and Ansty* (1942). Cork: Mercier, 1999.

Cross, Ira. *A History of the Labor Movement in California.* Berkeley: University of California Press, 1935.

Cross, Robert. *The Emergence of Liberal Catholicism in America.* Cambridge, Mass.: Harvard University Press, 1958.

Cullingford, Elizabeth Butler. *Ireland's Others: Ethnicity and Gender in Irish Literature and Popular Culture.* Notre Dame: University of Notre Dame Press, 2001.

Cunliffe, Marcus. *Chattel Slavery and Wage Slavery; The Anglo-American Context, 1830–1860.* Athens: University of Georgia Press, 1979.

Cunliffe, Marcus, and Robin Winks. *Pastmasters: Some Essays on American Historians.* New York: Harper and Row, 1969.

Curley, James Michael. *I'd Do It Again.* Englewood Cliffs: Prentice-Hall, 1957.

Curran, Robert. *Michael Augustine Corrigan and the Shaping of Conservative Catholicism in America, 1878–1902.* New York: Arno, 1978.

Curtis, L. Perry. *Apes and Angels: The Irishman in Victorian Caricature.* Washington, D.C.: Smithsonian Institution Press, 1997.

D'Agostino, Peter. *Rome in America.* Chapel Hill: University of North Carolina Press, 2004.

Daly, John Patrick. *When Slavery Was Called Freedom: Evangelicalism, Proslavery, and the Causes of the Civil War.* Lexington: University Press of Kentucky, 2002.

Dangerfield, George. *The Damnable Question: A History of Anglo-Irish Relations* (1976). New York: Barnes and Noble Books, 1999.

D'Arcy, William. *The Fenian Movement in the United States, 1858–1886* (1947). New York: Russell and Russell, 1971.

Darnton, Robert. *The Great Cat Massacre and Other Episodes in French Cultural History.* New York: Basic Books, 1984.

Davis, David Brion, ed. *The Fear of Conspiracy: Images of Un-American Subversion from the Revolution to the* Present. Ithaca: Cornell University Press, 1971.

Davis, Ronald L. *John Ford: Hollywood's Old Master.* Norman: University of Oklahoma Press, 1995.

Decker, Peter R. *Fortunes and Failures: White-Collar Mobility in Nineteenth-Century San Francisco.* Cambridge, Mass.: Harvard University Press, 1978.

Deloria, Philip. *Playing Indian.* New Haven: Yale University Press, 1998.

Demos, John. *The Unredeemed Captive: A Family Story from Early America.* New York: Alfred A. Knopf, 1994.

de Nie, Michael. *The Eternal Paddy: Irish Identity and the British Press, 1798–1882.* Madison: University of Wisconsin Press, 2004.

Dening, Greg. *The Death of William Gooch: A History's Anthropology* (1988). Honolulu: University of Hawai'i Press, 1995.

———. *Performances.* Chicago: University of Chicago Press, 1996.

Denning, Michael. *Mechanic Accents: Dime Novels and Working-Class Culture in America.* London: Verso, 1987.

de Paor, Maire. *Patrick: The Pilgrim Apostle of Ireland.* New York: Regan Books, 1998.

Derickson, Alan. *Workers' Health, Workers' Democracy: The Western Miners' Struggle, 1891–1925.* Ithaca: Cornell University Press, 1988.

Deutsch, Sarah. *No Separate Refuge: Culture, Class, and Gender on an Anglo-Hispanic Frontier in the American Southwest, 1880–1940.* New York: Oxford University Press, 1987.

Dickson, R. J. *Ulster Emigration to Colonial America, 1718–1785* (1966). London: Ulster Historical Foundation, 1996.

Digby, Margaret. *Horace Plunkett: An Anglo-American Irishman.* Oxford: Basil Blackwell, 1949.

Diner, Hasia. *Erin's Daughters in America: Irish Immigrant Women in the Nineteenth Century.* Baltimore: Johns Hopkins University Press, 1983.

Dolan, Jay. *In Search of an American Catholicism: A History of Religion and Culture in Tension.* New York: Oxford University Press, 2002.

Donnelly, James. *The Land and the People of Nineteenth-Century Cork: The Rural Economy and the Land Question.* London: Routledge and Kegan Paul, 1975.

———. *The Great Irish Potato Famine.* London: Sutton Publishing, 2001.

Doyle, David Noel. *Irish Americans, Native Rights and National Empires: The Structure, Divisions and Attitudes of the Catholic Minority in the Decade of Expansion, 1890–1901.* New York: Arno, 1976.

———. *Ireland, Irishmen, and Revolutionary America, 1760–1820.* Dublin: Mercier Press, 1981.

Doyle, David, and Owen D. Edwards, eds. *America and Ireland.* Westport: Greenwood, 1980.

Doyle, Roddy. *The Commitments.* New York: Vintage, 1989.

Drinan, Richard. *Facing West: The Metaphysics of Indian-Hating and Empire-Building* (1980). Norman: University of Oklahoma Press, 1997.

Dubofsky, Melvyn. *We Shall Be All: A History of the Industrial Workers of the World.* Chicago: Quadrangle Books, 1969.

Dubos, Rene, and Jean Dubos. *The White Plague: Tuberculosis, Man, and Society.* Boston: Little, Brown and Co., 1952.

Dumenil, Lynn. *Freemasonry and American Culture, 1880–1939.* Princeton: Princeton University Press, 1984.

Dungan, Myles. *How the Irish Won the West.* Dublin: New Island, 2006.

Dunne, Robert. *Antebellum Irish Immigration and Emerging Ideologies of "America": A Protestant Backlash.* Lewiston: Edwin Mellon, 2002.

Duratschek, Sister M. Claudia. *Builders of God's Kingdom: The History of the Catholic Church in South Dakota.* Sioux Falls: The Diocese, 1979.

Dwyer, John T. *Condemned to the Mines: The Life of Eugene O'Connell, 1815–1891.* New York: Vantage, 1976.

Edwards, Ruth Dudley. *Patrick Pearse: The Triumph of Failure.* New York: Taplinger Pub. Co., 1977.

Ellis, John Tracy. *American Catholicism.* 2nd revised ed. Chicago: University of Chicago Press, 1969.

Elson, Ruth. *Guardians of Tradition: American Schoolbooks of the Nineteenth Century.* Lincoln: University of Nebraska Press, 1972.

Emmons, David M. *Garden in the Grasslands: The Boomer Literature of the Central Plains.* Lincoln: University of Nebraska Press, 1969.

———. *The Butte Irish: Class and Ethnicity in an American Mining Town, 1875–1925.* Urbana and Chicago: University of Illinois Press, 1989.

Engeman, Thomas, and Michael P. Zuckert, eds. *Protestantism and the American Founding.* Notre Dame: University of Notre Dame Press, 2004.

Engh, Michael E., S.J. *Frontier Faiths: Church, Temple, and Synagogue in Los Angeles, 1846–1888.* Albuquerque: University of New Mexico Press, 1992.

Erickson, Charlotte. *Invisible Immigrants: The Adaptation of English and Scottish Immigrants in Nineteenth-Century America.* Coral Gables: University of Miami Press, 1972.

Erie, Steven. *Rainbow's End: Irish-Americans and the Dilemmas of Urban Machine Politics, 1840–1985.* Berkeley: University of California Press, 1988.

Etulain, Richard, ed. *Does the Frontier Experience Make America Exceptional?* Boston and New York: Bedford/St. Martin's, 1999.

Evans, E. Estyn. *The Personality of Ireland: Habitat, Heritage and History* (1973). Dublin: Lilliput Press, 1992.

Eyman, Scott. *Print the Legend: The Life and Times of John Ford.* New York: Simon and Schuster, 1999.

Fanning, Charles, ed. *The Exiles of Erin: Nineteenth-Century Irish-American Fiction.* Notre Dame: University of Notre Dame Press, 1987.

————. *The Irish Voice in America: Irish-American Fiction from the 1760s to the 1980s.* Lexington: University Press of Kentucky, 1990.

Farrell, James T. *Studs Lonigan: A Trilogy Comprising Young Lonigan, The Young Manhood of Studs Lonigan,* and *Judgment Day* (1932, 1934, 1935). Urbana: University of Illinois Press, 1993.

Faulkner, William. *The Sound and the Fury* (1929). New York: Vintage, 1990.

Feeney, Brian. *Sinn Féin: A Hundred Turbulent Years.* Madison: University of Wisconsin Press, 2002.

Fehrenbacher, Don. *The Dred Scott Case: Its Significance in American Law and Politics.* New York: Oxford University Press, 1978.

Fell, James. *Ore to Metals: The Rocky Mountain Smelting Industry.* Lincoln: University of Nebraska Press, 1979.

Ferguson, George. *Signs and Symbols in Christian Art.* New York: Oxford University Press, 1954.

Ferrie, Joseph. *Yankeys Now: Immigrants in the Antebellum United States, 1840–1860.* New York: Oxford University Press, 1999.

Fink, Leon. *Workingmen's Democracy: The Knights of Labor and American Politics.* Urbana: University of Illinois Press, 1985.

Finn, Janet. *Tracing the Veins: Of Copper, Culture, and Community from Butte to Chuquicamata.* Berkeley: University of California Press, 1998.

Fischer, David Hackett. *Albion's Seed: Four British Folkways in America.* New York: Oxford University Press, 1989.

Fitzgerald, F. Scott. *The Great Gatsby.* New York: Scribner's 1925.

————. *The Love of the Last Tycoon: A Western* (1941). Edited by Matthew Bruccoli. New York: Scribner, 1993.

Fitzgerald, Margaret, and Joseph King. *The Uncounted Irish in Canada and the United States.* Toronto: P. D. Meany, 1990.

Fitzgerald, Maureen. *Habits of Compassion: Irish Catholic Nuns and the Origins of the Welfare System, 1830–1920.* Urbana: University of Illinois Press, 2005.

Fitzpatrick, David. *Oceans of Consolation: Personal Accounts of Irish Migration to Australia.* Ithaca: Cornell University Press, 1994.

Fixico, Donald. *Termination and Relocation: Federal Indian Policy, 1945–1960.* Albuquerque: University of New Mexico Press, 1986.

Flanagan, Thomas. *The Year of the French.* New York: Henry Holt, 1979.

Fleming, Deborah. *"A Man Who Does Not Exist": The Irish Peasant in the Work of W. B. Yeats and J. M. Synge.* Ann Arbor: University of Michigan Press, 1995.

Fliegelman, Jay. *Prodigals and Pilgrims: The American Revolution against Patriarchal Authority, 1750–1800.* Cambridge: Cambridge University Press, 1982.

Fogarty, Gerald. *The Vatican and the Americanist Crisis: Denis J. O'Connell, American Agent in Rome, 1885–1903.* Rome: Gregorian University Press, 1974.

Foley, Neil. *The White Scourge: Mexicans, Blacks, and Poor Whites in Texas Cotton Culture.* Berkeley: University of California Press, 1997.

Foner, Eric. *Free Soil, Free Labor, Free Men: The Ideology of the Republican Party before the Civil War.* New York: Oxford University Press, 1970.

———. *Tom Paine and Revolutionary America.* New York: Oxford University Press, 1976.

———. *Politics and Ideology in the Age of the Civil War.* New York: Oxford University Press, 1980.

———. *Reconstruction: America's Unfinished Revolution, 1863–1877.* New York: Harper-collins, 1988.

Foster, Martha Harroun. *We Know Who We Are: Métis Identity in a Montana Community.* Norman: University of Oklahoma Press, 2006.

Foster, R. F. *Paddy and Mr. Punch: Connections in Irish and English History.* London: Penguin, 1993.

Franchot, Jenny. *Roads to Rome: The Antebellum Protestant Encounter with Catholicism.* Berkeley: University of California Press, 1994.

Fraysse, Olivier. *Lincoln, Land, and Labor, 1809–1860.* Translated by Sylvia Neely. Urbana: University of Illinois Press, 1994.

Fredrickson, George M. *The Inner Civil War: Northern Intellectuals and the Crisis of the Union.* New York: Harper Torchbooks, 1965.

———. *The Black Image in the White Mind: The Debate on Afro-American Character and Destiny, 1817–1914.* New York: Harper and Row, 1971.

———. *White Supremacy: A Comparative Study in American and South African History.* New York: Oxford University Press, 1982.

Freehling, William. *Prelude to Civil War: The Nullification Controversy in South Carolina, 1816–1836.* New York: Oxford University Press, 1992.

Friedheim, Robert. *The Seattle General Strike.* Seattle: University of Washington Press, 1964.

Fuchs, Lawrence. *John F. Kennedy and American Catholicism.* New York: Meredith Books, 1967.

———. *American Kaleidoscope: Race, Ethnicity, and the Civic Culture.* Hanover: Wesleyan University Press, 1990.

Funchion, Michael, ed. *Irish-American Voluntary Organizations.* Westport: Greenwood, 1983.

Furnas, J. C. *The Road to Harpers Ferry.* New York: William Sloane, 1959.

———. *The Life and Times of the Late Demon Rum.* New York: Capricorn, 1965.

Gallagher, Tag. *John Ford: The Man and His Films.* Berkeley: University of California Press, 1986.

Gates, Paul W. *Landlords and Tenants on the Prairie Frontier: Studies in American Land Policy.* Ithaca: Cornell University Press, 1973.

Gaustad, Edwin Scott. *A Religious History of America.* New York: Harper and Row, 1974.

Genovese, Eugene. *The Political Economy of Slavery: Studies in the Economy and Society of the Slave South.* New York: Pantheon, 1965.

———. *The World the Slaveholders Made: Two Essays in Interpretation.* New York: Pantheon, 1969.

———. *Roll, Jordan, Roll: The World the Slaves Made.* New York: Pantheon, 1970.

———. *The Southern Tradition: The Achievement and Limitations of an American Conservatism.* Cambridge, Mass.: Harvard University Press, 1994.

Gerschenkron, Alexander. *Economic Backwardness in Historical Perspective: A Book of Essays.* Cambridge, Mass.: Harvard University Press, 1962.

Gerteis, Louis S. *Morality and Utility in American Antislavery Reform*. Chapel Hill: University of North Carolina Press, 1987.

Gibbons, Luke. *Transformations in Irish Culture*. Notre Dame: University of Notre Dame Press, 1996.

Gienapp, *The Origins of the Republican Party, 1852–1856*. New York: Oxford University Press, 1988.

Gieske, Millard. *Minnesota Farmer-Laborism: The Third Party Alternative*. Minneapolis: University of Minnesota Press, 1979.

Gjerde, Jon. *From Peasants to Farmers: The Migration from Balestrand, Norway, to the Upper Middle West*. Cambridge: Cambridge University Press, 1985.

———, ed. *Major Problems in American Immigration and Ethnic History*. Boston: Houghton Mifflin, 1998.

———. *Minds of the West: Ethnocultural Evolution in the Rural Middle West, 1830–1917*. Chapel Hill: University of North Carolina Press, 1999.

Glassie, Henry. *Passing the Time in Ballymenone: Culture and History of an Ulster Community*. Philadelphia: University of Pennsylvania Press, 1982.

———, ed. *Irish Folk Tales*. New York: Pantheon, 1985.

Glazer, Nathan, and Daniel Moynihan. *Beyond the Melting Pot: The Negroes, Puerto Ricans, Jews, Italians, and Irish of New York City*. Cambridge, Mass.: MIT Press, 1963.

Glazier, Michael, ed. *The Encyclopedia of the Irish in America*. Notre Dame: University of Notre Dame Press, 1999.

Gleason, Philip. *Speaking of Diversity: Language and Ethnicity in Twentieth-Century America*. Baltimore: Johns Hopkins University Press, 1992.

Gleeson, David. *The Irish in the South, 1815–1877*. Chapel Hill: University of North Carolina Press, 2001.

Glickman, Lawrence. *A Living Wage: American Workers and the Making of Consumer Society*. Ithaca: Cornell University Press, 1997.

Glickstein, Jonathan A. *Concepts of Free Labor in Antebellum America*. New Haven: Yale University Press, 1991.

Golab, Caroline. *Immigrant Destinations*. Philadelphia: Temple University Press, 1977.

Golway, Terry. *Irish Rebel: John Devoy and America's Fight for Ireland's Freedom*. New York: St. Martin's, 1998.

Goodwyn, Lawrence. *Democratic Promise: The Populist Moment in America*. New York: Oxford University Press, 1976.

Goodykoontz, Colin. *Home Missions on the American Frontier: With Particular Reference to the Home Missionary Society*. Caldwell, Idaho: Caxton, 1939.

Gordon, Linda. *The Great Arizona Orphan Abduction*. Cambridge, Mass.: Harvard University Press, 1999.

Gordon, Michael. *The Orange Riots: Irish Political Violence in New York City, 1870 and 1871*. Ithaca: Cornell University Press, 1993.

Gordon, Milton. *Assimilation in American Life: The Role of Race, Religion, and National Origin*. New York: Oxford University Press, 1964.

Gould, Eliga. *The Persistence of Empire: British Political Culture in the Age of the American Revolution*. Chapel Hill: University of North Carolina Press, 2000.

Greeley, Andrew. *The Catholic Myth: The Behavior and Beliefs of American Catholics.* New York: Macmillan, 1990.

———. *The Catholic Imagination.* Berkeley: University of California Press, 2000.

Green, Archie. *Wobblies, Pile Butts, and Other Heroes: Laborlore Explorations.* Urbana: University of Illinois Press, 1993.

Green, James. *Grass-Roots Socialism: Radical Movements in the Southwest, 1895–1943.* Baton Rouge: Louisiana State University Press, 1978.

Griffin, Clifford. *Their Brothers' Keepers: Moral Stewardship in the United States, 1800–1865.* New Brunswick: Rutgers University Press, 1960.

Griffin, Patrick. *People with No Name: Ireland's Ulster Scots, America's Scots Irish, and the Creation of a British Atlantic World, 1689–1764.* Princeton: Princeton University Press, 2001.

Guinnane, Timothy. *The Vanishing Irish: Households, Migration, and the Rural Economy in Ireland, 1850–1914.* Princeton: Princeton University Press, 1997.

Gwynn, Denis. *Traitor or Patriot: The Life and Death of Roger Casement.* New York: Jonathan Cape and Harrison Smith, 1931.

Hafen, Leroy. *Broken Hand: The Life of Thomas Fitzpatrick, Mountain Man, Guide and Indian Agent.* Denver: Old West Publishing Co., 1931.

Handlin, Oscar. *The Uprooted.* Boston: Little, Brown, 1951.

———. *Boston's Immigrants: A Study in Acculturation.* Cambridge, Mass.: Harvard University Press, 1959.

Harrington, John P., ed. *Modern Irish Drama.* New York: W. W. Norton, 1991.

Hatch, Nathan. *The Democratization of American Christianity.* New Haven: Yale University Press, 1989.

Hays, Robert G. *A Race at Bay: New York Times Editorials on "the Indian Problem," 1860–1900.* Carbondale: Southern Illinois University Press, 1997.

Heaney, Seamus. *Selected Poems, 1966–1987.* New York: Noonday Press, 1990.

Hennessey, James. *American Catholics: A History of the Roman Catholic Community in the United States.* New York: Oxford University Press, 1981.

Herberg, Will. *Protestant, Catholic, Jew: An Essay in American Religious Sociology.* Garden City: Doubleday, 1955.

Hernon, Joseph M., Jr. *Celts, Catholics, and Copperheads: Ireland Views the American Civil War.* Columbus: Ohio State University Press, 1968.

Heski, Thomas M. *The Little Shadow Catcher, "Icastinyanka cikala hanzi": D. F. Barry, Photographer of Famous Indians.* Seattle: Superior Publishing Co., 1978.

Hicks, John. *The Populist Revolt: A History of the Farmers' Alliance and the People's Party* (1931). Lincoln: University of Nebraska Press, 1961.

Higham, John. *Strangers in the Land: Patterns of American Nativism, 1860–1925* (1963). New York: Atheneum, 1981.

Hill, Christopher. *The English Bible and the Seventeenth-Century Revolution.* London: Penguin, 1993.

Himmelfarb, Gertrude. *The New History and the Old: Critical Essays and Reappraisals.* Cambridge, Mass.: Harvard University Press, 1987.

Hine, Robert V. *Community on the American Frontier: Separate But Not Alone.* Norman: University of Oklahoma Press, 1980.

Hobsbawm, Eric. *Workers: Worlds of Labor.* New York: Pantheon Books, 1984.

Hochschild, Adam. *King Leopold's Ghost: A Story of Greed, Terror, and Heroism in Colonial Africa.* New York: Houghton Mifflin, 1999.

Hofstadter, Richard. *The Paranoid Style in American Politics.* New York: Knopf, 1965.

————. *The Progressive Historians: Turner, Beard, Parrington.* New York: Alfred A. Knopf, 1968.

Hofstadter, Richard, and Seymour Martin Lipset, eds. *Turner and the Sociology of the Frontier.* New York: Basic Books, 1968.

Holliday, J. S. *The World Rushed In: The California Gold Rush Experience* (1981). Norman: University of Oklahoma Press, 1999.

Holt, Marilyn Irvin. *The Orphan Trains: Placing Out in America,* Lincoln: University of Nebraska Press, 1992.

Holt, Michael F. *The Political Crisis of the 1850s.* New York: W. W. Norton, 1978.

Horgan, Paul. *Lamy of Santa Fe: His Life and Times.* New York: Farrar, Straus, Giroux, 1975.

Horsman, Reginald. *Race and Manifest Destiny: The Origins of American Racial Anglo-Saxonism.* Cambridge, Mass.: Harvard University Press, 1981.

Howard, Joseph Kinsey. *Montana: High, Wide, and Handsome.* New Haven: Yale University Press, 1943.

————. *Strange Empire: A Narrative of the Northwest.* New York: William Morrow and Co., 1952.

Howe, Daniel Walker. *The Political Culture of the American Whigs.* Chicago: University of Chicago Press, 1979.

Hoy, Suellen. *Good Hearts: Catholic Sisters in Chicago.* Urbana: University of Illinois Press, 2004.

Hubendorf, Shari. *Going Native: Indians in the American Cultural Imagination.* Ithaca: Cornell University Press, 2001.

Hunt, William. *Whiskey Peddler: Johnny Healy, North Frontier Trader.* Missoula: Mountain Press, 1992.

Ibsen, John Duffy. *Will the World Break Your Heart?: Dimensions and Consequences of Irish-American Assimilation.* New York: Garland, 1990.

Idriess, Ion. *The Silver City: The Saga of Broken Hill Mining.* Sydney: Angus and Robertson, 1956.

Ignatiev, Noel. *How the Irish Became White.* New York: Routledge, 1995.

Inglis, Brian. *Roger Casement.* New York: Harcourt Brace Jovanovich, 1973.

Irish-English/English-Irish Dictionary. Boulder: Roberts Rinehart, 1998.

Issel, William, and Robert W. Cherny. *San Francisco, 1865–1932: Politics, Power, and Urban Development.* Berkeley: University of California Press, 1986.

Jacobs, Wilbur. *On Turner's Trail: 100 Years of Writing Western History.* Lawrence: University Press of Kansas, 1994.

Jacobson, Matthew Frye. *Special Sorrows: The Diasporic Imagination of Irish, Polish, and Jewish Immigrants in the United States.* Cambridge, Mass.: Harvard University Press, 1995.

————. *Whiteness of a Different Color: European Immigrants and the Alchemy of Race.* Cambridge, Mass.: Harvard University Press, 1998.

————. *Barbarian Virtues: The United States Encounters Foreign Peoples at Home and Abroad.* New York: Hill and Wang, 2000.

James, Don. *Butte's Memory Book.* Caldwell, Idaho: Caxton Printers, 1980.

Jameson, Elizabeth. *All That Glitters: Class, Conflict, and Community in Cripple Creek.* Urbana and Chicago: University of Illinois Press, 1998.

Jasper, James. *Restless Nation: Starting Over in America.* Chicago: University of Chicago Press, 2000.

Jenkins, Philip. *The New Anti-Catholicism: The Last Acceptable Prejudice.* New York: Oxford University Press, 2003.

Jennings, Francis. *The Invasion of America: Indians, Colonialism, and the Cant of Conquest*. Chapel Hill: University of North Carolina Press, 1975.

Jensen, Richard. *The Winning of the Midwest: Social and Political Conflict, 1888–1896*. Chicago: University of Chicago Press, 1971.

Jensen, Vernon. *Heritage of Conflict: Labor Relations in the Nonferrous Metals Industry Up to 1930*. Ithaca: Cornell University Press, 1950.

Johanningsmeier, Edward. *Forging American Communism: The Life of William Z. Foster*. Princeton: Princeton University Press, 1994.

Johnson, Paul. *A Shopkeepers' Millennium: Society and Revivals in Rochester, New York, 1815–1837*. New York: Hill and Wang, 1978.

Johnson, Susan Lee. *Roaring Camp: The Social World of the California Gold Rush*. New York: W. W. Norton, 1999.

Johnston, Patricia Condon. *Minnesota's Irish*. Afton, Minn.: Johnston Pub., 1984.

Jordan, Donald, and Timothy O'Keefe, eds. *The Irish in the San Francisco Bay Area: Essays on Good Fortune*. San Francisco: Irish Literary and Historical Society, 2005.

Jordan, Winthrop. *White over Black: American Attitudes toward the Negro, 1550–1812*. Chapel Hill: University of North Carolina Press, 1969.

Joyce, James. *A Portrait of the Artist as a Young Man* (1916). New York: Penguin Classics, 2003.
———. *Ulysses* (1934). New York: Vintage International, 1990.

Joyner, Charles. *Down by the Riverside: A South Carolina Slave Community*. Urbana: University of Illinois Press, 1984.

Kammen, Michael. *A Season of Youth: The American Revolution and the Historical Imagination*. Ithaca: Cornell University Press, 1978.

Kamphoefner, Walter, Wolfgang Helbich, and Ulrike Sommer, eds. *News from the Land of Freedom: German Immigrants Write Home*. Ithaca: Cornell University Press, 1991.

Kasson, John F. *Civilizing the Machine: Technology and Republican Values in America, 1776–1900*. New York: Viking, 1976.

Kazin, Michael. *Barons of Labor: The San Francisco Building Trades and Union Power in the Progressive Era*. Urbana: University of Illinois Press, 1987.

Keane, John. *Durango: A Novel*. Cork: Mercier, 1992.

Kearney, Richard, ed. *Migrations: The Irish at Home and Abroad*. Dublin: Wolfhound Press, 1990.

Kearns, R. H. B. *Broken Hill, 1883–1893*. Vol. 1. Broken Hill, New South Wales: Broken Hill Historical Society, 1973.

Kee, Robert. *The Green Flag: A History of Irish Nationalism* (1972). London: Penguin, 2000.

Kelley, Robert. *The Transatlantic Persuasion: The Liberal-Democratic Mind in the Age of Gladstone*. New York: Alfred Knopf, 1969.

Kelly, Mary C. *The Shamrock and the Lily: The New York Irish and the Creation of a Transatlantic Identity, 1845–1921*. New York: Peter Lang, 2005.

Kelly, Mary Gilbert, O.P. *Catholic Immigrant Colonization Projects in the U.S., 1815–1860*. New York: Columbia University Press, 1939.

Kemp, David. *The Irish in Dakota*. Sioux Falls: Rushmore House, 1992.

Keneally, Thomas. *The Great Shame and the Triumph of the Irish in the English-Speaking World*. New York: Doubleday, 1998.

Kennedy, J. H. *Jesuit and Savage in New France*. New Haven: Yale University Press, 1955.

Kenny, Kevin. *Making Sense of the Molly Maguires.* New York: Oxford University Press, 1998.

————. *The American Irish.* Harlow, England: Longman, 2000.

————, ed. *New Directions in Irish-American History.* Madison: University of Wisconsin Press, 2003.

Kiberd, Declan. *Inventing Ireland: The Literature of the Modern Nation.* Cambridge, Mass.: Harvard University Press, 1995.

Kilkenny, John. *Shamrocks and Shepherds: The Irish of Morrow County.* Portland: Oregon Historical Society, 1981.

Kinzer, Donald. *An Episode in Anti-Catholicism: The American Protective Association.* Seattle: University of Washington Press, 1964.

Klein, Kerwin. *Frontiers of Historical Imagination: Narrating the European Conquest of Native America, 1890–1990.* Berkeley: University of California Press, 1997.

Kleppner, Paul. *The Cross of Culture: A Social Analysis of Midwestern Politics, 1850–1900.* New York: Free Press, 1970.

Kluger, James R. *The Clifton-Morenci Strike: Labor Difficulty in Arizona, 1915–1916.* Tucson: University of Arizona Press, 1970.

Knight, Robert. *Industrial Relations in the San Francisco Bay Area, 1900–1918.* Berkeley: University of California Press, 1960.

Knobel, Dale. *Paddy and the Republic: Ethnicity and Nationality in Antebellum America.* Middletown, Conn.: Wesleyan University Press, 1986.

Knox, Oliver. *Rebels and Informers: Stirrings of Irish Independence.* New York: Palgrave Macmillan 1998.

Kornbluh, Joyce. *Rebel Voices: An IWW Anthology.* Ann Arbor: University of Michigan Press, 1964.

Kraditor, Aileen. *The Radical Persuasion: Aspects of the Intellectual History and the Historiography of Three American Radical Organizations.* Baton Rouge: Louisiana State University Press, 1981.

Landes, David. *The Unbound Prometheus: Technological Change and Industrial Development in Western Europe from 1750 to the Present.* Cambridge: Cambridge University Press, 1969.

Lankton, Larry. *Cradle to Grave: Life, Work, and Death at the Lake Superior Copper Mines.* New York: Oxford University Press, 1991.

————. *Beyond the Boundaries: Life and Landscape at the Lake Superior Copper Mines, 1840–1875.* New York: Oxford University Press, 1997.

Larkin, Emmet. *The Roman Catholic Church and the Creation of the Modern Irish State, 1878–1886.* Philadelphia: American Philosophical Society, 1975.

————. *The Historical Dimensions of Irish Catholicism* (1976). Washington, D.C.: Catholic University of America Press, 1997.

————. *The Roman Catholic Church and the Plan of Campaign, 1886–1888.* Cork: Cork University Press, 1978.

————. *The Roman Catholic Church and the Fall of Parnell, 1888–1891.* Chapel Hill: University of North Carolina Press, 1979.

————. *The Consolidation of the Roman Catholic Church in Ireland, 1860–1870.* Chapel Hill: University of North Carolina Press, 1987.

————, ed. and trans. *Tocqueville's Journey in Ireland, July–August, 1835.* Washington, D.C.: Catholic University of America Press, 1990.

Larson, Erik. *The Devil in the White City: Murder, Magic, and Madness at the Fair That Changed America*. New York: Crown, 2003.

Larson, T. A. *History of Wyoming*. Lincoln: University of Nebraska Press, 1990.

Lasch, Christopher. *The New Radicalism in America, 1889–1963: The Intellectual as a Social Type*. New York: Knopf, 1965.

———. *The True and Only Heaven: Progress and Its Critics*. New York: W. W. Norton, 1991.

Laslett, John H. M., and Seymour Martin Lipset, eds. *Failure of a Dream?: Essays in the History of American Socialism*. Rev. ed. Berkeley: University of California Press, 1984.

Laughlin, Helen Rose, and Margaret Laughlin. *A Century of Memories: A History of St. Patrick's Catholic Church, Imogene, Iowa, 1880–1980*. Red Oak, Iowa: Nishna Printing Co., 1981.

Laurie, Bruce. *Artisans into Workers: Labor in Nineteenth-Century America*. New York: Noonday, 1989.

Lears, Jackson Turner. *No Place of Grace: Antimodernism and the Transformation of American Culture, 1880–1920*. New York: Pantheon, 1981.

Lee, J. J., and Marion R. Casey, eds. *Making the Irish American: History and Heritage of the Irish in the United States*. New York: New York University Press, 2006.

Lee, Joseph. *The Modernization of Irish Society, 1848–1918*. Dublin: Gill and Macmillan, 1983.

Levine, Edward. *The Irish and Irish Politicians: A Study of Cultural and Social Alienation*. Notre Dame: University of Notre Dame Press, 1966.

Lewis, Oscar. *The Silver Kings: The Lives and Times of Mackay, Fair, Flood, and O'Brien* (1947). Reno: University of Nevada Press, 1986.

Lewis, R. W. B. *The American Adam: Innocence, Tragedy, and Tradition in the Nineteenth Century*. Chicago: University of Chicago Press, 1967.

Leyburn, James G. *The Scotch-Irish: A Social History*. Chapel Hill: University of North Carolina Press, 1962.

Licht, Walter. *Working for the Railroad: The Organization of Work in the Nineteenth Century*. Princeton: Princeton University Press, 1983.

Limerick, Patricia. *Legacy of Conquest: The Unbroken Past of the American West*. New York: W. W. Norton, 1987.

Lingenfelter, Richard. *The Hardrock Miners: A History of the Mining Labor Movement in the American West, 1863–1893*. Berkeley: University of California Press, 1974.

Lipset, Seymour, and Gary Marks. *It Didn't Happen Here: Why Socialism Failed in the United States*. New York: W. W. Norton, 2000.

Luebke, Frederick, ed. *European Immigrants in the American West: Community Histories*. Albuquerque: University of New Mexico Press, 1998.

Lukas, Tony. *Common Ground: A Turbulent Decade in the Lives of Three American Families*. New York: Knopf, 1985.

———. *Big Trouble: A Murder in a Small Western Town Sets Off a Struggle for the Soul of America*. New York: Simon and Schuster, 1997.

MacDonagh, Oliver. *States of Mind: Two Centuries of Anglo-Irish Conflict, 1780–1980*. London: Pimlico, 1983.

MacDonagh, Oliver, and W. F. Mandle, eds. *Ireland and Irish-Australia: Studies in Cultural and Political History*. London and Sydney: Croom Helm, 1986.

Madsen, Brigham. *Glory Hunter: A Biography of Patrick Edward Connor*. Salt Lake City: University of Utah Press, 1990.

Maffly-Kipp, Laurie F. *Religion and Society in Frontier California.* New Haven: Yale University Press, 1994.

Maier, Pauline. *From Resistance to Revolution: Colonial Radicals and the Development of American Opposition to Britain, 1765–1776.* New York: Vintage Edition, 1974.

Malone, Michael. *The Battle for Butte: Mining and Politics on the Northern Frontier, 1864–1906.* Seattle: University of Washington Press, 1981.

Mansergh, Nicholas. *The Irish Question, 1840–1921: A Commentary on Anglo-Irish Relations and on Social and Political Forces in Ireland in the Age of Reform and Revolution* (1940). London: Allen and Unwin, 1965.

Marcosson, Isaac. *Anaconda.* New York: Dodd, Mead, 1957.

Mardock, Robert W. *The Reformer and the American Indians.* Columbia: University of Missouri Press, 1974.

Marsden, George. *The Outrageous Idea of Christian Scholarship.* New York: Oxford University Press, 1997.

Marty, Martin. *Righteous Empire: The Protestant Experience in America.* New York: Harper, 1970.

Marx, Leo. *The Machine in the Garden: Technology and the Pastoral Ideal in America.* New York: Oxford University Press, 1964.

Massa, Mark, S.J. *Anti-Catholicism in America: The Last Acceptable Prejudice.* New York: Crossroad, 2003.

May, Henry F. *Protestant Churches and Industrial America.* New York: Harper Torchbooks, 1967.

McCaffrey, Lawrence. *The Irish Diaspora in America.* Bloomington: Indiana University Press, 1976.

———. *Textures of Irish America.* Syracuse: Syracuse University Press, 1992.

McCarthy, Cormac. *Blood Meridian, or the Evening Redness in the West* (1985). New York: Vintage, 1992.

———. *No Country for Old Men.* New York: Random House, 2005.

McClelland, David. *The Achieving Society.* Princeton: Van Nostrand, 1961.

McCloskey, Robert G. *American Conservatism in the Age of Enterprise.* New York: Harper and Row, 1964.

McDiarmid, Lucy, and Michael J. Durkan. *Writing Irish: Selected Interviews with Irish Writers from "The Irish Literary Supplement."* Edited by James P. Myers, Jr. Syracuse: Syracuse University Press, 1999.

McFeely, William S. *Frederick Douglass.* New York: W. W. Norton, 1991.

McGrath, Eamonn. *The Charnel House.* Belfast: Blackstaff Press, 1990.

McGrath, Roger. *Gunfighters, Highwaymen, and Vigilantes: Violence on the Frontier.* Berkeley: University of California Press, 1984.

McGreevy, John. *Catholicism and American Freedom: A History.* New York: W. W. Norton, 2003.

McKivigan, John. *War against Proslavery Religion: Abolitionism and the Northern Churches, 1830–1865.* Ithaca: Cornell University Press, 1984.

McLysaght, Edward. *Irish Families: Their Names, Arms, and Origins.* New York: Crown Publishers, 1972.

McMath, Robert. *American Populism: A Social History, 1877–1898.* New York: Hill and Wang, 1993.

McMurry, Donald. *Coxey's Army: A Study of the Industrial Army Movement of 1894,* Boston: Little, Brown, 1929.

McWhiney, Grady, and Perry Jamieson. *Attack and Die: Civil War Military Tactics and the Southern Heritage*. University: University of Alabama Press, 1982.

McWilliams, Carey. *California: The Great Exception*. New York: Current Books, 1949.

Meagher, Timothy. *Inventing Irish America: Generation, Class, and Ethnic Identity in a New England City, 1880–1928*. Notre Dame: University of Notre Dame Press, 2001.

———. *The Columbia Guide to Irish American History*. New York: Columbia University Press, 2005.

Meinig, D. W. *Transcontinental America, 1850–1915*. Vol. 3 of *The Shaping of America: A Geographical Perspective on 500 Years of History*. New Haven: Yale University Press, 1998.

Mellinger, P. J. *Race and Labor in Western Copper: The Fight for Equality, 1896–1918*. Tucson: University of Arizona Press, 1995.

Menand, Louis. *The Metaphysical Club: A Story of Ideas in America*. New York: Farrar, Straus, and Giroux, 2002.

Messbarger, Paul. *Fiction with a Parochial Purpose: Social Uses of American Catholic Literature, 1884–1900*. Boston: Boston University Press, 1971.

Meyers, Jeffrey. *Scott Fitzgerald: A Biography*. New York: HarperCollins, 1994.

Miller, J. R. *Shingwauk's Vision: A History of Native Residential Schools*. Toronto: University of Toronto Press, 2003.

Miller, Kerby. *Emigrants and Exiles: Ireland and the Irish Exodus to North America*. New York: Oxford University Press, 1985.

———. *Ireland and Irish America: Culture, Class, and Transatlantic Migration*. Dublin: Field Day, 2008.

Miller, Kerby, Arnold Schrier, Bruce Boling, and David N. Doyle. *Irish Immigrants in the Land of Canaan: Letters and Memories from Colonial and Revolutionary America, 1675–1815*. New York: Oxford University Press, 2003.

Miller, Randall M., Harry S. Stout, and Charles Reagan Wilson, eds. *Religion and the American Civil War*. New York: Oxford University Press, 1998.

Miller, Robert Ryal. *Shamrock and Sword: The Saint Patrick's Battalion in the U.S.-Mexican War*. Norman: University of Oklahoma Press, 1989.

Miller, William Lee. *Arguing about Slavery: The Great Battle in the United States Congress*. New York: Alfred A. Knopf, 1997.

Milner, Clyde, Carol O'Connor, and Martha Sandweiss, eds. *The Oxford History of the American West*. New York: Oxford University Press, 1994.

Mink, Gwendolyn. *Old Labor and New Immigrants in American Political Development: Union, Party, and State, 1875–1920*. Ithaca: Cornell University Press, 1986.

Mokyr, Joel. *Why Ireland Starved: An Analytical and Quantitative History of the Irish Economy, 1800–1850*. London: Allen and Unwin, 1985.

Montgomery, David. *Beyond Equality: Labor and the Radical Republicans, 1862–1872*. New York: Alfred A. Knopf, 1967.

———. *The Fall of the House of Labor*. Cambridge: Cambridge University Press, 1987.

Moore, Barrington. *Social Origins of Dictatorship and Democracy: Lord and Peasant in the Making of the Modern World*. Boston: Little, Brown, 1966.

Moore, Brian. *Black Robe* (1985). London: Penguin, 1997.

Moore, R. Laurence. *Religious Outsiders and the Making of Americans*. New York: Oxford University Press, 1986.

Moran, Gerard. *Sending Out Ireland's Poor: Assisted Emigration to North America in the Nineteenth Century.* Dublin: Four Courts Press, 2004.

Morgan, Philip. *Slave Counterpoint: Black Culture in the Eighteenth-Century Chesapeake and Low Country.* Chapel Hill: University of North Carolina Press, 1998.

Morlan, Robert. *Political Prairie Fire: The Nonpartisan League, 1915–1922* (1955). St. Paul: Minnesota Historical Society Press, 1985.

Morris, Charles. *American Catholic: The Saints and Sinners Who Built America's Most Powerful Church.* New York: Vintage, 1997.

Morris, Thomas. *Rights of Catholic Initiation for Adults: Transforming the Church.* New York: Paulist Press, 1989.

Morrison, Michael A. *Slavery and the American West: The Eclipse of Manifest Destiny and the Coming of the Civil War.* Chapel Hill: University of North Carolina Press, 1997.

Moses, L. G. *The Indian Man: A Biography of James Mooney.* Urbana: University of Illinois Press, 1984.

Moynihan, James. *The Life of Archbishop John Ireland.* New York: Harper and Bros., 1953.

Mulder, John. *Woodrow Wilson: The Years of Preparation.* Princeton: Princeton University Press, 1978.

Muldoon, Paul. *Poems, 1968–1998.* New York: Farrar, Straus, and Giroux, 2001.

Murdoch, David. *The American West: The Invention of a Myth.* Reno: University of Nevada Press, 2002.

Murphy, Mary. *Mining Cultures: Men, Women, and Leisure in Butte, 1914–1941.* Urbana: University of Illinois Press, 1997.

Nabokov, Peter. *A Forest of Time: American Indian Ways of History.* Cambridge: Cambridge University Press, 2000.

Neufeld, Maurice, Daniel Leab, and Dorothy Swanson, eds. *American Working Class History: A Representative Bibliography.* New York: R. R. Bowker Co., 1983.

Noble, David. *Historians against History: The Frontier Thesis and the National Covenant in American Historical Writing since 1830.* Minneapolis: University of Minnesota Press, 1965.

———. *The Eternal Adam and the New World Garden.* New York: Grosset and Dunlap, 1968.

Nolan, Frederick. *The West of Billy the Kid.* Norman: University of Oklahoma Press, 1999.

———. *The Billy the Kid Reader.* Norman: University of Oklahoma Press, 2007.

Nolan, Janet. *Ourselves Alone: Women's Emigration from Ireland, 1885–1920.* Lexington: University Press of Kentucky, 1989.

Noll, Mark, ed. *God and Mammon: Protestants, Money and the Market, 1790–1860.* New York: Oxford University Press, 2001.

———. *The Civil War as a Theological Crisis.* Chapel Hill: University of North Carolina Press, 2006.

North, Douglass C. *The Economic Growth of the United States, 1790–1860* (1961). New York: W. W. Norton, 1965.

Novick, Peter. *That Noble Dream: The "Objectivity Question" and the American Historical Profession.* Cambridge: Cambridge University Press, 1988.

Nugent, Walter. *Crossings: The Great Transatlantic Migrations, 1870–1914.* Bloomington: Indiana University Press, 1992.

———. *Into the West: The Story of Its People.* New York: Knopf, 1999.

O'Brien, John, and Pauric Travers, eds. *The Irish Emigrant Experience in Australia.* Dublin: Poolbeg, 1991.

O'Brien, M. J. *A Hidden Phase of American History: Ireland's Part in America's Struggle for Liberty.* New York: American Irish Historical Society, 1919.

————. *Pioneer Irish in New England.* New York: American Irish Historical Society, 1937.

————. *Irish Settlers in America: A Consolidation of Articles from the Journal of the American Irish Historical Society.* 2 vols. Baltimore: Genealogical Publishing Co., 1979.

O'Broin, Leon. *Fenian Fever.* New York: New York University Press, 1971.

O'Connell, Marvin. *John Ireland and the American Catholic Church.* St. Paul: Minnesota Historical Society Press, 1988.

O'Connor, Edwin. *The Last Hurrah.* New York: Bantam, 1956.

O'Connor, Stephen. *Orphan Trains: The Story of Charles Loring Brace and the Children He Saved and Failed.* New York: Houghton Mifflin, 2001.

O'Connor, Thomas. *The Boston Irish: A Political History.* Boston: Northeastern University Press, 1996.

O'Dea, John. *History of the Ancient Order of Hibernians and Ladies' Auxiliary.* 3 vols. (1923). Notre Dame: University of Notre Dame Press, 1991.

O'Dwyer, Riobard. *Who Were My Ancestors? A Genealogy of Eyeries Parish, Castletownbere County Cork.* Astoria, Ill.: Stevens Pub. Co., 1976.

Oestreicher, Richard. *Solidarity and Fragmentation: Working People and Class Consciousness in Detroit, 1875–1900.* Urbana: University of Illinois Press, 1989.

O'Faolain, Julia. *No Country for Young Men* (1980). New York: Carroll and Graf, 1987.

O'Faoláin, Seán. *King of the Beggars: A Life of Daniel O'Connell.* New York: Viking Press, 1938.

————. *The Story of the Irish People* (1949). New York: Avenel Books, 1982.

O'Farrell, Patrick. *Ireland's English Question: Anglo-Irish Relations, 1534–1970.* New York: Schocken Books, 1971.

————. *England and Ireland since 1800.* New York: Oxford University Press, 1975.

————. *The Irish in Australia.* New South Wales: New South Wales University Press, 1993.

Ó Gráda, Cormac. *Ireland before and after the Famine: Explorations in Economic History, 1800–1925.* 2nd ed. Manchester: Manchester University Press, 1993.

————. *Black '47 and Beyond: The Great Irish Famine in History, Economy, and Memory.* Princeton: Princeton University Press, 1999.

O'Leary, Elizabeth L. *At Beck and Call: The Representation of Domestic Servants in Nineteenth-Century American Painting.* Washington, D.C.: Smithsonian Institution Press, 1996.

O'Malley, Padraig. *Biting at the Grave: The Irish Hunger Strikes and the Politics of Despair.* Boston: Beacon Press, 1990.

O'Meara, Walter. *Cloquet: The Trees Went Forth.* New York: Crown Pub., 1947.

————. *We Made It through the Winter: A Memoir of North Minnesota Boyhood.* St. Paul: Minnesota Historical Society Press, 1974.

O'Neill, William L., ed. *Echoes of Revolt: The Masses, 1911–1911.* Chicago: Ivan Dee, 1989.

Ostler, Jeffrey. *Prairie Populism: The Fate of Agrarian Radicalism in Kansas, Nebraska, and Iowa, 1880–1892.* Lawrence: University Press of Kansas, 1993.

O'Toole, Fintan. *The Ex-Isle of Erin: Images of a Global Ireland.* Dublin: New Island Books, 1996.

————. *The Lie of the Land: Irish Identities.* London: Verso, 1997.

Palmer, Bryon. *Descent into Discourse: The Reification of Language and the Writing of Social History.* Philadelphia: Temple University Press, 1990.

Palmer, Norman. *The Irish Land League Crisis.* New York: Octagon, 1978.

Paludan, Phillip Shaw. *"A People's Contest": The Union and Civil War, 1861–1865.* New York: Harper and Row, 1988.

Parker, Dorothy. *Singing an Indian Song: A Biography of D'Arcy McNickle.* Lincoln: University of Nebraska Press, 1992.

Parman, Donald. *Indians and the American West in the Twentieth Century.* Bloomington: Indiana University Press, 1994.

Peck, Gunther. *Reinventing Free Labor: Padrones and Immigrant Workers in the North American West, 1880–1930.* Cambridge: Cambridge University Press, 2000.

Phillips, Kevin. *The Cousins' Wars: Religion, Politics, and the Triumph of Anglo-America.* New York: Basic Books, 1999.

Pole, J. R. *The Pursuit of Equality in American History.* Berkeley: University of California Press, 1979.

Porter, John. *The Vertical Mosaic.* Toronto: University of Toronto Press, 1965.

Potter, David. *The South and the Sectional Conflict.* Baton Rouge: Louisiana State University Press, 1968.

———. *The Impending Crisis, 1848–1861.* New York: Harper and Row, 1976.

Potter, George. *To the Golden Door: The Story of the Irish in Ireland and America.* Boston: Little, Brown and Co., 1960.

Prendergast, Thomas F. *Forgotten Pioneers: Irish Leaders in Early California* (1942). Freeport, N.Y.: Books for Libraries, 1972.

Prucha, Francis Paul. *The Great Father: The United States Government and the American Indians.* 2 vols. Lincoln: University of Nebraska Press, 1984.

Purdy, John L., ed. *The Legacy of D'Arcy McNickle: Writer, Historian, Activist.* Norman: University of Oklahoma Press, 1996.

Quinlan, Kieran. *Strange Kin: Ireland and the American South.* Baton Rouge: Louisiana State University Press, 2005.

Quinn, David B. *The Elizabethans and the Irish.* Ithaca: Cornell University Press, 1966.

Quinn, Peter. *Banished Children of Eve.* New York: Viking, 1994.

Quintelli-Neary, Marguerite. *The Irish American Myth of the Frontier West.* Dublin: Academica Press, 2008.

Rawley, James. *Race and Politics: "Bleeding Kansas" and the Coming of the Civil War.* New York: J. B. Lippincott, 1969.

Rees, Jim. *A Farewell to Famine.* Arklow: Arklow Enterprise Center, 1994.

Reichek, Elaine *Home Rule.* Dublin: Irish Museum of Modern Art, 1993.

Rice, Madeleine Hooke. *American Catholic Opinion on the Slavery Controversy.* New York: Columbia University Press, 1944.

Richards, Leonard L. *The California Gold Rush and the Coming of the Civil War.* New York: Alfred Knopf, 2007.

Richardson, Heather Cox. *The Greatest Nation of the Earth: Republican Economic Policies during the Civil War.* Cambridge, Mass.: Harvard University Press, 1997.

———. *West from Appomattox: The Reconstruction of America after the Civil War.* New Haven: Yale University Press, 2007.

Ridge, Martin. *Ignatius Donnelly: Portrait of a Politician* (1963). St. Paul: Minnesota Historical Society Press, 1991.

Robbins, William. *Hard Times in Paradise: Coos Bay, Oregon, 1850–1986.* Seattle: University of Washington Press, 1988.

Robertson, David. *Capital, Labor, and State: The Battle for American Labor Markets from the Civil War to the New Deal.* Lanham, Md.: Rowman and Littlefield, 2000.

Rodgers, Daniel T. *The Work Ethic in Industrial America, 1850–1920*. Chicago: University of Chicago Press, 1978.

———. *Atlantic Crossings: Social Politics in a Progressive Age*. Cambridge, Mass.: Harvard University Press, 1998.

Roediger, David. *The Wages of Whiteness*. London: Verso, 1991.

Rolle, Andrew. *Immigrant Upraised: Italian Adventurers and Colonists in an Expanding America*. Norman: University of Oklahoma Press, 1968.

Rolvaag, Ole Edvart. *Giants in the Earth*. New York: Harper and Bros., 1929.

Ronan, Margaret. *Frontier Woman: The Story of Mary Ronan* (1932). Edited by H. G. Merriam. Missoula: University of Montana Publications in History, 1973.

Rosenszweig, Roy. *Eight Hours for What We Will: Workers and Leisure in an Industrial City, 1870–1920*. Cambridge: Cambridge University Press, 1983.

Rostow, W. W. *The Stages of Economic Growth: A Non-Communist Manifesto*. Cambridge, Mass.: Harvard University Press, 1960.

———. *The Economics of Take-off into Sustained Growth: Proceedings of a Conference Held by the International Economic Association*. New York: The Association, 1965.

Roy, Jody. *Rhetorical Campaigns of the Nineteenth Century: Anti-Catholicism and Catholics in America*. Lewiston: Edwin Mellon Press, 1999.

Rumpf, Erhard, and A. C. Hepburn. *Nationalism and Socialism in Twentieth-Century Ireland*. New York: Harper and Row, 1977.

Ryan, Mary P. *Cradle of the Middle Class: The Family in Oneida County, New York, 1790–1865*. New York: Cambridge University Press, 1983.

———. *Civic Wars: Democracy and Public Life in the American City during the Nineteenth Century*. Berkeley: University of California Press, 1997.

Ryan, Paul. *On the Drumhead: A Selection from the Writings of Mike Quin* (1935). San Francisco: Pacific Publishing Foundation, 1948.

———. *Dangerous Thoughts*. New York: People's World, 1940.

Rydell, Robert. *All the World's a Fair: Visions of Empire at America's International Expositions, 1876–1916*. Chicago: University of Chicago Press, 1987.

Salvatore, Nick. *Eugene V. Debs: Citizen and Socialist*. Urbana: University of Illinois Press, 1982.

Sampson, Robert. *John L. O'Sullivan and His Times*. Kent: Kent State University Press, 2003.

Sanford, Charles. *The Quest for Paradise: Europe and the American Moral Imagination*. Urbana: University of Illinois Press, 1961.

Sarbaugh, Timothy J., and James P. Walsh, eds. *The Irish in the West*. Manhattan, Kans.: Sunflower University Press, 1992.

Saveth, Edward. *American Historians and European Immigrants, 1875–1925* (1948). New York: Russell and Russell, 1965.

Saxton, Alexander. *The Indispensable Enemy: Labor and the Anti-Chinese Movement in California*. Berkeley: University of California Press, 1975.

———. *The Rise and Fall of the White Republic: Class Politics and Mass Culture in Nineteenth-Century America*. London: Verso, 2003.

Sayers, Peig. *Peig: The Autobiography of Peig Sayers of the Great Blasket Island* (1936). Syracuse: Syracuse University Press, 1991.

Scally, Robert. *The End of Hidden Ireland: Rebellion, Famine, and Emigration*. New York: Oxford University Press, 1995.

Schaefer, Jack. *Shane* (1949). New York: Houghton-Mifflin, 2001.

Schlesinger, Arthur, Jr. *A Pilgrim's Progress: Orestes A. Brownson.* Boston: Little, Brown, 1966.

Schrier, Arnold. *Ireland and the American Emigration, 1850–1900* (1958). Chester Springs, Pa.: Dufour Editions, 1997.

Schultz, Nancy Lusignan. *Fire and Roses: The Burning of the Charlestown Convent, 1834.* New York: Free Press, 2000.

Schwantes, Carlos. *Radical Heritage: Labor, Socialism, and Reform in Washington and British Columbia, 1885–1917.* Seattle: University of Washington Press, 1979.

———. *Coxey's Army: An American Odyssey.* Lincoln: University of Nebraska Press, 1985.

Scott, James. *Weapons of the Weak: Everyday Forms of Peasant Resistance.* New Haven: Yale University Press, 1985.

Sellers, Charles. *The Market Revolution: Jacksonian America, 1815–1846.* New York: Oxford University Press, 1991.

Senkewicz, Robert M. *Vigilantes in Gold Rush San Francisco.* Stanford: Stanford University Press, 1985.

Shain, Barry Alan. *The Myth of American Individualism: The Protestant Origins of American Political Thought.* Princeton: Princeton University Press, 1994.

Shannon, James P. *Catholic Colonization on the Western Frontier.* New Haven: Yale University Press, 1957.

Shannon, William. *The American Irish: A Political and Social Portrait.* New York: Macmillan, 1963.

Singleton-Gates, Peter, and Maurice Girodias. *The Black Diaries: An Account of Roger Casement's Life and Times with a Collection of His Diaries and Public Writings.* New York: Grove Press, 1959.

Slotkin, Richard. *Regeneration through Violence: The Mythology of the American Frontier, 1600–1860.* Middletown: Wesleyan University Press, 1973.

———. *The Fatal Environment: The Myth of the Frontier in the Age of Industrialization, 1800–1890.* New York: Atheneum, 1985.

———. *Gunfighter Nation: The Myth of the Frontier in Twentieth-Century America.* New York: Atheneum, 1992.

Smith, Henry Nash. *Virgin Land: The American West as Symbol and Myth.* New York: Vintage Books, 1962.

Smith, Rogers M. *Civic Ideals: Conflicting Visions of Citizenship in U.S. History.* New Haven: Yale University Press, 1997.

Socolofsky, Homer. *The Landlord William Scully.* Lawrence: University Press of Kansas, 1979.

Solnit, Rebecca. *A Book of Migrations: Some Passages in Ireland.* London: Verso, 1997.

Spence, Clark. *Territorial Politics and Government in Montana, 1864–1889.* Urbana: University of Illinois Press, 1975.

Sproat, John. *The Best Men: Liberal Reformers in the Gilded Age.* New York: Oxford University Press, 1968.

Starr, Kevin. *Americans and the California Dream, 1850–1915.* New York: Oxford University Press, 1973.

The Statistical History of the United States from Colonial Times to the Present. 2 vols. in 1. Stamford, Conn.: Fairfield Publishers, 1965.

Steckmesser, Kent. *The Western Hero in History and Legend.* Norman: University of Oklahoma Press, 1965.

Stegner, Wallace. *Mormon Country* (1942). Lincoln: University of Nebraska Press, 2003.

————. *Where the Bluebird Sings to the Lemonade Springs: Living and Writing in the West*. New York: Random House, 1992.

Stephanson, Anders. *Manifest Destiny: American Expansion and the Empire of Right*. New York: Hill and Wang, 1995.

Stone, Lawrence. *The Past and the Present*. London: Routledge and Kegan Paul, 1981.

Suggs, George. *Colorado's War on Militant Unionism: James H. Peabody and the Western Federation of Miners* (1972). Norman: University of Oklahoma Press, 1990.

Sullivan, Mary Connelly. *Our Yesterdays: A Montana Saga*. Great Falls: Helen Sullivan Pannell, 1984.

Tansill, Charles. *America and the Fight for Irish Freedom, 1866–1922*. New York: Devin-Adair, 1957.

Tatum, Steven. *Inventing Billy the Kid: Visions of the Outlaw in America, 1881–1981*. Tucson: University of Arizona Press, 1997.

Tawney, R. H. *Religion and the Rise of Capitalism* (1926). London: Penguin, 1938.

Taylor, Lawrence. *Occasions of Faith: An Anthropology of Irish Catholics*. Philadelphia: University of Pennsylvania Press, 1995.

Taylor, Philip. *The Distant Magnet: European Emigration to the United States of America*. New York: Harper's, 1973.

Thelen, David, and Frederick E. Hoxie, eds. *Discovering America: Essays on the Search for an Identity*. Urbana: University of Illinois Press, 1994.

Thomas, John, ed. *Slavery Attacked: The Abolitionist Crusade*. Englewood Cliffs: Prentice-Hall, 1965.

————. *Alternative America: Henry George, Edward Bellamy, Henry Demarest Lloyd and the Adversary Tradition*. Cambridge, Mass.: Harvard University Press, 1983.

Thompson, E. P. *The Making of the English Working Class* (1963). New York: Vintage Books, 1966.

Tierney, Evelyn. *But of Course They Were Irish*. Moravia, Iowa: Moravia Printing Co., 1984.

Trachtenberg, Alan. *The Incorporation of America: Culture and Society in the Gilded Age*. New York: Hill and Wang, 1982.

Tracy, David. *The Analogical Imagination*. New York: Crossroads, 1982.

Trennert, Robert. *Alternative to Extinction: Federal Indian Policy and the Beginnings of the Reservation System, 1846–1851*. Philadelphia: Temple University Press, 1975.

Tygiel, Jules. *Workingmen in San Francisco, 1880–1901*. New York: Garland, 1992.

Tyler, Alice Felt. *Freedom's Ferment: Phases of American Social History from the Colonial Period to the Outbreak of the Civil War*. Minneapolis: University of Minnesota Press, 1944.

Tyler, Robert. *Rebels of the Woods: The IWW in the Pacific Northwest*. Eugene: University of Oregon Books, 1967.

Udall, Stewart. *The Forgotten Founders: Rethinking the History of the Old West*. Washington, D.C.: Island Press, 2002.

Urgo, Joseph. *Willa Cather and the Myth of American Migration*. Urbana: University of Illinois Press, 1995.

Utley, Robert. *Frontier Regulars: The United States Army and the Indian, 1866–1891*. New York: Macmillan, 1973.

————. *Billy the Kid: A Short and Violent Life*. Lincoln: University of Nebraska Press, Bison Books, 1991.

Van Nuys, Frank. *Americanizing the West: Race, Immigrants, and Citizenship, 1890–1930*. Lawrence: University Press of Kansas, 2002.

Van Tyne, Claude H. *The Causes of the War of Independence.* New York: Peter Smith, 1951.

Vaughan, W. E., and A. J. Fitzpatrick, eds. *Irish Historical Statistics: Population, 1821–1971.* Dublin: Royal Irish Academy, 1978.

Voss, Kim. *The Making of American Exceptionalism: The Knights of Labor and Class Formation in the Nineteenth Century.* Ithaca: Cornell University Press, 1993.

Walker, Peter. *Moral Choices: Memory, Desire, and Imagination in Nineteenth-Century American Abolition.* Baton Rouge: Louisiana State University Press, 1978.

Walkowitz, Daniel. *Worker City, Company Town: Iron and Cotton-Worker Protest in Troy and Cohoes, New York, 1855–1885.* Urbana: University of Illinois Press, 1981.

Wall, Eamonn. *From the Sin-é Café to the Black Hills.* Madison: University of Wisconsin Press, 1999.

Walsh, James, ed. *The San Francisco Irish, 1850–1976.* San Francisco: Irish Literary and Historical Society, 1978.

Walters, Ronald. *American Reformers, 1815–1860.* New York: Hill and Wang, 1978.

Ward, Alan, *Ireland and Anglo-American Relations, 1899–1921.* Toronto: University of Toronto Press, 1969.

Ward, Leo. *God in an Irish Kitchen.* New York: Sheed and Ward, 1939.

———. *Holding Up the Hills: The Biography of a Neighborhood.* New York: Sheed and Ward, 1941.

———. *All Over God's Irish Heaven.* Chicago: Henry Regnery, 1964.

———. *Irish Portraits and Other Poems.* Notre Dame, Ind.: Fides, 1978.

Warren, Louis. *Buffalo Bill's America: William Cody and the Wild West.* New York: Knopf, 2005.

Way, Peter. *Common Labour: Workers and the Digging of North American Canals, 1780–1860.* New York: Cambridge University Press, 1993.

Weber, Fr. Francis J , ed. *Documents of California History, 1784–1963.* Los Angeles: L. A. Dawson Book Shop, 1965.

———, ed. *Readings in California Catholic History, 1784–1963.* Los Angeles: L. A. Dawson Book Shop, 1965.

Welter, Rush. *The Mind of America, 1820–1860.* New York: Columbia University Press, 1975.

West, Elliott. *The Saloon on the Rocky Mountain Mining Frontier.* Lincoln: University of Nebraska Press, 1979.

West, Trevor. *Horace Plunkett: Co-operation and Politics.* Washington, D.C.: Catholic University Press, 1986.

Whelan, Kevin. *The Tree of Liberty: Radicalism, Catholicism and the Construction of Irish Identity.* Notre Dame: University of Notre Dame Press; Cork: Cork University Press, 1996.

White, G. Edward. *The Eastern Establishment and the Western Experience: The West of Frederic Remington, Theodore Roosevelt, Owen Wister* (1968). Austin: University of Texas Press, 1989.

White, Richard. *"It's Your Misfortune and None of My Own": A New History of the American West.* Norman: University of Oklahoma Press, 1991.

———. *Remembering Ahanagran: Storytelling in a Family's Past.* New York: Hill and Wang, 1998.

Wiebe, Robert. *The Segmented Society: An Historical Preface to the Meaning of America.* New York: Oxford University Press, 1974.

———. *The Opening of American Society from the Adoption of the Constitution to the Eve of Disunion.* New York: Vintage, 1985.

Wilentz, Sean. *Chants Democratic: New York City and the Rise of the American Working Class, 1788–1850.* New York: Oxford University Press, 1984.

Williams, Hal A. *The Democratic Party and California Politics, 1880–1896*. Stanford: Stanford University Press, 1973.

Williams, William H. A. *'Twas Only an Irishman's Dream: The Image of Ireland and the Irish in American Popular Song Lyrics, 1800–1920*. Urbana: University of Illinois Press, 1996.

Wills, Gary. *Inventing America: Jefferson's Declaration of Independence*. New York: Doubleday, 1978.

Wilson, D. A. *United Irishmen, United States: Immigrant Radicals in the Early Republic*. Ithaca: Cornell University Press, 1998.

Wingerd, Mary. *Claiming the City: Politics, Faith, and the Power of Place in St. Paul*. Ithaca: Cornell University Press, 2003.

Winn, Kenneth. *Exiles in a Land of Liberty: Mormons in America, 1830–1846*. Chapel Hill: University of North Carolina Press, 1987.

Wister, Fanny Kemble, ed. *Owen Wister Out West: His Journals and Letters*. Chicago: University of Chicago Press, 1958.

Wittke, Carl. *The Irish in America*. Baton Rouge: Louisiana State University Press, 1956.

Women and Irish Migration. Vol. 4 of *The Irish World Wide*. Edited by Patrick O'Sullivan. London: Leicester University Press, 1995.

Woodham-Smith, Cecil. *The Great Hunger: Ireland, 1845–1849*. London: Hamish Hamilton, 1962.

Woods, Lawrence. *British Gentlemen in the Wild West: The Era of the Intensely English Cowboy*. New York: Free Press, 1989.

Woodward, C. Vann. *Tom Watson: Agrarian Rebel*. New York: Oxford University Press, 1938.

———. *Origins of the New South, 1877–1913*. Baton Rouge: Louisiana State University Press, 1951.

Works Progress Administration (WPA). *Copper Camp: Stories of the World's Greatest Mining Town, Butte, Montana* (1943). New York: Hastings House, 1976.

Wrobel, David. *The End of American Exceptionalism: Frontier Anxiety from the Old West to the New Deal*. Lawrence: University Press of Kansas, 1993.

———. *Promised Lands: Promotion, Memory, and the Creation of the American West*. Lawrence: University Press of Kansas, 2002.

Wylie, Paul. *The Irish General: Thomas Francis Meagher*. Norman: University of Oklahoma Press, 2007.

Wyman, Mark. *Hardrock Epic: Western Miners and the Industrial Revolution*. Berkeley: University of California Press, 1979.

Yans-McLaughlin, Virginia, ed. *Immigration Reconsidered: History, Sociology, and Politics*. New York: Oxford University Press, 1990.

Yeats, William Butler. *The Poems of W. B. Yeats*. Edited by Richard Finneran. New York: Macmillan, 1983.

Zahler, Helene. *Eastern Workingmen and National Land Policy* (1941). New York: Greenwood, 1969.

Zeitlin, Irving M. *Liberty, Equality and Revolution in Alexis de Tocqueville*. Boston: Little, Brown and Co., 1971.

Zipser, Arthur. *Working-class Giant: The Life of William Z. Foster*. New York: International Publishers, 1981.

Articles

Abbott, Carl. "The Urban West and the Twenty-First Century." *Montana, the Magazine of Western History* 43 (Spring 1993): 62–68.

Abell, Aaron. "The Reception of Leo XIII's Labor Encyclical in America, 1891–1919." *Review of Politics* 7 (October 1945): 464–95.

Aiken, Katherine. "'It May Be Too Soon to Crow': Bunker Hill and Sullivan Company Efforts to Defeat the Miners' Union." *Western Historical Quarterly* 24 (August 1993): 309–32.

Akenson, Donald H. "The Historiography of the Irish in the United States." In *The Irish World Wide: History, Heritage, Identity,* vol. 2, *The Irish in the New Communities,* edited by Patrick O'Sullivan, 99–127. Leicester: Leicester University Press, 1992.

Anderson, Douglas Firth. "Protestantism, Progress, and Prosperity: John P. Clum and 'Civilizing' the U.S. Southwest, 1871–1886." *Western Historical Quarterly* 33 (Autumn 2002): 315–36.

Arnesen, Eric. "Whiteness and the Historians' Imagination." *International Labor and Working Class History* 60 (2001): 3–32.

Bailyn, Bernard. "Religion and Revolution: Three Biographical Studies." *Perspectives in American History* 4 (1970): 85–172.

Baritz, Loren. "The Idea of the West." *American Historical Review* 66 (April 1961): 618–40.

Barkan, Elliott. "Race, Religion and Nationality in American Society: A Model of Ethnicity —From Contact to Assimilation." *Journal of American Ethnic History* 14 (Winter 1995): 38–75.

———. "America in the Hand, Homeland in the Heart: Transnational and Translocal Immigrant Experiences in the American West." *Western Historical Quarterly* 25 (Autumn 2004): 331–54.

———. "Introduction: Immigration, Incorporation, Integration, and Transnationalism: Interdisciplinary and International Perspectives." Special Issue of *Journal of American Ethnic History* 25 (Winter/Spring 2006).

Barrett, James. "Americanization from the Bottom Up: Immigration and the Remaking of the Working Class in the United States, 1880–1930." In *Discovering America: Essays on the Search for an Identity,* edited by David Thelen and Frederick E. Hoxie, 162–86. Urbana and Chicago: University of Illinois Press, 1994.

Barrett, James, and David Roediger, "Inbetween Peoples: Race, Nationality and the 'New Immigrant' Working Class." *Journal of American Ethnic History* 16 (Spring 1997): 3–44.

Bean, William G. "An Aspect of Know-Nothingism—the Immigrant and Slavery." *South Atlantic Quarterly* 23 (1924): 319–34.

———. "Puritan versus Celt, 1850–1860." *New England Quarterly* 7 (1934): 70–89.

Beck, William O. "The Journeys of a Victorian Jason: Moreton Frewen's Western American Mining Investments, 1890–1896." *Journal of the West* 9 (July 1972): 513–30.

Beckett, Edward F., S.J. "Listening to Our History: Inculturation and Jesuit Slaveholding." *Studies in the Spirituality of Jesuits* 28 (November 1996): 1–15.

Bellah, Robert. "Religion and the Shape of National Culture." *America* 181 (July 31– August 7, 1999): 9–14.

Berlin, Ira, and Herbert Gutman. "Natives and Immigrants, Free Men and Slaves: Urban Workingmen in the Antebellum American South." *American Historical Review* 88 (December 1983): 1175–1200.

Berthoff, Rowland. "Peasants and Artisans, Puritans and Republicans: Personal Liberty and Communal Equality in American History." *Journal of American History* 69 (December 1982): 579–98.

Bewley, Marius. "Scott Fitzgerald's Criticism of America." In *F. Scott Fitzgerald: A Collection of Critical Essays,* edited by Arthur Mizener, 125–41. Englewood Cliffs: Prentice-Hall, 1963.

Bhreathneach-Lynch, Síghle. "Revisionism, the Rising, and Representation." *New Hibernia Review* 3 (Spring 1999): 83–96.

Blessing, Patrick. "Culture, Religion and the Activities of the Committee of Vigilance, San Francisco, 1856." Cushwa Center for the Study of American Catholicism, University of Notre Dame, Working Paper Series, series 8, no. 3, Fall 1980.

———. "The Irish." In *Encyclopedia of American Ethnic Groups,* 528–45. Cambridge, Mass.: Harvard University Press, 1980.

———. "Irish Emigration to the United States, 1800–1920: An Overview." In *The Irish in America: Emigration, Assimilation and Impact,* edited by P. J. Drudy, 11–38. Cambridge: Cambridge University Press, 1985.

Bodnar, John. "Remembering the Immigrant Experience in American Culture." *Journal of American Ethnic History* 15 (Fall 1995): 3–27.

Bourne, Francis Cardinal. "Pastoral Letter on Catholics and Social Reform." In *The Church and Labor,* edited by John A. Ryan and Joseph Husslein, 187–203. New York: Macmillan, 1924.

Brady, Ciarán. "Spenser's Irish Crisis: Humanism and Experience in the 1590s." *Past and Present* 3 (1986): 16–49.

Brayer, Herbert. "The 76 Ranch on the Powder River." *American West* 8 (December 1950): 73–80.

Breen, T. H. "Ideology and Nationalism on the Eve of the American Revolution: Revisions Once More in Need of Revising." *Journal of American History* 84 (June 1997): 13–39.

Brown, Richard Maxwell. "Pivot of American Vigilantism: San Francisco's Vigilance Committee of 1856." In *Reflections of Western Historians,* edited by John Carroll, 108–11. Tucson: University of Arizona Press, 1969.

Browne, Henry J. "Archbishop Hughes and Western Colonization." *Catholic Historical Review* 36 (October 1950): 257–85.

Brundage, David. "Irish Land and American Workers: Class and Ethnicity in Denver, Colorado." In *"Struggle a Hard Battle": Essays on Working-Class Immigrants,* 46–70. De Kalb: Northern Illinois University Press, 1986.

Buckley, Frank. "Thoreau and the Irish." *New England Quarterly* 13 (1940): 389–400.

Bullock, Kurt. "Possessing Wor(l)ds: Brian Friel's *Translations* and the Ordnance Survey." *New Hibernia Review* 4 (Summer 2000): 98–115.

Bullough, William. "Christopher Buckley and San Francisco: The Man and the City." In *San Francisco Irish,* edited James Walsh, 27–41. San Francisco: Irish Literary and Historical Society, 1978.

Burrows, Edwin, and Michael Wallace. "The American Revolution: The Ideology and Psychology of National Liberation." *Perspectives in American History* 6 (1972): 167–306.

Busby, Mark, David Mogen, and Paul Bryant. "Introduction: Frontier Writing as a 'Great Tradition' of American Literature." In *The Frontier Experience and the American Dream: Essays on American Literature,* edited by Mogen, Busby, and Bryant, 3–12. College Station: Texas A&M University Press, 1989.

Califano, Joseph. "Who's a Catholic to Vote For?" *America,* September 9, 2000.

Campbell, Malcolm. "The Other Immigrants: Comparing the Irish in Australia and the United States." *Journal of American Ethnic History* 14 (Spring 1995): 3–22.

———. "Immigrants on the Land: Irish Rural Settlement in Minnesota and New South Wales, 1830–1890." *New Hibernia Review* 2 (Spring 1998): 43–61.

———. "Ireland's Furthest Shores: Irish Immigrant Settlement in Nineteenth-Century California and Eastern Australia." *Pacific Historical Review* 71 (February 2002): 59–90.

Canny, Nicholas. "The Ideology of English Colonization: From Ireland to America." *William and Mary Quarterly* 30 (1973): 575–98.

Carey, Patrick. "Republicanism within American Catholicism, 1785–1860." *Journal of the Early Republic* 3 (Winter 1983): 413–37.

Cashman, Roy. "The Heroic Outlaw in Irish Folklore and Popular Fiction." *Folklore* 5 (October 2000): 191–215.

"A Centennial Symposium on the Significance of Frederick Jackson Turner." *Journal of the Early Republic* 13 (Summer 1993): 133–250.

Chiles, Frederick. "General Strike: San Francisco, 1934." *Labor History* 22 (1981): 430–65.

Clinch, Thomas A. "Coxey's Army in Montana." *Montana, the Magazine of Western History* 15 (1965): 2–11.

Coburn, Carol, and Martha Smith. "'Pray for Your Wanderers': Women Religious on the Colorado Mining Frontier." *Frontiers: A Journal of Women's Studies* 15.3 (1995): 27–52.

Coleman, Michael C. "The Responses of American Indian Children and Irish Children to the School, 1850s–1920s." *American Indian Quarterly* 23 (Summer 1999): 1–23.

Conrad, Jane. "Charles Collins: The Sioux City Promotion of the Black Hills." *South Dakota History* 2 (Spring 1972): 131–71.

Conzen, Kathleen Neils. "Historical Approaches to the Study of Rural Ethnic Communities." In *Ethnicity on the Great Plains,* edited by Frederick C. Luebke, 1–18. Lincoln: University of Nebraska Press, 1980.

———. "Mainstreams and Side Channels: The Localization of Immigrant Cultures." *Journal of American Ethnic History* 11 (Fall 1991): 5–20.

Conzen, Kathleen, David Gerber, Ewa Morawska, George Pozzetta, and Rudolph Vecoli. "The Invention of Ethnicity: A Perspective from the U.S.A." *Journal of American Ethnic History* 12 (Fall 1992): 3–41.

Cornford, Daniel. "To Save the Republic: The California Workingmen's Party in Humboldt County." In *Working People of California,* edited by Cornford, 287–310. Berkeley: University of California Press, 1995.

Cosgrove, Kevin P. "Paul Muldoon's Explorer Myth: From Madoc to Raleigh." *New Hibernian Review* 4 (Summer 2000): 67–83.

Crane, Paul, and Alfred Larson. "The Chinese Massacre." *Annals of Wyoming* (1940): 47–55.

Cronon, William, George Miles, and Jay Gitlin. "Becoming West: Toward a New Meaning for Western History." In *Under an Open Sky: Rethinking America's Western Past,* edited by Cronon, Miles, and Gitlin, 3–27. New York: W. W. Norton, 1992.

Cummings, Kathleen. "'Not the New Woman?': Irish American Women and the Creation of a Useable Past, 1890–1900." *U.S. Catholic Historian* 19 (Winter 2001): 37–52.

Curcan, Paul. "Foreword." In E. E. Evans, *The Personality of Ireland: Habitat, Heritage, and History* (1973). Dublin: Lilliput Press, 1992.

Curtis, L. Perry, Jr. "The Greening of Irish History." *Éire-Ireland* 31 (Summer 1994): 7–28.

———. "The Four Erins: Feminine Images of Ireland, 1780–1900." *Éire-Ireland* 33 and 34 (Fall/Winter 1998; Spring 1999): 70–102.

———. "Comment: The Return of Revisionism." *Journal of British Studies* 44 (January 2005): 3–24.

Daly, Mary. "Revisionism and Irish History: The Great Famine." In *The Making of Modern Irish History: Revisionism and the Revisionist Controversy,* edited by D. George Boyce and Alan O'Day, 71–89. London: Routledge, 1996.

Daniel, Cletus. "Wobblies on the Farm: The IWW in the Yakima Valley." *Pacific Northwest Quarterly* 65 (1974): 166–75.

———. "In Defense of the Wheatland Wobblies: A Critical Analysis of the IWW in California." *Labor History* 19 (1978): 485–509.

Darby, Paul. "'Without the Aid of a Sporting Safety Net?': The Gaelic Athletic Association and the Irish Emigre in San Francisco." *International Journal of the History of Sport* 26 (January 2009): 63–83.

D'Arcy, F. A. "The National Trades, Political Union and Daniel O'Connell." *Éire-Ireland* 17 (Fall 1982): 7–16.

Davis, David Brion. "Some Themes of Counter-Subversion: An Analysis of Anti-Masonic, Anti-Catholic, and Anti-Mormon Literature." In *The Fear of Conspiracy: Images of Un-American Subversion from the Revolution to the* Present, edited by Davis, 9–23. Ithaca: Cornell University Press, 1971.

Delay, Cara. "The Devotional Revolution on the Local Level: Parish Life in Post-Famine Ireland." *U.S. Catholic Historian* 22 (Summer 2004): 41–60.

de Nie, Michael. "Curing 'the Irish Moral Plague.'" *Éire-Ireland* 32 (Spring 1997): 63–85.

Derickson, Alan. "Industrial Refugees: The Migration of Silicotics from the Mines of North America and South Africa in the Early 20th Century." *Labor History* 29 (1988): 66–89.

Deverell, William F. "To Loosen the Safety Valve: Eastern Workers and Western Lands." *Western Historical Quarterly* 19 (August 1988): 269–86.

———. "Fighting Words: The Significance of the American West in the History of the United States." *Western Historical Quarterly* 25 (Summer 1994): 185–206.

Diggins, John Patrick. "Comrades and Citizens: New Mythologies in American Historiography." *American Historical Review* 90 (June 1985): 614–38.

Dionne, E. J. "We're All Liberals Now." *Commonweal* 126 (November 19, 1999).

Doan, James E. "How the Irish and Scots Became Indians: Colonial Traders and Agents and the Southeastern Tribes." *New Hibernian Review* 3 (Autumn 1999): 9–19.

Donnelly, James, Jr. "The Land Question in Nationalist Politics." In *Perspectives on Irish Nationalism,* edited by Thomas Hachey and Lawrence McCaffrey, 90–93. Lexington: University Press of Kentucky, 1989.

———. "The Marian Shrine of Knock: The First Decade." *Éire-Ireland* 28 (Summer 1993): 54–97.

——— "The Great Famine and Its Interpreters, Old and New." *History Ireland* 1 (Autumn 1993): 27–33.

———. "The Construction of the Memory of the Famine in Ireland and the Irish Diaspora, 1850–1900." *Éire-Ireland* 31 (Spring/Summer 1996): 26–61.

Dorrity, D. T. "'Monkeys in a Menagerie': The Imagery of Unionist Opposition to Home Rule, 1886–1903." *Éire-Ireland* 16 (September 1981): 19–20.

Dowling, William. "John Ford's Festive Comedy: Ireland Imagined in *The Quiet Man.*" *Éire-Ireland* 36 (Fall/Winter 2001): 190–211.

Doyle, David. "Catholicism, Politics and Irish America since 1890: Some Critical Considerations." In *The Irish in America,* edited by P. J. Drudy, 191–230. Cambridge: Cambridge University Press, 1985.

———. "The Irish as Urban Pioneers in the United States, 1850–1870." *Journal of American Ethnic History* 10 (Fall 1990–Winter 1991): 36–59.

Doyle, Donald Harrison. "Social Theory and New Communities in Nineteenth-Century America." *Western Historical Quarterly* 8 (April 1977): 151–66.

———. "The Social Function of Voluntary Associations in a Nineteenth-Century American Town." *Social Science History* 1 (Spring 1977): 338–43.

Drewniany, Peter. "Not Marionettes: The American Irish in *The Damnation of Theron Ware.*" *Éire-Ireland* 16 (Winter 1981): 48–58.

Dubofsky, Melvyn. "The Leadville Strike of 1896–97: An Appraisal." *Mid-America* 48 (1966): 99–118.

———. "The Origins of Western Working-Class Radicalism, 1890–1905." In *The Labor History Reader,* edited by Daniel J. Leab, 230–53. Urbana: University of Illinois Press, 1985.

Dunne, Robert. "A Plea for a *Protestant* American Dream: Lyman Beecher's *A Plea for the West.*" *Old Northwest* 16 (1992): 189–97.

D'Urso, Joe. "Mass Strike in Minneapolis, 1934: Interviews with Strikers." *Red Buffalo* 2 and 3 (1972): 55–90.

Eagan, Catherine. "White, If 'Not Quite': Irish Whiteness in the Nineteenth-Century Irish-American Novel." *Éire-Ireland* 36 (Spring/Summer 2001): 66–82.

Edwards, Heather. "The Irish New Woman and Emily Lawless's *Grania: The Story of an Island:* A Congenial Geography." *English Literature in Transition, 1880–1920* 51 (2008): 421–38.

Edwards, Owen Dudley. "The American Image of Ireland: A Study of Its Early Phases." *Perspectives in American History, IV.* Cambridge, Mass.: Harvard University Press, 1970.

Eid, Leroy. "Irish-American Backwoods Culture: D. H. Fischer's *Albion's Seed.*" *New Hibernia Review* 1 (Summer 1997): 83–96.

Elliott, Michael. "Ethnography, Reform, and the Problem of the Real: James Mooney's *Ghost Dance Religion.*" *American Quarterly* 50 (June 1998): 201–33.

Elliott, Russell. "Labor Troubles in the Mining Camp at Goldfield, Nevada, 1906–1908." *Pacific Historical Review* 19 (1950): 369–84.

Ellis, Kirk. "On the Warpath: John Ford and the Indians." *Journal of Popular Film and Television* 8 (Summer 1975): 34–41.

Emmons, David M. "The Influence of Ideology on Changing Environmental Images: The Case of Six Gazetteers." In *Images of the Plains: The Role of Human Nature in Settlement,* edited by Brian Blouet and Merlin Lawson, 125–36. Lincoln: University of Nebraska Press, 1975.

———. "'A Spleene to Drayne Ill Humors': Directed Immigration as an Instrument of Social Control." In *A Taste of the West: Essays in Honor of Robert G. Athearn,* edited by Duane A. Smith, 32–48. Boulder: University of Colorado, 1983.

———. "Immigrant Workers and Industrial Hazards: The Irish Miners of Butte, 1880–1919." *Journal of American Ethnic History* 5 (1985): 41–64.

———. "The Orange and the Green in Montana: A Reconsideration of the Clark-Daly Feud." *Arizona and the West* 28 (Autumn 1986): 225–45.

———. "Social Myth and Social Reality." *Montana, the Magazine of Western History* 39 (Autumn 1989): 2–9.

———. "Constructed Province: History and the Making of the Last American West." *Western Historical Quarterly* 25 (Winter 1994): 437–60.

———. "The Strange Death of Thomas Francis Meagher: Tribal Politics in Territorial Montana." In *Thomas Francis Meagher,* edited by John Hearne, 223–40. Dublin: Irish Academic Press, 2006.

Erie, Steven. "Politics, the Public Sector, and Irish Social Mobility: San Francisco, 1870–1900." *Western Political Quarterly* 31 (1978): 274–89.

Evans, Thomas G. "Peasant Beliefs in 19th Century Ireland." In *Views of the Irish Peasantry, 1800–1916,* edited by Daniel Casey and Robert Rhodes, 37–57. Hamden, Conn.: Archon Books, 1977.

———. "The American Motif in the Irish Literary Renaissance: The Old Lady's Lost Children." *Éire-Ireland* 22 (Fall 1987): 4–14.

Faragher, John Mack. "'A Nation Thrown Back on Itself': Frederick Jackson Turner and the Frontier." In *Rereading Frederick Jackson Turner: "The Significance of the Frontier in American History" and Other Essays,* edited by Faragher, 1–10. New York: Henry Holt, 1994.

Farrell, John T. "Archbishop Ireland and Manifest Destiny." *Catholic Historical Review* 33 (1947): 269–30.

Fellman, Michael "Theodore Parker and the Abolitionist Role in the 1850s." *Journal of American History* 61 (1974): 666–84.

Ferreira, Patricia J. "Frederick Douglass in Ireland: The Dublin Edition of His *Narrative.*" *New Hibernia Review* 5 (Spring 2001): 53–67.

Fessenden, Tracy. "F. Scott Fitzgerald's Catholic Closet." *U.S. Catholic Historian* 23 (Summer 2005): 19–40.

Fitzhugh, George. "Selections from *A Sociology for the South, or the Failure of Free Society*" (1854). In *Ante-Bellum: Writings of George Fitzhugh and Hinton Rowan Helper on Slavery,* edited by Harvey Wish, 41–96. New York: Capricorn Books, 1960.

Fitzpatrick, David. "'That beloved country, that no place else resembles': Connotations of Irishness in Irish-Australasian Letters, 1841–1915." *Irish Historical Studies* 27 (November 1991): 324–50.

Flaherty, Stacy. "Boycott in Butte: Organized Labor and the Chinese Community, 1896–97." *Montana, the Magazine of Western History* 37 (Winter 1987): 34–47.

Foner, Eric. "Class, Ethnicity, and Radicalism in the Gilded Age: The Land League and Irish-America." In Foner, *Politics and Ideology in the Age of the Civil War,* 150–200. New York: Oxford University Press, 1980.

Ford, Lacy K. "Frontier Democracy: The Turner Thesis Revisited." *Journal of the Early Republic* 13 (Summer 1993): 144–63.

Fox, John, "Revisiting Eugene MacNamara's Irish Colony Scheme in California." *California Territorial Quarterly* 2 (Winter 2003): 36–43.

Fox-Genovese, Elizabeth, and Eugene Genovese. "The Political Crisis of Social History: A Marxian Perspective." *Journal of Social History* 10 (1976): 205–20. Reprinted in Fox-Genovese, *Fruits of Merchant Capital: Slavery and Bourgeois Property in the Rise and Expansion of Capitalism,* 179–212. New York: Oxford University Press, 1983.

Fredrickson, George. "The Coming of the Lord: The Northern Protestant Clergy and the Civil War Crisis." In *Religion and the American Civil War,* edited by Randall Miller, Harry Stout, and Charles Reagan Wilson, 110–30. New York: Oxford University Press, 1998.

Friedheim, Robert. "Prologue to a General Strike: The Seattle Shipyard Strike of 1919." *Labor History* 6 (1965): 121–42.

Friel, Brian. "Translations." In *Modern Irish Drama,* edited by John P. Harrington, 319–74. New York: W. W. Norton, 1991.

Gabaccia, Donna. "Is Everywhere Nowhere? Nomad, Nations, and the Immigrant Paradigm of United States History." *Journal of American History* 86 (December 1999): 1115–34.

Gaboury, William. "From Statehouse to Bull Pen: Idaho Populism and the Coeur d'Alene's Troubles of the 1890s." *Pacific Northwest Quarterly* 58 (1967): 14–22.

Gedicks, Al. "Ethnicity, Class Solidarity and Labor Radicalism among Finnish Immigrants in Michigan Copper Country." *Politics and Society* 7 (1977): 127–56.

Geertz, Cifford. "Religion as a Cultural System." Chapter 4 in Geertz, *The Interpretation of Cultures: Selected Essays,* 87–125. New York: Basic Books, 1973.

Genovese, Eugene. "Religion in the Collapse of the American Union." In *Religion and the American Civil War,* edited by Randall Miller, Harry Stout, and Charles Reagan Wilson, 74–88. New York: Oxford University Press, 1998.

Gerber, David. "The Immigrant Letter between Positivism and Populism: The Uses of Immigrant Personal Correspondence in Twentieth-Century American Scholarship." *Journal of American Ethnic History* 16 (Summer 1997): 3–34.

———. "Heartland Pluralism: Middle Western Ethnicities and Mentalities." *Journal of American Ethnic History* 18 (Fall 1998): 93–102.

———. "Epistolary Ethics: Personal Correspondence and the Culture of Emigration in the Nineteenth Century." *Journal of American Ethnic History* 19 (Summer 2000): 3–23.

Gerstle, Gary. "Liberty, Coercion, and the Making of Americans." *Journal of American History* 84 (September 1997): 524–58.

———. "Theodore Roosevelt and the Divided Character of American Nationalism." *Journal of American History* 84 (December 1999): 1280–1307.

Gerteis, Louis S. "Slavery and Hard Times: Morality and Utility in American Antislavery Reform." *Civil War History* 29 (December 1983): 316–31.

Gibbons, Luke. "Race against Time: Racial Discourse and Irish History." In *Transformations in Irish Culture,* 149–64. Notre Dame: University of Notre Dame Press, 1996.

———. "Unapproved Roads: Post-Colonialism and Irish Identity." In *Distant Relations: A Dialogue among Chicano, Irish, and Mexican Artists,* edited by Trisha Ziff, 56–67. Santa Monica: Smart Art Press, 1996.

Gilley, Sheridan. "The Roman Catholic Church and the Nineteenth-Century Irish Diaspora." *Journal of Ecclesiastical History* 35 (April 1984): 188–207.

Gingrich, Arnold. "Introduction." In F. Scott Fitzgerald, *Pat Hobby Stories,* 3–18. New York: Scribner's, 1962.

Gitlin, Jay. "On the Boundaries of Empire: Connecting the West to Its Imperial Past." In *Under an Open Sky: Rethinking America's Western Past,* edited by William Cronon, George Miles, and Jay Gitlin, 71–89. New York: W. W. Norton, 1992.

Gjerde, Jon. "New Growth on Old Vines: The State of the Field: The Social History of Immigration to and Ethnicity in the United States." *Journal of American Ethnic History* 18 (Summer 1999): 40–65.

———. "Following the Chain: New Insights into Migration." *Immigration and Ethnic History Newsletter* 33 (May 2001): 1, 8.

Glassie, Henry. "The Practice and Purpose of History." *Journal of American History* 81 (December 1994): 961–68.

Gleason, Philip. "The Melting Pot: Symbol of Fusion or Confusion." *American Quarterly* 16 (Fall 1964): 20–46.

———. "Crevecoeur's Question: Historical Writing on Immigration, Ethnicity, and National Identity." In *American Historians Interpret the Past,* edited by Anthony Molho and Gordon Wood, 120–43. Princeton: Princeton University Press, 1998.

———. "Trouble in the Colonial Melting Pot." *Journal of American Ethnic History* 20 (Fall 2000): 3–17.

Gleeson, David. "Parallel Struggles: Irish Republicanism in the American South, 1798–1876." *Éire-Ireland* 34 (Summer 1999): 109.

Gorn, Elliot. "Introduction." In *The McGuffey Readers: Selections from the 1879 Edition,* edited by Gorn, 1–36. Boston: Bedford/St. Martin's, 1998.

Gregory, James N. "The West and Workers, 1870–1930." In *A Companion to the American West,* edited by William Deverell, 240–55. Malden, Mass.: Blackwell Pub., 2004.

Gribble, Richard. "Advocate for Immigrants: The Church and State Career of Archbishop Edward J. Hanna." *Southern California Quarterly* 83 (2001): 285–316.

Grossman, James. "Introduction." In Richard White and Patricia Limerick, *The Frontier in American Culture,* 1–6. Berkeley: University of California Press, 1994.

Grow, Matthew. "The Whore of Babylon and the Abomination of Abominations: Nineteenth-Century Catholic and Mormon Mutual Perceptions and Religious Identity." *Church History* 73 (March 2004): 139–67.

Guilfoyle, James. "The Religious Development of Daniel O'Connell, I: From Deist to Roman Catholic." *New Hibernia Review* 2 (Autumn 1998): 89–101.

———. "The Religious Development of Daniel O'Connell, II: The Making of a Devotional Catholic." *New Hibernia Review* 2 (Winter 1998): 114–32.

Gutman, Herbert. "Work, Culture, and Society in Industrializing America, 1815–1919." In *Work, Culture and Society in Industrializing America: Essays in American Working-Class and Social History,* edited by Gutman, 3–78. New York: Vintage Books, 1977.

Hand, Wayland. "Nicknames of Butte Miners." *California Folklore Quarterly* 5 (July 1946): 307–309.

———. "The Cowboy's Lament." *Western Folklore* 17 (1958): 200–205.

Hannan, Robbie. "*An Ball Uaigneach Seo:* Attachment to Place in Gaelic Literature." *Éire-Ireland* 26 (Summer 1991): 19–31.

Hansen, Klaus. "The Millennium, the West, and Race in the Antebellum American Mind." *Western Historical Quarterly* 3 (October 1972): 373–90.

Harris, Ruth-Ann. "'Where the Poor Man Is Not Crushed Down to Exalt the Aristocrat': Vere Foster's Programmes of Assisted Emigration in the Aftermath of the Irish Famine." In *The Irish World Wide: History, Heritage, Identity,* vol. 6, *The Meaning of the Famine,* edited by Patrick O'Sullivan, 172–94. London: Leicester University Press, 1997.

Hauptman, Laurence M. "Mythologizing Westward Expansion: Schoolbooks and the Image of the American Frontier before Turner." *Western Historical Quarterly* 8 (July 1977): 269–82.

Hawkins, Maureen, S.G. "'We Must Learn Where We Live': Language, Identity, and the Colonial Condition in Brian Friel's *Translations.*" *Éire-Ireland* 38 (Spring/Summer 2003): 23–36.

Heaney, Seamus. "Correspondences: Emigrants and Inner Exiles." In *Migrations: The Irish at Home and Abroad,* edited by Richard Kearney, 21–32. Dublin: Wolfhound Press, 1990.

———. "From Ocean's Love to Ireland." In *Poems, 1965–1975,* 201–202. New York: Noonday, 1995.

Henretta, James. "The Study of Social Mobility: Ideological Assumptions and Conceptual Bias." In *The Labor History Reader,* edited by Daniel Leab, 28–41. Urbana: University of Illinois Press, 1985.

Herron, Thomas. "The Spanish Armada, Ireland, and Spenser's *The Faerie Queene.*" *New Hibernian Review* 6 (Summer 2002): 82–105.

Higgins, Michael, and Declan Kiberd. "Culture and Exile: The Global Irish." *New Hibernia Review* 1 (1997): 9–22.

Higham, John. "Integrating America: The Problem of Assimilation in the Nineteenth Century." *Journal of American Ethnic History* 1 (Fall 1981): 7–25.

Holt, Michael F. "The Politics of Impatience: The Origins of Know-Nothingism." *Journal of American History* 60 (1973): 309–31.

Hooper, Glenn. "Unsound Plots: Culture and Politics in Spenser's *A View of the Present State of Ireland*." *Éire-Ireland* 32 (Summer/Fall 1997): 117–36.

Hotten-Somers, Diane. "Relinquishing and Reclaiming Independence: Irish Domestic Servants, American Middle-Class Mistresses, and Assimilation, 1850–1920." *Éire-Ireland* 36 (Spring/Summer 2001): 166–84.

Howe, Daniel Walker. "The Social Science of Horace Bushnell." *Journal of American History* 70 (September 1983): 305–22.

Hoy, Suellen. "The Journey Out: The Recruitment and Emigration of Irish Religious Women to the United States, 1812–1914." *Journal of Women's History* 6 (Winter/Spring 1995): 64–98.

Hughes, Eamonn. "Tradition and Modernity" (review of Seamus Deane, *Strange Country: Modernity and Nationhood in Irish Writing since 1790*). *Irish Literary Review* 16 (Fall 1997).

Ibsen, John Duffy. "Virgin Land or Virgin Mary?: Studying the Ethnicity of White Americans." *American Quarterly* 33 (1981): 284–308.

Igler, David. "The Industrial Far West: Region and Nation in the Late Nineteenth Century." *Pacific Historical Review* 69 (May 2000): 159–92.

Ingersoll, Earl. "The Psychic Geography of Joyce's *Dubliners.*" *New Hibernian Review* 6 (Winter 2002): 98–107.

Issel, William. "Class and Ethnic Conflict in San Francisco Political History: The Reform Charter of 1898." *Labor History* 18 (Summer 1977): 34–59.

Jensen, Richard. "'No Irish Need Apply': A Myth of Victimization." *Journal of Social History* 36 (Winter 2002): 405–29.

Jockers, Matthew. "A Window Facing West: Charles Driscoll's *Kansas Irish.*" *New Hibernia Review* 8 (Autumn 2004): 100–113.

Johnson, Susan Lee. "'A Memory Sweet to Soldiers': The Significance of Gender in the History of the American West." *Western Historical Quarterly* 24 (November 1993): 495–518.

Johnston, Edith Mary. "Violence Transported: Aspects of Irish Peasant Society." In *Ireland and Irish-Australia: Studies in Cultural and Political History,* edited by Oliver MacDonagh and W. F. Mandle, 137–54. London: Croom Helm, 1986.

Jones, Maldwyn A. "The Scotch-Irish in British America." In *Strangers within the Realm: Cultural Margins of the First British Empire,* edited by Bernard Bailyn and Philip D. Morgan, 284–313. Chapel Hill: University of North Carolina Press, 1991.

Kane, Katherine. "Nits Make Lice: Drogheda, Sand Creek, and the Poetics of Colonial Extermination." *Cultural Critique* 42 (Spring 1999): 85–108.

———. "'Will Come Forth in Tongues and Fury': Relocating Irish Cultural Studies." *Cultural Studies* 15 (2001): 98–123.

Karson, Marc. "The Catholic Church and the Political Development of American Trade Unionism (1900–1918)." *Industrial and Labor Relations Review* 4 (July 1951): 527–42.

Kazal, Russell. "Revisiting Assimilation: The Rise, Fall, and Reappraisal of a Concept in American Ethnic History." *American Historical Review* 100 (April 1995): 437–71.

Kazin, Michael. "The Great Exception Revisited: Organized Labor and Politics in San Francisco and Los Angeles, 1870–1940." *Pacific Historical Review* 55 (1986): 371–402.

Kelly, Joseph. "Charleston's Bishop John England and American Slavery." *New Hibernia Review* 5 (Winter 2001): 48–56.

Kenny, Kevin. "Diaspora and Comparison: The Global Irish as a Case Study." *Journal of American History* 90 (June 2003): 134–62.

Kiberd, Declan. "White Skin, Brown Masks: Celticism and Negritude." *Éire-Ireland* 31 (1996): 1–63.

King, Joseph. "The Murphys and Breens of the Overland Parties to California, 1844 and 1846." In *The Irish World Wide: History, Heritage, Identity,* vol. 1, *Patterns of Migration,* edited by Patrick O'Sullivan, 84–109. London: Leicester University Press, 1997.

Kleppner, Paul. "Voters and Parties in the Western States." *Western Historical Quarterly* 14 (January 1983): 49–68.

Kolchin, Peter. "Whiteness Studies: The New History of Race in America." *Journal of American History* 89.1 (2002): 154–73.

Koppes, Clayton. "The Kansas Trial of the IWW, 1917–1919." *Labor History* 16 (1975): 338–58.

Krause, David. "Connolly and Pearse: The Triumph of Failure?" *New Hibernia Review* 3 (Winter 1999): 56–84.

Lamar, Howard. "From Bondage to Contract: Ethnic Labor in the American West, 1600–1890." In *The Countryside in the Age of the Capitalist Transformation: Essays in the Social History of Rural America,* edited by Steven Hahn and Jonathan Prude, 293–326. Chapel Hill: University of North Carolina Press, 1985.

Larkin, Emmet. "The Devotional Revolution in Ireland, 1850–1875." In *The Historical Dimensions of Irish Catholicism,* 57–84. Washington, D.C.: Catholic University of America Press, 1984.

———. "Myths, Revisionism and the Writing of Irish History." *New Hibernia Review* 2 (Summer 1998): 57–70.

Lauck, Jon. "'You can't mix wheat and potatoes in the same bin': Anti-Catholicism in Early Dakota." *South Dakota History* 38 (Spring 2008): 1–46.

Lawner, Lynne. "Introduction." In Antonio Gramsci, *Letters from Prison,* translated by Lawner. New York: Harper and Row, 1973.

Le Beau, Bryan. "'Saving the West from the Pope': Anti-Catholic Propaganda and the Settlement of the Mississippi River Valley." *American Studies* 32 (1991): 101–14.

Lebow, Ned. "British Images of Poverty in Pre-Famine Ireland." In *Views of the Irish Peasantry, 1800–1916,* edited by Daniel Casey and Robert Rhodes, 57–85. Hamden, Conn.: Archon Books, 1977.

Lindquist, John. "The Jerome Deportation of 1917." *Arizona and the West* 11 (1969): 233–46.

Lindquist, John, and James Fraser. "A Sociological Interpretation of the Bisbee Deportation." *Pacific Historical Review* 38 (1968): 401–22.

Lochlainn, Alf Mac. "Gael and Peasant—A Case of Mistaken Identity?" In *Views of the Irish Peasantry, 1800–1916,* edited by Daniel Casey and Robert Rhodes, 17–36. Hamden, Conn.: Archon Books, 1977.

Lovin, Hugh. "Idaho and the 'Reds,' 1919–1926." *Pacific Northwest Quarterly* 69 (1978): 1–15.

Luebke, Frederick. "Ethnic Group Settlement on the Great Plains." *Western Historical Quarterly* 8 (October 1977): 405–30.

———. "Turnerism, Social History, and the Historiography of European Ethnic Groups in the United States." In *Germans in the New World: Essays in the History of Immigration,* edited by Luebke, 138–56. Urbana: University of Illinois Press, 1990.

Lynch-Brennan, Margaret. "Ubiquitous Bridget: Irish Immigrant Women in Domestic Service in America, 1840–1930." In *Making the Irish American: History and Heritage of the Irish in the United States,* edited by J. J. Lee and Marion Casey, 332–53. New York: New York University Press, 2006.

MacDonagh, Oliver. "The Irish Famine Emigration to the United States." *Perspectives in American History* 10 (1976): 357–447.

MacLeod, William C. "Celt and Indian: Britain's Old World Frontier in Relation to the New." In *Beyond the Frontier: Social Process and Cultural Change,* edited by Paul Bohannan and Frederick Plog, 25–42. New York: Natural History Press, 1967.

Mageean, Deirdre M. "Emigration from Irish Ports." *Journal of American Ethnic History* 13 (Fall 1993): 6–30.

Maizlich, Stephen. "The Meaning of Nativism and the Crisis of the Union: The Know-Nothing Movement in the Antebellum North." In *Essays on Antebellum Politics, 1840–60,* edited by Maizlich and John Kushma, 166–98. College Station: Texas A&M University Press, 1982.

Malone, Michael. "The 'New Western History': An Assessment." *Montana, the Magazine of Western History* 40 (Summer 1990): 65–67.

Mason, Matthew E. "'The Hands Here Are Disposed to be Turbulent': Unrest among the Irish Trackmen of the Baltimore and Ohio Railroad, 1829–1851." *Labor History* 39 (August 1998): 253–72.

McCaffrey, L. "Irish-American Politics: Power with or without Purpose?" In *The Irish in America,* edited by P. J. Drudy, 169–90. Cambridge: Cambridge University Press, 1985.

McClymer, John. "Gender and the 'American Way of Life': Women and the Americanization Movement." *Journal of American Ethnic History* 10 (Spring 1991): 3–20.

McCurry, Jacqueline. "'S'crap': Colonialism Indicted in the Poetry of Paul Muldoon." *Éire-Ireland* 27 (Fall 1992): 92–109.

———. "A Land 'Not Borrowed' But 'Purloined': Paul Muldoon's Indians." *New Hibernia Review* 1 (Autumn 1997): 40–51.

McGovern, Bryan. "John Mitchell: Ecumenical Nationalist in the Old South." *New Hibernia Review* 5 (Summer 2001): 99–110.

Meinig, D. W. "The Mormon Culture Region: Strategies and Patterns in the Geography of the American West, 1847–1964." *Annals of the Association of American Geography* 55 (June 1965): 191–220.

Merrill, Karen. "Whose Home on the Range?" *Western Historical Quarterly* 27 (Winter 1996): 433–52.

Meyn, Susan Labry. "Mutual Infatuation: Rosebud Sioux and Cincinnatians." *Queen City Heritage* 52 (Spring/Summer 1994): 30 48.

Miller, Kerby. "Emigrants and Exiles: Irish Cultures and Irish Emigration to North America, 1790–1922." *Irish Historical Studies* 22 (September 1980): 97–125.

———. "Assimilation and Alienation: Irish Emigrants' Responses to Industrial America, 1871–1921." In *The Irish in America: Emigration, Assimilation and Impact,* edited by P. J. Drudy, 87–112. Cambridge: Cambridge University Press, 1985.

———. "Class, Culture, and Immigrant Group Identity in the United States: The Case of Irish-American Ethnicity." In *Immigration Reconsidered: History, Sociology, and Politics,* edited by Virginia Yans-McLaughlin, 96–129. New York: Oxford University Press, 1990.

———. "Emigration, Capitalism, and Ideology in Post-Famine Ireland." In *Migrations: The Irish at Home and Abroad,* edited by Richard Kearney, 91–108. Dublin: Wolfhound, 1990.

———. "For 'Love and Liberty': Irishwomen, Migration, and Domesticity in Ireland and America, 1815–1920s." In Miller, *Ireland and Irish America: Culture, Class, and Transnational Migration,* 300–326. Dublin: Field Day, 2008.

———. "From the Gaeltacht to the Prairie: Tom Brick's Ireland and America, 1881–1979." In Miller, *Ireland and Irish America: Culture, Class, and Transatlantic Migration,* 346–69. Dublin: Field Day, 2008.

Miller, Kerby, and Bruce Boling. "Golden Streets, Bitter Tears: The Irish Image of America during the Age of Mass Migration." *Journal of American Ethnic History* 10 (Fall 1990/Winter 1991): 16–35.

Miller, Kerby, Bruce Boling, with Liam Kennedy. "The Famine's Scars: William Murphy's Ulster and American Odyssey." In *New Directions in Irish-American History,* edited by Kevin Kennedy, 36–60. Madison: University of Wisconsin Press, 2003.

Milner, Clyde. "The Shared Memories of Montana's Pioneers." *Montana, the Magazine of Western History* 37 (Winter 1987): 2–13.

Mogen, David. "The Frontier Archetype and the Myth of America: Patterns That Shape the American Dream." In *The Frontier Experience and the American Dream: Essays on American Literature,* edited by David Mogen, Mark Busby, and Paul Bryant, 15–30. College Station: Texas A&M University Press, 1989.

Montgomery, David. "The Irish and the American Labor Movement." In *America and Ireland, 1776–1976: The American Identity and the Irish Connection,* ed. David N. Doyle and Owen D. Edwards, 205–18. Westport, Conn.: Greenwood, 1980.

———. "The Irish Influence in the American Labor Movement." Hibernian Lecture, October 11, 1984. Cushwa Center for the Study of American Catholicism, University of Notre Dame.

———. "Why Is There No Socialism in the United States? Report on Conference in Paris." *International Labor and Working Class History* 26 (1984): 67–68.

Moran, Gerard. "'In Search of the Promised Land': The Connemara Colonization Scheme to Minnesota, 1880." *Éire-Ireland* 31 (Fall/Winter 1996): 130–48.

Morris, Christopher. "The Articulation of Two Worlds: The Master-Slave Relationship Reconsidered." *Journal of American History* 85 (December 1998): 982–1007.

Moynihan, Humphrey. "Archbishop Ireland's Colonies." *Acta et Dicta* 6 (1931): 212–31.

Muldoon, James. "The Indian as Irishman." *Essex Institute Historical Collections* 3 (October 1975): 265–87.

Muldoon, Paul. "Seanchas." In *Poems,* 20–21. New York: Farrar, Straus and Giroux, 2001.

Muller, Dorothea R. "Church Building and Community Making on the Frontier—A Case Study: Josiah Strong, Home Missionary in Cheyenne, 1871–1873." *Western Historical Quarterly* 10 (April 1979): 191–216.

Myers, James P., Jr. "'Till their . . . bog-trotting feet get *talaria*': Henry D. Thoreau and the Immigrant Irish." In *The Irish World Wide: History, Heritage, Identity,* vol. 3, *The Creative Migrant,* edited by Patrick O'Sullivan, 44–56. Leicester: Leicester University Press, 1994.

Ní Dhomhnaill, Nuala. "Why I Choose to Write in Irish, the Corpse That Sits Up and Talks Back." *New York Times Book Review,* January 8, 1995.

———. "Cé Leis Tú?" *Éire-Ireland* 30 (Spring/Summer 2000): 39–78.

Niebuhr, H. R. "The Protestant Movement and Democracy in the United States." In *The Shaping of American Religion,* edited by J. W. Smith and A. L. Jamison, 20–71. Princeton: Princeton University Press, 1961.

Nolan, Janet. "Education and Women's Mobility in Ireland and Irish America, 1880–1920: A Preliminary Look." *New Hibernia* Review 2 (Autumn 1998): 78–88.

Nolan, Willie. Review of P. J. Duffy, *Landscapes of South Ulster. Irish Literary Supplement* 16 (Spring 1997): 30.

Noll, Mark. "The Bible and Slavery." In *Religion and the American Civil War,* edited by Randall Miller, Harry Stout, and Charles Reagan Wilson, 43–73. New York: Oxford University Press, 1998.

Nugent, Walter. "Frontiers and Empires in the Late Nineteenth Century." In *Trails: Toward a New Western History,* edited by Patricia Nelson Limerick, Clyde A. Milner II, and Charles E. Rankin, 161–81. Lawrence: University Press of Kansas, 1991.

———. "Where Is the American West?: Report on a Survey." *Montana, the Magazine of Western History* 42 (Summer 1992): 2–23.

O'Connell, Maurice. "Daniel O'Connell and Irish-Americans." *Éire-Ireland* 16 (Summer 1981): 7–15.

O'Connor, Frank. "Guests of the Nation." In *Collected Stories,* 3–12. New York, Vintage, 1981.

Oestreicher, Richard. "Industrialization, Class, and Competing Cultural Systems: Detroit Workers, 1875–1900." In *German Workers in Industrial Chicago, 1850–1910: A Comparative Perspective,* edited by Hartmut Keil and John B. Jentz, 49–72. DeKalb: Northern Illinois University Press, 1983.

————. "Urban Working-Class Political Behavior and Theories of American Electoral Politics, 1870–1940." *Journal of American History* 74 (1988): 1257–86.

O'Fahey, C. J. "Reflections on the St. Patrick's Day Orations of John Ireland." *Ethnicity* 2 (Summer 1975): 244–57.

Ó Gráda, Cormac. "Irish Emigration to the United States in the 19th Century." In *America and Ireland,* edited by David Doyle and Owen D. Edwards, 97–101. Westport: Greenwood, 1980.

————. "Making History in the 1940s and 1950s: The Saga of *The Great Famine.*" In *Interpreting Irish History: The Debate on Historical Revisionism,* edited by Ciaran Brady, 26–61. Dublin: Irish Academic Press, 1994.

O'Neill, Daniel P. "The Development of an American Priesthood: Archbishop John Ireland and the St. Paul Diocesan Clergy, 1884–1918." *Journal of American Ethnic History* 4 (Spring 1985): 33–52.

Onkey, Lauren. "Celtic Soul Brothers." *Éire-Ireland* 28 (Fall 1993): 147–58.

————. "'Not Quite White'?: Black 47's Funky Céili." *Éire-Ireland* 31 (Spring/Summer 1996): 45–60.

Orser, Charles E., Jr. "The Illinois and Michigan Canal: Historical Archaeology and the Irish Experience in America." *Éire-Ireland* 27 (Winter 1992): 122–34.

Ó Síocháin, Séamus. "Roger Casement, Ethnography, and the Putumayo." *Éire-Ireland* 29 (Summer 1994): 29–41.

Osofsky, Gilbert. "Abolitionists, Irish Immigrants, and the Dilemmas of Romantic Nationalism." *American Historical Review* 80 (October 1975): 889–912.

Palmer, William. "Borderlands and Colonies: Tudor Ireland in the Perspective of Colonial America." *Éire-Ireland* 29 (Fall 1994): 37–51.

Parker, Michael. "Gleanings, Leavings: Irish and American Influences on Seamus Heaney's *Wintering Out,* 1972." *New Hibernia Review* 2 (Autumn 1998): 18–19.

Pascoe, Peggy. "Western Women at the Cultural Crossroads." In *Trails: Toward a New Western History,* edited by Patricia Nelson Limerick, Clyde A. Milner II, and Charles E. Rankin, 40–58. Lawrence: University Press of Kansas, 1991.

Peck, Gunther. "Divided Loyalties: Immigrant Padrones and the Evolution of Industrial Paternalism in North America." *International Labor and Working-Class History* 53 (Spring 1998): 49–68.

————. "Mobilizing Community: Migrant Workers and the Politics of Labor Mobility in the North American West, 1900–1920." In *Labor Histories: Class, Politics, and the Working-Class Experience,* edited by Eric Arnesen, Julie Greene, and Bruce Laurie, 175–200. Urbana: University of Illinois Press, 1998.

Perl, Paul, and Jonathon Wiggins. "Don't Call Me Ishmael: Religious Naming among Protestants and Catholics in the United States." *Journal for the Scientific Study of Religion* 43 (June 2004): 209–28.

Peterson, Charles. "Imprint of Agricultural Systems on the Utah Landscape." In *The Mormon Role in the Settlement of the West,* edited by Richard Jackson, 91–106. Provo: Brigham Young University Press, 1978.

Peterson, Susan Carol. "Religious Communities of Women in the West: The Presentation Sisters' Adaptation to the Northern Plains Frontier." *Journal of the West* 21 (April 1992): 65–77.

Pinheiro, John. "'Religion without Restriction': Anti-Catholicism, All Mexico, and the Treaty of Guadalupe Hidalgo." *Journal of the Early Republic* 23 (Spring 2003): 69–96.

Regan, Ann. "The Irish." In *They Chose Minnesota: A Survey of the State's Ethnic Groups,* edited by June Drenning, 130–52. St. Paul: Minnesota Historical Society Press, 1981.

Richardson, Ernest M. "Moreton Frewen: Cattle King with a Monacle." *Montana, the Magazine of Western History* 40 (Winter 1961): 37–45.

Ridge, Martin. "Introduction." In *Frederick Jackson Turner's History, Frontier, and Section: Three Essays.* Albuquerque: University of New Mexico Press, 1993.

Riley, Glenda. "Frederick Jackson Turner Ignored the Ladies." In *Does the Frontier Experience Make America Exceptional?* edited by Richard Etulain, 65–80. Boston: Bedford/St. Martin's, 1999.

Riordan, John, "Garret McEnerney and the Pursuit of Success." In *The San Francisco Irish, 1850–1976,* edited by James Walsh, 73–78. San Francisco: Irish Literary and Historical Society, 1978.

Rischin, Moses. "Beyond the Great Divide: Immigration and the Last Frontier." *Journal of American History* 55 (June 1968): 42–53.

———. "Creating Crevecoeur's 'New Man': He Had a Dream." *Journal of American Ethnic History* 1 (Fall 1981): 26–42.

Robbins, William. "Western History: A Dialectic on the Modern Condition." *Western Historical Quarterly* 20 (November 1989): 419–34.

Rocha, Guy. "Radical Labor Struggles in the Tonopah-Goldfield Mining District, 1901–1922." *Nevada Historical Society Quarterly* 20 (1977): 3–45.

Roediger, David. "Ira Steward and the Anti-Slavery Origins of American Eight Hour Theory." *Labor History* 27 (Summer 1986): 410–26.

———. "Race and the Working-Class Past in the United States: Multiple Identities and the Future of Labor History." *International Review of Social History* 38 (1993): 127–43.

Rolston, Bill. "From King Billy to Cú Chulainn: Loyalist and Republican Murals, Past, Present, and Future." *Éire-Ireland* 33 (Winter/Spring/Summer 1997/1998): 6–28.

Roy, James Charles. "Celtic Soul—Some People Have It." *Irish Literary Supplement* 15 (Spring 1996): 27.

Ryan, George E. "Shanties and Shiftlessness: The Immigrant Irish of Henry Thoreau." *Éire-Ireland* 13 (1978): 54–78.

Said, Edward. "Yeats and Decolonization" (1988). In *The Edward Said Reader,* edited by Moustafa Bayoumi and Andrew Rubin, 291–313. New York: Vintage, 1996.

Salvatore, Nick. "Response." *International Labor and Working Class History* 26 (1984): 25–28.

Saposs, David. "The Catholic Church and the Labor Movement." *Modern Monthly* (May/June 1933).

Sarbaugh, Timothy. "Ireland of the West." *Pacific Historian* 28 (1984): 48–52.

———. "Exiles of Confidence: The Irish-American Community of San Francisco, 1880–1920." In *From Paddy to Studs: Irish-American Communities in the Turn of the Century Era, 1880–1920,* edited by Timothy J. Meagher, 161–80. New York: Greenwood, 1986.

Saum, Lewis. "Private John F. Donohue's Reflections on the Little Bighorn." *Montana, the Magazine of Western History* 50 (Winter 2000): 40–53.

Saxton, Alexander. "San Francisco Labor and the Populist and Progressive Insurgencies." *Pacific Historical Review* 34 (1965): 421–38.

Schwantes, Carlos. "Leftward Tilt on the Pacific Slope: Indigenous Unionism and the Struggle against AFL Hegemony in the State of Washington." *Pacific Northwest Quarterly* 70 (1979): 24–34.

———. "Protest in a Promised Land: Unemployment, Disinheritance, and the Origin of Labor Militancy in the Pacific Northwest, 1885–1886." *Western Historical Quarterly* 13 (1982): 388–404.

———. "The Concept of the Wageworkers' Frontier: A Framework for Future Research." *Western Historical Quarterly* 18 (1987): 36–53.

Shannon, James P. "Bishop Ireland's Connemara Experiment." *Minnesota History* 37 (March 1957): 205–13.

———. "The Irish Catholic Immigration." In *Roman Catholicism and the American Way of Life,* edited by Thomas T. McAvoy, 204–205. University of Notre Dame Press, 1960.

Smith, Timothy. "Religion and Ethnicity in America." *American Historical Review* 83 (Winter 1978): 1165–68.

Smyth, W. J. "The Western Isle of Ireland and the English Seaboard of America—England's First Frontiers." *Irish Geography* 2 (1978): 1–22.

Socolofsky, Homer. "William Scully's Irish and American Lands." *Western Historical Quarterly* 9 (April 1978): 149–61.

Sofchalk, Donald. "Organized Labor and the Iron Ore Miners of Northern Minnesota, 1907–1936." *Labor History* 12 (1971): 214–42.

Spence, Clark. "The Landless Man and the Manless Land." *Western Historical Quarterly* 16 (October 1985): 397–412.

Suggs, George. "Strike Breaking in Colorado: Governor James Peabody and the Telluride Strike, 1903–04." *Journal of the West* 5 (1966): 454–76.

———. "Catalyst for Industrial Change: The WFM, 1893–1903." *Colorado Magazine* 45 (1968): 322–39.

———. "Religion and Labor in the Rocky Mountain West: Bishop Nicholas C. Matz and the Western Federation of Miners." *Labor History* 11 (1970): 190–206.

Susman, Warren. "The Frontier Thesis and the American Intellectual." In Susman, *Culture as History: The Transformation of American Society in the 20th Century,* 27–38. New York: Pantheon, 1984.

Sweeney, Fionnghuala. "'The Republic of Letters': Frederick Douglass, Ireland, and the Irish *Narratives.*" *Éire-Ireland* 36 (Spring/Summer 2001): 47–65.

Sweeney, George. "Irish Hunger Strikes and the Cult of Self-Sacrifice." *Journal of Contemporary History* 28 (June 1993): 421–36.

Takaki, Ronald. "*The Tempest* in the Wilderness: The Racialization of Savagery." *Journal of American History* 79 (December 1992): 892–912. Reprinted in Takaki, *A Different Mirror: A History of Multicultural America,* 24–45. Boston: Little, Brown, 1993.

Taylor, Lawrence. "Colonialism and Community Structure in Western Ireland." *Ethnohistory* 27 (Spring 1980): 169–81.

———. "The Priest and the Agent: Social Drama and Class Consciousness in the West of Ireland." *Comparative Studies in Society and History* 27 (October 1985): 696–712.

Tilly, Charles. "Review of Robert Glen, *Urban Workers in the Early Industrial Revolution*" (1984). *Labor History* 32 (Summer 1991): 467–69.

———. "Retrieving European Lives." In *Reliving the Past: The Worlds of Social History,* edited by Olivier Zunz, 11–52. Chapel Hill: University of North Carolina Press, 1985.

———. "Transplanted Networks." In *Immigration Reconsidered: History, Sociology, and Politics,* edited by Virginia Yans-McLaughlin, 79–95. New York: Oxford University Press, 1990.

Tygiel, Jules. "Where Unionism Holds Undisputed Sway: A Reappraisal of San Francisco's Union Labor Party." *California History* 62 (1983): 196–215.

Tyler, Robert. "The IWW and the West." *American Quarterly* 12 (1960): 175–87.

Unterecker, John. "Countryman, Peasant, and Servant in the Poetry of W. B. Yeats." In *Views of the Irish Peasantry, 1800–1916,* edited by Daniel J. Casey and Robert Rhodes, 178–91. Hamden, Conn.: Archon Books, 1977.

Van der Linden, Marcel. "Transnationalizing American Labor History." *Journal of American History* 86 (December 1999): 1078–92.

Van Dussen, D. Gregory. "American Methodism's *Christian Advocate* and Irish Catholic Immigration, 1830–1870." *Éire-Ireland* 26 (Winter 1991): 76–99.

Vedder, Richard, and Lowell Gallaway, "The Geographical Distribution of British and Irish Emigrants to the United States after 1899." *Scottish Journal of Political Economy* 19 (1972): 19–35.

Wagaman, David. "The Industrial Workers of the World in Nebraska." *Nebraska History* 56 (1975): 295–337.

Wall, Eamonn. "The Black Hills, the Gorey Road." *New Hibernia Review* 2 (Winter 1998): 9–23.

———. "Poetry." *New Hibernian Review* 3 (Spring 1999): 61–70.

Walsh, James. "Father Peter Yorke of San Francisco." *Studies: An Irish Quarterly Review* 62 (1973): 19–34.

———. "Peter Yorke and Progressivism in California, 1908." *Éire-Ireland* 10 (Summer 1975): 73–81.

———. "Introduction." In *The Irish: America's Political Class,* edited by Walsh. New York: Arno, 1976.

———. "Peter C. Yorke: San Francisco's Irishman Reconsidered." In *San Francisco Irish,* edited by Walsh, 42–57. San Francisco: Irish Literary and Historical Society, 1978.

———. "The Irish in the New America: 'Way Out West.'" In *America and Ireland,* edited by David Doyle and Owen D. Edwards, 165–76. Westport: Greenwood, 1980.

Walsh, James, and Timothy Foley. "Father Peter C. Yorke: Irish-American Leader." *Studies Hibernica* 14 (1974): 90–103.

Wangler, T. E. "The Birth of Americanism: Westward the Apocalyptic Candlestick." *Harvard Theological Review* 65 (1972): 425–31.

Warren, Louis. "Buffalo Bill Meets Dracula: William F. Cody, Bram Stoker, and the Frontiers of Racial Decay." *American Historical Review* 107 (October 2002): 1124–57.

Welter, Barbara. "From Maria Monk to Paul Blanshard: A Century of Protestant Anti-Catholicism." In *Uncivil Religion: Interreligious Hostility in America,* edited by Robert N. Bellah and Frederick E. Greenspahn, 43–71. New York: Crossroad, 1987.

West, Elliott. "Reconstructing Race." *Western Historical Quarterly* 34 (Spring 2003): 7–26.

West, William. "Chattel Slavery versus 'Wages Slavery.'" In *Antebellum American Culture: An Interpretative Anthology,* edited by David Brion Davis, 432–34. Lexington: D. C. Heath, 1979.

White, Richard. "The Winning of the West: The Expansion of the Western Sioux in the Eighteenth and Nineteenth Centuries." *Journal of American History* 65 (September 1978): 319–43.

————. "Outlaw Gangs of the Middle Border: American Social Bandits." *Western Historical Quarterly* 12 (October 1981): 387–408.

————. "Howard Lamar." In *Historians of the American Frontier,* edited by John Wunder, 660–81. New York: Greenwood, 1988.

————. "Frederick Jackson Turner and Buffalo Bill." In *The Frontier in American Culture,* edited by James Grossman, 7–66. Berkeley: University of California Press, 1994.

————. "Comments." *Perspectives* (newsletter of the American Historical Association) (April 1999): 11–13.

Whitten, Woodrow. "The Wheatland Episode." *Pacific Historical Review* 17 (1948): 37–42.

Wiebe, Robert. "*Imagined Communities,* Nationalist Experiences." *Journal of the Historical Society* 1 (Spring 2000): 33–63.

Wiemers, Amy. "Rural Irish Women: Their Changing Role, Status, and Conditions." *Éire-Ireland* 29 (Spring 1994): 76–91.

Wilentz, Sean. "Industrializing America and the Irish: Towards the New Departure." *Labor History* 20 (1979): 579–95.

————. "Against Exceptionalism: Class Consciousness and the American Labor Movement, 1790–1920." *International Labor and Working Class History* 26 (1984): 1–24.

Wilgus, D. K. "The *Aisling* and the Cowboy: Some Unnoticed Influences of Irish Vision Poetry on Anglo-American Balladry." *Western Folklore* 44 (1985): 255–300.

Williams, Leslie. "'Rint' and 'Repale': *Punch* and the Image of Daniel O'Connell, 1842–1847." *New Hibernia Review* 1 (Autumn 1997): 74–93.

Wilson, Major L. "The Controversy over Slavery Expansion and the Concept of the Safety Valve: Ideological Confusion in the 1850s." *Mississippi Quarterly* 24 (Spring 1971): 135–53.

Wingerd, Mary Lethert. "Rethinking Paternalism: Power and Parochialism in a Southern Mill Village." *Journal of American History* 83 (December 1996): 872–902.

Wohl, R. Richard, "'The Country Boy' Myth and Its Place in American Urban Culture: The Nineteenth-Century Contribution." In *Perspectives in American History,* vol. 3, edited by Moses Rischin, 77–156. Cambridge, Mass.: Harvard University Press, 1969.

Woods, Betty. "Cleveland, Trip of the Month." *New Mexico Magazine* 40 (August 1962): 2.

Woodward, C. Vann. "The Irony of Southern History." In *The Burden of Southern History,* 187–212. Rev. ed. Baton Rouge: Louisiana State University Press, 1968.

————. "A Second Look at the Theme of Irony." In *The Burden of Southern History,* 213–34. Rev. ed. Baton Rouge: Louisiana State University Press, 1968.

Worster, Donald. "Beyond the Agrarian Myth." In *Trails: Toward a New Western History,* edited by Patricia Nelson Limerick, Clyde A. Milner II, and Charles E. Rankin, 3–25. Lawrence: University Press of Kansas, 1991.

Wortman, Roy. "Denver's Anti-Chinese Riot, 1880." *Colorado Magazine* 42 (Fall 1965): 275–91.

Zuckerman, Michael. "Tocqueville, Turner, and Turds: Four Stories of Manners in Early America." *Journal of American History* 85 (June 1998): 13–42.

INTERVIEWS, RECORDINGS, AND FILM

Green Fields of America. Compact Disc 1072. Danbury, Conn.: Green Linnet, 1987.

O'Sullivan, Father Sarsfield. Interviews with David Emmons, November 19, 1984, Whitehall, Montana; and June 5, 1997, Butte, Montana. Notes in possession of the author.

Parker, Alan, dir. *The Commitments*.

Shannon, Kevin. Interview in Brendan Ferriter's documentary film *Sceal ar Butte, Montana*.

Zeller, Eileen, and Barra O'Donovan. Irish Language Class sponsored by the Montana Gaelic Culture Society, Missoula, January 16, 1999. Notes in possession of the author.

DISSERTATIONS, THESES, AND UNPUBLISHED PAPERS

Blessing, Patrick. "West among Strangers: Irish Migration to California, 1800 to 1880." Ph.D. dissertation, University of California, Los Angeles, 1977.

Brundage, David. "The Road from the Land League: Irish Workers and Labor Conflict in Denver, 1897–1905." North American Labor History Conference, Wayne State University, 1987.

————. "After the Land League: The Persistence of Irish-American Labor Radicalism in Denver, 1897–1905." Conference of the Western Historical Association, Denver, October 1998.

Butler, Mary. "The Lynch Family Chronicles." Typescript, n.d. Copy in possession of the author.

————. "They invented whiskey so the Irish couldn't rule the world." Typescript history of the Connolly family, Shonkin, Montana, n.d. Copy in possession of the author.

Callahan, Robert. "The Myth of the Uncolonized West in Ireland and America." American Conference for Irish Studies meeting, Roanoke, May 13, 1999.

Chambers, Clarke. "Social Welfare Policies and Programs on the Minnesota Iron Range, 1880–1930." Copy available in Minnesota Historical Society.

Coughlin, Jason. "The History of Helmville." Typescript, n.d. Copy in possession of the author.

Cullingford, Elizabeth. "Are We the Cowboys or Are We the Indians?" American Conference of Irish Studies meeting, Roanoke, May 13, 1999.

Delury, John F. "Irish Nationalism in Sacramento, 1850–1890." M.A. thesis, University of San Francisco, 1990.

Emmons, David. "Faction Fights: Another Look at the Irish Immigrant Upraised." Hibernian Lecture, University of Notre Dame, October 1991.

Hennings, Robert. "James D. Phelan and the Wilson Progressives of California." Ph.D. dissertation, University of California, Berkeley, 1961.

Jockers, Matthew Lee. "In Search of Tir-na-Nog: Irish and Irish-American Literature in the West." Ph.D. dissertation, Southern Illinois University, 1997.

Kane, Katherine (Katie). "Irish and Indians." Lecture at University of Montana, February 27, 2009. Notes in possession of the author.

————. "To Hell or Pine Ridge." MS. University of Montana, Missoula, 2009.

Miller, Kerby. "The Black and the Green: Irish-American/Afro-American Interaction since Colonial Times." Unpublished article in possession of the author.

Mulligan, William. "Irish Miners in the Michigan Copper Country: New Home or Way Station on the Way West." Mining History Association, June 14–18, 2001, Butte, Montana.

Murray, Patrick F. "Calendar of the Overseas Missionary Correspondence of All Hallows College, Dublin, 1842–1877." Master's thesis, Department of History, University College, Dublin, 1956.

O'Fahey, Charles. "John Ireland's Rhetorical Vision of the Irish in America." M.A. thesis, University of Minnesota, 1973.

Rodechko, James P. "Patrick Ford and His Search for America: A Case Study of Irish-American Journalism, 1870–1913." Ph.D. dissertation, University of Connecticut, 1967.

Stanton, Kevin. "The Fighting Irish: Irish Soldiers Serving in the American West from 1850–1890." Ph.D. dissertation prospectus, University of Colorado, 1997.

Acknowledgments

I have accumulated many debts in compiling this book. To try to acknowledge all of them would be futile, but to fail to acknowledge the most important of them would make me—as the Irish would say—*an duine gan anam*, a person without a soul. Traolach Ó Ríordáin gave me that Irish phrase as well as the many layers of meaning that go with it, so I begin with him. He was my Irish language instructor; I was not his best student. Fortunately, that did not keep him from joining with Katie Kane and others to form the University of Montana's Irish Studies Program. All involved in that grand effort deserve the thanks of the American Irish wherever found, but particularly the descendants of the two-boat Irish. There were far more of those two-boat riders than has been previously thought, and for that happy description of them, I thank Jim Rogers, now of the Irish Studies Center at the University of St. Thomas, formerly secretary of the Irish American Cultural Institute. That the institute awarded a grant that allowed me to research the lives of these people of the two boats must also be acknowledged.

So must the encouragement given me by Thomas Archdeacon and Jim Donnelly of the University of Wisconsin. Both of them strongly encouraged me to deal not just with the Irish who were in the West but with the Irish and the West, specifically the perceptions that Americans had of both and the common nativist fear that a Catholic Irish presence on America's western border jeopardized the nation's future. For a significant number of Americans, the first boatloads of Irish were unwelcome, but the second and subsequent boats were a profanation. The two-boat people were also an outlandish people. They were beyond the American pale. That a great number of these Irish preferred to be beyond the pale and that the West allowed them the privilege of staying there gave added meaning to all the boat rides, both the ones to America and the ones within it. Having Tom and Jim's enthusiastic endorsement of that idea meant more to me than they could have known. It is a pleasure for me to let them know it now.

Historians never work alone. Every book is collaborative. In my case, seven superb scholars read various drafts, gently corrected my interpretive excesses, and saved me from countless errors. Tom Archdeacon read the entire manuscript—likely more times than he could count. In addition to his encouragement and good ideas, I thank him for his patience and understanding. Two of my colleagues at the University of Montana, Bill Farr and Katie Kane, read large sections of the manuscript; Tim Meagher, Walter Nugent, Richard White, and Kerby Miller read the whole of it. In Kerby Miller's case, I thank him not only for his critical reading but also for his extraordinary generosity in letting me use some of his vast personal collection of letters from Irish American immigrants. Much of whatever merit this book possesses exists because these good and careful readers gave it the attention they did.

Chuck Rankin of the University of Oklahoma Press liked this project from the beginning, when it was just a relatively uncomplicated account of western Irish. Chuck took a risk when he signed on to the additional and cluttered story-line of a people beyond a cultural as well as a geographical pale. He quickly made his peace with that more ambitious project and then doubled his bet by providing me with a word limit sufficient to the larger task we had set for ourselves. In my first contact with him, Steven Baker of the Press introduced himself as the "project editor who is shepherding your manuscript through editing." He was a most learned, patient, and kind shepherd. I know he would join me in saying that Kathy Lewis made both our jobs not only easier but possible. Kathy was much more than the copyeditor—although she is unquestionably the keenest-eyed and most thorough of those. Since herding is the metaphor of choice here, Kathy could herd cats; in this case, more than a few feral cats. She did it with unfailing grace and good humor; her Iowa Irish ancestors would have praised her. So do I.

I want as well to acknowledge the assistance of my son Mike and my daughter Ann, a one-time historian who backslid into literature but retained all of her good historians' instincts. That she also knows how to use a computer allowed her to convert the endnotes into a bibliography. Mike, another English major, had the daunting task of preparing the index. He performed heroically, listening to me when I left him no choice and pretending to listen but ignoring me when common sense was called for. As for Mari and John, they had only to lead cheers; but I heard them, and I'm grateful for their encouragement. Like every research historian, I had the indispensable assistance of some very efficient archivists. I visited archives from the Bancroft in Berkeley to the Minnesota Historical Society in St. Paul, with stopovers in Notre Dame, St. Louis, Pierre, Topeka, Lincoln,

Denver, Boulder, Helena, Missoula, Moscow, Reno, Seattle, and Portland. To the staffs of all of these university and state archives, I extend my sincere thanks. My debt to them is in no way diminished when I offer very special thanks to Ellen Crain of Butte/Silver Bow Archives. Ellen presides over the best local archive in America. When her new building is completed, the Butte Archives will be an even greater treasure than it is now. The real treasure, however, will still be Ellen and her staff. I think every American who can should visit Butte and see what much of America—including, and contrary to myth, its western reaches—once was. That grand tour should begin with a visit to the archives, the mother lode for the study of that city's remarkable history.

Finally, I thank Carol. She put up with this project longer than anyone and never lost confidence in my ability to get it finished and in working order. The granddaughter of immigrants from Ireland's Counties Offaly and Leix, she seems to know instinctively what the Irish mean by *cara anam*, soul friend. She has been that for me for more than thirty years. This book is dedicated to her as a very partial and very inadequate expression of gratitude for those years.

Index